COMMUNITY-BASED CORRECTIONS

FOURTH EDITION

Paul F. Cromwell
Wichita State University

Rolando V. del Carmen
Sam Houston State University

WEST/WADSWORTH
I(T)P® AN INTERNATIONAL THOMSON PUBLISHING COMPANY

Belmont, CA ■ Albany, NY ■ Boston ■ Cincinnati ■ Johannesburg ■ London ■ Madrid ■ Melbourne
Mexico City ■ New York ■ Pacific Grove, CA ■ Scottsdale, AZ ■ Singapore ■ Tokyo ■ Toronto

Editorial Assistant: Cherie Hackelberg
Marketing Manager: Mike Dew
Marketing Assistant: Shannon Ryan
Project Editor: Debby Kramer
Print Buyer: Karen Hunt
Permissions Editor: Robert Kauser
Production: Matrix Productions Inc.
Designer: Karen Hopkins
Copy Editor: Meg McDonald
Compositor: Shepherd Inc.
Printer: R. R. Donnelley, Crawfordsville
Cover Printer: Phoenix Corp.

Printed in the United States of America
3 4 5 6 7 8 9 10

For more information, contact Wadsworth Publishing Company, 10 Davis Drive, Belmont, CA 94002, or electronically at http://www.wadsworth.com

INTERNATIONAL THOMSON PUBLISHING EUROPE
Berkshire House
168-173 High Holborn
London, WC1V 7AA, United Kingdom

NELSON ITP, AUSTRALIA
102 Dodds Street
South Melbourne
Victoria 3205 Australia

NELSON CANADA
1120 Birchmount Road
Scarborough, Ontario
Canada M1K 5G4

INTERNATIONAL THOMSON EDITORES
Seneca, 53
Colonia Polanco
11560 México D.F. México

INTERNATIONAL THOMSON PUBLISHING ASIA
60 Albert Street
#15-01 Albert Complex
Singapore 189969

INTERNATIONAL THOMSON PUBLISHING JAPAN
Hirakawa-cho Kyowa Building, 3F
2-2-1 Hirakawa-cho, Chiyoda-ku
Tokyo 102 Japan

INTERNATIONAL THOMSON PUBLISHING SOUTHERN AFRICA
Building 18, Constantia Square
138 Sixteenth Road, P.O. Box 2459
Halfway House, 1685 South Africa

Library of Congress Cataloging-in-Publication Data

Cromwell, Paul F.
Community-based corrections
/ Paul F. Cromwell, Rolando V. del Carmen. — 4th ed.
p. cm.
Includes indexes.
ISBN 0-534-54639-0 (alk. paper)
1. Probation—United States. 2. Parole—United States.
3. Alternatives to imprisonment—United States. I. Del Carmen, Rolando V. II. Title.
KF9750.P77 1998
345.73'077—dc21 98-7435

This book is printed on acid-free recycled paper.

DEDICATION

In loving memory of my father, Paul F. Cromwell, Sr., and my father-in-law, John Thomas "Buck" Douglas.

Paul Cromwell

To my wife, Josie, and daughter, Jocelyn, and to my many colleagues and students in the College of Criminal Justice, Sam Houston State University.

Rolando V. del Carmen

Brief Contents

PART III: INTERMEDIATE SANCTIONS AND SPECIAL ISSUES 251

Contents

Chapter 7: Probation Revocation 159

Preface

By 1998, the number of adults under some form of correctional supervision in the United States had reached an all-time high of 5 million persons. More than 3.4 million of these were being supervised by probation, parole, and other community-based correctional programs. Clearly, most offenders serve their sentences in the community, and even those who are incarcerated eventually return to the community, often on parole. This book examines these community-based methods of corrections.

The goal of this fourth edition of *Community-Based Corrections* has been to provide students with comprehensive, up-to-date, objective knowledge of the procedures, practices, and personnel that constitute probation, parole, and other community-based sanctions. We have sought to present community-based correctional programs in their historical, philosophical, social, and legal context and to integrate theory and practice to the greatest extent possible.

Because we want this book to be as practical as possible, we have provided many examples of community-based programs, laws, and procedures from state and federal jurisdictions across the nation. In this edition, as in previous ones, we wrestled with the problem of using examples and laws from as many states as possible in order to make the materials relevant to a broad audience. However, the states' systems vary widely in their programs, laws, and sophistication. We decided we would not do students justice if we included laws and examples from only the large, populous states, and we could not possibly incorporate examples and laws from every jurisdiction. We therefore decided to use the federal system, a model system, as our primary point of reference. We have cited state laws and programs throughout the book nonetheless.

ORGANIZATION OF THE BOOK

Community-Based Corrections, Fourth Edition, is divided into three parts. Part I examines **probation.** Chapter 1 discusses the historical, social, and legal foundations of probation. Chapter 2 addresses sentencing and the decision to grant probation. Various forms of probation are discussed and analyzed. Chapter 3, "The Presentence Investigation Report," considers the purposes, contents, and legal issues of this important document. Examples of two types of presentence report are presented. Chapter 4 examines the terms and conditions of probation. Recent court decisions are discussed. Chapter 5 provides a review of the organization and administration of probation services. Chapter 6 is a comprehensive analysis of probation and parole supervision. Chapter 7 considers probation revocation and presents important court decisions.

Part II examines **parole.** Chapter 8 begins with a history of the concept and practice of parole and reviews the past and present controversies regarding the use of parole and analyzes the issues currently being debated. Chapter 9 examines the parole board and parole decision making. Chapter 10 provides an overview of parole conditions and of the issues involved in parole revocation.

Part III is a review and analysis of **intermediate sanctions and special issues.** Chapter 11 provides overviews of intensive supervision, boot camps, house arrest, electronic monitoring, restitution, community service, and fines. Supplementary readings provide more comprehensive examinations of the major intermediate sanctions. Chapter 12, "Juvenile Probation and Parole," is a new chapter for this edition. This chapter reviews the laws and practices of community-based corrections for juveniles. Chapter 13 is a review of research examining the effectiveness of intermediate sanctions. Chapter 14 is unique for a textbook of probation, parole, and other community sanctions. It is a review of the collateral consequences of conviction. Probationers and parolees often face indirect, unanticipated sanctions: the loss of civil and political rights following conviction. The rights lost include not only basic citizenship rights such as the right to participate in our democracy by voting, but more subtly the losses of "good character," of occupational and professional licenses, of the right to be bonded, and so on. These losses frequently work against the offender's efforts to put his or her life in order and to obtain and maintain employment. Chapter 15 examines the means by which the offender may regain some of these lost rights, taking a close look at pardons. We believe that the information presented in these two chapters can be of enormous benefit to probation and parole officers and the probationers and parolees under their supervision.

FEATURES AND LEARNING TOOLS

Community-Based Corrections makes use of **supplemental readings.** Most chapters are followed by one or more readings from articles on research in community corrections, digests of relevant court decisions, documents encountered in the community-based corrections field, or articles from recent criminal justice literature. These readings broaden the book's scope and allow the student to consult important sources directly.

Each chapter begins with an **outline,** a list of **key terms,** and a brief statement of the **learning objectives** in the chapter. Key terms are defined in the margins of the text and in the **glossary** at the end of the book. Each chapter is followed by **discussion questions** that will encourage students to think critically about the materials presented in the chapter. These questions could also serve as written exercises in many cases or as topics for essays or research papers. Most chapters contain **boxed features** that amplify particular issues, events, and processes. The book contains many **photographs, tables,** and **figures** that will help students to visualize the phenomena and processes under discussion. An Instructor's Manual with Test Bank and a computerized Test Bank are also available. The following supplements are available for bundling to aid student comprehension:

- **Crime Scenes: An Interactive Criminal Justice CD ROM** The first introductory criminal justice CD ROM available. This interactive CD ROM places students in various roles as they explore all aspects of the CJ system: Policing/Investigations, Courts, Sentencing, and Corrections.
- **InfoTrac College Edition** Gives students access to full-length articles from over 600 scholarly and popular periodicals. Students can print complete articles or use

the cut/paste and email techniques. Includes readings from *U.S. News and World Report, Corrections Today, Prison Journal, American Criminal Law Review* and much more.

- **Internet Investigator II** Includes new Criminal Justice related web sites categorized by course for ease of use: policing, investigations, courts, corrections, research, juvenile delinquency, and much, much more! Save students money by bundling with the book.

ACKNOWLEDGMENTS

This book could not have been written without the generous assistance of many colleagues and corrections professionals. Rolando del Carmen would like to acknowledge the help and support given by Dan Beto, Director of the Correctional Management Institute of Texas, in providing materials for some chapters of this book. Thanks are also due to colleagues in the probation and parole field who have given me the necessary background in field training that has been invaluable in writing chapters in the book. Among those are Rick Faulkner, Program Specialist of the National Institute of Corrections; Ron Corbett, Deputy Commissioner of the Massachusetts Department of Probation; and Todd Jermstad, Assistant Legal Counsel of the Texas Department of Criminal Justice. Paul Cromwell would like to acknowledge a long-time colleague and friend, John Byrd, Chief United States Pretrial Services Officer, Western District of Texas, who generously served as a source of information and referral. Professor Frederic Faust of the School of Criminology and Criminal Justice at Florida State University, a mentor and friend for many years, read and commented on the manuscript at various stages of completion. His advice and suggestions have improved the book immeasurably.

We leaned heavily on various documents published by the Administrative Office of the U.S. Courts and the U.S. Probation Service and on materials from the *Federal Probation Quarterly*. We also drew on published materials from the Bureau of Justice Statistics and the National Institute of Justice. These materials were essential to our effort.

In any undertaking of this sort, the extant literature in the field is relied upon for guidance and reference. In this regard we have benefited from the work of Howard Abadinsky, Joan Petersilia, Wesley Krause, Dean Champion, Belinda McCarthy, Bernard McCarthy, Velmer Burton, Frances Cullen, Lawrence Travis III, John Ortiz Smykla, Harry Allen, Chris Eskridge, Edward Latessa, Gennaro Vito, Norval Morris, Michael Tonry, Carl Klockars, Todd Clear, George Cole, Doris Layton MacKenzie, Edward Rhine, William R. Smith, and Ronald Jackson.

Sabra Horne, Criminal Justice Editor, and Claire Masson, Project Development Editor at Wadsworth Publishing Company, were stalwart and supportive guides. They did a superb job of keeping us on track and on schedule and encouraging us when our energy and enthusiasm occasionally waned.

Finally, we express our special appreciation to our colleagues who reviewed drafts of the book. Their insightful comments and suggestions proved invaluable. In particular, we appreciate the work of Paul Lawson, Montana State University; Thomas Tomlinson, Western Illinois University; Godpower Okereke, Fayetteville State University; Thomas Sullenberger, Southeastern Louisiana University; and Paul Paquette, University of Toledo.

Paul F. Cromwell
Rolando V. del Carmen

About the Authors

Paul F. Cromwell is Professor of Criminal Justice and director of the Hugo Wall School of Urban and Public Affairs at Wichita State University. He received his Ph.D. in criminology from Florida State University in 1986. He also holds a B.S. in sociology, an M.A. in criminal justice from Sam Houston State University in Texas, and a Master of Public Administration from Texas Christian University. He has previously taught at the University of Texas–Permian Basin and the University of Miami.

His extensive experience in the criminal justice system includes service as a U.S. probation and parole officer, chief juvenile probation officer, and commissioner and chairman of the Texas Board of Pardons and Paroles. His primary research interest is in corrections, criminal decision making, and crime prevention through environment design—a crime prevention methodology that stresses the manipulation of the physical environment (land use, roads, building design) to reduce opportunities for criminal activity.

Paul Cromwell is author and editor of 16 books and 35 articles and book chapters in the academic literature in the field of criminal justice and criminology, including *Breaking and Entering: An Ethnographic Analysis of Burglary*, *In Their Own Words: Criminals on Crime*, and *Crime and Justice in America*.

Rolando V. del Carmen is Distinguished Professor of Criminal Justice in the Criminal Justice Center, Sam Houston State University, in Huntsville, Texas. He holds a B.A. and a Bachelor of Laws degree from the Philippines; a Master of Comparative Law from Southern Methodist University; a Master of Laws from the University of California at Berkeley; and a Doctor of Science of Law from the University of Illinois.

Del Carmen was assistant dean and associate professor of a school of law in the Philippines and has held various administrative and academic positions in the United States. He has taught in various universities and has written extensively. His publications include more than ten books and numerous articles in several journals on law-related topics in criminal justice. His books include: *Criminal Procedure: Law and Practice* 4th edition, *Civil Liabilities of Law Enforcement Personnel, Texas Probation Law and Practice,* and *Potential Liabilities of Probation and Parole Officers.*

Rolando del Carmen travels and lectures extensively and has served as a consultant to criminal justice agencies in various states. He was appointed to a six-year term in the Texas Commission on Jail Standards. In 1986, he won the Faculty Excellence in Research Award at Sam Houston State University, the first such award ever to be given by the university. The Academy of Criminal Justices Sciences named Dr. del Carmen as the recipient of the 1990 Academy Fellow Award during the national convention in Denver, Colorado. In 1996, he was the recipient of the Bruce Smith Award, given each year by the Academy of Criminal Justice Sciences, for his contributions to the field of criminal justice education.

I

PROBATION

THE CONCEPT UNDERLYING A SENTENCE TO PROBATION IS SIMPLE. SENTENCING is in large part concerned with avoiding future crimes by helping the defendant to live productively in the community that he or she has offended. Probation proceeds on the theory that the best way to pursue this goal is to orient the criminal sanction toward the community setting in those cases where it is compatible with the other objectives of sentencing. Other things being equal, a given defendant is more likely to learn how to live successfully in the general community if he is dealt with in that community, rather than shipped off to the artificial, atypical environment of a correctional institution. Banishment from society, in a word, is not the way to integrate someone into society. Yet, imprisonment constitutes just such banishment—albeit a temporary one in most cases.

This is of course not to say that probation should be used in all cases, or that it will produce better results. There are many goals of sentencing, some of which may require the imposition of a sentence to imprisonment in a given case. And, there are defendants for whom forced removal from the environment that may have contributed to their offense can be the best beginning to a constructive, useful life.

By the same token, however, probation is a good bit more than the "matter of grace" or "leniency" that characterizes the philosophy of the general public and many judges and legislatures. Probation is an affirmative correctional tool, a tool that is used not because it offers maximum benefit to the defendant (though, of course, this is an important side product), but because it offers maximum benefit to the public that is supposed to be served by the sentencing of criminals. The automatic response of many in the criminal justice system that imprisonment is the best sentence for crime unless particular reasons exist for "mitigating" the sentence is not a sound starting point in framing criminal sanctions. Quite the opposite ought to be the case; the automatic response in sentencing situations ought to be probation, unless particularly aggravating factors emerge in the case at hand. At least, if such aggravating factors cannot be advanced as the basis of a more repressive sentence, probation offers more hope than imprisonment that the defendant will not become part of the depressing cycle in which the gates of our prisons are more like revolving doors than barriers to crime.

It must be realized that this thesis cannot be practiced in a vacuum. Too often a sentencing judge is faced with the "Hobson's choice" of sentencing the defendant to an overcrowded prison that almost guarantees that he will emerge a more dangerous person or to an essentially unsupervised probation that is little more than a release without sanction, and without incentive to avoid committing a new offense. Such a state of affairs represents a failure of the legislative process in the highest order. The U.S. criminal justice system has failed more for this reason than for any other; not enough attention has been paid to providing adequate correctional choices to those who must operate the system. An effective correctional system places great reliance on adequately funded and staffed probation services. Within such a context, probation can lead to significant improvement in the preventive effects of the criminal law at much lower cost than the typical prison sentence. This has been proven in jurisdictions where it has been given a chance to work. We should not treat lightly an approach to crime control that offers the hope of better results at less cost. This, in a sentence, is the hope of probation.

Source: American Bar Association Project on Minimum Standards and Goals, *Probation* (Chicago, n.d.).

INTRODUCTION

The United States currently has over 5 million persons under the supervision of the criminal justice system. More than 1.6 million of them are incarcerated in local, state, and federal institutions. The remainder are on probation or parole. Billions of dollars are spent annually to support the criminal justice system, yet the solution to crime continues to elude us.[1] Furthermore, it is becoming increasingly apparent that confinement has no positive effect on recidivism; rather, it may contribute to further criminality. What are we to do?

Advocates of sentencing reform are calling for an expanded range of sentencing options that provide control but do not impose confinement for many offenses. Many believe that **community-based corrections** may hold some of the answers. Community-based corrections are sanctions imposed on offenders that allow them to remain in the community while participating in one or more programs aimed at controlling criminal behavior and reintegrating them into the community.

Community-based programs are not new. Traditional probation and parole, the oldest and best-known programs of community corrections, have been part of the criminal justice system since the mid-19th century. (See chapters 1 and 8 for detailed discussions of the history of probation and parole.) Recent years have witnessed the development and growth of many new community-based programs. These programs share two primary goals and objectives: to protect the public and to reintegrate the offender back into the community.

GOALS OF COMMUNITY-BASED CORRECTIONAL PROGRAMS

Protection of the Public

Most offenders have shown by their offenses that they cannot easily conform to the norms of society. One of the goals of community-based corrections, therefore, is to help offenders conform to behavioral expectations and monitor their progress toward that goal. Perhaps the major criticism of traditional probation and parole has been their failure to protect the public from further criminal acts by individuals under supervision in the community. In order for probation or any other community-based program to be effective and accepted by policymakers and the public, it must first demonstrate that the offenders under supervision are adequately monitored and that the public has nothing to fear from their actions.

Control may be accomplished in a variety of ways. First, offenders should be assessed to determine the degree of risk posed by their participation in community programs. Community-based programs are not generally appropriate for violent offenders or those with extensive criminal records. Second, those who supervise offenders in community-based programs must accept responsibility to protect the public by monitoring compliance with court orders and conditions of release. Finally, violations of supervised conditions must be taken seriously. If the programs are to become credible sanctions, courts and paroling authorities must be willing to revoke probation or parole for those who cannot or will not comply with the conditions of release.[2]

Reintegration of the Offender Back into the Community

Thirty years ago the President's Commission on Law Enforcement and Administration of Justice introduced the term **reintegration.**[3] The report stated,

> Institutions tend to isolate offenders from society, both physically and psychologically, cutting them off from schools, jobs, families, and other supportive influences and increasing the probability that the label of criminal will be indelibly impressed upon them. The goal of reintegration is likely to be furthered much more readily by working with offenders in the community than by incarceration.[4]

Reintegration stresses adaptation to the community by requiring the offender to participate in programs that develop legitimate skills and opportunities and allow the offender to use and refine those skills in a community setting.[5] The role of the community in providing needed services and opportunities is also emphasized. The President's Commission called for mobilization and change of the community and its institutions. The commission said that communities must develop employment, recreational, and educational opportunities for all its citizens. Belinda and Bernard McCarthy conclude that to achieve the objectives of reintegration, community-based correctional programs must meet the following criteria:

- A location and interaction within a community that offers opportunities that fit offender's needs
- A nonsecure environment—the offender's home, a surrogate home, or a communal residence in which the offender lives as a responsible person with minimal supervision
- Community-based education, training, counseling, and support services
- Opportunities to assume (or learn) the normal social roles as citizen, family member, and student or employee
- Opportunities for personal growth[6]

Community correctional workers, such as probation and parole officers, act as advocates and resource brokers, linking offenders to programs and monitoring their progress once the contact has been established. (See chapter 6 for a more detailed discussion of supervision as brokerage of services.)

COMMUNITY-BASED CORRECTIONAL PROGRAMS

Community-based programs include traditional probation and parole as well as other noninstitutional sanctions such as intensive supervision probation, restitution, community service, fines, boot camps, house arrest, and others. The following section briefly examines some of the major community-based correctional programs. They will each be discussed in greater detail later in the book.

Probation

At one end of the continuum of sanctions lies **probation,** defined as the release of a convicted offender under conditions imposed by the court for a specified period during which the court retains authority to modify the conditions or to resentence the offender if he or she violates the conditions. Probation is the most widely used punishment in the United States; nearly 60 percent of all convicted offenders are under some form of probation supervision. Probation is most appropriate for nonviolent first offenders who do not represent a threat to the community but require structure, supervision, and assistance. Offenders sentenced to a term of probation are supervised by a probation officer, who enforces the conditions of release, reports violations of the conditions to the sentencing authority, and uses community resources to let the offender participate in self-improvement programs, including drug and alcohol treatment, job training, and educational opportunities.

Parole

Parole is the release of an offender before the expiration of his or her sentence under conditions established by the paroling authority. Parole is in most ways like probation. Both involve supervised release in the community and the possibility of revocation should the parolee or probationer violate the conditions of release. While there are some technical differences that will be discussed in later chapters, the primary difference is that probation is supervision in the community *instead of* incarceration and parole is supervised release *after* a portion of the sentence in prison has been served.

Intermediate Sanctions

Because of the perceived failure of probation and parole to protect the public from further crimes by those under supervision, a continuum of community-based punishments called **intermediate sanctions** has been developed. These sanctions, which fall between probation and prison on a scale of severity and control, are most appropriately used on low-risk and nonviolent offenders. They offer graduated levels of supervision and harshness with simple probation at one end and prison at the other. In between are a variety of community-based options such as fines, restitution, community service, work release, halfway houses, electronic monitoring, and boot camps. By developing these new sentencing alternatives, policymakers seek to

- make sentencing more just and effective
- enhance public safety
- control the growth of prison populations
- reduce costs

One commentator explains:

> Using a sentencing scheme of this sort enables authorities to maintain expensive prison cells to incapacitate violent criminals. At the same time, less restrictive community-based programs and restitution-focused sentences punish nonviolent offenders while teaching them accountability for their actions and heightening their chance for rehabilitation.[7]

This approach treats prison as the sentencing option of last resort rather than the sentencing option of choice. Intermediate sanctions impose much greater levels of surveillance, supervision, and monitoring than traditional probation. They may require as many as 30 contacts per month between the supervising officer and the offender, his or her family and employer, and others. Most also require the offender to participate in treatment or educational programs, do unpaid community service, pay restitution, and work or attend school or vocational training. Some require the offender to wear electronic monitoring devices or to live under "house arrest," leaving home only to work.[8] A full range of sentencing options gives judges greater latitude to select punishments that more closely fit the circumstances of the crime and the offender.[9] Figure 1 illustrates the range of sanctions from probation at one end to incarceration at the other.

Intensive Supervision Probation (ISP)

Intensive supervision probation (ISP) is a form of probation for offenders who require more structure and surveillance than ordinary probationers but for whom incarceration may be too severe a sanction. ISP involves considerable restrictions on the offender's freedom of movement and many other aspects of autonomy. ISP allows offenders to live at home under severe restrictions. They see their probation officers three to five times each week and may have to submit to curfews, drug and alcohol testing, and employment checks.

Intensive supervision probation (ISP) emphasizes control. Offenders are supervised in small caseloads, sometimes by a team of two probation officers. A national survey reported that the average ISP caseload was 29 in 1994,[10] compared to over 100 for traditional probation.

Restitution

Restitution is a monetary penalty paid to victims by offenders to compensate for their losses while teaching offenders responsibility for their actions. Restitution is one of the oldest punishments. The Code of Hammurabi (1792–1750 B.C.) established elaborate restitution schemes for crimes ranging from theft to murder. Today, 3700 years later, restitution remains a mainstay among the range of punishments available to the courts. However, because most people feel that restitution alone is insufficient punishment, it is frequently coupled with another penalty such as probation, ISP, or community service.

Restitution may be paid either directly to the victim or, as in some jurisdictions, to a state or federal restitution fund that passes the funds on to the victim. Some states have established secure facilities called *rehabilitation centers* or *restitution centers,* where offenders live until a restitution debt is paid. Residents work at a regular job and submit their pay directly to the center director, who deducts the amounts for room and board, support for dependents, supervision fees, and restitution to the victim. The remainder is returned to the resident upon release.

Several studies have examined the success or failure of restitution as a correctional sanction. Most have noted that 80 to 98 percent of restitution orders were completed before release. Others have shown that those who made restitution had fewer new convictions upon completion than a matched group who did not have restitution orders.[11]

Community Service

Community service, a form of symbolic restitution, is defined as unpaid service to the public to compensate society for some harm done by the crime. It usually consists of working for a tax-supported or nonprofit agency such as a hospital or library, an antipoverty agency, or a public works program. It may involve picking up roadside litter or removing graffiti. In community-service restitution the offender repays the community he or she offended by performing some service for it rather than by repaying money.

Like monetary restitution, community-service restitution is both punitive and rehabilitative. It is punitive in that the offender's time and freedom are restricted until the

Figure 1 **ESCALATING PUNISHMENTS TO FIT THE CRIME**

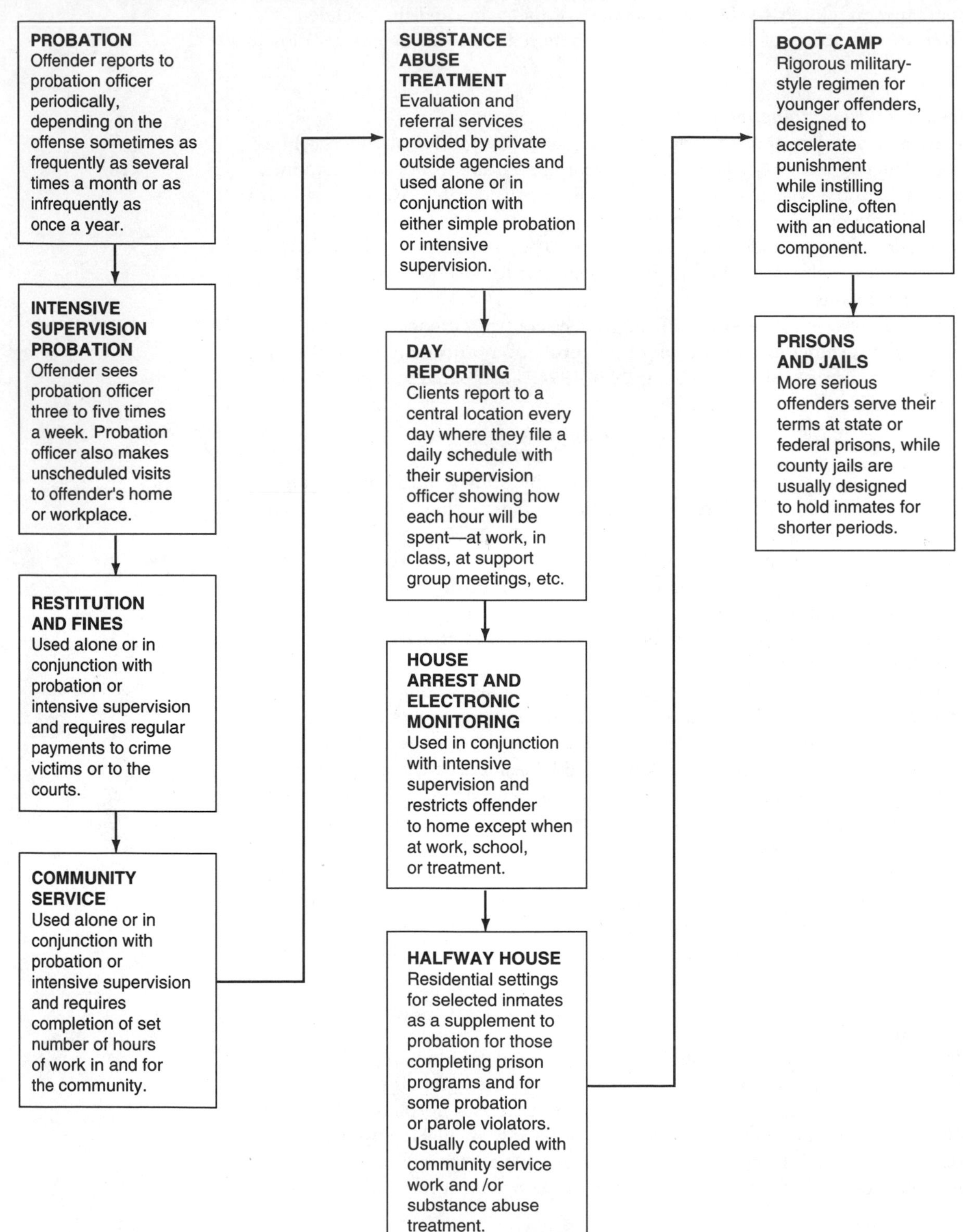

Source: William DiMascio, *Seeking Justice: Crime and Punishment in America* (New York: Edna McConnell Clark Foundation, 1997). Used with permission of the Edna McConnell Clark Foundation.

work is completed. It is rehabilitative in the same way as monetary restitution: it allows offenders to do something constructive, to increase their self-esteem, to reduce their isolation from society, and to benefit society through their efforts. Further, community service provides an alternative form of restitution both for offenders who are unable to make meaningful financial restitution and for those whose financial resources are so great that monetary restitution has no punitive or rehabilitative effect. As the search continues for less costly and more effective methods of dealing with offenders, community service is a major trend in U.S. corrections.

Fines

Fines are routinely imposed for offenses ranging from traffic violations to drug trafficking. It is estimated that well over $1 billion in fines is collected annually by courts across the country.[12] Fines are used more extensively in lower courts (fines in 86 percent of cases) than in higher courts (fines in 42 percent of cases). However, higher courts are assessing fines more frequently in conjunction with other penalties, such as probation or imprisonment. The federal Comprehensive Crime Control Act of 1984, effective November 1, 1987, specifies that for every sentence to probation, the court must also order the defendant to "pay a fine, make restitution, and/or work in community service."[13] Presently, patterns in the use of fines vary widely. Observers predict greater emphasis on fines in the future, however, both as a sentence in itself and in conjunction with other sentences.

House Arrest and Electronic Monitoring

House arrest is a condition, not a form, of probation. Electronic monitoring is a means of assuring that certain conditions of probation are met. Both have found acceptance in many jurisdictions because of their potential to satisfy the goals of imprisonment without the social and financial costs associated with incarceration.[14]

House arrest is viewed as an alternative to incarceration and a means of easing prison overcrowding. Programs vary, but most require that offenders remain within the confines of their home during specified hours, ranging from 24-hour-per-day confinement to imposition of late-night curfews only.

Electronic monitoring—a correctional technology rather than a correctional program—provides verification of an offender's whereabouts. Electronic monitoring is useful at many points on the correctional continuum, from pretrial release to parole.

Boot Camps

Recent innovations such as **boot camps** provide that the convicted offender reside in a correctional facility and participate in a program designed to instill discipline and responsibility. Most boot camp programs, designed for young, nonviolent offenders who have no prior incarcerations, provide an experience much like that of military basic training with intensive physical training, hard work, and little or no free time. After a specified period, typically 90–120 days, the probationer is released to regular probation supervision. Boot camps provide the court with an alternative disposition that is stricter and more structured than regular probation yet less severe than a prison sentence.

Boot camps have strong public appeal, and their use appears to be increasing.[15] Supporters of the concept cite evidence that the boot camp experience may be more positive than incarceration in traditional prisons. Moreover, they state, those who have completed such programs describe the experience as "difficult, but constructive." They assert that recidivism rates for those who complete boot camp programs are approximately the same as for those who serve longer periods in traditional prisons or on probation.[16] Others, however, have argued that boot camps hold potential for negative outcomes. Many boot camp environments are characterized by inconsistent standards, contrived stress, and leadership styles that are likely to reduce self-esteem, increase the potential for violence, and encourage the abuse of power.[17]

Despite the controversy, boot camps have the support of the public, the media, and most correctional policymakers. There is every likelihood that boot camp programs will continue to proliferate and will become an integral part of the correctional continuum.

SUMMARY

The cost in money and human potential of the unprecedented growth of the nation's prison population has caused policymakers to seek alternative solutions to control criminal behavior. Intermediate sanctions are a valuable resource to lessen these problems. They allow nonviolent offenders to repay their victims and the community and in doing so promote rehabilitation—all at a relatively low cost.[18] Providing a range of community-based sanctions allows the use of expensive prison beds to hold the most intractable and violent offenders while offering hope that others, less committed to a criminal lifestyle, may become useful citizens of the communities in which they live. This is the hope and promise of community corrections.

ENDNOTES

1. William M. DiMascio, *Seeking Justice: Crime and Punishment in America* (New York: Edna McConnell Clark Foundation, 1997).
2. Norval Morris and Michael Tonry, *Between Prison and Probation: Intermediate Punishments in a Rational Sentencing System* (New York: Oxford University Press, 1990).
3. President's Commission on Law Enforcement and Administration of Justice, *The Challenge of Crime in a Free Society* (Washington, D.C.: U.S. Government Printing Office, 1967), 169. Also see Belinda Rogers McCarthy and Bernard J. McCarthy Jr., *Community-Based Corrections,* 2nd ed. (Pacific Grove, Calif.: Brooks/Cole, 1995), 2.
4. President's Commission, *The Challenge of Crime,* 165.
5. Edward J. Latessa and Harry E. Allen, *Corrections in the Community* (Cincinnati: Anderson, 1997), 28.
6. McCarthy and McCarthy, *Community-Based Corrections,* 3.
7. Joan Petersilia, Susan Turner, James Kahan, and Joyce Peterson, *Granting Felons Probation: Public Risks and Alternatives* (Santa Monica, Calif.: RAND, 1985), 24.
8. DiMascio, *Seeking Justice,* 24.
9. Ibid.
10. C. Camp and G. Camp, *The Corrections Yearbook: Probation and Parole—1994* (South Salem, NY: Criminal Justice Institute, 1994).
11. Marilyn D. McShane and Wesley Krause, *Community Corrections* (New York: Macmillan, 1993).
12. George Cole, *The American System of Criminal Justice,* 6th ed. (Pacific Grove, Calif.: Brooks/Cole, 1992).
13. 18 U.S.C. 3563 (a) (2).

14. Howard Abadinsky, *Probation and Parole: Theory and Practice,* 5th ed. (Englewood Cliffs, N.J.: Prentice-Hall, 1997).

15. Doris Layton MacKenzie, Robert Brame, David McDowell, and Claire Souryal, "Boot Camp Prisons and Recidivism in Eight States," *Criminology* 33(3):328–57 (1995).

16. Doris Layton MacKenzie, "Boot Camp Prisons Grow in Number and Scope," *National Institute of Justice Reports* (1990).

17. Merry Morash and Lila Rucker, "A Critical Look at the Idea of Boot Camp as a Correctional Reform," *Crime and Delinquency* (April 1990): 204–22.

18. DiMascio, *Seeking Justice,* 41.

1
HISTORY AND LEGAL FOUNDATIONS OF PROBATION

What You Will Learn in This Chapter

You will become familiar with the social and legal history of probation in both Europe and America. You will learn how probation grew out of early efforts by judges to mitigate the harsh punishments prescribed by law. You will learn how distinctly American practices evolved, including the origins of both adult and juvenile probation.

KEY TERMS

- **Amercement**
- **Benefit of clergy**
- **"Neck verse"**
- **Sanctuary**
- **Abjuration**
- **Judicial reprieve**
- **Security for good behavior**
- **Filing**
- **Bail**
- **Motion to quash**
- ***Commonwealth v. Chase***
- **Recognizance**
- **Suspended sentence**
- **Suspension of imposition of sentence**
- **Suspension of execution of sentence**
- ***Killets* case**
- **Peter Oxenbridge Thacher**
- **Matthew Davenport Hill**
- **John Augustus**
- **Illinois Juvenile Court Act of 1899**

INTRODUCTION

We begin with an examination of early European criminal law and briefly describe the various efforts to mitigate the harsh punishments characteristic of the times. Early American law is then discussed with an emphasis on the means by which judges relieved selected offenders from the full effects of the excessive, and often inappropriate, punishments prescribed by statute. Two of the methods, recognizance and suspended sentence, are addressed in detail. Early state, federal, and juvenile probation legislation is then reviewed.

EARLY CRIMINAL LAW

Probation, as it is known and practiced today, evolved out of ancient precedents in England and the United States devised to avoid the mechanical application of the harsh penal codes of the day.[1] Early British criminal law, which was dominated by the objectives of retribution and punishment, imposed rigid and severe penalties on offenders. The usual punishments were corporal: branding, flogging, mutilation, and execution. Capital punishment was commonly inflicted upon children and animals as well as men and women. At the time of Henry VIII, for instance, more than 200 crimes were punishable by death, many of them relatively minor offenses against property.

Methods used to determine guilt—what today we would call *criminal procedure*—also put the accused in danger. Trial might be by combat between the accused and the accuser, or a person's innocence might be determined by whether he or she sank when bound and thrown into a deep pond—the theory being that the pure water would reject wrongdoers. Thus the choice was to drown as an innocent person or to survive the drowning only to be otherwise executed. Sometimes the offender could elect to be tried "by God," which involved undergoing some painful and frequently life-threatening ordeal, or "by country," a form of trial by jury for which the accused first had to pay an **amercement** to the king. The accepted premise was that the purpose of criminal law was not to deter or rehabilitate but to bring about justice for a past act deemed harmful to the society.

AMERCEMENT

A monetary penalty imposed upon a person for some offense, he being *in mercy* for his conduct. It was imposed arbitrarily at the discretion of the court or the person's lord. *Black's Law Dictionary* distinguishes between amercements and fines in that fines are certain, are created by some statute, and can be assessed only by courts of record; amercements are arbitrarily imposed.

EARLY EFFORTS TO MITIGATE PUNISHMENT

The early Middle Ages saw efforts to mitigate the severity of punishment. Royal pardons, usually paid for by the accused, were sometimes granted. Judges could choose to interpret statutes narrowly or fail to apply them. Juries sometimes devalued stolen property so as to bring its value below that which required capital punishment. Prosecutors dismissed charges or charged offenders with lesser offenses. Devices such as "benefit of clergy" and "judicial reprieve" benefited some defendants, while "sanctuary" and "abjuration" enabled some criminals to gain immunity from punishment. Courts began to release certain offenders on good behavior for a temporary period, which allowed them time to seek a pardon or commutation of sentence. Gradually, an "inherent" power of certain courts to suspend sentences was recognized, although the existence and limits on that power were almost at once the subject of controversy.

BENEFIT OF CLERGY

An exemption for members of the clergy that allowed them to avoid being subject to the jurisdiction of secular courts.

Benefit of clergy was a privilege originally given to ordained clerics, monks, and nuns accused of crimes. Benefit of clergy required representatives of the church to be delivered to church authorities rather than secular courts, for punishment. Although the ecclesiastical courts had the power to imprison for life, they seldom exacted such severe punishment. Thus the benefit of clergy served to mitigate the harsh (frequently capital) punishments prescribed by English law. Benefit of clergy was later extended to protect ordinary citizens. Judges used the benefit as a means of exercising discretion when the prescribed punishment for a crime seemed too severe in particular cases. A person could qualify for benefit of clergy by demonstrating that he or she could read—a skill that only the clergy and some of the upper classes possessed. Over time the courts began to require these defendants to read in court the text of Psalm 51 as a test of their literacy. The psalm came to be known as the *neck verse,* and many criminals soon memorized it and pretended to read it in court, using its protection to escape being hanged. The benefit was practiced in the United States for a brief period, but the procedure became so technical and legalistic that it was almost unworkable. It was finally abolished in 1827.

SANCTUARY

In old English law, a consecrated place, such as a church or abbey, where offenders took refuge because they could not be arrested there.

ABJURATION

An oath to forsake the realm forever taken by an accused person who claimed sanctuary.

Sanctuary referred to a place (usually a church or vestry) the king's soldiers were not permitted to enter for the purpose of taking an accused into custody. Offenders were accorded sanctuary until negotiations with the accusers could be accomplished or arrangements could be made to smuggle the accused out of the country. Offenders who confessed their crimes while in sanctuary were allowed **abjuration**—they promised to leave England under pain of immediate punishment if they returned without the king's permission. One legal historian wrote, "For a man to take sanctuary, confess his crime, and abjure the realm was an everyday event. If the man who had taken sanctuary would neither confess to a crime nor submit to a trial, the state could do no more against him. It tried to teach the clergy that their duty was to starve him into submission, but the clergy resented this interference with holy things."[2]

JUDICIAL REPRIEVE

Withdrawal of a sentence for an interval of time during which the offender was at liberty and imposition of other sanctions was postponed.

Judicial reprieve (from *reprendre,* "to take back") was another method by which judges who recognized that not all offenders are dangerous, evil persons avoided imposing the prescribed punishment for crimes. Judicial reprieve amounted to a withdrawal of the sentence for some interval of time—similar to what today is called *suspension of sentence.* During the period of judicial reprieve the offender was at liberty, and the imposition of other criminal sanctions was postponed. At the expiration of the specified time, the accused could apply to the Crown for a pardon.

Psalm 51: "The Neck Verse"

1. Have mercy upon me, O God, according to thy lovingkindness: according unto the multitude of thy tender mercies blot out my transgressions.
2. Wash me thoroughly from mine iniquity, and cleanse me from my sin.
3. For I acknowledge my transgressions: and my sin is ever before me.
4. Against thee, thee only, have I sinned, and done this evil in thy sight: that thou mightest be justified when thou speakest, and be clear when thou judgest.
5. Behold, I was shapen in iniquity; and in sin did my mother conceive me.
6. Behold, thou desirest truth in the inward parts: and in the hidden part thou shalt make me to know wisdom.
7. Purge me with hyssop, and I shall be clean: wash me, and I shall be whiter than snow.
8. Make me to hear joy and gladness; that the bones which thou has broken may rejoice.
9. Hide thy face from my sins, and blot out all mine iniquities.
10. Create in me a clean heart, O God; and renew a right spirit within me.
11. Cast me not away from thy presence; and take not thy holy spirit from me.
12. Restore unto me the joy of thy salvation; and uphold me with thy free spirit.
13. Then will I teach transgressors thy ways; and sinners shall be converted unto thee.
14. Deliver me from bloodguiltiness, O God, thou God of my salvation: and my tongue shall sing aloud of thy righteousness.
15. O Lord, open thou my lips; and my mouth shall shew forth thy praise.
16. For thou desirest not sacrifice; else would I give it: thou delightest not in burnt offering.
17. The sacrifices of God are a broken spirit: a broken and a contrite heart, O God, thou wilt not despise.
18. Do good in thy good pleasure unto Zion: build thou the walls of Jerusalem.
19. Then shalt thou be pleased with the sacrifices of righteousness, with burnt offering and whole burnt offering: then shall they offer bullocks upon thine altar.

EARLY AMERICAN LAW

Recognition of the doctrine of benefit of clergy was never widespread in the American colonies. Instead, distinct American practices developed, such as "security for good behavior" and a practice known in Massachusetts as *filing.*[3] **Security for good behavior,** also known as *good abearance,* was a fee paid to the state as collateral for a promise of good behavior. Much like the modern practice of bail, security for good behavior allowed the accused to go free in certain cases either before or after conviction. Under **filing** the indictment was "laid on file" in cases where justice did not require an immediate sentence; however, the court could impose certain conditions on the defendant. The effect was that the case was laid at rest without either dismissal or final judgment and without the necessity of asking for final continuances.

SECURITY FOR GOOD BEHAVIOR

A recognizance or bond given the court by a defendant before or after conviction conditioned on his or her being "on good behavior" or keeping the peace for a prescribed period.

FILING

A procedure under which an indictment was "laid on file," or held in abeyance, without either dismissal or final judgment in cases where justice did not require an immediate sentence.

Massachusetts judges also often granted a *motion to quash* after judgment, using any minor technicality or the slightest error in the proceedings to free the defendant in cases where they thought the statutory penalties inhumane. Some early forms of *bail* had the effect of suspending final action on a case, although the chief use of bail then (as now) was for the purpose of insuring appearance for trial. Because the sureties "went bail" and became responsible for the action of the defendant, they

A criminal is granted sanctuary.

assumed supervision of the defendant, at least to the extent of keeping track of his or her whereabouts. The continuous availability of the defendant for further action by the court was one of the conditions of liberty.

All of these methods had the common objective of mitigating punishment by relieving selected offenders from the full effects of the legally prescribed penalties that substantial segments of the community, including many judges, viewed as excessive and inappropriate to their offenses. They were precursors to probation as it is known today. The procedures most closely related to modern probation, however, are recognizance and the suspended sentence.

RECOGNIZANCE AND SUSPENDED SENTENCE

As early as 1830 Massachusetts courts had begun to release some offenders through the use of innovative and possibly extralegal procedures instead of imposing the prescribed punishments. In the 1830 case of ***Commonwealth v. Chase,***[4] often cited as an example of the early use of release on **recognizance** (from *recognocere,* "to call to mind"), Judge Peter Oxenbridge Thacher found the defendant guilty on her plea, suspended the imposition of sentence, and ruled that the defendant was permitted, "upon her recognizance for her appearance in this court whenever she should be called for, to go at large."[5] Recognizance came to be used often in Massachusetts as a means of avoiding a final conviction of young and minor offenders in hope that they would avoid further criminal behavior. The main thrust of recognizance was to humanize criminal law and mitigate its harshness.[6] Recognizance is used today to ensure a defendant's presence at court and is not a disposition in itself.

RECOGNIZANCE

Originally a device of preventive justice that obliged persons suspected of future misbehavior to stipulate with and give full assurance to the court and the public that the apprehended offense would not occur. Recognizance was later used with convicted or arraigned offenders with conditions of release set. Recognizance was usually entered into for a specified period.

Suspended sentence is a court order, entered after a verdict, finding, or plea of guilty, that suspends or postpones the filing, imposition, or execution of sentence during the good behavior of the offender. Although suspension of sentence is, in a few jurisdictions, a form of disposition of the criminal offender that is separate from and in addition to probation,[7] we consider it here chiefly in its close historical and legal relationship to probation.

Where suspension of sentence exists independent of probation, it is distinguished from probation in that the offender is released without supervision. The only condition is the implicit, or sometimes explicit, imperative that the withholding or postponement of sentence will be revoked or terminated if the offender commits a new crime. As a disposition, suspension of sentence also differs from probation in that no term is specified. It is generally held, however, that the period of suspension of sentence is limited by the maximum period of commitment permitted by statute for the offense.

Two Kinds of Suspended Sentence

There are two kinds of suspended sentence—suspension of *imposition* of sentence and suspension of *execution* of sentence. In the case of *suspension of imposition of sentence,* there may be a verdict or plea and a judgment, but no sentence is pronounced. In the case of *suspension of execution of sentence,* the sentence is pronounced, but its execution is suspended; in other words, the defendant is not committed to a correctional institution or otherwise taken into custody. As we will see, the form of the suspension—whether of imposition or of execution of sentence—has different legal consequences, and it directly impacts whether suspension of sentence is considered as a separate disposition of the offender or as the basis for or equivalent to probation. The distinction is critical and may affect such later issues as the following:

SUSPENDED SENTENCE

An order of the court after a verdict, finding, or plea of guilty that suspends or postpones the imposition or execution of sentence during a period of good behavior.

- ▲ Whether the offender has been convicted
- ▲ What civil rights he or she has forfeited
- ▲ The term for which he or she may be committed upon resentence after revocation of the suspension
- ▲ Whether probation is a part of the criminal prosecution
- ▲ Whether the probationer on revocation of probation is entitled to counsel under the holding in *Mempa v. Rhay*[8] or the right to counsel rules announced in *Morrissey v. Brewer*[9] and *Gagnon v. Scarpelli*[10]

The Power to Suspend Sentence

Several variables must be considered in discussions of the power to suspend sentence. For instance, it makes a difference whether:

- ▲ we are talking about the power to withhold or delay sentencing indefinitely, or for only a temporary period or a specific purpose.
- ▲ we are referring to a power inherent in the courts to suspend sentence, or to a power granted to the courts by a legislative act.
- ▲ we mean power to suspend imposition of sentence, power to suspend execution of sentence, or both.
- ▲ suspended sentence is a separate disposition or sentencing alternative, or connected with probation.
- ▲ probation depends upon the existence of the power to suspend sentence, or does not have the suspended sentence aspect.
- ▲ probation is actually deemed to be a sentence.

"The Killets Case"

EX PARTE UNITED STATES, 242 U.S. 27 (1916)

The defendant, John Killets, was convicted of embezzling nearly $5,000 from a bank in Toledo, Ohio. A first offender with a good reputation in the community, Killets had made full restitution, and the bank did not wish to prosecute. The trial court suspended sentence indefinitely, and the prosecution appealed, alleging that the court did not have the power to suspend either the imposition or execution of sentence indefinitely.

It is generally conceded that at common law the English courts had the power to suspend sentence for a limited period or for a specified purpose. This power was used, for example, in judicial reprieve, where there was a temporary suspension of imposition or execution of sentence and in which the defendant—with neither the right of appeal nor the right to a new trial—could apply to the Crown for an absolute or conditional pardon.

Whether the common law recognized the inherent right of the courts to suspend sentence indefinitely is a matter of considerable dispute. Certain practices in both England and the American colonies support the view that such a right was recognized. Recognizance, used as early as 1830 in Massachusetts, permitted one Jerusha Chase, "upon her own recognizance for her appearance in this court whenever she was called for, to go at large."[11] Judicial reprieve was also cited as proof of a court's inherent right to suspend sentence indefinitely, particularly because in some cases the temporary suspension became indefinite when the court subsequently refused or failed to proceed with the case.

CONSEQUENCE OF THE *KILLETS* DECISION

When the Supreme Court decided that the federal courts, in the absence of permissive legislation by Congress, were without power to suspend sentence, some 2,000 convicted offenders previously released on unauthorized federal suspensions were pardoned by the President on the Court's recommendation.

As far as the United States is concerned, the matter was resolved in 1916 in the so-called ***Killetts* case,** in which the Supreme Court held that the federal courts have no power to suspend indefinitely the imposition or execution of a sentence.[12] The Court recognized that the temporary suspension of imposition or execution of sentence was frequently resorted to in both England and the colonies because errors in the trial or miscarriage of justice could not be corrected by granting a new trial or by appeal under the existing system. Many of these temporary suspensions became indefinite because of a court's failure to proceed further in a criminal case. The Supreme Court pointed out, however, that

> neither of these conditions serve to convert the mere exercise of a judicial discretion to temporarily suspend for the accomplishment of a purpose contemplated by law into the existence of an arbitrary judicial power to permanently refuse to enforce the law.[13]

The Court went on to hold that the practice was inconsistent with the Constitution because

> its exercise in the very nature of things amounts to a refusal by the judicial power to perform the duty resting on it, and, as a consequence thereof, to an interference with both the legislative and executive authority as fixed by the Constitution.[14]

Suspended Sentence and Probation

The Supreme Court indicated, somewhat inconsistently, that Congress had adequate power to authorize both temporary and indefinite suspension by statute. An earlier New York court had, indeed, upheld the power of a court to suspend sentences indefinitely where this right had been conferred upon the court by statute.[15] The *Killets* case recognized the right of the legislative authority to grant the power of indefinite suspension to the courts by making probation as now defined and practiced in the United States largely a creature of statute.

The early controversy about the court's authority to suspend sentence has also resulted in differing ideas about the relationship between probation and suspended sentence. Depending upon the jurisdiction, four views are commonly held:

1. Probation may be granted on suspension of imposition of sentence.
2. Probation may be granted on suspension of imposition or of execution of sentence.
3. Suspended sentence is probation.
4. Probation does not have the suspended sentence aspect.

Supporting the fourth view, the *American Bar Association Standards Relating to Probation* states that probation should not involve or require suspension of any other sentence.[16] The matter is also complicated by the problem of whether probation itself is a sentence and by the varying definitions of "conviction." In 1984 the federal Sentencing Reform Act[17] abolished the authority of U.S. courts to suspend the imposition or execution of sentence in order to impose a term of probation. Instead, the act recognized probation as a sentence in itself.

Suspended Sentence as "Conviction"

Conviction has two definitions. By the narrow definition, which follows popular usage, conviction denotes a plea, finding, or verdict of guilt. By the broad definition, it is a plea, finding, or verdict of guilt followed by a final judgment of conviction and sentence. Conviction in the narrow sense is followed by the imposition of criminal sanctions, but a determination of guilt is not accompanied by loss of civil rights and privileges. Conviction in the broad sense is followed by the imposition of criminal sanctions *and* loss of civil rights and privileges.

Whether there is a conviction if sentence is suspended often turns on the question of what is suspended. A conviction is more likely reached if the execution—rather than the imposition—of sentence has been suspended, although this is not always true.

EARLY PROBATION

The increasing awareness that prisons were not accomplishing their stated purpose of reforming the offender and that suspension of sentence without supervision was not a satisfactory alternative brought about the development of probation as we know it today. Although judges such as **Peter Oxenbridge Thacher** in Massachusetts introduced probation-like practices such as recognizance and suspension of sentence in the early 19th century, the credit for founding probation is reserved for John Augustus, a

PETER OXENBRIDGE THACHER

Massachusetts judge who introduced probation-like practices in the early 19th century.

Boston bootmaker, and Matthew Davenport Hill, an English lawyer who held the judicial position of Recorder of Birmingham.

The development of probation in England has been traced to specialized practices for dealing with young offenders. Some judges sentenced youthful offenders to a term of one day on the condition that they return "to the care of their parents or master, to be by him more carefully watched and supervised in the future."[18] **Matthew Davenport Hill** had witnessed this practice as a young attorney, and when he became the Recorder of Birmingham (a judicial post), he employed a similar practice when he perceived "that the individual was not wholly corrupt—when there was reasonable hope of reformation—and when there could be found persons to act as guardians kind enough to take charge of the young convict."[19] Under Hill's direction, police officers visited the guardians from time to time, "recording the progress of the offender and keeping a regular account."[20]

MATTHEW DAVENPORT HILL

As Recorder of Birmingham (England) established probation-like practices with young offenders.

It was not until 1887 that a probation law was adopted in England that authorized the use of recognizance for first offenders. It did not provide for special conditions of probation or for supervision of those released.

It is generally agreed that the first true probation law was enacted in the United States in 1878. This legislation grew out of the work of **John Augustus,** the first person to apply the term *probation* to his new method. For this reason he is regarded as the "Father of Probation," and probation is said to be of U.S. origin.[21] Augustus was a member of the Washington Total Abstinence Society, an organization devoted to the promotion of temperance.[22] In August 1841 this interest led him to bail out a "common drunkard" by permission of the Boston Police Court. Augustus later wrote of this first "probationer" in his journal, which appeared in 1852:

JOHN AUGUSTUS

The "father of probation."

> He was ordered to appear for sentence in three weeks from that time. He signed the pledge and became a sober man; at the expiration of this period of probation, I accompanied him into the court room; his whole appearance was changed and no one, not even the scrutinizing officers, could have believed that he was the same person who less than a month before had stood trembling on the prisoner's stand.[23]

It is evident that he viewed probation as a selective process, although his first probationer was selected on his behavior, his manner of speech, and his protestation of a "firm resolve to quit liquor." In his journal Augustus wrote the following:

> Great care was observed, of course, to ascertain whether the prisoners were promising subjects for probation, and to this end it was necessary to take into consideration the previous character of the person, his age, and the influences by which he would in [the] future be likely to be surrounded.[24]

John Augustus continued his work in the Boston courts for 18 years, during which he received some financial aid from other citizens of the community interested in the offender. His journal reports that of the first 1,100 probationers on whom he kept records, only one forfeited bond. As to reformation, he stated that if "only one-half of this number have become reformed, I have ample cause to be satisfied."[25]

As is true today, probation was not universally accepted. Augustus repeated over and over that "the object of the law is to reform criminals and to prevent crime, and not to punish maliciously or from a spirit of revenge," and he did not hesitate to castigate the police, the judges, and others who did not share his views.[26] As a result, a newspaper of the time described him as a "fellow who is called John Augustus" who "seems to have a great itching for notoriety, and dollars" and "hangs and loafs about the Police and Municipal Courts, almost every day, and takes more airs upon himself than all the judges and officers."[27] The newspaper continued:

> We know something about this Peter Funk Philanthropist, and peanut reformer, and unless he conducts himself henceforth with a great deal more propriety, we shall take it upon ourself to teach him decency.[28]

John Augustus and his immediate successors were not officials of the court and hence lacked official status, although Massachusetts had passed a law in 1689 that authorized an agent of the State Board of Charities to investigate cases of children tried before the criminal courts. In 1878, almost 20 years after the death of John Augustus, adult probation in Massachusetts was sanctified by statute. A law was passed authorizing the mayor of Boston to appoint a paid probation officer to serve in the Boston criminal courts as a member of the police force. For the first time the probation officer was recognized as an official agent of the court. The statute made probation available to "such persons as may reasonably be expected to be reformed without punishment." No other restrictions were inserted. Probation was thus available in the city of Boston to men and women, felons and misdemeanants, and juveniles and adults, regardless of the nature of the offense or the amount or kind of punishment assessed.

Early Probation Legislation—State

Statewide probation was first enacted in Massachusetts in 1891 with a provision that appears in many modern statutes: that the probation officer should not be an active member of the regular police force. Although this early legislation provided for probation officers, it did not specifically give courts the power to grant probation. Missouri in 1897 and Vermont in 1898 remedied this omission, although the Missouri statute was labeled "an Act relating to the parole of prisoners" and used the words *probation* and *parole* interchangeably.

Several other states passed probation laws in the late 19th and early 20th centuries. The statutes varied in their provisions. Illinois and Minnesota provided for juvenile probation only; Rhode Island placed restrictions on eligibility and excluded persons guilty of certain offenses. Some states provided for statewide probation, while others followed the example set by Vermont in adopting the county plan.[29]

Early Probation—Federal

As we have noted, the Supreme Court held in 1916 that the federal courts had no inherent power to suspend indefinitely the imposition or execution of a sentence.[30] The Court indicated, however, that the power to suspend sentence could be given to the courts by statute.[31] Between 1916 and 1925, several attempts were made to pass laws authorizing federal judges to grant probation. In the closing days of the session in 1925, Congress enacted the National Probation Act, which authorized each federal district court, except in the District of Columbia, to appoint one salaried probation officer. In 1930 judges were empowered to appoint without reference to the civil service list, and the limitation of one officer to each district was removed. The attorney general was charged with the duty of coordinating the probation system, and probation officers were given certain duties with respect to parolees. The objectives of the probation law were stated by Chief Justice Taft as follows:

> The great desideratum was the giving to young and new violators of law a chance to reform and to escape the contaminating influence of association with hardened or veteran criminals in the beginning of imprisonment. Probation is the attempted saving of a man who has

> taken one wrong step and whom the judge thinks to be a brand who can be plucked from the burning at the time of imposition of sentence.[32]

By virtue of the statute, the courts in the federal system had (until 1984) the power to suspend the imposition or execution of sentence. By 1925 probation was authorized by statutes in all 48 states, and it is now so authorized in all 50 states and in the federal system.

Early Probation—Juvenile

There is a tendency to think of juvenile probation only in connection with a juvenile court. Since the first juvenile court and apparently the use of the term *juvenile delinquency* were established in Illinois in 1899, some writers trace the development of juvenile probation from that date. However, as we have seen previously, some English courts put into practice many of the principles, characteristics, and procedures that today we equate with juvenile courts long before any separate tribunals for the handling of juveniles were established in the United States.

As early as 1630 a guidebook that sanctioned special treatment of juveniles was prepared for justices of the peace in England. One provision read as follows:

> And yet if an infant shall commit larceny, and shall be found guilty thereof before the Justice of the Peace, it shall not be amiss for them to respite the judgment and so hath it often beene [sic] done by the Judges.[33]

A report of criminal trials from the Old Bailey Sessions in London, 1686–93, contains an account of the trial of Chollis Searl, "a little youth, aged about twelve years," who was acquitted of picking pockets in a proceeding that would be familiar in today's juvenile courts.[34] One of the justices of the peace for the county of Warwick, writing between 1820 and 1827, proposed the appointment of legal guardians to children without supervision to supply the place of their own relatives.

Between 1866 and 1871 a boy's "beadle" or "persuader" was employed as an unofficial probation officer by the Reformatory and Refuge Union in London. In 1881 an article on the "Massachusetts Method of Dealing with Juvenile Offenders," which advocated placing them on probation, was given wide publicity by the Howard Association of London.

Although the need for separate treatment of juveniles was recognized in the early 19th century in the United States, special children's institutions developed more rapidly than did special procedures and separate courts. Unfortunately, many of the special institutions came to be nothing more than children's prisons, and a system of contracting the labor of the children to private employers led to extremely harsh treatment and outright exploitation of children's labor. To protect children from this exploitation, late in the 19th century the New York Children's Aid Society shipped wholesale lots of Manhattan street urchins to farmers in the West; otherwise, they would have been committed to the House of Refuge. In 1890 the Children's Aid Society of Pennsylvania offered to place in foster homes delinquents who would otherwise be sent to reform school. Known as *placing out,* this practice was an early form of juvenile probation.[35] The system of apprenticeship was another early form of probation of children. It was used chiefly to detach poor children from their parents and attach them to masters who would teach them a trade.

The First Juvenile Court

The **Illinois Juvenile Court Act of 1899** combined the Massachusetts and New York systems of probation with several New York laws to provide delinquents with special court sessions and separate detention facilities.[36] In an article that appeared in the *Harvard Law Review* in 1909, Julian W. Mack declared that juvenile court legislation

> has assumed two aspects. In Great Britain and in New York, and in a few other jurisdictions, the protection [of children] is accomplished by suspending sentence and releasing the child under probation, or, in case of removal from the home, sending it to school instead of to a jail or penitentiary. But in Illinois, and following the lead of Illinois, in most jurisdictions, the form of proceeding is totally different. Proceedings are brought to have a guardian or representative of the state appointed to look after the child, to have the state intervene between the natural parent and child because the child needs it, as evidenced by some of its acts, and because the parent is either unwilling or unable to train the child properly.[37]

ILLINOIS JUVENILE COURT ACT OF 1899

Established the first juvenile court in the United States.

Mack continued with an analysis of the main principles of juvenile court legislation. The first was that child offenders should be kept separate from adult criminals and should receive a treatment differentiated to suit their special needs. That is, the courts should be agencies for the rescue as well as the punishment of children. The second principle was that parents of offenders must be made to feel more responsible for their children's wrongdoing. Third, no matter what offense they have committed, placing children in the common jails was an unsuitable penalty. The fourth principle stated that removing children from their parents and sending them even to an industrial school should as far as possible be avoided, and

> that when it is allowed to return home it should be under probation, subject to the guidance and friendly interest of the probation officer, the representative of the court. To raise the age of criminal responsibility from seven or ten to sixteen or eighteen without providing for an efficient system of probation, would indeed be disastrous. *Probation is, in fact, the keynote of juvenile court legislation.* [Emphasis added.][38]

Mack further related,

> Whenever juvenile courts have been established, a system of probation has been provided for, and even where as yet the juvenile court system has not been fully developed, some steps have been taken to substitute probation for imprisonment of the juvenile offender. What they need, more than anything else, is kindly assistance; and the aim of the court, appointing a probation officer for the child, is to have the child and the parents feel, not so much the power, as the friendly interest of the state; to show them that the object of the court is to help them to train the child right, and therefore the probation officers must be men and women fitted for these tasks.[39]

SUMMARY

Probation grew out of efforts to mitigate the harsh punishments demanded by early English law. At the time of Henry VIII more than 200 offenses were punishable by death, many of them relatively minor offenses against property. Judges interpreted statutes narrowly or failed to apply them. Juries placed lower value on stolen property (to bring the value below that which required imposition of the death penalty). Prosecutors dismissed charges or charged offenders with lesser offenses. Devices such as benefit of clergy, judicial reprieve, banishment, and sanctuary reduced the otherwise unrelenting severity of the penal code.

In the American colonies, where English law prevailed, distinct American practices developed. Filing, security for good behavior, recognizance, and suspension of imposition of sentence were procedures by which American judges exercised discretion to reduce the severity of punishment in cases where the circumstances of the crime or characteristics of the offender warranted leniency. These were the direct precursors of modern probation.

With the foundation laid by early judges in America and England, the later work of Matthew Davenport Hill, an English judge, and John Augustus, an American reformer, brought about the practice of probation as we know it today. The modern concept of probation depends on the power of the courts to suspend sentence. This power was the subject of much controversy in the early years of probation's use. The issue was eventually settled by the U.S. Supreme Court in the *Killets* case in 1916. In this case the Court held that courts did not have an inherent power to suspend sentences indefinitely, but that power might be granted to the judiciary by the legislature. This aspect of the *Killets* case—recognition of legislative authority to grant the power of indefinite suspension to the courts—made probation as now defined and practiced in the United States largely statutory.

Although most writers trace the origins of juvenile probation to the creation of the first American juvenile court in Chicago in 1899, English courts had put into practice many of its principles, characteristics, and procedures long before. As early as 1630 a guidebook for English justices of the peace recommended "respite of judgement" for crimes committed by "infants." Numerous accounts attest to procedures and practices of the 17th and 18th centuries that would be familiar to juvenile courts today. By 1899 the concept that crimes committed by children and those committed by adults should be dealt with differently, with special courts and special facilities for juveniles, was formalized by the creation of the first juvenile court in Illinois.

ENDNOTES

1. Edgardo Rotman, "The Failure of Reform," in *The Oxford History of the Prison,* ed. Norval Morris and David Rothman (New York: Oxford University Press, 1995), 71–197.
2. Sol Rubin, Henry Weihofen, George Edwards, and Simon Rosenzweig, *The Law of Criminal Corrections* (St. Paul: West, 1963), 16. They cite Stephen, *A History of the Criminal Law in England* (1883), 491–92.
3. Rubin et al, *The Law of Criminal Corrections.*
4. *Commonwealth v. Chase,* in *Thacher's Criminal Cases,* 267 (1831), recorded in vol. 11 of the *Records of the Old Municipal Court of Boston,* 199.
5. *Commonwealth v. Chase.*
6. Todd Clear and George Cole, *American Corrections* (Belmont, Calif.: Wadsworth, 1997), 178.
7. Sol Rubin advocated a greater use of suspended sentence without probation, arguing that this would provide an additional sentencing alternative of particular value in situations where apprehension and conviction have so thorough a corrective impact on the offender that supervision by probation is unnecessary. Sol Rubin, *The Law of Criminal Corrections,* 2nd ed. (St. Paul: West, 1973), 197–200.
8. *Mempa v. Rhay,* 389 U.S. 128, 88 S. Ct. 254, 19 L. Ed. 2d 336 (1967).

9. *Morrissey v. Brewer,* 408 U.S. 471, 92 S. Ct. 2593, 33 L. Ed. 2d 484 (1972).
10. *Gagnon v. Scarpelli,* 411 U.S. 778, 93 S. Ct. 1756, 36 L. Ed. 2d 656 (1973).
11. *Commonwealth v. Chase,* note 3.
12. *Ex parte* United States, 242 U.S. 27, 37 S. Ct. 72, 61 L. Ed. 129 (1916).
13. See note 12.
14. See note 12.
15. People *ex rel. Forsyth v. Court of Sessions,* 141 N.Y. 288, 36 N.E. 386 (1894).
16. ABA, *Standards, Probation* § 1.1(b) reads: "In this report, the term 'probation' means a sentence not involving confinement which imposes conditions and retains authority in the sentencing court to modify the conditions of the sentence or to resentence the offender if he violates the conditions. *Such a sentence should not involve or require suspension of the imposition or the execution of any other sentence.*" [Emphasis added.]
17. 18 U.S.C.A. § 3561.
18. Paul Tappan, *Crime, Justice, and Correction* (New York: McGraw-Hill, 1960), 542.
19. Tappan, *Crime, Justice, and Correction,* 542.
20. Tappan, *Crime, Justice, and Correction,* 542.
21. See John Augustus, *A Report of the Labors of John Augustus, for the Last Ten Years, in Aid of the Unfortunate* (Boston: Wright and Hasty, 1852); reprinted as *John Augustus, First Probation Officer* (New York: National Probation Association, 1939). See also this chapter's supplemental reading, "John Augustus: The First Probation Officer."
22. Augustus, *First Probation Officer.*
23. Augustus, *First Probation Officer.*
24. Augustus, *First Probation Officer,* 34.
25. Augustus, *First Probation Officer,* 96.
26. Augustus, *First Probation Officer,* 23.
27. Augustus, *First Probation Officer,* 78–79.
28. Augustus, *First Probation Officer,* 78–79.
29. *Attorney General's Survey, Digest,* vol. 1. (Washington, DC: 1938).
30. *Ex parte* United States, 242 U.S. 27, 37 S. Ct. 72, 61 L. Ed. 129 (1916).
31. See note 30.
32. *United States v. Murray,* 275 U.S. 347, 48 S. Ct. 146, 72 L. Ed. 309 (1928).
33. Frederic L. Faust and Paul J. Brantingham, *Juvenile Justice Philosophy* (St. Paul: West, 1974), 44.
34. Faust and Brantingham, *Juvenile Justice Philosophy,* 45.
35. Faust and Brantingham, *Juvenile Justice Philosophy,* 62.
36. Faust and Brantingham, *Juvenile Justice Philosophy,* 63.
37. Julian W. Mack, "The Juvenile Court," *Harvard Law Review* 23 (1909): 102, as quoted in Faust and Brantingham, *Juvenile Justice Philosophy,* 159–69.
38. Mack, "The Juvenile Court," 162.
39. Mack, "The Juvenile Court," 163.

DISCUSSION QUESTIONS

1. How did the existence of extremely harsh penal laws in early England influence the evolution of probation?
2. Explain benefit of clergy. What was its original purpose, and how did it come to be used?

3. Why is Psalm 51 referred to as the neck verse?
4. What was judicial reprieve? How is it related to modern probation?
5. Explain the use of filing and security for good behavior in the American colonies.
6. What is the importance for probation of the ruling in *Commonwealth v. Chase*?
7. What are the two kinds of suspended sentence? Why is the distinction critical to an understanding of modern probation?
8. What is the *Killets* case? What was its impact on modern probation?
9. Distinguish between the narrow and broad definitions of conviction. What consequences arise from each?
10. Who were Matthew Davenport Hill and John Augustus? What did each contribute to modern criminal justice practices?

John Augustus: The First Probation Officer

The first probation law in the new world was passed in Massachusetts in 1878. This law, Chapter 198, Acts in 1878, authorized the mayor of Boston to appoint from the police force or from the city at large a person to attend the criminal courts in Suffolk County, to investigate the cases of those charged with or convicted of crimes, and to recommend to the courts the placing on probation of those who might be reformed without punishment. The act provided for the compensation of the first statutory probation officer from public funds.

It is important to remember that the act of 1878 did not create probation or initiate the probation movement. It created no new judicial power but provided only for the appointment and payment of a special officer in order that the courts might exercise more fully and broadly what had become a well-established, well-recognized, approved usage. Defendants had been placed on probation in Boston as early as 1830. By judicial experiment and the use of volunteer probation officers, the probation movement came into being. In the act of 1878 the general court reflected public opinion that for nearly 50 years had favored placing defendants on probation.

The probation movement as it developed before legislation is the story of devoted men and women of Massachusetts, many of them volunteers, who saw in probation an opportunity for rehabilitation. Of these, John Augustus made the first great contribution.

When on an August day in 1841 John Augustus appeared in the police court of Boston and the court bailed into his custody a poor inebriate who would otherwise have been committed to jail, probation was ready for development. The courts were prepared, there was no lack of the human beings with whom probation is concerned, and John Augustus had the vision and the consecration necessary to give probation life.

Probation was not discovered by John Augustus; the idea was apparent in the enlightened legal thought of Boston judges in the decade before him. But there could be no real development of probation until, in addition to the legal thought and practice that made it possible, a demonstration showed its possibilities and value as a treatment process, which would gain the interest, understanding, and respect of the courts and of the public, and which would attract other workers to the field. John Augustus, the bootmaker of Boston, made such a demonstration from 1841 until his death in 1859. It was Augustus's practice to bail, after conviction, an offender in whom there was hope of reformation. The man would be ordered to appear before the court at a stated time, at which Augustus would accompany him to the courtroom. If the judge was satisfied with Augustus's account of his stewardship, the offender, instead of being committed to the House of Correction, would be fined one cent and costs. The one cent and costs, which generally amounted to three to four dollars, Augustus paid.

Who was John Augustus? What was it that took him from boot factory to the police court in 1841? How did he do his work? Who financed it? How was he received by the personnel of the courts, by the press, and by the people of Boston? What were his accomplishments?

John Augustus was born in Burlington, Massachusetts (then part of Woburn), in 1785. About 1806 he moved to Lexington and carried on a shoe manufactory in part of his home. He apparently prospered, as he owned a large tract of land on both sides of Bedford Street. His old home, now renovated and restored at One Harrington Road and known as the Jonathan Harrington House, faces the Lexington Common.

Although John Augustus was in business in Boston as early as 1820, he continued to maintain his Lexington home and possibly his Lexington business until 1829, when the *Boston Directory* lists him as living in Boston on Chambers Street. It was in his shop at 5 Franklin Avenue near the police court, now only an alley, that Augustus received from 1841, according to his own account of his work, frequent calls from those who sought his help. His business there suffered owing to the time he was required to spend away from it bailing people in the courts or attending to their needs elsewhere.

All of Augustus's residences from 1841 on are of particular interest because as soon as he began his work in the courts, his home became a refuge for people he had bailed until more permanent plans could be made for them. From 1845 until his death in 1859, Augustus lived at 65 Chambers Street, in the West End of Boston. Nothing remains today of this old house.

There can be no doubt it was the Washingtonian temperance reform movement that led Augustus to the police court and later to the municipal court in Boston. It was the conviction of the Washingtonians that drunkards could be saved through understanding, kindness, and moral suasion rather than through commitment to prison.

The movement resulted in the formation of the Washington Total Abstinence Society in Boston on April 25, 1841. Its members pledged not only not to use intoxicating liquors themselves but to reclaim and to restore to temperance those who were addicted to drunkenness.

The members were soon in the police court doing the work to which they were pledged; and some of them were there before Augustus, as the first quarterly report of the society's auditor, published in July 1841, indicates:

> I take this opportunity, in the name, and in behalf of this Society, of tendering to the Justices and Clerks of the Police Court, my hearty thanks for their kindness in affording (as far as consistent with duty) every facility to our members in their attempts to rescue and bring back to the paths of temperance, the *poor, forsaken, heartbroken* Drunkard, who came under their cognizance. Many, very many, have been taken from this Court and restored to their families and friends, who do not appear in the Reports from the Houses of Correction and Industry. Thus it will be seen that a heavy expense has been saved to the city, and many a person has been brought back to usefulness, unknown to the public.

The First Probationer

Let Augustus describe in his own words the moving story of his first probationer:

> In the month of August, 1841, I was in court one morning, when the door communicating with the lock-room was opened and an officer entered, followed by a ragged and wretched looking man, who took his seat upon the bench allotted to prisoners. I imagined from the man's appearance that his offence was that of yielding to his appetite for intoxicating drinks, and in a few moments I found that my suspicions were correct, for the clerk read the complaint, in which the man was charged with being a common drunkard. The case was clearly made out, but before sentence had been passed, I conversed with him a few moments, and found that he was not yet past all hope and reformation, although his appearance and his looks precluded a belief in the minds of others that he would ever become a *man* again. He told me that if he could be saved from the House of Correction, he never again would taste intoxicating liquors; there was such an earnestness in that tone, and a look expressive of firm resolve, that I determined to aid him; I bailed him, by permission of the Court. He was ordered to appear for sentence in three weeks from that time. He signed the pledge and became a sober man; at the expiration of this period of probation, I accompanied him into the court room; his whole appearance was changed and no one, not even the scrutinizing officers, could have believed that he was the same person who less than a month before, had stood trembling on the prisoner's stand. The Judge expressed himself much pleased with the account we gave of the man, and instead of the usual penalty—imprisonment in the House of Correction—he fined him *one cent and costs,* amounting in all to $3.76, which was immediately paid. The man continued industrious and sober, and without doubt has been, by this treatment, saved from a drunkard's grave.[1]

With this encouragement, Augustus continued to appear in court to receive on probation alcoholics who appeared likely prospects for reformation, to rehabilitate them and then to return with them to court for a report on their progress. By January 1842 he had bailed 17 other alcoholics. His real consecration to this work occurred in August 1842, when he could say

> I had labored about a year when it became evident that much, much good had been and might be performed, by laboring in the field in which I had commenced operations, and to promote this object, several kind and philanthropic individuals placed in my hands donations of various sums, which enabled me to accomplish a much greater amount of good than I could have done from my own limited means alone.

From this time on, Augustus's record is one of dedication to a cause, understood by some and misunderstood by others, to which he devoted the remainder of his life, much of his own financial resources, as well as the money contributed by Boston people. John Augustus set the general pattern to be followed by succeeding voluntary and official probation officers. During the first year, Augustus bailed only men, but thereafter, year by year until 1859, his probationers were men, women, boys, and girls whose offenses represented every bailable crime.

When in December 1851 John Augustus consulted his records preparatory to publishing an account of his labors in behalf of unfortunates during the preceding ten years, he found he had bailed in the police or municipal courts 1,102 persons, 674 males and 428 females. He had become bail for them to the amount of $19,464, and he had paid $2,417.65 for fines and costs.

Although this alone may be considered an impressive record, he continued such work in the courts for about seven and one-half years more; in addition, he responded to calls for assistance from many in need of social services who were not court offenders. Up to 1858 we know that he had bailed 1,946 persons, 1,152 males and 794 women and girls.

Opposition to Be Overcome

In the conduct of his work inside and outside the court, John Augustus faced opposition, misunderstanding, and even physical abuse. Charges were made that he was profiting financially from those whom he bailed even though many of

1. John Augustus, *A Report of the Labors of John Augustus, for the Last Ten Years, in Aid of the Unfortunate* (Boston: Wright and Hasty, 1852), reprinted as *John Augustus, First Probation Officer* (New York: National Probation Association, 1939).

them were so poor they were unable to pay the fine and costs. Much of the opposition and misunderstanding he gradually overcame. Some of it remained, and Augustus expressed it in words that have been used in reference to probation from time to time up to this day:

> There is, however, much opposition to the plan of bailing on probation. Those who are opposed to this method tell us that it is rather an incentive to crime and, therefore, instead of proving salutary, it is detrimental to the interest of society, and so far from having a tendency to reform the person bailed, it rather presents inducements for them to continue a career of crime; the law is robbed of its terrors, and its punishments, and there is nothing, therefore, to deter them from repeating the offense with which they were previously charged.

To such thinking, Augustus replied

> The premise upon which such reasoning is based is incorrect. Individuals and communities generally are but too prone to infer evil of a class, if they but occasionally observe it in individuals; if a person who has been bailed, or received the leniency of the court, proves false to his promises of amendment, people are ever ready to predict that all others will conduct in a similar manner; and this they persist in believing, although instances are very frequent, even three to one, where such persons have become good citizens, and regain their former station and relation in society. I shall leave the matter for others to discuss and decide, but I am content, feeling as I do, that by such humane means hundreds of the fallen have been raised even by my humble instrumentality.

Augustus varied his answers to his critics. To some he said that for each person bailed to him, a commitment to a house of correction was prevented. To those who understood social progress and justice only in terms of a dollar saved, he pointed out that the public was saved the greater expense of caring for the person in jail. When he was charged with cheating the jails of their rightful tenants, he replied that his form of treatment was more effective; that it saved the offender for his family and for society and did not disgrace him forever as a commitment would. How modern is the sound of some of these charges that Augustus had to answer!

It was the court officers—the clerk, the turnkeys, and the process servers—who were the first to oppose Augustus and who remained strongest in their opposition. Because their financial security was threatened in every case for which Augustus became bail, they lost no time or opportunity to show their displeasure over his work. For every person bailed by Augustus, the officer lost the fee of either 75 cents or 62 cents payable on the taking of the offender to jail; the clerk lost 25 cents, and the turnkey was out 40 cents. But Augustus was not deterred.

Although the opposition of the court officers was discouraging, the judges and the press were friendly, and influential people in the community gave him both moral and financial support.

Securing Funds

There is no evidence that Augustus was anything more than a man of limited means. To accomplish the work he felt called to do, more money was necessary than he could provide alone. Much of it had to come from others. It did not come, as was charged, from his probationers. In December 1851 Augustus wrote

> The first two years, 1841–42, I received nothing from any one except what I earned by my daily labor; in 1843, I received from various persons in aid of my work, seven hundred and fifty-eight dollars; in 1844–45–46, I received twelve hundred and thirteen dollars each year. I then gave up business at my shop, and for the last five years, my receipts have averaged, yearly, seventeen hundred and seventy-six dollars, all of which I have expended, and have not a dollar of this sum. The money which I have thus received came from kind friends to the cause in which I was engaged.

The busy life of the first career man in the field of probation came to a close on June 21, 1859. The morning after his death, the *Boston Herald* summed up the meaning of his life and work in these words:

> DEATH OF A WELL-KNOWN CITIZEN
>
> Mr. John Augustus died at his residence in Chambers Street, this city, last evening after a somewhat protracted and lingering illness, superinduced by old age and a general prostration of the system from overtaxation of its powers. The deceased was well known in this community in connection with his benevolent exertions in behalf of poor criminals, the latter years of his life being almost entirely spent in ameliorating their condition by becoming bondsman for their good behavior, and providing means and opportunities that would tend to a reformation. . . . Possessed of a living income from means accumulated in business pursuits, the deceased was in a position to carry out the dictates of a generous heart, and those who knew him best give him credit for sincerity of purpose, although there are many who saw nothing in his conduct toward criminals that was not the offspring of selfish motives. Undoubtedly, Mr. Augustus was the means of doing much good in his daily walks through our courts and penal institutions, and a charitable community will not be backward in revering his memory with this fact in remembrance.

Source: Excerpted from a paper presented by John Moreland at the 35th Annual Conference of the National Probation Association, Boston, Mass., May 29, 1941.

2

THE DECISION TO GRANT PROBATION

KEY TERMS

Regular probation
Intensive supervision probation
Electronic surveillance
Deferred adjudication
Pretrial diversion
Net-widening
Sentencing
Sentence
Privilege theory
Model Adult Community Corrections Act
Presentence investigation report
Right of allocation
Sentencing guidelines

What You Will Learn in This Chapter

You will learn the various types of probation, including regular probation, intensive supervision probation, deferred adjudication, and pretrial diversion. We will examine the factors that affect the decision to grant probation. Variations in sentencing policy will also be addressed in terms of their effect on the decision to grant or deny probation.

INTRODUCTION

In recent years the United States has responded to the public's fear of crime by incarcerating more offenders for longer periods. Prisoners are entering our prisons and jails in record numbers. Every week over 1600 new prison beds are needed—the equivalent of 50 large, new prisons each year.[1] By June 1996 the nation's prison population had risen to 1.16 million, an increase of 5.3 percent over 1995. Federal and state prisons and local jail authorities held in their custody 615 persons per 100,000 population in the United States—up from 461 per 100,000 in 1990.[2] A recent report by the Edna McConnell Clark Foundation revealed that a greater percentage of convicted felons are being imprisoned than ever before in our nation's history and that at the same time, budget limitations have made it impossible to build prisons fast enough to keep pace with the influx of new inmates.[3] The report concluded,

> Billions of taxpayer dollars are spent each year to support the burgeoning corrections industry, and yet, crime and the uncertainty of what to do with those who commit crime, remains. The problem is vexing and persistent.[4]

Many incorrectly assume that growth in prison populations will result in fewer persons under supervision in the community and that those remaining in the community will have become increasingly less serious and in need of less supervision. Unfortunately, this is not true.[5] In fact, the number of convicted offenders sentenced to probation grew nearly as fast as the prison population, totaling 3.09 million on January 1, 1996. (See Table 2.1).[6] Over one-half were on probation for a felony.

Judging by prior criminal records, current conviction crimes, and substance abuse histories, it is apparent that the crimes of the population of persons sentenced to probation supervision have become increasingly serious. The truth is that the overall U.S. population has grown, more citizens are being convicted, and all correctional populations have grown simultaneously.[7] (See Table 2.2 and Table 2.3.)

Despite the fact that over two-thirds of all convicted offenders are on probation or some other form of community corrections supervision, little attention or public discourse is directed at the community corrections process. Politicians and governmental officials find that it is more politically attractive to seek resources for prosecutors, police, and prisons than to appear to be "soft on crime" by proposing more support for community-based programs such as probation.[8]

The little attention that is focused on probation tends to be negative. Probation has been seriously criticized as lenient and as a threat to public safety. Some of these criticisms are warranted—not so much due to the unviability of probation as a correctional tool, but because the population of persons sentenced to probation is

Table 2.1 **ADULTS ON PROBATION, 1995**

Region and jurisdiction	Beginning probation population, 1/1/95	DURING 1995 Entries	Exits	Ending probation population, 12/31/95	Percent change in probation population during 1995	Number on probation on 12/31/95 per 100,000 adult residents
U.S. total	2,981,400	1,501,589	1,381,636	3,090,626	3.7%	1,593
Federal	42,309	18,601	22,404	38,506	9.0%	20
State	2,939,091	1,482,988	1,359,232	3,052,120	3.8%	1,573
Northeast	526,375	232,686	214,444	544,620	3.5%	1,402
Connecticut	53,453	37,135	36,081	54,507	2.0%	2,201
Maine	8,638			8,641		923
Massachusetts	46,670	34,611	37,601	43,680	–6.4%	941
New Hampshire	4,323	3,432	3,408	4,347	0.6%	509
New Jersey	125,299	59,376	57,552	127,123	1.5%	2,125
New York	163,613	45,061	35,175	173,499	6.0%	1,276
Pennsylvania	99,524	39,764	32,465	106,823	7.3%	1,166
Rhode Island	18,179	9,813	9,314	18,678	2.7%	2,483
Vermont	6,676	3,494	2,848	7,322	9.7%	1,672
Midwest	642,924	341,567	316,851	671,094	4.4%	1,472
Illinois	104,664	63,862	61,723	109,489	4.6%	1,258
Indiana	83,555			83,555		1,936
Iowa	15,902	10,456	9,779	16,579	4.3%	783
Kansas	17,256	11,831	7,726	16,547	–4.1%	884
Michigan	142,640	68,000	62,338	148,377	4.0%	2,110
Minnesota	81,972	55,911	57,131	83,778	2.2%	2,490
Missouri	36,295	21,887	18,453	40,595	11.8%	1,030
Nebraska	18,639	15,485	14,697	19,427	4.2%	1,627
North Dakota	2,036	1,474	1,219	2,291	12.5%	486
Ohio	90,190	68,077	59,558	99,603	10.4%	1,201
South Dakota	3,874	4,393	4,643	3,624	–6.5%	693
Wisconsin	45,901	20,191	19,584	47,269	3.0%	1,254
South	1,214,375	618,343	573,402	1,254,817	3.3%	1,846
Alabama	31,284	4,696	4,498	31,416	0.4%	990
Arkansas	19,606	8,431	5,656	22,381	14.2%	1,220
Delaware	15,507	7,395	6,555	16,347	5.4%	3,036

Table 2.1 **ADULTS ON PROBATION, 1995**

Region and jurisdiction	Beginning probation population, 1/1/95	DURING 1995		Ending probation population, 12/31/95	Percent change in probation population during 1995	Number on probation on 12/31/95 per 100,000 adult residents
		Entries	Exits			
South—*Continued*						
District of Columbia	11,306	4,733	5,777	10,262	–9.2%	2,334
Florida	247,014	146,989	133,585	255,550	3.5%	2,367
Georgia	140,694	69,102	67,228	142,453	1.3%	2,699
Kentucky	11,417	2,558	5,500	11,499	0.7%	398
Louisiana	33,604	11,431	11,282	33,753	0.4%	1,088
Maryland	76,940	35,530	41,441	71,029	–7.7%	1,884
Mississippi	9,042	3,511	2,958	9,595	6.1%	496
North Carolina	90,418	49,804	42,301	97,921	8.3%	1,815
Oklahoma	26,285	14,195	13,029	27,866	6.0%	1,161
South Carolina	40,005	16,643	14,482	42,166	5.4%	1,545
Tennessee	34,896	20,431	18,594	36,733	5.3%	931
Texas	396,276	200,365	181,144	415,497	4.9%	3,119
Virginia	24,089	19,394	19,219	24,264	0.7%	485
West Virginia	5,992	111	153	6,085	1.6%	433
West	555,417	290,392	254,535	581,589	4.7%	1,397
Alaska	2,899	960	1,296	2,563	–11.6%	619
Arizona	34,365	15,514	10,728	32,532	–5.3%	1,076
California	277,655	142,560	133,229	286,986	3.4%	1,259
Colorado	39,065	25,042	21,840	42,010	7.5%	1,519
Hawaii	13,088	6,620	6,385	13,323	1.8%	1,518
Idaho	5,770	6,110	5,711	6,169	5.9%	757
Montana	5,656	2,022	1,833	5,845	3.3%	922
Nevada	9,410	6,043	5,377	10,076	7.1%	890
New Mexico	8,063	7,727	7,514	8,276	2.6%	698
Oregon	38,086	13,397	11,758	39,725	4.3%	1,695
Utah	7,714	4,136	3,372	8,478	9.9%	664
Washington	110,279	58,476	43,640	122,306	10.9%	3,048
Wyoming	3,367	1,785	1,852	3,300	–2.0%	960

Source: Bureau of Justice Statistics, *Correctional Population in the United States, 1995* (U.S. Department of Justice, 1997).

Figure 2.1 **NUMBER OF PERSONS UNDER SUPERVISION PER 100,000 ADULT U.S. RESIDENTS**

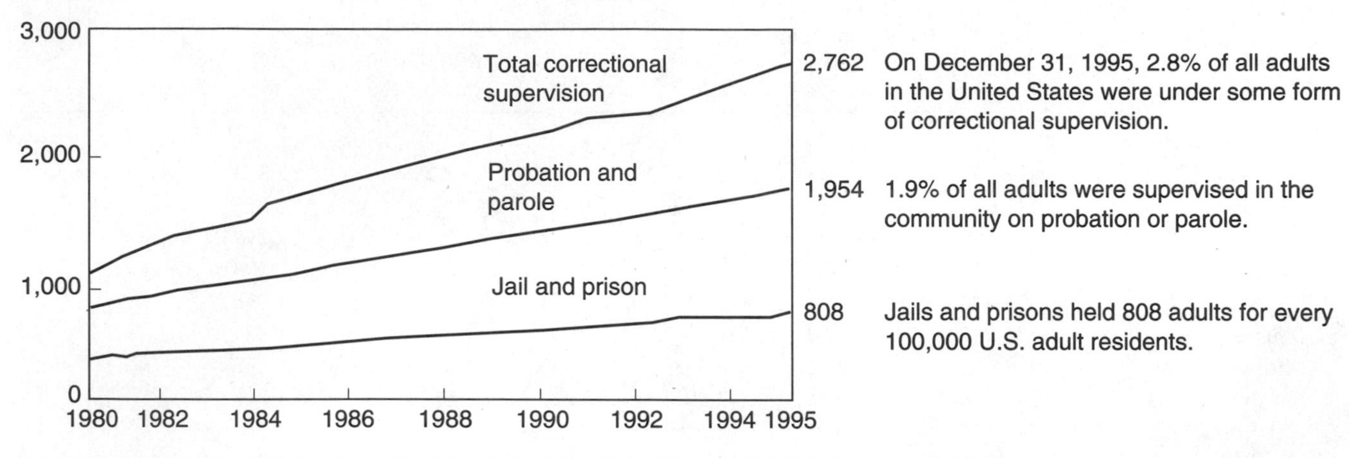

Source: Bureau of Justice Statistics, *Correctional Population in the United States, 1995* (U.S. Department of Justice, 1997).

Table 2.2 **ADULTS UNDER COMMUNITY SUPERVISION OR INCARCERATED, 1980–95**

Year	Total estimated correctional population	COMMUNITY SUPERVISION		Incarcerated	Percentage of U.S. adults under supervision
		Probation	Parole		
1980	1,840,400	1,118,097	220,438	501,886	1.1%
1985	3,011,500	1,968,712	300,203	742,579	1.7%
1990	4,348,000	2,670,234	531,407	1,146,401	2.3%
1991	4,535,600	2,728,472	590,442	1,216,664	2.4%
1992	4,762,600	2,811,611	658,601	1,292,347	2.5%
1993	4,944,000	2,903,061	676,100	1,364,881	2.6%
1994	5,147,100	2,981,400	690,371	1,475,329	2.7%
1995	5,357,800	3,090,626	700,174	1,567,000	2.8%
Percentage change					
1994–95	4%	4%	1%	6%	
1980–95	191%	176%	218%	212%	
Annual average change					
1990–95	4%	3%	6%	6%	
1980–95	7%	7%	8%	8%	

Source: Bureau of Justice Statistics, *Correctional Population in the United States, 1995* (U.S. Department of Justice, 1997).

Table 2.3 **NUMBER OF INMATES HELD IN STATE OR FEDERAL PRISONS OR IN LOCAL JAILS, 1985, 1990–95**

		NUMBER OF STATE AND FEDERAL PRISONERS ON DECEMBER 31			
Year	Total inmates in custody	Jurisdiction	Custody	Number of inmates held in local jails on June 30th	Incarceration rate, 1995
1985	744,208	502,507	487,593	256,615	313
1990	1,148,702	773,919	743,382	405,320	461
1991	1,219,014	825,559	792,535	426,479	483
1992	1,295,150	882,500	850,566	444,584	508
1993	1,369,185	969,301	909,381	459,804	528
1994	1,478,086	1,055,073	991,612	486,474	562
1995	1,585,401	1,127,132	1,078,357	507,044	600
Percentage change, 1994–95		**7.3%**	**6.8%**	**8.7%**	**4.2%**
Percentage change, 1985–95		**113.0%**	**124.3%**	**121.2%**	**97.6%**
Annual average increase, 1985–95		**7.9%**	**8.4%**	**8.3%**	**7.0%**

Source: Bureau of Justice Statistics, *Correctional Population in the United States, 1995* (U.S. Department of Justice, 1997).

growing rapidly while resources and funding have not kept pace. Only 11 cents of every correctional dollar is directed to probation and parole, although they account for over 70 percent of all persons under correctional supervision. Due to a lack of funding, probation caseloads are high and continue to grow larger. While most correctional authorities agree that a probation officer should not supervise more than 50 probationers, national averages now exceed 115 cases per officer (see Figure 2.2). In some areas the number is even higher. Petersilia reports that 60 percent of all Los Angeles probationers are tracked solely by computer and have no contact with officers.[9] Further, as prison populations swell to the bursting point, more serious and potentially dangerous offenders are placed on probation by judges who have few alternatives due to lack of available prison beds.

The many problems faced by probation and other community-based correctional programs create a pressing need to focus on the role that community corrections can and should play in managing crime and criminal offenders. This chapter will examine various forms of probation and discuss how and when probation, rather than incarceration, is an appropriate sentence.

In 1995 the nation's prisons and jails held nearly 1.6 million inmates, or 600 inmates per 100,000 U.S. residents

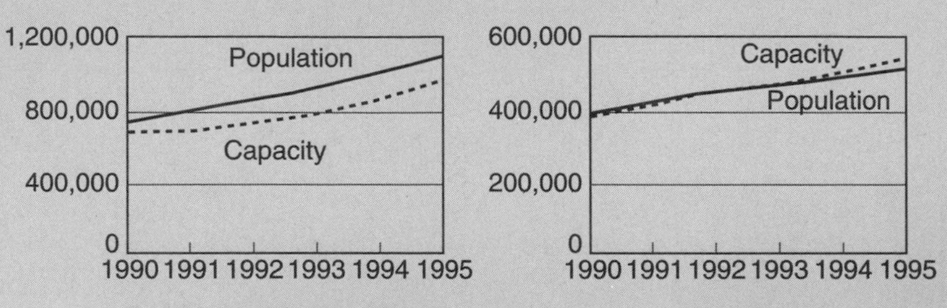

Federal and state prisons
(holding persons with longer sentences)

Local jails
(holding unconvicted persons and those with shorter sentences)

On December 31, 1995—

- 1,127,132 prisoners were under the jurisdiction of correctional authorities of the 50 states and the District of Columbia (together holding 1,026,882) and of the federal government (100,250).
- Over the 12 preceding months, the nation's prison population grew by 72,059 prisoners—an increase of 6.8% since yearend 1994.
- State prison systems were operating between 14% and 25% over their reported capacity; the federal system, 26% over the reported capacity.
- Nearly 30% of all prisoners in the United States were incarcerated in California (135,646), Texas (127,766), and New York (68,484).

On June 30, 1995—

- The nation's local jails held or supervised an estimated 541,913 persons. Of that total, 34,869 were in community supervision programs such as electronic monitoring, house detention, and day reporting.
- From midyear 1994, the number of persons held in local jails grew 4.2%—from 486,474 to 507,044.
- An estimated 7,888 juveniles (under age 18) were held in local jails, an increase of 17% from 12 months before. Over three-quarters were tried or awaiting trial as adults.
- Over the 12 preceding months, local jails added space for 41,439 inmates, an annual increase of 8%. This added space allowed local jails to operate at 7% below their rated capacity.

Source: C. Camp and G. Camp, *The Correction Yearbook, 1995.* (South Salem, NY: The Criminal Justice Institute, 1995).

Figure 2.2 **AVERAGE SIZE OF PROBATION AND PAROLE OFFICER'S CASELOADS DURING 1996**

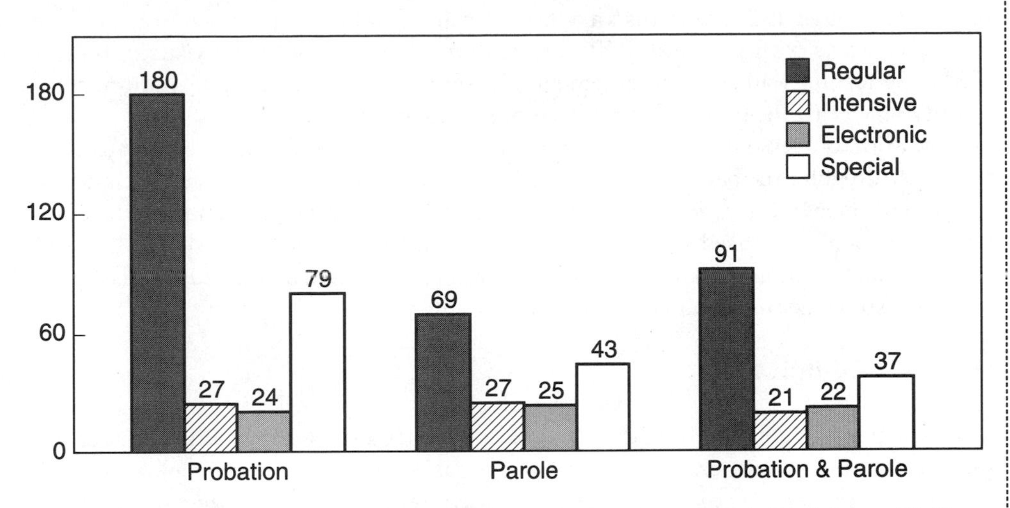

Source: C. Camp and G. Camp, *The Corrections Yearbook, 1997 Probation and Parole* (South Salem, NY: The Criminal Justice Institute, 1997), 22.

WHAT IS PROBATION?

Although there are no authoritative classifications by law, probation may be generally classified in four categories:[10]

1. Regular probation
2. Intensive supervision probation
3. Deferred adjudication probation
4. Pretrial diversion probation

Regular Probation

Regular probation can be defined as the release of a convicted offender under conditions imposed by the court for a specified period during which the court retains authority to modify the conditions of sentence or to resentence the offender if he or she violates the conditions. Regular probation is used in both misdemeanor and felony cases and is the type most often used, accounting for about 90 percent of all probation sentences.

REGULAR PROBATION

The release of a convicted offender by a court under court-imposed conditions for a specified period.

Intensive Supervision Probation

Intensive supervision probation, for offenders who are too antisocial for the relative freedom afforded by regular probation yet not so seriously criminal as to require incarceration, has sprung up around the country since 1980.[11] Intensive supervision probation in some form had been adopted nationwide by 1990. Although ISP was originally designed to enhance rehabilitation and to ensure public safety by affording greater contact between probation officers and probationers, the purposes of newer programs include those of reducing costs and alleviating prison overcrowding.

INTENSIVE SUPERVISION PROBATION (ISP)

A form of probation for offenders who require more structure and surveillance than ordinary probationers but for whom incarceration may be too severe a sanction. ISP involves considerable restrictions on the offender's freedom of movement and limits many other aspects of his or her autonomy.

Intensive supervision programs are also seen as "socially cost-effective" in that they are less likely to contribute to the breakup of offenders' families than incarceration, they allow offenders to remain employed, and they lack the stigmatizing effects of prison. Although ISP programs vary between jurisdictions, most require multiple weekly contacts with probation officers, random night and weekend visits, unscheduled drug testing, and strict enforcement of probation conditions. Many require community service restitution and some form of **electronic surveillance.**

Probation officers who work with ISP clients generally have smaller caseloads than those with regular probation clients. Smaller caseloads allow for greater assistance to the probationer in his or her rehabilitation efforts and greater protection to the community through increased surveillance and control. One writer has observed that ISP is what most communities want all probation to be.[12] A more detailed discussion of intensive supervision appears in chapter 11.

ELECTRONIC SURVEILLANCE

A correctional technology that involves the wearing, by a probationer or parolee, of an electronic device that allows authorities to verify his or her whereabouts.

Deferred Adjudication

Most states and the federal system also provide for **deferred adjudication** under the general probation statutes. In this form of probation, the court, after a plea of guilty or nolo contendere (French "do not wish to contend"), defers further proceedings without entering an adjudication of guilt and places the defendant on probation, usually ordering some form of community service and restitution. Defendants who successfully complete the probation term have their charges dropped. Failure to comply with the terms of the deferred adjudication agreement may result in incarceration.

DEFERRED ADJUDICATION

A form of probation that, after a plea of guilty or nolo contendere, defers further proceedings without an adjudication of guilt.

Pretrial Diversion

Pretrial diversion is another form of probation authorized by most states and in the federal system. Criminal sanctions would be excessive for many persons who come to the attention of the criminal justice system because of their need for treatment or supervision. Programs that provide these needed services without the stigma of criminal prosecution have proved quite attractive. Pretrial diversion is like deferred adjudication in that there is no finding of guilt. The difference is that probation is imposed *before* a plea of guilty in pretrial diversion, whereas deferred adjudication is imposed after a plea of guilty or nolo contendere.[13] Pretrial diversion has been criticized based on research indicating that many persons who are diverted would not have been arrested or prosecuted in the first place were it not for the existence of a diversion program. Such "net-widening" increases the number of persons involved in the criminal justice process.

PRETRIAL DIVERSION

A form of probation imposed before a plea of guilty that can result in dismissal of the charges. Pretrial diversion is used primarily with offenders who need treatment or supervision and for whom criminal sanctions would be excessive.

NET WIDENING

The tendency for social control mechanisms to encompass a larger (or different) population than originally planned.

THE DECISION TO GRANT PROBATION

Sentencing

Sentencing has long been considered the most difficult decision in the criminal justice process. **Sentencing** can be defined as the postconviction stage of the criminal process in which the defendant is brought before the court for the imposition of a sentence. A **sentence** is the formal judgment pronounced by a court or a judge after conviction that imposes some degree of punishment. Problems abound when the issue of fair, just sentencing is addressed. Sentencing demands choosing among a

SENTENCING

The postconviction stage of the criminal process in which the defendant is brought before the court for the imposition of a sentence.

SENTENCE

The formal judgment pronounced by a court or a judge after conviction that imposes some degree of punishment.

Convicted offender exercising her right of allocution at the sentencing hearing.

number of alternatives. Figure 2.3 illustrates the typical outcomes of 100 felony arrests brought by police for prosecution.

Sentencing decisions may be the most important decisions made in the criminal justice process. They are affected by the judge's sentencing philosophy, the types of sentences available, plea bargaining between the defendant and the prosecutor, recommendations of probation officers, and many other factors.

Factors That Affect The Probation Grant

The decision to grant probation to an individual offender must consider such factors as the following:

- the offender's eligibility for probation
- whether probation or incarceration is the preferred disposition
- the conditions of probation as fixed by statute
- the availability and quality of probation services
- the availability and quality of other sentencing dispositions
- the methods of developing sentencing information
- whether probation is appropriate for the offender

Eligibility for Probation

Courts have consistently held that probation is a privilege, not a right. The **privilege theory** considers probation a matter of grace and places the question of whether it should be granted in a particular instance entirely with the court. To phrase it differently, the decision to grant or withhold probation is a discretionary act of the trial court, and an offender has neither a constitutional nor statutory right to probation. Statutes provide for probation, however, and an eligible offender has the right to be

PRIVILEGE THEORY

Probation is a privilege, not a right.

Figure 2.3 **TYPICAL OUTCOME OF 100 FELONY ARRESTS BROUGHT BY POLICE FOR PROSECUTION**

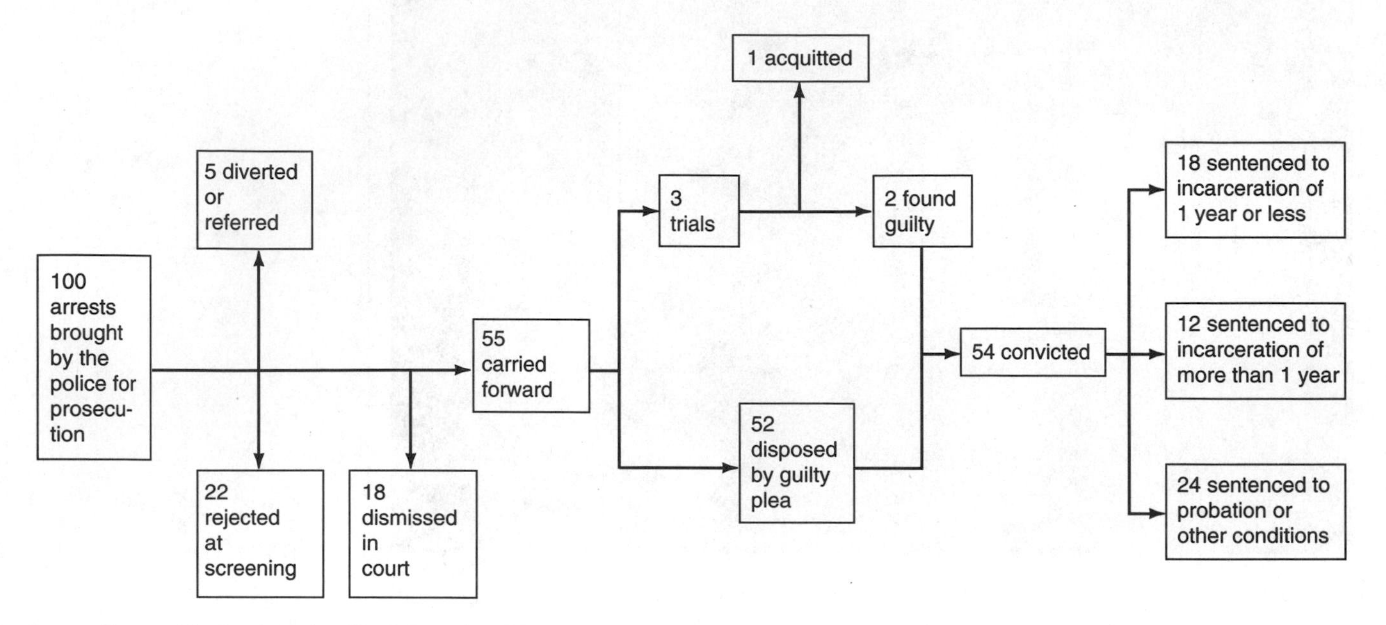

Source: Bureau of Justice Statistics, *The Prosecution of Felony Arrests, 1986* (Washington, D.C.: USGPO, June 1989), cover page.

considered for it. When the statute provides that a class of offenders is to be considered for probation, the defendant is entitled to fair treatment and is not to be made the victim of whim or caprice. Thus it has been held that a judge was in error for considering probation only for defendants who pleaded guilty and for refusing to consider probation for a defendant who pleaded not guilty and stood trial. The court in the one case pointed out that there is nothing to bar the judge who entertains an application for probation from considering (among other things) whether the defendant pleaded guilty or stood trial, especially when the defendant has presented only a frivolous defense. The error occurred when the judge refused to consider as a class all defendants who had stood trial.[15] A judge who announced that he could "never grant probation to a drug pusher" committed a similar error.[16]

States sometimes legislate restrictions on the use of probation. Restrictions on eligibility tend to declare ineligible defendants convicted of certain specified offenses (usually crimes of violence), those upon whom a term longer than a specified number of years is assessed, and those with a prior felony conviction. New York, for example, precludes probation for anyone with a prior felony conviction. Minnesota sentencing guidelines, on the other hand, direct judges to grant probation for persons convicted of larceny regardless of their prior convictions and requires judges who depart from the guidelines to justify the sentence. Generally, probation is more likely to be granted to first-time offenders who have committed less serious offenses. A survey of felony convictions in 1988 in the nation's 75 largest counties found that 37 percent of defendants with no prior felony convictions received probation, compared to 15 percent of repeat offenders.[17] However, some observers have noted that more and more serious felony offenders are being placed on probation due to plea bargaining and because of prison overcrowding.[18]

Federal statutes provide that probation may be used as an alternative to incarceration where the terms and conditions of probation can be fashioned so as to meet fully the statutory purposes of sentencing, including promoting respect for law, providing just punishment for the offense, achieving general deterrence, and protecting the public from further crime by the defendant.

Probation as the Preferred Disposition

In jurisdictions where the ordinary and expected disposition of the offender is commitment to an institution, the problem is to meet criteria for *granting* probation. In jurisdictions where probation is deemed to be the preferred and expected disposition of the offender, the problem is to meet criteria for *denying* probation. With regard to adult offenders, the former type of sentencing statute is more frequently found. However, model statutes and standards for probation emphasize the latter type of statute and recommend that sentencing statutes make probation preferable to incarceration, which should be ordered only when the welfare of the offender or the safety of society clearly demonstrates the need for withholding probation and sentencing imprisonment. The American Bar Association's **Model Adult Community Corrections Act** makes the rebuttable presumption that a community-based sanction, such as probation, is the most appropriate penalty for individuals convicted of nonviolent felonies or misdemeanors. The act attempts to "foster the development of policies and funding for programs that encourage jurisdictions to minimize the use of incarceration where other sanctions are appropriate."[19]

MODEL ADULT COMMUNITY CORRECTIONS ACT

A model code developed in 1992 by the American Bar Association that states could use as a model, if they wished, when they undertook to revise or modernize their laws regarding community-based corrections.

The criteria for probation are often stated in general terms. The California statute, for example, provides that "[i]f the court shall determine that there are circumstances in mitigation of punishment prescribed by law, or that the ends of justice would be subserved by granting probation to the defendant, the court shall have the power in its discretion to place the defendant on probation as hereinafter provided."[20]

New York follows its general statement with more specific criteria. Probation is allowed if the court believes that institutional confinement of the defendant is not necessary for the protection of the public; the defendant is in need of guidance, training, or other assistance, which, in the defendant's case, can be effectively administered through probation; and such disposition is not inconsistent with the ends of justice.[21]

Conditions of Probation Fixed by Statute

The conditions of probation as fixed by statute also must be considered in the probation-granting decision. If the presentence information about the defendant shows that he or she cannot meet the statutory conditions that must be imposed, then it is useless to grant probation. An example that readily comes to mind is that of the chronic alcoholic whose history indicates an inability to abstain from intoxicating beverages. Yet the nature of the crime may require as a condition of probation complete abstinence from the use of alcohol. Such a situation imposes both legal and practical dilemmas on the court. Has the court the right to assume that this time the defendant "won't make it" simply because he or she has been unable to abstain on previous occasions? Conversely, can the court ignore the intractable nature of alcoholism, the lack of treatment facilities, and the discouraging statistics about "cures"? In such a situation the court's duty is probably to take all the factors into consideration, to assign such weight to each factor as in its best judgment the situation seems to require, and then to grant or withhold probation accordingly.

To avoid confronting the court with dilemmas of this sort, many authorities recommend that statutes refrain from making specific conditions for probation, leaving

Model Adult Community Corrections Act

I. Overview
  A. Goals and Objectives
    1. To enhance public safety and achieve economies by encouraging the development and implementation of community sanctions as a sentencing option;
    2. To enhance the value of criminal sanctions and ensure that the criminal penalties imposed are the most appropriate ones by encouraging the development of a wider array of criminal sanctions;
    3. To increase the community's awareness of, participation in, and responsibility for the administration of the corrections system;
    4. To ensure that the offender is punished in the least restrictive setting consistent with public safety and the gravity of the crime;
    5. To provide offenders with education, training, and treatment to enable them to become fully functional members of the community upon release from criminal justice supervision;
    6. To make offenders accountable to the community for their criminal behavior, through community service programs, restitution programs, and a range of locally developed sanctions; and
    7. To foster the development of policies and funding for programs that encourage jurisdictions to minimize the use of incarceration where other sanctions are appropriate

the matter open for the judge based on the most up-to-date information that can be obtained by competent presentence investigations about the defendant and available treatment facilities and programs.

Availability and Quality of Probation Services

The decision to grant probation is also affected by the availability and quality of community and probation services. A judge may consider it useless to grant probation if there are no organized probation services in the locality, if the probation department gives no supervision whatever to the misdemeanant placed on probation, or if the probation officers' caseloads are so large that meaningful and consistent supervision is not possible. On the other hand, efficient and effective probation services may be overused.

The organizational structure of probation services and the training and ability of the probation officers are important determinants of the availability and quality of probation services. In some states probation is part of the judicial branch of government, whereas in others it is part of the executive branch. Probation may be administered on a local or statewide basis and may or may not be combined with parole services. Juvenile and adult probation may be under a single administration, or they may be in separate departments. The trend seems to be toward establishing statewide probation departments in the executive branch of government. This structure provides greater uniformity of services statewide and allows for standardization of services, training, and probation officer qualifications.

Quality of probation service is also determined by the qualifications required of probation officers. These vary widely even when minimum qualifications are set out in the probation statute. The American Probation and Parole Association recommends that all probation and parole officers have fully completed a baccalaureate degree at an accredited college or university supplemented by a year of graduate study or full-time field experience. The American Correctional Association requires entry-level probation officers to possess a minimum of a bachelor's degree. Latessa and Allen report that a majority of the jurisdictions in the United States now require a bachelor's degree or higher.[22] In addition, many require additional training or experience.

Unfortunately, neither statutory requirements nor recommended qualification standards for probation officers assure that adequate probation services will be available to the sentencing court. In some areas no probation department exists. Under such circumstances it is not uncommon for the judge to act as his or her own probation officer by setting up conditions and requiring that defendants report to the court at regular intervals. Police and prosecution officials are sometimes pressed into service as unofficial probation officers, although placing released persons in custody of police or prosecution officials is considered an unwise practice. The use of probation varies widely throughout the country and even within a single state. This is so partially because of the unavailability of probation services and also because of differing sentencing philosophies and differing degrees of community acceptance and involvement in probation.

A recent study of probation utilization showed that the southern states utilized probation to a greater extent than other areas.[23] The South reported 1,846 probationers per 100,000 adult residents. This ratio surpassed the West (1,397), the Midwest (1,472), and the Northeast (1,402). Washington reported the highest rate of persons on probation (3,048). Texas and Delaware had more than 3,000 persons on probation per 100,000 persons in the population, while Connecticut, New Jersey, Rhode Island, Michigan, Minnesota, the District of Columbia, Florida, and Georgia had more than 2,000 persons on probation for every 100,000 adult males in the population. States that utilize probation less generously include New Hampshire (509), North Dakota (486), Kentucky (398), Mississippi (496), Virginia (485), and West Virginia (433). (See Table 2.1.) This suggests that among the factors that determine whether an offender will receive probation or a prison sentence is not only *what* he or she does but *where* he or she does it.

Other Available Sentencing Dispositions

Granting probation also depends upon the availability and quality of other sentencing dispositions. In the past two decades state and federal statutes have provided a range of sentencing alternatives, including boot camps, restitution, community service, monitored home confinement, and intensive supervision programs. These intermediate sanctions have gained approval in the courts and have become popular adjuncts to regular probation. Where such programs exist, probation is more widely utilized. (Intermediate sanctions are discussed in greater detail in chapter 11.) The court may also be influenced toward granting probation by its knowledge of overcrowding or deplorable conditions in the adult prison system or of lack of treatment in youth institutions, or by the fact that specialized facilities—such as those needed for sex offenders or narcotic addicts—are not available in the community or in state institutions. Juvenile dispositions are also influenced by the programs being offered in juvenile institutions and, even more, by the lack of juvenile probation services in some areas. The rate of commitment to state juvenile institutions is routinely higher from counties where commitment is the only viable disposition.

In its Model Adult Community Corrections Act (1992) the American Bar Association takes a strong stand in favor of increasing the dispositional alternatives available to the sentencing judge.[24] The Act recommends that the sentencing court should be provided in all cases with a wide range of alternatives, with gradations of supervisory, supportive, and custodial facilities at its disposal so as to permit a sentence appropriate for each case.

Increased use of diversion strategies will tend to reduce the use of regular probation, but it may not reduce the need for probation services because many diversion programs involve probation-type supervision of the offender. Halfway houses, day care centers, and specialized institutions for the care of alcohol and drug abusers provide the sentencing authority with additional dispositional alternatives, which may tend to reduce the use of probation. On the other hand, making probation the preferred disposition places new burdens on probation services. It is evident that the frequency with which probation and other sentencing dispositions are selected is changing as sentencing philosophy changes and other dispositional alternatives for the care and custody of offenders become available.

Methods of Developing Sentencing Information

The information required to enable a judge to impose an appropriate sentence is developed in a postconviction hearing or a presentence investigation. In the case of jury sentencing, the jury is furnished with information about the defendant's general reputation and character at a sentencing hearing.

If probation is one of the dispositions being considered, there is a particular need for accurate, complete information. Not all offenders can benefit from probation. Some offenders must be incarcerated, either for the public good or because they need specialized treatment that is not available with probation. In some cases the nature and circumstances of the crime dictate incarceration of the offender, especially if the public's ideas of fairness and justice in the criminal process are to be upheld and vindicated. Granting probation thus demands an investigative process that will inform the sentencing authority of the circumstances of the offense and the nature of the offender.

Of the three methods of obtaining sentencing information, the one most closely identified with the granting of probation is the *presentence investigation report*. In fact, the origins of the presentence investigation report can be traced to the use of probation as a disposition. (See chapter 3, "The Presentence Investigation Report," for a detailed discussion.) Many states require a presentence investigation only when the offender is to be placed on probation. In such cases the statutory authority and requirements for the presentence investigation and report are contained in the probation statutes. In juvenile court the judge is routinely furnished with a social history report (also termed *predispositional report*) prior to the dispositional hearing.

Presentence reports are seldom required or used in misdemeanor probation. In some instances this is because no provision is made for misdemeanor probation. When a presentence report is prepared in a misdemeanor case, it is shorter and more summarized. In practice, the judge who sentences for a misdemeanor relies on the police officer for information about the defendant's criminal history and the circumstances of the offense. The defendant is usually given a **right of allocution,** a common-law privilege to speak to the question of sentencing. The defendant may also be given the right to submit a written memorandum that sets forth any information that may be pertinent to the question of sentence.

RIGHT OF ALLOCUTION

The right to speak in one's own behalf at sentencing.

Appropriateness of Probation

Probably the most important factor in the decision to grant probation is whether probation is an appropriate sentence for the particular offender. When probation is a statutory alternative, the decision to grant or deny it is seldom clear-cut. Individualized justice—that noble ideal of the criminal justice system—demands that the penalty fit the criminal as well as the crime. The needs of the offender, the protection of society, and the maintenance of social order must all be carefully weighed. This balancing of the best interests of both the offender and society is the crux of the probation decision process.

Such factors as the offender's age, criminal history, and potential for rehabilitation must be considered in probation decisions. The offender's history of substance abuse, potential for violence, community and family stability, and employment record also affect the judge's choice between prison and probation. Social and political attitudes in a community may affect the decision. The recommendations and advice of police, prosecutors, and victims can be significant considerations. Probation officer recommendations are frequently relied on. Seemingly extraneous factors such as overcrowded prison conditions may play a role. The defendant's attitude toward the offense and the existence or lack of remorse are often weighed in the decision. The judge's own biases, prejudices, and emotional responses toward the crime, the offender, and the victim(s) may affect the choice. In the final analysis, the decision is often subjective, and this has often led to sentencing disparity—markedly different sentences for individuals whose crimes and criminal history are similar.

Sentencing Guidelines

In recent years the advent of **sentencing guidelines** has introduced a completely new variable into the decision whether to grant probation. Sentencing reformers have criticized current sentencing practices as abusive and as rooted in untenable assumptions. Although many different approaches have been suggested, none has yet satisfied the need to reduce or eliminate unjustifiable disparity in sentencing. Just what *does* constitute inequity or unjustified disparity in sentencing? The point is arguable, depending on one's philosophy. One writer has stated that

SENTENCING GUIDELINES

Standardized instruments designed to provide clear and explicit direction to the court in determining the appropriate sentence. Guidelines typically consider offense severity and the offender's prior record. A matrix that relates these factors may be used.

> Inequity exists when significant differences in sentencing occur which cannot be justified on the basis of the severity of the crime, the defendant's prior criminal history, or characterological considerations which have a demonstrable bearing upon the appropriate penalty or disposition.[25]

According to this, it is not uniformity in sentencing that should be the goal, but rather a fair and rational approach to arriving at a sentence that allows for variability within a constantly applied framework.

Sentencing guidelines represent attempts to reduce sentencing disparity. Although guideline systems vary greatly from jurisdiction to jurisdiction, they generally establish an "appropriate" sentence based upon the severity of the offense and the offender's criminal history. In some jurisdictions the use of the guidelines is voluntary. Judges are not obligated to follow their recommendations. They merely provide the judge with information about the "usual" sentence for the offense and offender.

Figure 2.4 **MINNESOTA SENTENCING GUIDELINES GRID**

Presumptive Prison Sentence Lengths in Months

LESS SERIOUS ⟵ ⟶ MORE SERIOUS (criminal history)

LESS SERIOUS ⟷ MORE SERIOUS (severity of offense)

SEVERITY OF OFFENSE (Illustrative Offenses)	**CRIMINAL HISTORY SCORE**						
	0	**1**	**2**	**3**	**4**	**5**	**6 or more**
Sale of simulated controlled substance	12*	12*	12*	13	15	17	19 *18–20*
Theft-related crimes ($2500 or less) Check forgery ($200–$2500)	12*	12*	13	15	17	19	21 *20–22*
Theft crimes ($2500 or less)	12*	13	15	17	19 *18–20*	22 *21–23*	25 *24–26*
Nonresidential burglary Theft crimes (over $2500)	12*	15	18	21	25 *24–26*	32 *30–34*	41 *37–45*
Residential burglary Simple robbery	18	23	27	30 *29–31*	38 *36–40*	46 *43–49*	54 *50–58*
Criminal sexual conduct, 2nd degree	21	26	30	34 *33–35*	44 *42–46*	54 *50–58*	65 *60–70*
Aggravated robbery	48 *44–52*	58 *54-62*	68 *64–72*	78 *74–82*	88 *84–92*	98 *94–102*	108 *104–112*
Criminal sexual conduct, 1st degree Assault, 1st degree	86 *81–91*	98 *93–103*	110 *105–115*	122 *117–127*	134 *129–139*	146 *141–151*	158 *153–163*
Murder, 3rd degree Murder, 2nd degree (felony murder)	150 *144–156*	165 *159–171*	180 *174–186*	195 *189–201*	210 *204–216*	225 *219–231*	240 *234–246*
Murder, 2nd degree (with intent)	306 *299–313*	326 *319–333*	346 *339–353*	366 *359–373*	386 *379–393*	406 *399–413*	426 *419–433*

(Shaded cells: Sale of simulated controlled substance, columns 0–5; Theft-related crimes, columns 0–5; Theft crimes ($2500 or less), columns 0–3; Nonresidential burglary, columns 0–3; Residential burglary, columns 0–2; Criminal sexual conduct 2nd degree, columns 0–2.)

[Shaded] At the discretion of the judge, up to a year in jail and/or other nonjail sanctions can be imposed instead of prison sentences as conditions of probation for most of these offenses. If prison is imposed, the presumptive sentence is the number of months shown.

[Unshaded] Presumptive commitment to state prison for all offenses.

Notes: 1. Criminal history score is based on offender's prior record and seriousness of prior offenses. 2. Numbers in italics represent the range of months within which a judge may sentence without the sentence being deemed a departure from the guidelines. 3. First degree murder is excluded from the guidelines by law and carries a mandatory life sentence.

*One year and one day

Source: Minnesota Sentencing Guidelines Commission. Effective August 1, 1994.

Judges in some other jurisdictions—such as Minnesota, Pennsylvania, Washington, and the federal courts—have only limited discretion to sentence outside the ranges established by the guidelines. The federal sentencing guidelines, for example, state that if the minimum term of imprisonment specified by the guideline range in the Sentencing Table is more than six months, probation may not be granted. Minnesota's sentencing guidelines are shown in Figure 2.4. The range and form of the prescribed sentence can vary significantly from state to state, as the cases of Minnesota and Pennsylvania demonstrate. In Minnesota probation is the recommended sentence for most property crimes when the offender's criminal history is not extensive. Pennsylvania guidelines, in contrast, generally specify nonconfinement only for misdemeanor offenses when mitigating circumstances are involved. For normal misdemeanor cases, minimum ranges of 0 to 6 or 0 to 12 months are specified, regardless of offenders' prior records. Furthermore, Minnesota sentencing guidelines provide judges with a relatively narrow sentence range for a given severity level of offense and a given criminal history score. From this range one fixed term is chosen. Pennsylvania sentencing guidelines, however, are broad, and they specify a minimum range, an aggravated minimum range, and a mitigated minimum range from which the judge chooses a minimum term (the maximum term being set by statute).

A sentencing commission in each jurisdiction monitors the use of the guidelines and departures from the recommended sentences by the judiciary. Written explanations are required from judges who depart from guidelines ranges. The Minnesota Sentencing Commission rules state that although the sentencing guidelines are advisory to the sentencing judge, departures from their established presumptive sentences should occur only when substantial, compelling circumstances exist. Pennsylvania sentencing guidelines stipulate that court failure to explain sentences deviating from the recommendations is grounds for vacating the sentence and resentencing the defendant. Furthermore, if the court does not consider the guidelines or it inaccurately or inappropriately applies them, an imposed sentence may be vacated upon appeal to a higher court by either the defense or the prosecution.

SUMMARY

Since 1970 the number and rate of offenders sentenced to prison have increased alarmingly. As the nation's prisons have become critically overcrowded, courts have been forced to consider alternative sentences. Probation has emerged as a viable alternative. In fact, the number of persons sentenced to probation has expanded nearly as fast as the number sentenced to prison. Probation may generally be classified into four categories: regular probation, intensive supervision probation, deferred adjudication probation, and pretrial diversion probation. Each category of probation is regarded as appropriate for specific types of offenders. The decision to grant probation to an individual offender must consider many factors, one of the most critical being the jurisdiction's and the judge's philosophy of sentencing. Historically sentencing has been influenced by philosophical justifications based on retribution, incapacitation, deterrence, rehabilitation, and "just deserts." The extent to which probation is utilized in a jurisdiction is at least partially determined by these considerations. Other factors include the eligibility of the individual offender for probation as fixed by statute, whether probation or imprisonment is the preferred disposition, the conditions of probation as fixed by statute, the availability and quality of probation services, the availability and quality of other sentencing dispositions, the methods of developing sentencing information, and whether probation is appropriate for the particular offender. The use of sentencing guidelines is another variable recently introduced to reduce sentencing inequality and thus to ensure fairness.

ENDNOTES

1. Edna McConnell Clark Foundation, *Seeking Justice: Crime and Punishment in America* (New York, 1997).
2. Bureau of Justice Statistics, *Prison and Jail Inmates at Midyear 1996* (U. S. Department of Justice, January, 1997).
3. Edna McConnell Clark Foundation, *Seeking Justice,* 2.
4. Edna McConnell Clark Foundation, *Seeking Justice,* 2.
5. Joan Petersilia, "A Crime Control Rationale for Reinvesting in Community Corrections," *The Prison Journal* 75 (4) (December 1995).
6. Bureau of Justice Statistics, *Probation and Parole Population Reaches Almost 3.8 Million* (U.S. Department of Justice, June 30, 1996).
7. Petersilia, "A Crime Control Rationale."
8. Edna McConnell Clark Foundation, *Seeking Justice,* 35.
9. Petersilia, "A Crime Control Rationale."
10. Rolando del Carmen, Betsy Witt, Thomas Caywood, and Sally Layland, *Probation Law and Practice in Texas* (Criminal Justice Center, Sam Houston State University, 1989), 29–35.
11. Joan Petersilia, Susan Turner, James Kahan, and Joyce Peterson, *Granting Felons Probation: Public Risks and Alternatives* (Santa Monica, Calif.: RAND, January 1985).
12. Joan Petersilia, *Expanding Options for Criminal Sentencing* (Santa Monica, Calif.: RAND, November 1987).
13. Del Carmen et al, *Probation Law and Practice in Texas,* 35.
14. Howard Abadinsky, *Probation and Parole: Theory and Practice,* 5th ed. (Englewood Cliffs, N.J.: Prentice Hall, 1994).
15. *United States v. Wiley,* 267 F. 2d 453 (7th Cir.1959), on remand 184 F. Supp. 679 (N.D. Ill. E.D. 1960).
16. *Burns v. United States,* 287 U.S. 216, 53 S. Ct. 154, 77 L. Ed. 266 (1953).
17. Patrick A. Langan and Mark Cunniff, "Recidivism of Felons on Probation, 1986–1989," *Special Report,* Bureau of Justice Statistics (February 1992).
18. Larry Siegel, *Criminology,* 5th ed. (St. Paul: West, 1995).
19. Lynn S. Branham, "The Model Adult Community Corrections Act," *Community Corrections Report* 1(3):4 (February 1994).
20. Cal. Penal Code, sec. 1203 (West).
21. New York Penal Law sec. 65.00–1 (McKinney).
22. Edward J. Latessa and Harry E. Allen, *Corrections in the Community* (Cincinnati: Anderson, 1997), 268.
23. Bureau of Justice Statistics, *Correctional Populations in the United States, 1995* (United States Department of Justice, 1997).
24. Branham, "The Model Adult Community Corrections Act."
25. James Stanfiel, "Criminal Justice Decision Making: Discretion vs. Equity," *Federal Probation* (June 1983).

DISCUSSION QUESTIONS

1. How do diversion and deferred adjudication differ? How are they alike?
2. Discuss net-widening. How does it relate to pretrial diversion programs?
3. Discuss the "right" versus the "privilege" theory of probation.
4. What should be the purpose of sentencing—rehabilitation, deterrence, incapacitation, or retribution?
5. Is it more important that sentences be consistent or that they be individualized to the characteristics and needs of particular offenders?
6. What are sentencing guidelines? How might they affect the decision whether to grant probation?
7. What are the two positions with regard to criteria for granting or withholding probation? Which position is more prevalent in practice? Which position is recommended by both the Model Penal Code and the American Bar Association? Explain your position on this issue.
8. What major factors determine the availability and quality of probation services? How might the existence of highly professional services result in "overuse" of the justice system?
9. In your opinion, should probation services be administered on a local or a statewide basis? Should they be provided by the executive or judicial branch of government? Ask a judge or probation administrator in your area for his or her opinion on this issue.
10. How might the availability and quality of other sentencing dispositions affect the decision whether to grant probation? Give examples.
11. What are the three major methods by which a judge obtains sentencing information? Which do you believe is the most useful in establishing just and fair sentences? Why?

American Probation and Parole Association: Position Statement—Probation

The purpose of probation is to assist in reducing the incidence and impact of crime by probationers in the community. The core services of probation are to provide investigation and reports to the court, to help develop appropriate court dispositions for adult offenders and juvenile delinquents, and to supervise those persons placed on probation. Probation departments in fulfilling their purpose may also provide a broad range of services including, but not limited to, crime and delinquency prevention, victim restitution programs, and intern/volunteer programs.

Position

The mission of probation is to protect the public interest and safety by reducing the incidence and impact of crime by probationers. This role is accomplished by:

- ▲ assisting the courts in decision making through the probation report and in the enforcement of court orders;
- ▲ providing services and programs that afford opportunities for offenders to become more law-abiding;
- ▲ providing and cooperating in programs and activities for the prevention of crime and delinquency;
- ▲ furthering the administration of fair and individualized justice.

Probation is premised upon the following beliefs:

Society has a right to be protected from persons who cause its members harm, regardless of the reasons for such harm. It is the right of every citizen to be free from fear of harm to person and property. Belief in the necessity of law to an orderly society demands commitment to support it. Probation accepts this responsibility and views itself as an instrument for both control and treatment appropriate to some, but not all, offenders. The wise use of authority derived from law adds strength and stability to its efforts.

Offenders have rights deserving of protection. Freedom and democracy require fair and individualized due process of law in adjudicating and sentencing the offender.

Victims of crime have rights deserving of protection. In its humanitarian tradition, probation recognizes that prosecution of the offender is but a part of the responsibility of the criminal justice system. The victim of criminal activity may suffer loss of property, emotional problems, or physical disability. Probation thus commits itself to advocacy for the needs and interests of crime victims.

Human beings are capable of change. Belief in the individual's capability for behavioral change leads probation practitioners to a commitment to the reintegration of the offender into the community. The possibility for constructive change of behavior is based on the recognition and acceptance of the principle of individual responsibility. Much of probation practice focuses on identifying and making available those services and programs that will best afford offenders an opportunity to become responsible, law-abiding citizens.

Not all offenders have the same capacity or willingness to benefit from measures designed to produce law-abiding citizens. Probation practitioners recognize the variations among individuals. The present offense, the degree of risk to the community, and the potential for change can be assessed only in the context of the offender's individual history and experience.

Intervention in an offender's life should be the minimal amount needed to protect society and promote law-abiding behavior. Probation subscribes to the principle of intervening in an offender's life only to the extent necessary. Where further intervention appears unwarranted, criminal justice system involvement should be terminated. Where needed intervention can best be provided by an agency outside the system, the offender should be diverted from the system to that agency.

Punishment. Probation philosophy does not accept the concept of retributive punishment. Punishment as a corrective measure is supported and used in those instances in which it is felt that aversive measures may positively alter the offender's behavior when other measures may not. Even corrective punishment, however, should be used cautiously and judiciously in view of its highly unpredictable impact. It can be recognized that a conditional sentence in the community is, in and of itself, a punishment. It is less harsh and drastic than a prison term but more controlling and punitive than release without supervision.

Incarceration may be destructive and should be imposed only when necessary. Probation practitioners acknowledge society's right to protect itself and support the incarceration of offenders whose behavior constitutes a danger to the public through rejection of social or court mandates. Incarceration can also be an appropriate element of a probation program to emphasize the consequences of criminal behavior and thus effect constructive behavioral change. However, institutions should be humane and required to adhere to the highest standards.

Where public safety is not compromised, society and most offenders are best served through community correctional programs. Most offenders should be provided services within the community in which they are expected to demonstrate acceptable behavior. Community correctional programs generally are cost-effective, and they allow offenders to remain with their families while paying taxes and, where applicable, restitution to victims.

3
THE PRESENTENCE INVESTIGATION REPORT

What You Will Learn in This Chapter

You will learn the purposes of the presentence investigation report, how the presentence report is prepared, and what information goes into a presentence report. You will learn the difference between "offender-based" reports and "offense-based" presentence reports. The process of writing a presentence investigation report is examined, with emphasis on the initial interview with the offender, the investigation and verification, and the evaluative summary. Legal issues and criticisms regarding the presentence investigation report are also considered.

KEY TERMS

Presentence investigation report (PSI)
Presentence investigation
Offender-based PSI
Recidivism
Indeterminate sentencing
Determinate sentencing
Offense-based PSI
Victim impact statement
Disclosure
Hearsay evidence
Exclusionary rule

INTRODUCTION

The **presentence investigation report (PSI)** has long been the major source of information on which courts base sentences and is one of the major contributions of probation to the administration of criminal justice. This is especially true in indeterminate-sentencing jurisdictions, where judges have considerable discretion in imposing sentence. The original function of presentence investigation reports was to assist the court in resolving the issue of whether to grant probation. Over the years, however, many other uses for the report's information have been found. Presentence reports are now used in the entire range of correctional programs. We will also examine how the presentence report has changed with the shift in correctional philosophy from rehabilitation to punishment and from indeterminate to determinate sentencing. Associated legal and philosophical issues are also addressed.

PRESENTENCE INVESTIGATION REPORT (PSI)

A report prepared from the presentence investigation and provided to the court before sentencing that serves a number of purposes.

PURPOSES OF THE PRESENTENCE REPORT

The primary purpose of the presentence investigation report is to provide the sentencing court with timely, relevant, and accurate data on which to base a rational sentencing decision. The PSI also assists correctional institutions in their classification of inmates, institutional programming, and release planning. Paroling authorities use the PSI to obtain information that is pertinent to considerations of parole. Probation and parole officers use it in their supervision efforts. The PSI may also serve as a source of information for research.[1]

CONTENTS OF THE PRESENTENCE REPORT

What are the essentials of a good presentence report? The philosophy guiding the preparation of presentence reports may be characterized as either primarily offender-based or primarily offense-based.

Offender-Based Reports

PRESENTENCE INVESTIGATION (PSI)

An investigation undertaken by a probation officer at the request of the court for the purpose of obtaining information about the defendant that may assist the court in arriving at a rational, fair sentence.

Traditionally presentence investigation reports have been "offender-based." That means that the probation officers have been guided in their **presentence investigations** by a philosophy that attempts to understand the causes of an offender's antisocial behavior and to evaluate the offender's potential for change. One of the earliest references to the investigation states that its purpose is to learn the character and ability of the person under consideration, the influences that surround him or her, and those that may be brought to bear in the event of probations.[2]

Another writer asserted,

> What the investigation seeks is a full understanding of the offender from the point of view of his possible *reintegration* into society as a self-sufficient and permanently useful member.[3]

Another source states that a satisfactory PSI is one that

> describes a defendant's character and personality, evaluates his or her problems and needs, helps the reader understand the world in which the defendant lives, reveals the nature of his or her relationships with people, and discloses those factors which underline the defendant's specific offense and conduct in general. It suggests alternatives for sentencing and the supervision process.[4]

These statements make little or no reference to the nature of the offense. They are wholly centered on the offender.

There are several excellent models on which a traditional (offender-based) presentence report might be based. We believe that the PSI prepared by U.S. probation officers for the federal courts in the pre–sentencing guidelines era (before 1984) was and is a model for jurisdictions with an offender-based sentencing philosophy. The format of a comprehensive **offender-based presentence report** is shown in the Box on page 53.[5]

OFFENDER-BASED PRESENTENCE INVESTIGATION REPORT

A presentence investigation report that seeks to understand the offender and the circumstances of the offense and to evaluate the offender's potential as a law-abiding, productive citizen.

A Shift from Rehabilitation to Punishment

In the mid-1970s the corrections system's failure to curb rapidly growing crime rates or to reduce **recidivism** brought about public disillusionment with the existing emphasis on rehabilitation. One of the foundations of the "rehabilitative ideal" was an **indeterminate sentencing** structure. Under such a system judges were authorized to impose a sentence from within a wide range, with a maximum sentence stated, but release to be determined by a paroling authority based upon its determination of the offender's readiness to return to society. Richard Singer writes,

RECIDIVISM

The repetition of criminal behavior.

INDETERMINATE SENTENCE

A model of sentencing that encourages rehabilitation through the use of relatively unspecific sentences such as a prison term of 2 to 10 years with release to be determined by a parole board based upon evaluation of the offender's readiness to return to society.

> This system was called indeterminate because the prisoner's actual time in prison would not be known, or determined, until release by a parole board. The system of indeterminate sentencing could be justified on a number of bases, but its primary theoretical rationale was that it permitted sentencing and parole release decisions to be individualized, often on the basis of an offender's rehabilitative progress or prospects.[6]

By 1985 the philosophy of rehabilitation and the indeterminate sentence were under heavy attack from advocates of a "get tough" approach to crime control. Rehabilitation and indeterminate sentences were chief among the targets selected for abolition. "Get tough" proponents advocated determinate sentencing in which judges were given little discretion in sentencing options and offenders little opportunity to reduce their sentences through participation in prison programs. (A more detailed discussion of the "get tough on crime" movement is found in chapter 8.)

Contents of an Offender-Based Presentence Report

1. Offense
   - Official version
   - Defendant's version
   - Codefendant information
   - Statement of witnesses, complainants, and victims
2. Prior record
   - Juvenile adjudications
   - Adult arrests
   - Adult convictions
3. Personal and family data
   - Defendant
   - Parents and siblings
   - Marital
   - Education
   - Employment
   - Health
   - Physical
   - Mental and emotional
   - Military service
   - Financial condition
   - Assets
   - Liabilities
4. Evaluative summary
   - Alternative plans
   - Sentencing data
5. Recommendation

With the emphasis on punishment, many courts focused not on the individual and the factors that may have led to his or her crime, but rather on the crime itself. Some jurisdictions limited judges' discretion in sentencing by sentencing guidelines that established a sentence based on the nature of the crime itself and the offender's criminal history. Personal and social variables, previously considered important in the sentencing decision, either were no longer considered or played a minor role in the sentence determination.

Offense-Based Reports

In **determinate-sentencing** jurisdictions—those in which the statutes specify a similar sentence for every offender convicted of a particular offense—the emphasis is on an **offense-based presentence report,** which is very different from the traditional document. Here also certain information about the offender is considered relevant (prior criminal record, employment history, family ties, health, and drug use), but the dominant focus is on the offense. The sentencing court is concerned with the offender's culpability in the offense, whether anyone was injured, whether a firearm was used, the extent of loss to the victim(s), and other aspects of the offense. In jurisdictions where the court uses sentencing guidelines to determine appropriate sentences, the emphasis of the PSI is on applying the particular guidelines to the facts of the case.[7] In federal court, for example, the presentence report provides "solid, well-researched, verifiable information that will aid the court in selecting the proper guideline range."[8] The *Federal Sentencing Guidelines Handbook* advises:

> Among the only offender characteristics taken into consideration by the [federal sentencing] guidelines are the defendant's criminal record and criminal livelihood, which will enhance the sentencing range, and the defendant's acceptance of responsibility for the crime, which will lower the range.[9]

DETERMINATE SENTENCE

A sentencing model that establishes a specific punishment for a specific crime. Under such a model, all persons convicted of the same offense would receive essentially the same punishment.

OFFENSE-BASED PRESENTENCE INVESTIGATION REPORT

A presentence investigation report that focuses primarily on the offense committed, the offender's culpability, and the offender's criminal history.

Contents of an Offense-Based Presentence Report

1. The offense
   - Charge(s) and conviction(s)
   - Related cases
   - The offense conduct
   - Adjustment for obstruction of justice
   - Adjustment for acceptance of responsibility
   - Offense level computation
2. The defendant's criminal history
   - Juvenile adjudications
   - Criminal convictions
   - Criminal history computation
   - Other criminal conduct
   - Pending charges (include if pertinent)
3. Sentencing options
   - Custody
   - Supervised release
   - Probation
4. Offender characteristics
   - Family ties, family responsibilities, and community ties
   - Mental and emotional health
   - Physical condition, including drug dependence and alcohol abuse
   - Education and vocational skills
   - Employment record
5. Fines and restitution
   - Statutory provisions
   - Guideline provisions for fines
   - Defendant's ability to pay
6. Factors that may warrant departure (from sentence guidelines)
7. The impact of plea agreement (if pertinent)
8. Sentencing recommendation

Although offender characteristics are not completely ignored, it is obvious that the crime, not the criminal, is the primary emphasis. Probation officers in some jurisdictions where sentencing guidelines are used no longer write presentence reports; they are responsible only for completing a guidelines worksheet and calculating the presumptive sentence.[10] This, of course, deprives other agencies of the criminal justice system of valuable information about the offender.

The current federal PSI is offense-based, with primary emphasis upon providing the court with the necessary information to accurately apply the sentencing guidelines. The Box, "Contents of an Offense-Based Presentence Investigation Report," shows the format of the offense-based presentence report used in federal court. It addresses all the significant issues of the sentencing guidelines.[11]

What constitutes a good presentence report depends to some extent on whether the jurisdiction utilizes offender-based or offense-based sentencing. Certain criteria apply to all types of presentence reports, however; all presentence reports should be factual, germane, precise, and succinct. Certainly a concise report, fully read, is more effective than a lengthy one that is not considered or used.[12] The effectiveness of a presentence report is directly related to the success with which the findings are communicated and the extent to which it is used. The report's length and content should be appropriate to the seriousness of the offense; the greater the consequences of a judgment, the more likely is the court or a subsequent decision-making body to need more information. Where an individual has committed a violent or potentially violent offense, consideration of release on probation, prison

A Typical Victim Impact Statement

Ms. Karen Mercer of Charlotte, N.C., was the victim in the instant offense in which the defendant hit her over the head and stole her purse. The purse contained $90, her driver's license, credit cards, and her car keys. The defendant also stole her car. The offense occurred at gunpoint outside Ms. Mercer's apartment. Ms. Mercer's 1995 Mazda was discovered by local police a month later in damaged condition in New York City.

Although Ms. Mercer was covered by insurance, she was not compensated for the damage to her car by her insurance company because her car was recovered and she did not have comprehensive coverage. Damages to her car included a broken windshield, two flat tires, and a smashed right front fender. Further, she had to travel to New York City at her own expense in order to pick up her car. Ms. Mercer was also hospitalized for a slight concussion and as a result lost two weeks' work. Ms. Mercer certified by receipts (with the exception of the cash) that her total loss, because of the defendant's offense, was as follows:

Hospital bill (deductible costs)	$100.00
Bus ticket to New York	85.00
Gasoline (return trip)	28.50
Loss of two weeks' work at $6.70 per hr.	536.00
Two tires at $45 each	90.00
Windshield	250.00
Right front fender/ paint job	500.00
Cost of new driver's license	20.00
Cash loss (unable to verify)	90.00
Replacement of purse/ keys	125.00
TOTAL	1,824.50

In addition to Ms. Mercer's loss, the hospital bill paid by International Casualty Insurance Co. was $950.00. Ms. Mercer also stated that she now suffers from anxiety attacks when she considers leaving her apartment at night. She would like to attend counseling for this problem but presently does not have the money for this expense. It would not be covered by her health insurance. An estimate of the cost of such counseling is $90 per session. Ms. Mercer thought she might need as many as 10 counseling sessions to clear up this anxiety problem.

Ms. Mercer has no savings, and even though she is employed, she is earning only $6.70 per hour. Thus the probation officer's assessment of Ms. Mercer's financial situation is that she is in dire need of being compensated for her financial losses and of receiving the money for 10 counseling sessions.

Source: Adapted and updated from Administrative Offices of the United States Courts, *The Presentence Investigation Report,* monograph no. 105.

classification committee decisions, and parole release decisions will all require more knowledge of the individual than if he or she were a situational, nonviolent first offender. Above all other considerations, the PSI report must be objective and completely accurate.

Several aspects of the new federal PSI report are worthy of comment. In the 1984 Criminal Fine Enforcement Act, Congress cited the need to determine a defendant's ability to pay fines and restitution.[13] The federal presentence report and those of several states now include an analysis of the defendant's financial status for the purpose of imposing fines, ordering restitution, and assessing probation fees. The federal presentence report also contains a **victim impact statement** in the offense section. The use of victim impact statements stems from renewed interest in victim rights in the 1980s. Restoring the victim's wholeness has become an integral part of

VICTIM IMPACT STATEMENT

Information in a presentence investigation report about the impact of the offense on identifiable victims or the community.

Probation officer interviewing convicted offender for purposes of preparing the presentence investigation report.

the sentencing process. The victim impact statement is to include "information about the impact of the offense conduct on identifiable victims or the community."[14] It assesses the financial, social, psychological, and medical impact upon any individual victim. An example of a victim impact statement in a presentence report is given in the Box on page 55.

PREPARING THE PRESENTENCE REPORT

Preparing the PSI is one of the most critical and imposing duties of a probation officer. Many probation officers also consider it their most interesting task. It requires many important skills, including interviewing, investigating, and writing. The probation officer's responsibility is to search out the facts about the offense and the offender, verify the information received, and present it in an organized and objective format.[15]

When Should the PSI Be Prepared?

The preferred practice is to conduct the presentence investigation and prepare the presentence report after adjudication of guilt. The American Bar Association's *Standards Relating to Sentencing Alternatives and Procedures* gives four reasons the presentence investigation should not be undertaken until after a finding of guilt.

1. The investigation invades the defendant's privacy if he or she is later acquitted. The defendant's friends, employers, and relatives must be questioned, and potentially embarrassing questions must be asked.

2. Certain information is sought from the defendant that can place him or her in an awkward position before the trial.
3. The material in the presentence report is not admissible at the trial on the question of guilt, and there is a chance that it may come to the attention of the court before guilt is determined.
4. It is economically unfeasible to compile a report that may never be used.[16]

Exceptions to this rule are allowed when the defendant's attorney consents that the report may be prepared before conviction and plea. This recognizes the fact that under certain circumstances prompt preparation of the report is advantageous to the defendant. In many cases the presentence investigation report is actually prepared before the defendant pleads or is found guilty by the court. In such cases the report may be more accurately referred to as the Pretrial/Plea Report.

The Pretrial/Plea Investigation Report

This is most common in the case of a plea bargain. Many cases are settled without a trial through negotiation between the prosecution and defense. In many jurisdictions the plea bargain specifies an agreed-upon sentence. This has led in some jurisdictions to a pretrial/preplea investigation report. Judges may require a pretrial investigation before agreeing to the plea and sentence negotiated by the parties. In some areas the pretrial investigation is more common than the traditional PSI. These of necessity are short reports that contain information about the defendant's prior criminal record, details about the circumstances of the offense for which he or she is being sentenced, and some facts about the defendant's present social, employment, family, and economic circumstances.

The Initial Interview

The first task in preparing the PSI is to interview the newly convicted offender. This meeting usually occurs in the probation office or, if the defendant has not been released on bail, in jail. In some cases the initial interview takes place at the defendant's home, which allows the officer to observe the offender's home environment and thus adds an additional dimension to his or her understanding of the defendant. The home visit may also allow the probation officer to verify information gained from the offender with family members. The officer may also assess the offender's standard of living and relationships with family members.

The initial interview, wherever conducted, is usually devoted to completing a worksheet that elicits information about the offender, his or her criminal history, education, employment, physical and emotional health, family, and other relevant data. The officer also uses this time to develop some initial sense of the offender's character, personality, needs, and problems.

Investigation and Verification

Following the initial interview, the probation officer begins investigating and verifying information supplied by the offender and obtaining employment, military, education, and criminal history records from local, state, and federal agencies. Many of these records are protected by state and federal privacy laws, and obtaining them may require the defendant's written permission. Friends, family, and employers are also excellent sources of information, and they are frequently contacted to assist in developing a well-rounded, accurate depiction of the offender. The probation officer is interested in information that might influence the sentencing decision but that is omitted during the trial, particularly any aggravating or mitigating circumstances. When obtaining information from any source—particularly from relatives, friends, acquaintances, and employers—the probation officer must be careful to distinguish between facts and conclusions. Much of the information given to the probation officer during the investigation will be opinions and conclusions that may have little basis in fact. As a general rule the report should contain only information the probation officer knows to be accurate. In some cases information may be presented that the officer has been unable to verify. When that is necessary, the information should be clearly denoted as "unconfirmed" or "unverified."

The Evaluative Summary

Writing the evaluative summary is perhaps the most difficult and painstaking task in preparing the presentence report—particularly in offender-based reports—as this has a significant bearing on the future course of the defendant's life. In writing the evaluative summary, probation officers call into play their analytical ability, diagnostic skills, and understanding of human behavior. They must bring into focus the kind of person that is before the court, the basic factors that brought the person into trouble, and the special assistance the defendant needs for resolving those difficulties.

LEGAL PROBLEMS CONCERNING THE PRESENTENCE REPORT

Several legal issues have been addressed by various courts concerning the PSI. The most important among these legal issues are as follows:

- Does the defendant have a constitutional right to disclosure of the PSI?
- Are inaccuracies in the PSI legal grounds for resentencing?
- Is hearsay information in the PSI allowable?
- Does the exclusionary rule apply to the PSI?
- Must the Miranda warnings be given when a defendant is asked questions by the probation officer for the PSI?
- Does the defendant have a right to counsel during the PSI interview?

Disclosure of the PSI

DISCLOSURE

The right of a defendant to read the presentence investigation report prior to sentencing.

Should the defendant be permitted to see the presentence report—that is, be permitted **disclosure**—and have the opportunity to refute any statements contained therein? Compulsory disclosure has generally been opposed by judges and probation officers. The main argument against allowing disclosure is that persons having knowledge about the offender may refuse to give information if they know that they can be called into court and subjected to cross-examination and that the defendant will know they have given information about him or her. The concern is that disclosure of the presentence report to the defendant will dry up the sources of information. In the words of one court, there is fear that disclosure of the report "would have chilling effect on the willingness of various individuals to contribute information that would be incorporated into the report".[17] A second concern is that permitting the defendant to challenge the presentence report could unduly delay the proceedings. The fear is that the defendant will challenge everything in the report and transform the sentencing procedure virtually into a new trial. A third concern is that it could be harmful to the defendant himself or herself to have some of the report's information—such as the evaluation of a psychiatrist or even of the probation officer who is to be the defendant's probation supervisor. A fourth concern is protecting the confidential nature of the information in the report. Given all these concerns, some maintain that the report should be a completely private document; others would permit disclosure at the discretion of the trial judge.

The opposite view—advocating disclosure of the presentence report—is rooted in due process, meaning fundamental fairness. Because the PSI might have a big influence on the type and length of sentence to be imposed, due process demands that convicted persons should have access to the information on which their sentence is to be based so that they can correct inaccuracies and challenge falsehoods. It is pointed out that in jurisdictions where the accused has access to the reports, the sources of information have not dried up, nor have sentencing hearings turned into prolonged adversarial proceedings. Supporters of this position also argue that the defendants' attorneys cannot properly perform their constitutional duty to assure the accuracy of the information used in sentencing without access to the information on which judges are expected to act.

The United States Supreme Court has held that there is no denial of due process of law when a court considers a presentence investigation report without disclosing its contents to the defendant or giving the defendant an opportunity to rebut it.[18] A defendant may have such right, however, if disclosure is required by state law or court decisions in that jurisdiction.

There is a trend toward a "middle position" on the question of disclosure of the presentence report. Although the entire report—which contains the names of informants—is not disclosed to the defendant, it may be shown to his or her attorney. Also, the defendant and his or her attorney may be told about any adverse information in the report and given the opportunity to challenge its accuracy.

After an exhaustive consideration of the reasons for and against disclosure, the authors of the American Bar Association *Standards Relating to Sentencing Alternatives and Procedures* took a position in favor of disclosure.[19] The Model Penal Code would require that the court advise the defendant or the defendant's counsel of the factual contents and the conclusions of any presentence investigation or psychiatric examination and afford fair opportunity, if the defendant so requests, to controvert them. The sources of confidential information need not, however, be disclosed.[20]

In federal jurisdictions the *Federal Rules of Criminal Procedure,* Rule 32(c)(3), requires that the PSI be disclosed to the defendant and his or her counsel and to the attorney for the government, except in three instances:

1. When disclosure might disrupt rehabilitation of the defendant
2. When the information was obtained on a promise of confidentiality
3. When harm may result to the defendant or to any other person from such disclosure

The same rule also provides that should the accuracy of the presentence report be challenged by a defendant or attorney, the court must either make a finding as to that allegation or conclude that such finding was unnecessary because the controverted matter would not be considered by the sentencing court.

When withheld information is used in determining sentence, the court must provide the defendant and counsel with a summary of the withheld information and give the defendant or counsel the opportunity to comment on such information.

The above federal rules represent an intermediate position between complete disclosure and complete secrecy. In states practicing disclosure and in federal districts, the release of the presentence report has not resulted in the problems that have been anticipated by the opponents of the practice. Rather, it seems to have led probation services to develop skills for analyzing the offense and the offender more objectively. With greater objectivity has come greater reliance on the reports by the courts and a resultant increase in the number of reports requested and persons granted probation. These analytical rather than judgmental presentence reports are not only more useful to the courts, they are also more acceptable to the offender, for in them the offender may see that perhaps someone understands or at least attempts to understand his or her problems. This latter effect might result in a closer relationship between the offender and the probation officer. Further, disclosure is a requirement for fairness to the defendant. Thus the presentence investigation report is an integral part of the correctional system and should be made available to the defendant or his or her counsel.

Inaccuracies in the PSI

Two federal circuit courts that have recently addressed this issue say that inaccuracies in the PSI are not grounds for automatic revocation of the sentence imposed.[21] Both courts based their decisions on a determination by the appellate court of whether the inaccuracies are harmful or harmless. If the inaccuracies are harmful (meaning that the error would have affected the outcome of the sentencing proceeding), then there is reason for reversal; however, if the error is harmless, then reversal is not justified. Moreover, the defendant has the burden of establishing that the error was harmful. On the other hand, when a defendant is sentenced on the basis of a report that is materially false or unreliable, that person's due process right is violated.[22] The usual remedy in these cases is vacating the sentence imposed and remanding the case to the trial court for resentencing.

Hearsay in the PSI

HEARSAY EVIDENCE

Information offered as a truthful assertion that does not come from the personal knowledge of the person giving the information but from knowledge that person received from another.

Hearsay is information offered as a truthful assertion that does not come from the personal knowledge of the person giving the information but from knowledge that person received from another. In general, hearsay is not admissible in trial because the truth of the facts asserted cannot be tested by cross-examination of the witness: the witness simply heard what somebody else said. Decided cases are clear, however, that hearsay is not by itself constitutionally objectionable in a PSI report. The reason is that the purpose of the report is to help the judge determine an appropriate sentence for the defendant. It is important that the judge be given every opportunity to obtain relevant information during sentencing without rigid adherence to rules of evidence. Because the report is usually not compiled and written by a person with legal training, it is up to the judge to exercise proper discretion as to the sources and types of information he or she might want to use. This does not vest the court with unlimited discretion, however. By state or case law, the defendant is usually given the opportunity to rebut information that is claimed to be false.

The Exclusionary Rule

EXCLUSIONARY RULE

Evidence received in violation of the Fourth Amendment's prohibition against unreasonable search and seizure is not admissible in a court of law.

The **exclusionary rule** provides that evidence seized in violation of the Fourth Amendment prohibition against unreasonable searches and seizures is not admissible in a court of law. This rule does not apply, however, to the PSI. Courts have consistently resisted efforts to extend the exclusionary rule to proceedings other than the trial itself and only in instances when the misconduct was by the police. Some might argue that sentencing is so closely related to the trial itself that the use of illegally obtained evidence should not be allowed to influence the sentencing proceedings. Courts, however, have rejected this argument.

An interesting issue is whether the exclusionary rule applies in cases where the illegally obtained evidence is acquired by the probation officer or the police solely for use in a PSI and not in connection with an investigation for a criminal act. This will likely be an issue for local courts to decide based on state rules rather than on a possible violation of a constitutional right. Evidence illegally seized cannot be used in the PSI if its use is prohibited by state or case law.

Miranda Warnings for the PSI

The case of *Miranda v. Arizona*[23] holds that the Miranda Warning must be given whenever a suspect is under custodial interrogation. The warning is as follows:

1. You have a right to remain silent.
2. Anything you say can be used against you in a court of law.
3. You have the right to the presence of an attorney.
4. If you cannot afford an attorney, one will be appointed for you prior to questioning.
5. You have the right to terminate this interview at any time.

Should the Miranda warning be given by the probation officer when interviewing a defendant in connection with the PSI? Courts say no, holding that the PSI does not trigger the defendant's right to be free from self-incrimination even if the defendant is in custody and facing serious punishment.[24]

Counsel During PSI Questioning

Courts have held that the defendant does not have a Sixth Amendment right to have an attorney present during the PSI interview.[25] The reasons are that during the PSI the probation officer acts as an agent of the court charged with assisting the court in arriving at a fair sentence rather than as an agent of the prosecution. In most cases guilt has already been determined, so the adversarial situation that requires the assistance of a lawyer is absent. Moreover, the PSI interview is not considered by the courts as a critical stage of the criminal proceeding that requires the presence of a lawyer.

CRITICISMS OF THE PRESENTENCE REPORT

Some critics argue that judges place too much weight on the PSI in sentencing, which effectively shifts the sentencing decision from the court to the probation officer. Many studies have shown a high correlation between PSI sentence recommendation and the actual sentence imposed by the court. A study by the American Justice Institute, for example, demonstrated that the probation officer's recommendation was adopted by the sentencing judge in 66 to 95 percent of the cases.[26] Among the factors that might explain this high correlation is that probation officers may make their recommendations in anticipation of what the judge desires. One of the authors of this book served as a U.S. probation officer for several years. He suggests that probation officers who work with judges for a while come to know the judges' biases and predispositions regarding offenses and offenders. They know, for example, that Judge X always sentences drug-sale defendants to the maximum allowable penalty and that Judge Y almost always grants probation to first offenders. In time the officers' recommendations reflect the inevitability of the situation. A federal judge once told this author, "Never give me a recommendation for probation in a drug case. I don't want to see it."

Other studies have suggested that prosecutors suggest a recommended sentence to the probation officer after making a plea agreement with the defendant.[27] Florida State University criminology professor Eugene Czajkoski, himself a former U.S. probation officer, suggests that prosecuting attorneys often find a way to communicate the plea agreement to the probation officer, who responds with a conforming recommendation.[28] He writes,

> Like the judge's role, the probation officer's role in sentencing is diminishing. If it has become the judicial role of the judge to simply certify the plea bargaining process, then the probation officer's role is quasi-judicial in that he does the same thing. . . . [T]he probation officer does a perfunctory presentence report and aims his recommendation toward what he already knows will be the plea bargaining sentence.[29]

Other commentators suggest that judges vary widely in their reliance on the PSI report. Abraham Blumberg reports that some judges do not read the report at all, whereas others carefully select passages from the report to read aloud in court to justify their sentence.[30] Other judges discount the PSI because of the report's hearsay nature.[31] Howard Abadinsky points out that in many jurisdictions the probation officer is overburdened with presentence investigations and "does not have the time to do an adequate investigation and prepare a (potentially) useful report. In courts where the judge usually pays little or no attention to the contents of the report, the PO will not be inclined to pursue the necessary information and prepare well-written reports."[32]

SUMMARY

The ultimate merit of probation as a correctional tool depends to a great extent on the nature and quality of the presentence report. Probation is in essence a method of individualization and is predicated on the proper selection of offenders to be accorded this community-based correctional treatment. Although the primary purpose of a presentence investigation report is to examine and expose the factors that will mitigate for or against successful community adjustment in lieu of incarceration, use of the report should not be limited to the courts. It should also be made available to prison authorities for classification and treatment purposes and to the parole board to aid in the determination of parole grants and future needs of the offender.

ENDNOTES

1. *The Presentence Investigation Report,* Monograph no. 105 (Washington, D.C.: Administrative Office of the U.S. Courts, 1978).

2. A. Bolster, "Adult Probation, Parole, and Suspended Sentence," *J.Crim.L.* 444 (1910).

3. G. Ferris, "The Case History in Probation Service," in S. Glueck, *Probation and Criminology* (New York: Arno Press, 1933).

4. *The Presentence Investigation Report,* Monograph no. 103 (Washington, D.C.: Administrative Office of the U.S. Courts, 1965).

5. These categories were excerpted from *The Presentence Investigation Report,* monograph no. 105.

6. Richard Singer, "Sentencing," *Crime File* (U.S. Department of Justice, n.d.), 1.

7. *The Presentence Investigation Report,* monograph no. 105, 6.

8. *Presentence Investigation Reports under the Sentencing Reform Act of 1984,* monograph no. 107 (Division of Probation, Administrative Office of the U.S. Courts, September 1987).

9. *Federal Sentencing Guidelines Handbook: Text, Analysis, Case Digests* (New York: Shepard's/McGraw-Hill, 1990), 5.

10. Andrew E. Doom, Connie M. Roerich, and Thomas H. Zoey, "Sentencing Guidelines in Minnesota: the View from the Trenches," *Federal Probation* 52 (1988), 34–38.

11. *Presentence Investigation Reports under the Sentencing Reform Act of 1984.*

12. *Presentence Investigation Report,* Monograph no. 105, 6.

13. Howard Abadinsky, *Probation and Parole: Theory and Practice,* 5th ed. (Englewood Cliffs, N.J.: Prentice Hall, 1994), 102.

14. Abadinsky, *Probation and Parole,* 21–22.

15. *Presentence Investigation Reports under the Sentencing Reform Act of 1984,* 6.

16. ABA, *Standards Relating to Sentencing Alternatives and Problems* (Chicago: American Bar Association).

17. *United States v. Trevino,* 89 F. 3d 187, U.S. [4th Cir. July 1996].

18. *Williams v. Oklahoma,* 358 U.S. 576 (1959); *Williams v. New York,* 337 U.S. 241 (1949).

19. ABA, *Standards Relating to Sentencing Alternatives and Procedures,* Sections 4.3 and 4.4.

20. Model Penal Code, Sec. 7.07 (5). (American Law Institute, 1962).

21. *United States v. Rivera,* 96 F. 3rd 41 [2nd Cir. Sept. 1996] and *United States v. Lockhart,* 58 F. 3d 86 [4th Cir. June 1995].

22. *United States v. Lasky,* 592 F.2d 5670 [9th Cir. 1979] and *Moore v. United States,* 571 F. 2d 179 [3rd Cir. 1978].

23. *Miranda v. Arizona,* 384 U.S. 436 [1966].

24. *United States v. Allen,* 13 F. 3d 105 [U.S. 4th Cir. Dec. 1993] and *United States v. Washington,* 11 F. 3d 1510 [U.S. 10th Cir. Nov. 1993].

25. *United States v. Gordon,* 4 F. 3d 1567 [U.S. 10th Cir. Sept. 1993] and *United States v. Washington,* 11 F. 3d 1510 [U.S. 10th Cir. Nov. 1993].

26. *Presentence Investigation Report Program* (Sacramento, Calif.: American Justice Institute, 1981).

27. Rodney Kingsnorth and Louis Rizzo, "Decision Making in the Criminal Court: Continuities and Discontinuities," *Criminology* 17 (May 1979).

28. Eugene Czajkoski, "Exposing the Quasi-Judicial Role of the Probation Officer," *Federal Probation* 37 (September 1973).

29. Czajkoski, "Exposing the Quasi-Judicial Role of the Probation Officer," 120.

30. Abraham Blumberg, *Criminal Justice* (Chicago: Quadrangle Books, 1970).

31. Abadinsky, *Probation and Parole,* 118.
32. Abadinsky, *Probation and Parole,* 121.

DISCUSSION QUESTIONS

1. Discuss the importance of the presentence investigation report for the criminal justice system.
2. What is the primary purpose(s) of the PSI? How might other agencies in the criminal justice system use it?
3. How has the introduction of sentencing guidelines affected the use and nature of the PSI?
4. How do the PSI prepared in a jurisdiction with offender-based sentencing and the PSI prepared in an offense-based sentencing jurisdiction differ?
5. What is the purpose of the victim impact statement in a PSI? What factors brought about the use of this victim impact statement?
6. What is the federal rule regarding disclosure of the PSI? What are the arguments for and against disclosure? What is the middle-ground approach to disclosure?
7. Is hearsay evidence admissible in a presentence investigation report? Why or why not?
8. Is the probation officer required to give the Miranda Warning to a defendant before the presentence investigation interview? Why or why not?
9. What factor(s) might explain why probation officers' recommendations are so highly correlated with actual sentences imposed by judges?
10. Discuss some of the other criticisms of the PSI. Do you believe these criticisms are valid? Why or why not?

An Offender-Based Presentence Report

Offense

Official Version. Herman Hesse is the subject of two separate indictments, one in the District of Massachusetts and one in the Western District of Texas. On August 20, 1983, the Massachusetts Grand Jury returned an indictment against Hesse and Nancy Rooney, charging that they conspired between May 28, 1983, and July 30, 1983, to distribute a quantity of heroin and that they distributed that heroin on June 23, 1983.

On August 26, 1983, a grand jury in El Paso, Texas, returned an indictment against Hesse and Rooney, charging that they imported 101.7 grams of heroin into the United States on or about July 30, 1983, and that they distributed

UNITED STATES DISTRICT COURT
PRESENTENCE REPORT

NAME (Last, First, Middle) Hesse, Herman P.		DICTATION DATE October 14, 1983
ADDRESS Hampden County House of Correction	LEGAL RESIDENCE 71 Lee Avenue Holyoke, Mass.	SCHEDULED SENT. DATE
		DOCKET NO. 83-00I24-01
		CITIZENSHIP U.S.
AGE 28 · RACE Caucasian · DATE OF BIRTH 11-15-54	PLACE OF BIRTH Boston, Mass. · SEX Male	EDUCATION 10th Grade
MARITAL STATUS Divorced	DEPENDENTS One, in custody of former wife	SOC.SEC.NO 987-65-4321
FBI NO. 999-888 H	U.S. MARSHALL NO.	OTHER IDENTIFYING NO.
OFFENSE D/Mass.—Consp. & Dist. heroin, 21:USC. 841(a)(1) & 846		
PENALTY 0–15 yrs. and/or $25,000 and SPT of at least 3 yrs. on each count		
CUSTODIAL STATUS In custody in lieu of 100,000 surety bond since 8-15-83.		DATE OF ARREST
PLEA Guilty to Mass. Ind, 9-29-83; will plead under Rule 20 to W/D Tx. Ind.		
VERDICT		
DETAINERS OR CHARGES PENDING Rule 20, W/D Tx. Doc. #83-00135-01. Violation of 21:USC, 952(a) & 960(a)(1) & 841(a)(1), same penalty.		
OTHER DEFENDANTS Nancy Rooney, in local custody in Mexico		
ASSISTANT U.S. ATTORNEY David Crawford, Esq.	DEFENSE COUNSEL Philip Pratt. Esq. 981 Main Street Springfield, Mass. (413) 555-4321 (Retained)	
DISPOSITION		
SENTENCING JUDGE	DATE	PROBATION OFFICER

that heroin on the same date at El Paso, Texas. Hesse appeared on September 29, 1983, and pleaded guilty to the Massachusetts indictment. He has indicated his intention to plead guilty to the Texas indictment under Rule 20.

This investigation began in May 1983, when the Drug Enforcement Agency received information that Hesse was looking for a buyer for a large quantity of heroin. On May 28, 1983, an undercover agent was introduced to Hesse at a bar in Springfield, and Hesse acknowledged that he was looking for a buyer for a kilo of heroin. He was initially reluctant to deal with a stranger, but after four meetings he offered to make the agent a partner if the agent agreed to purchase the heroin as soon as it came across the border into Texas. The agent accepted the offer but insisted on first receiving a sample of the heroin.

On June 23, 1983, the agent and Hesse met in Springfield and drove to a shopping mall where they met Hesse's girlfriend, Nancy Rooney. After receiving instructions from Hesse, Rooney went to her car and returned with a sample of 2.70 grams of heroin, which she gave to the agent. The latter paid Hesse $300. The substance was tested and found to contain 31.7 percent heroin.

On July 21, 1983, the agent informed Hesse that the sample was of acceptable quality. On July 24, Hesse instructed the agent to meet him on July 29 in El Paso, Texas. The agent flew to El Paso, where he met with Hesse and Nancy Rooney at the Yellow Rose Hotel. At 8:15 A.M. on July 30, Hesse and Rooney crossed the border into Juarez. They returned two hours later, and Hesse told the agent that he was able to obtain only a quarter kilogram of heroin. The agent expressed disappointment, but Hesse said that the heroin was of very high quality and could be cut many times. Hesse then sold the agent the first installment of 101.7 grams for $4,000. Tests determined that this substance contained 44.6 percent heroin. Hesse explained that Rooney and he would return to Mexico that afternoon to obtain the balance.

Hesse and Rooney crossed into Juarez and were arrested by Mexican police later in the day. Nancy Rooney had 147.3 grams of heroin in her possession. No heroin was found on Hesse, who was released after two days in custody. Rooney was held for trial. Hesse returned to Massachusetts, where he was arrested on August 15, 1983.

Defendant's Version. "I was going to Mexico on a vacation, and Nancy decided to come with me. This guy she met in Springfield was pestering her to get him some heroin. I had seen him a couple of times in June. All of a sudden he shows up in El Paso and demands to know where the stuff is. She finally agreed to get him some and she asked me to come, in case anything happened. I was there, so I guess I'm guilty. All of a sudden I was arrested by the Mexican cops, but they let me go because they didn't have anything on me. Then, all of a sudden, I'm arrested up here. My lawyer says entrapment is hard to prove, so I guess I'm guilty. But I didn't say all those things the narc claims. I don't deserve to go to jail."

Prior Record

Juvenile Adjudications

11-05-68 Age 14	Using motor vehicle without authority	Springfield, Mass., Juvenile Court	1 year probation

Mr. Hesse was represented by counsel. He and two other juveniles stole a car and went on a "joy ride." Mr. Hesse made a good adjustment on probation during the initial months but became increasingly uncooperative thereafter.

10-28-69 Age 15	Breaking and entering	Holyoke District Ct.	Committed, Youth Service Board

Mr. Hesse was represented by counsel. He and another juvenile broke into a home in Holyoke. The Youth Service Board sent him to the Industrial School at Shirley, Massachusetts, where he remained until June 1964, when he was paroled. He was discharged one year later. His institutional performance was routine. He participated in a woodworking course and was placed on report on one occasion for fighting in the dining hall.

Adult Record

12-23-74 Age 20	Shoplifting	Springfield P.D.	Dismissed, lack of prosecution

Hesse was arrested after he allegedly attempted to steal several jewelry items from a department store. The store manager declined to press charges.

5-11-75 Age 20	Receiving stolen property	Holyoke District Ct.	4 mos. County Jail ss; prob. 2 years

Mr. Hesse was represented by counsel. He was arrested after he sold a stolen television set to a pawn shop. The probation officer reports that he had little success with Mr. Hesse, who was constantly on the borderline of violation.

9-15-76 Age 21	Burglary and entering in the nighttime	Northampton District Ct.	6 mos. County Jail

Mr. Hesse was represented by counsel. He was apprehended at 2:15 A.M., inside a drugstore. He had activated a silent alarm when he entered the building. Jail officials recall that Mr. Hesse attempted to be reclusive while incarcerated. He voluntarily spent several months in segregation because of his fear of attack by other inmates.

6-27-82 Age 25	Larceny over $100 and forgery	Hampden Cty. Superior Ct.	2 yrs. prison ss; 18 mos. prob. w/ restitution

Mr. Hesse was represented by counsel. He withdrew $500 from a bank account, using a stolen passbook and forged withdrawal slips. He was identified through bank photographs. Mr. Hesse paid $310 in restitution, and the balance was remitted. He performed well under probation supervision.

Personal and Family Data

Defendant. Herman Hesse was born on October 15, 1954, in Boston, Massachusetts. His parents, natives of Austria, came to the United States as displaced persons after World War II. The family has lived for the last fifteen years at their present residence in Holyoke. The defendant's early years were turbulent because of many violent arguments between his parents. Mrs. Hesse attributes these difficulties to her husband's excessive drinking. She summoned police assistance on several occasions, although no arrests were made. In 1961 Mrs. Hesse contracted tuberculosis. She was hospitalized for almost one year, and the father was unable to keep the family together. The defendant and his siblings were placed in the Western Massachusetts Home for Children, and the family was reunited when Mrs. Hesse recovered. The defendant remained with his family until he married at the age of twenty. He returned to the family home after his divorce three years later.

The defendant's parents picture their son as a well-intentioned individual whose difficulties with the law have been due to his unwise selection of associates. They are bitter toward codefendant Nancy Rooney, whom they believe was responsible for this offense. They view his previous juvenile and adult transgressions as minor matters that were treated with undue harshness by police and the courts. His parents describe the defendant as an intelligent and ambitious individual who values financial success above all else. They are proud of the fact that, in recent years, the defendant has acquired such material possessions as an expensive automobile and a boat. They also note that he has been especially generous with his younger brother and sister.

Parents and Siblings. The father, Henry Hesse, age 59, resides with his family and for the last seventeen years has been employed as a machine operator, earning a moderate salary. The home atmosphere improved considerably when Mr. Hesse stopped drinking approximately five years ago. The mother, Geraldine Ericksen Hesse, age 58, resides with her husband and is a housewife. Her health is poor due to respiratory ailments.

There are two siblings. Stanley Hesse, age 24, resides with his parents and is unemployed. Stanley believes that his brother is the victim of harassment by law enforcement authorities. Audrey Hesse, age 19, resides with her parents and is a community college student.

Marital. Herman Hesse married Barbara Raymond in a civil ceremony in Hartford, Connecticut, on November 22, 1974. Both parties were twenty years old at the time, and she was pregnant. The couple had one child, Herman, Jr., who was born on April 29, 1975. Mrs. Hesse reports that the marriage was troubled from the start by financial problems, since the defendant was unemployed. He turned to illegal means of supporting the family, and his subsequent arrests caused even more strain on the couple's relationship. There were several brief separations during 1975 and 1976 and a longer separation when the defendant was sentenced to serve six months in September of 1976. When he was released, Mrs. Hesse found him a "different man" and that it was impossible to reconstitute their relationship. The Hampden County Probate Court granted a divorce on December 28, 1977, on grounds of incompatibility and awarded her custody of the child. The defendant was required to pay $20 a week child support. Mrs. Hesse is employed as a telephone operator. She reports that her ex-husband's support payments have been sporadic. He often goes for months without visiting the child or making any payments, but he will then arrive with lavish gifts for his son and lump-sum support payments. Mrs. Hesse says that her relationship with the defendant is now amicable, but they see each other infrequently.

Mr. Hesse asserts that he has no plans to marry again. He stated that Nancy Rooney was merely a friend.

Education. Mr. Hesse was educated in local public schools. He left junior high school in October 1969, when he was committed to the Youth Service Board. He returned to Baran High School in Holyoke in the fall of 1970 and dropped out of the eleventh grade in November 1971.

School officials describe Mr. Hesse as an intelligent individual who never worked up to his capabilities. His grades were generally C's and D's. Mr. Hesse left school because he was older than most of his classmates and wanted to get a job.

Employment. Between November 1982 and the time of his arrest, Mr. Hesse was unemployed and collected unemployment compensation of $72 a week. From August 1980 to November 1982, he was a forklift operator at the Smith Chemical Company in Northampton. He earned $5.10 an hour, but he was subject to frequent layoffs. Company officials described him as an uncooperative employee with a high degree of tardiness. He would not be considered for reemployment.

Between March 1978 and December 1979, Mr. Hesse worked in the warehouse of the United Rug Company in East Hampton, Massachusetts. He earned $4.75 an hour and he quit after a disagreement over hours. Between 1974 and 1977, Mr. Hesse was sporadically employed in the roofing business. This work paid well, but he seldom was able to get more than three or four months' work in any year.

After he left high school, Mr. Hesse worked on a delivery truck for Central Bakery, Inc., of Holyoke. He held this job between April 1972 and October 1974 and earned the minimum wage. He lost this job when the company went out of business.

Mr. Hesse said that he would like someday to open his own business. He had no clear ideas about the nature of this business, but stressed that he saw himself in a managerial capacity and would hire others to do the menial labor.

Health

Physical. Mr. Hesse is in good physical condition. He denies having used drugs of any kind, and he specifically disclaims the use of heroin. Discussion with family members as well as with law enforcement sources revealed no information that would contradict Mr. Hesse's assertions in this respect. A physical examination and urinalysis test performed at the jail were negative for heroin use.

Mental and Emotional. On two occasions Mr. Hesse was tested in public schools and received I.Q. scores of 102 and 113.

Mr. Hesse has been examined by mental health professional on two occasions. The first examination occurred shortly after Mr. Hesse was committed to the Youth Service Board in 1969. At that time a psychologist described him as "a person whose anxiety is stimulated by a frustrated need for affection," adding that "Herman has developed no healthy conscience. His response to social demands is not based on any close commitment to moral principles."

Mr. Hesse was examined once again as a result of this court's pretrial order. Dr. Robert Land administered a battery of psychological tests. Dr. Land wrote that the results suggested that Mr. Hesse "seems to be unusually fearful of being overpowered and destroyed. It is obvious that he has been unable to resolve childhood problems and continues to feel quite rejected. He tends to view threatening environmental forces as coming outside his control."

Financial Condition

Assets. Mr. Hesse lists two main assets. One is a 1982 Cadillac purchased in January of this year for $18,640. This automobile was confiscated by the Drug Enforcement Administration. The other asset is a 19-foot fiberglass speedboat with a 115-horsepower Mercury outboard engine worth approximately $6,000.

Mr. Hesse's parents displayed to the probation officer a savings account passbook with a present balance of $7,146.23. The account was in the names of Mr. Hesse and his mother, but the parents made it clear that the defendant had made the deposits. When questioned about this, Mr. Hesse asserted that the account in fact belonged to his mother and that his name was on it only as a matter of convenience. His mother subsequently contacted the probation officer and retracted her earlier statement. She said that she made a mistake and that the money in the account belonged to her.

Liabilities. The only debt Mr. Hesse lists is a loan from GMAC to finance the purchase of his 1982 Cadillac. The loan balance is presently $9,200, and Mr. Hesse plans to make no further payments until such time as his car is returned to him by the government.

Evaluation

Although he attempts to shift responsibility to his codefendant, Mr. Hesse was the principal figure in the importation and sale of more than 100 grams of high-quality heroin. Were it not for the intervention of the Mexican authorities, he would have completed the sale of a quarter-kilogram to an undercover agent. Mr. Hesse is not a user of the drug. He apparently values financial success to the point that he made a calculated decision that heroin trafficking was profitable. His lack of concern about the moral aspects of his decision confirms the observation of mental health professionals that his personality lacks some of the constraints under which most people operate. For Mr. Hesse, participation in this offense, as well as in earlier offenses, was a logical means of satisfying his economic motives.

The members of Mr. Hesse's family are intensely loyal to him and they have an unrealistic view of his participation in criminal activities. They do not question the sources of his assets, which are surprisingly large for a person with his employment history. The family cannot be counted upon to exert the pressure that might convince Mr. Hesse to conform to law-abiding behavior. Mr. Hesse himself is unrealistic in his personal goals. Without much education or skill, he expects a high degree of financial compensation, but he has not thus far shown a willingness to work toward that goal. It is unlikely that Mr. Hesse will attempt conventional paths to economic success until he is convinced that illegal means are too hazardous.

Alternative Plans. Adult sentencing provisions apply in this case, and a special parole term of at least three years is required. Under any sentence imposed, Mr. Hesse will eventually come under the supervision of the probation office. An appropriate supervision plan would require immediate attention to Mr. Hesse's lack of marketable skills. The first step would be participation in a GED program, either in an institution or in the community. This would prepare him to accept more specialized training under the auspices of the Massachusetts Rehabilitation Commission. At least during the first six months of supervision, he would require maximum supervision with weekly reporting. The probation office suggests a requirement that he reside in Northrop House, where a highly structured environment is available. Northrop House has a contract with the Division of Legal Medicine and could provide Mr. Hesse with professional mental attention. Over the long term, the probation officer would pay particular attention to Mr. Hesse's financial dealings. He would also be encouraged to live independently of his family.

Recommendation

The probation office recommends commitment to the custody of the Attorney General and a mandatory special parole term of three years. This recommendation considers the quantity and quality of the heroin involved and the defendant's prior record.

The court may wish to consider imposing sentence under 18 U.S.C. 4205(b)(2) so that the Parole Commission can release him in the event that institutional conditions present a critical hazard to his mental health. The court might also consider recommending commitment to a minimum-security institution, where Mr. Hesse would feel less threatened.

Respectfully submitted,

Matilda Gormally
U.S. Probation Officer

Information Excluded from the Presentence Report as Potentially Exempt from Disclosure: Rule 32(c)(3)(A)

Marital. The defendant's ex-wife reported that when he was released from jail in early 1977 he showed no interest in resuming sexual relations with her. His behavior was also unusual in other respects, and he exhibited great tension and insomnia. Mrs. Hesse began to suspect that he had some experience in jail that had affected his sexual function. She questioned him about this on several occasions, and he responded with bitter denials. Mrs. Hesse became convinced that it was impossible to save the marriage and she filed for divorce. Mrs. Hesse was adamant that her husband not learn that she provided this information.

Officials of the Hampshire County Jail confirmed that Mr. Hesse was the victim of a homosexual assault in the jail. He refused to identify his attackers, but he asked to be moved to an isolated cell. This request was granted.

Officials of the Hampden County Jail, where Mr. Hesse is now lodged, report that he has displayed acute anxiety during his confinement. They are not aware of the reasons for this, but they note that Mr. Hesse has requested a transfer to the administrative segregation section. The jail has not complied with this request because of overcrowding.

Mental and Emotional. The latest psychological report suggests that Mr. Hesse will continue to experience acute anxiety whenever he is placed in a situation that threatens recurrence of the homosexual assault. The psychologist believes that Mr. Hesse is not overtly homosexual, but that his sexual orientation is ambiguous. Since the attack, Mr. Hesse has reportedly experienced complete sexual dysfunction.

Summary of Withheld Factual Information. If the court is of the view that the above information is excludable under Rule 32(c)(3)(A), and if the court intends to rely on that information in determining sentence, a summary of the withheld factual information is provided for disclosure to the defendant or his counsel:

> The court has received information about experiences of the defendant while previously incarcerated that caused him to have serious emotional problems. Subsequent psychological examination confirmed this existence.

Source: Updated and adapted from *The Presentence Investigation Report*, Monograph 105 (Administrative Office of the U.S. Courts, 1978).

SUPPLEMENTAL READINGS

An Offense-Based Presentence Report

PART A. THE OFFENSE

Charge(s) and Convictions(s)

1. Frank Jones was named in a three-count indictment filed by a Western District of Atlantis grand jury on November 1, 1991. Counts one through three charge that the defendant attempted to evade a total of $60,000 income tax due and owed by him and his wife for calendar years 1988, 1989, and 1990, respectively, in violation of 26 U.S.C. § 7201. On November 15, 1991, superceding information was filed by the United States Attorney's Office in the Western District of Atlantis. The information charges that on October 15, 1990, Jones evaded income tax due and owed by him

UNITED STATES DISTRICT COURT
PRESENTENCE REPORT

NAME (Last, First, Middle) Jones, Frank		DICTATION DATE May 25, 1992
ADDRESS	LEGAL RESIDENCE 1701 Seagull Lane Breaker Bay, AT 11111	SCHEDULED SENT. DATE
		DOCKET NO. CR 91-002-01-KGG
		CITIZENSHIP U.S.
AGE 56 · RACE Caucasian · DATE OF BIRTH 1-1-35	PLACE OF BIRTH · SEX Male	EDUCATION BS Degree
MARITAL STATUS	DEPENDENTS Two	SOC.SEC.NO 111-11-1111
FBI NO. 111-11-11A	U.S. MARSHALL NO. 11111-111	OTHER IDENTIFYING NO.
OFFENSE Tax Evasion (26 U.S.C. § 7201)		
PENALTY 5 years/$250,000 fine		
CUSTODIAL STATUS At liberty on a $50,000 personal recognizance bond with pretrial supervision (No pretrial custody)		DATE OF ARREST
PLEA		
VERDICT		
DETAINERS OR CHARGES PENDING		
OTHER DEFENDANTS		
ASSISTANT U.S. ATTORNEY Mr. Robert Prosecutor United States Courthouse Breaker Bay, Atlantis (123) 111-1212	DEFENSE COUNSEL Mr. Arthur Goodfellow 737 North 7th Street Breaker Bay, Atlantis (123) 111-1313	
DISPOSITION		
SENTENCING JUDGE	DATE	PROBATION OFFICER

and his wife for the calendar year 1990 by writing a check to the American Medisearch Organization in the amount of $20,000 for which he received 90 percent back in cash, and by filing a false tax return in which he deducted as a charitable contribution the entire amount of $20,000, in violation of 26 U.S.C. § 7201.

2. On November 21, 1991, Jones appeared before a U.S. magistrate judge and pled not guilty to all of the charges. He was released after posting bond and was ordered to report to the Pretrial Services Agency. According to his supervising pretrial services officer, Jones made satisfactory adjustment while under pretrial services supervision and reported as directed. On December 1, 1991, in accordance with the terms of a written plea agreement, the defendant pled guilty as charged in the superceding information. The terms of the plea agreement call for the dismissal of the original indictment. Jones is scheduled to be sentenced on June 5, 1992.

The Offense Conduct

3. The American Medisearch Organization is a not-for-profit national corporation that supervises fungus research. Across the country, the American Medisearch Organization derives its funds from 50 charter divisions that are separately incorporated not-for-profit organizations. The American Medisearch Organization, Atlantis Division, Inc., located in Breaker Bay, Atlantis, is one of the charter divisions employing salaried individuals and volunteers, which supports the goals of the American Medisearch Organization and are authorized to use the name of the American Medisearch Organization in fund-raising, educational programming, the issuance of grants in fungus research, and other activities. In late 1980 the Atlantis Medisearch Organization began to raise funds through an annual fall dinner dance, casino night.

4. Nancy Oscar began employment with the Atlantis Medisearch Organization in 1975 as a field services representative. Oscar, who created the dinner dance fund-raising event, was responsible for the fund-raising activities of the Atlantis Medisearch Organization. Three schemes developed from the dinner dance, all of which were aimed at enabling various "contributors" to inflate or falsify the "charitable" donations, which could then be reported and, where applicable, deducted on personal, corporate, partnership, or private foundation federal income tax returns. Oscar and other participants collected checks made payable to the American Medisearch Organization and returned 90 percent of the face value of the checks, either in the form of cash, or later in the form of chips that could be converted to cash or merchandise sold by the vendors at the dinner dance.

5. At least as early as 1985, in connection with the annual dinner dance, Oscar instituted a "check cashing" procedure whereby an individual was permitted to write a check payable to the American Medisearch Organization and send it to Oscar in advance of the affair. However, only 10 percent of the value of the check was retained by the Atlantis Medisearch Organization as a donation to the American Medisearch Organization, and 90 percent of the value of the check was returned to the "contributor" in cash either before or at the dinner dance.

6. At the dinner dance, which was usually held in October or November, guests were permitted to write checks, payable to the American Medisearch Organization, to purchase gambling chips. Ten percent of the value of each check was retained by the Atlantis Medisearch Organization as a donation, but 90 percent was returned to the "contributor" in the form of gambling chips. At the end of the evening all outstanding chips could be redeemed for cash or merchandise. Also at the dance, boutiques sold merchandise and gift certificates at fair market value, which were paid for by checks payable to the American Medisearch Organization, with chips or cash. No portion of the purchase price was a contribution to the organization; however, it did receive a small donation from the vendors.

7. Although the Atlantis Medisearch Organization raised money from other fund-raising events, its major source of income was from the annual dinner dance. Over the years, the number of people attending the dinner dance increased, the amount of advance "check-cashing" increased, the amount of checks written for gambling chips increased, and the amount of money Atlantis Medisearch Organization raised for the American Medisearch Organization increased. In 1987 the organization raised $73,000, and in 1990 the organization raised $360,000.

8. This scheme was in essence a "check cashing" operation, allowing "contributors" to draw checks to the American Medisearch Organization several weeks before the dinner dance affair. Specifically, before each dinner dance, Oscar told the members of the Atlantis Medisearch Organization if they or their invited guests wished to write a check to the American Medisearch Organization over $3,000, the check would have to be

received approximately two weeks before the affair, and 90 percent of the face value would be returned in cash. When the checks were collected in this manner they were deposited into the Atlantis Medisearch Organization bank account.

9. After the checks cleared the account, Oscar and other employees at her direction would arrange for the bank to ship cash to the dinner dance site. Oscar and some of the officers and members of the Atlantis Medisearch Organization would meet in rooms at the dinner dance site, where they took the cash and placed it in envelopes in amounts corresponding to 90 percent of the face value of the checks sent in advance of the dinner dance by the "contributors." Oscar also arranged for additional cash to be available at the dinner dance for those members who chose to redeem their chips for cash. Other "contributors" who did not attend the dinner dance were permitted to cash checks so long as they purchased a ticket for the affair. Those nonattending "contributors" who bought tickets and cashed checks were assigned to a nonexistent "dummy table" that was actually added to the dinner dance guest list.
10. The scheme was able to continue and flourish not only because of the greed of the "contributors" but also due to Oscar's bookkeeping methods. Oscar instructed officers of the organization who were preparing financial reports on the annual dinner to conceal the source of the funds raised through the check cashing schemes by including those funds in other categories of the financial report, such as gambling receipts.
11. In support of their income tax submissions, "contributors" often attached to their tax returns copies of the fraudulent checks they wrote to the American Medisearch Organization, and during routine audits "contributors" furnished the original copy of the fraudulent check to agents of the Internal Revenue Service and directly or indirectly misrepresented that the full amounts of the checks were charitable contributions to the American Medisearch Organization.
12. Over the years, the number of participants in this scheme substantially increased. According to available records, while the dinner dance attendees increased from approximately 65 in 1986 to approximately 650 in 1990, the government has only sought prosecution of those "contributors" who participated in the various kickback schemes and filed fraudulent tax returns when the total amount of the checks written to the American Medisearch organization was $30,000 or more over several years or $20,000 in one given year. To date, the government has prosecuted Nancy Oscar, who was the organizer and creator of this scheme. She has recently pled guilty to a three-count indictment charging her with mail fraud, income tax evasion, and wire fraud, along with five "contributors," namely the defendant, Frank Jones, together with Samuel James, Brian McDonald, Vincent St. James, and Donald Goodman. In total, the government expects to obtain indictments for approximately 37 additional "contributors." Although the value of the checks written to the American Medisearch Organization varied from "contributor" to "contributor," they are equally culpable.
13. Frank Jones participated in this false deduction scheme involving the Atlantis division of the American Medisearch Organization and filed fraudulent income tax returns for the years 1988, 1989, and 1990. During each of the years, Jones made contributions of $20,000 but received 90 percent of the contribution (or $18,000) back in cash, or in gambling chips, some of which he used to gamble with, but the majority of which he redeemed for cash. However, on each of his individual income tax returns, filed jointly with his wife, Jones deducted the full amount of $20,000 as "charitable contributions" even though he was only entitled to deduct $2,000 in each tax year, which represents the 10 percent retained by the Atlantis Medisearch Organization as a contribution to the American Medisearch Organization.
14. Jones was invited to attend the dinner dance by the former chairman of the board of the Sigma Systems Company, John Adams. In 1988 and 1990 Jones drew personal checks to the American Medisearch Organization for $20,000 each year and attended the dinner dance. At the dance, Jones received $18,000, or 90 percent of his check, back in gambling chips of which the' majority was later redeemed for cash. In 1989 Jones did not attend the dance but learned that he could draw the personal check and still receive the 90 percent return. As a result, Jones drew the check and gave it to Adams. Several weeks later, Adams gave Jones $18,000 in cash. Jones used the $18,000 he received each year from the Atlantis Medisearch Organization for personal expenditures and did not redeposit any of the funds into his personal bank account.

Victim Impact Statement

15. The Internal Revenue Service is the victim. In each tax year, Frank Jones deducted $20,000 as a charitable contribution from his taxable income, when in fact he was entitled to deduct a total of only $2,000 as a charitable contribution during each of the tax years. As a

result, Jones underreported his taxable income by $54,000. According to the results of an Internal Revenue Service audit, Jones had outstanding tax liabilities, not including interest and penalties, in the amount of $27,000, which he has paid in full.

Adjustment for Obstruction of Justice

16. The probation officer has no information to suggest that the defendant impeded or obstructed justice.

Adjustment for Acceptance of Responsibility

17. During an interview with Internal Revenue Service agents, and later during an interview with the probation officer, Jones readily admitted his involvement in this offense. Jones explained that he falsely claimed the charitable deductions on his personal tax returns because everyone else who attended the dinner dance was claiming the deductions.
18. Jones added that his involvement in this offense has had an adverse effect on his career, and in retrospect he never envisioned the potential impact such wrongdoing would have on his life. He expressed feelings of both embarrassment and regret and assumes full responsibility for his criminal conduct, as supported by his recent tax payment to the Internal Revenue Service in the amount of $27,000. Jones indicates that he will immediately pay the balance of his tax liabilities once the IRS has assessed interest and penalties.

Offense Level Computation

19. The 1991 edition of the *Guidelines Manual* has been used in this case. In accordance with the provisions found in U.S.S.G. § 1B1.3(a)(1), the total amount of evaded taxes has been taken into account in determining the sentencing guideline range.
20. **Base Offense Level:** The guideline for a 26 U.S.C. § 7201 offense is found in U.S.S.G. § 2T1.1. That section provides that the base offense level for tax offenses is determined in accordance with the tax table found in U.S.S.G. § 2T4.1 that corresponds to the tax loss. In this offense, the total amount of evaded taxes is $27,000. According to U.S.S.G. § 2T4.1(E), the base offense level for tax losses of more than $20,000 is ten. 10
21. **Specific Offense Characteristic:** Pursuant to the provision found in U.S.S.G § 2T1.1(b)(1), because defendant failed to report or to correctly identify the source of income exceeding $10,000 in any year from criminal activity, the offense level is increased by two levels. +2
22. **Adjustment for Role in the Offense:** None 0
23. **Victim-Related Adjustments:** None 0
24. **Adjustment for Obstruction of Justice:** None 0
25. **Adjusted Offense Level** (Subtotal): 12
26. **Adjustment for Acceptance of Responsibility:** The defendant has shown recognition of responsibility for his conduct and a reduction of two levels for Acceptance of Responsibility is applicable under U.S.S.G. § 3E1.1. -2
27. **Total Offense Level:** 10
28. **Chapter Four Enhancements:** None 0
29. **Total Offense Level:** 10

PART B. THE DEFENDANT'S CRIMINAL HISTORY

Juvenile Adjudication(s)

30. None

Adult Criminal Conviction(s)

31. None

Criminal History Computation

32. A check with the FBI and the local police authorities reveal no prior convictions for Frank Jones. Therefore, Jones has a criminal history score of zero. According to the sentencing table (chapter five, part A), 0 to 1 criminal history points establish a criminal history category of I.

PART C. OFFENDER CHARACTERISTICS

Personal and Family Data

33. Frank Samuel Jones was born on January 1, 1935, in Breaker Bay, Atlantis, to the union of Samuel and Patricia Jones, nee DeAngelo. Jones is an only child and was raised by his parents in the upper river section of Breaker Bay in an upper-middle-class socioeconomic setting. Jones has fond memories of his developmental years, advising that he was reared under Roman Catholic traditions by concerned, loving parents who emphasized hard work, respect, and honesty.
34. The defendant's father was a partner in the Atlantis Tallow Company, a refinery and exporting company which manufactured tallow, the main ingredient in soap. When the defendant was 18 years old, his father became critically ill with tuberculosis and was not expected to recover. Jones withdrew from his daytime studies at college and worked in the father's business. According to the defendant, his father fully recovered

approximately three years later, and eventually returned to the tallow business, allowing the defendant to pursue other interests.

35. According to the defendant, his father died in 1974 at the age of 68, following a massive heart attack. While reporting a positive relationship with his father, Jones advised us that he felt much closer to his mother, who died of natural causes in 1983 at the age of 80. Prior to her retirement and failing health, the defendant's mother was employed by the Breaker Bay Electric Company as a secretary. According to Jones, after his father's death, he assisted his mother financially, and she moved into an apartment in Breaker Bay, closer to the defendant's residence, in view of her declining health. As her health continued to decline, Jones eventually placed his mother in a retirement home, where she eventually died.
36. Jones married the former Nancy Lipson Smith on June 17, 1967, in Spring Hill, Atlantis. This union produced two children: Frank, Jr., and Mellisa, ages 13 and 15, respectively, who both attend boarding schools in Central City, Atlantis. According to Mrs. Jones, the couple were married in 1967. For the past 13 years, the defendant and his family have resided at 1701 Seagull Lane, in a rather reclusive, wooded, upper-class area in Breaker Bay. A home investigation found this five-bedroom, bilevel, ranch-style home to be impeccably maintained and tastefully furnished. Prior to the birth of their children, Mrs. Jones was employed by the Breaker Bay school system and later employed by an investment banking firm in Bodega Bay, Atlantis. Mrs. Jones has not been employed outside the home in over 15 years although in recent years she has participated in charities and other volunteer work.
37. Mrs. Jones describes her marriage in harmonious terms and states that the defendant is a kind, considerate, and devoted husband and father. Jones, for the most part, is a private person, and has suffered embarrassment as a result of the publicity in this case. The defendant's wife believes that her husband's actions "were not very well thought out," adding that "he never thinks about the impact his actions may have on his life or family," although Mrs. Jones considers the defendant's conduct in this offense as an isolated incident contrary to his otherwise "law-abiding lifestyle." According to Mrs. Jones, her husband has been described by his children as a "workaholic," but he never allows himself to neglect the needs or concerns of his family. Mrs. Jones added that she rarely attended functions, such as one described in this offense, and considered her husband's involvement as a business-related activity.

Physical Condition

38. The defendant is 5'10" tall and weighs 180 pounds. He has brown eyes and slightly graying brown short hair. At our request, the defendant's private physician, John W. Brown, M.D., provided a summary of Jones' overall health, which was described as excellent and free from hospitalizations.

Mental and Emotional Health

39. The defendant states that he has never been seen by a psychiatrist and describes his overall mental and emotional health as good. We have no information to suggest otherwise. Jones was polite and cooperative during the presentence process and presented himself as a professional and soft-spoken businessman, voicing normal stress and concerns affiliated with pending legal difficulties.

Substance Abuse

40. Jones states that he rarely drinks alcohol and has never used narcotics. A urine specimen collected by the probation officer tested negative for illicit drug use.

Educational and Vocational Skills

41. The defendant graduated from the Breaker Bay Military Academy in 1953 and continued his education at Atlantis University, where he received a bachelor of science degree in marketing on June 12, 1958. Jones advised that he received a master's in business administration (MBA) from Atlantis University in 1959; however, according to university records, Jones enrolled in the MBA program in September 1958 but left the program without completing the requirements in February 1963. Jones maintains that he completed the requirements but "failed to pick up the degree."

Employment Record

42. Since March 1978 Jones has been employed by the commodity and securities firm, Greater Life Securities, Inc., in Breaker Bay, where he earns approximately $700,000 a year as senior vice president in charge of the commodities division.
43. From December 1970 until March 1978 Jones was a senior vice president and director of the commodity division at Bruger Securities, where he earned $275,000 per year until he resigned. According to

Bruger Securities president, John Bruger, the defendant was a talented commodities broker, who was an asset to the firm. From October 1957 until December 1970 Jones was employed by the Marshall, Jones, and LaBelle securities firm in Breaker Bay as the company's vice president and director of commodity research. Jones earned approximately $65,000 a year and resigned to accept employment with Bruger. In the late 1950s Jones worked for an economic consulting firm and an economic forecasting firm as a price index analyst. Jones also worked at his father's tallow business for several years, where he was responsible for the purchase of raw materials, such as animal carcasses, used in the production of tallow.

Financial Condition: Ability to Pay

44. A review of the defendant's amended personal income tax returns for 1988 through 1990 (which now reflect the $57,000 in additional income previously reported as charitable deductions) reveals that the defendant earned $616,973 in 1988; $652,751 in 1989; and $704,448 in salary and wages from Greater Life Securities. In addition, interest income ranging from $1,231 (1987) to $22,013 (1988) is also shown. In each tax year Jones appears to have noteworthy long- and short-term capital losses, and in each year he takes the maximum loss allowed ($3,000) on his Schedule D. In addition, Jones reports substantial losses from tax shelters (set up in the form of limited partnerships and trusts), ranging from $91,234 (1988) to $221,008 (1989).
45. Jones submitted a signed joint financial statement and accompanying documentation, which supported the following verified financial profile summarized below:

Assets	
Cash	
Cash on hand	$5,000
Bank accounts (4)	206,000
Securities	250,000
Subtotal:	$461,000
Unencumbered Assets	
1987 Mercedes Benz 450	$45,000
1988 BMW	30,000
1988 Nissan Stanza	15,000
1964 Camaro	20,000
Subtotal:	$110,000
Equity in Other Assets	
1701 Seagull Lane Breaker Bay, Atlantis (family residence)	$580,000 (See Note A)
1471 Vermont Avenue Lake Shore, Atlantis (vacation residence)	$150,000 (See Note A)
Subtotal:	$730,000
Total Assets:	$1,301,000
Unsecured Debts	
Credit cards (3)	$13,000
Total Unsecured Debts:	$13,000
NET WORTH:	$1,288,000
Monthly Cash Flow	
Income	
Defendant's net salary	$11,038
Stocks and securities	10,000
Interest income	20,000
Total income:	$41,038
Necessary Living Expenses	
Property mortgages	$1,100
Food	750
Utilities	900
Telephone	300
Credit cards	300
Life insurance	800
Car insurance	1,200
Health insurance	200
School tuition	700
Other expenses	5,000
Total Expenses:	$11,250
Net Monthly Cash Flow:	$29,788

Note A: The market value of the family residence is $650,000, and the market value of the vacation home is $160,000 based on sales of comparable homes in the property areas. The outstanding mortgage balance on the family home is $70,000, and the vacation home has a $10,000 mortgage balance.

46. The defendant retained counsel in this offense and states that his attorney's fees have been paid in full. Based on the defendant's financial condition he has the ability to pay a fine within the guideline range.

PART D. SENTENCING OPTIONS

Custody

47. **Statutory Provisions:** The maximum term of imprisonment for this offense, a Class D felony, is 5 years, pursuant to 26 U.S.C. § 7201.
48. **Guideline Provisions:** Based on an offense level of 10 and a criminal history category of I, the guideline range of imprisonment is 6 to 12 months.

Impact of Plea Agreement

49. Under the plea agreement, Jones has entered a plea to one count of tax evasion in return for the dismissal of two other tax evasion counts. Pursuant to U.S.S.G. § 3D1.2(a), counts involving the same transaction are grouped together into a single group. Because all of the evaded taxes have been taken into account in determining the sentence guideline range, a conviction on the additional accounts would not affect the offense level or any other guideline calculation.

Supervised Release

50. **Statutory Provisions:** If a term of imprisonment is imposed, the court may impose a term of supervised release of not more than three years, pursuant to 18 U.S.C. § 3583(b)(2), since this is a Class D felony.
51. **Guideline Provisions:** If the defendant is sentenced to a term of imprisonment of less than one year, a term of supervised release is optional, pursuant to U.S.S.G. § 5D1.1(a). The authorized term of supervised release for this offense is not less than two years nor more than three years, pursuant to U.S.S.G. § 5D1.2(b)(2).

Probation

52. **Statutory Provisions:** The defendant is eligible for a term of probation in this offense, pursuant to 18 U.S.C. § 3561(a). The authorized term for a felony is not less than one nor more than five years, pursuant to 18 U.S.C. § 3561(b)(1). In accordance with the provisions found in 18 U.S.C. § 3563(a)(2), absent extraordinary circumstances, the court shall impose one of the following as a special condition of probation: a fine, restitution, or community service.
53. **Guideline Provisions:** The defendant is eligible for a term of probation, pursuant to U.S.S.G. § 5B1.1(a)(2), provided that the court impose a condition or combination of conditions requiring intermittent confinement, community confinement, or home confinement, provided that at least one-half on the minimum term is satisfied by a term of imprisonment. Pursuant to section 5B1.2(a)(1), the authorized term of probation is at least one year but not more than five years because the offense level is greater than six.

Fines

54. **Statutory Provisions:** The maximum fine for this offense is $250,000, pursuant to 18 U.S.C. § 3571(b).
55. A special assessment of $50 is mandatory, pursuant to 18 U.S.C. § 3013.
56. **Guideline Provisions:** According to U.S.S.G. § 5E1.2(c)(3), the minimum fine for this offense is $2,000 and the maximum fine in this offense is $20,000.
57. Subject to the defendant's ability to pay, the court shall impose an additional fine amount that is at least sufficient to pay the costs to the government of any imprisonment, probation, or supervised release, pursuant to U.S.S.G. § 5E1.2(i). The most recent advisory from the Administrative Office of the U.S. Court suggests that a monthly cost of $1,210.05 be used for imprisonment, a monthly cost of $91.66 for supervision, and a monthly cost of $938.44 for community confinement.

Restitution

58. **Statutory Provisions:** Pursuant to 18 U.S.C. § 3563, restitution may be ordered. If the defendant is sentenced to a term of probation or supervised release, restitution shall be a condition of supervision. In this case the defendant's outstanding tax obligation has been paid. Interest and penalties are outstanding to the Internal Revenue Service, and can be forwarded to the following address:
    Internal Revenue Service
    111 IRS Tower
    Breaker Bay, Atlantis 11111
    Attention: Mr. Sam Claim
59. **Guideline Provisions:** In accordance with the provisions of U.S.S.G. § 5E1.1, restitution shall be ordered.

PART E. FACTORS THAT MAY WARRANT DEPARTURE

60. The probation officer has no information concerning the offense or the offender that would warrant a departure from the prescribed sentencing guidelines.

Respectfully submitted,

Chief U.S. Probation Officer

by ____________________

Craig T. Doe
U.S. Probation Officer

Approved:

____

Mark T. Clark Date
Supervising U.S. Probation Officer

SENTENCING RECOMMENDATION

UNITED STATES DISTRICT COURT FOR THE WESTERN DISTRICT OF ATLANTIS
UNITED STATES V. FRANK JONES, DKT. # CR 91-002-01-KGG

TOTAL OFFENSE LEVEL: 10
CRIMINAL HISTORY CATEGORY: I

	Statutory Provisions	Guideline Provisions	Recommended Sentence
CUSTODY.	5 years	6 to 12 months	3 months
PROBATION:	1–5 years	1–5 years	Not Applicable
SUPERVISED RELEASE:	2–3 years	2–3 years	2 years, 3 months home confinement
FINE:	$250,000	$2,000–$20,000	$20,000
RESTITUTION:	$0	$0	$0
SPECIAL ASSESSMENT:	$50	$50	$50

Justification

Frank Jones is a successful and respected businessman who appears to be a situational offender, having been motivated by opportunistic greed. While his acceptance of responsibility and remorse are reflected in the guideline calculation, Jones has also paid restitution to the Internal Revenue Service prior to sentencing. As such, a sentence in the lower end of the guideline range is recommended.

The defendant earns a considerable income, has accumulated an impressive financial portfolio of over $1,000,000, and is employed with a reputable commodities firm. Given his financial acumen, his evasion of the payment of taxes by participation in a fraudulent scheme in the guise of charity merits a sentence reflective of the seriousness of the offense. While he is eligible for probation, a split sentence of three months in custody followed by three months in community confinement as a condition of supervised release is the recommended sentence in order to reflect the seriousness of the defendant's conduct and to provide just punishment.

In view of Jones's financial profile, a fine of $20,000 is also recommended to be paid immediately with the $50 penalty assessment. Inasmuch as he does not appear to pose a risk to the community nor to be in need of correctional treatment, the minimum term of supervised release of two years will be sufficient. Since the defendant will owe interest and penalties to the Internal Revenue Service as soon as they are calculated, it is recommended that collection of these monies be a condition of supervised release. A restriction against incurring any new debts until the criminal sanctions are paid is an additional recommended condition.

Voluntary Surrender

Jones has no prior criminal record and solid ties to the community, and he appears to be a good candidate for voluntary surrender.

Recommendation

It is respectfully recommended that sentence in this case be imposed as follows:

Pursuant to the Sentencing Reform Act of 1984, it is the judgment of the court that the defendant, Frank Jones, is hereby committed to the custody of the United States Bureau of Prisons to be imprisoned for a term of 3 months.

Upon release from imprisonment, the defendant shall be placed on supervised release for a term of two years. Within 72 hours of release from the custody of the Bureau of Prisons, the defendant shall report in person to the probation office in the district to which the defendant is released.

While on supervised release the defendant shall not commit any federal, state, or local crimes, and he shall be prohibited from possessing a firearm or other dangerous device. In addition, the defendant shall not possess a controlled substance, and he shall comply with the standard conditions of supervised release as recommended by the United States Sentencing Commission.

In addition, the defendant shall comply with the following special conditions: The defendant shall be confined continuously to a community corrections center for a period of three months, pursuant to 18 U.S.C. § 3563(b)(12); said placement shall commence on a date to be determined by the probation officer. Subject to the approval of the court or the probation officer, the defendant may not leave the community corrections center except to maintain employment. In addition, the defendant shall pay any fine that is imposed by this judgment and that remains unpaid at the commencement of the term of supervised release. The defendant shall incur no new debts or open additional lines of credit without the permission of the probation officer unless the fine has been paid in full.

THE COURT FINDS that the defendant has the ability to pay a fine, and it is further ordered that the defendant shall pay to the United States a fine of $20,000. This fine, including any interest required by law, shall be paid in full within 30 days. In addition, the defendant is ordered to pay a special assessment in the amount of $50, which shall be due immediately.

Respectfully submitted,

Chief U.S. Probation Officer

by ____________________

Craig T. Doe
U.S. Probation Officer

Approved:

____

Mark T. Clark Date
Supervising U.S. Probation Officer

ADDENDUM TO THE PRESENTENCE REPORT

UNITED STATES DISTRICT COURT FOR THE WESTERN DISTRICT OF ATLANTIS
UNITED STATES V. FRANK JONES,
DKT. # CR 91-002-01-KGG

OBJECTIONS

By the Government

On May 21, 1991, Assistant U.S. Attorney Robert Prosecutor advised the probation officer that he had no objections to the presentence report.

By the Defendant

On May 23, 1991, defense counsel Arthur Goodfellow advised the probation officer that he had no objections to the presentence report.

Respectfully submitted,

Chief U.S. Probation Officer

by ____________________

Craig T. Doe
U.S. Probation Officer

Approved:

____

Mark T. Clark Date
Supervising U.S. Probation Officer

Source: *The Presentence Investigation Report,* Monograph 107 (Administrative Office of the U.S. Courts, March 1992).

4

CONDITIONS AND LENGTH OF PROBATION

KEY TERMS

- Reform conditions
- Control conditions
- Standard conditions
- Special conditions
- Clear conditions
- "Scarlet letter" conditions
- Reasonable conditions
- First Amendment rights
- Freedom of religion
- Right against unreasonable searches and seizures
- Privilege against self-incrimination
- Early termination
- Shock probation
- Split sentencing
- Intensive supervision
- Electronic monitoring
- Fine
- Restitution
- Community service

What You Will Learn in This Chapter

The imposition of conditions is at the heart of probation because conditions are the means whereby the goals of probation are achieved. In this chapter you will learn that the court imposes the various types of conditions, but there are limitations to the exercise of this power by the courts. Conditions may be modified, but modification must also be done by the court and not by the probation officer. Most states have provisions for early termination of probation. This takes place when the court feels that the offender has behaved well and further supervision is unnecessary. The chapter concludes with a discussion of the various special programs that are usually established to carry out the conditions imposed.

INTRODUCTION

Offenders are granted probation if they agree to abide by a set of rules or conditions for release. These conditions might apply to all persons released under supervision, or they may be tailored to the needs of particular offenders. Probation conditions determine the degree of freedom a probationer enjoys and are also the primary means by which societal objectives of control and rehabilitation are served.

The imposition of conditions can be a challenging function, particularly in jurisdictions where the prevailing sentencing philosophy is that conditions should fit the offender. The imposition of conditions varies greatly from state to state and even in jurisdictions within a state, in both theory and practice. Variations abound in the types of conditions imposed, whether these conditions are required by law or imposed by courts on their own, and the degree to which these conditions are enforced before revocation ensues.

This chapter looks at the role of the court in the imposition of conditions, the types of conditions imposed, and examples of conditions imposed. It looks at modification of conditions and discusses some of the common types of programs that carry out imposed conditions.

THE COURT IMPOSES CONDITIONS OF PROBATION

The power to impose conditions of probation is vested in the courts. In general, judges enjoy immense discretion when imposing conditions of probation, subject only to the four limitations discussed in this chapter. Although conditions are usually recommended by the probation officer, the judge has the final say as to which conditions are to be imposed on an offender, the justification being that judges are in the best position, by virtue of their authority and contact with the offender, to determine what conditions best serve the aims of probation.

Judges can be creative in imposing conditions because of the immense discretion usually given to them. For example, one judge required a man who beat up his wife to publicly apologize to her, with the wife's consent, in front of a dozen television cameras on the steps of the Houston City Hall during the lunch hour as a condition of probation.[1] Another judge ordered an offender with AIDS to obtain written informed consent from all future sex partners as a condition of probation for a car theft conviction. That form read:

> (Defendant's name) has advised me that he has been diagnosed as positive for the HIV virus in his body and may be symptomatic for the disease of acquired immune deficiency syndrome. Although I realize I am potentially risking my own life, I nonetheless desire to engage in sexual relations with the above named individual.[2]

Courts are generally split on the validity or constitutionality of creative conditions. In general, however, these conditions are considered valid if they are reasonably related to the rehabilitation of the individual or the protection of society. Moreover, in case of doubt, the authority of the court to impose conditions is upheld by appellate courts.

In some states conditions imposed are set by the state legislature; in others they are imposed by the judge without legislative guidance. But even in states where some conditions are required by law, judges can usually set additional conditions as they see fit, given the nature of the offense and the offender. In other states where conditions to be imposed are enumerated by law, judges are nonetheless given the discretion to impose all, some, or none of the conditions. In sum, except in rare cases where their authority is specifically limited by the legislature, judges have vast discretion to do as they please when imposing conditions of probation.

PURPOSE OF PROBATION CONDITIONS

Based on purpose, probation conditions may be categorized into two types: reform conditions and control conditions. **Reform conditions** are designed to facilitate the offender's rehabilitation, while **control conditions** are designed to facilitate monitoring the offender's behavior and attitude. These categories reflect what in most states are the twin goals of probation: rehabilitation and protection of society.[3]

REFORM CONDITIONS

Probation conditions designed to facilitate the offender's rehabilitation.

CONTROL CONDITIONS

Probation conditions designed to facilitate monitoring the offender's behavior and attitude.

Whether probation is more rehabilitative than placing an offender in prison or jail has not been conclusively established. While some believe that probationers recidivate less and therefore probation is more rehabilitative, the lower rate of recidivism may in fact be attributed to the type of offenders (usually minor and first offenders) who are less likely to recidivate anyway. A clear benefit of probation, however, is that it is less expensive than incarceration. In many states the cost of imprisonment is 10 to 15 times more than the cost of probation. Moreover, probation leaves the offender in the community where he or she can be a contributing member of society instead of depending on it for support.

TYPES OF PROBATION CONDITIONS

Probation conditions may be further classified into two types: standard conditions and special conditions. Some writers call these required conditions and discretionary conditions. These terms can be confusing, however, because in most jurisdictions the imposition of conditions is usually left to the discretion of the judge; so even if state law provides that certain conditions are required to be imposed, they are still somewhat discretionary.

*Mandatory Conditions of Probation—Federal Probation**

Mandatory conditions. The court shall provide, as an explicit condition of a sentence of probation

1. for a felony, a misdemeanor, or an infraction, that the defendant not commit another federal, state, or local crime during the term of probation;
2. for a felony, that the defendant also abide by at least one condition set forth in subsection (b)(2), (b)(3), or (b)(13), unless the court finds on the record that extraordinary circumstances exist that would make such a condition plainly unreasonable, in which event the court shall impose one or more of the other conditions set forth under subsection (b);
3. for a felony, a misdemeanor, or an infraction, that the defendant not unlawfully possess a controlled substance; and
4. for a domestic violence crime as defined in section 3561(b) by a defendant convicted of such an offense for the first time that the defendant attend a public, private, or private nonprofit offender rehabilitation program that has been approved by the court, in consultation with a State Coalition Against Domestic Violence or other appropriate experts, if an approved program is readily available within a 50-mile radius of the legal residence of the defendant.
5. for a felony, a misdemeanor, or an infraction, that the defendant refrain from any unlawful use of a controlled substance and submit to one drug test within 15 days of release on probation and at least 2 periodic drug tests thereafter (as determined by the court) for use of a controlled substance, but the condition stated in this paragraph may be ameliorated or suspended by the court for any individual defendant if the defendant's presentence report or other reliable sentencing information indicates a low risk of future substance abuse by the defendant.

***Source:** Federal Criminal Code and Rules, Title 18, Chapter 227, Section 3563(a).

STANDARD CONDITIONS

Conditions imposed on all offenders in a jurisdiction.

Standard Conditions

Standard conditions are conditions imposed on all probationers in a jurisdiction. They are either prescribed by law or set by judicial practice. These usually require that the probationer will

- commit no criminal offense
- work regularly and support dependents
- submit to drug testing
- not change residence or employment without first notifying or obtaining permission from the probation officer
- report regularly to the probation officer as directed
- not leave the jurisdiction without permission
- allow the probation officer to visit at any time
- not associate with persons who have criminal records
- allow the probation officer to visit the probationer's residence

Discretionary Conditions of Probation—Federal Probation*

Discretionary conditions. The court may provide, as further conditions of a sentence or probation, to the extent that such conditions are reasonably related to the factors set forth in section 3553(a)(1) and (a)(2) and to the extent that such conditions involve only such deprivations of liberty or property as are reasonably necessary for the purposes indicated in section 3553(a)(2), that the defendant

1. support his dependents and meet other family responsibilities;
2. pay a fine imposed pursuant to the provisions of subchapter C;
3. make restitution to a victim of the offense under sections 3663 and 3664 (but not subject to the limitations of section 3663(a));
4. give to the victims of the offense the notice ordered pursuant to the provisions of section 3555;
5. work conscientiously at suitable employment or pursue conscientiously a course of study or vocational training that will equip him for suitable employment;
6. refrain, in the case of an individual, from engaging in a specified occupation, business, or profession bearing a reasonably direct relationship to the conduct constituting the offense, or engage in such a specified occupation, business, or profession only to a stated degree or under stated circumstances;
7. refrain from frequenting specified kinds of places or from associating unnecessarily with specified persons;
8. refrain from excessive use of alcohol, or any use of a narcotic drug or other controlled substance, as defined in section 102 of the Controlled Substances Act (21 U.S.C. 802), without a prescription by a licensed medical practitioner;
9. refrain from possessing a firearm, destructive device, or other dangerous weapon;
10. undergo available medical, psychiatric, or psychological treatment, including treatment for drug or alcohol dependency, as specified by the court, and remain in a specified institution if required for that purpose;
11. remain in the custody of the Bureau of Prisons during nights, weekends, or other

continued

Special Conditions

Special conditions are conditions tailored to fit the needs of an offender and therefore vary from one offender to another. Judges are given much discretion in determining what conditions should be imposed so that the conditions can be individualized for a particular offender. Judges usually impose conditions based on their assessment in court of an offender's needs, or they rely on recommendations made by a probation officer, particularly in cases where the probation officer prepared and submitted a presentence report. These conditions are suggested by law for certain offenses or are imposed by the judge on his or her own.

Special conditions may require the probationer to

- attend counseling sessions for substance abusers
- attend literacy classes
- obtain a high school diploma
- serve time in jail

SPECIAL CONDITIONS

Conditions tailored to fit the needs of an offender.

*Discretionary Conditions of Probation—Federal Probation**

intervals of time, totaling no more than the lesser of one year or the term of imprisonment authorized for the offense, during the first year of the term of probation;

12. reside at or participate in the program of a community corrections facility (including a facility maintained or under contract to the Bureau of Prisons) for all or part of the term of probation;
13. work in community service as directed by the court;
14. reside in a specified place or area, or refrain from residing in a specified place or area;
15. remain within the jurisdiction of the court, unless granted permission to leave by the court or a probation officer;
16. report to a probation officer as directed by the court or the probation officer;
17. permit a probation officer to visit him at his home or elsewhere as specified by the court;
18. answer inquiries by a probation officer and notify the probation officer promptly of any change in address or employment;
19. notify the probation officer promptly if arrested or questioned by a law enforcement officer;
20. remain at his place of residence during non-working hours and, if the court finds it appropriate, that compliance with this condition be monitored by telephonic or electronic signaling devices, except that a condition under this paragraph may be imposed only as an alternative to incarceration;
21. comply with the terms of any court order or order of an administrative process pursuant to the law of a state, the District of Columbia, or any other possession or territory of the United States, requiring payments by the defendant for the support and maintenance of a child or of a child and the parent with whom the child is living; or
22. satisfy such other conditions as the court may impose.

***Source:** Federal Criminal Code and Rules, Title 18, Chapter 227, Section 3563(b).

- participate in drug or alcohol treatment
- refrain from entering designated areas
- pay restitution
- seek mental health treatment
- perform community service
- support dependents
- obtain gainful employment

LIMITATIONS ON THE POWER OF COURTS TO IMPOSE CONDITIONS

Courts generally enjoy wide discretion in imposing conditions of probation because imposing probation conditions is solely a judicial function. Unless certain conditions are mandated by law, judges can be selective and impose any condition they deem proper. There are, however, some limitations to the immense power of judges to impose conditions. Based on decided cases, these limitations may be divided into four general categories: the condition must be clear; the condition must be reasonable; the condition must protect society and/or rehabilitate the offender; and the condition must be constitutional.

Clarity

Clear conditions of probation are explicit, precise, and easily understood. Unclear conditions are invalid because they are unfair to the offender and therefore violate the offender's right to due process. Actual cases help illustrate the problem. For example, a condition saying that the probationer must not associate with "a person of disreputable character" would be unfair unless that phrase is defined and explained to the probationer—which is done in some jurisdictions. In one case a court said that the "probation condition must be sufficiently explicit so as to inform a reasonable person of the conduct to be avoided."[4] In another case a state court held that probation conditions must be "sufficiently precise and unambiguous to inform the probationer of the conduct that is essential so that he may retain his liberty."[5] In another case a condition that the probationer not be within three blocks of a "high drug area" as defined by his probation officer was deemed too vague and was struck down because it could be violated by the probationer unintentionally.[6] Another court declared as too vague a condition that prohibited a probationer from residing in "Central Florida."[7] A condition that provided that the probationer "live honorably" was rejected on appeal by the court as vague and imprecise.[8] A condition that prohibited the probationer from "frequenting" establishments selling alcoholic drinks was declared unconstitutional because there was no evidence that the probationer understood what the term "frequenting" meant.[9]

CLEAR CONDITIONS

Conditions that are sufficiently explicit so as to inform a reasonable person of the conduct that is required and/or prohibited.

Reasonableness

A **reasonable condition** is one that can reasonably be complied with by the offender; conversely, an unreasonable condition is one that is likely to fail because the probationer cannot possibly comply with it. What is reasonable or unreasonable will likely depend on an offender's circumstances. For example, it is reasonable to require a rich offender to pay $1000 each week in restitution fees, but such a condition would be unreasonable if imposed on an indigent probationer. A condition that prohibits a drug addict from using drugs might be challenged as unreasonable because chances are high that such a condition would fail. However, courts have upheld the validity of this condition because using drugs violates the law, and violation of the law by probationers cannot be tolerated. There is also the belief, right or wrong, that the use of drugs starts with the exercise of free will and hence is preventable, and that addiction can be cured if the offender submits to treatment and resolves to refrain from using drugs.

REASONABLE CONDITIONS

Probation conditions that can reasonably be complied with by the offender.

In one case, however, a defendant was placed on probation for five years on condition that he refrain from the use of all alcoholic beverages. His probation was revoked when he violated the condition. He appealed, alleging that a psychiatric examination would have shown that he was a chronic alcoholic and that he was not responsible at the time of the act. The appellate court remanded the case on the ground that the district court may have imposed an impossible condition, particularly if psychiatric testimony established that his alcoholism had destroyed his power of volition and prevented his compliance with the condition.[10] This case appears to be the exception, however, rather than the rule.

What is reasonable or unreasonable, however, cannot be defined with precision and usually depends on the perception of the court. What may be reasonable to one judge may appear unreasonable to another. Usually, however, courts will consider a condition as reasonable and therefore valid, the benefit of the doubt being given to the judge who imposed the condition. This explains why relatively few conditions have been struck down as unreasonable.

Protection of Society and Rehabilitation of the Offender

Protection of society and rehabilitation of the offender are generally considered the two major goals of probation; therefore probation conditions must be reasonably related to these goals. In reality, these may not limit the power of the judge by much because both goals are so broad as to include just about any condition that is not way out of line or violative of basic constitutional rights. Nonetheless, appellate courts have limited what trial courts can set as conditions. For example, in a burglary case the court declared invalid two conditions that prohibited the defendant from living with a member of the opposite sex who was not a relative and from being in a certain area, saying that these conditions were not reasonably tailored to prevent future criminal conduct by the probationer.[11] In another case a state court invalidated a probation condition that imposed a 9:00 P.M. curfew on a defendant for five years, saying that the condition was not reasonably related to the defendant's rehabilitation.[12]

It is questionable whether a probationer who has never had a drinking problem and whose crime is unrelated to use of alcohol can be ordered to refrain from the use of alcoholic beverages.[13] The Federal Court of Appeals for the First Circuit has held, however, that the trial court could require that a defendant totally abstain from using alcohol during the defendant's three years of probation. In that case the defendant pleaded guilty to several counts of possession of stolen mail, theft of property used by the U.S. Postal Service, and other offenses resulting from a crime spree. The defendant later challenged the condition, saying that it was not related in any way to the circumstances of his offense. The court upheld the condition, saying that the defendant's family had an active history of alcohol abuse and that the defendant's record indicated that substance abuse was and continued to be a serious problem for him.[14]

In a 1997 case a defendant was placed on probation for tax-related offenses. One of the conditions imposed prohibited the defendant from leaving the judicial district without the permission of the court or the probation officer. The defendant thrice sought permission to travel to Russia; permission was denied. The Federal Court of Appeals for the Second Circuit concluded that the denial of the travel request was not reasonably related to the defendant's rehabilitation or the protection of the public and was therefore invalid.[15] And in a 1996 case the Federal Court of Appeals for the Tenth Circuit remanded a case to the district court to determine whether the condition prohibiting the defendant from contacting his son was reasonably related to the offense of making threatening telephone calls, saying that while a court enjoys broad discretion in setting conditions of supervised release, the condition must be reasonably related to the nature and circumstances of the offense and the history and characteristics of the defendant.[16]

SCARLET LETTER CONDITIONS

Conditions that, in effect, brand the offender.

The issue of **scarlet letter conditions** (conditions that in effect "brand" a probationer) has recently been viewed with disfavor by the courts based on the expressed purpose of probation in that jurisdiction. In one case a defendant pleaded guilty to

DWI and was placed on probation. Noting that this was the defendant's sixth DWI offense since 1971, the court imposed as a condition that the defendant affix to the license plates of any vehicle he drove a fluorescent sign saying "CONVICTED DWI." Defendant claimed this condition was unlawful. The New York court of appeals held the condition invalid because by law probation in New York is primarily a rehabilitative tool. Therefore, any condition imposed should be directed toward a defendant's rehabilitation rather than toward punitive or deterrent goals.[17] In another case the Tennessee Supreme Court in 1996 struck down a scarlet letter condition because it was not authorized by state law. In the Tennessee case the defendant was convicted of sexual battery and placed on probation. One of the special conditions of his probation required that he place this sign in his front yard:

> Warning, all children. Wayne Burden is an admitted and convicted child molester. Parents beware.

The appellate court reasoned that Tennessee law enumerates conditions for probation and that the statute did not allow substantial departures from conventional principles of probation. Saying that the primary goal of probation under Tennessee law was rehabilitation, the court struck down the condition because the sign was not consistent with that goal.[18]

Constitutionality

Courts have invalidated conditions that violate constitutionally protected activity. Probationers, by virtue of a criminal conviction, have diminished constitutional rights, but they nonetheless enjoy some rights, particularly those considered basic and fundamental. When basic, fundamental rights are alleged to have been violated courts are likely to hold that the condition is valid only if the government can establish a compelling state interest that would justify the condition. **First Amendment rights** are considered basic and fundamental and are therefore better protected by the courts than Fourth, Fifth, or Sixth Amendment Rights. The burden of proof is on the government to establish that a compelling state interest exists. Again, however, that term is subjective, and its meaning may vary from one judge to another. What follows is a discussion of some cases involving constitutional rights.

FIRST AMENDMENT RIGHTS

Basic and fundamental rights guaranteed by the first amendment to the U.S. Constitution to freedom of religion, press, assembly and to petition the government for redress of grievances.

FREEDOM OF RELIGION: Freedom of religion is a First Amendment right that is highly protected by the courts. The First Amendment provides as follows:

> Congress shall make no law respecting an establishment of religion, or prohibiting the free exercise thereof; or abridging the freedom of speech, or of the press; or the right of people peaceably to assemble, and to petition the Government for a redress of grievances.

Based on this provision, the following are considered basic, fundamental rights that deserve protection by the courts:

1. Freedom of religion
2. Freedom of speech
3. Freedom of assembly
4. Freedom of the press
5. Freedom to petition the government for redress of grievances

In *Jones v. Commonwealth* a Virginia court held that an order of a juvenile court requiring regular attendance at Sunday school and church was unconstitutional because "no civil authority has the right to require anyone to accept or reject any religious belief or to contribute any support thereto."[19] The Court of Appeals for the 11th Circuit has reviewed a condition requiring a probationer to participate in an "Emotional Maturity Instruction" program. The probationer claimed the condition violated his First Amendment freedom of religion due to the program's religious content. The court stated,

> A condition of probation which requires the probationer to adopt religion or adopt any particular religion would be unconstitutional. . . . It follows that a condition of probation which requires the probationer to submit himself to a course advocating the adoption of religion or a particular religion also transgresses the First Amendment.[20]

An issue related to freedom of religion is required participation in an Alcoholics Anonymous (A.A.) program. In one case a defendant pleaded guilty to a third alcohol-related driving offense within a one-year period. He was placed on probation on condition that he attend Alcoholics Anonymous at the direction of his probation officer. The probationer, an atheist, complained that A.A. was a religious program and therefore violated his freedom of religion. The court reviewed the Twelve-Step Program (for which A.A. has become famous) and concluded that the concept of a "higher power" is at the center of the 12 steps. Moreover, much of the literature of A.A. refers to God and encourages prayer, leading the court to conclude that the meetings tended to establish a form of religion; therefore, requiring A.A. meeting attendance as a condition of probation was unconstitutional.[21]

Not all courts agree. Some courts have concluded that A.A., although bearing a religious flavor, is basically a secular treatment program that does not violate a probationer's freedom of religion. The issue has not been decided authoritatively by the U.S. Supreme Court.

PRIVACY: The right to privacy is not found in any specific amendment; instead, it is derived from other amendments such as the Fourth, Fifth, and the Ninth Amendments. Nonetheless, it is considered a fundamental right, particularly when applied to certain types of conditions. The right to privacy has been the basis of arguments challenging conditions that restrict relationships with family members, prohibit child-bearing, and limit sexual intercourse.[22] A condition is usually not invalidated merely because it invades the fundamental right to privacy. Only where no compelling state interest exists to overcome the individual's right to privacy does the condition fail. The state therefore bears the burden of establishing that a compelling state interest justifies such a condition. This varies depending upon the offense involved. For example, a condition that prohibits child-bearing would doubtless be unconstitutional if imposed for driving while intoxicated but would likely be constitutional if the crime were the killing of one's own infant child.

PROCREATION: Although not found in any specific amendment, the right to procreation is considered fundamental and may be limited only if there is a compelling state interest to justify the limitation. In a California case, a probation condition prohibiting a woman, convicted of robbery, from becoming pregnant without being married was struck down.[23] The court said that there was no relationship between robbery and pregnancy.

In *Rodriguez v. State* a Florida court placed a defendant convicted of aggravated child abuse on probation for ten years, provided she (1) not have custody of her children, (2) not become pregnant, and (3) not marry without the consent of the court. The appellate court ruled that although trial courts have broad discretion to impose various

The Alcoholics Anonymous "Twelve-Step Program"—Is It Religious?*

1. We admitted we were powerless over alcohol—that our lives had become unmanageable.
2. Came to believe that a Power greater than ourselves could restore us to sanity.
3. Made a decision to turn our will and our lives over to the care of God as we understood Him.
4. Made a searching and fearless moral inventory of ourselves.
5. Admitted to God, to ourselves and to another human being the exact nature of our wrongs.
6. Were entirely ready to have God remove all these defects of character.
7. Humbly ask Him to remove our shortcomings.
8. Made a list of all persons we had harmed and became willing to make amends to them all.
9. Made direct amends to such people wherever possible, except when to do so would injure them or others.
10. Continued to take personal inventory and when we were wrong promptly admitted it.
11. Sought through prayer and meditation to improve our conscious contact with God as we understood Him, praying only for knowledge of His will for us and the power to carry that out.
12. Having had a spiritual awakening as the result of these steps we tried to carry this message to alcoholics, and to practice these principles in all our affairs.

*In *Warner v. Orange County Department of Probation*, 870 F.Supp. 69 (S.D.N.Y.), a federal district court in New York declared that A.A. meetings, using the above tenets, were the equivalent of a religious exercise and therefore violated an atheist probationer's freedom of religion.

conditions of probation, a special condition of probation cannot be imposed if it is so punitive as to be unrelated to rehabilitation. Applying these criteria to the case, the court held that a condition prohibiting custody of children has a clear relationship to the crime of child abuse and is therefore valid. However, probation conditions relating to marriage and pregnancy had no relationship to the crime of child abuse and were related to noncriminal conduct. The conditions prohibiting marriage and pregnancy did nothing to decrease the possibility of future child abuse or other criminality.[24]

THE RIGHT AGAINST UNREASONABLE SEARCHES AND SEIZURES: The Fourth Amendment **right against unreasonable searches and seizures** is not as highly protected by the courts as First Amendment rights. Several courts have held that conditions of probation that required probationers to submit to searches with or without a warrant were valid. In *People v. Mason* the court ruled that the waiver of Fourth Amendment rights can be a probation condition and that by such waiver a probationer has no reasonable expectation of privacy.[25] The reasonableness standard of the Fourth Amendment has generally been held to apply, however, and probation and parole officers must have reasonable grounds to believe that searches are necessary to the performance of their duties relating to the probationer or parolee.[26]

RIGHT AGAINST UNREASONABLE SEARCHES AND SEIZURES
Rights guaranteed under the fourth amendment of the U.S. Constitution.

In *Griffin v. Wisconsin* the U.S. Supreme Court addressed the issue of searches by probation officers. In *Griffin* a probation officer searched the home of a probationer under his supervision without having obtained a search warrant. The probation officer had received a tip from a police officer that guns might be found in the probationer's home. A gun was found, and the probationer was subsequently convicted on a firearms charge. At his trial the probationer moved to suppress the gun evidence, saying that the search was a violation of his Fourth Amendment protection from unreasonable searches and seizures. The motion was denied, and the conviction was later affirmed by the Wisconsin Supreme Court. In making the search, the probation officer relied on a Wisconsin probation regulation that allows the search of a probationer's home without a warrant but with the approval of a supervisor. The regulation also required that there be reasonable grounds (which is lower in certainty than probable cause) to believe contraband is present in violation of the conditions of probation. Declaring the search valid, the U.S. Supreme Court described probation as a form of sanction, like incarceration, where warrant requirements are impractical because of the necessity for quick decisions. The Court also found that the regulation permitting the search, on which the probation officer had relied, was consistent with the Fourth Amendment's "reasonableness" requirement.[27]

PRIVILEGE AGAINST SELF-INCRIMINATION

Constitutional right guaranteed by the fifth amendment to the U.S. Constitution.

THE PRIVILEGE AGAINST SELF-INCRIMINATION: The Fifth Amendment guarantees the **privilege against self-incrimination.** Does a probation condition that compromises this right violate the Constitution? The answer is uncertain. In a 1996 case the Vermont Supreme Court held that a condition requiring a probationer to admit guilt as part of a sex offender therapy program violated the probationer's right to be free from self-incrimination. The court added that a person in a probation setting cannot be forced to incriminate himself without first receiving immunity from criminal prosecution as a result of such admission.[28] The Montana Supreme Court has also ruled that the Fifth Amendment privilege against compelled self-incrimination bars a state from conditioning probation upon the probationer's successful completion of a therapy program in which probationer would be required to admit responsibility for the criminal acts of which he was convicted.[29] The Alaska Supreme Court has held, however, that a probationer cannot validly invoke the privilege to be free from self-incrimination unless there is "real or substantial hazard of incrimination."[30] The issue of whether a probationer can refuse to admit guilt in cases where such is required for participation in a treatment program was accepted for decision by the U.S. Supreme Court in 1992, but the Court subsequently changed its mind and dismissed the case from its docket.[31] Various courts have decided this issue differently, so unless the U.S. Supreme Court resolves the issue, jurisdictions will continue to differ as to its constitutionality.

The condition that the probationer "tell the truth" does not violate the right against self-incrimination, particularly if the evidence is used in a revocation proceeding and not in a subsequent criminal trial.

LENGTH OF PROBATION

The power to determine the length of probation is vested in the judge, although maximum and minimum limits are usually set by statute. These limits are sometimes similar to the terms fixed by statute for the offense if the offender were committed to a penal institution instead of placed on probation. The modern trend is to specify limits for probation that are less than the limits for commitment. In some states the court is empowered to extend the length of probation during the original term, but within a specified limit. For example, a five-year probation term may be extended but not to exceed seven years.

Modern standards for probation recommend that probation terms be fixed and relatively short and that the court be given authority to terminate the probation at any time during the probation period. Extended periods of probation are viewed with disfavor, perhaps because they may be ineffective after a while and can be subject to abuse. In some jurisdictions that impose a probation fee, an extended period of probation without supervision may become a revenue-raising scheme instead of a genuine effort at rehabilitation or public protection.

Short and more definite periods of probation are favored by many corrections groups. For example, the Model Penal Code suggests a probation of five years on conviction of a felony and of two years on conviction of a misdemeanor or petty misdemeanor.[32] The American Bar Association *Standards Relating to Probation* provides that neither supervision nor the power to revoke it should be permitted to extend beyond a legislatively fixed time, which should in no event exceed two years for a misdemeanor and five years for a felony.[33] Section 3561 of the latest *Sentencing Reform Act, Sentencing Guidelines, and Parole* for the federal government provides for the following terms of probation: for a felony, not less than one nor more than five years; for a misdemeanor, not more than five years; and for an infraction, not more than one year.

MODIFICATION OF CONDITIONS OF PROBATION

The length and conditions of probation may be modified in two ways: shortening the term or easing restrictions, and extending the term or imposing additional restrictions. Authority to modify the term of probation by decreasing the term and discharging the offender before completion of the term is also given to the court. The court can modify the conditions of probation on application of the probationer or the probation officer or on its own. The probationer can ask the court and the probation officer to clarify the probation conditions. The power to modify conditions underlines the flexibility of probation as a correctional tool.

The court can modify the term and conditions of probation in response to changing circumstances during the probation term. Controversy sometimes arises over the technical issues of determining when a probation period has ended and the policy issues of what procedures should be required before the court can modify the original term and conditions of probation. This is particularly true if the modification is to extend the term or impose more restrictive conditions. Shorter and more favorable conditions are not challenged by the probationer and therefore do not raise legal concerns.

PROCEDURES FOR MODIFYING THE CONDITIONS AND LENGTH OF PROBATION

It can be argued that the procedure for modifying the term or conditions of probation should be similar to those associated with the granting of the probation. However, no such procedures may be impractical and unnecessary. For example, requiring an appearance of all parties before the court, together with a lawyer, in order to change the reporting day (say, from Friday to Wednesday) or to change a treatment program would be a waste of time and resources. Changes that impose longer, harsher, or more restrictive conditions on the offender might demand more formal procedures, but even these may not justify a full-blown hearing as in probation revocation cases.

The American Bar Association committee working with sentencing and probation standards distinguishes between modifications in probation conditions that may lead to the defendant's confinement and those that would not. The standards recommend that, when necessary, there should be a review of the conditions and a formal or informal conference with the probationer to reemphasize the necessity of complying with the conditions of probation.[34] A request for clarification provides an avenue for resolving disputes between probationer and probation officer about the meaning of a condition. Such disputes are generally resolved without court intervention.[35]

Where a modification in the terms and conditions of probation may lead to confinement, procedures should correspond to those required for revocation of probation.[36] Whether this would include the "on-site hearing" demanded by *Gagnon v. Scarpelli*[37] as well as the probation revocation hearing before the court is still an open question. If the suggested modifications are so extensive as to raise this question, the matter should probably be identified as a revocation hearing. Instead of the procedures for a modification of term or conditions, the revocation procedures would be followed.

WHO CAN MODIFY CONDITIONS AND LENGTH OF PROBATION

Setting and modifying the conditions and length of probation is a judicial function and cannot be performed by the probation officer. The only exception is if such authority is specifically given to the probation officer by law, which seldom happens. Neither can the judge delegate the power to set and modify conditions to the probation officer. The wording, usually at the end of the list of probation conditions, that the probationer is to "abide by any or other conditions as the probation officer may deem wise and proper to impose," is an outright delegation of authority by the judge and should be avoided unless such wording is provided for by law.

A distinction must be made, however, between *setting* conditions of probation and *implementing* conditions of probation. In the words of one court, a judge "can set general probation conditions and a probation officer can then set specific rules to implement the general condition."[38] For example, a judge may prescribe that the offender be required to submit to psychological treatment, the specific treatment to be determined by the probation officer. This is generally valid (unless specifically prohibited by state law) because it sets a condition but does not implement it. Similarly, a condition that sets restitution at a certain amount but leaves the method of payment to be determined by the probation officer would likely be valid because specifying the method of payment is implementation. The only possible exception is if this is specifically prohibited by state law. Leaving the restitution amount, however, to the discretion and final decision of the probation officer is likely to constitute an illegal delegation of judicial authority. In most jurisdictions the judge asks the probation officer to investigate and recommend a restitution amount, but the judge retains the authority to set the final amount.

EARLY TERMINATION OF PROBATION

EARLY TERMINATION

Termination of probation at any time during the probation period or after some time has been served.

In many states the court is given authority to terminate probation at any time during the probation period or after some time has been served. For example, Texas state law provides that for felony offenses a probationer may apply for **early termination** after having satisfactorily served one-third of the probation term or two years, whichever is less.[39] Article 3564 of the Federal Rules of Criminal Procedure states that the court may "terminate a term of probation previously ordered and discharge the defendant at any time in the case of a misdemeanor or an infraction or at any time after the expiration of one year of probation in the case of a felony, if it is satisfied that such action is warranted by the conduct of the defendant and the interest of justice."[40]

The authority to terminate probation early is usually vested in the judge, who acts upon recommendation of the probation officer. Early termination is usually discretionary with the judge, who reviews the record of the probationer before granting or rejecting the request. Some states authorize early termination without providing statutory guidelines as to when the power should be exercised. A significantly larger number permit early termination upon the satisfaction of statutory criteria, such as good behavior during the period of probation. The motion for early termination can be initiated by the probationer or the probation officer.

Giving the court power to terminate probation early manifests legislative recognition that many probationers do not need probation services for the full term. It removes from probation offenders whose reintegration into the community is complete or at least sufficiently acceptable to not warrant continued supervision.

SPECIAL PROGRAMS TO CARRY OUT PROBATION CONDITIONS

Probation conditions require that programs or arrangements be established to carry out the conditions imposed. Treatment-oriented conditions require the probationer to undergo treatment in-house or be referred to existing programs in the community. Control-oriented conditions may require the availability of programs that are not otherwise a part of regular probation. Discussed next are some programs or arrangements available in many jurisdictions. Many of these programs are discussed in greater detail in the chapter on intermediate sanctions (chapter 11).

Prison Time

In some jurisdictions the court may order a brief period of incarceration as a condition of probation. Known in various states as **shock probation** or shock incarceration or **split sentencing,** the practice is based on the assumption that if offenders are given a taste of prison (the "shock"), they will be less likely to violate the conditions of probation upon their release. The federal probation statute allows the court to impose intermittent confinement as a condition of probation during the first year of probation.[41]

SHOCK PROBATION/SPLIT SENTENCING

A period of incarceration imposed as a condition of probation.

Combining a jail sentence with probation, in effect making a jail sentence a condition of probation, is used widely in various states. The Bureau of Justice Statistics reports that in 1995 15 percent of adults on probation from state or federal courts (248,379 out of 1,616,004 adults on state and federal probation) were on split sentences, meaning incarceration with probation.[42]

The Model Penal Code permits a 30-day period of imprisonment in connection with a probated term for a person convicted of a felony or misdemeanor.[43] The American Bar Association's *Standards Relating to Sentencing Alternatives and Procedures* includes among the range of sentencing alternatives "[c]ommitment to an institution for a short, fixed period followed by automatic release under supervision."[44] The commentary on this section recognizes widespread opposition to combining jail with probation. The National Advisory Commission recommended against the practice, arguing that the goal of probation should be to maintain in the community all persons who, with support, can perform there acceptably and to select for some type of confinement only those who cannot complete probation successfully, even with optimal support. Because of this, the commission recommended that the practice of commitment to an institution for the initial period of probation should be discontinued, saying that it defeats the purpose of probation. Those who reject jail as a condition of probation assert that short-term commitment subjects the probationer to the destructive effects of institutionalization, disrupts his or her life in the community, and stigmatizes the probationer for having been in jail.[45]

The effectiveness of shock probation has not been conclusively proved. Moreover, treatment-oriented critics see the practice as undermining the basic meaning and objective of probation. By contrast, others believe that an initial period of incarceration makes the offender more receptive to probation supervision and improves the person's chances of making successful community adjustment. In many cases the outcome may depend not so much on the approach used as it does on the type of offenders exposed to this approach. Shock probation does not work for offenders familiar with detention systems or for those who commit crimes for reasons unrelated to free will. It may, however, be a deterrent for others.

Intensive Supervision

INTENSIVE SUPERVISION

A form of probation for offenders who require more structure and surveillance than ordinary probation for whom incarceration may be too severe a sanction.

Intensive supervision is a form of probation where the caseload is low and the probationer is supervised closely. Regular probation caseload may vary from 100 to 250 probationers for each probation officer; by contrast, the ideal intensive supervision caseload is 25. One or more probation officers are assigned to monitor a group, depending on how the system is structured. Intensive supervision differs from regular supervision mainly in the intensity of the supervision and the clientele involved. Probationers placed in intensive supervision are usually higher-risk offenders who would otherwise have been sent to jail or prison.[46]

Two legal issues are raised in intensive supervision: possible violations of the constitutional rights to equal protection and the prohibition against cruel and unusual punishment. Equal protection requires that people be treated in the same manner unless there is justification for treating them differently. Critics assert that placing some probationers in intensive supervision, while others are not as closely supervised, treats them differently in violation of the U.S. Constitution. It is also alleged that the Eighth Amendment ban on cruel and unusual punishment prohibits supervision that is overly intrusive on individual privacy. Both objections have been rejected by the courts, primarily because probationers have diminished constitutional rights and because offenders on intensive supervision would likely have been sent to prison anyway, where restrictions are more severe and privacy is virtually nonexistent. Besides, equality in supervision does not exist in probation anyway because the treatment approach that undergirds many probation conditions requires individualized treatment based on what may best rehabilitate the offender.

The Bureau of Justice Statistics reports that 97,737 probationers were on intensive supervision in 1995 (out of a total adult probation population of 3,096,529).[47] It is estimated that in 1995 the average daily cost for regular supervision in the United States was $2.12, while the cost for intensive supervision was $10.63.[48] Intensive supervision

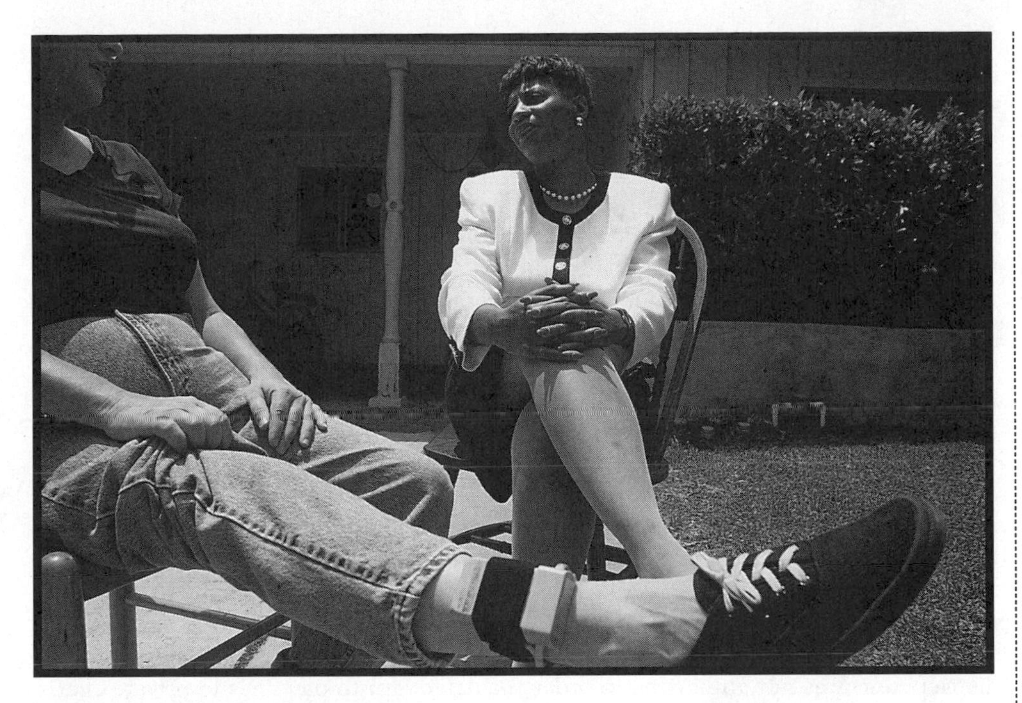

Probation officer counsels probationer wearing electronic monitoring device.

is unquestionably more expensive than regular probation, but it is seen as better protective of society and is still much less expensive than incarceration.

Electronic Monitoring

Electronic monitoring has become popular as a condition of probation because it is efficient, is less expensive than intensive supervision or incarceration, and is definitely high-tech. It involves linking a monitor attached to the probationer's wrist or ankle to a home telephone, which is linked to a computer at the probation agency. This gives the probation officer greatly enhanced surveillance capacity. In most states electronic monitoring may be imposed by a judge as a special condition; in some states it is specifically provided for by law.

ELECTRONIC MONITORING

A correctional technology which involves linking a monitor attached to the offender's wrist or ankle to a home telephone which is linked to a computer at the probation agency.

In 1995 the Bureau of Justice Statistics reported that 15,373 probationers (out of a total of 3,096,529) were on electronic monitors.[49] Another source reports that during that same year at least 20 states were using electronic monitors (a total of 3,507 devices) to supervise probationers.[50]

Fines

A **fine** is "a pecuniary (monetary) punishment imposed by lawful tribunal upon a person convicted of crime or misdemeanor."[51] Federal sentencing guidelines specifically state, "The amount of the fine should always be sufficient that the fine, taken together with the other sanctions imposed, is punitive."[52] Both federal and state court judges frequently impose fines as a condition of probation. The use of fines has been criticized as causing a greater burden on the poor than on the wealthy, so many of the laws regarding fines have been revised. Revisions are needed to ensure equality in the

FINE

A pecuniary penalty imposed upon a person convicted of a crime or misdemeanor.

imposition of fines, although that may be an elusive goal primarily because circumstances surrounding offenses and offenders are never the same.

New York and some other jurisdictions have experimented with the European system of "day fines." Day fines are assessed as some multiple of the offender's daily wage, or "unit." For example, if an offender earns $100 per day and the fine is 5 units, the offender would be required to pay 5 times his or her daily wage, or $500. A day fine of 5 units imposed on an offender with an income of $1,000 a day would be $5,000. Failure to pay a fine imposed as a probation condition may result in revocation and incarceration. However, probation is seldom revoked for failure to pay fines alone.

In the 1983 case of *Bearden v. Georgia* the U.S. Supreme Court held that probation cannot be revoked solely because of an offender's inability to pay a fine or restitution.[53] The Court said that such revocation based on indigency violates the equal protection clause of the Fourteenth Amendment. The Court distinguished, however, between indigency (inability) and unwillingness (refusal) to pay. Unwillingness to pay court-ordered restitution or fines, despite a probationer's ability to do so, may result in revocation. Statutes in most states and the federal system provide for allowing a flexible payment schedule if the defendant is unable to pay the entire fine immediately, modifying the sentence to reduce the fine, and in some cases forgoing the fine and imposing an alternative sanction.

In a 1996 federal case the Seventh Circuit Court of Appeals held that the federal district court was not authorized to order the defendant to pay fines to private charities. The court could not require a defendant to pay a fine to private charities because fines are paid to the government, not to private parties.[54]

Restitution

RESTITUTION

An equitable penalty under which an offender is required to restore the victim to his or her position prior to loss or injury.

Restitution is defined as "an equitable remedy under which a person is restored to his or her position prior to a loss or injury . . . compensation for the wrongful taking of property."[55] The main distinction between restitution and fines is that restitution is paid to the victim while fines are paid to the government. Restitution requires offenders to compensate their victims for damages or loss of property and may take the form of either direct monetary restitution to the victim or symbolic restitution, as in the case of community service. In recent years restitution has become widely accepted and popular as a condition of probation; however, it can be abused. John Ortiz Smykla warns that

> Restitution is not without its dangers. Because litigation has not contested its use, there is potential for abuse; the due process rights of probationers can be ignored in placing them in restitution programs, or they can be sentenced to prolonged periods of community service or to unfair amounts of restitution. For example, victims frequently exaggerate the amount of property damage inflicted upon them by offenders.[56]

Generally, however, restitution benefits the probationer, the victim, and society as a whole. In a National Institute of Justice report Douglas McDonald writes

> Victim restitution . . . forces offenders to see firsthand the consequences of their deeds and thus may encourage the development of greater social responsibility and maturity.[57]

A 1992 Bureau of Justice Statistics study reported that in a sample of 79,000 probationers, 50 percent of all property offenders and 24 percent of all violent offenders were ordered restitution as a condition of probation. The average restitution ordered was $3,368. The study also reported that 60 percent of the offenders had completed their restitution by the time they completed their sentence.[58] A recent survey in Texas found that restitution was "always ordered" in 49 percent of probation cases statewide, while it was "frequently ordered" in 50 percent of the cases.[59] Other studies have found that probationers receiving restitution orders have equal or lower recidivism rates than control groups receiving no restitution orders.[60]

The validity of restitution as a condition of probation has been upheld. In a recent case a defendant was convicted of criminally negligent homicide and was placed on probation. Among the conditions of probation was that the defendant was to "pay restitution to the victim, perform 100 hours of community service, and write a letter of apology to the victim's girlfriend and family." The State Court of Appeals held that "a trial court has discretion to order a probationer to pay restitution to the victim as a condition of probation, so long as the amount set by the court has a factual basis in the record and is just."[61] Another state court of appeals has held, however, that the court cannot delegate to the probation department the responsibility of determining the amounts of the loss and the restitution: this is a judicial function.[62]

Community Service

Many offenders coming through the criminal justice system are poor and cannot reasonably be expected to pay monetary restitution. Moreover, even if the offender is able to pay, unpaid personal service by the offender is often a welcome form of restitution to the community. Thus, **community service,** defined as the performance of unpaid work for civic or nonprofit organizations, is popular as an alternative means of restitution. In a study of 79,000 felons sentenced in 1986, Langan and Cunniff (1992) reported that 14 percent had a special condition requiring community service.[63] A more recent survey in Texas shows that 59 percent of respondents said that community service was "always imposed" as a condition in felony cases, and 40 percent said that it was "always imposed" in misdemeanor cases.[64] Some states, by statute, require community service as a condition of probation for just about any offense. The number of hours of community service vary depending on the nature and seriousness of the offense. For example, one state provides for the following community service hours for probation:[65]

COMMUNITY SERVICE

Performance of unpaid work for civic or nonprofit organizations as an alternative means of restitution.

Punishment range	Maximum hours	Minimum hours
1st degree felony	1000	320
2nd degree felony	800	240
3rd degree felony	600	160
State jail felony	400	120
Class A misdemeanor	200	80
Class B misdemeanor	100	24
Class C misdemeanor	No range	No range

In *Higdon v. United States,* the Ninth Circuit Court of Appeals rejected a probation condition that required the probationer to do 6,200 hours of volunteer work over a three-year period. The court held that the condition, which was essentially full-time charity work, was "much harsher than necessary." The court reasoned as follows:

> First we consider the purpose for which the judge imposed the conditions. If the purposes are permissible, the second step is to consider whether the conditions are reasonably related to the purposes. In conducting the latter inquiry the court examines the impact . . . the conditions have on the probationer's rights. If the impact is substantially greater than is necessary to carry out the purposes, the conditions are impermissible.[66]

Drug Testing

Drug testing, usually in the form of urinalysis (urine testing), is widely used as a condition of probation as an easy and efficient way to determine if an offender has used drugs during probation. It is prescribed by law in some states and left to the discretion of the probation agency or probation officer in other states. A urine sample is obtained from the probationer, usually at random during an office visit, under the supervision of a probation officer. The sample is either tested in-house or sent to a laboratory for analysis. A recent survey shows that in one state drug testing was "always imposed" as a condition of probation in 78 percent of the departments surveyed. Among those departments, 92 percent conducted drug testing of probationers at random instead of on schedule.[67]

Drug testing of offenders may be authorized in a number of ways: by state law, by agency policy, by agency practice, or as imposed by the judge in the absence of any specific authorization. Some courts have held that urine testing can be conducted by an officer even if it is not specifically prescribed as a condition of probation[68] because one of the required conditions of probation in practically all jurisdictions is that the offender not violate the law. Because using drugs is a violation of law, urine tests are justified even without being specifically prescribed as a condition.

Legal challenges have arisen concerning drug testing, among them the possible violation of the constitutional right to privacy, the right against unreasonable searches and seizures, the privilege against self-incrimination, the right to due process, and the right to equal protection. Courts, however, have upheld drug testing against constitutional challenges, saying that these rights are not infringed because probationers have diminished constitutional rights anyway. Besides, these rights are waived when the probationer consents to drug testing as a condition of probation. Courts have generally required, however, that obtaining a sample not be unnecessarily humiliating and that the test used to determine the presence of drugs be accurate and reliable.[69]

SUMMARY

Probationers typically agree to abide by a set of rules or conditions of release. The power to fix these conditions lies with the court. Conditions may generally be classified into standard conditions and special conditions. Standard conditions are those imposed on all probationers in a jurisdiction, while special conditions are tailored to fit the needs of each offender and therefore vary.

Although courts have broad powers to impose other conditions of probation, there are nonetheless four limitations: each condition must be clear, reasonable, related to the protection of society and the rehabilitation of the offender, and constitutional. Constitutional rights that might be violated by probation conditions are freedom of religion, privacy, the right to procreate, the right against unreasonable search and seizure, and the right against self-incrimination.

The court has the power to modify the conditions and the term of probation. The power to set or modify conditions is exercised by the judge and cannot be delegated to the probation officer. Courts are also empowered in many jurisdictions to terminate probation early once it is determined that further supervision is no longer warranted.

Conditions imposed result in such special programs as prison time as part of the term of probation, intensive supervision, electronic monitoring, fines, restitution, community service, and drug testing. Each of these programs raises constitutional issues, but courts have generally upheld them.

ENDNOTES

1. *Houston Chronicle,* July 30, 1996, 11A.
2. *Dallas Morning News,* March 9, 1996, 1.
3. James J. Gobert and Neil P. Cohen, *The Law of Probation and Parole* (Deerfield, Ill.: Clark, Boardman, Callaghan, 1983), 186.
4. *People v. Howland,* 108 AD 2d 1019 (Sup. Ct. App. Div. 1985).
5. *Rich v. State,* 640 P2d 159 (Alaska Ct. App. 1982).
6. *Huff v. State,* 554 So. 2d 616 (Fla. Dist. Ct. App. 1989).
7. *Almond v. State,* 350 So. 2d 810 (Fla. 4th DCA 1977).
8. *Norris v. State,* 383 So. 2d 691 (Fla. Dist. Ct. App. 1980).
9. *Panko v. McCauley,* 473 F. Supp. 325 (C.D. Wisc. 1979).
10. *Sobell v. Reed,* 327 F. Supp. 1294 (S.D. N.Y. 1971).
11. *Huff v. State,* 554 So. 2d 616 (Fla. Dist. Ct. App. Dec 1989).
12. *State v. Labure,* 427 S. 2d 855 (La. 1983).
13. Gobert and Cohen, *The Law of Probation and Parole,* 189.
14. *United States v. Thurlow,* 44 F. 3d 46 (U.S. 1st Cir. 1995).
15. *United States v. Porotsky,* 105 F. 2d 69 (U.S. 2nd Cir. 1997).
16. *United States v. Edgin,* 92 F. 3d 1044 (U.S. 10th Cir. 1996).
17. *People v. Letterlough,* 631 N.Y.S. 2d 105 (N.Y. App. 1995).
18. *State v. Burden,* 924 S.W. 2d 82 (Tenn. Sup. 1996).
19. *Jones v. Commonwealth,* 185 Va. 335 (1946).
20. *Owens v. Kelly,* 681 F. 2d 1362 (11th Cir. 1982).
21. *Warner v. Orange County Department of Probation,* 870 F. Supp. 69 (S.D.N.Y. 1994).
22. Rolando V. del Carmen, *Potential Liabilities of Probation and Parole Officers* (Cincinnati, Ohio: Anderson, 1985), 1102.
23. *People v. Dominquez,* 64 Cal. Rptr. 290 (1967).
24. *Rodriguez v. State,* 378 So. 2d 7 (Fla. Dist. Ct. App. 1979).
25. *People v. Mason,* 488 P. 2d 630 (1971).
26. *United States v. Scott,* 678 F. 2d 32 (5th Cir. 1982).
27. *Griffin v. Wisconsin,* 483 U.S. 868 (1987).
28. *State v. Cate,* 683 A. 2d 1010 (Vt. Sup. 1996).
29. *Montana v. Imlay,* 813 P. 2d 979 (1991).
30. *State v. Gonzalez,* 853 P. 2d 526 (Alaska, 1993).
31. *Houston Chronicle,* November 4, 1992, 5A.
32. Model Penal Code, Sec. 301.2.
33. ABA, *Standards Relating to Probation,* Sec. 1.1(d); and *Standards, Sentencing Alternatives, and Procedures,* Sec. 2.4.
34. ABA, *Standards Relating to Probation,* Sec. 5.1(b). (Chicago, n.d.).
35. ABA, *Standards Relating to Probation,* Sec. 3.1.
36. See chapter 7 of this book on revocation of probation.
37. *Gagnon v. Scarpelli,* 411 U.S. 778 (1973).

38. *Costa v. State,* 58 Md. App. 474 (1984).
39. Texas Code of Criminal Procedure, Art. 42.12, Sec. 20.
40. Federal Rules of Criminal Procedure, Art. 3564.
41. 18 U.S.C.A., Sec. 3563 (b) (11); and *Federal Sentencing Guidelines Handbook: Text, Analysis, Case Digests.*
42. Bureau of Justice Statistics, *Correctional Populations in the United States, 1995,* 32.
43. Model Penal Code, Sec. 301.1(3).
44. ABA, *Standards Relating to Sentencing Alternatives and Procedures,* Sec. 2.4(a)iii.
45. National Advisory Commission, *Standards, Corrections,* 321.
46. See Rolando V. del Carmen, *Criminal Procedure: Law and Practice,* 3rd ed. (Belmont, Calif.: Wadsworth, 1995), 433.
47. Bureau of Justice Statistics, *Correctional Populations in the United States, 1995,* 40–41.
48. Camille Graham Camp and George M. Camp, *Corrections Yearbook, 1996* (Criminal Justice Institute), 142.
49. Bureau of Justice Statistics, *Correctional Populations in the United States, 1995,* 41.
50. Camp and Camp, *Corrections Yearbook, 1996,* 160.
51. *Black's Law Dictionary,* 5th ed. (St. Paul, Minnesota: West, 1979), 568.
52. *Federal Sentencing Guidelines Handbook,* 335.
53. *Bearden v. Georgia,* 461 U.S. 660 (1983).
54. *United States v. Wolff,* 90 F. 3d 191 (7th Cir. 1996).
55. *Black's Law Dictionary,* 118.
56. John Ortiz Smykla, *Probation and Parole: Crime Control in the Community* (New York: MacMillan, 1984), 222.
57. Douglas C. McDonald, *Restitution and Community Service* (Washington, D.C.: National Institute of Justice), 192.
58. Patrick A. Langan and Mark Cunniff, "Recidivism of Felons on Probation, 1986–1989," *Bureau of Justice Statistics Special Report,* February 1992.
59. Rolando V. del Carmen, Jeffrey D. Dailey, and Lance Emerson, *Community Supervision: Law and Practice in Texas* (Huntsville, Tex.: SHSU Press, 1996), 106.
60. Larry Siegel, *Criminology,* 4th ed. (St. Paul, Minnesota: West, 1992), 561.
61. *Todd v. State,* 911 S.W. 2d 807 (Tex. App. 1995).
62. *State v. Toups,* 499 S. 2d 1149 (La. Ct. App. 1987).
63. Langdan and Cunniff, "Recidivism of Felons on Probation," 7.
64. Del Carmen, Dailey, and Emerson, *Community Supervision,* 105.
65. Texas Code of Criminal Procedure, Art. 42.12 Sec. 22(a)(1).
66. 627 F. 2d 893 (9th Cir. 1980).
67. Del Carmen, Dailey, and Emerson, *Community Supervision,* 103.
68. *United States v. Duff,* 831 F. 2d 176 (9th Cir. 1987).
69. For a collection of cases on the legality of drug testing as a condition of probation, see *Drug Testing Guidelines and Practices for Adult Probation and Parole Agencies,* a monograph published by the Bureau of Justice Assistance (July 1991), 87–108.

DISCUSSION QUESTIONS

1. Discuss the extent of the power of the court to impose conditions. Can judges impose creative conditions? Give some examples. Are creative conditions constitutional?

2. What are the twin goals of probation? How does one differ from the other?
3. Based on purpose, what are the two types of conditions? Distinguish one from the other.
4. Distinguish between standard and special conditions of probation. What do you suggest should be the only conditions of probation? Justify your answer in terms of the goals of probation.
5. What are the four limitations on the power of courts to impose conditions? Discuss each.
6. Identify five constitutional rights that might be violated by probation conditions. Discuss each.
7. What are scarlet letter conditions? Are they constitutional?
8. Are all constitutional rights protected equally by the courts? Discuss the implications of a yes or no answer.
9. Does a condition that requires attendance in an Alcoholics Anonymous program violate an offender's constitutional rights? Discuss your answer.
10. Does a condition that requires participation in a treatment program that requires admission of guilt as a prerequisite violate a probationer's right against self-incrimination? Discuss.
11. "A probation officer has power to impose and modify conditions of probation." Is that statement true or false? Justify your answer.
12. What is early termination of probation? When is it usually given and for what purpose?
13. Name five special programs discussed in this chapter and briefly discuss the essence of each program.
14. What is restitution, and how does it differ from a fine?
15. Identify five legal challenges that can arise from drug testing.

Court Decisions on Probation Conditions

A. Cases Holding Probation Conditions Valid

A condition that a defendant totally abstain from the use of alcohol is valid.

United States v. Thurlow, 44 F. 3d 46 (U.S. 1st Cir. Jan. 1995). The district court could properly impose a condition of the defendant's probation that he *totally abstain from the use of alcohol during the defendant's three-year term of supervised release.* The defendant had entered a guilty plea to several counts of possession of stolen mail, theft of property used by the United States Postal Service, and other offenses resulting from a crime spree. *Although the defendant claimed that the condition of alcohol abstention was not related to circumstances of his offense, the court noted that the defendant came from a family with an active history of abuse. Furthermore, the defendant's record indicated that substance abuse was and continued to be a serious problem for him.* Indeed, the defendant's attorney admitted as much in the presentence conference before the district court. Finally, the record revealed that the defendant used the proceeds from the crime spree to purchase alcohol on several occasions. Under these circumstances the court could find no abuse of discretion and affirmed the imposition of the special condition of the defendant's probation.

A trial court has discretion to order a probationer to pay restitution to the victim as a condition of probation, so long as the amount has a factual basis in the record and is just.

Todd v. State, 912 S.W. 2d 807 (Tex. App. Nov. 1995) After the defendant was convicted of criminally negligent homicide, he was placed on probation. Among the conditions of probation, the defendant was required to pay restitution to the victim, perform 100 hours of community service, and write letters of apology to the victim's girlfriend and family. The defendant's appeal claimed, inter alia, that these conditions of probation were improper.

On review by the Texas Court of Appeals, the court disagreed. A trial court has discretion to order a probationer to pay restitution to the victim as a condition of probation, so long as the amount set by the court has a factual basis in the record and is just. Although the defendant in this case testified that his insurance company had tendered an offer of $20,000 to the victim's family, there was no evidence that the family refused that offer. Thus, the order requiring the defendant to pay approximately $15,000 in restitution to the family of the victim was not improper. Nor could the court agree that the requirement that defendant perform 100 hours of community service in a place where the aftermath of automobile accidents could be observed was improper. The trial court is authorized to require the appellant to serve community service as a condition of probation. While somewhat unusual, the requirement in this case that the service be performed in a place where the defendant would observe the effects of automobile accidents was reasonably related to the defendant's rehabilitation.

As a final matter, the court could not say that requiring the defendant to write letters of apology was improperly imposed. The trial court heard extensive evidence during the punishment phase of the trial, both as to the character of the defendant as well as the impact of his actions on secondary victims. The court found that the imposition of this condition would make it less likely that appellant would commit his crime in the future. Of greater significance, the condition would serve to make the defendant appreciate the nature and consequences of his actions.

The conditions were affirmed.

Probation condition to pay restitution is proper.

United States v. Haggard, 41 F. 3d 1320 (U.S. 9th Cir. Dec. 1994). The defendant was convicted of activity in which he fraudulently represented that he had information about a kidnap and murder victim. After his fraud was brought to light, the effect on the victim's family was traumatic. The district court imposed restitution in the amount of $6,836 for the income lost by the natural mother as a result of losing her job and going on disability. The defendant claimed on appeal that this order of restitution was improper.

On review by the Ninth Circuit Court of Appeals, the court disagreed. The court found nothing in the statutory scheme which restricted the availability of restitution to the victim specified in the offense of conviction. In a case such as this, in which the defendant deliberately targeted an unsuspecting family as the victim of his crimes, the defendant should be held to answer for the family's loss of income. Moreover, even if the defendant was unable to pay the fine and restitution at the time of sentencing, they were nonetheless appropriately imposed. The defendant made no showing of future inability to pay.

SUPPLEMENTAL READINGS

A. Conditions Held Valid

The condition of the defendant's probation that he not participate in anti-abortion protests was valid and did not infringe on his First Amendment rights.

Markley v. State
507 So. 2d 1043 (Ala. Ct. Crim. App. 4/14/87)

The defendant, a priest, was found guilty of burglary and criminal mischief because of incidents involving his participation in an anti-abortion demonstration. The trial court suspended the imposition of sentence and placed the defendant on probation. Among the special conditions of probation was a condition that the defendant refrain from knowingly going within 500 yards of any clinic that performed abortive surgery. The defendant was subsequently found in violation of this condition and he appealed, claiming that the condition infringed upon his First Amendment rights.

Rejecting the defendant's claim, the court cited *Persall v. State,* 16 So. 2d 332 (1944) for the proposition that a defendant has the right to accept the terms and conditions of probation or to reject them and serve out his sentence. In this case, by accepting the conditions of probation, the defendant was bound by the terms of that probation. While conditions of probation must serve the dual objectives of rehabilitation and public safety, there is no presumption that limitations on constitutional rights are impermissible. *United States v. Consuelo-Gonzalez,* 521 F. 2d 259 (1975). Furthermore, a convicted criminal may be subjected, as a condition of his probation, to restrictions on his expression and associations. *Malone v. United States,* 502 F. 2d 554 (9th Cir.) 1974, cert. denied, 419 U.S. 1124, 95 S. Ct. 809, 42 L. Ed. 2d 824 (1975). In line with the above cases, the court found no violation whatsoever of the appellant's constitutional rights.

As a second matter, the court went on to find that the trial court carefully scrutinized the appellant's actions in light of his First Amendment rights. The appellant was not precluded from attending church or, indeed, going near certain places of worship, provided he was not at the same point engaged in some type of activity which had been restricted. His testimony at the revocation hearing indicated that the appellant was knowingly in violation of the terms of his probation and had participated in abortion protest activities without hesitation.

The revocation was affirmed.

The condition requiring the defendant to submit to polygraph testing at the request of his probation officer was not unconstitutional.

People v. Miller
265 Cal. Rptr. 587 (Cal. App. Feb. 1989)

After being convicted of committing lewd and lascivious acts upon a child under the age of 14, the defendant was placed on probation. One of the conditions of probation was that he have no contact with the victim or any other minor females unless in the presence of the minor's parent or with the express approval of his probation officer. It was further required that he submit to a polygraph examination at the direction of his probation officer. The probation officer asserted that the polygraph condition was necessary to monitor the defendant's compliance with other conditions of probation, especially the condition forbidding his unsupervised contact with young girls. The defendant's appeal claimed that the polygraph requirement violated his privilege against self-incrimination.

On review by the California Court of Appeals, the court disagreed. The mere requirement of taking the test in itself did not constitute an infringement of the privilege. Although the defendant had a duty to answer the polygraph examiner's questions truthfully, unless he invoked the privilege or demonstrated a realistic threat of self-incrimination and was nevertheless required to answer, there would be no violation of his right against self-incrimination.

Nor could the court agree that the defendant would be entitled to *Miranda* warnings prior to the administration of the polygraph examination. Stated the court [footnotes omitted],

> The polygraph condition is designed to help evaluate the truthfulness of defendant's reports and "[t]he purpose and objectives of probation would be frustrated if a convicted defendant could maintain . . . a right to silence at the time of his . . . report to the probation officer. . . ." (*People v. Hamilton* (1968) 260 Cal. App. 2d 103, 105, 66 Cal. Rptr. 831)
>
> When subject to a polygraph examination as an investigative tool alone, a probationer is not placed in any worse position than he would otherwise be were there no polygraph condition. In either case, the probation officer may fully investigate the probationer's compliance with conditions whether or not the polygraph is used.
>
> The trial court did not abuse its discretion by including the polygraph requirement as a condition of probation for the limited use as an investigative tool.

The judgment of the trial court was affirmed.

B. Cases Holding Probation Conditions Invalid

Scarlet letter condition of probation held not proper because it was not authorized by law.

State v. Burdin, 924 S.W. 2d 82 (Tenn. Sup. May 1996). After being convicted on a charge of sexual battery) the defendant was placed on probation. One of the special conditions of his probation required that he place a sign in his front yard stating "Warning, all children. Wayne Burden is an admitted and convicted child molester. Parents beware." The defendant's appeal claimed that this condition was invalid. On review by the Court of Appeals, the court agreed with the defendant. The state sought review by the Tennessee Supreme Court.

On review by the Tennessee Supreme Court, the court agreed with the Court of Appeals that the condition was not statutorily authorized. The authority to impose conditions of probation is granted under Section 40-35-303(d). That section provides:

> Whenever a court sentences an offender to supervised probation, the court shall specify the terms of the supervision and may require the offender to comply with certain conditions which may include, but are not limited to: (1) Meet the offender's family responsibilities; (2) Devote the offender to a specific employment or occupation; (3) Perform without compensation services in the community for charitable or governmental agencies; (4) Undergo available medical or psychiatric treatment . . . (5) Pursue a prescribed secular course of study or vocational training; (6) Refrain from possessing a firearm or other dangerous weapon; (7) Remain within prescribed geographical boundaries and notify the court or the probation officer of any change in the offender's address or employment; (8) Submit to supervision by an appropriate agency or person, and report as directed by the court; (9) Satisfy any other conditions reasonably related to the purpose of the offender's sentence and not unduly restrictive of the offender's liberty, or incompatible with the offender's freedom of conscience, or otherwise prohibited by this chapter; or (10) Make appropriate and reasonable restitution to the victim or the family of the victim involved pursuant to § 40-35-304.

The court noted that the enumerated conditions in the above section were closely related to conventional societal duties, i.e., family support, productive employment, community service, personal health, vocational training, avoidance of dangerous instruments, cooperation with supervising agencies, and restitution. The conditions offer no dramatic departures from traditional principles of rehabilitation. The court found that the statute did not allow substantial departures from conventional principles of probation.

Federal court did not have authority to order defendant deported. Federal law only authorized court to turn over offender to Immigration and Naturalization Service for deportation.

United States v. Phommachanh, 91 F. 3d 1383 (U.S. 10th Cir. July 1996). The Tenth Circuit Court of Appeals disagreed with the result reached by the Eleventh Circuit Court of Appeals in *United States v. Oboh,* above. *The Tenth Circuit held that a district court did not have the authority to order, as a condition of supervised release, that a defendant be deported. Rather, the court found that 18 U.S.C. § 3583(d) simply authorized the district court to order, as a condition of supervised release, that a defendant be turned over to the Immigration and Naturalization Service for the deportation process.* The court found that Congress had authorized the Immigration and Naturalization Service to make determinations as to whether an alien was subject to deportation. Thus, the court held that Section 3583(d) simply allowed the sentencing court to order, as a condition of supervised release, that an alien defendant who is subject to deportation be surrendered to immigration officials for deportation proceedings.

Probation condition imposed must be reasonably related to the nature and circumstances of the offense.

United States v. Edgin, 92 F. 3d 1044 (U.S. 10th Cir. Aug. 1996). *Ordinarily, a court enjoys broad discretion in setting a condition of supervised release. The general requirements are that a condition of supervised release must be reasonably related to the nature and circumstances of the offense and the history and characteristics of the defendant. Furthermore, a condition must involve no greater deprivation of liberty than is reasonably necessary given the needs to afford adequate deterrence to criminal conduct, to protect the public from further crimes of the defendant, and to provide the defendant with educational and vocational training, medical care, or other correctional treatment in the most effective manner.*

In this case the defendant was convicted of making threatening telephone calls. One of the special conditions of his supervised release prohibited the defendant from contacting his son. On review by the Tenth Circuit Court of Appeals, the court found that remand was required for the district court to make findings of fact with regard to the relationship of this condition to the defendant's offense.

Condition requiring probationer to admit guilt as part of sex offender therapy violated probationer's right to be free from self-incrimination.

State v. Cate, 683 A. 2d 1010 (Vt. Sup. Aug. 1996). The condition that required the probationer to admit his guilt as part of sex offender therapy violated the probationer's right to be free from self-incrimination. The court held that a person in a probation setting cannot be forced to incriminate himself without first receiving immunity from criminal prosecution as a result thereof. Although a probationer may not assert the privilege against self-incrimination where his statements pose no realistic threat of incrimination in a criminal proceeding, in the present case the prosecution had failed to eliminate the threat of future prosecution in relation to any of the defendant's admissions. The proper remedy in these circumstances, found the court, was to grant judicial use immunity that would make any statements required for successful completion of a rehabilitative program inadmissible against the probationer at a subsequent criminal proceeding. The court further held that the sentencing court had to advise the probationer that statements required for further successful completion of probation, and their fruits, would not be admissible against him at any subsequent criminal proceeding.

The conditions prohibiting the defendant from living with a member of the opposite sex who was not a relative and from being within three blocks of a known "high drug area" as determined by his probation officer were invalid.

Huff v. State
554 So. 2D 616 (Fla. Dist. Ct. App. Dec. 1989)

Defendant was convicted of burglary and was as placed on probation. One of the conditions of probation required that he not live with a member of the opposite sex who was not his relative. The defendant was subsequently charged with various violations of probation. The trial court revoked probation and sentenced the defendant to nine years in prison followed by six years' probation. The trial court then reimposed the condition of probation that appellant not live with a member of the opposite sex who was not his relative. Another condition required that appellant not be within three blocks of a known "high drug area" as determined by the probation officer. Neither of these conditions was announced at the sentencing hearing.

On review, the court held that the conditions were invalid. Stated the court:

> The condition that Appellant not live with a member of the opposite sex has been held to be invalid because it relates to noncriminal conduct. See *Brodus v. State,* 449 So. 2d 941 (Fla. 2d DCA 1984); *Wilkinson v. State,* 388 So. 2d 1322 (Fla. 5th DCA 1980).
>
> We find that the condition that Appellant not be within three blocks of a "high drug area" as defined by his probation officer is too vague to advise appellant of the limits of his restrictions and can be easily violated unintentionally. The validity of this condition may depend on whether or not the probation officer apprised Appellant of which areas he was to avoid prior to a violation. Since the conditions were not announced at sentencing, there is nothing in the record to suggest that these areas were defined specifically or in writing. See *Almond v. State,* 350 So. 2d 810, 811 (Fla. 4th DCA 1977) (striking as too vague a condition of probation prohibiting defendant from residing in "central Florida").
>
> Further, it has not been shown that either of these conditions has any relationship to the crime of burglary or is reasonably tailored to prevent future criminal conduct by the appellant. Therefore, pursuant to *Rodriguez v. State,* 378 So. 2d 7 (Fla. 2d DCA 1979) (requiring conditions of probation to be reasonably related to prevention of similar criminal acts), we strike the conditions of probation. We also strike the finding of violation based upon his cohabitation with a woman. In all other respects the judgment and sentence are affirmed.

5

ORGANIZATION AND ADMINISTRATION OF PROBATION SERVICES

What You Will Learn in This Chapter

Probation is both a disposition and a process. In this chapter we will be especially concerned with the process of probation, that is, the way probation services are organized, administered, and delivered. You will review early probation organizational structures and consider modern organizational systems. The major organizational issues in the late 1990s are whether probation should be administered at the state or local level and whether the judicial or executive branch of government should have operational control of probation services. We will also discuss the qualifications and appointment of probation officers, probation and parole officer salaries, and policies and issues related to the carrying of weapons by probation and parole officers. The Interstate Compact on Probation will be examined and problems associated with transferring probationers and parolees from state to state will be discussed.

KEY TERMS

Court of general jurisdiction
Court of record
Community Corrections Act
Interstate Compact for the Supervision of Parolees and Probationers
Sending state
Receiving state

INTRODUCTION

The operation of a probation system is best understood when we distinguish between probation as a disposition and probation as a process. Thus we make that distinction in this chapter. The *disposition* is the aspect of probation that leads to granting and revocation of probation. The *process* of probation is the furnishing of probation services. The two functions are closely related and frequently overlap. As we shall see, different jurisdictions have different probation systems, and there is significantly less diversity in probation as a disposition than in the way probation services are provided.

Probation as a Disposition

Probation as a disposition is court-related; that is, statutory limits laid down by the legislature place the power to grant it and to revoke it in a court. The federal government permits all courts having jurisdiction of the offenses for which probation may be used to place defendants on probation.[1] This is generally true in state jurisdictions also. Thus if the state provides only for felony probation, **courts of general jurisdiction** with power to try felony cases have the authority to grant and revoke probation. If misdemeanor probation is provided for, courts with misdemeanor jurisdiction may grant and revoke misdemeanor probation. In a few states the power to probate is limited to **courts of record.**

That the authority to grant probation resides with a court is not surprising, especially when we consider that probation developed out of the court's power to sentence criminal offenders and (depending on the point of view) from either its inherent or its legislatively granted power to suspend the imposition or execution of sentence. The power to revoke probation, quite logically, accompanies the power to grant it.

Opinions differ as to the exact nature of probation—for example, whether it is a sentence or a conviction and whether it rests on suspension of *imposition* of sentence

COURT OF GENERAL JURISDICTION

A court with jurisdiction that extends to all controversies that may be brought before a court. A trial court.

COURT OF RECORD

A court that is required to make a record of its proceedings and that may fine or imprison.

or of *execution* of sentence or both. Nonetheless, there is almost unanimous agreement that granting and revoking probation is a judicial responsibility.

Probation as a Process

The probation process encompasses the organization, administration, and delivery of probation services. The administration of probation services in the 50 states and the federal government differs in philosophy, organization, and procedures. In many cases the differences have arisen more by historical accident than anything else.

EARLY PROBATION ORGANIZATION

As the states enacted probation legislation, they did not do it uniformly. They followed Vermont's *local* organizational pattern or Rhode Island's *state* organizational pattern; some states combined *adult* and *juvenile* probation services; some states combined probation with *parole* services; they developed joint or separate agencies for *felony* and *misdemeanor* probation services; they placed probation services in the *executive* branch or the *judicial* branch of the state government. Various organizational combinations were adopted. For example, Massachusetts enacted the nation's first probation statute in 1878, although the law related only to Suffolk County (Boston). The statute gave to the mayor of Boston the power to appoint the probation officer, subject to confirmation by the board of aldermen, and it placed the officer under the general control of Boston's chief of police, although the officer was paid from the county treasury. The probation officer was considered an arm of the court, however, and had the power to investigate cases and recommend probation for "such persons as may reasonably be expected to reform without punishment."[2] Two years later, a law was enacted that permitted other cities and towns in Massachusetts to appoint probation officers. Statewide probation did not begin until 1891, when a statute transferred the power of appointment from the municipalities to the courts and made such appointment mandatory rather than permissive.[3]

Vermont was the second state to pass a probation statute, adopting a county plan of organization in 1898. The county judge in each county was given the power to appoint a probation officer to serve all of the courts in the county.[4] The following year (1899) Rhode Island adopted a statewide and state-controlled probation system.[5] A state agency, the Board of Charities and Correction, was given the power to appoint a probation officer and assistants, with the requirement that at least one of the assistants be a woman. California enacted a probation statute in 1903 following the Vermont pattern of county-based probation administration. The California law provided for adult as well as juvenile probation.[6]

In New York probation began in 1901 under a law that empowered all justices of courts having original criminal jurisdiction in all cities to appoint officers to investigate and report cases to the courts that might deserve mitigation of punishment by probation. The first independent commission for supervising probation was established in 1907. By 1939 the probation system was made up of probation officers appointed by the local courts and paid by local governments, but under state supervision. Later the Division of Probation in the charge of a director of probation was located in the Department of Correction. Subsequently New York established a state Department of Correctional Services, which has as one of its divisions the Division of Probation.

The first juvenile court (and juvenile probation) statute was passed in Illinois in 1899. Illinois did not provide for adult probation until 1911, when the circuit and city courts of Illinois were authorized to appoint probation officers and place adult offenders on probation. A state probation office was created in 1923, but it did not begin to function until 1929, and in 1933 it was abolished.[7]

ORGANIZATION OF PROBATION SERVICES IN THE 1990s

The Controversy over Probation Organizational Patterns

The major arguments center on the issues of (1) whether probation should be administered at the state or local level and (2) whether the executive branch or the judicial branch of government should administer probation services.[8] Table 5.1 illustrates the branch of government administering probation services and whether probation is under state or local control in each state.

State versus Local Administration

Probation services in the United States are administered by more than 2,000 separate agencies. Adult probation is exclusively state-administered in 25 states. In an additional 11 states, a state agency is the primary but not the exclusive provider of probation services. Seventeen states have some form of mixed state and local administration.[9] In the states with mixed state and local administration, the mixture takes different forms. The National Institute of Corrections reports that larger cities may have municipal courts provide their own probation services, primarily for misdemeanants, while the state agency handles all other cases.[10] Other situations are more complex. In Ohio, for example, 38 of the states' 88 counties have county probation departments. In 40 counties probation services are provided contractually by the Ohio Adult Parole Authority, an agency of the state corrections department. The remaining 10 counties have a combination of county and state probation services. Municipal court agencies also provide adult misdemeanant supervision in 21 cities.

There are arguments pro and con for statewide administration of probation services. The arguments *for* state-administered probation contend that a state-administered system is free of local political considerations and can recommend new programs without approval by local political bodies. Furthermore, a state-administered system provides greater assurance that goals and objectives can be met and uniform policies and procedures developed. Moreover, it allows more efficiency in the disposition of resources. It is also argued that county probation agencies are small and thus lack resources for providing staff training, research programs, and services to probationers.[11] The arguments *against* a state-administered probation system emphasize the need for local conditions and resources to be taken into account. The probationer remains in the local community and can be best supervised by a person thoroughly familiar with that community. Proponents also claim that local agencies are best equipped to experiment with new procedures and better methods because of their smaller size: mistakes are not so costly and far-reaching. They also argue that state policies are often rejected by local communities that then refuse to cooperate with the

Table 5.1 **STATE OR LOCAL BRANCH OF GOVERNMENT ADMINISTERING PRIMARY PROBATION SERVICES**

	EXECUTIVE BRANCH		JUDICIAL BRANCH	
	State Level	Local Level	State Level	Local Level
Alabama	✔			
Alaska	✔			
Arizona				✔
Arkansas				✔
California		✔		
Colorado			✔	
Connecticut			✔	
Delaware	✔			
District of Columbia			✔	
Florida	✔			
Georgia	✔			
Hawaii				✔
Idaho	✔			
Illinois				✔
Indiana				✔
Iowa		✔		
Kansas			✔	
Kentucky	✔			
Louisiana	✔			
Maine	✔			
Maryland	✔			
Massachusetts				✔
Michigan	✔ (felony)			
Minnesota		✔		✔ (CCA counties)
Mississippi	✔			
Missouri	✔			

probation system, which undermines operational efficiency and success.[12] When probation is centralized at the state level under the department of corrections, probation administrators often decry what appears to be an emphasis on the institutional division to the detriment of the community corrections component. The president of the Texas Probation Association recently argued that community corrections in Texas should be deconsolidated from the Texas Department of Criminal Justice, which also oversees the vast institutional division. He wrote,

> In my opinion, this relationship has not been in the best interest of community corrections. . . . Under the direction of the prior agency, the Texas Adult Probation Commission, the State of Texas was at least sensitive to the needs of the local level, where the roots of our criminal justice system should be focused. Communication with our state agency was open and productive. The ideas we had were heard with open ears, and the frustrations we felt were shared. The current system, whose priority is justifiably centered about the Institu-

Table 5.1 ***(Continued)***

	EXECUTIVE BRANCH		JUDICIAL BRANCH	
	State Level	Local Level	State Level	Local Level
Montana	✔			
Nebraska				
Nevada	✔			
New Hampshire	✔			
New Jersey				
New Mexico	✔			
New York				✔
North Carolina	✔			
North Dakota	✔			✔ (CCA counties)
Ohio				✔
Oklahoma	✔			
Oregon	✔			
Pennsylvania				
Rhode Island	✔		✔	
South Carolina	✔			✔
South Dakota				
Tennessee	✔			
Texas				
Utah	✔			
Vermont	✔			✔
Virginia	✔			
Washington	✔			
West Virginia				13
Wisconsin	✔		6	
Wyoming	✔	4	✔	
Total	30	✔		
	✔			

Source: LIS, Inc. *State and Local Probation Systems in the United States: A Survey of Current Practice.* Used with permission of LIS, Inc., Longmont, CO.

tional Division of the Department of Criminal Justice, has not proven beneficial to our community corrections system, nor to our constituency.[13]

The American Bar Association's *Standards* do not favor any particular formula for allocating administrative authority for probation services between local and state governments. They agreed with the National Council on Crime and Delinquency[14] that adequate services can be developed through various approaches.[15]

The evidence on this issue appears to support state-administered probation services in some form. Few states where probation is a local function have provided any leadership for probation services. Where probation is a local function, tremendous variations exist in the quantity and quality of services, the qualifications of probation personnel, and the emphasis on service to the court and probationers.[16]

State–County Shared Responsibility

In some jurisdictions the system is said to be *mixed*—that is, the state and counties share responsibility for delivering probation services. The development of Community Corrections Acts that provide state funding for increased local services appears to have many advantages. This alternative arrangement usually involves a state executive-branch agency with the authority to develop standards for local probation systems that provide a minimum acceptable level of functioning. The state agency is also responsible for establishing policies, defining statewide goals, providing staff training, assisting in fiscal planning and implementation, collecting statistics and other data to monitor the operations of local probation agencies, and enforcing changes when necessary. This organizational structure recognizes the need for local control while allowing local governments to benefit from the greater revenue-generating capacity of state government.[17] Minimum standards of service delivery and the benefits of service uniformity may thus be established and enforced under threat of withdrawal of state funds.

Community Corrections Acts

COMMUNITY CORRECTIONS ACT

Statewide legislation which creates a mechanism through which funds are granted to local units of government to plan, develop, and deliver correctional services and sanctions.

A **Community Corrections Act** is defined as a statewide mechanism through which funds are granted to local units of government to plan, develop, and deliver correctional sanctions and services. The overall purpose of this mechanism is to provide local sentencing options in lieu of imprisonment in state institutions.[18] The specifics of these state–local partnerships vary.[19] Oregon's legislation is typical. The act, which became operative on January 1, 1997, states,

> Because counties are in the best position for the management, oversight, and administration of local criminal justice matters and for determining local resource priorities, it is declared to be the legislative priority of this state to establish an ongoing partnership between the state and counties and to finance with appropriations from the General Fund statewide community correction programs on a continuing basis. The intended purposes of this program are to:
>
> 1. Provide appropriate sentencing and sanctioning options including incarceration, community supervision, and services;
> 2. Provide improved local services for persons charged with criminal offenses with the goal of reducing the occurrence of repeat criminal offenses;
> 3. Promote local control and management of community corrections programs;
> 4. Promote the use of the most effective criminal sanctions necessary to protect public safety, administer punishment to the offender, and rehabilitate the offender;
> 5. Enhance, increase, and support the state and county partnership in the management of offenders; and
> 6. Enhance, increase, and encourage a greater role for local government and the local criminal justice system in the planning and implementation of local public safety measures.[20]

By 1993, 18 states had passed CCA legislation. However, most jurisdictions continue to operate either state or local probation services with few, if any, cooperative programs. And despite the success of CCAs, the controversy over how probation services should be organized and administered continues.

Judicial versus Executive Administration

In the debate over the appropriate governmental branch for the probation system, those who favor the executive branch argue that placing responsibility for probation in the branch that holds responsibility for other human services and correctional services is a more rational alignment. Those who favor executive-branch control point out that it allows program budgeting to be better coordinated because of that branch's greater ability to negotiate in the resource allocation process. Moreover, they claim that it facilitates a better-coordinated continuum of services to offenders. These advocates of executive-branch administration argue that judges are trained in law, not administration, and are thus not equipped to administer probation services. They fear that under judicial authority, services to the court will have higher priority than services to persons.

Some independent observers support placing probation in the judicial branch. They stress that probation is more responsive to the courts, to whom it provides services, when it is administered by the judiciary. When probation is in the executive branch, it is often a branch of the department of corrections, and thus probation services might have lower priority than when they are part of the judiciary. These people also argue that courts are more aware of the resource needs of probation than the executive branch, and that the relationship of probation staff to the courts provides automatic feedback on the effectiveness of probation services.[21]

At present, probation services are the responsibility of an executive-branch agency at the state or local level in 34 states. All but four of these states administer probation services at the state level, making this the most common administrative arrangement.[22]

The Impact of Changing Concepts of Probation on Administration

As we have noted, the nature and objectives of probation have undergone considerable change—and they continue to change. Regular probation is increasingly perceived as ineffective and as a threat to public safety. The public has had to redefine the role probation should play as a sanction for convicted felons. Increasingly, the response has been to develop intensive-supervision programs that emphasize surveillance, control, and risk management. This shift of emphasis from routine supervision to intensive surveillance has implications for probation administration and organization. In their book *Between Prison and Probation,* Norval Morris and Michael Tonry discuss these organizational and philosophical issues.[23] Typically, they assert, the central questions are, To whom is the probation officer accountable, to whom does he or she look for promotion, and thus, who has the power to influence his or her priorities?

When probation is a branch of the judiciary, the probation officer's duties are more likely to be preparing presentence reports than supervising probationers, because the officer's relationship with his or her superior—the judge—is centered on the presentence function. If, however, new duties such as intensive supervision and other risk-control responsibilities are assigned, the probation department and the individual officer will be forced to devote more time and higher priority to supervision. Under the control of the judiciary, it is often difficult for the probation officer to shift priorities from servicing the court's presentencing needs to supervising high-risk probationers.

Even when the court supports and encourages the shift from court service to supervision, the judiciary seldom has the political clout to provide the necessary additional resources for such a change in priorities.

Placing probation administration under local executive-branch administration seldom resolves the dilemma. Except in large, prosperous counties, few local communities can provide the additional resources necessary to supervise and control the type and volume of offenders being served if intermediate punishments are to be effective. The sheer volume of offenders overwhelms the resources of most communities.

In a state probation system, however, there is at least the possibility of allocating the staff and funding necessary for the task.[24] Such placement can facilitate a more rational allocation of probation staff services, increase interaction and administrative coordination with corrections and allied human services, increase access to the budget process and establishment of priorities, and remove from the courts an inappropriate responsibility.

THE SELECTION AND APPOINTMENT OF PROBATION OFFICERS

The selection of probation officers is similar to that used to select other public employees. Depending upon the particular laws and policies in a jurisdiction, one of three systems for employment of probation officers is employed; the appointment system, the merit system, or a combined system.[25]

Appointment System

Depending on the situs of probation services in the judicial or executive branch of government, probation officers are appointed either by the courts authorized to grant probation or by the director of the executive department or agency in which probation services are housed. If there is only one felony trial court in the county, the probation officer is selected by the judge that tries felony cases. Where two or more probation officers are needed, the usual pattern is that the judge or judicial body appoints a chief probation officer, who in turn selects assistants, subject to the approval of the advisory body. Salary scales are fixed, and broad policy matters are determined by the judicial body that selects the chief probation officer.

In the federal system, for example, the judges of each federal district court appoint a chief probation officer, who is under the overall supervision of the Probation Division of the Administrative Office of the United States. Collectively, the probation officers in the federal system are called the *United States Probation Service*. The chief probation officer selects subordinate probation officers.[26] Salary and minimum qualifications are fixed by statute or determined by the Administrative Office of the United States Courts. Federal probation officers also supervise parolees. Parolees are assigned for supervision to the appropriate chief probation officer by the United States Parole Commission,[27] the Justice Department agency that is responsible for administering the federal parole system. The assignment is based primarily on geographic considerations. The chief probation officer assigns particular parolees to individual officers on the basis of each probationer or parolee's special needs and each officer's special skills, with due consideration to caseload, geographic location, and other matters. A U.S. probation officer also supervises offenders at liberty under supervised release (those not released on parole), as required by the Comprehensive Crime Control Act of 1984, and those on military parole.

In a state where probation services are locally administered and parole services are statewide, there are usually two sets of supervisory officers. Parole officers are appointed by an administrative department or the board that supervises the department. Power to appoint the chief probation officer is usually in the judiciary, although it may rest with the county governing body, the governor, a state board upon nomination by a judge, or the judiciary from a list supplied by a state agency.

Where juvenile and adult probation services are administered locally and separately, the chief probation officer for adult probationers may be chosen by the judges of the criminal courts, and the chief probation officer for juveniles by the juvenile judge or a juvenile board. Sometimes the juvenile board can also designate which court is to be the juvenile court for the particular geographic area.[28]

Merit System

Merit systems were developed to remove public employees from political patronage. In a merit system, applicants who meet minimum employment standards are required to pass a competitive exam. Persons who score above a specified minimum grade are placed on a ranked list. Candidates are selected from the list by their order of rank. In some systems applicants are also graded by their education and employment history. The merit system is also used in some states to determine promotions.[29] A merit or civil service system exam is required in four states (Delaware, Indiana, Rhode Island, and Wisconsin).

Combined System

Elements of both systems are used in some jurisdictions. Applicants are screened through an exam, and candidates are then selected by the agency after a process similar to the appointment system.[30]

QUALIFICATION AND TRAINING OF PROBATION AND PAROLE OFFICERS

Education and Experience

Selection criteria for probation and parole officers generally include education, experience, or a combination of the two.[31] Some jurisdictions may also require psychological evaluations, physical fitness tests, and drug screening. A baccalaureate degree is usually the minimum educational requirement. Some jurisdictions also specify that the degree must be in a social or behavioral science. Many states allow a combination of education and experience as a substitute for the bachelor's degree, while others require additional course work above the bachelor's degree. Seven states (California, Connecticut, Delaware, Idaho, Kansas, Minnesota, and Wisconsin) do not specify any particular educational background beyond high school as a prerequisite to selection as a probation officer.[32] One state (Hawaii) requires a master's degree, and others require graduate training or equivalent experience. Table 5.2 contains a state-by-state listing of selection and training requirements for probation officers.

Table 5.2 **PROBATION OFFICER SELECTION AND TRAINING REQUIREMENTS**

	ENTRY-LEVEL REQUIREMENTS		TRAINING REQUIREMENTS	
	Bachelor's degree	Other	Preservice hours	Inservice hours
Alabama	✔		320	(Not indicated)
Alaska	✔	Experience	40	40
Arizona	✔		40	16
Arkansas	✔	Experience	68	20
California		High school diploma: experience	200	40
Colorado	✔		32	40
Connecticut		(Not specified)	200	20
Delaware		State merit system test	160	(Not indicated)
District of Columbia	✔	Experience; if candidate has an M.A., less experience required	(Not indicated)	40
Florida	✔		380	(Not indicated)
Georgia	✔		(Not indicated)	40
Hawaii		Master's degree plus experience	(Not specified)	(Not indicated)
Idaho		(No specific qualifications)	240	40
Illinois	✔		40	20
Indiana	✔	State merit system test	40	12
Iowa		Associate of arts degree	(Not specified)	0
Kansas		(Not specified)	(Not specified)	0
Kentucky	✔		40	40
Louisiana	✔		(Not indicated)	40
Maine	✔	Experience	(Not specified)	0
Maryland	✔	May substitute experience or graduate work	209	20
Massachusetts	✔	Experience	(Not specified)	(Not specified)
Michigan	✔		440	40
Minnesota		(No statewide standards)	(Not specified)	0
Mississippi	✔	May substitute experience	100	(Not specified)
Missouri	✔	May substitute experience	160	0

(continued)

Preservice and In-Service Training

Thirty states and the federal probation system require some preservice training before the probation or parole officer assumes his or her duties. Preservice training requirements range from 32 hours in Maryland to 520 hours in Oklahoma. The average preservice training requirement is 173 hours.[33]

Twenty-seven states and the federal system require annual in-service training, as well. Probation officers are expected to keep current with new developments in the field, and in-service training offers an opportunity to accomplish this goal. Forty hours annually appears to be the most common requirement. While 23 states do not require inservice training, the requirement for in-service training has grown more popular in the past several years.

Table 5.2 **(*Continued*)**

	ENTRY-LEVEL REQUIREMENTS		TRAINING REQUIREMENTS	
	Bachelor's degree	Other	Preservice hours	Inservice hours
Montana	✔		80	16
Nebraska	✔		(Not specified)	0
Nevada	✔	May substitute combination of education and experience	200	40–60
New Hampshire	✔		286	(Not indicated)
New Jersey	✔		(Not specified)	0
New Mexico	✔		40	40
New York	✔		(Not specified)	0
North Carolina	✔	Experience	0	0
North Dakota	✔		440	(Not indicated)
Ohio	✔	Experience/training	(Not specified)	0
Oklahoma	✔		520	40
Oregon	✔	Experience; may substitute experience for degree	160	64
Pennsylvania	✔		(Not indicated)	40
Rhode Island	✔	State merit system test	(Not indicated)	(Not indicated)
South Carolina	✔		128	(Not indicated)
South Dakota	✔	May substitute combination of education and experience	(Not indicated)	16
Tennessee	✔	May substitute experience	(Not indicated)	0
Texas	✔	State certification process	(Not indicated)	40
Utah	✔	Experience (paid employment)	(Not indicated)	(Not indicated)
Vermont	✔	Experience; may substitute education/experience for degree	40	(Not indicated)
Virginia	✔	May substitute training/experience	80	40
Washington	✔	Graduate training or experience	80	20
West Virginia	✔		(Not indicated)	24–30
Wisconsin		State civil service examination	360	(Not indicated)
Wyoming	✔	May substitute experience	80	40

Source: LIS, Inc. *State and Local Probation Systems in the United States: A Survey of Current Practice.* Used with permission of LIS, Inc., Longmont, CO.

SALARIES OF PROBATION AND PAROLE OFFICERS

For jurisdictions in which probation and parole services are performed by a single agency, starting salaries for probation and parole officers range from a low of $17,964 in Kentucky to $32,673 in Rhode Island. In 1996 the average starting salary nationwide for probation and parole officers was $23,963. In states with separate probation and parole services, parole officers earn somewhat more than probation officers. The average starting salary for parole officers was $26,813 and $25,205 for probation officers. The highest beginning salary for parole officers was $39,257 in New York. The highest beginning salary for probation officers was $32,975 in Connecticut.[34] The

Table 5.3 **PROBATION AND PAROLE OFFICERS' STARTING, AVERAGE, AND MAXIMUM SALARIES ON JANUARY 1, 1997**

Probation	Start	Salaries Average	Maximum
Arizona[1]	$24,929	$26,456	$31,642
Arkansas	$20,140	$22,951	$31,891
Colorado	$28,128	$39,576	$48,108
Connecticut	$32,975	$50,885	$59,060
Dist. of Col.	$22,744	$37,034	$51,324
Georgia	$22,260	$33,852	$44,136
Hawaii	$32,544		$46,356
Illinois[1]	$25,000		
Kansas	$23,916		$33,660
Massachusetts[2]	$38,206		$60,346
Nebraska	$22,257	$27,997	$35,911
New Jersey	$25,500	$37,500	$53,300
South Dakota[3]	$22,700	$29,700	$32,531
Tennessee	$16,752	$18,960	$29,952
West Virginia	$20,004	$30,045	$50,496
Average	**$25,204**	**$32,269**	**$43,480**
Parole	Start	Salaries Average	Maximum
Arizona	$22,568	$26,003	$37,998
Arkansas	$20,140	$26,251	$36,582
California[4]	$39,588	$54,000	$58,236
Colorado	$27,528	$40,800	$49,416
Connecticut	$35,635	$39,180	$41,542
Dist. of Col.	$29,500	$42,406	$50,821
Georgia	$22,260	$28,282	$42,852
Hawaii	$30,084	$36,665	$50,136
Illinois	$24,744		$43,152
Indiana	$20,332	$25,697	$30,368
Kansas	$23,920	$28,392	$37,107
Massachusetts	$36,960	$47,316	$47,316
Nebraska	$22,257	$29,114	$37,528
New Jersey	$34,207	$41,580	$58,216
New York[5]	$39,257	$43,900	$48,557
South Dakota	$21,000	$25,000	$27,000
Tennessee	$18,960	$23,892	$34,128
Texas[6]	$22,032	$26,019	$30,588
West Virginia	$18,468	$23,000	$36,856
Average	**$26,813**	**$33,750**	**$42,021**

[1]Entry salaries vary, figure is an average. [2]Highest is 1st Assistant Chief Probation Officer (since Chief Probation Officer is considered supervisory). [3]High salary is for nonsupervision/manager. [4]Annual salaries based on monthly wages. [5]Avg. salary est. [6]Entry-level and avg. salary excl. hazardous duty and benefit retirement pay.

Table 5.3 **(continued)**

Probation and Parole	Start	Salaries Average	Maximum
Alabama	$22,820	$43,000	$55,328
Alaska[7]	$30,144	$39,600	$82,000
Delaware[8]	$24,078	$28,104	$36,870
Florida[9]	$23,270	$26,664	$45,495
Idaho	$26,000	$31,000	$41,500
Iowa	$27,997	$35,000	$41,434
Kentucky	$17,964	$25,973	$53,069
Louisiana[10]	$19,308	$28,110	$36,912
Maine	$23,670	$30,000	$32,115
Maryland	$20,449	$30,618	$35,800
Michigan	$27,700		$46,900
Minnesota	$25,996	$33,909	$47,961
Mississippi	$19,932		$37,736
Missouri	$23,616	$26,520	$31,860
Montana	$24,902	$24,000	$36,108
Nevada	$31,442	$37,326	$40,932
New Hampshire	$25,700	$35,500	$42,500
New Mexico	$26,390	$31,599	$35,869
North Carolina	$20,967	$26,806	$38,503
North Dakota	$20,856	$30,660	$40,788
Ohio	$24,669	$41,225	$46,820
Oklahoma	$21,525	$27,331	$35,184
Rhode Island	$32,673	$35,045	$36,888
South Carolina	$19,375	$22,771	$35,332
Utah	$22,905	$30,684	$43,911
Vermont	$22,406	$31,300	$40,346
Virginia	$25,582	$35,237	$43,661
Washington	$24,936	$37,080	$40,440
Wisconsin	$22,258		$38,000
Wyoming	$18,960	$24,508	$35,052
Federal[11]	$24,350		$66,750
Average	**$23,963**	**$31,466**	**$42,647**

[7]In the Northern region of the state, PO's receive a cost of living allowance of up to 42% above base. [8]Salaries are based on existing pay scale and may vary according to time served. [9]High is for Senior Corporal, highest for corporal level was $42,026. [10]High is officer class 3. Officer class 1 and 2 highest salary was $32,244. [11]Salaries as of 1/1/96 for Admin. Office of U.S. Courts.

Probation and Parole Administrators' Salaries

- The average probation administrator earned $80,024 per year; the average parole administrator earned $110,291 per year; and the average probation and parole administrator earned $68,511 per year.

Source: Camp and Camp, *Corrections Yearbook—1997.* Used with permission.

overall average salary for probation and parole officers was $31,466. Parole officers averaged $33,750 and probation officers $32,269. The average high salary for probation and parole officers was $42,647; for parole officers the average high salary was $42,021; and for probation officers the average high salary was $43,480.[35] See Table 5.3 for a state-by-state listing of probation and parole officer salaries.

FIREARMS POLICIES FOR PROBATION AND PAROLE OFFICERS

Probation and parole officers are increasingly calling for the right to carry a firearm while on duty. In the past most probation and parole officers viewed themselves as therapeutic agents whose primary duties were oriented toward rehabilitation. Few officers in that period carried firearms or wished to. However, the past two decades have witnessed a shift from the medical model to a surveillance–control orientation, and many probation and parole officers now view their job and their role differently. Also, it is becoming clear that the probation and parole caseloads include more dangerous offenders, and some evidence suggests that client violence against supervising officers is escalating.[36] The hazards of probation and parole work are clearly illustrated in a study by the Federal Probation and Pretrial Officers Association in 1993.[37] This study revealed the following assaults or attempted assaults against probation, parole, and pretrial services officers nationwide between 1980 and 1993:

Murder or attempted murder	16
Rape or attempted rape	7
Other sexual assaults	100
Shot or wounded or attempts	32
Use or attempted use of blunt instrument or projectile	60
Slashed or stabbed or attempt	28
Car used as weapon or attempt	12
Punched, kicked, choked	1,396
Use or attempted use of caustic substance	3
Use or attempted use of incendiary device	9
Abduction or attempt	3
Attempted or actual unspecified assaults	944
TOTAL	2,610

Dean Champion argues that whether probation and parole officers should arm themselves may be a moot question because many arm themselves anyway, regardless of law or agency policy. Our experience supports Champion's assertion. When surveyed, 59 percent of officers believed they should have the legal option to carry a firearm on the job. However, when asked if they would endorse a requirement to carry a firearm as a part of the job, 80 percent of the female and 69 percent of the male officers opposed such a requirement. Yet 80 percent of all officers said they would carry a firearm if required to do so.[38]

Law and agency policy differs between jurisdictions, and it is difficult to determine which states allow probation and parole officers to arm themselves. One method of determining whether an officer has the legal right to carry a firearm is to examine statutes to find whether probation and parole officers are considered peace officers under state law. Even this method is not foolproof because agency policy may prohibit carrying firearms even if state law defines the officer as a peace officer. A recent survey of state laws reports that probation officers are peace officers in eight states,[39] parole officers are peace officers in eight states,[40] and probation and parole officers are peace officers in 16 states.[41]

The American Probation and Parole Association (APPA) neither supports nor opposes the carrying of weapons by probation and parole officers. The association argues that should officers be authorized to carry weapons, that decision should be made within the framework of actual need and officer safety demands and must be consistent with laws and policies.[42]

The APPA has established guidelines for agencies implementing a decision to allow officers to carry weapons:

> In the event an agency determines that officers should carry a weapon or that specific job functions require that an officer be armed, it is mandatory that exceptional care be given to the implementation of such a decision. This decision to arm staff must be decisively made by the agency's leadership based on a clearly delineated and comprehensive plan responding to issues of staff safety. Once this decision is made, the agency must dictate all choices as to equipment, training, and procedures related to carrying a weapon. Nothing should be left to the discretion of individual officers except perhaps whether they want to accept an assignment which requires carrying a weapon. Standards must be established and monitored closely for compliance.[43]

The APPA also recommends clear policies, training in the handling of firearms, legal issues and liability, and selection procedures that minimally include a physical and psychological examination.[44]

INTERSTATE COMPACTS ON PROBATION

Our consideration of probation administration would not be complete if we failed to discuss the interstate compacts for supervising adult and juvenile probationers and parolees. At one time there was no way to supervise a probationer or parolee outside the state where he or she was convicted, in spite of the fact that many transient offenders are arrested and convicted far from where they have relatives and community ties. As a result, there was often no way to provide the offender with supervision in the very place that would offer the best chance for success on probation or parole. Pursuant to the Crime Control Consent Act passed by Congress in 1936, a group of states entered into an agreement by which they would supervise probationers and parolees for each other. Known as the **Interstate Compact for the Supervision of Parolees and Probationers,** the agreement was originally signed by 25 states in 1937. By 1951 it had been ratified by all the states.

A similar agreement, the Interstate Compact on Juveniles, provides for return of juvenile runaways, escapees, and absconders and for cooperative supervision of juvenile probationers and parolees. An amendment to this compact provides for out-of-state confinement of juveniles. Each state enacts the compact as part of its state laws.[45]

The compacts identify the **sending state**—the state of conviction—and the **receiving state**—the state that undertakes the supervision. The offender must meet certain residence requirements of the receiving state. Ordinarily the probationer or parolee must be a resident of the receiving state, have relatives there, or have employment there. The receiving state agrees to accept the offender and to provide the same supervision it accords other probationers or parolees in the state. The offender who obtains

INTERSTATE COMPACT FOR THE SUPERVISION OF PAROLEES AND PROBATIONERS

An agreement signed by all 50 states which allows for the supervision of parolees and probationers in a state other than the state of conviction.

SENDING STATE

Under the Interstate Compact, the state of conviction.

RECEIVING STATE

Under the Interstate Compact, the state that undertakes the supervision.

the benefits of out-of-state supervision waives extradition. The sending state may enter the receiving state to take custody of the probationer or parolee who has violated the terms of release without going through extradition proceedings, and a supplementary agreement permits the violator to be incarcerated in the receiving state at the expense of the sending state if both states agree.[46]

Parole boards usually designate one member to be the interstate compact administrator. That person handles the details of arranging the supervision of parolees who are either sent out of the state for supervision or received into the state after conviction in another state. Where probation is locally administered, the compact does not work as smoothly for probation supervision as it does for parole supervision. Some exchanges take place, however, and probation supervision or detention and care of runaways and absconders is provided by the receiving state.

Problems with Interstate Compacts

Under the interstate compacts, states agree to provide "courtesy supervision" of probationers and parolees from other states. Some requests are problematic and thus are not approved. In the past some probation and parole agencies have alleged that certain local departments and some states practiced "dumping"—transferring difficult cases to other states with little or no justification other than the desire to rid themselves of the problem individuals. In addition, some states are asked to accept far more interstate-compact supervision cases than they send out. However, the vast majority of requests for transfer of supervision are legitimate, and when it appears that a case will not unreasonably burden the receiving department, the state usually complies.

SUMMARY

Probation is both a disposition and a process. As a disposition, probation is court-related; that is, the power to grant and to revoke it is in a court. As a process, it is the organization, administration, and delivery of probation services. There is little uniformity to probation organizational patterns in the United States. Probation services may be combined with parole or kept separate. Adult and juvenile probation may be combined or entirely separate. Probation may be administered by the executive branch of government or by the judiciary. Probation services may be organized at the state level or at the local level. There are arguments for and against each of these organizational schemes. Generally, however, the evidence seems to support state executive-branch control of probation services as the most effective and efficient approach. Recent developments such as Community Corrections Acts, which provide state funding to local probation agencies for enhancement of existing services and development of a wider range of sanction alternatives, appear to be increasing in use and interest. This chapter also discussed the provisions for selecting probation officers, initial qualifications, and both preservice and in-service training, as well as whether probation and parole officers should be allowed to carry weapons. Interstate agreements for supervision were also discussed in relation to the issue of probation administration.

ENDNOTES

1. 18 U.S.C.A. 3651.
2. Cited in Howard Abadinsky, *Probation and Parole: Theory and Practice,* 5th ed. (Englewood Cliffs, N.J.: Prentice Hall, 1994), 28.
3. *Attorney General's Survey: Probation,* vol. 2 (Washington, D.C.: U.S. Department of Justice, 1939), 24.
4. *Attorney General's Survey,* 22–23, n. 75.
5. *Attorney General's Survey,* 25.
6. *Attorney General's Survey,* 105–106.
7. *Attorney General's Survey,* "Digest," 299–300.
8. *Attorney General's Survey,* 2.
9. *Attorney General's Survey,* 7.
10. *Attorney General's Survey,* 7.
11. Paraphrased from the National Advisory Commission, *Standards, Corrections* (Washington, D.C.: Government Printing Office, 1973): 315–316.
12. National Advisory Commission, *Standards, Corrections,* 315–316.
13. Jim Scott, "Deconsolidation, Design for the Future Stolen from the Past," *Journal of the Texas Probation Association,* 9(1):1 (January 1997).
14. National Council on Crime and Delinquency, *Standard Probation and Parole Act,* § § 3.3, 7.7.
15. ABA, *Standards, Probation,* Commentary, 75–76.
16. National Advisory Commission on Criminal Justice Standards and Goals, *Report on Corrections* (Washington, D.C.: Government Printing Office, 1973).
17. John Ortiz Smykla, *Probation and Parole: Crime Control in the Community* (New York: Macmillan, 1984), 90.
18. Patrick D. McManus and Lynn Zeller Barclay, *Community Corrections Act: Technical Assistance Manual* (College Park, Md.: American Correctional Association, 1994).
19. The states that have passed CCAs include Alabama, Arizona, Colorado, Connecticut, Florida, Indiana, Iowa, Kansas, Michigan, Minnesota, Montana, New Mexico, Ohio, Oregon, Pennsylvania, Tennessee, Texas, and Virginia.
20. *The Community Corrections Act,* Oregon Revised Statutes 423.505, Oregon Laws 1995.
21. NAC. See also E. Kim Nelson, Howard Ohmart, and Nora Harlow, *Promising Strategies in Probation and Parole* (Washington, D.C.: Government Printing Office, 1978).
22. NAC, 5.
23. Norval Morris and Michael Tonry, *Between Prison and Probation: Intermediate Punishments in a Rational Sentencing System* (New York: Oxford University Press, 1990).
24. Morris and Tonry, *Between Prison and Probation,* 230–231.
25. Abadinsky, *Probation and Parole,* 353.
26. The selection is, however, subject to the approval of the chief U.S. district judge of the judicial district, who officially appoints all U.S. probation officers.
27. The U.S. Parole Commission was abolished by the Comprehensive Crime Control Act of 1984. Although the Commission was scheduled to be phased out by 1992, it was extended for an additional 5 years.
28. This is the situation in Texas. Tex. Fam. Code Ann. § 51.04 (Vernon).
29. Abadinsky, *Probation and Parole,* 353.
30. Abadinsky, *Probation and Parole,* 353.
31. NAC, 12.

32. NAC.
33. LIS, Inc. *State and Local Probation Systems in the United States* (Longmont, CO.: 1995).
34. Camp and Camp, *The Corrections Yearbook—1997*, 178.
35. Camp and Camp, *The Corrections Yearbook—1997*, 178.
36. Dean Champion, *Probation, Parole, and Community Corrections,* 2nd ed. (Englewood Cliffs, NJ: Prentice-Hall, 1996).
37. Phillip J. Bigger, "Officers in Danger: Results of the Federal Probation and Pretrial Services Association's National Study on Serious Assaults," *APPA Perspectives* 17, 14–20.
38. Reported in Champion, *Probation, Parole, and Community Corrections,* 429–430.
39. Arizona, California, Connecticut, Delaware, Georgia, Illinois, Nebraska, and New York.
40. California, Colorado, Georgia, Illinois, Kansas, Massachusetts, New Jersey, and New York.
41. Alabama, Alaska, Arkansas, Florida, Idaho, Kentucky, Louisiana, Maine, Montana, Nevada, North Dakota, Oklahoma, Oregon, Pennsylvania, South Carolina, and Utah.
42. American Probation and Parole Association, *APPA Position Statement: Weapons.* Approved 1994.
43. *APPA Position Statement: Weapons.*
44. *APPA Position Statement: Weapons.*
45. See, for example, Interstate Parole Reciprocal Agreement, Ill. Ann. Stat. ch. 38, § § 123–25, 123–26 (Smith-Hurd).
46. California Interstate Compact on Juveniles, Cal. Welf. and Inst. Code, § § 1300–1308 (West).

DISCUSSION QUESTIONS

1. Distinguish between probation as a disposition and as a process.
2. Early probation legislation followed one of the two existing organizational plans—that of Vermont or Rhode Island. How were these two organizational structures different?
3. What are the major patterns of administering probation services?
4. What are the advantages and disadvantages of placing responsibility for probation in the executive branch of government?
5. What are the advantages and disadvantages of administering probation services at the state level rather than the local level?
6. What is a mixed organizational structure, and what are its advantages?
7. According to Morris and Tonry the trend in probation is toward the development of intermediate sanctions such as intensive supervision programs. How might this trend affect probation administration?
8. How are probation officers selected in your jurisdictions? What are some alternative methods?
9. What are Community Corrections Acts? What are the major advantages of such an organizational structure?
10. Discuss the various methods of probation and parole officer selection. What are some advantages of each? Disadvantages?
11. What are the issues regarding weapons being carried by probation and parole officers?

Model Adult Community Corrections Act

I. Overview

A. Goals and Objectives

(1) To enhance public safety and achieve economies by encouraging the development and implementation of community sanctions as a sentencing option;

(2) To enhance the value of criminal sanctions and ensure that the criminal penalties imposed are the most appropriate ones by encouraging the development of a wider array of criminal sanctions;

(3) To increase the community's awareness of, participation in, and responsibility for the administration of the corrections system;

(4) To ensure that the offender is punished in the least restrictive setting consistent with public safety and the gravity of the crime;

(5) To provide offenders with education, training and treatment to enable them to become fully functional members of the community upon release from criminal justice supervision;

(6) To make offenders accountable to the community for their criminal behavior, through community service programs, restitution programs, and a range of locally developed sanctions; and

(7) To foster the development of policies and funding for programs that encourage jurisdictions to minimize the use of incarceration where other sanctions are appropriate.

B. Definitions

(1) **Community.** Any local jurisdiction, or any combination of jurisdictions, the government(s) of which undertake(s) joint efforts and shared responsibilities for purposes of providing community corrections options in the jurisdiction(s) in accordance with the purposes and requirements of this Act.

(2) **Community Corrections.** Any number of sanctions which are served by the offender within the community in which the offender committed the offense or in the community in which the offender resides.

(3) **Incarceration.** Any sanction which involves placement of the offender in prison, jail, boot camp, or other secure facility.

Commentary

The goals and objectives set forth in Section 1(A) of this Act reflect three broad purposes: more effective sentencing, more effective use of public resources allocated for correctional purposes, and more extensive involvement of local communities in developing and implementing correctional programs for offenders whose criminal conduct does not require utilization of scarce prison and jail space.

All too often, judges have in the past been faced with very limited sentencing options: either a sentence of incarceration in prison or jail, placement on unsupervised probation, or imposition of a fine without regard to the offender's financial means. In recent years, a number of innovative sentencing options have been developed in the United States, giving some judges a broader range of choice as they strive to impose sentences that are cost-efficient, effective, and responsive to public safety concerns. The Model Act encourages use of these options, not only to help relieve problems of prison and jail crowding, but to help achieve appropriate purposes of criminal sanctions. The community-based sentencing options authorized in the Model Act can be used to achieve the full range of sentencing purposes: punishment (or "just desserts") deterrence (both specific and general), rehabilitation, and incapacitation.

II. Sanctions

A. This Model Community Corrections Act provides for local implementation of the following community-based sanctions (the list is not intended to be exclusive of other community-based sanctions):

(1) Standard probation;

(2) Intensive supervision probation;

(3) Community service;

(4) Home confinement with or without electronic monitoring;

(5) Electronic surveillance (including telephone monitoring);

(6) Community-based residential settings offering structure, supervision, surveillance, drug/alcohol treatment, employment counseling and/or other forms of treatment or counseling;

(7) Outpatient treatment;

(8) Requirement of employment and/or education/training;

(9) Day reporting centers;

(10) Restitution; and

(11) Means-based fines.

B. Definitions

(1) Standard Supervised Probation. A judicially imposed criminal sanction permitting court supervision of the offender within the community.

(2) Intensive Supervision Probation. An organized program of probation which includes a combination of conditions such as training, community service, home confinement, or counseling and treatment, and is characterized by frequent and close monitoring of the offender.

(3) Community Service. A program of specific work assigned to the offender which substantially benefits the community in which the offense was committed.

(4) Home Confinement. A judicially or administratively imposed condition requiring an offender to remain at home for some portion of the day. There are three types of home confinement.

  (a) Curfew. A type of home confinement requiring the offender to be home during established hours.

  (b) Home Detention. A type of home confinement requiring offenders to remain at home except during periods of work or study or other permitted absence; and

  (c) Home Incarceration. A type of home confinement requiring the offender to remain at home at virtually all times.

(5) Electronic Surveillance. A means of utilizing telephonic or telemetry technology to monitor the presence or absence of an individual at a particular location from a remote location.

(6) Community-based residential settings offering structure, supervision, surveillance, drug/alcohol treatment, employment counseling and/or other forms of treatment or counseling. A program of organized treatment or counseling designed to assist the offender in overcoming any psychological and/or physical conditions which may have contributed to his or her prior criminal behavior while also providing structure, supervision and/or surveillance.

(7) Outpatient Treatment. This option is identical to subsection (6) above with the exception that such treatment would be offered on an outpatient basis.

(8) Requirement of Employment and/or Education/Training. A judicially imposed requirement that the offender remain employed or participate in an educational training course as a condition of his or her sentence.

(9) Day Reporting Centers. A center where an offender serving a community-based sentence in a community corrections setting would be required to report as a condition of his or her sentence.

(10) Restitution. Reparation by the offender for personal or property damages incurred by the victim as a result of the offense.

(11) Means-based Fines. A monetary sanction imposed on an offender which is proportional to the crime(s) committed and the offender's ability to pay within a reasonable period of time.

Commentary

Section II(A) of the Act lists a range of sanctions to become available as sentencing options under the Act. As is indicated, the list is not all-inclusive. The Act contemplates, facilitates, and encourages the further development of effective and cost-efficient community-based sanctions.

All of the community-based sanctions listed in Section II(A) have been tried in at least some American jurisdictions and some of them (e.g., day reporting centers and means-based fines) have a long history of successful utilization in other countries. See, e.g., S. Hillsman, J. Sichel & B. Mahoney, Fines in Sentencing: A Study of the Use of the Fine as Criminal Sanction—Executive Summary 5 (1984) (two-thirds of offenders in West Germany and one-half in England and Sweden are fined for committing crimes against a person). A growing body of research has found that these sanctions take a wide variety of forms in different communities and has begun to identify factors that are essential for their successful implementation. See, e.g., N. Morris and M. Tonry, Between Prison and Probation: Intermediate Punishments in a Rational Sentencing System (1990); Freed and Mahoney, Between Prison and Probation: Using Intermediate Sanctions Effectively, 29 The Judges' Journal 6 (Winter, 1990); D. Parent, Day Reporting Centers for Criminal Offenders—A Descriptive Analysis of Existing Programs (National Institute of Justice, 1990); Knapp, Next Step: Non-Imprisonment Guidelines, Perspectives (Winter, 1988); P. Hofer and B. Meierhoefer, Home Confinement: An Evolving Sanction in the Federal Criminal Justice System (1987); Intermediate Punishments: Intensive Supervision, Home Confinement and Electronic Surveillance (B. McCarthy, ed., 1987); J. Petersilia, Expanding Options for Criminal Sentencing (1987); P. DuPont, Expanding Sentencing Options: A Governor's Perspective (National Institute of Justice, 1985).

The community-based sanctions listed in the Act share a number of advantages, including the following: (1) offenders, if employed in the community, can continue to support their families; (2) taxes can be collected on the earnings of these offenders; (3) offenders will be better able to pay restitution; (4) families can remain intact; and (5) offenders can avoid the criminogenic influences of prison or jail. In addition, the flexibility afforded by this array of sentencing options permits them to be used with a large and varied population of offenders. Some offenders, for example, could be required to perform community service and/or receive drug dependency treatment while also serving a period of home confinement.

The sanctions also can be both punitive and structured to meet offenders' rehabilitation needs and guard the public's safety. For example, intensive supervised probation ("ISP") provides for more frequent supervision and intensive treatment of offenders than is normally afforded by traditional probation programs. Day reporting centers are also a useful means of ensuring that offenders comply with the terms of their sentences. Such centers provide a central location where offenders can spend the day and attend classes; receive vocational training; participate in substance-abuse, family, and other types of counseling sessions; and undergo urinalysis tests for evidence of drug or alcohol use.

Although the Act does not address the use of community-based sanctions as conditions of parole, many of these sanctions, such as those of intensive supervision and day reporting centers discussed above, can also be used to provide parolees with the supervision and treatment needed to successfully complete their parole terms.

III. State Criminal Justice Council

A. The Community Corrections Act shall be administered by a State Criminal Justice Council that has oversight responsibility for state criminal justice policies and programs. The Council shall be responsible for ensuring that policies and activities undertaken by State or local governmental units or other organizations in furtherance of the purposes of the Act are consistent with those purposes and with the statewide community corrections plan required under Section III(D)(1).

B. Not later than 90 days after the effective date of this Act, the governor shall appoint, and the legislature shall confirm, the 15 members of the Council as follows:
   (1) One member shall be a county sheriff;
   (2) One member shall be a chief of a city police department;
   (3) One member shall be a judge of a general jurisdiction trial court;
   (4) One member shall be a judge from an appellate level court;
   (5) One member shall be a county commissioner or county board head;
   (6) One member shall be a city government official;
   (7) One member shall represent an existing community corrections program;
   (8) One member shall be the director of the department of corrections or his or her designee;
   (9) One member shall be a county prosecutor;
   (10) One member shall be a criminal defense attorney;
   (11) One member shall be the head of a probation department;
   (12) Four members shall be representatives of the general public.

C. The governor shall ensure that there is a fair geographic representation on the State board and that minorities and women are fairly represented.

D. The Council shall:
   (1) Develop a plan for statewide implementation of the Act that incorporates the purposes and objectives of the Act; ensures consistency of community corrections programs and requirements with other applicable State laws and regulations; and establishes goals, criteria, timetables, and incentives for initiation of community corrections programs;
   (2) Establish standards and guidelines for community development of plans to implement the Act in local jurisdictions, as described in Section IV of this Act;
   (3) Review initial community plans, require revisions as necessary, and monitor implementation of approved plans to ensure consistency with the statewide plan;
   (4) Award, administer and monitor grants, loans or other State funding mechanisms that the State Legislature establishes for assisting communities in implementing their community corrections plans, as provided in Section VI of this Act;
   (5) Review community plans and their implementation at least annually to ensure consistency with the statewide plan and require modification of plans as necessary to ensure compliance with the objectives of this Act;
   (6) Evaluate annually the effectiveness of policies and programs carried out under the Act and report to the Legislature on evaluation findings;
   (7) Monitor and evaluate the effect of the Act's implementation on offenders of different races;
   (8) Take steps to ensure that the community corrections program is adequately funded by the Legislature;

(9) Provide technical assistance and training to provide community corrections services in local jurisdictions;

(10) Provide guidance to local Community Corrections Boards, as defined in Section IV(A) of the Act, in educating the public concerning the purposes of the Act, the types of programs and activities to be undertaken under the Act, the possible impacts of the Act on local jurisdictions, and other matters that may assist the local Boards in establishing and carrying out their community corrections programs;

(11) Maintain records on the number of offenders who met the eligibility criteria in Section V(l)(a) through V(A)(1)(c) but who were incarcerated;

(12) Monitor the results of appeals of offenders who met the eligibility criteria in Section V(1)(a) through V(A)(1)(c) but who were incarcerated;

(13) Assess user fees against communities that incarcerate eligible offenders based on the per inmate incarceration cost formula described in Section VI(C)(1); and

(14) Hire an executive director who shall serve at the pleasure of the Council.

E. The Legislature shall appropriate such funds as are necessary for the Council to carry out its responsibilities under the Act, including funds to hire an executive director and necessary staff to implement the program. Appropriations shall be provided in a way and an amount to ensure program continuity and stability.

Commentary

The provisions of Section III reflect the drafters' view that implementation of an effective, statewide community corrections program requires the active involvement of a broad range of policymakers, criminal justice practitioners from different institutions and agencies, and the general public. The State Criminal Justice Council contemplated by this Act is much like the State community corrections board established by the Michigan Community Corrections Act. That board is composed of a wide array of criminal justice professionals and members of the public. See Mich. Comp. Laws Sec. 791.403. The Criminal Justice Council under the Model Act carries out much the same role as the board identified in the Michigan statute.

Although some States currently operate community corrections programs through established entities, such as probation and parole departments or departments of corrections, the objectives of a community corrections program are broader, and in some instances different from those of other criminal justice departments or agencies in a State. An entity that is separate from those departments or agencies would therefore generally be most able to coordinate implementation of a community corrections program among all affected departments and agencies. In addition, a Criminal Justice Council would be able to handle funding administration, training and education, local program oversight, and other responsibilities that often would not fall within the purview of other departments or agencies, but that are essential to the operation of a successful community corrections program.

It is possible, however, that in some states, existing bodies might be able to assume the implementation, administrative, coordinating, and oversight functions for a statewide community corrections program. Minnesota and Oregon, for example, administer community corrections programs through their Departments of Corrections. Oregon's community corrections program is actually a hybrid model. It allows for varying levels of local participation, ranging from local administration of all community corrections sanctions and supervision programs to centralized State administration of those sanctions and programs with local advisory input. Or. Rev. Stat. Sec.s 423.540 and 423.545 (1990).

In Section III(B) of the Model Act, a county sheriff is listed as one of the members of the Criminal Justice Council. The intent of the Act is to have the chief correctional officer from a county serve on the Council. Usually, this person would be the sheriff. In those jurisdictions in which individuals other than the sheriffs are responsible for county corrections systems, i.e., the county jails, one of those individuals should be on the Council rather than the sheriff.

Although not required by this Act, jurisdictions should also consider adding members of the legislature as ex officio members of the Council. These legislators could be helpful advocates for the community corrections program within the legislature and could help to ensure that the program is properly funded. Other State officials, such as a parole board member and a member of the State sentencing commission, might also bring helpful expertise to the Council.

The development of a statewide community corrections plan by the State Criminal Justice Council, as provided by Section III(D)(1) of the Model Act, is important to the furthering of the goals and objectives of the Act. A plan will result in the establishment of minimum standards, will ensure that there is some consistency in local program operations statewide, and will provide a means for encouraging community support of community corrections. In addition, the State plan win provide a means for gauging progress in the implementation of the Act and for measuring the effectiveness of both individual programs and the statewide county corrections model as a whole.

The broad range of Council functions set forth in Section III(D) necessarily requires staff to administer the programs. The staff would assist in providing technical assistance and training, monitoring and evaluating the implementation of the program in local communities, and ensuring sound fiscal management of appropriated funds. Provision is made for appropriation of funds to hire an executive director and staff to implement the program, as well as for funds for direct program operations at the local level (Section III(E)). Because of the time required to design, build support for, and implement a community corrections program, as well as the time that must elapse before any assessment of program effectiveness is possible, a State legislature must commit itself to supporting the community corrections program over a period of time long enough to permit thorough, thoughtful and coordinated planning.

IV. Community Corrections Boards

A. Every city and county in the State shall establish a community corrections program by applying individually or as part of grouping designated as a "community," as defined in Section I of this Act, to participate in programs and activities, including grant and other financial assistance programs, authorized by this Act and the statewide plan described in Section III(D)(1) of this Act.

B. Each community shall establish a local Community Corrections Board that shall be responsible for developing and implementing a community corrections plan for the community (including locating suitable sites for community correctional programs). Each Board shall be comprised, at minimum, of representatives of the following categories:

(1) Local prosecutor;
(2) Local public defender;
(3) Local member of the criminal defense bar;
(4) Local judges from limited and general jurisdiction courts including courts with jurisdiction over criminal matters;
(5) Local law enforcement official;
(6) Local corrections official;
(7) Local representative from the probation department;
(8) Local government representative;
(9) Local health, education, and human services representatives;
(10) Nonprofit community corrections services provider; and
(11) Three or more representatives of the general public.

C. Each Community shall ensure that minorities and women are fairly represented on the Community Corrections Board.

D. In accordance with such rules, regulations, or other policies as the State Council establishes under Section III(D) of this Act, each Board shall develop a comprehensive community corrections plan that, consistent with the objectives and requirements of the Act:

(1) Offers programs for the placement of offenders in the community rather than in correctional institutions; specifies the type(s) and scope of community-based sentencing options to be offered and the type(s) of offenders to be included in the program; describes the community's capacity to carry out the specified community-based sanction; and identifies the means by which the Board intends to provide the sentencing option;
(2) Addresses projected program costs and identifies sources of funds, including grants, loans or other financial assistance available through the Council to meet those costs;
(3) Provides for monitoring and annual reporting of program results to the Council;
(4) Provides for annual review of the plan and for its revision, as necessary or desirable;
(5) Includes a commitment to carry out the plan in cooperation and coordination with other governmental entities and to conduct the program in a manner designed to ensure public safety and the program's efficacy;
(6) Addresses the need for involvement and education of the community regarding the purposes and objectives of the Act generally and the local community corrections program specifically; and
(7) Identifies the extent to which its plan will affect the number of individuals who are incarcerated.

E. Each Board shall submit its plan to the State Council for review. An approved plan shall serve as the basis for subsequent Board activity and for the Council's determination of the extent of funding assistance to be provided for community corrections in that Board's community.

Commentary

The Model Act is intended to establish community corrections programs for all local jurisdictions so that qualified offenders in every part of the State can be placed in community corrections programs and so that criminal justice system responsibilities are borne by communities throughout the State. At the same time, however, geography, resources, or other constraints may make community corrections programs impractical or infeasible in some locales. The Act therefore permits jurisdictions to join together as a single "community" for purposes of the Act, provided that all jurisdictions in the community commit themselves fully to shared responsibility for and cooperative support of the local programs.

Because the success of community corrections on a broad scale depends upon the community commitment and involvement, the Act places responsibility for decisions about local program operations with a local entity comprised of individuals who represent the diverse constituencies affected by community corrections program decisions. Although the community corrections board would not make offender placement decisions, it would determine the types and locations of community corrections programs and facilities in the community. It also would be responsible for generating and, through oversight activity, maintaining the necessary community support for community corrections in the jurisdiction(s) it represents.

The membership of the community corrections boards may vary somewhat from jurisdiction to jurisdiction. For example, some jurisdictions do not have public defenders. The critical requirement, however, is that the community corrections board be comprised of a broad array of criminal justice professionals and members of the public.

The board's actions and decisions would be based upon a local plan containing sufficient detail to confirm that the planned program is in compliance with the Act and the statewide plan. The board would be accountable both to the community and to the State, for both monies spent and programs operated.

V. Program Criteria

A. Offender Eligibility.
   (1) The following offender groups shall be eligible for sentencing to community-based sanctions:
      (a) misdemeanants;
      (b) nonviolent felony offenders. including drug abusers and other offenders with special treatment needs;
      (c) parole, probation, and community corrections condition violators whose violation conduct is either non-criminal or would meet either criterion (a) or (b) above had it been charged as a criminal violation;
      (d) offenders who, although not eligible under criteria (a) through (c) above, are found by the court to be the type of individuals for whom such a sentence would serve the goals of the Act. In making such a determination, the judge shall consider factors that bear on the danger posed and likelihood of recidivism by the offender, including but not limited to the following:
         (i) that the offender has a sponsor in the community;
         (ii) that the offender either has procured employment or has enrolled in an educational or rehabilitative program; and
         (iii) that the offender has not demonstrated a pattern of violent behavior and does not have a criminal record that indicates a pattern of violent offenses.

Commentary

The provisions of this section are intended to strongly encourage the sentencing of offenders who meet the eligibility requirements of Sections V(A)(1)(a)-(V)(A)(1)(c) to a community corrections program. The section is meant to comport with ABA Standard for Criminal Justice 18-22, which provides that "[t]he sentence imposed in each case shall call for the minimum sanction which is consistent with the protection of the public and the gravity of the crime."

VI. Funding Mechanism

A. Eligibility. A community shall apply for State funding by submitting a community corrections plan to the State Criminal Justice Council. The plan will provide information on a community's demonstrated need for community corrections. The plan also will establish program criteria consistent with this Act. Once the Council has approved a proposed corrections plan, that community will be eligible to receive a grant payment for part of the plan's cost.

B. Funding.
   (1) Communities will be allocated grant funds to ensure program continuity and stability.
   (2) To allocate funds appropriated by the State to implement the Community Corrections Act, the Council will equitably apportion funds to communities.

(3) The Council will redetermine periodically each community's appropriate level of funding, taking into account the community's proven commitment to the implementation of this Act.

(4) The funds provided under this Act shall not supplant current spending by the local jurisdiction for any existing community corrections program.

C. Chargeback Provision.

(1) Commencing two years after the approval of a community's corrections plan, the Criminal Justice Council will charge each community a user fee equivalent to 75 percent of the per-inmate cost of incarceration for each offender who has met the eligibility criteria in Sections V(A)(1)(a) through V(A)(1)(c) but who has been either:

(a) Committed to a State correctional facility by a sentencing authority in the community; or

(b) Committed by a sentencing authority in the community to a county or regional jail facility.

(2) The amount charged to a community under this Section shall not exceed the amount of financial aid received under Section VI(B).]

D. Audit. Every two years, the State's general auditor will audit all community financial reports related to Community Corrections Act projects.

E. Continual Grant Funding. To receive aid, communities must comply with the requirements established by this Act and the standards promulgated by the State Criminal Justice Council under it. A community corrections program will be evaluated two years after the approval of the community's correction plan and every year thereafter.

F. Notice. If a community fails to meet the standards of the Act, the Council shall notify the community that it has 60 days to comply or funding will be discontinued. The community shall have the opportunity to respond within 30 days after receipt of such notice.

Commentary

The eligibility requirements found in Section VI(A) for State funding of community corrections programs will help ensure that community plans correspond to the basic goals of the Act. Further, by reviewing such plans, the Criminal Justice Council will become more aware of the variety of community corrections program which exist within each community.

Adequate funding is essential to the successful implementation of any community corrections act. The funding mechanism included in Section VI(B) envisions State funding of community corrections programs. Such funding would be based on each community's need. Determination of a community's financial need would be based on a variety of factors, such as: (a) the population of the community; (b) the percentage of the community's total population which is in prison or jail or on probation; (c) the community's per capita income; (d) the number of offenders from the community committed to correctional institutions for violent and nonviolent crimes; and (e) the availability, conditions, and capacity of community corrections programs, facilities, and resources. This Act does not attempt to resolve how these and other factors would be balanced; each State would decide on its own how to balance the factors and assess a community's financial need. See, e.g., Minn. Stat. Sec. 401.06; Ohio Rev. Code Ann. Sec. 5149.31-5149.36; Tenn Code Ann. Sec. 40-36-301 and 304-305; Tex. Crim. Pro. Code Ann Sec. 6166a-4.

The Act requires that the grants be allocated to ensure program continuity and stability. Ideally, this would involve multi-year grants by the legislature, particularly at the program's start, to allow time for its establishment. Three or more years of committed funds would be preferable. The Act recognizes that this may be neither feasible nor permissible under most jurisdictions' granting processes. This Act avoids identifying a minimum funding period for this reason. Instead, it imposes a commitment on the jurisdiction to recognize that establishing a community corrections program is a multi-year undertaking requiring the long-term commitment of resources.

The chargeback provisions of Section VI(C) are a means of encouraging the development and use of community-based sanctions and of further ensuring that an offender for whom a community-based sanction or sanctions is appropriate will be so sentenced. The figure of 75% of the cost of incarceration as a charge to a community that fails to use community-based sanctions for eligible offenders is high enough to provide communities with a substantial incentive to punish those offenders within the community. See Ind. Code Sec. 11-2-2-9 (1988). The actual amount of the fee would be calculated by multiplying 75% of the cost of incarcerating the inmate in a correctional institution by the length of the incarcerative sentence imposed. The fee would not be assessed the community if, because of the results of an appeal, an offender sentenced to a period of incarceration is not actually incarcerated.

The chargeback provision provides communities with an incentive to develop and implement effective community corrections programs. The potentially harsh effect of the provision is ameliorated by the limit on the amount that may be charged back to the community under Section VI(C)(2). In addition, the chargeback provision does not apply until after communities have had time to develop their community corrections programs.

Some jurisdictions, notably Oregon, have avoided the use of a chargeback provision by adopting sentencing guidelines to ensure that community-based sanctions are imposed on offenders who fall within the target population. Sentencing guidelines that govern the imposition of community-based sanctions can help ensure their appropriate use while avoiding the criticism often leveled at chargeback provisions that they penalize city and county governments for decisions made by judges over whom they have little or no control. The ABA Standards for Criminal Justice call for the adoption of sentencing guidelines to govern sentencing decisions. See Standard 18-3.1. If those guidelines include community based sanctions, as is recommended by Section VII(D)(1) of this Act, reliance on the chargeback provisions of Section VI(C) would be unnecessary, which is why that Section has been placed in brackets.

VII. Sentencing Determinations

A. Presentence Report.

(1) All presentence reports shall be required to specifically address whether a community-based sanction is a viable sentencing option.

B. Judicial Sentencing Statement.

(1) The sentencing judge must consider the community-based sanctions set out in this statute before sentencing any eligible offender as defined in Section V(A).

(2) Where the judge has decided that community-based sanction is inappropriate, the judge must state on the record at the time of sentencing that the court considered community correction sentencing options and must explain why such sentencing options were rejected.

C. Appellate Review.

(1) All individuals sentenced under this State's criminal statutes shall have a right of review of their sentence for conformity with the provisions of this Act, provided that such grounds for appeal are raised on direct appeal of the conviction.

D. Relationship Between Community Corrections Sanctions and Sentencing Guidelines in Jurisdictions with Sentencing Guidelines.

(1) The [State legislature] in those jurisdictions with sentencing guidelines shall appoint a committee for the purpose of fashioning sentencing guidelines that incorporate community corrections sentences in a manner consistent with the provisions of this Act.

(2) Under guidelines drafted pursuant to Section VII(D)(1), nonincarceration sanctions will be the presumptively appropriate sentence for offenders meeting the criteria of Section V(A)(1)(a)-V(A)(1)(c).

Commentary

Section VII(A) requires that presentence reports include a discussion of whether a community-based sanction is appropriate in each case. This provision will ensure that parties involved in the sentencing process—judges, probation personnel, prosecutors, and defense attorneys—are aware of community-based sentencing options during the sentencing process.

Section VII(B) then encourages judges to take advantage of such sentencing options by requiring them to explain why they did not utilize a community-based sanction in sentencing an offender who fits within the target population as defined in Section V(A). This requirement will encourage judges to use the sentencing options set out in this Act so that, consistent with ABA policy, the sentence is the minimum sanction which is consistent with the protection of the public and the gravity of the crime.

Section VII(D) is included to accommodate those jurisdictions that either have in place or are enacting or authorizing concurrently with this Community Corrections Act a set of sentencing guidelines. Community corrections sanctions should be included in such guidelines and referenced by the nature of the current criminal conduct and the offender's criminal history, just as other sanctions are.

Any State sentencing guidelines should be consistent with the eligibility criteria in Section V(A). Application of the guidelines would then generally lead to a community corrections sanction when the offender has met the criteria in Section V(A)(1)(a)-V(A)(1)(c) and would permit a community corrections sanction when the offender meets the criteria of Section V(A)(1)(d).

Section VII(D) requires the incorporation of community-based sanctions in the sentencing guidelines of State which have them. The reference to the State legislature in Section VII(D)(1) has been placed in brackets because in some jurisdictions, the responsibility for drafting sentencing guidelines may not be the responsibility of the legislature. In those jurisdictions, Section VII(D)(1) can be modified to authorize whatever body is to be charged with the responsibility of drafting and recommending a set of guidelines to set about its task.

VII. Enabling Provision

A. Judges with jurisdiction over misdemeanors and felonies are authorized to sentence eligible offenders as defined by Section V(A)(1) of this Act.

B. Judges with jurisdiction over misdemeanors and felonies are authorized to use the sentencing options set out in Section II of this Act.

Commentary

These provisions recognize that there may be instances in which conflicts with preexisting statutes may limit or circumscribe the ability of courts to use the sentencing options included in this statute. These provisions make clear that courts with jurisdiction have the authority to use the sentencing sanctions created and authorized under this statute, notwithstanding any other provision of law.

6

SUPERVISION IN PROBATION AND PAROLE

What You Will Learn in This Chapter

This chapter reviews how the philosophy and practice of probation and parole supervision have changed from an emphasis on casework (rehabilitation) to one of monitoring court orders and determining that the probationer or parolee is following the conditions of release (surveillance). We then examine a middle-of-the-road approach to supervision that we call an "integrative approach to supervision." We will look at probation and parole officer roles and working styles. Caseload classification, risk assessment, and workload are also discussed in detail.

KEY TERMS

Supervision
Casework model
Brokerage model
Community resource management team model
Justice model
Integrated model
Classification
Risk assessment

INTRODUCTION

Supervision is the element that differentiates probation from suspended sentence and parole from other forms of early release. This chapter discusses both probation and parole supervision, distinguishing between them when necessary. Some authorities believe that parole supervision requires more intense supervision because parolees are more serious offenders—in that they have been to prison. Furthermore, the transition from rigidly controlled prison life to freedom requires major living adjustments not usually faced by probationers.

Others, however, consider probationers and parolees essentially alike. Some probationers have been to prison as a result of earlier crimes. Others could have been sentenced to prison for their crimes had they not plea-bargained (pleaded guilty in exchange for a reduced penalty). Further, parolees know what prison is like and may exert extra effort while on supervision in order to remain free. Accordingly, with some exceptions, the supervision process is identical. In many states and in the federal system the same officers supervise both probationers and parolees.

In its simplest terms **supervision** may be defined as the oversight that an officer exercises over those committed to his or her custody. Whether in practice it is more effective than mere oversight depends on many conditions. Few offenders can be expected to transform themselves into law-abiding citizens without some assistance. However, probation or parole cannot be a constructive force in the administration of criminal justice if supervision amounts only to discipline directed toward holding in check antisocial tendencies during the period of supervision. Merely observing conditions of release or managing not to be arrested for a new offense does not indicate that an offender has been transformed. It is the element of *constructive* supervision that distinguishes probation and parole from both leniency and punishment. The concept of supervision has undergone much change in the past 50 years.

SUPERVISION

The oversight that a probation or parole officer exercises over those committed to his or her custody.

CHANGING CONCEPTS OF SUPERVISION

The Casework Era

In 1939 the *Attorney General's Survey: Probation* defined supervision as follows:

> In the conventional attitudes of the criminal law, it is a form of punishment, but the purpose of it is reformative, reconstructive, and educational; to use a scientific term, it is therapeutic.[1]

CASEWORK MODEL

Supervision oriented toward providing services to probationers or parolees to help them live productively in the community.

This philosophy of supervision flourished for the next 30 years. The supervision process was oriented toward **casework,** providing services to probationers or parolees (often referred to as *clients*) in an effort to help them live productively in the community. Probation and parole officers frequently viewed themselves as caseworkers, and the term *agent of change* was popular as a description of their role. The literature of probation and parole supervision during this period is fraught with medical and psychiatric terminology—such terms as *treatment* and *diagnosis,* for example. The National Advisory Commission on Criminal Justice Standards and Goals, reviewing the casework era, stated:

> The literature discussed the development of social work skills in interviewing, creating therapeutic relationships with clients, counseling, providing insight, and modifying behavior.[2]

A leading textbook of the period, *Probation and Parole in Theory and Practice,* reflected this orientation with chapters entitled "Social Casework," "Case Study and Diagnosis," and "Casework as a Means of Treatment."[3] The probation officer was viewed as a social worker engaged in a therapeutic relationship with the probationer "client."

Supervision as Brokerage of Services

In the early 1970s the casework approach began to break down. The National Advisory Commission on Criminal Justice Standards and Goals reported in 1973 that probation had failed to realize many of its goals.[4] The commission pointed out that many of the services needed by probationers and parolees could be more readily and effectively provided by specialized community agencies that provide mental health, employment, housing, education, private welfare, and other services. The commission report stated,

> Probation also has attempted to deal directly with such problems as alcoholism, drug addiction, and mental illness, which ought to be handled through community mental health and other specialized programs.[5]

BROKERAGE MODEL

Supervision that involves identifying the needs of probationers or parolees and referring them to an appropriate community agency.

This alternative strategy for delivering probation and parole services is referred to as the **brokerage of services** approach. The "service broker" type of probation or parole officer does not consider himself or herself as the primary agent of change as in the casework approach. Instead he or she attempts to determine the needs of the probationer or parolee and locates and refers the client to the appropriate community agency. Thus an unemployed parolee might be referred to vocational rehabilitation services, employment counseling, or the state employment office. Rather than attempting to counsel a probationer with emotional problems, the "broker of services" officer would locate and refer the probationer to agencies whose staff were skilled in working with problems such as those faced by the probationer. In this supervision strategy, developing linkages between the clients and appropriate agencies is considered one of the probation or parole officer's most important tasks. Probation and parole officers are encouraged to differentiate between services that can be provided internally (by the probation officer) and those that must be obtained from other social institutions. Under the brokerage model, the kinds of services that are provided directly to probationers through the probation system are those that

- relate to the reasons the offender was brought into the probation system,
- help him or her adjust to the status of probationer,
- provide information and facilitate referral to needed community resources,
- help create conditions permitting readjustment and reintegration into the community as an independent individual through full utilization of all available resources.

Probationers' needs that are related to employment, training, housing, health, and so on are the responsibility of other social agencies and should be provided by them.[6] By the middle to late 1970s the brokerage approach to probation and parole supervision was firmly entrenched.

Community Resource Management Team (CRMT)

Another approach to supervision, closely allied to the brokerage approach, is that of the **community resource management team (CRMT) model.** Using the CRMT strategy, individual probation and parole officers develop skills and linkages with community agencies in one or two areas only. One officer might be designated the drug abuse specialist and another the employment specialist, while another develops expertise in family counseling. The CRMT concept recognizes that the diverse needs of the probation or parole caseload cannot be adequately satisfied by one individual. Thus the caseload is "pooled," and the probationer might be assisted by not one but several officers. For example, Officer Mary Smith might assess the probationer's needs for drug treatment and refer him or her to the appropriate agency for assistance. Officer Sam Jones might work with him or her in obtaining job training and employment from other community social agencies. Each officer applies his or her particular skills and linkages in the community to serve the needs of the offender.

COMMUNITY RESOURCE MANAGEMENT TEAM (CRMT)

A supervision model in which probation or parole officers develop skills and linkages with community agencies in one or two areas only. Supervision under this model is a team effort, each officer utilizing his or her skills and linkages to assist the offender in their areas of expertise.

The Justice Model of Supervision

In recent years a new model of probation and parole supervision has come to dominate supervision philosophy. It is the **justice model,** which advocates an escalated system of sanctions corresponding to the social harm resulting from the offense and the offender's culpability. The justice model repudiates the idea that probation is a sanction designed to rehabilitate offenders in the community and, instead, regards a sentence of probation as a proportionate punishment that is to be lawfully administered for certain prescribed crimes.[7]

JUSTICE MODEL

A supervision model that specifically gears offender assistance to helping offenders comply with the conditions of probation.

In the justice model of probation, the probationary term is viewed not as an alternative to imprisonment but rather as a valid sanction in itself. The popular view that probation is an alternative to incarceration has led the public to regard probation as an expression of leniency, and the public often feels that the offender is "getting off." There is no question that justice and the community's welfare are best served when *some* offenders are imprisoned. But for the majority, who can safely remain in the community, the public must feel that appropriate penalties are imposed. Therefore, the justice philosophy regards probation as a separate, distinct sanction requiring

Supervision Objectives and Duties of Federal Probation Officers

The primary objectives of supervision are to enforce compliance with the conditions of release, to minimize risk to the public, and to reintegrate the offender into a law-abiding lifestyle. To accomplish these objectives, the officer has the following specific responsibilities.

DISCHARGE STATUTORY DUTIES. To comply with the requirements of 18 U.S.C. section 3603, probation officers shall [see Ch. IV. A.1A]:

- instruct the person under supervision as to the conditions specified by the sentencing court and provide him or her with a written statement clearly setting forth all such conditions;
- keep informed concerning the compliance with any condition of supervision and report thereon to the court or Parole Commission;
- keep informed as to the conduct and condition of a person under supervision and report his or her conduct and condition to the sentencing court or Parole Commission;
- use all suitable methods, consistent with the conditions specified by the court, to aid a person under supervision and to bring about improvements in his or her conduct and condition; and
- keep a record of the officers' work.

PROTECT THE COMMUNITY. To provide this most vital aspect of community supervision, the probation officer should [see Ch. IV.A.1B]:

- establish a plan of supervision consistent with the level of risk posed by the offender to the community;
- utilize risk control supervision activities, including verification of employment and sources of income, financial investigation, monitoring of associates, record checks, urinalysis, and restrictions on travel;
- request modification of the conditions of supervision if necessary to reduce risk. Such modifications may include home detention, community confinement, provisions for search and seizure, and requirements for financial disclosure; and
- systematically review the conduct and condition of offenders and revise supervision plans in accordance with changes in risk levels.

ADDRESS RELEVANT PROBLEMS OF OFFENDERS. To assist the offender in becoming a law-abiding and productive member of the community, the probation officer should [see Ch. IV. A.1C]:

- assess the relevant problems of the offender that are likely to be associated with further criminal conduct and develop a supervision plan to address those problems;
- utilize community resources to provide the offender with the opportunity to participate in substance-abuse and/or mental-health treatment, employment assistance, and educational opportunities; and
- ensure that the offender's response to treatment is consistent with risk-control supervision.

Source: *Supervision of Federal Offenders,* Monograph no. 109 (Washington, D.C.: Probation and Pretrial Services Division, Administrative Offices of the U.S. Courts, June 1991).

penalties that are graduated in severity and duration corresponding to the seriousness of the crime.[8]

The Role of the Justice Model Probation Officer

A justice model probation penalty has two major components—some degree of deprivation of personal liberty and reparation to the victim or the community.[9] Advocates of the justice model hold that practices of counseling, surveillance, and reporting accomplish very little and have minimal impact on recidivism. On the other hand, they favor probation that consists of monitoring court orders for victim restitution or community service and that ensures that the imposed deprivation of liberty is carried out.[10]

Justice model probation specifically gears offender assistance to helping probationers comply with the conditions of their probation. Other services such as mental health counseling, alcohol and drug treatment, and such should be available for probationers who express a need or desire for them, and these should be brokered through social agencies in the community. As already noted, the primary responsibility of the probationer is to complete the conditions imposed by the court satisfactorily. Likewise, the primary task of the probation officer is to assist the probationer in satisfactorily completing the conditions. The probation agency should be prepared, however, to assist those individuals who voluntarily request rehabilitative assistance.[11]

Most probation and parole agencies in the United States now subscribe to the general tenets of the justice model. For example, the 1991 edition of the federal probation system supervision manual, *Supervision of Federal Offenders,* states:

> The primary objectives of supervision are to enforce compliance with the conditions of release, to minimize risk to the public, and to reintegrate the offender into a law-abiding life style.[12]

As recently as eight years earlier, the federal probation system's supervision philosophy had been a "community resource manager" approach. The 1983 edition of the supervision handbook stated,

> The most important goal of the supervision process is to engage the available community resources or provide assistance directly to aid offenders in organizing their lives to successfully meet the challenges of life in conformity with law.[13]

The shift in philosophy in probation and parole systems throughout the country was obvious and abrupt. The primary impetus for this change can be traced to the philosophical and political movements of the late 1970s and early 1980s that placed greater emphasis on punishment and the failure of corrections to live up to its promises to rehabilitate, reintegrate, and restore offenders to productive, law-abiding lives.[14] One particular event contributed more than any other to the shift to a more punitive role for probation and parole: the publication by Robert Martinson and his associates of a national study of treatment programs. In this study more than 200 correctional treatment programs were carefully evaluated and declared failures.[15] The work was persuasive, and it was soon followed by other studies that reported similar results.[16] As Larry Siegel states,

> These less than enthusiastic reviews of correctional rehabilitation helped develop a more conservative view of corrections, which holds that prisons are places of incapacitation and punishment and should not be used for treatment.[17]

The so-called "medical model" of corrections, which stressed diagnosis and treatment, ended with the "nothing works" findings by Martinson and others—a more conservative approach that stressed "deserved punishment," incapacitation, and reparation to the victim replaced it.

Thus, we now find ourselves in a conservative era of criminal justice history. Probation and parole are at a crossroads, redefining their mission and role from therapeutic correctional treatment toward control, deserved punishment, and risk management.

AN INTEGRATED MODEL OF SUPERVISION

In practice, probation and parole supervision usually lies between the two extremes of the casework approach and the justice model. Effective supervision has elements of control *and* treatment; neither will suffice alone. The justice model of corrections has been, we believe, correctly described as "a solution . . . of despair, not hope."[18] Because we cannot show that treatment programs have been successful in bringing about long-term change in the offender, we have assumed that they have no value and that a strategy that emphasizes control and punishment is therefore more efficacious. However, research has not shown the justice model approach to be any more successful in reducing recidivism than the approach it replaced.

Control and treatment are not mutually exclusive in supervision, and we can draw an analogy to child-rearing practices. In their widely acclaimed 1990 book, *A General Theory of Crime,* Michael Gottfredson and Travis Hirschi attribute crime to deficiencies in self-control. They explore the nature and sources of self-control, locating it largely in family child-rearing practices. They then use self-control as the basis for a general theory of crime.[19] They report that low self-control tends to ensue in the absence of nurturance, discipline, and training.[20] Good child-rearing practices—which develop self-control—contain elements of all three. It is not too great an intellectual step to move from child-rearing practices to probation and parole supervision strategies. Many authorities have commented on the commonalities of behavior between criminals and children; namely, the pursuit of immediate pleasures, lack of ability to defer gratification, immature judgment, impulsiveness, and short attention span. Discipline, nurturance, and training socialize the child and develop the self-control and maturity of judgment necessary for successful integration into society. A child who experiences only discipline is not likely to develop into a mature, contributing member of society. So too, the child who is nurtured and trained, but not disciplined, is equally unlikely to become a contributing member of society. Probation and parole supervision, too, must contain all three. Current philosophy does not negate the nurturing and training elements; it merely assigns them much less priority than the discipline (control) element.

The strategy we recommend involves an active treatment function (nurturing and training) within a broad framework of control (discipline). This is referred to as an **integrated model.** We recall an argument between the directors of treatment and security in a large state prison on the subject of the relative importance of rehabilitation and institutional security. The treatment director charged that the institution's security regulations undermined his efforts to treat and rehabilitate the inmates. The head of security, an assistant warden of many years' experience, drawled, "Doctor, no matter how good your programs are, you can't treat 'em if we can't keep 'em." It is in this context that we view probation and parole supervision.

INTEGRATED MODEL

A supervision model that integrates a concern for control with a concern for treatment.

The Surveillance Function in Supervision

Supervision must first involve surveillance, which is defined as "a watch kept over a person, group, etc."[21] Probation and parole are expected to provide a means of ascertaining whether those released live up to the conditions imposed by the court or the parole board. Failure to maintain proper surveillance can only bring the officer and the system into disrepute. Furthermore, an officer's failure to require the offender to adhere to the terms of release complicates the officer's task. Supervision cannot exist in a lax, haphazard manner without arousing contempt in the offender. In addition, public support and cooperation are difficult to obtain for any probation or parole system that does not assure the community of at least minimal protection against renewed criminal activities by those under supervision.[22]

The Treatment Function in Supervision

The rehabilitative function of supervision includes both nurturing and training. Treatment-oriented supervision, conducted within a context of discipline and control, must be directed toward removing or reducing individual and social barriers that may result in recidivism. Carrying out a supervisory process that can accomplish this end is an extraordinarily difficult task. Offenders can be dealt with effectively only on an individual basis and according to their special conditions and needs. Much of the effectiveness of supervision depends on the personal relationship between the officer and the offender. An honest, direct relationship between the officer and the offender is the most effective means of promoting change and ensuring successful completion of the term of probation. The authoritative nature of the relationship should be made clear to the offender, but the spirit of encouragement and helpfulness should also be apparent. Most probationers and parolees have problems they must overcome if they are to succeed in complying with the terms and conditions of release and remaining crime free. Among the most critical problems are employment and drug or alcohol abuse.

Employment Services

It is not unreasonable to suggest that meaningful employment is the most important issue for most probationers and parolees. Not only does employment provide financial support for the offender and his or her family, but it is also crucial for establishing and maintaining self-esteem and personal dignity—qualities that are seen by most authorities as essential to successful reintegration into the community.[23] In a study of employment services provided by the New York State Division of Parole, Joy Davidoff-Kroop concluded:

> Two recent parole follow-up studies showed a high rate of unemployment amongst parolees returned to prison.[24]

Experienced probation and parole officers know this to be true, and most probation and parole conditions require the offender to maintain employment during the period of supervision. However, finding and maintaining employment is not a simple task. Offenders are often the last to be hired and the first to be terminated. Many of them are unskilled, and many have poor work habits. Some are barred from employment in their chosen fields due to regulatory and licensing laws that preclude persons with a criminal conviction.

Because of the critical relationship between success on parole or probation supervision and meaningful employment, the supervising officer must assess the employment status of each person under his or her supervision and work with each to locate a job. In many cases the probationer or parolee will require a vocational assessment to determine employability, interests, capabilities, and any barriers to employment. Many will require vocational or job readiness training before they can seek jobs. Ideally these services are obtained from external agencies and organizations such as state employment offices or vocational rehabilitation services. The probation or parole officer's job is to locate the existing service, refer the supervisee to the service, assist him or her in obtaining the service, and monitor progress and participation. Ideally the

Figure 6.1 **FEDERAL INMATES BY OFFENSE CATEGORY**

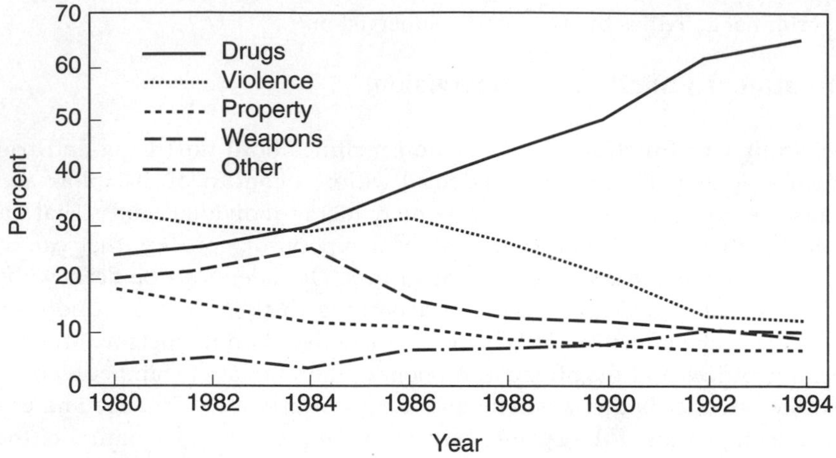

Source: Frank Schmalleger, *Criminal Justice Today,* 4th ed. (Upper Saddle River, N.J.: Prentice-Hall, 1997), 569.

probation or parole agency would have funds available for purchasing these services if they are not available otherwise.

Drug and Alcohol Treatment Services

Drug and alcohol abuse has a negative effect on every aspect of an offender's life; it contributes to employment, marital, and other personal and social problems. For many, if not most, substance abuse contributed directly or indirectly to the crime(s) that led to their conviction. As Figure 6.1 indicates, approximately 65 percent of inmates in the United States Bureau of Prisons were incarcerated for drug-related offenses in 1994.[25] Figure 6.2 illustrates recent findings from the drug use monitoring program of the U.S. Department of Justice showing that over 60 percent of all newly arrested adult male offenders tested positive for drug use through urinalysis.[26] Evidence today suggests that most imprisoned offenders were using drugs or alcohol when they committed the offense for which they are serving time. Because these findings are obtained primarily from self-reports or from drug testing as much as 48 hours after arrest, they should be interpreted conservatively. The true figure is likely much higher.

In light of these data, probation and parole officers must consider drug and alcohol monitoring and treatment a major aspect of their job. None of the goals of supervision can be met when the releasee is using and abusing alcohol or drugs. The federal probation manual, *The Supervision Process,* states,

> In the United States alcohol is the principal drug of abuse. Alcoholism represents a unique problem in the supervision of offenders in that often alcohol is not identified as a primary problem having a direct effect on all other aspects of an individual's life. A probation officer may address an offender's lack of employment, marital difficulties, or other social problems when, in fact, they are all secondary to the problem of alcoholism.[27]

and,

> One of the most important functions of the probation officer is the identification of drug abuse from available historical data, recognition of physical symptoms, and urinalysis.[28]

Figure 6.2 **PERCENTAGE OF ARRESTEES TESTING POSITIVE FOR ANY DRUG**

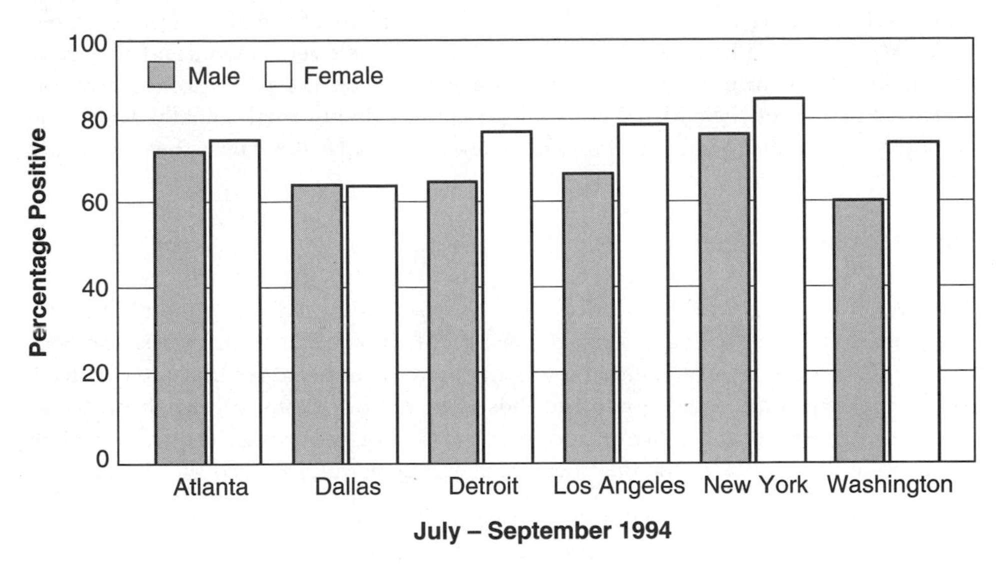

Note: Data for New York City cover only Manhattan.

Source: Frank Schmalleger, *Criminal Justice Today*, 4th ed. (Upper Saddle River, N.J.: Prentice-Hall, 1997), 592.

As in the case of employment problems, few probation and parole officers possess the expertise necessary to provide drug and alcohol assessment, urinalysis monitoring, and treatment. Once again, the releasee should have ready access to external agencies and organizations. To carry out his or her duties, the probation or parole officer helps the probationer or parolee obtain the needed services by assessing needs, being aware of available community resources, contacting the appropriate resources, referring the probationer for services, and monitoring compliance.

A TYPOLOGY OF PROBATION OFFICER WORK STYLES

The broadest component of probation supervision is the role that officers set for themselves and the logic and rationale they develop to explain what they do or what they ought to do. Carl Klockars developed a typology of probation officers that defines four basic work styles on the "probation *is not* casework" versus "probation *is* casework" continuum.[29]

The Law Enforcer

At the "probation is not casework" pole are officers who stress the legal authority and enforcement aspects of the position. These officers' philosophies dictate firmness, authority, and rule abidance as essentials of social life. Of prime importance to such officers are the court order, authority, and decision-making power.

The Time Server

Time-serving officers are nearly the functional equivalent of the law enforcers. They see their jobs as fulfilling certain requirements until their retirement, and they have little aspiration to improve their skills. Their conduct on the job is to abide by the rules, and they meet their job responsibilities minimally but methodically. Rules and regulations are upheld but unexamined. They don't make the rules; they just work there.

The Therapeutic Agent

At the other pole are officers who consider themselves therapeutic agents. They see their role as administering a form of treatment, introducing the probationer or parolee to a better way of life, and motivating patterns of behavior that are constructive. They give guidance and support to those who are unable to solve their problems by themselves and provide them an opportunity to work through their ambivalent feelings. The philosophy of the therapeutic agent may be summarized as follows:

1. I take conscious pains in every contact with offenders to demonstrate my concern for them and my respect for them as human beings.
2. I seize every opportunity to help offenders come to understand the nature of the shared problem solving, aiding the process by actually experiencing it.
3. I recognize, bring into the open, and deal directly with offenders' negative attitudes toward me as the representative of social authority.
4. I partialize the total life problems confronting offenders.
5. I help individuals perceive the degree to which their behavior has and will result in their own unhappiness.

The Synthetic Officer

The fourth and final work style in Klockars's typology is distinguished by recognition of both the treatment and law enforcement components of probation officers' roles. These officers' attempts at supervision reflect their desire to balance the needs for therapy and law enforcement. Thus they set for themselves the task of combining the paternal, authoritarian, and judgmental with the therapeutic. Theirs is a dilemma—combining treatment and control—that is found throughout the field of corrections.

From the foregoing, it is obvious that probation and parole supervision is a multifaceted problem that depends not only on the quality of the particular administrative organization and the officers' education and experience, but also—and to a great degree, more importantly—upon the way in which the officers view their job and their role within the system.

CLASSIFICATION: THE FIRST STEP IN SUPERVISION

CLASSIFICATION

A procedure consisting of assessing the risks posed by the offender, identifying the supervision issues, and selecting the appropriate supervision strategy.

The first step in the supervision process is to classify the offender's case. **Classification** consists of assessing the risks posed by the offender, identifying the supervision issues, and selecting the appropriate supervision strategies. The resulting supervision plan serves as a blueprint for "enforcing the conditions of supervision, controlling the risk posed by the offender, and selecting the appropriate supervision strategies."[30]

The Supervision Planning Process—Federal Probation Model[31]

The federal probation system manual, *Supervision of Federal Offenders,* emphasizes the need to create a strategy-based plan of action to address specific issues. It requires that all supervision activities be structure to ensure (1) compliance with the conditions of supervision, (2) protection of the public, and (3) correctional treatment. Such a supervision plan emphasizes what is accomplished by a particular supervision activity rather than the frequency of contacts.

Supervision planning is the initial phase of the supervision process. It begins with an initial assessment period during which the supervising officer obtains and evaluates information regarding the conditions of release, the degree and type of risk the offender poses to the community, and the traits of the offender that indicate a need for treatment. Based on these factors, the officer will identify as supervision issues those conditions of supervision and case problems that require direct action by the officer during the period and then select the supervision strategies necessary to address those problems.[32]

Reviewing the Conditions of Probation

The first stage of the planning process requires the officer to become familiar with the conditions of release and to understand their purpose. He or she must then develop a plan to ensure compliance with the conditions. Some offenders will have special conditions imposed, such as a requirement to participate in drug or alcohol treatment, or to avoid certain persons or places, or to not work in certain occupations. For example, a person convicted of violating Security and Exchange Commission regulations may not be allowed to work as a stockbroker or in investment banking.

Assessing Risk

Risk assessment provides a measure of the probationer or parolee's propensity to further criminal activity and indicates the level of officer intervention that will be required to deal with this problem. Most risk assessment instruments consider (1) the degree of risk of recidivism posed by the offender and (2) the amount of assistance the offender requires from the probation or parole agency. Together these variables predict the level of supervision the offender needs.

RISK ASSESSMENT

A procedure which provides a measure of the offender's propensity for further criminal activity and indicates the level of officer intervention that will be required.

Most jurisdictions have developed some form of risk prediction scale to assist them in developing supervision plans and in caseload classification. These instruments differ in some respects, but all of them place offenders in groups with a known statistical probability of committing new crimes or violating the conditions of supervision. As illustrated in Figure 6.3, Pennsylvania assesses 11 risk variables to determine the level of supervision required by the offender. Pennsylvania also assesses 13 needs variables that provide a standardized means of discerning problem areas that should be addressed in the supervision process. The probationer is assigned to one of several levels of supervision on the basis of the two scores.

The federal probation system employs the Risk Prediction Scale (RPS-80) for classifying and developing supervision plans for probationers and the Salient Factor Score (SFS-81) for parolees. The RPS-80 is shown in Figure 6.4. (The SFS-81 for parolee risk assessment is found in chapter 9, "The Parole Board and Parole Selection," Figure 9.1.)

Figure 6.3 PENNSYLVANIA'S INITIAL CLIENT ASSESSMENT FORM

COMMONWEALTH OF PENNSYLVANIA
BOARD OF PROBATION AND PAROLE
PBPP-20 (1/85)

INITIAL CLIENT ASSESSMENT

CLIENT NAME (Last, First, Middle Initial)	PAROLE NO.	AGENT NAME	OFFICE	DATE

RISK ASSESSMENT

1. Age at First Conviction: (or juvenile adjudication)
- 24 or older 0
- 20-23 2
- 19 or Younger 4

2. Number of Prior Probation/Parole Revocations: (adult or juvenile)
- None 0
- One or more 4

3. Number of Prior Felony Convictions: (or juvenile adjudications)
- None 0
- One 2
- Two or more 4

4. Convictions or Juvenile Adjudications for:
(Select applicable and add for score. Do not exceed a total of 5. include current offense.)
- Burglary, theft, auto theft, or robbery 2
- Worthless checks or forgery 3

5. Number of Prior Periods of Probation/Parole Supervision:
(Adult or Juvenile)
- None 0
- One or more 4

6. Conviction or Juvenile Adjudication for Assaultive Offense within Last Five Years: (An offense which involves the use of a weapon, physical force or the threat of force.)
- Yes 15
- No 0

7. Number of Address Changes in Last 12 Months:
(Prior to incarceration for parolees)
- None 0
- One 2
- Two or more 3

8. Percentage of Time Employed in Last 12 Months:
(Prior to incarceration for parolees)
- 60% or more 0
- 40%-50% 1
- Under 40% 2
- Not applicable 0

9. Alcohol Usage Problems: (Prior to incarceration for parolees)
- No interference with functioning 0
- Occasional abuse; some disruption of functioning 2
- Frequent abuse; serious disruption; needs treatment 4

10. Other Drug Usage Problems: (Prior to incarceration for parolees)
- No interference with functioning 0
- Occasional abuse; some disruption of functioning 1
- Frequent abuse; serious disruption; needs treatment 2

11. Attitude:
- Motivated to change; receptive to assistance 0
- Dependent or unwilling to accept responsibility 3
- Rationalizes behavior; negative; not motivated to change 5

TOTAL

INITIAL ASSESSMENT SCALES

Risk Scale		Needs Scale
0-5	Reduced Supervision	8-10
6-18	Regular Supervision	1-10
19-30	Close Supervision	11-25
31 & above	Intensive Supervision	26 & above

SCORING AND OVERRIDE

Score Based Supervision Level	Intensive ☐	Regular ☐
	Close ☐	Reduced ☐
Score Override	No ☐	Yes ☐
FINAL GRADE OF SUPERVISION	Intensive ☐	Regular ☐
Override Explanation:	Close ☐	Reduced ☐

NEEDS ASSESSMENT

1. Academic/Vocational Skills
- High school or above skill level .... −1
- Adequate skills; able to handle everyday requirements 0
- Low skill level causing minor adjustment problems .... +2
- Minimal skill level causing serious adjustment problems .... +4

2. Employment
- Satisfactory employment for one year or longer .... −1
- Secure employment; no difficulties reported; or homemaker, student or retired 0
- Unsatisfactory employment; or unemployed but has adequate job skills .... +3
- Unemployed and virtually unemployable; needs training .... +6

3. Financial Management
- Long-standing pattern of self-sufficiency; e.g., good credit rating .... −1
- No current difficulties .... −0
- Situational or minor difficulties .... +3
- Severe difficulties; may include garnishment, bad checks or bankruptcy .... +5

4. Marital/Family Relationships
- Relationships and support exceptionally strong .... −1
- Relatively stable relationships 0
- Some disorganization or stress but potential for improvement .... +3
- Major disorganization or stress .... +5

5. Companions
- Good support and influence .... −1
- No adverse relationships 0
- Associations with occasionally negative results .... +2
- Associations almost completely negative .... +4

6. Emotional Stability
- Exceptionally well adjusted; accepts responsibility for actions .... −2
- No symptoms of emotional instability; appropriate emotional responses 0
- Symptoms limit but do not prohibit adequate functioning; e.g., excessive anxiety .... +4
- Symptoms prohibit adequate functioning; e.g., lashes out or retreats into self .... +7

7. Alcohol Usage
- No interference with functioning 0
- Occasional abuse; some disruption of functioning .... +3
- Frequent abuse; serious disruption; needs treatment .... +6

8. Other Drug Usage
- No interference with functioning 0
- Occasional substance abuse; some disruption of functioning .... +3
- Frequent substance abuse; serious disruption; needs treatment .... +5

9. Mental Ability
- Able to function independently 0
- Some need for assistance; potential for adequate adjustment; mild retardation .... +3
- Deficiencies severely limit independent functioning; moderate retardation .... +6

10. Health
- Sound physical health; seldom ill 0
- Handicap or illness interferes with functioning on a recurring basis .... +1
- Serious handicap or chronic illness; needs frequent medical care .... +2

11. Sexual Behavior
- No apparent dysfunction 0
- Real or perceived situational or minor problems .... +3
- Real or perceived chronic or severe problems .... +5

12. Recreation/Hobby
- Constructive 0
- Some constructive activities .... +1
- No constructive leisure-time activities or hobbies .... +2

13. Agent's Impression of Client's Needs
- Minimum .... −1
- Low 0
- Medium .... +3
- Maximum .... +5

TOTAL

Source: Board of Probation and Parole, Commonwealth of Pennsylvania.

Figure 6.4 **RISK PREDICTION SCALE**

RISK PREDICTION SCALE (RPS 80)

NAME	PROBATION OFFICER	DATE

I. Automatic Assignment

If "yes" is checked for both A and B, place in Low Activity Supervision.

A) Individual has completed high school education YES ☐ NO ☐

B) Individual has history free of opiate usage YES ☐ NO ☐

II. Risk Score Determination

If not automatically assigned, use items C through G to determine risk score and supervision activity level.

C) Twenty-eight years or older at time of instant conviction..........(7) ——

D) Arrest-free period of five (5) or more consecutive years..........(4) ——

E) Few prior arrests (none, one, or two)..........(10) ——

F) History free of opiate usage..........(9) ——

G) At least four (4) months steady employment prior to arraignment for present offense..........(3) ——

SUM OF POINTS (33) ——

RISK SCORE RANGE	SUPERVISION LEVEL
Automatic Assignment or 20-33	Low Activity ☐
0-19	High Activity ☐

Source: Administrative Office of the U.S. Courts.

The RPS-80 and SFS-81 are based on variables that have been correlated empirically with probation success or failure. For example, on the RPS-80, two variables have been found to predict a low level of required supervision. The probationer is automatically assigned to "low-activity" supervision if he or she has completed high school *and* has a history free of opiate usage. If the offender is not automatically assigned to low-activity supervision, the officer assigns points for the presence of five risk variables:

1. Twenty-eight years or older at time of instant offense: 7 points
2. Arrest-free for five or more consecutive years: 4 points

3. Few prior arrests (none, 1, or 2): 10 points
4. History free of opiate use: 9 points
5. At least four months' steady employment prior to arraignment for present offense: 3 points

The maximum possible score is 33 points. An offender is automatically assigned to low-activity supervision if his or her score is 20 to 33 points. A score of 0 to 19 points places the offender in high-activity supervision.

While objective, statistics-based devices such as the RPS provide educated predictions of risk, the federal system uses an additional, subjective method to assist the probation officer in determining whether the risk posed by the offender is greater than that predicted by the risk prediction instrument. If the offender has already been identified as a risk, this subjective method helps to identify the type of risk involved. Such indications include the following:

- ▲ Substance abuse related to criminal conduct
- ▲ Current or prior violent behavior or use of weapons
- ▲ Participation in continuing criminal conspiracies (such as wholesale drug distribution or organized crime offenders)
- ▲ Unexplained assets or current lifestyle incompatible with reported income
- ▲ Pattern of similar criminal conduct
- ▲ Serious mental health problems

The combination of the risk prediction score and the presence or absence of these factors will assist the officer in determining which, if any, risk control factors must be addressed.

Identifying Treatment Needs

The officer must also identify those characteristics, conditions, or behavioral problems that limit the offender's motivation or ability to function within the conditions of supervision. Treatment activities are defined as actions taken by the supervising officer intended to bring about a change in the offender's conduct or condition for the purpose of rehabilitation and reintegration into the law-abiding community.[33]

Here are some sources of information that may be used to identify treatment needs:

- ▲ The presentence report
- ▲ Prison records and the prerelease plan
- ▲ Physical or medical health evaluations
- ▲ Information from family or other collateral sources
- ▲ Records of drug or alcohol abuse and other related criminal conduct
- ▲ Financial history
- ▲ Residential history

The importance of careful gathering and evaluation of the offender's history cannot be overstated, for past behavior is the best predictor of future behavior.[34]

Developing the Case Plan

After reviewing the conditions of probation, assessing the offender's risk, and determining treatment concerns, the officer may then identify specific supervision issues and select appropriate strategies for addressing the issues identified. Supervision issues may involve any or all of the three areas—conditions, risk control, and treatment.

Identifying Supervision Issues

A supervision issue is a condition or offender characteristic or pattern of conduct that requires intervention by the officer to correct or control. When an issue is identified, the officer should then develop a strategy to deal with or monitor that issue. In the supplemental reading accompanying this chapter, the probation officer has identified a history of drug abuse as a supervision issue in the case of Joe R. Recognizing that Joe R. may need drug treatment in the community at some point, the supervising officer has elected to monitor drug use through random urinalyses.

Levels of Supervision and Caseload Contacts

Although various names are used to differentiate the levels of supervision, most are essentially similar to the traditional *maximum, medium,* and *minimum supervision* classes. Practically all classification systems specify contact requirements for each level. Unfortunately, these requirements are usually specified in terms of number of contacts per month or some other time interval, or by the contact type or location (home, telephone, office, or other). Few specify the quality or content of the contact. The federal probation system requires that the frequency, place, and nature of supervision contacts be determined by the supervision plan and be directly related to the supervision issues. The supervision manual states,

> If the primary purpose of a supervision contact is to secure information or verify compliance with a special condition or correctional treatment program, the officer should make such contact by phone, mail, or office visit. If personal observation is necessary to verify compliance with conditions or to control risk, the officer should make a field contact.[35]

In most instances the supervision plan optimistically looks toward gradual reduction of the level of supervision if the offender manages to avoid further transgressions of rules or laws. In many instances the final, minimum level is that of no supervision or level of assistance other than that specifically requested by the client or necessitated by a new arrest. See the Box on page 150, "Typical Contact Standards by Supervision Level."

Caseloads and Workloads

Traditionally, 35 to 50 cases has been considered the ideal caseload for a probation or parole officer. However, there is no empirical evidence to show that this range is ideal or that it is regarded as such any longer. In practice, caseloads vary widely. *The Corrections Yearbook* reported that in 1993 the average caseload of adult probationers was 124. Caseloads ranged from 58 in Missouri to 400 in California. Intensive supervision probation caseloads averaged 26 offenders, ranging from 13 in Arizona to 40 in Texas.[36] The report also stated that the average number of face-to-face contacts between officer and probationer was 15 in 1992. Offenders under intensive supervision averaged 114 contacts per year.[37]

The American Probation and Parole Association (APPA) argues that the issue is not one of numbers alone:

> Simply stated, not every offender needs the same type or amount of supervision to achieve the goals of probation or parole. There are a number of proven and accepted methods for determining the type and amount of supervision, but the key is that in order to be most effective and efficient, there must be varying amounts of supervision provided to offenders.

Typical Contact Standards by Supervision Level

MAXIMUM/INTENSIVE SUPERVISION

- One face-to-face contact and one collateral contact monthly.
- Monthly report; one home visit; one face-to-face (in addition to home) visit; one employment verification; one special condition.
- Two face-to-face contacts monthly; one collateral contact monthly; one home visit every 45 days.
- Four face-to-face contacts monthly; one collateral contact monthly; one home call within 30 days of placement on caseload and within two weeks after each reported move; verification of residence every three months; criminal history check after first year of supervision.
- Two face-to-face contacts monthly, one of which must be in the field; two collateral contacts per month.

MEDIUM/MODERATE SUPERVISION

- One face-to-face contact monthly and one collateral contact per quarter.
- One home visit per quarter; one monthly report; one residence verification; one face-to-face contact; one employment verification; one special condition, if applicable.
- One face-to-face contact and one collateral contact monthly; one home visit every 90 days.
- Two face-to-face contacts monthly with unemployed offenders; one contact if verified full-time employment/training; one collateral contact per month; home call within 30 days of placement on caseload and within two weeks after each reported move; verification of residence every three months and employment/training monthly; criminal history check after first year of supervision.
- One face-to-face contact per month; one collateral contact monthly; one field visit every three months.

MINIMUM SUPERVISION

- One face-to-face semiannual contact and one collateral contact quarterly.
- One home visit, as needed; one monthly report; one face-to-face contact per quarter; one employment verification per quarter.
- One face-to-face contact monthly, unless quarterly reporting.
- One face-to-face contact monthly, verification of residence once every three months.
- Mail-in report monthly; one face-to-face contact every three months; one collateral contact every three months.

Source: Edward E. Rhine, William R. Smith, and Ronald W. Jackson, *Paroling Authorities: Recent History and Current Practice* (Laurel, Md.: American Correctional Association, 1991). Reprinted with permission of the American Correctional Association.

> This concept is crucial to the discussion of ideal caseload size because it states as a given that cases will be treated differently in terms of the amount and type of supervision they will receive. This means that the caseload officer will be expected to give differing amounts of time and types of attention to different cases.[38]

The APPA recommends a workload standard rather than a caseload standard. It does not make sense, the APPA argues, to count every case as equal. A case requiring maximum supervision effort may require, for example, four hours of the probation or parole officer's time per month. A medium supervision case may require two hours per month to effectively supervise. A minimum supervision case may require only one hour or less per month of the probation or parole officer's time. Depending on the

Table 6.1 **AVERAGE CASELOAD PER OFFICER DURING 1996 BY TYPE**

Probation	Regular	Intensive	Electronic	Special
Arizona[1]	60	13		
Arkansas	173	15		
California[2]	900	43	43	53
Connecticut	213	25		
Dist. of Col.[3]	108	11		68.5
Florida	76	25	25	56
Georgia	218	23		
Hawaii	190	79	2.5	
Illinois	125	12		40
Kansas	71	7		
Michigan[4]	88			
Nebraska[5]	85	20		
New Jersey[6]	152	20		
New Mexico	71	20		25
Rhode Island	302	66		267
Tennessee[3]	85	21		
Texas[7]		33		40
Vermont	137			
Average	**180**	**27**	**24**	**79**
Parole	**Regular**	**Intensive**	**Electronic**	**Special**
Arizona	49		15	
Arkansas[8]	65	10		
California	88	59		35
Colorado[3]	60	20		
Connecticut[9]	50			20
Dist. of Col.	176	54		118
Georgia	60		25	
Hawaii	80	38		30
Indiana[10]	67			
Kansas[11]	63			
Massachusetts	60	15		19
Michigan[4]	95			
Nebraska	40	3		
New Jersey	86	25	16	25
New Mexico	71	20		25
New York[12]	100	40		65
Rhode Island	95		39	
South Dakota	31	15		
Tennessee[13]	54			
Texas	80	28	28	47
Vermont	10			
West Virginia	30			
Average	**69**	**27**	**25**	**43**

[1]Int. based on answer of "2:25." [2]Reg. Supv. is 800–1000 cases. Int. Supv. and Elec. Supv. are 25–60 cases. Spec. Off. is 25–80 cases. [3]Int. incl. Elec. [4]Avg. caseload is a combined quarterly avg. beginning 10/1/96–12/31/96. [5]Excl. juveniles. [6]Caseload for Spec. Off. varies. [7]Int. is avg. of 25–40. [8]Int. as of 12/31/96. [9]Elec. and Spec. Off. are 15–25. Spec. Off. incl. Elec. [10]Incl. juvenile caseloads. [11]Based on Kansas caseload ADP (incl. probationers). Dept. leases 30 elec. monitoring units. [12]First year of parole is considered Int. Time after that is considered Reg. [13]Reg. supv. is the overall avg. caseload per officer.

Table 6.1 **AVERAGE CASELOAD PER OFFICER DURING 1996 BY TYPE—*Continued***

Probation and Parole	Regular	Intensive	Electronic	Special
Alabama	165	20	20	
Alaska	59	15		
Delaware	113	40	19	20
Idaho	72		30	30
Iowa[14]	100	25		
Kentucky	87			
Louisiana	95			
Maine	152			
Maryland	98			
Minnesota	89	11		
Mississippi	118		17	
Missouri	66			
Montana	118			
Nevada	75	30	30	
New Hampshire	80	2		18
North Carolina	90	25		60
North Dakota	97	15		
Ohio	53			
Oklahoma[15]	80			
Oregon	100			
Pennsylvania	72			
South Carolina	97			
Utah[16]		22	25	55
Virginia[17]	76	28		
Washington	98			
Wisconsin	72	25		
Wyoming	69	10	10	
Federal[18]	70	26	26	
Average	**91**	**21**	**22**	

Face-to-Face Contacts with Probation and Parole Officers During 1996

- Annually, probation officers had an average of 13 face-to-face contacts with probationers on regular supervision, 76 contacts with probationers on intensive supervision, 98 contacts with probationers on electronic monitoring, and 48 face-to-face contacts with probationers on special caseloads.
- Parole officers had an annual average of 19 face-to-face contacts with parolees on regular supervision, 62 contacts with parolees on intensive monitoring, 69 contacts with parolees on electronic monitoring, and 53 contacts with parolees on special caseloads.
- Probation and parole officers had an annual average of 30 face-to-face contacts with offenders on regular supervision, 141 contacts with offenders on intensive supervision, 115 contacts with offenders on electronic monitoring, and 67 contacts with offenders on special caseloads.

[14]Avg. Reg. caseload is based on a range from 80–120. [15]Active cases only. [16]Spec. Off is avg. of 50 and 60. [17]Int. is avg. of a range from 24–32. [18]Reg. incl. parole. All fig. 1995.

Source: Camp and Camp, *Corrections Yearbook—1997.* Used with permission.

makeup of the caseload, the officer could effectively and efficiently supervise 30 to 40 maximum supervision cases, 60 medium supervision cases, or as many as 120 minimum supervision cases. In practice, caseloads contain offenders at every level of supervision need. The "ideal" caseload, then, is calculated by determining how many hours are available to the officer and adjusting the caseload to account for the various supervision requirements of the persons being supervised.[39] Table 6.1 portrays the average caseload per officer by caseload type in 1996.

Using workload rather than caseload allows time for duties other than supervision. Many probation officers have presentence report responsibilities as well as supervision duties. A workload computation method allows for the time required to complete a presentence investigation report. Other factors such as geography can also play a part in determining the number of cases an officer can effectively supervise. One of the authors of this book, while a U.S. probation officer in the Western District of Texas in the 1970s, supervised a caseload dispersed geographically from San Antonio to Midland, a distance of over 300 miles. At the same time one of his colleagues in New York City was able to visit his entire caseload within the confines of 12 city blocks.

It is clear that there can be no "magic number" for the optimal caseload size.[40] However, development of a workload standard should be a goal for the future of community corrections. It would allow for comparison between jurisdictions, guide research in probation and parole effectiveness, and help probation administrators interpret their work to legislators and other policymakers.

Specialized Caseloads

The use of specialized caseloads has proven to be effective in improving supervision quality and effectiveness. Offenders with certain characteristics can often benefit from supervision by a specialist—a probation or parole officer who has specialized education, training, or experience in a certain area. These specialized caseloads are used with such groups as youthful offenders, drug addicts, alcoholics, dangerous offenders, sex offenders, and emotionally disturbed offenders.[41] Rhine, Smith, and Jackson found that specialized parole caseloads were being used in 25 states by 1990. Fourteen states were using specialized caseloads for sex offenders, and 12 states did the same for drug offenders; ten jurisdictions used specialized caseloads for offenders with mental disabilities, five for "career criminals," and two for violent criminals.[42] Specialized caseloads for DWI (Driving While Intoxicated) offenders were established in Texas in 1983 and now exist in virtually every medium-to-large probation department in the nation. Although there are few empirical studies of the efficacy of specialized caseloads, anecdotal evidence supports the concept.

SUMMARY

The most vital aspect of the probation and parole process in the criminal justice system is supervision. In its simplest terms, supervision is the oversight that is exercised over those who have been placed on probation and parole. A supervisory process that is highly individualized and purposefully reconstructive can meet the needs of an adequate probation or parole system. The personality, training, and experience of the supervisory officer largely determines the adequacy of the process. Lax supervision and failure to deal firmly with those who persistently violate the terms of release can bring an entire system into disrepute. Adequate probation and parole supervision must deal with all phases of an offender's life, including the offender's family and the community in which he or she lives. Although probation and parole professionals may disagree on the value and propriety of many specific techniques of supervision, all recognize the need for a plan of supervision that is based on the needs, capacities, and limitations of each offender. Physical and mental health, the offender's home and family, and his or her leisure activities, education, vocational training, economic status, work habits, and capacity for discipline and self-control must all be considered by those who are attempting to help him or her become a law-abiding citizen.

In order to deal affirmatively with all aspects of the probationer or parolee's life that require aid, the officer cannot act entirely alone. The officer must whenever possible endeavor to secure the assistance and cooperation of community agencies and facilities. Responsibility for securing this assistance and for monitoring and evaluating the results of these agencies rests with the probation or parole officer. This is an indispensable part of the officer's duty; if it is neglected, the officer's work will be unsatisfactory.

Probation and parole supervision necessitates frequent and continuous contact with the offender. This contact should be characterized by a positive relationship of mutual respect and trust and the officer's willingness to see his or her role as multifaceted, not as a singularly therapeutic or enforcement-oriented role.

Good probation service is not easily accomplished when officers are compelled to supervise too many cases. A supervision caseload of 35 to 50 offenders per officer has been suggested as desirable. Research has indicated, however, that the total workload, based on a properly classified caseload, should determine the ratio of offenders to officers.

Our discussion of supervision in probation and parole may be summarized by paraphrasing from the American Bar Association's Standards for Criminal Justice project:

> The basic idea underlying probation and parole is to help the offender learn to live productively in the community that has been offended.[43]

ENDNOTES

1. *Attorney General's Survey: Probation,* vol. 2 (Washington, D.C.: U.S. Department of Justice, 1939), 261.
2. National Advisory Commission on Criminal Justice Standards and Goals, *Report on Corrections* (1973). Cited in *Corrections in the Community,* 2nd ed., edited by George Killinger and Paul Cromwell (St. Paul, Minn.: West, 1978), 108 (cited as NAC).
3. Helen D. Pidgeon, *Probation and Parole in Theory and Practice* (New York: National Probation and Parole Association, 1942), 105.
4. NAC, *Report on Corrections* (1973).
5. Cited in "Probation Standards and Goals" in Killinger and Cromwell, *Corrections in the Community,* 107–108.
6. "Probation Standards and Goals" in Killinger and Cromwell, *Corrections in the Community,* 115.
7. Robert Gemignani, "Rethinking Probation," *Change* 5(4)(1983).
8. Gemignani, "Rethinking Probation," 2.
9. Gemignani, "Rethinking Probation," 2.
10. Gemignani, "Rethinking Probation," 3.

11. Gemignani, "Rethinking Probation," 3.
12. *Supervision of Federal Offenders,* Monograph no. 109 (Washington, D.C.: Administrative Office of the U.S. Courts, 1991), 2.
13. *The Supervision Process,* Publication no. 106 (Washington, D.C.: Administrative Office of the U.S. Courts, 1983), 2.
14. See Robert G. Culbertson and Thomas Ellsworth, "Treatment Innovations in Probation and Parole," in Lawrence W. Travis III, ed., *Probation, Parole, and Community Corrections* (Prospect Heights, Ill.: Waveland Press, 1985).
15. D. Lipton, Robert Martinson, and Judith Wilks, *The Effectiveness of Correctional Treatment: A Survey of Treatment Evaluation Studies* (New York: Praeger, 1975).
16. See Charles Murray and Louis Cox, *Beyond Probation: Juvenile Corrections and the Chronic Delinquent* (Beverly Hills: Sage, 1979).
17. Larry J. Siegel, *Criminology,* 4th ed. (St Paul, Minn.: West, 1992), 575.
18. Willard Gaylin and David Rothman, "Introduction," in Andrew von Hirsch, *Doing Justice: The Choice of Punishments* (New York: Hill and Wang, 1976), xxi–xli.
19. Michael R. Gottfredson and Travis Hirschi, *A General Theory of Crime* (Stanford, Calif.: Stanford University Press, 1990), xv.
20. Gottfredson and Hirschi, *A General Theory of Crime,* 95.
21. *Webster's Third New International Dictionary* (Springfield, Mass.: Merriam-Webster, 1986).
22. *Supervision of Federal Offenders,* 2.
23. *The Supervision Process.* Materials in this section rely heavily on "Systematic Approach to Supervision Responsibilities" in this manual.
24. Joy Davidoff-Kroop, *An Initial Assessment of the Division of Parole's Employment Services* (Albany, N.Y.: New York State Division of Parole, 1983), 1.
25. Bureau of Justice Statistics, *Federal Inmates by Offense Category—1980–1994* (U.S. Department of Justice, 1995).
26. National Institute of Justice, *Drug Use Forecasting—1996* (Washington, D.C.: U.S. Department of Justice, 1997).
27. *The Supervision Process,* 29.
28. *The Supervision Process,* 32.
29. Carl B. Klockars, Jr., *Journal of Criminal Law, Criminology, and Police Science* 63 (4)(1974).
30. *Supervision of Federal Offenders,* 13.
31. The following discussion relies heavily on the federal probation manual, *Supervision of Federal Offenders,* Monograph no. 109 (Washington, D.C.: Administrative Office of the United States Courts, 1991).
32. *Supervision of Federal Offenders.*
33. *Supervision of Federal Offenders,* 18.
34. *Supervision of Federal Offenders,* 18.
35. *Supervision of Federal Offenders.*
36. George M. Camp and Camille G. Camp, *The Corrections Yearbook—1993* (South Salem, N.Y.: The Criminal Justice Institute, 1994).
37. Camp and Camp, *The Corrections Yearbook—1993,* 24.
38. American Probation and Parole Association (APPA), *Position Statement—Caseload Standards* (Lexington, Ky.: American Probation and Parole Association, n.d.). Cited as APPA.
39. APPA, *Caseload Standards.*
40. APPA, *Caseload Standards.*
41. See Howard Abadinsky, *Probation and Parole: Theory and Practice,* 5th ed. (Englewood Cliffs, N.J.: Prentice-Hall, 1994).
42. Edward E. Rhine, William R. Smith, and Ronald W. Jackson, *Paroling Authorities: Recent History and Current Practice* (Laurel, Md.: American Correctional Association, 1991), 112.
43. American Bar Association, *Standards Relating to Probation,* (Chicago, IL, 1990) p. 1.

DISCUSSION QUESTIONS

1. Discuss how the concept of supervision has changed over the past half-century. What factors have brought about the change?
2. How do the casework and brokerage of service supervision models differ?
3. What are the probation or parole officer's major functions under the justice model?
4. What is case classification? What are the advantages?
5. Discuss the use of risk prediction scales. What is their purpose? How might they be used in case management?
6. Discuss the concept of caseload and workload computation. What is the traditional position? Why might workload be a better method of allocating probation and parole officer resources?
7. How does a specialized caseload differ from a traditional caseload?
8. Explain the analogy of child rearing to probation supervision.
9. Discuss Klockars's typology of probation officers.
10. Why is it critical for probation and parole officers to assess clients' needs regarding substance abuse and employment? How are they related to the other needs and risks in probation supervision?

SUPPLEMENTAL READING

A Day in the Life of a Federal Probation Officer

It's Tuesday, and I've got my work cut out for me on this cold January day in West Texas. On the way in to work I mentally review the upcoming scheduled events for the day: 8:30 A.M. meet with assistant U.S. attorney regarding a probation revocation hearing on John D.; 9:00 A.M. revocation hearing in Judge B's court—contested; thereafter, head for the counties to do field supervision and collateral work. This will be an overnighter, so I'll be back in the office on Thursday—another court day.

I'm almost at the office, but I need to make a quick stop at Joe R. to collect a random urinalysis (UA). He's been out a month now and seems to be doing all right. He's working, home is stable, and the UA will address the primary supervision issue in this case—history of drug abuse. I'm almost ready to complete an initial supervision plan in this case. Although he participated in drug treatment in the institution, he may need treatment in the community. Time will tell; but for right now random UAs will do.

Well, I caught him before he left for work, and things seem solid. The wife seemed happy, the job is stable, and there was no problem with the UA. It's going to be a great day! I love this job! On to the office.

Oops, I spoke too soon. Telephone voice mail—David S. got arrested for DWI—he's still locked up at County. I'll swing by the county jail on the way out of town. Other than that, no other emergencies.

The assistant U.S. attorney is ready for a contested hearing. That's fine; five dirty UAs and failure to participate in drug treatment will get you every time. The supervision file is well documented, and I'm prepared to testify as to chain of custody on the dirty UAs. Our contract provider was subpoenaed and will testify on the failure to participate violation. We're in Judge B's court, and the AUSA tells me the defendant has decided to plead true and throw himself on the mercy of the court—good luck. Sure enough, the judge revokes John D.'s probation and sentences him to 24 months custody. John takes it all right, but his mother doesn't. If he had taken the judge's advice and "lived at the foot of the cross," he'd still be on probation—instead, he's locked up, and his mother is crying in court. It's always harder on the family. I'll talk to her—maybe it will help. John couldn't do it on the street, so maybe he will get the help he needs inside. [The federal correctional institution in] Fort Worth has an excellent treatment program—I'll tell her that and maybe she will feel better. I hate this job!

Well, it's midmorning and time to hit the road. Fort Stockton is 100 miles down the road, but I've got to stop at the county jail on the way out of town. I'll check out the GSA vehicle with the four-wheel drive in case the roads get bad; cellular phone 1; pepper spray; sidearm; and laptop in case I have time to do chronos. Gosh times have changed; in the good old days I'd be leaving town in my personal vehicle with a smile on my face.

At the county lockup David S. advises he was arrested by the P.D. for DWI—but he really only "had a couple." Of course, he forgot he was supposed to abstain completely from alcohol. When I get back in town I'll get the offense report, staff the case with the boss, and decide what type of action to take. David has been on supervision for over a year and has done exceptionally well. Graduated sanctions may be in order, and if so, I'll ask the court to place him in the halfway house with a required treatment condition.

On the road again. This is what I've got to do in Fort Stockton: check in with the sheriff—he knows everything that is going on in his county; go by our drug contractor's office and visit with the therapist regarding Mary J.; go by the county clerk's office and finish this collateral request out of the Northern District; and conduct home inspections on Bob S. and Joe R. Talk about time management—the boss will love this! Sheriff B. is in a great mood, and he says all my people have been behaving themselves. Over coffee I advise him John D. will be getting out on parole—for the second time—and will be coming back home to Fort Stockton. That didn't make his day. At the drug treatment facility the contractor gives me a good report on Mary J. She's keeping all her appointments and has not submitted any dirty UAs. Her participation in treatment is good, and her mother has also attended a couple of counseling sessions. Great report!

The county clerk was busy, but she did have the judgments I had called ahead about—that was a quick and easy collateral, not like the last one that took two hours to find an old judgment. These people in Fort Stockton are great to work with; they really know how to help you. Man I love this job!

Well, there's Bob S.'s house. I think I'll drive past and around the block—just in case. Everything looks cool, and his car is in front, so he should be home.

Bob was surprised to see me, advising it was his day off since the day before he had pulled a double on the rig he works. Oil field work is steady, but the cold weather is hard, and it shows on Bob's face. The wife seems to be doing well, and the house is neat and clean. Things look solid, but I know better than to start bragging. This offender has a history of drug violations, which presents certain risk control issues. Risk control issues never go away!

At Joe R.'s no one comes to the door, but I thought I heard someone inside. I leave my card, drive around the block, and call Joe on the cellular phone. It amazes me how sneaky I can get when I have to. Sure enough, Joe's girlfriend answers the phone and advises Joe is still at work. Work is 15 miles out of town at a ranch, so I'll try to catch him first thing in the morning.

I'm running a little ahead of schedule, so I'll stop by and see Mary J. She should be home from work; if she's not her mother will be, and she'll let me know how her daughter is really doing. The supervision issues here are enforcing court-ordered sanctions and drug treatment. Sure enough, Mary J. is there and seems to be doing really well. She gives me her community service hours documentation and discusses her progress in the drug treatment program. Her mother is obviously very satisfied with her daughter's progress and is a good supervision resource to me.

Before I check into the motel, I call the office on the cellular to check my voice mail. David S. called to advise he bonded out of jail. I call him back and set up an appointment for him to come in on Thursday. We'll staff him at that time. I'm glad now that I brought the laptop—I can catch up on some chronos. Since I lucked out and saw all the people I needed to, I won't need to go out tonight—it's getting too cold out here in West Texas anyway. What a day—win a few, lose a few. Gosh I love this job!

The next morning comes early, and I catch breakfast before I hit the road. I figure I'll work my way back to the office and try to catch Joe R. at the ranch before he gets busy. I'm positive his girlfriend told him I was by the house, so he should be expecting me. I'm not quite comfortable with this offender because he does have some violence in his background. Therefore, officer safety and risk control are the primary supervision issues I am addressing. Wouldn't you know it, he locked the main gate on me—but what he doesn't know is the rancher previously gave me a key to the gate. As I drive up to the ranch headquarters, I can see my man out by the horse corral. He seems surprised to see me. We visit, and he convinces me he is making a "good hand." I try not to be too obvious, but I'm looking for any signs of contraband or a weapon. Ranch hands and rifles seem to go hand in hand—no pun intended. Nothing is obvious, although Joe just seems to be nervous. As I drive back down the road to the main gate, I call the Border Patrol sector headquarters and check in with the duty agent. Joe is clean as far as they know, but they agree to drive by in the next few days. They'll let me know. The agent advised they have received recent intelligence of illegal aliens working in the area where Joe works.

Well, I'm almost home, and it's a beautiful day. In fact, it looks like it will warm up. The only pressing issue I know of is the staffing on David S. You know what, I really do love this job!

Written especially for this volume. The author, Richard V. Russell, is Supervising U.S. Probation Officer for the Western District of Texas. He is headquartered in Midland, Texas.

7 PROBATION REVOCATION

KEY TERMS

- Technical violations
- Law violations
- Exclusionary rule
- Equal protection
- Indigency
- Due process

What You Will Learn in This Chapter

You will learn why the decision to revoke probation is significant but discretionary. Revocation has implications for the probationer, the probation officer, and the community. You will learn about the two types of violations and the procedure followed after the decision to revoke probation is made. The rights given to probationers during revocation are listed, and other issues related to revocation are explored. Alternatives to revocation are also discussed.

INTRODUCTION

Placing an offender on probation implies that, in the best judgment of the court, the probationer will respect and abide by the law and observe the conditions of release. Unfortunately, this is not true in many cases. For example, from a study of felony probation in California, the Rand Corporation found that over a 40-month period 65 percent of a sample of felony probationers were rearrested, and 34 percent received a new prison term.[1] Research by Patrick Langan and Mark Cunniff on probation rearrest, published in 1992, used a sample of 79,000 felons sentenced to probation in 1986.[2] They reported that 43 percent had been rearrested for a felony within three years of being placed on probation. An additional 19 percent had a disciplinary hearing for violating the conditions of their supervision (technical violations). Another study shows that "50 percent of probationers did not comply with court-ordered terms of their probation; 50 percent of known violators went to jail or prison for their noncompliance."[3] A 1995 survey in Texas shows that the revocation rates in that state's probation departments reached a maximum of 60 percent for felony probation and 78 percent for misdemeanor probation.[4] These figures indicate that probation reoffense rates are high.

When probation is unsuccessful, the probation officer must revoke probation or modify the conditions of supervision. This chapter explores the various facets of probation revocation, including the authority to revoke probation, the types of probation violation, revocation procedures, rights during revocation, and other legal issues related to probation revocation. It concludes by discussing the various alternatives to revocation and situations that arise under the interstate probation compact.

THE DECISION TO REVOKE

Probation release is conditional. The probationer's liberty is not absolute; it is subject to compliance with specified conditions. Violation of conditions can cause revocation of probation and incarceration of the offender. Revocation is obviously a serious matter to the probationer because it denotes failure and loss of freedom. It is also important for society because the offender will now serve time in jail or prison and will therefore become a financial drain on the public treasury.

Although a probationer is subject to court-imposed restrictions, the probationer's freedom is often similar to that enjoyed by persons who have not been charged with

Probation officer interviewing inmate.

or convicted of an offense. The probationer continues to live in the community (albeit with some restrictions), can work at suitable employment, enjoys the association of family and friends, can participate in community activities, and partakes of the benefits enjoyed by nonoffending members of the community. In other words, the probationer can live basically the same kind of life as the other members of the community. The big difference comes when conditions are violated and the probationer becomes accountable for what he or she failed to do. The probationer's status after revocation changes dramatically, so revocation is not taken lightly by either the offender or the court.

Court Authority to Revoke Probation

Although the probation officer or the probation department can recommend revocation, only the court has authority to revoke probation. This authority remains with the court that granted probation[5] unless the case has been transferred to another court that is given the same powers as the sentencing court.[6] The federal probation statute and all state statutes provide for transfer of jurisdiction in appropriate cases to allow the probationer, with the court's permission, to change residence. This may be from one part of the state to another or, in the case of a federal offender, from one part of the country to another. Transfer of *jurisdiction* to another court is distinguished from the provision of interstate compacts for the transfer of *responsibility for supervision* to another state's probation department. When transfer occurs under the interstate compact, authority to modify the conditions of probation, revoke probation, or terminate probation remains with the court in the sending state.

Revocation Is Discretionary

The authority to revoke probation is *discretionary,* meaning that whether the probationer is to be revoked is up to the court. The only exception occurs if the law provides for mandatory revocation in certain cases. Examples of discretionary and mandatory revocation can be found in federal probation, where federal law provides for discretionary revocation as follows:

> If a defendant violates a condition of probation at any time prior to the expiration or termination of the term of probation, the court may, after a hearing pursuant to Rule 32.1 of the Federal Rules of Criminal Procedure, and after considering the factors set forth in section 3553(a) to the extent that they are applicable—
>
> (1) continue him on probation, with or without extending the term or modifying or enlarging the conditions; or
> (2) revoke the sentence of probation and resentence the defendant.[7]

This provision for discretionary revocation is followed by a provision for mandatory revocation, which states that revocation is mandatory for federal probationers in three types of violation: (a) if the probationer is found to possess a controlled substance; (b) if the probationer possesses a firearm; or (c) if the probationer refuses to comply with drug testing. In these cases the "court shall revoke the sentence of probation and resentence the defendant . . . to a sentence that includes a term of imprisonment."[8]

Some departments provide general guidelines for revocation, but these guidelines are seldom strictly followed because the probation department realizes that the court has the final say. Even in cases where the probationer is convicted of another crime, revocation is often optional unless state law provides otherwise, which is rare. Conversely, however, some jurisdictions simply revoke probation if the probationer commits a new crime instead of prosecuting the offender for the new crime. Revocation is a more convenient option that achieves the same results: the incarceration of the offender and his or her removal from society.

DIFFERING PERCEPTIONS OF REVOCATION BY PROBATION OFFICERS

Revocation of probation is a serious matter not only to the probationer and the public but also to the probation officer. The officer's supervision orientation often determines how he or she perceives the revocation.

The *traditional probation officer* is likely to view revocation as a "failure."[9] Before the officer–probationer relationship has deteriorated to the point where revocation is considered, the officer will have invested considerable time and effort to rehabilitate the probationer. Sometimes an officer develops a genuine interest in the probationer and becomes acquainted with his or her family. The officer may feel strongly that imprisonment will hinder rather than facilitate the probationer's rehabilitation and reintegration into society.

The *community resource manager officer* sees probation revocation in terms of his or her own failure to identify and arrange for the probationer's needs, or as the community's failure to provide the necessary resources. Revocation is viewed as society's failure rather than that of the offender. Often decision makers are blamed for not providing sufficient support to enable the probationer to succeed.

The *justice model officer* attributes the revocation decision to the probationer's failure to live up to the terms of the contract or agreement with the court. This officer knows that despite the officers' efforts, a percentage of probationers will fail. These are not failures of the system, the community, or the probation officer, but rather the failure of probationers to respond positively to an opportunity to remain free and rehabilitate themselves.

REVOCATION AND THE COMMUNITY

Revocation is also a matter of concern to the community. Incarcerating the offender increases the cost to the community because keeping an offender under probation supervision costs much less than providing care and treatment in a correctional institution. A study in 1993 showed that it cost one state $639 a year to keep an offender in probation, while the yearly cost for imprisonment was $16,681.[10] The costs in most states are much higher and will continue to climb.

Imprisoning offenders who otherwise would have been in probation may force their families to go on welfare or make greater demands on community resources. The offender ceases to be a contributing member of society and instead becomes dependent on the state. Revocation, however, protects the community from offenders who continue to commit criminal acts or fail to abide by conditions designed to rehabilitate. It is also needed so offenders will take the conditions imposed seriously, thus ensuring a higher likelihood of compliance. The public needs reassurance that persistent offenders are incapacitated by incarceration so they cannot continue to prey on society.

TYPES OF PROBATION VIOLATION

Revocation of probation is generally triggered in two ways: law violations and technical violations. A **law violation** occurs if a probationer commits another crime and hence violates an almost universal condition for the probationer not to break the law. **Technical violations** are infractions that do not involve law violations.

LAW VIOLATIONS

Violations of probation or parole conditions which involve the commission of a crime.

TECHNICAL VIOLATIONS

Violations of the conditions of probation that do not involve law violations.

Violation of the Condition to Obey All Laws

Most jurisdictions provide that the offender "commit no offense against the laws of this state or of any other state or of the United States."[11] In rare instances when this condition is not specified, it is usually deemed an implicit condition of probation because law violation is a form of conduct society condemns. Even if the offender commits a new crime, however, revocation is not automatic and is left to the discretion of the court. Most courts require the probation officer to report any violation of law and to make a recommendation regarding the issuance of a warrant and the initiation of revocation proceedings. But whether or not to revoke remains a prerogative of the court.

The 1995 guidelines manual for federal probation classifies violations into three categories:

1. Grade A Violations—conduct constituting a federal, state, or local offense punishable by a term of imprisonment exceeding one year that is a crime of violence, is a controlled substance offense, or involves possession of a firearm or destructive device . . . or any other federal, state, or local offense punishable by a term of imprisonment exceeding twenty years;

2. Grade B Violation—conduct constituting any other federal, state, or local offense punishable by a term of imprisonment exceeding one year;
3. Grade C Violations—conduct constituting a federal, state, or local offense punishable by a term of imprisonment of one year or less; or a violation of any other condition of supervision.[12]

Even in cases of law violations, revocation is often discretionary with the judge and the department, except in cases where revocation is mandated by law. Conviction of an offense, particularly if the offense is a misdemeanor, does not necessarily lead to revocation. Even felony convictions may not lead to revocation, particularly if the sentence for the second offense is lengthy and makes incarceration for the first offense unnecessary, and especially in states where service of sentence is concurrent instead of consecutive. On the other hand, acquittal for a new offense may nonetheless lead to revocation. This is because conviction of an offense requires guilt beyond reasonable doubt, while revocation needs only a preponderance of the evidence or even less—such as reasonable grounds or reasonable suspicion. What may not suffice for conviction may suffice for revocation. There is no double jeopardy because revocation is merely an administrative and not a criminal proceeding, although it results in incarceration.

Technical Violations

Most violations come under the category of technical violations. They include conditions that require the offender to report regularly to the probation or parole officer, not move from or leave the jurisdiction without obtaining permission, support dependents, refrain from excessive use of alcohol, work regularly at a lawful occupation, pay a fine or restitution, and other similar conditions. One jurisdiction reports that the three most commonly alleged technical violations are failure to report to the probation officer (89 percent); failure to pay probation fees (76 percent); and substance abuse (37 percent).[13]

Courts have upheld revocation for technical violations under a wide variety of circumstances. These are representative:

- ▲ Engaging in a scuffle with campus police during a demonstration in violation of the condition that the probationer not participate in demonstrations[14]
- ▲ Failure to pay off civil judgments for fraud although the probationer was able to pay[15]
- ▲ Failure to make child support payments[16]
- ▲ Failure to report[17]
- ▲ Failure to pay supervision fees although financially able[18]
- ▲ Associating with persons who were not "law-abiding"[19]
- ▲ Driving a motor vehicle when condition specified license to drive was suspended[20]

As a general rule probation is not revoked for occasional violations of technical conditions. Probation officers are urged to address these violations promptly and to take whatever action is necessary to ensure compliance. Revocation, however, is the last resort for dealing with technical violations. Revocation policy in most jurisdictions is generally consistent with the federal guideline, which states:

> When a violation is detected, the officer is to respond with the least restrictive measures necessary to bring the offender into compliance in light of the seriousness of the violation, its implications for public safety, and the type and frequency of supervision strategies that were being employed at the time of the violation.[21]

The measures contemplated by the guideline range from a simple admonition from the probation officer to revocation and incarceration.

In many jurisdictions only a series of or particularly serious violations lead to revocation. The reasons are that revocation, in cases where the violation is minor or simple, may be a waste of time and resources. Moreover, revocation means incarceration and the high cost that goes with it. In jurisdictions where a probation fee is imposed, revocation means not getting money from the probationer and the state supporting the offender while he or she is in jail or prison. Because revoking probation means high costs for the community, it is used with caution in many states.

REVOCATION PROCEDURE

Revocation procedures are governed by constitutional rules and in some cases by state law and agency policy. Constitutional requirements, such as the right to a hearing and basic due process, are binding on all jurisdictions and must be given to the probationer. In the absence of constitutional requirements, procedures vary greatly from state to state or even from court to court within a state. Unless these rules violate the rights of probationers, they are valid and considered the law in that jurisdiction.

How It Begins

Revocation proceedings usually begin with a violation report. This report is prepared by the probation officer and becomes the basis for revocation. The decision to initiate revocation is usually made by the officer or in some cases by the probation chief or immediate supervisor. Jurisdictions differ as to who files the motion to revoke probation. A survey in one state shows that while the violation report is usually initiated by the probation officer (96 percent of the time), it can also be initiated by the officer's immediate supervisor or by the probation director.[22]

The prosecutor files the motion to revoke after reviewing the probation violation report. The prosecutor's authority to file a motion to revoke is discretionary, meaning that the prosecutor makes the final decision to file or not to file for revocation.

Most states have no guidelines for initiating a violation report. Whether to initiate revocation is a decision made by the probation officer or the department after a review of the alleged violation. Neither is there any guideline as to when a prosecutor should file the motion to revoke. Some judges set guidelines for probation officers to follow, but most judges do not. The discretionary nature of the revocation authority discourages the structuring of guidelines by which decisions to revoke or not to revoke are made. Because of this, practices vary greatly from one state to another and even among departments within a state. A study by Peggy B. Burke for the National

Institute of Corrections, released in 1997, shows that probation officers nationwide file motions to revoke for the following violations:[23]

Types of Violation	Percentage
Positive urinalysis	27.0%
Failure to participate in treatment	20.0%
Abscond	18.5%
New felony	12.0%
Failure to report	10.0%
New misdemeanor	4.0%
All other technical violations	8.5%

The Warrant to Revoke

In just about all states the warrant to revoke is issued by a court, usually the court that granted probation, and is served by law enforcement officers or by probation officers. Federal law has the following provision for federal probationers:

> If there is probable cause to believe that a probationer or a person on supervised release has violated a condition of his probation or release, he may be arrested, and upon arrest, shall be taken without unnecessary delay before the court having jurisdiction over him. A probation officer may make such an arrest wherever the probationer or releasee is found, and may make the arrest without a warrant.[24]

Other states have similar provisions, except that the degree of certainty required for warrant issuance may vary. While probable cause is used in many states, a lower degree of certainty (such as reasonable grounds or reasonable suspicion) is allowed in others.

The Power to Arrest Probationers

In some states probation officers are authorized to make an arrest with or without a warrant. In other states probation officers are not authorized to make an arrest at all. In these states arrests are made by the police or other law enforcement officers. In still other states probation officers are authorized to make an arrest, but only if a warrant has been issued by the court. In these states warrantless arrests are prohibited.

These differences in the arrest powers given to probation officers reflect the treatment or surveillance orientation of probation departments in each state. Those with treatment orientation do not want their officers to be viewed as law enforcement agents because it lessens their effectiveness as treatment agents, so the power to arrest is denied. By contrast, states with a surveillance orientation believe that law enforcement is a part and a necessary function of probation. In these states it is not unusual for probation officers to be armed and certified as law enforcement officers.

Proceedings after Arrest

After arrest, the probationer is taken to jail to await a court hearing. How long that jail detention lasts varies from one state to another. Some states specify by law how long a probationer can be detained before a revocation hearing must be given. Other states prescribe no limitation; or, if one is prescribed, there is no provision for auto-

Examples of Results of Statistical Analysis of Violation Practice

LENGTH AND COMPLEXITY OF THE REVOCATION PROCESS

How long does it take to move from detection of a violation through court disposition?	Estimated average ranges from 44 to 64 days
Who is involved in the process?	Probation Officer, Supervisor, Prosecutor, Judge, Law Enforcement, Jail Administration, Service Providers
What mechanism is used to bring probationer into the violation process?	18% receive summons 82% have warrants issued against them

DISPOSITIONS OF MOTIONS TO REVOKE

Disposition	Number	Percentage of Dispositions	Percentage of Total Probation Population
Prison	94	36.0	2.5
Jail	8	3.0	.21
Jail with Probation	56	21.0	1.5
Probation with Conditions	4	1.5	.1
Probation	100	38.0	2.6
Incarcerative Sanctions	158	60	4.2
Nonincarcerative Sanctions	104	40	2.7

FOR WHAT VIOLATIONS DO PROBATION OFFICERS FILE MOTIONS TO REVOKE?

Types	Percentage
Positive Urinalysis	27.0
Failure to Participate in Treatment	20.0
Abscond	18.5
New Felony	12.0
Failure to Report	10.0
New Misdemeanor	4.0
All Other Technical	8.5

Source: Peggy B. Burke, *Policy-Driven Responses to Probation and Parole Violations* (National Institute of Corrections, March 1997), 12.

matic release if the limit is exceeded. This is usually because the probationer has already been convicted and could have been sent to prison at that time anyway. Bail prior to hearing is usually discretionary with the judge. A hearing must be given before the probationer is finally sent to prison to serve whatever incarceration term may have been originally imposed.

Time Served on Probation Is Not Credited

If probation is revoked, time served on probation is not credited as jail or prison time. In essence, it is "wasted time" for the probationer. For example, Probationer X has served one year probation for a five-year prison term that was suspended. If probation is revoked, Probationer X goes to prison for the original five years even if the revocation took place with a few months left to go on the five-year probation term.

The 1995 guidelines manual for federal probation provides as follows: "Upon revocation of probation, no credit shall be given (toward any sentence of imprisonment imposed) for any portion of the term of probation served prior to revocation."[25] In some states, however, judges may reduce the original sentence imposed, but the sentence cannot be increased.

Most offenders on probation either have been convicted of or have pleaded guilty to an offense. In some states, however, offenders may be placed on deferred adjudication or suspended sentence, which means that the finding of guilt is deferred and the offender placed on probation just like those who have been found guilty. If the offender serves out the probation period successfully, charges are dismissed and the finding of guilt is never made. It is as though the offender was never in probation, except that in some states the prior record of probation can be used to increase the sentence if the offender subsequently commits another offense.

THE RIGHTS OF PROBATIONERS DURING REVOCATION PROCEEDINGS

Offenders are entitled to only diminished or reduced constitutional rights while on probation. Among these rights are those given to probationers prior to and during revocation. These rights were granted by the U.S. Supreme Court in the case of *Gagnon v. Scarpelli,*[26] arguably the most important probation case ever to be decided by the Court.

Gagnon v. Scarpelli—The Facts

Gerald Scarpelli was on probation for a felony when he was arrested for burglary. He admitted involvement in the burglary but later claimed that his admission was made under duress and was therefore invalid. His probation was revoked without a hearing and without a lawyer present. After serving three years of his sentence, Scarpelli sought release through a writ of habeas corpus. He claimed violations of two constitutional rights: the due process right to a hearing and the right to a lawyer during the hearing.

The Right to a Hearing

The right to a hearing prior to revocation was the more significant and far-reaching issue in the *Scarpelli* case. The Court held that probationers, like parolees, are entitled to a hearing prior to revocation. The Court said that, like parolees, probationers were entitled to a two-stage hearing consisting of a preliminary hearing and a final revocation hearing. More importantly, however, the Court ruled that probationers are entitled to the following due process rights during the hearings:

1. Written notice of the alleged probation violation
2. Disclosure to the probationer of the evidence of violation
3. The opportunity to be heard in person and to present evidence as well as witnesses
4. The right to confront and cross-examine adverse witnesses, unless good cause can be shown for not allowing this confrontation
5. The right to judgment by a detached and neutral hearing body
6. A written statement of the reasons for revoking probation, as well as of the evidence used in arriving at that decision

(The case of *Gagnon v. Scarpelli* is reproduced at the end of this chapter.)

These due process rights are exactly the same as those given to parolees in parole revocation proceedings in the case of *Morrissey v. Brewer,* decided by the Court one year earlier.[27] The Court said in *Scarpelli* that there was no difference between probation and parole revocation because both of them resulted in loss of liberty; therefore, rights in both revocation proceedings should be the same.

Although *Gagnon v. Scarpelli* provides for preliminary and formal revocation hearings prior to revocation, as was mandated in *Morrissey v. Brewer* for parolees, most courts uphold as valid probation revocations after just a single hearing. Courts consider it important that the probationer be given a hearing. But even more important is that the due process rights listed above must be given to probationers in these hearings.

The Right to a Lawyer

On the right to a lawyer during the revocation hearing, the Court said that this issue should be decided on a case-by-case basis. This means that although the state is not constitutionally obliged to provide counsel in all revocation cases, it should do so where the indigent probationer may have difficulty in presenting his or her version of the facts without the examination or cross-examination of witnesses or the presentation of complicated documentary evidence. The Court said that the introduction of counsel into every revocation proceeding will "alter significantly the nature of the proceeding" and make it "more akin to that of a judge at a trial, and less attuned to the rehabilitative needs of the individual probationer." Many states by law, however, provide counsel to indigent probationers in revocation proceedings.

OTHER LEGAL ISSUES IN PROBATION REVOCATION

Gagnon v. Scarpelli is the leading case in probation revocation. It addressed two issues: the right to a hearing and the right to a lawyer during probation revocation. Lower courts have explored other issues not raised in *Scarpelli;* some of these issues are discussed next.

Sufficiency of Notice

In accordance with heightened due process consciousness among probationers, recent cases are requiring an increasing degree of specificity in notices of intended revocation of probation. Allowing sufficient time for preparation of a defense is mandated. In a Texas case the defendant was served with notice of a motion to revoke probation on the day of the hearing and was told orally that one of the bases for the revocation would be "theft by false pretext" instead of "felony theft" as set out in the written notice. The court held that the defendant was denied due process by the court's failure to give him adequate and prior notice to prepare his defense.[28] In another case the state's motion to revoke probation alleged that the defendant had "violated paragraphs (a), (b), and (c) of his Conditions of Probation." The defendant claimed the pleadings were insufficient; the denial of his motion by the trial court was reversed on appeal. The appellate court stated that the state's pleadings were not sufficient to give the defendant fair notice of the conduct or acts for which the state intended to offer evidence to prove a violation of the conditions of probation.[29]

Nature of the Hearing

The requirements of minimum due process in a revocation hearing have not changed the basic character of the probation revocation hearing—which is that it is not a criminal trial. In *Morrissey v. Brewer* the U.S. Supreme Court said, "We begin with the proposition that the revocation of parole is not part of a criminal prosecution, and thus the full panoply of rights due a defendant does not apply to parole revocation." Similarly, a hearing on probation revocation is a hearing and not a trial. As such, it is not governed by the rules concerning formal criminal trials.[30] Not all technical provisions in criminal procedure must be followed. The result of a probation hearing is not a conviction but a finding upon which the trial court may exercise discretion by revoking or continuing probation.[31] The defendant is not constitutionally entitled to a jury in revocation proceedings.[32] Some states by law provide a jury hearing, particularly in juvenile cases.

Standard of Proof Required in Revocation Proceedings

What standard of proof is needed to revoke probation? The standard varies widely among the states because this issue has not been decided by the U.S. Supreme Court. For example, Georgia requires only "slight evidence" for revocation,[33] whereas Oklahoma requires that the decision be supported by a preponderance of evidence.[34] A Texas appellate court in 1996 also held that the state need only prove through a preponderance of the evidence that the terms of probation were violated.[35] Similarly, the Fifth Circuit Court of Appeals held in 1995 that a federal court may revoke probation if it finds by a preponderance of the evidence that a condition of release has been violated.[36] Most courts require "preponderance of the evidence" as the standard for revocation, but the U.S. Supreme Court has not set that standard. Whether a lower standard than probable cause (such as reasonable grounds, reasonable suspicion, slight evidence, or suspicion) would suffice for revocation has yet to be addressed by the Court. In the meantime different revocation standards are used in various states. Even within a state the standard needed to revoke probation may vary from one court to another. The standard is the same within a state only if one standard is set by law or by a state supreme court decision. Not many state legislatures or state supreme courts have done that.

Nature of Proof Required

Illinois has held that once a defendant has admitted violating probation, the admission eliminates the need on the part of the government to present proof of the violation.[37] Louisiana, on the other hand, has held revocation improper where the only evidence was the probationer's guilty plea without counsel.[38]

The testimony of the probation officer is often crucial at a revocation proceeding. Whether such testimony—unsupported by any other evidence—is sufficient to revoke varies. In Texas a court has held that revocation cannot be based merely on the statement of a probation officer that the probationer failed to report at least once a month as directed.[39] Oklahoma did not permit revocation based solely on an officer's testimony, without supporting evidence, that the defendant had moved to another state.[40] North Carolina reached the opposite result, holding that the uncontradicted testimony of a probation officer—that the defendant had been fired from his job and had not made payment toward his probation costs—was sufficient to support a revocation.[41] In Georgia (where only "slight evidence" is needed to revoke) probation revocation was upheld based solely on the testimony of an arresting officer that in his opinion the probationer was driving while intoxicated.[42]

The Exclusionary Rule

The **exclusionary rule** states that any evidence obtained by the government in violation of the Fourth Amendment guarantee against unreasonable searches and seizures is not admissible in a criminal prosecution to prove a defendant's guilt.[43] The main purpose of the exclusionary rule is to deter police misconduct, the assumption being that if evidence illegally seized is not admissible in court, then the police will be deterred from behaving illegally. This rule has been applied in federal courts since 1914 but was not extended to prosecutions in state courts until 1961.

EXCLUSIONARY RULE

Evidence that is obtained in violation of the Fourth Amendment guarantee against unreasonable searches and seizures is not admissible in a criminal prosecution to prove the defendant's guilt.

Is evidence illegally seized admissible in a revocation proceeding? At the federal level, the courts of appeals are split on the issue. Most federal courts of appeals that have considered the issue allow use of this type of evidence in revocation proceedings. In a recent case a federal district court decided that absent some evidence in the record that the defendant was targeted or harassed by the police, the evidence should be admitted.[44] Of the federal courts of appeals that admit illegally seized evidence, two exclude its use in cases of police harassment,[45] and one does not permit the use of such evidence if the police knew the person was a probationer.[46]

State cases reflect the same uncertainty over the admissibility in revocation proceedings of evidence obtained in violation of the Fourth Amendment. A few states provide full Fourth Amendment protection, and the evidence obtained is excluded. In a recent Kansas case, for example, an appeals court applied the exclusionary rule to exclude the evidence. The court said that the law enforcement officer knew the subject was on probation and therefore may have had an incentive to carry out the illegal search because he knew that if the evidence obtained was not admissible in a criminal prosecution, it could still be used in a revocation hearing.[47] In most states, however, the exclusionary rule does not apply, so the evidence obtained is admissible in probation revocation.[48]

Equal Protection

In *Bearden v. Georgia*[49] an offender pleaded guilty in a Georgia court to burglary and theft by receiving stolen property. The court did not enter a judgment of guilt; instead, the court sentenced the petitioner to probation on condition that he pay a $500 fine and $250 in restitution, with $100 payable that day, $100 the next day, and the $550 balance within four months. The probationer borrowed money and paid the first $200, but a month later he was laid off from work, and despite repeated effort was unable to find other work. Shortly before the $550 balance became due, he notified the probation office that his payment was going to be late. Thereafter, the State of Georgia filed a petition to revoke probation because the probationer had not paid the balance. The trial court, after a hearing, revoked probation, entered a conviction, and sentenced the probationer to prison. The record of the hearing disclosed that the probationer had been unable to find employment and had no assets or income.[50] On appeal, the U.S. Supreme Court held that a sentencing court cannot properly revoke a defendant's probation for failure to pay a fine and make restitution, absent evidence and findings that he was somehow responsible for the failure or that alternative forms of punishment were inadequate to meet the state's interest in punishment and deterrence.

INDIGENCY

The state of being without the financial resources to defend oneself in court or other legal proceedings.

The burden of proving **indigency** is with the probationer. This means that the state does not have to prove that the probationer can pay; instead, it is up to the probationer to prove as a defense that he or she cannot pay. It is clear from *Bearden,* however, that a distinction must be made between failure to pay because of indigency and refusal to pay. While failure to pay because of indigency cannot lead to revocation, refusal to pay can result in revocation or a possible contempt proceeding.

Due Process

DUE PROCESS

Laws applied in a fair and equal manner. Fundamental fairness.

In *Black v. Romano*[51] the U.S. Supreme Court addressed the issue of whether the U.S. Constitution requires a judge to consider alternatives to incarceration before revoking probation. In this case Nicholas Romano pleaded guilty in a Missouri state court to several controlled substance offenses; he was placed on probation and given suspended prison sentences. Two months later he was arrested for and subsequently charged with leaving the scene of an automobile accident, a felony under Missouri law. After a hearing the judge revoked his probation, and Romano was sent to prison. Romano appealed, saying that the judge violated his constitutional right to **due process** (meaning fundamental fairness) by revoking his probation without considering alternatives to incarceration. On appeal the U.S. Supreme Court held that the due process clause of the Fourteenth Amendment does not generally require a sentencing court to indicate that it has considered alternatives to incarceration before revoking probation. The procedures for revocation of probation, first laid out in *Morrissey v. Brewer* and then applied to probation cases in *Gagnon v. Scarpelli,* do not include an express statement by the fact finder that alternatives to incarceration were considered and rejected. The Court reiterated that the procedures specified in *Gagnon v. Scarpelli* adequately protect the probationer against unfair revocation.[52]

REVOCATION AFTER THE TERM OF PROBATION HAS EXPIRED

The general rule is that probation can be revoked only during the probation term. After that the court loses authority unless an extension is provided by law. In the absence of such authorization, the power of the court to revoke ends. For example, in a 1996 case an appellate court in Arkansas set aside an order of revocation, saying that "the general rule is that the trial court may revoke a defendant's suspension of sentence [probation] only prior to the expiration of the period of suspension." The court's ruling was based on Arkansas state law, which says that the court may revoke probation after the expiration of the probation period in only two instances: when (1) the defendant is arrested for violation of probation or (2) a warrant is issued for the probationer's arrest before the period of probation expires.[53]

The exceptions in Arkansas law are found in other state laws, as well. Federal law also authorizes delayed revocation, saying that "the power of the court to revoke a sentence of probation for violation of a condition of probation, and to impose another sentence, extends beyond the expiration of the term of probation for any period reasonably necessary for the adjudication of matters arising before its expiration if, prior to its expiration, a warrant or summons has been issued on the basis of an allegation of such a violation."[54]

Probation may also be revoked after the term of probation has expired if the probationer absconds supervision before completing the sentence. Probation statutes usually provide that the term of probation is "tolled" if the defendant either is charged with a violation of probation or flees the jurisdiction (or cannot be found) and a warrant is issued. To toll the running of a sentence or a period of time limitation is to interrupt it, to "stop the clock." The Illinois statute, for example, provides that when a petition is filed charging a violation of a probation condition, the court may order a summons for the offender to appear or a warrant for the offender's arrest:

> The issuance of such warrant or summons shall toll the sentence of probation or of conditional discharge until the final determination of the charge, and the term of probation or conditional discharge shall not run so long as the offender has not answered the summons or warrant.[55]

ALTERNATIVES TO REVOCATION

Not every violation of probation conditions results in revocation; in fact, most violations do not. Probation departments use various alternative programs instead of outright revocation. These programs vary, but they usually take the form of more severe restrictions on the offender or a different type of treatment. The attitude in most probation departments is one of adjustment and accommodation, primarily because of the high costs to the probationer and the state if probation is revoked.

Federal guidelines for reporting violations of probation conditions—which are similar to those in many states—require the probation officer (except for certain specified serious incidents) to "consider whether or not a modification of the conditions of supervision would bring the offender into compliance and serve the relevant purposes of sentencing."[56]

Sometimes the probation officer will tolerate a whole series of minor violations before taking the offender before the court. While in court, the officer may recommend modifying the imposed conditions in hopes that a change in the conditions will increase the chance of successful adjustment. Some courts will hear a motion for revocation, postpone a violation finding, and continue probation—but the next time the probationer violates another condition of probation, the probation is revoked without a hearing based on the earlier violation. This gives a probationer one more chance at probation but allows revocation without any further hearing (thus saving the court time) if another violation occurs.

Probation officers have considerable discretion to handle probation violations without referral to the court so long as the infractions do not develop into a pattern or threaten public safety. Carl Klockars suggests that much probation work is conducted by threats of revocation.[57] For most probationers a warning or admonition is sufficient. In some jurisdictions probationers are brought back to court to show cause why the probation should not be revoked. This return to court to face the judge has a more sobering effect on the defendant than a simple admonition in the probation officer's office.

A controversial alternative to revocation is *jail therapy*. This consists of placing a probationer in jail without holding a subsequent revocation hearing. The period of incarceration is usually short. The "therapy" has two purposes: (1) to impress upon the probationer the seriousness of the offense and the possible consequences of continued violation, and (2) to provide a realistic comparison between life in the community and life in jail. Opponents of jail therapy reject it as punitive, saying it does not contribute to the probationer's rehabilitation. They also believe that the relationship between the probation officer and the probationer may be permanently damaged by such action.

In other cases circumstances might warrant modification of conditions that appear impossible to meet, unreasonable, or inappropriate.

In sum, probation departments can use many alternatives to revocation courts. These vary from state to state and often from court to court within a state. Many states do not provide for automatic revocation, so judges can create innovative alternatives to use before revoking probation and sending the offender to jail or prison.

PROBATION REVOCATION AND THE INTERSTATE COMPACT

Special problems arise after a probationer is revoked while supervised in a state other than the state of conviction. The *Interstate Compact for the Supervision of Parolees and Probationers* provides that any state that has signed the compact will accept supervision of a parolee or probationer who meets the residence requirements set forth in the compact; that state will supervise the probationer at the same level of supervision that it gives to its own cases. The sending state may retake a person being supervised in another state simply by having its officer present appropriate credentials and proving the identity of the person to be retaken. When requesting and accepting out-of-state supervision, the probationer waives extradition prior to leaving the sending state, although formal extradition procedures may be resorted to if necessary.

The sending state can retake a probation violator being supervised under the compact without resorting to formal extradition procedures. The receiving state is obligated to surrender the probationer unless a criminal charge is pending against the individual in the receiving state. In such a case the probationer cannot be retaken without the receiving state's consent until he or she is discharged from prosecution or from any imprisonment for such offense. The effect is that the sending state cannot retake the probationer into custody until all local charges are disposed of. Some states admit a probationer to bail pending disposition of charges for revocation of probation. Other states hold that the right to bail does not apply to persons who have been tried and convicted.

The validity of extradition waivers has been upheld against a challenge that they violate an offender's constitutional rights and are invalid because they would not become operative until some future date. It is also generally held that the sending state alone has authority to determine upon what basis a violator may be returned. The reasons for return are not reviewable by the receiving state.[58]

SUMMARY

The decision to revoke is important for the probationer, the probation officer, and the community. The authority to revoke lies with the court and is discretionary. There are two types of probation violation: violation of the condition to obey all laws and technical violation. Technical violations are violations of conditions other than the condition to obey the law.

The revocation procedure begins with a violation report filed by the probation officer. The motion to revoke is usually filed by the prosecutor; the court then issues the warrant to revoke. After arrest, the probationer is kept in detention pending a hearing. Time served on probation is not credited as jail or prison time if the probation is revoked.

The case of *Gagnon v. Scarpelli* provides that probationers must be given a hearing and certain due process rights prior to revocation. Other legal issues in probation revocation include sufficiency of notice, nature of the hearing, standard of proof in revocation proceedings, the applicability of the exclusionary rule, and whether probationers have equal protection and due process rights prior to the final decision to revoke. The general rule is that probation can be revoked only during the probation term, not after it has expired. There are several alternatives to revocation, usually limited only by whatever arrangements the court might allow.

ENDNOTES

1. Joan Petersilia, Susan Turner, James Kahan, and Joyce Peterson, *Granting Felons Probation: Public Risks and Alternatives* (Santa Monica, Calif.: RAND, 1985).
2. Patrick Langan and Mark Cunniff, "Recidivism of Felons on Probation," *Special Report* (Washington, D.C.: Bureau of Justice Statistics, February 1992).
3. Patrick Langan, "Between Prison and Probation: Intermediate Sanctions," *Science* (1994), 791–93, as cited in Joan Petersilia, "Probation in the United States: Practices and Challenges," *National Institute of Justice Journal* (September 1997), 4.
4. Rolando V. del Carmen, Jeffrey D. Dailey, and Lance Emerson, *Community Supervision: Law and Practice in Texas* (Huntsville, Tex.: SHSU Press, 1996), 108.
5. Authority to grant probation lies with the court having jurisdiction to try the offense. 18 U.S.C.A. sec. 3561. State statutes often have similar provisions.
6. 18 U.S.C.A. sec. 3563. The court to which transfer is made has all the power previously possessed by the court from which transfer is made, except that the period of probation cannot be changed without the consent of the sentencing court.
7. Federal Code and Rules, Title 18, Ch. 227, Rule 3565(a).
8. Federal Code and Rules, Title 18, Ch. 227, Rule 35651(b).
9. The traditional officer's attitude toward revocation decisions reflects the rehabilitative rather than the punitive focus of the probation and parole systems. For example, here is a quote from *Gagnon v. Scarpelli,* 411 U.S. 778 (1973): "Revocation is, . . . if anything, commonly treated as a failure of supervision. While presumably it would be inappropriate for a field agent never to revoke, the whole thrust of the probation/parole movement is to keep [individuals] in the community, working with adjustment problems there, and using revocation only as a last resort where treatment has failed or is about to fail."

10. Carol Vance, "Imprisoning All Our Convicts on the Cheap Is a Myth," *Houston Chronicle,* October 31, 1993, 1F.
11. Texas Code of Criminal Procedure, Article 42.12, sec. 11(1).
12. 1995 Federal Guidelines Manual, sec. 7B1.1.
13. Langan, "Between Prison and Probation," 72.
14. *People v. King,* 267 Cal. App. 2d 814 (1968).
15. *People v. McClean,* 130 Cal. App. 2d 439 (1955).
16. *Olivas v. State,* 168 Tex. Crim. 437 (1959).
17. *House v. State,* 166 Tex. Crim. 41 (1958).
18. *Rinto v. State,* 628 S.W. 2d 159 (1982).
19. *United States v. Furukawa,* 596 F. 2d 921 (9th Cir. 1979).
20. *Baker v. State,* 428 So. 2d 684 (Fla. Dist. Ct. App. 1983).
21. *Supervision of Federal Offenders,* Monograph no. 109 (Washington, D.C.: Administrative Office of the U.S. Courts, Probation and Pretrial Services Division, 1991), 39–40. The guidelines require mandatory revocation for possession of a firearm or controlled substances.
22. Langan, "Between Prison and Probation," 74.
23. Peggy B. Burke, *Policy-Driven Responses to Probation and Parole Violations* (National Institute of Corrections, March 1997), 12.
24. Federal Criminal Code and Rules, 1995, chap. 229, sec. 3603.
25. 1995 Federal Guidelines Manual, sec. 7B1.5.
26. 411 U.S. 778 (1973).
27. 408 U.S. 471 (1972).
28. *Kuenstler v. State,* 486 S.W. 2d 367 (Tex. 1972).
29. *Burkett v. State,* 485 S.W. 2d 578 (Tex. 1972).
30. *People v. Sweeden,* 116 Cal. App. 2d 891 (1953).
31. *Soliz v. State,* 171 Tex. Crim. 376 (1961).
32. *People v. Price,* 24 Ill. App. 2d 364 (1960).
33. *Dickerson v. State,* 136 Ga. App. 885 (1975).
34. *Cooper v. State,* 599 P. 2d 419 (Okla. Crim. App. 1979).
35. *Smith v. State,* 932 S.W. 2d 279 (Tex. App. 1996).
36. *United States v. McCormick,* 54 F. 3d 214 (U.S. 5th Cir. 1995).
37. Rolando V. del Carmen, *Potential Liabilities of Probation and Parole Officers,* rev. ed. (Anderson, 1985), 144.
38. del Carmen, *Potential Liabilities of Probation and Parole Officers,* 144.
39. *Herrington v. State,* 534 S.W. 2d 311 (Tex. Crim. App. 1976).
40. *Meyer v. State,* 596 P. 2d 1270 (Okla. Crim. App. 1979).
41. *State v. Dement,* 42 N.C. App. 254 (1979).
42. *Gilbert v. State,* 150 Ga. App. 339 (1979).
43. Rolando V. del Carmen, *Criminal Procedure: Law and Practice* (Belmont, Calif.: Wadsworth, 1998).
44. *United States v. James,* 893 F. Supp. 649 (U.S.D. Tex. 1995).
45. *United States v. Wiygul,* 578 F. 2d 577 (5th Cir. 1978), and *United States v. Farmer,* 512 F. 2d 160 L (6th Cir. 1975).
46. *United States v. Vandemark,* 522 F. 2d 1019 (9th Cir. 1975).
47. *State v. Turner,* 873 P. 2d 208 (Kansas App. 1994).
48. del Carmen, *Potential Liabilities of Probation and Parole Officers,* 147.
49. 461 U.S. 660 (1983).
50. del Carmen, *Potential Liabilities of Probation and Parole Officers,* 147.
51. 471 U.S. 606 (1985).
52. del Carmen, *Potential Liabilities of Probation and Parole Officers,* 152.
53. *Jones v. State,* 916 S.W. 2d 766 (Ark. App. 1996).

54. Federal Criminal Code and Rules, 1995, Ch. 227, Sec. 3565.
55. Ill. Unified Code of Corrections sec. 1005-6-5(2).
56. *Supervision of Federal Offenders,* 39–40.
57. Carl Klockars, "A Theory of Probation Supervision," *Journal of Criminology, Criminal Law, and Police Science* 63(4):550–57 (1972).
58. *Gagnon v. Scarpelli,* 411 U.S. 778, *Standards Relating to Probation* 6.

DISCUSSION QUESTIONS

1. Support the statement, "The decision to revoke is important." What are revocation's implications for the probationer, the probation officer, and the community?
2. "Revocation is discretionary." Discuss what this means.
3. What are the two types of probation violation? Discuss each.
4. Discuss the revocation procedure. How does it start and what are the steps?
5. Do probation officers have the power to arrest probationers? Discuss your answer.
6. What is the leading case on probation revocation? Discuss what that case says.
7. There are six due process rights given to probationers during the revocation hearing. What are they?
8. What standard of proof is needed in revocation proceedings? Is one standard of proof prescribed?
9. What is the exclusionary rule? Does it apply in revocation proceedings?
10. What does the case of *Bearden v. Georgia* say?
11. "There is no way a probationer can be revoked after the probation term has expired." Is that statement true or false? Discuss.
12. Identify four alternatives to revocation and discuss each briefly.

SUPPLEMENTAL READING

Gagnon v. Scarpelli

JOHN R. GAGNON,
Warden, Petitioner, v.
GERALD H. SCARPELLI
411 US 778, 36 L Ed 2d 656, 93 S Ct 1756
[No. 71-1225]
Argued January 9, 1973. Decided May 14, 1973.

Summary

After the petitioner had pleaded guilty to a charge of armed robbery in Wisconsin and the trial court had sentenced him to 15 years' imprisonment, the judge suspended sentence, placed the petitioner on probation for seven years in the custody of the Wisconsin Department of Public Welfare, and authorized him to reside in Illinois, where, pursuant to an interstate compact, he was accepted for supervision by Illinois probation authorities. Subsequently, he and a companion were arrested in Illinois for a burglary. Several days later, the Wisconsin Department, without affording him either a hearing or counsel, revoked his probation on the grounds that by being involved in and arrested for the burglary, and by associating with his companion, a known criminal, he had violated his probation. Shortly thereafter, he was incarcerated in a Wisconsin prison to begin serving his 15-year sentence. In habeas corpus proceedings in the United States District Court for the Eastern District of Wisconsin, the petitioner contended that the revocation of his probation without affording him a hearing or counsel was a denial of due process. The District Court agreed with this contention and granted a writ of habeas corpus (317 F Supp 72), and the Court of Appeals for the Seventh Circuit affirmed (454 F 2d 416).

On certiorari, United States Supreme Court affirmed in part, reversed in part, and remanded the case. In an opinion by Powell, J., it was held (1) expressing the unanimous view of the court, that the petitioner was entitled to both a preliminary hearing to determine whether there was probable cause to believe that he had violated his probation and a final hearing prior to the ultimate decision whether his probation should be revoked, and (2) expressing the view of eight members of the court, that the state was not under a constitutional duty to provide counsel for indigents in all probation revocation cases, but that the decision as to the need for counsel must be made on a case-by-case basis in the exercise of a sound discretion by the state authority charged with responsibility for administering the probation system, and that certain general guidelines as to whether the assistance of counsel was constitutionally necessary should be applied in the first instance by those charged with conducting the revocation hearing.

Opinion of the Court

[411 US 779]

Mr. Justice Powell delivered the opinion of the Court.

This case presents the related questions whether a previously sentenced probationer is entitled to a hearing when his probation is revoked and, if so, whether he is entitled to be represented by appointed counsel at such a hearing.

I

Respondent, Gerald Scarpelli, pleaded guilty in July 1965, to a charge of armed robbery in Wisconsin. The trial judge sentenced him to 15 years' imprisonment, but suspended the sentence and placed him on probation for seven years in the custody of the Wisconsin Department of Public Welfare (the Department).[1]

[411 US 780]

After being apprised of his constitutional rights, respondent admitted that he and Kleckner had broken into the house for the purpose of stealing merchandise or money, although he now asserts that his statement was made under duress and is false. Probation was revoked by the Department on September 1, without a hearing. The stated grounds for revocation were that:

> "1. [Scarpelli] has associated with known criminals, in direct violation of his probation regulations and his supervising agent's instructions;"
>
> "2. [Scarpelli] while associating with a known criminal, namely Fred Kleckner, Jr., was involved in, and arrested for, a burglary . . . in Deerfield, Illinois." App 20.

On September 4, 1965, he was incarcerated in the Wisconsin State Reformatory at Green Bay to begin serving the 15 years to which he had been sentenced by the trial judge. At no time was he afforded a hearing.

Some three years later, on December 16, 1968, respondent applied for a writ of habeas corpus. After the petition had been filed, but before it had been acted upon, the

1. The Court's order placing respondent on probation provided, among other things, that "[i]n the event of his failure to meet the conditions of his probation he will stand committed under the sentence all ready [sic] imposed." App. 10. The agreement specifying the conditions of the probation, duly executed by respondent, obligated him to "make a sincere attempt to avoid all acts which are forbidden by law. . . ."

Department placed respondent on parole.[2] The District Court found that his status as parolee was sufficient custody to confer jurisdiction on the court and that the petition was not moot because the revocation carried "collateral consequences," presumably including the restraints imposed by his parole. On the merits, the District Court held that revocation without a hearing and counsel was a denial of due process. 317 F Supp 72 (ED Wis 1970). The Court of Appeals affirmed sub nom. *Gunsolus v. Gagnon,* 454 F 2d 416 (CA 7 1971),

[411 US 781]

and we granted certiorari, 408 US 921, 33 L Ed 2d 331, 92 S Ct 2490 (1972).

II

Two prior decisions set the bounds of our present inquiry. In *Mempa v Rhay,* 389 US 128, 19 L Ed 2d 336, 88 S Ct 254 (1967), the Court held that a probationer is entitled to be represented by appointed counsel at a combined revocation and sentencing hearing. Reasoning that counsel is required "at every stage of a criminal proceeding where substantial rights of a criminal accused may be affected," id., at 134, 19 L Ed 2d 336, and that sentencing is one such stage, the Court concluded that counsel must be provided an indigent at sentencing even when it is accomplished as a part of subsequent probation revocation proceeding. But this line of reasoning does not require a hearing or counsel at the time of probation revocation in a case such as the present one, where the probationer was sentenced at the time of trial.

Of greater relevance is our decision last Term in *Morrissey v Brewer,* 408 US 471, 33 L Ed 2d 484, 92 S Ct 2593 (1972). There we held that the revocation of parole is not a part of a criminal prosecution.

> "Parole arises after the end of the criminal prosecution, including imposition of sentence. . . . Revocation deprives an individual, not of the absolute liberty to which every citizen is entitled, but only of the conditional liberty properly dependent on observance of special parole restrictions." Id., at 480, 33 L Ed 2d 484.

Even though the revocation of parole is not a part of the criminal prosecution, we held that the loss of liberty entailed is a serious deprivation requiring that the parolee be accorded due process. Specifically, we held that a parolee is entitled to two hearings, one a

[411 US 782]

preliminary hearing at the time of his arrest and detention to determine whether there is probable cause to believe that he has committed a violation of his parole and the other a somewhat more comprehensive hearing prior to the making of the final revocation decision.

[1] Petitioner does not contend that there is any difference relevant to the guarantee of due process between the revocation of parole and the revocation of probation, nor do we perceive one.[3] Probation revocation, like parole revocation, is not a stage of a criminal prosecution, but does result in a loss of liberty.[4] Accordingly, we hold that a probationer, like a parolee, is entitled to a preliminary and a final revocation hearing, under the conditions specified in *Morrissey v Brewer,* supra.[5]

[411 US 783]

III

The second, and more difficult, question posed by this case is whether an indigent probationer or parolee has a due process right to be represented by appointed counsel at these hearings.[6] In answering that question, we draw heavily on the opinion in *Morrissey.* Our first point of reference is the character of probation or parole. As noted in *Morrissey* regarding parole, the "purpose is to help individuals reintegrate into society as constructive individuals as soon

2. Respondent was initially paroled to a federal detainer to serve a previously imposed federal sentence arising from another conviction. He was subsequently released from federal custody, but remains a parolee under the supervision of the Department.

3. Despite the undoubted minor differences between probation and parole, the commentators have agreed that revocation of probation where sentence has been imposed previously is constitutionally indistinguishable from the revocation of parole. *See, e.g.,* Van Dyke, *Parole Revocation Hearings in California: The Right to Counsel,* 59 Calif L Rev 1215, 1241–1243 (1971); Sklar, *Law and Practice in Probation and Parole Revocation Hearings,* 55 J Crim LC & PS 175, 198 n. 182 (1964).

4. It is clear at least after *Morrissey v. Brewer,* 408 US 471, 33 L Ed 2d 484, 92 S Ct 2593 (1972), that a probationer can no longer be denied due process. in reliance on the dictum in *Escoe v. Zerbst,* 295 US 490, 492, 79 L Ed 2d 1566, 55 S Ct 818 (1935), that probation is an "act of grace."

5. Petitioner argues, in addition, that the *Morrissey* hearing requirements impose serious practical problems in cases such as the present one in which a probationer or parolee is allowed to leave the convicting State for supervision in another State. Such arrangements are made pursuant to an interstate compact adopted by all of the States, including Wisconsin. Wis.Stat.Ann. § 57.13 (1957). Petitioner's brief asserts that as of June 30, 1972, Wisconsin had a total of 642 parolees and probationers under supervision in other States and that incomplete statistics as of June 30, 1971, indicated a national total of 24,693 persons under out-of-state supervision. Brief for Petitioner.

Some amount of disruption inevitably attends any new constitutional ruling. We are confident, however, that modifications of the interstate compact can remove without undue strain the more serious technical hurdles to compliance with *Morrissey.* An additional comment is warranted with respect to the rights to present witnesses and to confront and cross-examine adverse witnesses. Petitioner's greatest concern is with the difficulty and expense of procuring witnesses from perhaps thousands of miles away. While in some cases there is simply no adequate alternative to live testimony, we emphasize that we did not in *Morrissey* intend to prohibit use where appropriate of the conventional substitutes for live testimony, including affidavits, depositions, and documentary evidence. Nor did we intend to foreclose the States from holding both the preliminary and the final hearings at the place of violation or from developing other creative solutions to the practical difficulties of the *Morrissey* requirements.

6. In *Morrissey v Brewer,* we left open the question "whether the parolee is entitled to the assistance of retained counsel or to appointed counsel if he is indigent." 408 US, at 489, 33 L Ed 2d 484. Since respondent did not attempt to retain counsel but asked only for appointed counsel, we have no occasion to decide in this case whether a probationer or parolee has a right to be represented at a revocation hearing by retained counsel in situations other than those where the State would be obliged to furnish counsel for an indigent.

as they are able. . . ." 408 US, at 477, 33 L Ed 2d 484. The duty and attitude of the probation or parole officer reflect this purpose:

> While the parole or probation officer recognizes his double duty to the welfare of his clients and to the safety of the general community, by and large concern for the client dominates his professional attitude.

[411 US 784]

The parole agent ordinarily defines his role as representing his client's best interests as long as these do not constitute a threat to public safety.[7] Because the probation or parole officer's function is not so much to compel conformance to a strict code of behavior as to supervise a course of rehabilitation, he has been entrusted traditionally with broad discretion to judge the progress of rehabilitation in individual cases, and has been armed with the power to recommend or even to declare revocation.

In *Morrissey,* we recognized that the revocation decision has two analytically distinct components:

> "The first step in a revocation decision thus involves a wholly retrospective factual question: whether the parolee has in fact acted in violation of one or more conditions of his parole. Only if it is determined that the parolee did violate the condition does the second question arise: should the parolee be recommitted to prison or should other steps be taken to protect society and improve chances of rehabilitation?" *Morrissey v. Brewer,* supra, at 479–480, 33 L Ed 2d 484.[8]

[411 US 785]

The parole officer's attitude toward these decisions reflects the rehabilitative rather than punitive focus of the probation/parole system:

> "Revocation . . . is, if anything, commonly treated as a failure of supervision. While presumably it would be inappropriate for a field agent *never* to revoke, the whole thrust of the probation-parole movement is to keep men in the community, working with adjustment problems there, and using revocation only as a last resort when treatment has failed or is about to fail."[9]

[2] But an exclusive focus on the benevolent attitudes of those who administer the probation/parole system when it is working successfully obscures the modification in attitude which is likely to take place once the officer has decided to recommend revocation. Even though the officer is not by this recommendation converted into a prosecutor committed to convict, his role as counselor to the probationer or parolee is then surely compromised.

When the officer's view of the probationer's or parolee's conduct differs in this fundamental way from the latter's own view, due process requires that the difference be resolved before revocation becomes final. Both the probationer or parolee and the State have interests in the accurate finding of fact and the informed use of discretion—the probationer or parolee to insure that his liberty is not unjustifiably taken away and the State to make certain that it is neither unnecessarily interrupting a successful effort at rehabilitation nor imprudently prejudicing the safety of the community.

[411 US 786]

[3, 4] It was to serve all of these interests that Morrissey mandated preliminary and final revocation hearings. At the preliminary hearing, a probationer or parolee is entitled to notice of the alleged violations of probation or parole, an opportunity to appear and to present evidence in his own behalf, a conditional right to confront adverse witnesses, an independent decision maker, and a written report of the hearing. *Morrissey v. Brewer,* supra, at 487, 33 L Ed 2d 484. The final hearing is a less summary one because the decision under consideration is the ultimate decision to revoke rather than a mere determination of probable cause, but the "minimum requirements of due process" include very similar elements:

> (a) written notice of the claimed violations of [probation or] parole; (b) disclosure to the [probationer or] parolee of evidence against him; (c) opportunity to be heard in person and to present witnesses and documentary evidence; (d) the right to confront and cross-examine adverse witnesses (unless the hearing officer specifically finds good cause for not allowing confrontation); (e) a "neutral and detached" hearing body such as a traditional parole board, members of which need not be judicial officers or lawyers; and (f) a written statement by the fact finders as to the evidence relied on and reasons for revoking [probation or] parole. *Morrissey v. Brewer,* supra, at 489, 33 L Ed 2d 484.

---

7. F. Remington, D. Newman, E. Kimball, M. Melli and H. Goldstein, Criminal Justice Administration, Materials and Cases 910–911 (1969).

8. The factors entering into these decisions relate in major part to a professional evaluation, by trained probation or parole officers, as to the overall social readjustment of the offender in the community, and include consideration of such variables as the offender's relationship toward his family, his attitude toward the fulfillment of financial obligations, the extent of his cooperation with the probation officer assigned to his case, his personal associations, and—of course—whether there have been specific and significant violations of the conditions of the probation. The importance of these considerations, some factual and others entirely judgmental, is illustrated by a Wisconsin empirical study which disclosed that, in the sample studied, probation or parole was revoked in only 34.5% of the cases in which the probationer or parolee violated the terms of his release. S. Hunt, *The Revocation Decision: A Study of Probation and Parole Agents' Discretion 10* (unpublished thesis on file at the library of the University of Wisconsin 1964), cited in Brief for Petitioner, Addendum 106.

9. Remington, Newman, Kimball, Melli and Goldstein, supra n. 7, at 910.

[5] These requirements in themselves serve as substantial protection against ill-considered revocation, and petitioner argues that counsel need never be supplied. What this argument overlooks is that the effectiveness of the rights guaranteed by *Morrissey* may in some circumstances depend on the use of skills which the probationer or parolee is unlikely to possess. Despite the informal nature of the proceeding and the absence of technical

[411 US 787]

rules of procedure or evidence, the unskilled or uneducated probationer or parolee may well have difficulty in presenting his version of a disputed set of facts where the presentation requires the examining or cross-examining of witnesses or the offering or dissecting of complex documentary evidence.

[6] By the same token, we think that the Court of Appeals erred in accepting respondent's contention that the State is under a constitutional duty to provide counsel for indigents in all probation or parole revocation cases. While such a rule has the appeal of simplicity, it would impose direct costs and serious collateral disadvantages without regard to the need or the likelihood in a particular case for a constructive contribution by counsel. In most cases, the probationer or parolee has been convicted of committing another crime or has admitted the charges against him.[10] And while in some cases he may have a justifiable excuse for the violation or a convincing reason why revocation is not the appropriate disposition, mitigating evidence of this kind is often not susceptible of proof or is so simple as not to require either investigation or exposition by counsel.

The introduction of counsel into a revocation proceeding will alter significantly the nature of the proceeding. If counsel is provided for the probationer or parolee, the State in turn will normally provide its own counsel; lawyers, by training and disposition, are advocates and bound by professional duty to present all available evidence and arguments in support of their clients' positions and to contest with vigor all adverse evidence and views. The role of the hearing body itself, aptly described in *Morrissey* as being "predictive and discretionary" as well as fact-finding, may become more akin to that of a judge at a trial, and less attuned to the

[411 US 788]

rehabilitative needs of the individual probationer or parolee. In the greater self-consciousness of its quasi-judicial role, the hearing body may be less tolerant of marginal deviant behavior and feel more pressure to reincarcerate rather than to continue nonpunitive rehabilitation. Certainly, the decision-making process will be prolonged, and the financial cost to the State—for appointed counsel, counsel for the State, a longer record, and the possibility of judicial review—will not be insubstantial.[11]

[5, 7] In some cases, these modifications in the nature of the revocation hearing must be endured and the costs borne because, as we have indicated above, the probationer's or parolee's version of a disputed issue can fairly be represented only by a trained advocate. But due process is not so rigid as to require that the significant interests in informality, flexibility, and economy must always be sacrificed.

In so concluding, we are of course aware that the case-by-case approach to the right to counsel in felony prosecutions adopted in *Betts v Brady,* 316 US 455, 86 L Ed 1595, 62 S Ct 1252 (1942), was later rejected in favor of a per se rule in *Gideon v Wainwright,* 372 US 335, 9 L Ed 2d 799, 83 S Ct 792, 93 ALR 2d 733 (1963). See also *Argersinger v Hamlin,* 407 US 25, 32 L Ed 2d 530, 92 S Ct 2006 (1972). We do not, however, draw from *Gideon* and *Argersinger* the conclusion that a case-by-case approach to furnishing counsel is necessarily inadequate to protect constitutional rights asserted in varying types of proceedings: there are critical differences between criminal trials and probation or parole revocation

[411 US 789]

hearings, and both society and the probationer or parolee have stakes in preserving these differences.

In a criminal trial, the State is represented by a prosecutor; formal rules of evidence are in force; a defendant enjoys a number of procedural rights which may be lost if not timely raised; and, in a jury trial, a defendant must make a presentation understandable to untrained jurors. In short, a criminal trial under our system is an adversary proceeding with its own unique characteristics. In a revocation hearing, on the other hand, the State is represented, not by a prosecutor, but by a parole officer with the orientation described above; formal procedures and rules of evidence are not employed; and the members of the hearing body are familiar with the problems and practice of probation or parole. The need for counsel at revocation hearings derives, not from the invariable attributes of those hearings, but rather from the peculiarities of particular cases.

10. See Skar, supra, n. 3, at 192 (parole), 193 (probation).

11. The scope of the practical problem which would be occasioned by a requirement of counsel in all revocation cases is suggested by the fact that in the mid-1960s there was an estimated average of 20,000 adult felony parole revocations and 108,000 adult probation revocations each year. President's Commission on Law Enforcement and Administration of Justice, Task Force Report: The Courts 56 n. 28 (1967).

[8, 9] The differences between a criminal trial and a revocation hearing do not dispose altogether of the argument that under a case-by-case approach there may be cases in which a lawyer would be useful but in which none would be appointed because an arguable defense would be uncovered only by a lawyer. Without denying that there is some force in this argument, we think it a sufficient answer that we deal here, not with the right of an accused to counsel in a criminal prosecution, but with the more limited due process right of one who is a probationer or parolee only because he has been convicted of a crime.[12]

[411 US 790]

[10] We thus find no justification for a new inflexible constitutional rule with respect to the requirement of counsel. We think, rather, that the decision as to the need for counsel must be made on a case-by-case basis in the exercise of a sound discretion by the state authority charged with responsibility for administering the probation and parole system. Although the presence and participation of counsel will probably be both undesirable and constitutionally unnecessary in most revocation hearings, there will remain certain cases in which fundamental fairness—the touchstone of due process—will require that the State provide at its expense counsel for indigent probationers or parolees.

[11, 12] It is neither possible nor prudent to attempt to formulate a precise and detailed set of guidelines to be followed in determining when the providing of counsel is necessary to meet the applicable due process requirements. The facts and circumstances in preliminary and final hearings are susceptible of almost infinite variation, and a considerable discretion must be allowed the responsible agency in making the decision. Presumptively, it may be said that counsel should be provided in cases where, after being informed of his right to request counsel, the probationer or parolee makes such a request, based on a timely and colorable claim (i) that he has not committed the alleged violation of the conditions upon which he is at liberty; or (ii) that, even if the violation is a matter of public record or is uncontested, there are substantial reasons which justified or mitigated the violation and make revocation inappropriate, and that the reasons are complex or otherwise difficult to develop or present. In passing on a request for the appointment of counsel, the responsible agency also should consider,

[411 US 791]

especially in doubtful cases, whether the probationer appears to be capable of speaking effectively for himself. In every case in which a request for counsel at a preliminary or final hearing is refused, the grounds for refusal should be stated succinctly in the record.

IV

[13, 14] We return to the facts of the present case. Because respondent was not afforded either a preliminary hearing or a final hearing, the revocation of his probation did not meet the standards of due process prescribed in *Morrissey,* which we have here held applicable to probation revocations. Accordingly, respondent was entitled to a writ of habeas corpus. On remand, the District Court should allow the State an opportunity to conduct such a hearing. As to whether the State must provide counsel, respondent's admission to having committed another serious crime creates the very sort of situation in which counsel need not ordinarily be provided. But because of respondent's subsequent assertions regarding that admission, see supra, at 780, 36 L Ed 2d at 660, we conclude that the failure of the Department to provide respondent with the assistance of counsel should be reexamined in light of this opinion. The general guidelines outlined above should be applied in the first instance by those charged with conducting the revocation hearing.

Affirmed in part, reversed in part, and remanded.

Mr. Justice Douglas, dissenting in part.

I believe that due process requires the appointment of counsel in this case because of the claim that respondent's confession of the burglary was made under duress. See *Morrissey v. Brewer,* 408 US 471, 498, 33 L Ed 2d 484, 92 S Ct 2593 (opinion of Douglas, J.)

12. Cf. In re *Gault,* 387 US 1, 18 L Ed 2d 527, 87 S Ct 1428 (1967), establishing a juvenile's right to appointed counsel in a delinquency proceeding which while denominated civil, was functionally akin to a criminal trial. A juvenile charged with violation of a generally applicable statute is differently situated from an already-convicted probationer or parolee. and is entitled to a higher degree of protection. See In re *Winship,* 397 US 358, 25 L Ed 2d 368, 90 S Ct 1068 (1970) (the standard of proof in a juvenile delinquency proceeding must be "proof beyond a reasonable doubt").

II

PAROLE

AT PRESENT MOST STATES HAVE SOME FORM OF PAROLE STATUTES AND procedures for the discretionary release of most adult felony offenders from prisons and correctional institutions. Almost all jurisdictions have at least nominal programs for supervising offenders released to the community and procedures for their return to incarceration should they fail in community adjustment.

The structure of the paroling process—including the composition and selection of the parole board, caseloads, training, and authority of field staff and procedures used for the parole grant or revocation—varies considerably from jurisdiction to jurisdiction. The same is true for the *use* of parole. Some states parole virtually all adult prisoners, while in others legislative action has abolished discretionary release on parole.

These variations in the structure and use of the parole process, as well as the accompanying variations in sentencing structures from one jurisdiction to another, account in good part for the lack of agreement about the legal status of parole across the country. Where parole is the common, almost universal means of release from prison, it comes to be viewed as a right. Where it is granted reluctantly and rarely, and in jurisdictions with long statutory sentences and no other alternatives to mitigation of sentences, parole becomes crucially important to inmates.

This section focuses on parole as a subsystem of the entire field of criminal justice. The history and philosophy of parole are discussed in detail, as are current practices and legal issues and attempts to clarify the contemporary controversies involving parole and other forms of early release from incarceration. Parole is viewed in its relationship to sentencing, imprisonment, and other aspects of the correctional continuum.

8

THE HISTORY AND CONCEPT OF PAROLE

KEY TERMS

- Parole
- Mandatory release
- Probation
- Pardon
- *Parole d'honneur*
- Transportation
- Ticket-of-leave
- Ticket-of-leave man
- Alexander Maconochie
- Mark system
- Norfolk Island
- Sir Walter Crofton
- The Irish system
- Indeterminate sentence
- Zebulon R. Brockway
- Determinate sentence
- Medical model
- Just deserts
- Justice model
- Presumptive sentence
- Postrelease supervision
- Split sentence
- Good time
- Supervised release

What You Will Learn in This Chapter

In this chapter you will learn how parole differs from probation and pardon. You will examine the interesting history of parole, beginning with the work of Manuel Montesinos in Spain and Georg Michael Obermaier in Germany. We will survey the practices of transportation and ticket-of-leave and their influence on the development of parole. Particular emphasis will be placed on the work of Alexander Maconochie on the penal colony of Norfolk Island and the subsequent implementation of parole by Walter Crofton in Ireland and Zebulon R. Brockway in America. Finally, you will continue to trace the history of parole into the modern era, examining the various attacks on parole and the role parole plays in the latter years of the 20th century.

INTRODUCTION

The procedure now known as *parole* was first tried in the United States at Elmira Reformatory in 1876. Since then its use has extended to all parts of the country, and it is now the major device by which offenders are released from prisons and correctional institutions. Even after a century of use there is great misapprehension and misunderstanding about parole, much of which arises from a confusion in terminology. The general public often considers parole to be based on clemency or leniency and seldom distinguishes it from probation and pardon. The terms *parole, probation,* and *pardon* are used indiscriminately not only by the public but even by officials, judges, and in some state statutes. Because of this confusion in terminology and administration, parole is often charged with all the shortcomings of other release procedures, for which it is in no way responsible. It is evident, therefore, that a clear definition of the term is essential to any analysis of parole. **Parole** is the conditional release, by an administrative act, of a convicted offender from a penal or correctional institution, under the continued custody of the state, to serve the remainder of his or her sentence in the community under supervision.

PAROLE

Conditional release, by an administrative act, of a convicted offender from a penal or correctional institution, under the continual custody of the state, to serve the remainder of his or her sentence in the community under supervision.

Parole Distinguished from Mandatory Release

Mandatory release differs from parole in that mandatory releasees enter supervision in the community *automatically* at the expiration of their maximum term *minus* credited time off for good behavior. In many jurisdictions where parole-board authority has been abolished, most released prisoners return to the community via mandatory release. As with parole, mandatory release may be revoked for failure to comply with the conditions of release.

MANDATORY RELEASE

Conditional release to the community that is automatic at the expiration of the maximum term of sentence minus any credited time off for good behavior.

Parole Distinguished from Probation

Probation and parole are different methods of dealing with offenders, although their terms are often used interchangeably. Whereas parole is a form of release granted to a prisoner who has served a portion of a sentence in a correctional institution, **probation** is granted an offender without required incarceration. Parole is an administrative act of the executive or an executive agency, whereas probation is a judicial act of the court. Therefore, so-called bench parole—which is nothing more than a suspension of sentence without supervision—is not parole at all but a form of probation; the use of the word *parole* in this connection is improper and misleading and should thus be eliminated.

Parole Distinguished from Pardon

Parole may be distinguished from **pardon** as follows: Pardon involves forgiveness. Parole does not. Pardon is a remission of punishment. Parole is an extension of punishment. Pardoned prisoners are free. Parolees may be arrested and reimprisoned without a trial. Pardon is an executive act of grace; parole is an administrative expedient.[1]

PARDON

An executive act of clemency that absolves an individual from the legal consequences of a crime and conviction. A pardon is an act of grace or a remission of guilt. A *full* pardon freely and unconditionally absolves the party from the consequences of the crime and conviction. A *conditional* pardon becomes operative when the grantee has performed some specified act, or it becomes void after the occurrence of some specified event, or it remits only a portion of the penalties that are the legal consequences of a crime and conviction.

The distinction between parole and pardon was clearly drawn in an address before the American Prison Association in 1916:

> The whole question of parole is one of administration. A parole does not release the parolee from custody; it does not discharge or absolve him from the penal consequences of his act; it does not mitigate his punishment; it does not wash away the stain or remit the penalty; it does not reverse the judgment of the Court or declare him to have been innocent or affect the record against him. Unlike a pardon, it is not an act of grace or of mercy, of clemency or leniency. The granting of parole is merely permission to a prisoner to serve a portion of his sentence outside the walls of the prison. He continues to be in the custody of the authorities, both legally and actually, and is still under restraint. The sentence is in full force and at any time he does not comply with the conditions upon which he is released, or does not want to conduct himself properly, he may be returned, for his own good and in the public interest.[2]

It has been pointed out that there is no similarity between pardon and parole except that both involve release from an institution.[3] Release on parole is not based on any concept of clemency. Nor is it regarded as a lenient treatment of prisoners, even though they are released prior to the expiration of their sentences. Parole, as it functions today, is an integral part of the total correctional process. As such, it is a method of selectively releasing offenders from the institution and placing them under supervision in the community, whereby the community is afforded continuing protection while the offender is making adjustments and beginning to contribute to society.

THE ORIGINS OF PAROLE

The English word *parole* is derived from the French ***parole d'honneur,*** meaning "word of honor." This choice of word was unfortunate inasmuch as most people would distrust a released prisoner's word of honor. It is not surprising, therefore, that the French themselves prefer the term *conditional liberation* to the one we borrowed from their language.

PAROLE D'HONNEUR

French for "word of honor," from which the English word *parole* is derived.

In penal philosophy parole is part of the general 19th-century trend in criminology from punishment to reformation. In 1791, during the French Revolution, the Comte de Mirabeau (Honore-Gabriel Rigueti) anticipated modern penal theories when he published a report based on the idea of reformation and emphasizing the principles of labor, segregation, rewards under a mark system, conditional liberation, and aid on discharge.[4] Another Frenchman, Bonneville de Marsangy, public prosecutor of Versailles, published a book in 1847 in which he discussed a pardoning power, conditional liberation, police supervision of discharged convicts, aid upon discharge, and rehabilitation. This book was distributed by the government to the members of both chambers of Parliament. In 1864, in a further work on this subject, he used the following simile in his argument for what is now called *parole:*

> As a skillful physician gives or withholds remedial treatment according as the patient is or is not cured, so ought the expiatory treatment imposed by law upon the criminal to cease when his amendment is complete; further his detention is inoperative for good, an act of inhumanity, and a needless burden to the state. Society should say to the prisoner, "Whenever you give satisfactory evidence of your genuine reformation, you will be tested, under the operation of a ticket of leave; thus the opportunity to abridge the term of your imprisonment is placed in your own hands."[5]

Parole *as a practice* originated almost simultaneously with three European prison administrators: a Spaniard, Manuel Montesinos; a German, Georg Michael Obermaier; and an Englishman, Alexander Maconochie.

Manuel Montesinos

In 1835 Col. Manuel Montesinos was appointed governor of the prison at Valencia, Spain, which held about 1,500 convicts. He organized the institution on the basis of semimilitary discipline and encouraged vocational training and primary education of the prisoners. The novelty of his plan was that there were practically no guards to watch the prisoners, who nevertheless made few, if any, attempts to escape. The main reason for this was probably that each could earn a one-third reduction in the term of his sentence by good behavior and positive accomplishments. The number of recommitments while Montesinos was governor fell from 35 percent to "a figure which it would be imprudent to name, lest it should not be believed."

The law that allowed this program was subsequently repealed, and the system collapsed. Montesinos resigned, and in a pamphlet published in 1846 drew the following conclusions from his experiment:

> What neither severity of punishment nor constancy in inflicting them can secure, the slightest personal interest will obtain. In different ways, therefore, during my command, I have applied this powerful stimulant; and the excellent results it has always yielded, and the powerful germs of reform which are constantly developed under its influence, have at length fully convinced me that the most inefficacious methods in the prison, the most pernicious and fatal to every chance of reform, are punishments carried to the length of harshness. The maxim should be constant and of universal application in such places, not to degrade further those who come to them already degraded by their crimes. Self-respect is one of the most powerful sentiments of the human mind, since it is the most personal; and he who will not condescend, in some degree, according to circumstances, to flattery of it, will never attain his object by any amount of chastisement; the effect of ill treatment being to irritate rather than to correct, and thus turn from reform instead of attracting to it. The moral object of penal establishments should not be so much to inflict punishment as to correct, to receive men idle and ill-intentioned and return them to society, if possible, honest and industrious citizens.[6]

Georg Michael Obermaier

When Georg Michael Obermaier became governor of a prison in Munich, Germany, in 1842,[7] he found approximately 700 rebellious prisoners being kept in order by more than 100 soldiers. In a short time he gained the men's confidence, removed their chains, discharged nearly all of their guards, and appointed one of them superintendent of each of the industrial shops. His success in reforming prisoners was so great that reportedly only 10 percent relapsed into crime after their discharge. He was aided by two favorable circumstances: many of the men were sentenced to simple imprisonment with no fixed term; and discharged inmates were thoroughly supervised by numerous prison aid societies.

Alexander Maconochie and Walter Crofton

Chief credit for developing early parole systems, however, goes to Alexander Maconochie, who was in charge of the English penal colony at Norfolk Island, 1000 miles off the coast of Australia, and to Sir Walter Crofton, who directed Ireland's prisons. Crofton refined the scheme originated by Maconochie into what is known today as the *ticket-of-leave,* or *Irish system.* Inasmuch as the earliest known plan of conditional liberation was used in the Australian convict colonies, and because present-day parole is closely linked to these experiments, their tragic history is worthy of consideration. We discuss this next.

TRANSPORTATION AND TICKET-OF-LEAVE

The **transportation** of English criminals to the American colonies began in the early 17th century. The system evolved from a 1597 law that provided for the banishment of those who appeared to be dangerous. As early as 1617, reprieves and stays of execution were granted to persons convicted of robbery who were strong enough to work in the colonies. The government devised a plan to transport convicted felons to the American colonies as a partial solution to the labor shortage in the colonies and the poor economic conditions and widespread unemployment in England. The London, Virginia, and Massachusetts Companies and similar organizations supported the plan. The king approved the proposal to grant reprieves and stays of execution—pardons—to convicted felons who were physically able to be employed in the colonies.

Initially no specific conditions were imposed on those receiving pardons. Consequently many of them evaded transportation and returned to England before their terms expired, which made it necessary to impose certain restrictions on individuals who were granted pardons. About 1655 the form of pardon was amended to include specific conditions and to provide that the pardon would be nullified if the recipient failed to abide by the conditions.

Until 1717 the government had paid a fee to contractors for each prisoner transported. Under a new procedure adopted that year, the contractor was given "property in service," and the government took no interest in the welfare or behavior of the offender unless he or she violated the conditions of the pardon by returning to England before the sentence expired. Upon arrival in the colonies, the "services" of the prisoner were sold to the highest bidder, and thereafter the prisoner was an indentured servant.

TRANSPORTATION

The forced exile of convicted criminals. England transported convicted criminals to the American colonies until the Revolution and afterward to Australia. The foundations of the transportation system are found in the law of 1597, 39 Eliz. c.4, "An Acte for Punyshment of Rogues, Vagabonds, and Sturdy Beggars." The act declared that obdurate idlers "shall . . . be banished out of this Realm . . . and shall be conveyed to such parts beyond the seas as shall be . . . assigned by the Privy Council."

The system of indenture dates to 1512, and it originally had no relation to persons convicted of crimes. It usually applied to the indenture of apprentices to masters for a number of years. The indenture consisted of a contract stipulating the conditions of the relationship and was somewhat similar to the parole agreement of today.

The Revolutionary War brought an end to the practice of transporting criminals to America, but the transportation law was not repealed. Detention facilities in England became overcrowded, resulting in a more liberal granting of pardons. During a serious crime wave, the English public demanded enforcement of the transportation law, and Australia was designated as a convict settlement, with the first shipload arriving there in January 1788. Transportation to Australia differed from transportation to the American colonies in that the government incurred all expenses of transportation and maintenance, and the prisoners remained under government control instead of being indentured. The governor was given "the property and service" for the prisoners, and he assigned them to the free settlers, who assumed the property and service agreement. As early as 1790 the governor of New South Wales had the right to grant conditional pardons. He could set the convicts free and give them grants of land, afterward even assigning newly arrived convict laborers to them. Such was the original **ticket-of-leave** system that was regulated by statute in 1834. Originally there were no provisions for governmental supervision of **ticket-of-leave men.**

In 1811 a policy was adopted that required prisoners to serve specific periods of time before becoming eligible to receive ticket-of-leave. Strict enforcement of the policy was not seen until 1821, when an eligibility scale was formulated. Prisoners serving a sentence of 7 years became eligible for the ticket-of-leave after serving 4 years; those serving sentences of 14 years, after serving 6 years; and those serving life sentences, after 8 years.

In 1837 **Alexander Maconochie,** a former British naval captain and geographer, proposed to the House of Commons a system whereby the duration of the sentence would be determined not by time but by the prisoner's industry and good conduct. He proposed a **mark system** by which "marks" or credits would be credited to the prisoner daily in accordance with the amount of labor performed and his or her conduct. His system saw the prisoners passing through a series of stages from strict imprisonment through conditional release to final and complete restoration of liberty, with promotions being based on marks accredited.

Maconochie was given the opportunity to test his "mark system" in 1840, when he was appointed governor of the notorious penal colony on **Norfolk Island,** a thousand miles off the eastern coast of Australia. Under his mark system there, prisoners were able to progress through stages of custody, each less restrictive than the previous one:

1. Strict custody
2. Labor in work gangs
3. Freedom in certain areas of the island
4. Conditional release—ticket-of-leave
5. Complete freedom

Vocal and powerful detractors in Australia and in England railed against Maconochie's system, however. It was seen as radical and too liberal by many influential colonists in Australia, who believed that convicts should be kept in irons and not given any relief from their sentences. They lobbied the colonial governor of Van Dieman's Land (now Tasmania), who had appointed Maconochie to his post, for his dismissal. The governor was torn between his hope that Maconochie's experiment would succeed and his fear of the political power of the colonists who opposed the

TICKET-OF-LEAVE

A license or permit given to a convict as a reward for good conduct, which allowed him to go at large and labor for himself before his sentence expired, subject to certain restrictions and revocable upon subsequent misconduct. A forerunner of parole.

TICKET-OF-LEAVE MAN

A convict who has obtained a ticket-of-leave.

ALEXANDER MACONOCHIE

A British naval captain who served as governor of the penal colony on Norfolk Island, who instituted a system of early release that was the forerunner of modern parole. Maconochie is known as the "father of parole."

MARK SYSTEM

Credits for good behavior and hard work. In Alexander Maconochie's mark system on Norfolk Island, convicts could use the credits or *marks* to purchase either goods or time (reduction in sentence). In this system the prisoner progressed through stages from strict imprisonment, through conditional release, to final and complete restoration of liberty, with promotion being based on the marks accredited. One of the historical foundations of parole.

NORFOLK ISLAND

The notorious British penal colony 1000 miles off the coast of Australia.

project. Finally, however, partly due to the controversy over his methods and partly because of pressure in England to cut the costs of the transportation system, Maconochie was dismissed in 1844, and the "noble experiment" came to an end.

As the free settlers in Australia increased in number, they protested the use of the country as a dumping ground for prisoners. In response to the protest, England initiated a selection system whereby prisoners would undergo an 18-month training program before being transported to Australia. The selection experiment failed, but it was the first use of trained, experienced individuals for selecting prisoners who have profited by a training program. Three prison commissioners were appointed to make the selections, which may well have set the precedent for the three-member parole boards later established by prison reformers in America. In 1867 transportation of prisoners to Australia was terminated.

England's Experience with Ticket-of-Leave

Although England did not stop transporting prisoners to Australia until 1867, the English Penal Servitude Act of 1853, pertaining to English and Irish prisoners, substituted imprisonment for transportation. In accordance with the act, prisoners sentenced to 14 years or less were committed to prison, but the judge was given the option of ordering transportation or imprisonment for prisoners with sentences of more than 14 years. The law also specified how long prisoners must remain incarcerated before becoming eligible for conditional release on ticket-of-leave. This act legalized the ticket-of-leave system.

Prisoners released on a ticket-of-leave in England were subject to three general conditions:

1. The power of revoking or altering the license of a convict will most certainly be exercised in the case of misconduct.
2. If, therefore, he wishes to retain the privilege, which by his good behavior under penal discipline he has obtained, he must prove by his subsequent conduct that he is really worthy of Her Majesty's clemency.
3. To produce a forfeiture of the license, it is by no means necessary that the holder should be convicted of a new offense. If he associates with notoriously bad characters, leads an idle or dissolute life, or has no visible means of obtaining an honest livelihood, etc., it will be assumed that he is about to relapse into crime, and he will at once be apprehended and recommitted to prison under his original release.[8]

The British policy assumed that the prison program would be reformative, that the prisoners released on ticket-of-leave would have responded positively to prison training programs, and that those released would be adequately supervised. Such was not the case. The three years following the enactment of the Servitude Act saw an outbreak of serious crime attributed to a lack of supervision of the ticket-of-leave men. The British public thus came to regard the ticket-of-leave system as a menace to public safety and an absolute failure.

A series of prison riots in 1862, accompanied by another serious crime wave, again focused attention on prison administration and the ticket-of-leave system. A royal commission was appointed to investigate both areas. The commission's final report blamed poor training programs for the problems and gave the opinion that prisoners were released on ticket-of-leave without giving reliable evidence of their reformation. The royal commission's report resulted in policemen being given responsibility for supervising released prisoners. Later, a number of prisoners' aid societies, supported in part by the government, were established. These agencies aligned their methods of supervision with the method that had proven effective in Ireland.

Sir Walter Crofton and the Irish System

SIR WALTER CROFTON

An Irish prison reformer who established an early system of parole based on Alexander Maconochie's experiments with the mark system on Norfolk Island.

THE IRISH SYSTEM

Developed in Ireland by Sir Walter Crofton, the Irish system involved graduated levels of institutional control leading up to release under conditions similar to modern parole. The American reforms at Elmira Reformatory were partially based on the Irish system.

Sir Walter Crofton, who had studied Maconochie's innovations on Norfolk Island, became the administrator of the Irish Prison System in 1854, one year after the Penal Servitude Act was passed. He believed that the intent of the law was to make the penal institution more than just a house of incarceration. Crofton felt that prison programs should be directed more toward reformation and that tickets-of-leave should be awarded only to prisoners who had shown definite achievement and positive attitude changes.

Under Crofton's administration, the **Irish system** became renowned for its three classes of penal servitude: strict imprisonment, indeterminate sentence, and ticket-of-leave. Each prisoner's classification was determined by the marks he or she had earned for good conduct and achievement in industry and education, a concept borrowed from Maconochie's experience on Norfolk Island. So-called indeterminate sentences were employed, and institutional conditions for this class were made as near to normal as possible, the restraint exercised over the prisoner being no more than what was required to maintain order. The ticket-of-leave system was different from the one in England. The general written conditions of the Irish ticket were supplemented with instructions designed for closer supervision and control and thus resembled the conditions of parole in the United States today.

Ticket-of-leave men and women residing in rural areas were under police supervision, but those living in Dublin were supervised by a civilian employee called the *Inspector of Released Prisoners.* These persons had the responsibility of securing employment for the ticket-of-leave person, visiting the residence, and verifying employment. It was the Inspector of Released Prisoners or the designated local police officer to whom the ticket-of-leave man or woman periodically reported. The Irish system of ticket-of-leave had the confidence and support of the public and of convicted criminals.

DEVELOPMENT OF PAROLE IN THE UNITED STATES

INDETERMINATE SENTENCE

A sentence to imprisonment in which the duration is not fixed by the court but is left to be determined by some other authority (typically a parole board or other agency) after some minimum period is served. The basis of parole.

Three concepts underlie the development of parole in the United States: (1) a reduction in the length of incarceration as a reward for good conduct, (2) supervision of the parolee, and (3) imposition of the **indeterminate sentence.**

Release as a result of a reduction in the time of imprisonment was always accompanied by a written agreement in which the prisoner agreed to abide by the conditions specified by the authority authorizing the release. These documents would now be considered parole agreements. The agreement normally stipulated that any violation of the conditions would result in a return to the institution. The first legal recognition of shortening the term of imprisonment as a reward for good conduct in the United States was the 1817 "Good Time" law in New York.

Supervision of those released from prison was originally accomplished by volunteers. Members of prison societies were also among the first volunteer supervisors of adult offenders. The Philadelphia Society for Alleviating the Miseries of Public Prisons recognized the importance of caring for released prisoners as early as 1822. In

1851 the society appointed two agents to assist prisoners discharged from the Philadelphia County Prison and the penitentiary. The first public employees paid to assist released prisoners are believed to have been appointed by the State of Massachusetts in 1845.

Zebulon R. Brockway and the Elmira Reformatory

By 1865 American penal reformers were well aware of the reforms achieved by conditional release programs in the European prison systems, particularly in the Irish system. As a result, an indeterminate sentence law was passed in Michigan in 1869 at the instigation of **Zebulon R. Brockway.** (This law was subsequently declared unconstitutional, however.) Brockway later became superintendent of the newly constructed Elmira Reformatory in New York, and he succeeded in getting an indeterminate sentence law adopted in that state in 1876. The first parole system in the United States had come into being.

ZEBULON R. BROCKWAY

The American prison reformer who introduced modern correctional methods, including parole, to the Elmira Reformatory in New York in 1876.

The system established at Elmira included grading inmates on their conduct and achievement, compulsory education, and careful selection for parole. Volunteer citizens, known as *guardians,* supervised the parolees. A condition of parole was that the parolee report to the guardian the first day of each month. Written reports became required and were submitted to the institution after being signed by the parolee's employer and guardian.

Parole legislation spread much more rapidly than did indeterminate sentence legislation. By 1901, 20 states had parole statutes, but only 11 had indeterminate sentence laws. By 1944, however, every U.S. jurisdiction had adopted some form of parole release, and indeterminate sentencing had become the rule rather than the exception.[9]

PAROLE IN THE MODERN ERA

Parole continued to spread rapidly in the following decades. Parole was seen as a major adjunct to the rehabilitation philosophy that dominated American corrections in these years. This rehabilitative ideal, the so-called **medical model,** assumed that criminal behavior had its roots in environmental and psychosocial aspects of the offender's life and that corrections could, in fact, correct it. This meant that every offender would be dealt with on an individual basis in order to determine the causes of his or her criminal behavior. In their book *Reaffirming Rehabilitation,* Frank Cullen and Karen Gilbert wrote,

MEDICAL MODEL

The concept that given proper care and treatment, criminals can be changed into productive, law-abiding citizens. This approach suggests that people commit crimes due to influences beyond their control, such as poverty, injustice, and racism. Also called the *rehabilitation model.*

> Since the life experiences of one offender will inevitably differ from the next, the source of crime in any given instance could be expected to vary. This meant that every lawbreaker would have to be processed on a case-by-case basis. It would be necessary to study the offender closely and then to diagnose the particular criminogenic condition—perhaps the sordid influence of a slum home, perhaps a mental conflict—responsible for the person's waywardness. Once the cause of the problem was discovered, then the offender would be subjected to a treatment program specifically designed to eliminate the abnormality giving rise to the criminal inclinations in question.[10]

Under the old punitive model of corrections, the question asked was, What did he do? Under the medical model, the relevant questions were, Who is he? How did he come to be the person he is? What can be done to ameliorate his condition? One early commentator wrote,

> There can be no intelligent treatment until more is known than the fact that a man did a certain thing. It is as important to know why he did it. Diagnosis is as necessary in the treatment of badness as it is in the treatment of illness.[11]

If, in fact, prison staff could diagnose and treat "badness," then the lawbreaker should be released when "cured." The mechanisms for accomplishing this were the indeterminate sentence and parole. The theory held that the judge at the time of sentencing could tailor a sentence to the particular needs of the offender and provide, by means of an indeterminate sentence, an opportunity for release at the optimum time in the rehabilitative process. The release decision is thus shared between the court, which sets a minimum and a maximum period of incarceration, and the correctional system—typically a parole board. The parole board's responsibility is to determine, with the assistance of prison authorities, the optimal release moment—the time at which the inmate is most ready to reenter the community as a responsible citizen.

In 1933 the American Parole Association stated that fitness for release under parole supervision should be determined by the answers to the following questions:

> Has the institution accomplished all that it can for him; is the offender's state of mind and attitude toward his own difficulties and problems such that further residence [in prison] will be harmful or beneficial; does a suitable environment await him on the outside; can the beneficial effect already accomplished be retained if he is held longer to allow a more suitable environment to be developed?[12]

This philosophy assumes that correctional specialists have the ability to diagnose an offender's problems and develop a means of curing those problems. Because one cannot know at the time of diagnosis how long it will take to effect a cure, the indeterminate sentence makes it possible, in theory at least, to confine an offender as long as is necessary and to follow up that confinement with community supervision.

Changing Public Opinion

Although parole has generally drawn support from many sources and has a history of consensual acceptance, it has occasionally been subject to vigorous criticism and reexamination. In the early 20th century, particularly after World War I, parole administration came under attack. Critics claimed that parole was not fulfilling its promise. Antiparole groups believed that parole release was used primarily as a means of controlling inmates and that it failed to produce the desired lasting changes in their behavior and attitudes. This was a severe criticism at a time of increasing acceptance of the rehabilitative ideal with its emphasis on treatment and cure in criminal corrections.[13] Other critics of the system pointed out that release was granted after only a cursory review of the inmates' records and that paroling authorities had no criteria by which to measure rehabilitation and on which to base release decisions.

These criticisms led to two major changes in parole administration and organization. First, more emphasis was placed on postrelease supervision, and the number of parole conditions was increased. Second, there was a shift in parole authority from prison personnel to parole boards with independent authority and statewide jurisdiction.[14]

Attorney General's Survey of Release Procedures

By the mid-1930s the parole system's continuance as a viable part of the justice system again was being scrutinized. The *Attorney General's Survey of Release Procedures,* a monumental study of the correctional process, was established to review the efficacy of parole. The survey report stated,

> While there has never been a time when the functions and purpose of parole have been clearly understood, at no period has the entire institution been the object of so much controversy and attack or viewed with as much suspicion by the general public as it has been during the past four or five years.[15]

Mounting prison populations and rising recidivism rates aggravated the general uneasiness concerning early release via parole. Questions involving the value of rehabilitation as a goal of corrections arose, and without the philosophical underpinnings of reform and rehabilitation as purposes of punishment, parole has much less to offer the criminal justice system.

Both the concept of rehabilitation and the practice of parole survived the criticism, and in 1940 President Franklin D. Roosevelt declared, "We know from experience that parole, when it is honestly and expertly managed, provides better protection for society than does any other method of release from prison."[16]

Perhaps a bit optimistically, New York Parole Commissioner (later Director of the U.S. Bureau of Prisons) Sanford Bates, in a 1941 speech entitled "The Next Hundred Years," stated,

> Parole, as a method of release, will soon have become an indispensable part of this correctional process. We shall speak more accurately of *subjecting* a prisoner to parole than of *granting* him parole. We shall learn to speak of recidivists not as parole failures, but as unreformed inmates. We shall not shrink from the word, *parole,* as something involving weakness or venability, but shall recognize institution aftercare and supervision as a necessary sequel to a prison term. *Nevermore shall we talk about abolishing parole* any more than about abolishing police or commitment or discipline. [Emphasis added.][17]

Thus the medical model of corrections was born during the early years of the 20th century and grew into prominence in the late 1930s and early 1940s. This rehabilitative ideal viewed corrections as corrective and reformative, as opposed to punitive.

The years between World War II and 1970 saw the advent and development of classification systems, vocational training, academic training, group and individual therapy, conjugal visitation in some prisons, work release, and numerous other reforms. By 1967 (at the height of the reformative era), a Harris Poll of a nationwide sample found that 77 percent of the population believed that prisons should be *mainly corrective,* while only 11 percent believed they should be *mainly punitive.*[18] The belief that criminals could be changed if they were given the opportunity and if sufficient skills, funds, and personnel were available was the central philosophy of the rehabilitative model of corrections. Parole was once again considered a viable and necessary aspect of the American system of corrections.

A Philosophical Change

In the middle 1970s, with a suddenness remarkable in social change, there was a dramatic turnabout. Individualism, rehabilitation, sentence indeterminacy, and parole all seemed to fall from grace and, indeed, appeared to be on their way out.[19] By 1978 a Law Enforcement Assistance Administration publication stated, "One of the movements we are currently witnessing in the criminal justice field is the trend toward the establishment of **determinate** or 'fixed' **sentencing** of criminal offenders."[20]

DETERMINATE SENTENCE

A sentence to imprisonment for a fixed period of time as specified by statute; also known as *flat, fixed,* or *straight* sentence.

The correctional system's failure to reduce the steadily increasing crime rate and its obvious inability to reduce recidivism, rehabilitate offenders, or make predictive judgments about offenders' future behavior brought about public disillusionment, disappointment, and resentment. The pendulum began to swing, and by the late 1970s it seemed to have moved 180 degrees from the rehabilitative ideal to the "just deserts" approach to criminal correction.

JUST DESERTS

The concept that the goal of corrections should be to punish offenders because they deserve to be punished, and that punishment should be commensurate with the seriousness of the offense.

JUSTICE MODEL

The correctional practice based on the concept of just deserts. The justice model calls for fairness in criminal sentencing, in that all persons convicted of a like offense will receive a like sentence. Prisons are viewed as a place of even-handed punishment, not rehabilitation. This model of corrections relies on determinate sentencing and abolition of parole.

In contrast to the rehabilitative ideal, the **just deserts** or **justice model** denies the efficacy of rehabilitation and changes the focus of the system from the offender to the offense. The September 1977 issue of *Corrections Magazine*, for example, was devoted to the debate regarding the justice model and determinate sentencing. Even a brief review of the contents of this journal indicates that determinate sentencing and the abolition of parole were embraced by liberals and conservatives alike.

Prison reformers and police chiefs seemed to agree almost completely. Vietnam, Kent State, and Attica convinced many liberals that the state could not be trusted to administer rehabilitation in a just and humane manner. Popular movies such as *Clockwork Orange* and *One Flew Over the Cuckoo's Nest* depicted a less than benevolent government and the potential oppressiveness of deviant institutions. Furthermore, contemporary research such as the "Nothing Works" study by Robert Martinson found that few correctional treatment programs were successful in reducing recidivism or drug and alcohol readdiction, or in fostering personality and attitude change or community adjustment. Martinson concluded that "with few and isolated exceptions, the rehabilitative efforts which have been reported so far have had no appreciable effect on recidivism."[21] For liberals the indeterminate sentence was too vague and without due process protections to limit discretion. The just deserts approach was perceived as stressing fair punishment, which reduced the "more pernicious abuses that had arisen when state authorities were invested with the discretion 'to fit the punishment to the criminal.'"[22] For conservatives the indeterminate sentence, parole, and treatment programs were too "soft" on crime. They viewed determinate sentencing and the just deserts approach as consistent with their political and social agenda—a return to the "hard line" and a punishment-oriented correctional system.

The general aim of those favoring determinate sentencing was to abolish, or at least to tightly control, discretion. This included the discretion of the prosecutor to choose charges and plea-bargain, the discretion of judges to choose any sentence within a broad range of time, the discretion of prison administrators to decide what kind of treatment a prisoner needed in order to become law-abiding, and the discretion of parole boards to release or not to release prisoners without having to justify their decisions or render their decisions consistent. Determinate sentencing was the reformers' answer to this problem.[23] The proposals of the mid-1970s called for clear, certain, uniform penalties for all crimes, either through legislative action or the promulgation of guidelines to which prosecutors, judges, and parole boards would be required to adhere.

ORIGINS OF MODERN CONCEPTS OF DETERMINACY

Where did all this talk of determinate sentencing begin? John Irwin, an ex-prisoner and now an author and college professor, contends that inmates themselves, particularly inmates in California prisons in the 1960s, were the original advocates of determinacy.[24] California, Irwin believes, had the most indeterminate of all indeterminate sentencing structures and a parole board that was very "stingy with its favors." The situation in California prisons prompted the formation of a working group of the American Friends Service Committee, which produced the book *Struggle for Justice* in 1971.[25] In it the group denounced the very existence of U.S. prisons as well as the rehabilitative model of corrections, declaring coercion of prisoners for any purpose to be immoral. Although *Struggle for Justice* declared that all prisons should be shut down, it recognized that such a proposal was unrealistic. The book argued that the least that should be done was to repeal all indeterminate sentencing laws and design a system in which offenders convicted of similar crimes served roughly equal terms in prison.

David Greenberg, one of the primary authors of *Struggle for Justice,* was also a member of a group called the Committee for the Study of Incarceration. Together with Andrew von Hirsch, the committee's executive director, Greenberg persuaded the committee that the most important subject to study was not the conditions of incarceration but the haphazard and irrational manner in which offenders ended up—or did not end up—in prison, and the equally chaotic system of release. The committee's final report was published in 1976 under the title *Doing Justice: The Choice of Punishments.*[26] Written by von Hirsch, it was a heavily philosophical monograph whose thesis was that the motives underlying the treatment of criminal offenders at the time were all wrong.

The principal goals of the correctional system at the time were to rehabilitate and restrain offenders based on predictions of their future criminality or dangerousness. As a result the sanctions prescribed for particular crimes had little to do with the severity of criminal behavior. In fact, large numbers of widely disparate crimes were often punished with the same indeterminate term, with the actual setting of a release date left to parole boards, which judged particular offenders' potential rehabilitation and dangerousness.

Doing Justice pointed out that the goal of sentencing should be to punish offenders, that it is proper to punish the criminal because he or she "deserves" to be punished, and that each punishment should be commensurate with the gravity of the last offense or series of offenses. The committee recommended the adoption of a **presumptive sentence** for each crime or category of crimes, with the presumptive sentences graded according to the severity of the crime. The severity of the crime would be graded on two scales: the harm done by the offense, and the offender's culpability. The judgment of the degree of culpability would be based partly on the offender's prior record. The reasoning behind this was that a succession of criminal acts would imply calculation or deliberate defiance of the law, thus making the offender more culpable for the current offense.

PRESUMPTIVE SENTENCE

A statutorily determined sentence convicted offenders will presumably receive if convicted. Offenders convicted in a jurisdiction with presumptive sentences will be assessed this sentence unless mitigating or aggravating circumstances are found to exist.

Having proposed punishment as the main goal of sentencing, the committee then ruled out prison as the punishment for all but the most serious offenses, those in which bodily harm is threatened or done to the victim. The committee proposed alternatives such as periodic imprisonment, increased use of fines, and other lesser sanctions. In cases where prison is deemed necessary, the committee recommended that no prison sentence exceed five years except in some murder cases.

At about the same time *Doing Justice* was making the academic rounds, another determinate sentencing model was published in David Fogel's book: "*. . . We Are the Living Proof . . .*" *The Justice Model for Corrections.*[27] Fogel, former Minnesota Commissioner of Corrections, former head of the Illinois Law Enforcement Commission, and then a university professor, is considered by many the "father of determinate sentencing." As early as 1970 he had actively urged a narrowing of sentencing and parole discretion and had been among the most influential of the determinate sentencing advocates in the drafting of legislation in various states.

One of the main goals of Fogel's sentencing reforms was to humanize the internal operation of correctional institutions by extending much more freedom to inmates and "unhooking" their release date from their progress or participation in programs. He advocated abolishing parole boards and establishing "flat-time" sentencing—a single sentence for each class of felonies that could be altered slightly for aggravating or mitigating circumstances.[28]

In June 1977 then University of Chicago Law School Dean Norval Morris, speaking at a symposium on criminal sentencing, addressed the issues of determinacy and parole by asking, "Should the indeterminacy of parole discretion be preserved?" Morris responded to the six most common justifications for the parole board, rather than the judge, fixing the precise release date—that the parole board is able to

1. find the optimum moment for release;
2. provide an incentive for rehabilitation;
3. facilitate prison control and discipline;
4. share sentencing responsibility to maximize deterrence while reducing the time served;
5. control the size of the prison population; and
6. rectify unjust disparity in sentencing.[29]

Morris stated that the first justification—the parole board's ability to predict the optimum moment for release—has repeatedly failed to be proved empirically. The second justification, provision of an incentive for the offender's rehabilitation, has as its net effect the reliance on compulsory rehabilitation in the prison setting. "This type of coerced curing of crime is ineffective," Morris said, "and is wasteful of resources. We don't know enough to make that second purpose work." The third justification, facilitating prison control and discipline, is an important, latent, pragmatic justification of parole, but it is vulnerable to attack on grounds of injustice. The fourth claimed justification of parole is the sharing of sentencing responsibility between the court and the parole board in order to maximize deterrence. Although it is true that parole allows for judicial pronouncements of larger punishments than are in fact served, the charade, Morris claims, is so well known that court systems compensate for it. Judges and juries (where jury sentencing is applicable) routinely take parole laws into consideration when handing down sentences, knowing that, in most cases, the offender will serve less time than the sentence publicly announced. There still exists the question, however, of whether the parole experience has increased or reduced times served in the United States. The fifth justification, the ability to control the prison population, has occasionally been useful. Generally speaking, however, in times of community anxiety about crime and the pressures for law and order, there has been great pressure on parole boards to be more conservative in granting parole. When this has occurred, parole boards, rather than attempting to solve the problem by releasing more prisoners, have compounded the problem by tightening requirements for parole. To the last claimed justification of parole, that of rectifying unjust sentencing disparities, Morris responds as follows:

> In Illinois, and I believe the same is true in many states, crime for crime and criminal for criminal, sentences imposed by courts in Chicago are subsequently less severe than those imposed in downstate, small-town, and rural areas. The Illinois Parole Board, not incorrectly, in my view, exercises its releasing discretion so as to minimize the grosser disparities—it moves toward a regression to the mean.[30]

A question arises, however: Should we not develop other mechanisms for serving that purpose in place of parole? Morris believes we should, and he views the ultimate abolition of parole as inevitable. What alternatives are available, and what problems do these alternatives pose?

The trend of the 1978 symposium and of the public attitude prevalent at the time seemed inevitably to point to increasing determinacy in sentencing and ultimately to abolishing parole as a release mechanism. However, many theorists of the sentence reform movement urged caution before abolishing parole outright and instituting "real time" sentences in its place. In *The Question of Parole,* Andrew von Hirsch and Kathleen Hanrahan warned:

> Our culture has historically thought of prison time in huge quantities, and this has made it harder to justify the more modest actual confinements meted out by parole boards. The long-run objective should be the creation of a system that speaks in terms of moderate real sentences and banishes the long, fictional prison terms—through a gradual, slow phase-out of parole release.[31]

Their message was not heeded. Between 1976 and 1982 at least 15 states passed determinate sentencing legislation. Other states increased penalties and passed mandatory sentencing and career criminal laws. One observer wrote, "Even though no model came to predominate, the impact on parole, especially discretionary parole release, was dramatic."[32] In some states both parole release and postrelease supervision were abandoned. In other states parole release was abandoned but supervision was retained. In still other states parole guidelines were established to reduce and structure release decision making.

Parole, however, did not disappear from the correctional scene. Indeed, in most states today, a parole board or some similar body with a different name retains the power to alter the amount of time served in prison by releasing prisoners to community supervision before the completion of the maximum sentence.[33] The legislature has limited the releasing power of the parole board in some jurisdictions by requiring that prisoners serve a flat minimum or some proportion of the maximum sentence before becoming eligible for parole. In other jurisdictions parole board discretion is extensive—relatively unconstrained by law or not constrained at all.

The *American Corrections Association's Standards* continues to consider parole the preferred release mechanism and to recommend that such power be given to

> [a] single authority provided by statute which has parole decision-making power with respect to all offenders convicted of a felony who are sentenced to a term of imprisonment and are eligible for discretionary parole.[34]

Parole boards in most jurisdictions continue to handle revocations, and in some jurisdictions they also handle good-time decisions. Discretionary paroling may continue in these jurisdictions to a limited extent for persons sentenced to life imprisonment, persons sentenced before the current structure went into effect, or for youthful offenders.

A REPRIEVE AND A NEW ROLE FOR PAROLE

The abolition of discretionary parole release did not prove to be the panacea some had expected. During the 1970s and 1980s the nation's prison population grew dramatically, partly fueled by the reduction in parole discretion and the harsher sentences that came with determinate and mandatory sentencing. In 1970 there were 196,429 prisoners in state and federal prisons, with the rate of incarceration at 96 per 100,000. By 1980 the rate of incarceration had risen to 139 per 100,000. By June 30, 1990, the U.S. prison population had reached 755,425, and the incarceration rate was 289 per 100,000—a 300 percent increase since 1970. By mid-year 1996 the U.S. prison population had risen to 1,076,625 with an incarceration rate of 394.[35] Figure 8.1 documents this trend.

In some jurisdictions the rapid increase in prison populations brought about a reappraisal of the decision to abolish parole. Since 1976 Maine has had to build four new prisons to handle the increased population resulting from parole abolition. Other states have faced similar problems. Idaho adopted a hybrid scheme that permitted judges to impose either fixed sentences with no parole eligibility or indeterminate sentences, with the parole board setting release dates.[36] The U.S. Parole Commission, scheduled to be phased out by 1992, was given an extension until 1997. In 1985 Colorado reinstated parole, six years after abolition. North Carolina, which had severely limited the use of parole, has since allowed more discretion.

Prison Population Control

Parole boards have always been the "back doorkeeper" of America's prisons, often serving as the operators of safety valves to relieve crowded institutions.[37] Although this function is not consistent with the philosophy of parole as a tool of rehabilitation, and most paroling authorities do not believe that the management of prison populations is (or should be) their primary responsibility, it has become de facto if not a de jure function.[38] Recent years, however, have witnessed an institutionalization of this function. In a report for the National Institute of Corrections, Peggy Burke noted,

> There is no longer any question of whether paroling authorities will become involved in population issues, but rather . . . when.[39]

Some states have given legislative authority and direction to their parole boards to control prison populations. Others have done so through informal agreements among the governor, the director of corrections, and the parole board. Boards in states such as Michigan, Georgia, and Texas have become actively involved in prison population management out of necessity; prison populations in those states had risen to levels that threatened the correctional authorities' ability to maintain control of their institutions. In Georgia the governor cited an "atmosphere of tension, and potentially explosive violence."[40] Federal court orders established "caps" on the prison populations in Texas and Michigan. Through a variety of formal and informal methods, parole boards in each of these jurisdictions have been utilized in efforts to reduce and maintain the prison population, with varying and arguable degrees of success.

Most authorities agree, however, that it is not feasible, in the long term, to control prison populations by parole board action. The reductions achieved in those states that so use their paroling power are, at best, temporary—and have often achieved those results to the detriment of effective postrelease supervision due to escalating caseloads. Rhine, Smith, and Jackson concluded that where parole boards are used as

Figure 8.1 **STATE AND FEDERAL PRISON POPULATION, 1980–1994**

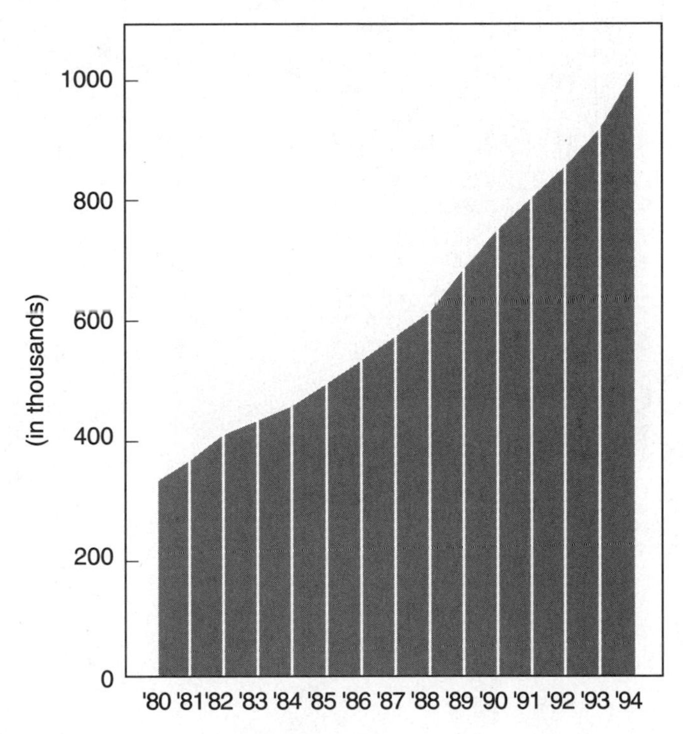

Source: Bureau of Justice Statistics

the "back door" for overcrowded prisons, the population crisis is often simply transferred from the institutional component of corrections to the community component. They report that many jurisdictions have increased and expanded community correctional facilities—such as halfway houses, work release centers, house arrest–electronic monitoring, and intensive supervision—to monitor the offenders who are granted early release. Furthermore, in some states the continuing escalation in prison populations has had another, albeit unanticipated effect on the ability of parole officers to revoke parole for anything other than serious criminal violations. In several states parole officers have experienced difficulty in revoking parolees for technical violations of the conditions of supervision, even when there are indications of deteriorating behavior on the part of the parolee.

POSTRELEASE SUPERVISION

Postrelease supervision has been maintained in most jurisdictions, even in states that have effectively abolished the parole board's discretion in release decisions. Only a very few jurisdictions have abolished postrelease supervision altogether. Others have limited postrelease supervision to a short period after release, generally one to three years. Kevin Krajick points out that in Maine and Connecticut many judges, unhappy with the abolition of postrelease supervision, began sentencing large numbers

Table 8.1 **PAROLEES UNDER ACTIVE SUPERVISION ON 1/1/97**

		PERCENTAGE OF TOTAL UNDER SUPERVISION							
		GENDER		RACE					
Parole	Total Under Supv.	Male	Female	Black	White	Asian/Pac. Is.	Nat. Am./AK	Other	Hispanic Ethnicity
Alabama	3,123								
Arizona	4,289	90.0	10.0	15.9	45.6	0.2	4.1	34.2	33.0
Arkansas	5,143	88.1	11.9	52.3	47.3	0.1	0.1	0.3	0.2
California	100,935	90.3	9.7	26.9	69.2	1.0	0.7	2.3	39.2
Colorado	2,311	91.0	9.0	21.7	75.5	0.3	2.0	0.5	25.2
Connecticut	1,145	92.8	7.2	46.1	26.4	0.4	0.2	26.9	26.9
Dist. of Col.	5,132	93.0	7.0	97.0	2.0	0.0	0.0	1.0	
Florida	8,240	92.2	7.8	54.8	42.4	0.0	0.0	2.8	6.9
Georgia	21,146	90.7	9.3	65.2	34.8	0.0	0.0	0.0	
Hawaii	1,464	91.7	8.3						
Idaho	714	90.2	9.8						
Illinois	30,336	91.9	8.1	68.9	23.2	0.1	0.1	7.6	7.6
Indiana	3,575	93.8	6.2						
Iowa	2,131	88.6	11.4	15.8	80.5	0.3	0.8	2.6	2.6
Kansas	4,494	88.6	11.4	36.0	61.7	0.6	1.6	0.1	5.3
Kentucky	4,621								
Louisiana	19,267	92.7	7.3	73.8	25.9	0.2	0.0	0.1	0.1
Maine	57	96.5	3.5						
Maryland	10,469	91.0	9.0	75.3	24.3	0.2	0.1	0.1	
Massachusetts	4,180	92.0	8.0	23.0	55.0	0.9	0.1	21.0	21.0
Michigan	12,713								
Minnesota	444	94.1	5.9	2.9	84.9	0.0	11.0	1.1	3.2
Mississippi	1,767	91.0	9.0	69.6	29.2	0.0	0.0	1.2	
Missouri	9,616	90.4	9.6	39.7	59.9	0.0	0.0	0.5	
Montana	881	91.0	9.0						
Nebraska	717	88.3	11.7	25.4	71.5	0.1	2.8	0.1	6.0
Nevada	3,216	91.1	8.9	29.9	58.2	0.5	1.3	10.1	8.9
New Hampshire	1,066	75.0	25.0	7.0	68.3	3.0	0.0	21.7	21.7
New Jersey	19,059	91.6	8.4	59.9	39.9	0.1	0.0	0.0	19.5
New Mexico	1,426	83.0	17.0	9.3	83.3	0.0	5.6	1.8	56.0
New York	46,411	91.6	8.4	50.5	15.3	0.0	0.0	34.1	32.3
North Carolina	11,540	90.4	9.6	63.2	33.3	0.2	2.2	1.1	
North Dakota	103	91.3	8.7	1.9	85.4	0.0	12.6	0.0	3.9
Ohio	6,101	90.9	9.1	58.3	39.9	0.1	0.1	1.6	1.5
Oregon	10,281	88.7	11.3	12.8	76.3	0.7	1.8	8.4	8.3
Rhode Island	960								
South Carolina	4,408	90.2	9.8	69.0	30.3	0.0	0.0	0.7	
South Dakota	725	87.3	12.7	4.3	81.2	0.0	14.5	0.0	1.4
Tennessee	8,934	90.6	9.4	55.1	40.9	0.5	0.0	3.6	
Texas	79,944	86.7	13.3	44.6	33.4	0.1	0.1	21.9	21.1
Utah	3,091	90.8	9.2	7.5	86.1	1.6	3.0	1.8	18.2
Vermont	635	92.6	7.4	1.6	98.4	0.0	0.0	0.0	
Virginia	9,918	88.0	12.0	64.0	35.3	0.2	0.0	0.5	0.5
West Virginia	831	91.9	8.1	15.0	85.0	0.0	0.0	0.0	0.0
Wisconsin	7,499	92.4	7.6	46.3	47.6	0.5	2.4	3.2	6.1
Wyoming	414	78.0	22.0	3.6	68.4	0.0	3.1	24.9	22.2
Federal	51,167	85.2	14.8	26.8	68.3	1.8	1.3	1.7	0.9
Total & Average	**526,639**	**89.9**	**10.1**	**37.9**	**53.5**	**0.4**	**1.9**	**6.3**	**13.8**
Percentage of Total		**89.6**	**10.4**	**44.5**	**45.5**	**0.5**	**0.6**	**8.9**	**20.1**

Source: C. Camp and George Camp, *The Correctional Yearbook–1997* (South Salem, New York: Criminal Justice Institute, 1997).

of prisoners to *split sentences*—that is, terms of jail or imprisonment to be followed by probation—in an effort to assure that inmates would not be released without some kind of supervision.[41] In Maine the proportion of split sentences has doubled since the abolition of parole supervision.

This means of circumventing the legislation was forecast by former U.S. Parole Board Chairman Maurice Sigler in 1975 when he spoke of the criminal justice system as having "hydraulic properties."[42] Sigler stated that "when discretion is artificially compressed at one level of the system, it is increased at another level in order that the decision makers, be they policemen, prosecutors, judges, or parole boards, are capable of individualizing justice and reducing injustice caused by ill-conceived laws."[43] Sigler spoke of a state that had introduced a mandatory sentence for nighttime burglary. Within the next year the filings by police and prosecutors for daytime burglary had increased by 90 percent, and nighttime burglary had all but disappeared. Had the burglars, in response to the new legislation, changed their nocturnal habits, or were the police and prosecutors maintaining their discretion by filing the cases as daytime burglary? The danger in such a situation is that the discretion, formerly out in the open, becomes less visible and not subject to scrutiny.

The supervision component was retained in other states that abolished parole by allowing release dates to be determined by *good-time laws*, with supervision for the period of the sentence. At the federal level the Sentencing Reform Act (1987), which implemented sentencing guidelines and paved the way for the abolition of parole, created a new form of postrelease supervision, **supervised release.** Courts may impose a term of supervised release as part of a sentence that includes imprisonment at the time of the initial sentencing. Unlike parole, supervised release does not replace a portion of the sentence of imprisonment. Rather, it orders supervision in addition to any term of imprisonment. The conditions of supervised release are the same as those of probation or parole.[44] Table 8.1 illustrates the 1995 status of parole supervision in the United States.

GOOD-TIME POLICIES

Most of the new laws have retained policies for **good time,** which award prisoners days off their minimum or maximum terms for maintaining good behavior or participating in various prison activities or programs. The amount of good time that can be accrued varies widely among states, ranging from 5 days to more than 30 days per month off an inmate's time in prison. Because a good-time policy can greatly reduce sentenced terms, it can be a real incentive for cooperative behavior.

GOOD TIME (OR GAIN TIME)

Reduction in sentence for institutional good conduct.

Good-time policies are written into many states' statutes, but they may also be nonstatutory, systemwide correctional policies. Good time is typically awarded and administered by a state's department of corrections or by individual prison wardens. Typically this credit is automatically awarded and subtracted from a prisoner's sentenced term at the time of prison entry and then rescinded in whole or in part for unsatisfactory behavior. In Oregon good-behavior credit is subtracted from the maximum sentence and does not affect a prisoner's parole eligibility date or actual time served unless the prisoner is not paroled and serves the maximum term. More typically, however, the minimum sentence is reduced by good time, so that good-time policies are a significant element in prison term length. This is particularly true in states that have eliminated discretionary parole release.

A few states award good-time credit in ways that do not reduce sentence length. In New Hampshire, for example, a number of disciplinary days are automatically added to the minimum term, and it is from this number that good-behavior days are subtracted. If the prisoner accrues all of his or her good time, the disciplinary days will cancel out, and the parole eligibility date will occur, as scheduled, on the completion of the minimum sentence. Otherwise the prisoner is penalized by a delay in the eligibility date.

Good-time reductions based on prisoners' positive actions are in effect in most states and the federal system. These reductions result from participating in various programs (such as work, school, rehabilitative counseling, medical research, or blood donation) or from meritorious conduct (including success under minimum security). In January 1983 the California Department of Corrections eliminated automatic time off for good behavior; prisoners sentenced after that date must earn all their good-time credit through work or school participation.

SUMMARY

Parole is different from other forms of release and community supervision, but the term *parole* is often used interchangeably with *probation, pardon,* and *mandatory release.* The misunderstanding and misapprehensions about parole today are to some extent due to this semantic confusion.

Parole has origins in the work of penal reformers in Germany, Spain, France, and on Norfolk Island in the early decades of the 19th century. The Norfolk Island experiments with ticket-of-leave and the mark system by a former British naval officer, Alexander Maconochie, constitute the origins of parole as we know it in the United States. Walter Crofton, head of the Irish prison system, studied Maconochie's work on Norfolk Island and implemented his ideas in Ireland. Crofton's efforts were noticed by the U.S. prison reformer Zebulon R. Brockway, and Brockway adopted them in 1876 at the Elmira Reformatory in New York. This program was the first to use parole in the United States.

Although the late 1990s find the criminal justice system embroiled in controversy, engaged in self-examination, and subjected to scrutiny by the public and the courts, the issues involved—prison overcrowding, the efficacy of probation and parole, sentencing disparity, parole release decision making, and indeed, the very continued existence of parole—are not new, and neither are the proposed solutions. The inertia of the criminal justice system is as great as is its failure to learn the lessons of history.

More than a century ago the leading penologists of the time met in Cincinnati to form the National Prison Association, now the American Correctional Association. The main objective of that first meeting in 1870 was to attempt to resolve the conflict between those who advocated the punishment-centered Pennsylvania and Auburn prison systems and those who advocated a progressive new system recently imported from Ireland. The new system, which appealed to progressive prison administrators, had three main factors: trade training, the indeterminate sentence, and parole.

What emerged was the remarkable "Declaration of Principles," a blueprint for the future of U.S. corrections. The concepts of vocational training, indeterminate sentencing, and parole were established and for the most part embraced by the leadership of the newly emerging discipline of corrections. Since that time these same issues have been scrutinized, rejected, embraced, modified, codified, outlawed, and reincarnated under new labels. Over a period of 50 years presidential commissions have alternatively recommended the extension of parole and indeterminacy of sentencing and the outright abolition of the same. The optimal solution is not yet at hand. History has taught us that all too often the unanticipated and unintended consequences of reform have aggravated rather than mitigated the problems they sought to solve. Prudence in reform efforts is advisable, and such lessons as can be learned from past efforts should be carefully evaluated.

ENDNOTES

1. Claire Wilcox, *Theory of Parole* (1927), 20; quoted in *Attorney General's Survey of Release Procedures: Parole,* vol. 4 (Washington, D.C.: U.S. Department of Justice, 1939).
2. Warren F. Spaulding, *Proceedings,* American Prison Association (1916), 548.
3. Justin Miller, "Evils of Confusion between Pardon and Parole," *Proceedings,* American Prison Association, 1932.
4. *Attorney General's Survey,* 6.
5. Quoted in Fredrick H. Wines, *Punishment and Reformation* (Crowell, 1895), 219.
6. Wines, *Punishment and Reformation,* 194.
7. Wines, *Punishment and Reformation,* 195.
8. Parker, *Parole: Origins, Development, Current Practices, and Statutes* (American Correctional Association, Corrections—Parole-MDT-Project, resource document no. 1, 1972).
9. The historical discussions in this chapter rely on three documents: *Attorney General's Survey;* Charles L. Whitehead, *Adult Parole in Texas,* unpublished M.A. thesis (Huntsville, Tex.: Sam Houston State University, May 1975); and Robert Hughes, *The Fatal Shore: The Epic of Australia's Founding* (New York: Vintage, 1986).
10. Francis T. Cullen and Karen E. Gilbert, *Reaffirming Rehabilitation* (Cincinnati: Anderson, 1982), 76.
11. Warren F. Spaulding, "The Treatment of Crime—Past, Present, and Future," *Journal of the American Institute of Criminal Law and Criminology* 3 (May 1912), 378.
12. Cited in Edwin H. Sutherland, Donald R. Cressey, and David F. Luckenbill, *Principles of Criminology,* 11th ed. (Dix Hills, N.J.: General Hall, 1992), 560.
13. Lawrence F. Travis III and Vincent O'Leary, *Changes in Sentencing and Parole Decision Making, 1976–1978* (Washington, D.C.: National Institute of Corrections, 1979)—a publication of the National Parole Institutes and Parole Policy Seminars.
14. Travis and O'Leary, *Changes in Sentencing and Parole,* 6.
15. *Attorney General's Survey.*
16. Quoted by Sanford Bates in his speech, "The Next Hundred Years," at the Thirty-Fifth Annual Conference of the National Probation Association, Atlantic City, N.J., 1941. Sanford Bates, then Commissioner for Parole for the State of New York, became the Director of the United States Bureau of Prisons. Bates reorganized the Bureau of Prisons, introduced psychologists and psychiatrists into the system, and is often recognized as the father of "the new prison."
17. Bates, "The Next Hundred Years."
18. "Harris Poll," *Los Angeles Times,* August 14, 1967.
19. National Advisory Commission on Criminal Justice Standards and Goals, *A National Strategy to Reduce Crime* (Washington, D.C.: Law Enforcement Assistance Administration, 1973).
20. National Advisory Commission on Criminal Justice Standards and Goals, *A National Strategy to Reduce Crime.*
21. Robert Martinson, "What Works? Questions and Answers About Prison Reform," *Public Interest* (Spring 1974), 25.

22. Cullen and Gilbert, *Reaffirming Rehabilitation,* xxvii.

23. David B. Griswold and Michael D. Wiatrowski, "The Emergence of Determinate Sentencing," *Federal Probation* (June 1983).

24. Reported in Michael S. Serrill, "Determinate Sentencing: The History, the Theory, the Debate," *Corrections Magazine* (September 1977). Much of the material on the history of the determinate sentencing movement drew liberally from this excellent paper.

25. American Friends Service Committee, *Struggle for Justice* (Hill and Wang, 1971).

26. Andrew von Hirsch, *Doing Justice: The Choice of Punishments* (Hill and Wang, 1976).

27. David Fogel, *". . . We Are the Living Proof . . ." The Justice Model for Corrections,* 2nd ed. (Cincinnati: Anderson, 1979).

28. Fogel, *The Justice Model for Corrections.*

29. Cited in Edward R. Rhine, William Smith, and Ronald W. Jackson, *Paroling Authorities: Recent History and Current Practice* (Laurel, Md.: American Correctional Association, 1991), 25.

30. "Conference Takes a Hard Look at Corrections," *Corrections Magazine* (September 1977), 67.

31. Andrew von Hirsch and Kathleen Hanrahan, *The Questions of Parole: Retention, Reform, or Abolition* (Cambridge, Mass.: Ballinger, 1981), 81.

32. Rhine, Smith, and Jackson, *Paroling Authorities,* 25.

33. After abolishing parole, some states were faced with burgeoning prison populations and were forced to reintroduce parole—usually by another name. California abolished parole and then introduced the Board of Prison Terms—with almost identical responsibilities as the former parole board. Florida abolished the Parole Commission and replaced it soon after with a Controlled Release Authority.

34. Rhine, Smith, and Jackson, *Paroling Authorities,* 26.

35. Bureau of Justice Statistics, "Prisoners in 1996," *Bulletin,* June 1997.

36. A. Keith Bottomley, "Parole in Transition: A Comparative Study of Origins, Developments, and Prospects for the 1990s." In Michael Tonry and Norval Morris, eds., *Crime and Justice: View of Research,* vol. 12 (Chicago: University of Chicago Press, 1990), 342.

37. Bottomley, "Parole in Transition," 27.

38. Rhine, Smith, and Jackson, *Paroling Authorities,* 96. Reporting on the ACA Parole Task Force survey, they stated, "Regardless of the pressure to release, most parole board chairs surveyed by the Task Force do not believe that the management of prison population levels should be an important responsibility of parole boards."

39. Peggy Burke, *Current Issues in Parole Decision Making: Understanding the Past, Shaping the Future* (Washington, D.C.: National Institute of Corrections, 1988), 31–32.

40. Cited in Rhine, Smith, and Jackson, *Paroling Authorities,* 97–98.

41. Kevin Krajick, "Abolishing Parole: An Idea Whose Time Has Passed," *Corrections Magazine* (June 1983).

42. Maurice Sigler, "Abolish Parole?" in a speech at Law Day Convocation, Culver-Stockton College, Canton, Missouri, May 1975.

43. Sigler, "Abolish Parole?"

44. 18 U.S. C. 3583 (e) (3).

DISCUSSION QUESTIONS

1. Define *parole* and *pardon* and distinguish between them.
2. Distinguish between *parole, mandatory release,* and *probation.*
3. Discuss the founders of parole and their contributions.
4. What is the mark system, and what is its relationship to the origins of parole?
5. What was a ticket-of-leave, and what is its relationship to the origins of parole?
6. What was transportation? What is the connection between transportation and parole?
7. What were the five stages in Maconochie's mark system? How did his system differ from the English practice of ticket-of-leave?
8. How did parole develop in the United States? Be sure to include discussions of the Irish system, Zebulon Brockway, the Elmira Reformatory, and the indeterminate sentence in your explanation.
9. Discuss the medical model of corrections. How do parole and indeterminacy relate to this model?
10. Why did the medical model fall out of favor? What factors were associated with this phenomenon?
11. What is the justice model of corrections? What factors were associated with its emergence in the 1970s?
12. What happened to parole under the justice model? Why?
13. How and why did parole acquire a new role in the 1980s and 1990s? What is that role? How do you feel about this new role?

Alexander Maconochie and the Origins of Parole

Alexander Maconochie wanted to shift the focus of penology from punishment to reform. Of course the state could and must punish crime, but punishment on its own, he argued, was a socially empty act without checks built into it: "Our penal science is . . . without precise rule, a mere balancing between conflicting impulses, severity for the supposed good of society on one hand, and leniency for the supposed good of the criminal on the other, in both frequently running into error." He saw no sense in punishing a criminal for his past while not training him with incentives for his future.

Because it was fixated on punishment alone, the old system had produced mainly crushed, resentful, and embittered men and women in whom the spark of enterprise and hope was dead, Maconochie argued. Exemplary punishment was only vindictive; it ran wild, degrading both convict and jailer. Terms like *mercy* and *remission of punishment* were to be dropped. "Let us offer our prisoners, not favors, but *rights,* on fixed and unalterable conditions."

But how was this to be done? How the corrosion of despair, the leakage of human possibility to be stopped? Maconochie never claimed to be an original penal thinker, but he had what more original men like Jeremy Bentham lacked—firsthand experience of prison and humane understanding of its inmates. The basic idea for his system had first been raised by the Cambridge theologian William Paley in his *Moral and Political Philosophy* (1785). In this early Utilitarian text, Paley suggested that the punishment of criminals should be measured not by raw time but by work "in order both to excite industry, and to render it more voluntary."

Within a few years this idea of punishment by task and not by time was rooted in America. It found another advocate in Richard Whately, soon to be appointed Archbishop of Dublin. In the *London Review* in 1829 Whately urged that convicts be sentenced to give the state a measurable amount of labor in expiation of their sins so that the quicker and better they worked, the sooner they would be free: "With each additional step they took on the treadmill they would be walking out of prison—by each additional cut of the spade they would be cutting a way to return to society."

Such ideas reached the Quaker missionaries James Backhouse and George Walker and went from them to Maconochie. They too advocated task rather than time punishment, arguing that as most convicts were morally childish, the penal reformer might take a cue from the discipline of "enlightened" schools, which offered rewards for good conduct rather than punishment for bad. At each monthly muster the diligent convict would get a "ticket," and the lazy would lose one or more; getting three tickets would shorten one's sentence by a month.

Such ideas of discipline by the carrot, not the stick, were the germ of Alexander Maconochie's mark system. Maconochie argued that sentences should be indefinite—no more stretches of 7, 10, 14 years or life. Instead the convicts would have to earn a certain number of marks, or credits for good behavior and hard work, before they got free. Six thousand marks would be the equivalent of a seven-year sentence; seven thousand would correspond to ten years, and ten thousand to life. They would buy their way out of prison with these marks. To buy, they must save.

Hence the length of sentence was, within limits, up to the convict. Marks could be exchanged for either goods or time. The prisoner could use marks to buy luxuries from the jail administration—extra food, tobacco, clothing, and the like. They were "just wages, and will equally stimulate to care, exertion, economy, and fidelity." Maconochie hoped to abolish rations, "whose moral effect is always bad, by taking the care of a man's maintenance out of his own hands." Ideally the convict would pay for everything beyond a bare subsistence diet of bread and water with the marks he earned.

Maconochie believed his mark system would be objective. As things stood, prisoners were at the mercy of their overseers for "indulgences," which "corrupt and debilitate the mind." Official freedom to remit sentences led the convicts to lie and curry favor. It made them servile or evasive, and usually both. Only measurable actions could measure reform:

> The term "remission of sentence" should be banished. . . . There should, in truth, be none whatever; but the duration of the sentences being made measurable by conduct under them, and not by time at all . . . no power should anywhere even exist in a subordinate authority to remit a fraction of it; but on the other hand, there should not be less certainty in the result of good conduct. The fate of every man should be placed unreservedly in his own hands. . . . There should be no favour anywhere.

As soon as a convict entered the system, then, he would begin with a short harsh stretch of confinement with hard labor and religious instruction. This was a moral aperient, punishment for the past.

The next phase, rehabilitation for the future, would begin with his advance through the stages of the mark system, where everything he had was bought with his labor and obedience, translated into marks and entered in the commandant's incorruptible ledgers. As the convict's behavior improved and the moral lesson of the mark system—nothing for nothing—sank in, so his environment altered by stages: first, solitary or separate imprisonment; then, "social labor" through the day and separate confinement at night; next, "social treatment both day and night"; and so on. He rose from one grade to the next automatically, with no interference from commandant or magistrates, depending on his total credit of marks. Some, of course, would slide back, losing marks or wasting them, which only reinforced the metaphor of real life. However, just as there would be no favors under Maconochie's system, so the only punishment would be the loss of marks—the mild, inescapable, all-seeing accountancy that drew its attentive parallels between time and money, units of labor and moral worth.

Once the prisoner was trained to see the relation between morality and self-interest, he stood ready for the third stage of the mark system: group therapy. Maconochie wanted to put "developed" prisoners in groups of six. They would work together and mess together. Each man in the group would be responsible for the marks of others as well as his own. If one backslid and lost marks, all would. In this way the prisoners would learn mutual dependence and social responsibility.

Nobody in England or America, let alone penal Australia, had tried such therapies on convicts before. This idea of prison as a moral hospital would not win full acceptance until well into the 20th century. The details of Maconochie's system—that prisoners should have direct access to the commandant through an ombudsman, for instance, or that officials should take a personal interest in individual convicts—were a century ahead of their time.

9

THE PAROLE BOARD AND PAROLE SELECTION

What You Will Learn in This Chapter

In this chapter we examine the qualities of an effective parole system. We also discuss the parole selection process, looking at traditional parole decision making as well as selection methods that rely on objective measures of potential risk. Particular attention is paid to the question of due process in parole selection, with an emphasis on appellate court decisions addressing the issue.

KEY TERMS

Paroling authority
Institutional model of organization
Autonomous model of organization
Consolidation model of organization
Parole guidelines
Graduated release
Parole eligibility
Salient Factor Score
Guiding principles
Grace or privilege theory
Continuing custody theory
Parens patriae
Liberty interest

INTRODUCTION

The first element of parole is the decision by a duly constituted **paroling authority** to determine the portion of the offender's sentence that he or she must complete before being released to complete the sentence outside the institution. This authority is granted to an executive-branch agency, a parole board (or parole commission) that is charged with administering parole policy. The board must work within the statutes of the particular jurisdiction but may adopt its own rules and regulations insofar as they do not conflict with the statutes. The scope of the board's authority and the consequences of its actions are enormous. No other part of the criminal justice system concentrates such power in the hands of so few.[1]

PAROLING AUTHORITY

An administrative body (usually 3–19 members) empowered to decide whether inmates shall be conditionally released from prison before the completion of their sentence, to revoke parole, and to discharge from parole those who have satisfactorily completed their terms.

THE PAROLE BOARD

Parole boards have two basic functions: to select prisoners for parole and to determine when revocation and return to prison is necessary. In a minority of states the parole board also supervises and provides continuing control of parolees in the community. In most jurisdictions, however, parolees are supervised by parole officers under the supervision of the department of corrections. These officers enforce the conditions of parole established by the parole board. Table 9.1 shows which agency provides probation and parole supervision in each state and the federal government.

ELEMENTS OF AN EFFECTIVE PAROLE SYSTEM

Parole board power and responsibility vary widely, but all effective parole systems have certain characteristics. The American Correctional Association lists the essential elements of an effective parole system:

1. Flexibility in sentencing and parole laws
2. A qualified parole board
3. A qualified parole staff
4. Freedom from political or improper influences
5. Workable position in the governmental administrative structure
6. Proper procedures
7. Prerelease preparation within the institution

TABLE 9.1 **PROBATION AND PAROLE SUPERVISION LOCATION BY STATE**

State	Function	State Agency	Local Agency	Judicial (J) or Executive (E) Branch
AL	Parole and Probation	Board of Pardons and Paroles		E
AK	Parole and Probation	Department of Corrections		E
AR	Parole	Department of Corrections		E
	Probation	Department of Community Punishment		E
AZ	Parole	Department of Corrections		E
	Probation	Administrative Office of the Courts	Court	J
CA	Parole	Department of Corrections		E
	Probation		Court	J
CO	Parole	Department of Corrections		E
	Probation		Court	J
CT	Parole	Parole Board		E
	Probation	Judicial Dept.		J
DE	Parole and Probation	Department of Corrections		E
DC	Parole	Parole Board		E
	Probation	Court		J
FL	Parole and Probation	Department of Corrections		E
GA	Parole	Parole Board		E
	Probation	Department of Corrections		E
HI	Parole	Parole Board		E
	Probation	Judiciary		J
IA	Parole and Probation		Judicial Districts	E
ID	Parole and Probation	Department of Corrections		E
IL	Parole	Department of Corrections		E
	Probation		Judicial Circuits	J
IN	Parole	Department of Corrections		E
	Probation		County Courts	J
KS	Parole	Department of Corrections		E
	Probation		Judicial Districts	J
KY	Parole and Probation	Department of Corrections		E
LA	Parole and Probation	Department of Public Safety and Corrections		E
ME	Parole and Probation	Department of Corrections		E
MD	Parole and Probation	Department of Public Safety and Correctional Services		E
MA	Parole	Parole Board		E
	Probation	Judicial Branch		J
MI	Parole and Probation	Department of Corrections		E
MN	Parole and Probation	Department of Corrections	Counties	E

TABLE 9.1 (***Continued***)

State	Function	State Agency	Local Agency	Judicial (J) or Executive (E) Branch
MS	Parole and Probation	Department of Corrections		E
MO	Parole and Probation	Department of Corrections		E
MT	Parole and Probation	Department of Corrections		E
NC	Parole and Probation	Department of Corrections		E
ND	Parole and Probation	Department of Corrections		E
NE	Parole	Department of Corrections		E
	Probation	Court		J
NH	Parole and Probation	Department of Corrections		E
NJ	Parole	Department of Corrections		E
	Probation		Courts	J
NM	Parole and Probation	Correction Department		E
NV	Parole and Probation	Department of Parole and Probation		E
NY	Parole	Division of Parole		E
	Probation		Counties	E
OH	Parole	Department of Corrections		E
	Probation	Department of Corrections	Courts	J/E
OK	Parole and Probation	Department of Corrections		E
OR	Parole	Department of Corrections	County Courts	J
	Probation	Department of Corrections	County Courts	J
PA	Parole	Board of Probation and Parole	County Courts	J
RI	Probation and Parole	Department of Corrections		E
SC	Probation and Parole	Department of Probation, Parole, and Pardon Services		E
SD	Parole	Department of Corrections		E
	Probation	Unified Judicial System		J
TN	Parole	Parole Board		E
	Probation	Department of Corrections		E
TX	Parole	Texas Department of Criminal Justice		E
	Probation		District Courts	J
UT	Parole and Probation	Department of Corrections		E
VA	Parole and Probation	Department of Corrections		E
VT	Parole and Probation	Department of Corrections		E
WA	Parole	Department of Corrections		E
	Probation	Department of Corrections	Courts	J
WV	Parole	Department of Public Safety		E
	Probation		Circuit Courts	J
WI	Parole and Probation	Department of Corrections		E
WY	Parole and Probation	Department of Corrections		E
US	Parole and Probation	Federal Court	Courts	J

Reprinted with permission of the American Correctional Association 1996 Directory.

8. Proper public attitude toward parole
9. Research and statistics on effectiveness[2]

Flexibility in Sentencing and Parole Laws

An effective parole system requires an indeterminate sentencing environment and that the release decision for most offenders be made by the paroling authority. This does not preclude statutes that require a minimum term to be served before parole eligibility for certain offenses or statutes that prohibit parole for some offenses. Public safety and accountability require some constraints on parole board discretion, particularly for violent offenders and those with long criminal histories and previous incarcerations. Most incarcerated offenders, however, are not violent and are not recidivists. Parole serves an important correctional purpose for these offenders in allowing for consideration of their individual circumstances, reducing unnecessary confinement, and ameliorating inequities in sentencing.

It is not possible to obtain agreement on a form of sentencing and parole law that would permit the release of a prisoner at the optimum time. Wide latitude and discretion were advocated in the past. Since the 1970s, however, there has been a movement toward the use of objective guidelines in the release decision. A national advisory commission reported, "The absence of written criteria by which decisions are made constitutes a major failing in virtually every parole jurisdiction."[3] The commission recommended that parole decisions be made visible and that parole authorities be made accountable for their decisions through the use of explicit parole selection policies. The American Correctional Association (ACA) recommends,

> The criteria which are employed by the parole authority in its decision making are available in written form and are specific enough to permit consistent application to individual cases.[4]

In an attempt to make parole selection decisions more rational and consistent, many paroling jurisdictions have established decision guidelines that structure discretion without removing it. By specifying the primary factors to be considered in parole selection and the weight to be assigned to each factor, the paroling authority gives judges, the public, and potential parolees a clearer idea of how it generally exercises its discretion.

Qualified Parole Board

Parole board members should be of such integrity, intelligence, and good judgment as to command respect and public confidence. Because of the importance of their quasi-judicial functions, they must possess the equivalent personal qualifications of a high judicial officer. They must be forthright, courageous, and independent. They should be appointed without reference to creed, color, or political affiliation. Board members should have sufficiently broad educational backgrounds that they have knowledge of those professions most closely related to parole administration—specifically, academic training that qualifies them for professional practice in fields such as criminology, education, psychiatry, psychology, law, social work, and sociology. It is essential that each member have the capacity and the desire to further his or her knowledge, as effective performance depends on understanding legal processes, the dynamics of human behavior, and cultural conditions contributing to crime.

Parole Board Hearing

Parole board members should have previous professional experience that has given them intimate knowledge of common situations and problems confronting offenders. This might be obtained from a variety of fields, such as probation, parole, the judiciary, law, social work, a correctional institution, or a delinquency prevention agency.[5]

Selection and Term of Board Members

In most jurisdictions the governor appoints parole board members.[6] In some jurisdictions the governor shares the appointing authority with another body. In others the secretary or commissioner of corrections appoints the parole board, and in one state the secretary of public safety makes the appointments.[7] As a rule parole board members are appointed for a term of years rather than serving at the pleasure of the governor. However, the ACA Parole Task Force survey found that in six states—Georgia, Michigan, Minnesota, Ohio, West Virginia, and Wisconsin—board members are not appointed for specific terms.[8] In 40 percent of the states board members serve four-year terms, and in 25 percent of the states they serve six years. Three- and five-year terms are less common.

Any parole decision is influenced by the board members' qualifications and expertise. Therefore, it is important that each member be qualified and possess expertise. Many parole officials are able and knowledgeable, but some have neither the qualifications nor the expertise. Statutes vary in the explicitness with which they specify the qualifications of a parole board member. A few require only that the member be of "good moral character." Rhine and his associates reported that over half of the jurisdictions had no requirement that board members possess any special professional qualifications. In these states the governor may nominate any person without regard for education, training, or experience. Others specify specific educational or special qualifications. For example, New York statutes require that each member of the board have graduated from an accredited college or university with a degree in criminology, criminal justice administration, law enforcement, sociology, law, social work, corrections, psychology, psychiatry, or medicine, plus five or more years of experience in one or more of those fields. Montana requires that at least one board member have "particular knowledge of Indian culture and problems."[9]

Many authorities view the part-time board of parole, often found in smaller states, as one of the most severe problems in corrections. Able to give only a limited amount of time to the job because of their business or professional concerns, part-timers cannot participate effectively in correctional decision making. Since the mid-1970s there has been a trend toward increasing the number of full-time boards. According to the ACA Parole Task Force survey, there are 31 full-time boards and seven boards with a mixture of full-time and part-time members. In the states with both full-time and part-time members, the chair is usually full-time and the other members serve on a part-time basis.[10]

Qualified Parole Staff

A parole officer is expected to perform three main functions:

1. Make investigations and write reports, and evaluate, interpret, and present data for the guidance of the court, the institution, or the paroling authority
2. Keep informed about the conduct and enforcement of parolees by personal contacts, and report any violation to the court or paroling authority
3. Interpret his or her work to the community by actively participating in civic and community organizations

In order to perform these functions a parole officer must possess certain basic qualifications and specialized knowledge. The minimum qualifications should be a working knowledge of the principles of human behavior, knowledge of the laws of the jurisdiction in which he or she will work and of the powers and limitations of the position, and familiarity with the operation of related law-enforcement agencies in the particular jurisdiction.

The minimum standards for employment as a probation or parole officer should include a bachelor's degree from a college or university with coursework in the social sciences, one year of paid full-time experience in employment for the welfare of others or one year of graduate work beyond the baccalaureate, and good character and a well-balanced personality.

Freedom from Political or Improper Influences

A parole system should be entirely free from political control, manipulation, or influence and also from improper influences of pressure groups of any type. The law should forbid parole board or staff participation in partisan political activities and coerced contributions to party campaign funds, and should give parole authorities the independence and security of tenure that they must have in order to resist interference successfully.[11]

Workable Position in Government

The parole system should be administered within the governmental structure that assures the most effective coordination of parole with other correctional services, such as institutional programs, and with community-based correctional agencies such as probation halfway houses, drug and alcohol treatment agencies, the courts, and police. Basically, four major parole structures exist:

1. The parole board serves as the administrative and policymaking board for a combined probation and parole system.
2. The parole board administers parole services only.
3. Parole services are administered by the department that administers the state correctional institutions.
4. Parole services are administered by the state correctional agency, which also administers the probation and institutional services.

The two dominant organizational patterns are the institutional model and the autonomous model. The **institutional model,** most prevalent in the juvenile field, centers parole decision making primarily in the institutions. The **autonomous model** prevails in the adult field; it centers parole decision making in an independent authority. Advocates of the institutional model believe that because the institutional staff are most familiar with the offender and his or her response to institutional programs, they are most sensitive to the optimum time for release. They see the autonomous board as (1) unconcerned with or insensitive to problems of the institutional programs and the staff's goals, (2) too preoccupied with issues other than the rehabilitative aspects of the offender's treatment to make appropriate case decisions, (3) lending unnecessary complications to decision making, and (4) infringing on the professional judgment of competent institutional staff.

On the other hand, proponents of the autonomous model believe that the institutional staff places undue emphasis on the offender's institutional adjustment. They see the institutional board as (1) being tempted to set release policies to fit the needs of the institution, to control population size, and to rid itself of problem cases; (2) extending confinement as a penalty for petty rule violations; and (3) having decision-making procedures that are so informal and lacking in visibility that questions arise concerning the board's ability to maintain fairness or even an appearance of fairness.

Although both the institutional and autonomous models are in practice, a **consolidation model** has gained popularity. This model is a result of the trend toward consolidating all correctional services—institutional and field programs—into a single department. In the consolidation model, parole decisions are made by a central authority that has independent powers although it is organizationally situated in the department of corrections. Advocates of this model contend that it (1) promotes greater concern for the entire corrections system, (2) provides greater sensitivity to institutional programs, and (3) separates parole decisions from the institution's immediate control, thereby giving appropriate weight to parole considerations beyond management of the institution.

Regardless of the organizational or administrative structure adopted by the jurisdiction, it is essential that it facilitate close coordination between the parole decision makers and all correctional programs. In so doing, sufficient autonomy should be retained to permit the parole board to serve as a check on the system.

INSTITUTIONAL MODEL OF PAROLE ORGANIZATION

An organizational pattern in which parole release decisions are made primarily within the institution. Advocates of the institutional model believe that because institutional staff are most familiar with the offender and his or her response to institutional programs, they are most sensitive to the optimal time for release. Most commonly used in the juvenile field.

AUTONOMOUS MODEL OF PAROLE ORGANIZATION

An organizational pattern in which parole decisions are made by an autonomous body not affiliated with other agencies of the criminal justice system. The most common pattern for adult paroling authorities.

CONSOLIDATION MODEL OF PAROLE ORGANIZATION

An organizational pattern in which parole decisions are made by a central authority that has independent powers but that is organizationally situated in the department of corrections.

Proper Procedures

Under traditional parole practice, the decision about a prisoner's release is deferred until well into his or her sentence; the prisoner is given a parole hearing shortly before completing the minimum term. If the prisoner is not granted parole at that time, another hearing is scheduled after some additional period. Consequently a prisoner may have several parole hearings before learning whether he or she will be granted parole and when he or she will actually be released. From the perspective of the traditional rehabilitative model, this practice is both necessary and desirable, because parole decisions are based primarily on rehabilitative concerns. The goal of the parole release authority is to identify the optimal time for release. Thus deferral of the release decision is necessary for monitoring the prisoner's rehabilitative progress.

Current thought has been shaped by empirical evidence. Research has failed to demonstrate that institutional rehabilitative programs are effective or that the optimal time for release can be ascertained. Behavior in prison has not been found to predict future criminal behavior. More and more jurisdictions are moving by statute or voluntarily toward the use of **parole guidelines** as explicit standards for determining the optimal length of a prison sentence without reference to the prisoner's institutional record, length of incarceration before parole, or other factors that have not been shown to correlate with prisoners' ability to live crime-free in the world outside prison.

PAROLE GUIDELINES

Guidelines to be followed in making parole release decisions. Most guidelines prescribe a presumptive term for each class of convicted inmate depending on both offense and offender characteristics.

Prerelease Preparation within the Institution

The Parole Plan

When a tentative or definite parole date has been set by the board, a parole plan should be developed for the future parolee. This specifies a satisfactory home or living arrangement for the individual and assesses his or her potential for employment. The plan is usually investigated and approved by the parole field staff.

Graduated Release

Direct, sudden release from confinement in a controlled environment to the free community often results in psychological and cultural shock to the releasee, and this may affect the person's ability to adjust. Whenever possible the inmate should be transferred to a minimum-security or open institution a few months before release. In such a setting the inmate may begin to exercise the necessary self-direction for living in free society. Work-release arrangements and furloughs are also helpful in gradually allowing the inmate short, yet important, opportunities to function without the strict regimen and all-encompassing discipline of the closed institution. The use of halfway houses or prerelease centers is increasing, and preliminary research indicates that inmates released to those settings are considerably less prone to recidivism.[12]

Release under a Firm, Helpful Supervisor

Parole supervision is a continuation of the correctional process. Its effectiveness in aiding the parolee's reintegration in society relies on the knowledge and experience of the field officer. This topic is discussed in chapter 6, "Supervision in Probation and Parole."

Proper Public Attitude toward Parole

The parole board and the institution have a large part to play in the matter of the parolee's return to society; however, the manner in which the public receives the parolee and the attitude it assumes is vital to that person's success.[13] Probation and parole officers should do all they can to increase public understanding of and appreciation for probation and parole. They should take advantage of opportunities to speak to educational and community groups and to use radio and television to foster public understanding of probation and parole and to explain their responsibilities and objectives. Most media stories about probation and parole are of the Parolee Arrested in Holdup variety. There are, however, many success stories that can and should be told.

Research and Statistics on Effectiveness

Full public acceptance of parole as a means of release from prisons and other correctional institutions can come only from rigorous research demonstrations of its effectiveness. Virtually all subjects connected with crime and criminal justice need further research. In 1927 Felix Frankfurter observed that the subject of crime was "overlaid with shibboleths and cliches" and that it was essential to "separate the known from the unknown, to divorce fact from assumption, to strip biases of every sort from their authority."[14] This statement is no less true today. Research must develop and validate parole prediction tables, recidivism outcome indices, and other instruments that aid boards in predicting the future behavior of those being considered for parole. Research into the causes of recidivism and subsequent revocation could be invaluable in equipping the parole officer with the tools necessary for aiding parolees in this area. Most importantly, research must examine which factors in inmates' backgrounds and present circumstances predict success or failure on parole.

Preconceived and outmoded prejudices and concepts of parole boards and staff can be modified or eliminated in light of statistical analyses of the outcomes of board decisions. Parole authorities know that the criminal justice system needs improvement, and gathering solid research data is the first step in bringing about improvement. As a subsystem of the criminal justice process, parole is inextricably interrelated with all other aspects of the system.

THE DECISION TO PAROLE

Who is to be paroled? This question has vital importance today. The parole selection process is of serious consequence to the effectiveness, perhaps even the survival, of the entire parole system. Because the selection process determines to a great extent the character of the system as a whole, it has inevitably received more criticism than any other aspect of the system.

Eligibility for Parole

Prisoners generally become eligible for parole at the completion of their minimum sentence. Early in their incarceration—often within the first few months—a **parole eligibility** date is fixed. The way the date is established varies from state to state. Many states require an inmate to have served one-third of the imposed sentence to be eligible for *consideration* for parole; thus a 15-year sentence would require that 5 years be served before parole eligibility. However, most statutes allow further reductions in the eligibility date through credit for time served in jail before sentencing and good-time credits.[15] Some states credit good time to the inmate upon arrival in prison and calculate the eligibility date by subtracting credited good time from the maximum sentence. An inmate who is serving a 15-year sentence and receiving standard good time of 20 days per month (50 days' credit on his or her sentence for each 30 days served) would be eligible for parole consideration after 40 months (2/3 × 15 × 1/3).

PAROLE ELIGIBILITY DATE

The point in a prisoner's sentence at which he or she becomes eligible to be *considered* for parole.

The Parole Release Decision

The decision to grant parole is a complicated one, and the consequences of the decision are of the gravest importance both for society and for the inmate. A decision to grant parole results in conditional release before the expiration of the maximum term of imprisonment; a denial results in continued imprisonment. The parole release decision is often more important than the court's sentence in determining how long the prisoner actually spends incarcerated. In the absence of clear legislative or judicial guidelines for parole decisions, vast responsibility has been placed on parole boards. Parole decisions traditionally have been regarded as matters that demand special expertise, matters that involve observation and treatment of offenders and release under supervision at a time that maximizes both the protection of the public and offenders' rehabilitation. This idealistic correctional goal of protecting society while rehabilitating the offender has served as additional justification for vesting broad discretionary powers in parole authorities.[16]

Statutes have usually directed parole boards to base their decisions on one or more of these criteria:

- The probability of recidivism
- The welfare of society
- The conduct of the offender while in the correctional institution
- The sufficiency of the parole plan

Such statutory language does not lend itself to workable decision making, so the parole boards have had to interpret and determine the best means by which to turn the legislative mandate into functioning administrative machinery. This broad discretion has brought criticism upon the paroling authority for making arbitrary, capricious, and disparate decisions. The lack of published standards to guide decision making, combined with the lack of written reasons for parole decisions, contribute to this perception.[17]

Traditional Parole Decision Making

Traditionally the hearing stage of parole decision making was thought to allow decision makers to speak with and observe the prospective parolee, to search for and intuit such indications of his or her rehabilitation as repentance, willingness to accept responsibility, and self-understanding. Parole decisions were based not on formally articulated criteria or policies but on the subjective, intuitional judgments of individual decision makers.[18] The courts, to the extent that they were willing to review the parole decision at all, agreed with the contentions of paroling authorities that to impose even minimal due-process constraints on the decisional process would interfere with the fulfillment of its duty to engage in diagnosis and prognosis.

> In 1970, in *Menechino v. Oswald*, the U.S. Court of Appeals held as follows:
> The Board has an identity of interest with [the inmate]. . . . It is seeking to encourage and foster his rehabilitation and readjustment to society. . . . In making this determination the Board is not restricted by rules of evidence developed for the purpose of determining legal or factual issues. It must consider many factors of a nonlegal nature [such as] medicine, psychiatry, criminology . . . psychology and human relations.[19]

In his book *Conscience and Convenience*, David Rothman discussed the issue of discretionary decision making by parole boards. He reported that in the early 20th century parole boards considered primarily the seriousness of the crime in determining whether to release an inmate on parole. However, there was no consensus on what constituted a serious crime. "Instead," Rothman wrote, "each member made his own decisions. The judgments were personal and therefore not subject to debate or reconsideration."[20] Rothman's evaluation of early parole decision making applies equally to many jurisdictions in the late 20th century. One of the authors of this book (Cromwell) has served on a parole board and observed situations in which board members' biases or preconceptions mitigated for or against a release decision—with little else factored in. One decision maker refused to vote to parole any person convicted of murder. Another member of the same paroling body regarded murder as a situational crime of passion and reminded his colleagues that "murderers have a very low recidivism rate." As Rothman states, "one man's nightmare case did not necessarily frighten another."[21] Another board member of our acquaintance looked only at the nature and seriousness of the offense in arriving at a release decision, whereas a colleague in the very next office was primarily concerned with an inmate's adjustment and behavior since being incarcerated. She commented, "A person can't do anything about what he did to get here [in prison]. I look at what they have done to get their life in order."

Growing recognition of the lack of fundamental fairness in such situations made obvious the need for research-based predictors of recidivism. The National Advisory Commission on Criminal Justice Standards and Goals spoke to the issue of parole decision making:

> The sound use of discretion and ultimate accountability for its exercise rests largely in making visible the criteria used in forming judgments. . . .[22]

Development of Parole Guidelines

At about the same time the U.S. Board of Parole[23] took a major step in the direction recommended by the National Advisory Commission. As part of a general reorganization plan, case decision making authority was delegated to panels of hearing examiners, using explicit parole selection guidelines established by the Board of Parole.[24] The guidelines were an attempt to structure discretion without removing it. By making explicit the primary factors to be considered in parole decisions, as well as the weight to be given to each, the Board of Parole provided judges, the public, and inmates with a clearer idea of how it intended to exercise its discretion.

Research had shown that parole decisions could be predicted by using specific variables. Three variables were identified as explaining a large number of the board's decisions:

- The seriousness of the offense
- The risk posed by the inmate (probability of recidivism)
- The inmate's institutional behavior (relatively less important than the first two)

The researchers produced a chart that related seriousness of offense and risk of recidivism to suggested terms of imprisonment. Based on this chart, the parole board constructed a matrix by placing the two dimensions—seriousness of offense and risk of recidivism—on the *X* and *Y* axes of a graph. Range of sentence length was then determined by plotting intersections of the dimensions on the graph.

SALIENT FACTOR SCORE

The parole guidelines developed and used by the United States Parole Commission for making parole release decisions; served as the model for parole guidelines developed in many other jurisdictions.

The Salient Factor Score

This actuarial device has been continually validated and evaluated for years and was revised several times, with the latest revision in 1981. Known as the **Salient Factor**

FIGURE 9.1 **SALIENT FACTOR SCORE (SFS/81)**

Item A.	PRIOR CONVICTIONS/ADJUDICATIONS (ADULT OR JUVENILE)	☐
	None . . . . = 3	
	One . . . . = 2	
	Two or three . . . . = 1	
	Four or more . . . . = 0	
Item B.	PRIOR COMMITMENT(S) OF MORE THAN THIRTY DAYS (ADULT OR JUVENILE)	☐
	None . . . . = 2	
	One or two . . . . = 1	
	Three or more . . . . = 0	
Item C.	AGE AT CURRENT OFFENSE/PRIOR COMMITMENTS	☐
	Age at commencement of the current offense:	
	26 years of age or more . . . . = 2*	
	20–25 years of age . . . . = 1*	
	19 years of age or less . . . . = 0	
	*EXCEPTION: If five or more prior commitments of more than thirty days (adult or juvenile), place an "x" here ____ and score this item . . . . = 0	
Item D.	RECENT COMMITMENT-FREE PERIOD (THREE YEARS)	☐
	No prior commitment of more than thirty days (adult or juvenile) or released to the community from last such commitment at least three years prior to the commencement of the current offense . . . . = 1	
	Otherwise . . . . = 0	
Item E.	PROBATION/PAROLE/CONFINEMENT/ESCAPE STATUS VIOLATOR THIS TIME	= ☐
	Neither on probation, parole, confinement, or escape status at the time of the current offense; nor committed as a probation, parole, confinement, or escape status violator this time . . . . = 1	
	Otherwise . . . . = 0	
Item F.	HEROIN/OPIATE DEPENDENCE	= ☐
	No history of heroin/opiate dependence . . . . = 1	
	Otherwise . . . . = 0	
TOTAL SCORE		☐

Source: United States Parole Commission, 1997.

Score (SFS/81), it provides explicit guidelines for release decisions based on a determination of the potential risk of parole violation. The SFS measures six offender characteristics and assigns a score to each (see Figure 9.1). Note in the figure that the first offender characteristic considered in the Salient Factor Score calculation is *Prior Convictions/Adjudications.* This offender characteristic has a score range of 0 to 3. Offenders with no prior convictions are assigned a score of 3; one prior conviction results in a score of 2; two to three prior convictions gives a score of 1; and so on. Each offender characteristic is scored in a similar manner, and the sum of the six items yields the *predictive score.* The higher the score (maximum of 10) the less likely is the probability of recidivism.

Decision makers then use decision-making guidelines (see Figure 9.2) to determine the customary time to be served for a range of offenses, based on the severity of the offense. Severity is based on eight categories, ranging from the least to the most severe. For example, an adult offender whose SFS/81 score was 5 and whose offense severity was rated in Category 2 would be expected to serve 12–16 months before being paroled.

Although the SFS/81 provided a method of summarizing research data on the relationship between offender characteristics and the likelihood of recidivism, its use with a guidelines system did not eliminate the need for clinical judgment. No prediction device can take into account all the variations in human behavior. Thus the decision maker was allowed to override the salient factor score, but only for articulated, written reasons. If the decision maker chose to make a clinical judgment outside the guidelines, he or she was required to explain the specific factors considered in the decision to override the SFS.[25]

Following the lead of the federal parole system, many states adopted guidelines for use in release decision making. Some states adopted a matrix guideline system similar to the SFS, while others adopted different types of guidelines. Most of these other systems feature a list of factors to be considered in making release decisions. Rhine and associates refer to this second category of guidelines as **guiding principles.** Joan Petersilia and Susan Turner[26] compiled a list of criteria (see Figure 9.3) used in both types of instruments—matrix and guiding principles.

Regardless of the form parole release guidelines take, they structure the exercise of discretion. Parole boards are free to deviate from their guidelines, but they generally must give reasons for doing so. Parole authorities are guided in decision making while retaining broad powers; deviations from these guides are held in check by the possibility of appeal.

Research indicates that guidelines have performed one of their intended functions, that of evening out obvious disparities so that prison time is more predictable. The main argument against them is that they do not address the questions of who is to go to prison in the first place and how wide the sentence ranges should be. These questions are addressed mostly by the courts, and many critics have pointed out that court sentencing is just as capricious, unpredictable, and fraught with disparities as parole decisions ever were.[27]

Prisoners' Perceptions of Parole Selection

Whether the length of incarceration before parole is any more predictable in guideline jurisdictions is still speculative. James Beck studied prisoners' perceptions of parole decision making in the federal parole system, which used a justice model guideline system, and in Pennsylvania, which used a rehabilitative nonmatrix guideline system.[28] The Pennsylvania board was generally treatment-oriented and strongly considered institutional behavior, recommendations of institutional staff, and parole release plans. The federal system, as we have discussed in detail, primarily considered offense severity and offender characteristics such as prior criminal history.

Contrary to expectations, Beck found no significant difference in the two groups' abilities to predict parole decisions, but he found that a significantly greater percentage of Pennsylvania inmates than federal inmates considered the parole procedure "basically fair" (48 percent of inmates as opposed to only 20 percent of the federal inmates). The major conclusion of the study was that the justice approach to parole

FIGURE 9.2 **GUIDELINES FOR DECISION MAKING**

Offense Characteristics: Offense Severity (Some Crimes Eliminated or Summarized)	OFFENDER CHARACTERISTICS: PAROLE PROGNOSIS			
	Very Good	Good	Fair	Poor
Category One *Low:* possession of a small amount of marijuana; simple theft under $1,000.	*Adult Range*			
	≤ 6 months	6–9 months	9–12 months	12–16 months
	(Youth Range)			
	(≤) 6 months	(6–9) months	(9–12) months	(12–16) months
Category Two *Low/Moderate:* income tax evasion less than $10,000; immigration law violations; embezzlement, fraud, forgery under $1,000	*Adult Range*			
	≤ 8 months	8–12 months	12–16 months	16–22 months
	(Youth Range)			
	(≤) 8 months	(8–12) months	(12–16) months	(16–20) months
Category Three *Moderate:* bribery; possession of 50 lb. or less of marijuana, with intent to sell; illegal firearms; income tax evasion $10,000 to $50,000; nonviolent property offenses $1,000 to $19,999; auto theft, not for resale	*Adult Range*			
	10–14 months	14–18 months	18–24 months	24–32 months
	(Youth Range)			
	(8–12) months	(12–16) months	(16–20) months	(20–26) months
Category Four *High:* counterfeiting; marijuana possession with intent to sell, 50 to 1,999 lb.; auto theft, for resale; nonviolent property offenses, $20,000 to $100,000	*Adult Range*			
	14–20 months	20–26 months	26–34 months	34–44 months
	(Youth Range)			
	(12–16) months	(16–20) months	(20–26) months	(26–32) months
Category Five *Very High:* robbery; breaking and entering bank or post office; extortion; marijuana possession with intent to sell, over 2,000 lb.; hard drugs possession with intent to sell, not more than $100,000; nonviolent property offenses over $100,000 but not exceeding $500,000	*Adult Range*			
	24–36 months	36–48 months	48–60 months	60–72 months
	(Youth Range)			
	(20–26) months	(26–32) months	(32–40) months	(40–48) months
Category Six *Greatest I:* explosive detonation; multiple robbery; aggravated felony (weapon fired—no serious injury); hard drugs, over $100,000; forcible rape	*Adult Range*			
	40–52 months	52–64 months	64–78 months	78–100 months
	(Youth Range)			
	(30–40) months	(40–50) months	(50–60) months	(60–76) months
Category Seven *Greatest II:* aircraft hijacking; espionage; kidnapping; homicide	*Adult Range*			
	52–80 months	64–92 months	78–110 months	100–148 months
	(Youth Range)			
	(40–64) months	(50–74) months	(70–86) months	(76–110) months
Category Eight	*Adult Range*			
	100+ months	120+ months	150+ months	180+ months
	(Youth Range)			
	(80+) months	(100+) months	(120+) months	(150+) months

Source: United States Parole Commission, 1997.

FIGURE 9.3 **CRITERIA USED IN PAROLE RELEASE RISK INSTRUMENTS**

MOST COMMONLY USED ITEMS (5)
(found in over 75% of instruments identified)
Number of parole revocations
Number of adult or juvenile convictions
Number of prison terms served
Number of incarcerations served
Current crime involves violence

SECOND MOST COMMONLY USED ITEMS (11)
(found in 50–74% of instruments identified)
Number of prior convictions
Number of previous felony sentences
Number of juvenile incarcerations
Number of jail terms served
Age at first incarceration
Commitment-free period shown
On parole at arrest
Victim injured
Current age
Drug use
Prison infractions

THIRD MOST COMMONLY USED ITEMS (15)
(found in 25–49% of instruments identified)
Number of adult or juvenile arrests
Age at first conviction
Repeat of conviction types
Length of current term
Total years incarcerated
Current crime is property crime
Current crime involved weapon
Current crime involved forcible contact
Educational level
Employment history
Living arrangements
Alcohol use/abuse
Program participation in prison
Parole release plan formulated
Escape history

Source: Joan Petersilia and Susan Turner, "Guideline-Based Justice: Prediction and Racial Minorities," in D. Gottfredson and M. Tonry, eds., *Prediction and Classification* (Chicago: University of Chicago Press, 1987).

does not result in greater perceived certainty for the offender, even though the criteria are made concrete and more sharply defined. The treatment model—based on institutional adjustment—allowed the offender a greater perceived influence over the parole decision and thus was viewed as basically more fair. Beck concluded that the justice approach to parole is still a useful tool for reducing sentence disparity and that the rehabilitation approach will remain suspect until some method of rehabilitating offenders has been proven effective. Offenders, however, seem to prefer the rehabilitation model of parole method of deciding when they should be released from prison. Beck's findings do not surprise us. While serving on the Texas Parole Board, author Paul Cromwell received hundreds of letters from inmates protesting the use of offense-related factors in making parole decisions. A letter received by the parole board from a Texas inmate illustrates this point:

> I can't do nothing about what I did. I did it and I'm sorry I did. Now I'm trying to show you people that I've changed and can be trusted out in the free world but you keep setting me off [denying parole] because of "nature and seriousness of the offense." Tell me what I can do to make parole. Please.[29]

Any system that totally ignores positive institutional behavior runs the risk of alienating offenders and increases the possibility of poor adjustment. Many, however, suggest that career criminals know how to do time; that is, they can manipulate the parole board by avoiding institutional violations and participating in rehabilitation programs that look good on their record when they are reviewed for parole.

So despite criticisms leveled at the use of guidelines, this procedure appears to offer the greatest degree of fairness to the parole-granting process. By making explicit the primary factors that the board should consider in parole selection and the weight that should be given to each, the unfettered discretion traditionally allowed parole boards should, at the very least, be structured and more predictable.

Due Process

One of the most striking aspects of the traditional parole release process has been the virtual inability to review parole decisions.[30] In recent years courts have provided some procedural protections and articulated criteria (1) for reviewing the conditions that parole boards have set on parolees' conduct and (2) for revoking parole and returning parolees to prison. Until very recently, federal and state courts almost invariably rejected claims that the denial of parole was subject to review because of procedural or substantive defects in the parole release decision process.[31]

The parole grant has long been analogized by courts to the grant of executive pardon, which makes it essentially an act of grace or the conferring of a privilege, neither of which gives rise to rights or expectations in need of due process.[32] In addition to the act of **grace** or **privilege** rationales, another theory for judicial passivity in this area has been the **continuing custody theory,** the argument that parole merely constitutes a change in the nature of custody, which places the parole decision in the area of administrative decision making.[33]

However, the theory of grace or privilege is inconsistent with the view that parole is merely a change in custody status because the former theory recognizes that a substantial benefit of conditional freedom is being conferred. The custody theory ignores the fact that a major purpose of parole is to provide a halfway point between incarceration and total freedom in the community in order to promote rehabilitation and to protect society.[34]

GRACE OR PRIVILEGE THEORY

The view that parole is a privilege and a matter of grace (mercy) by the executive. Under this theory parole confers no particular rights on the recipient and is subject to withdrawal at any time.

CONTINUING CUSTODY THEORY

The view that the parolee remains in custody of either the parole authorities or the prison and that his or her constitutional rights are limited. Release on parole is merely a change in the degree of custody.

Another rationale used to justify the vast and unreviewable discretion is that parole boards act as ***parens patriae*** (benevolent parents) with respect to the inmates. As such, the boards need be concerned only with promoting the inmates' rehabilitation through the exercise of their expert knowledge and judgment, which obviates any need for procedural protection.[35] This rationale reflects the pervasive view that release decisions are part of the rehabilitation process. In support of this view, courts have emphasized that parole boards possess an administrative expertise in evaluating "nonlegal" factors relevant to the release decision.[36] The courts acquiesced in the board's assertion that the proper moment for parole can be determined only after an inmate has been observed for a period of time and attempts have been made to treat the inmate within the rehabilitative institutional context.[37]

PARENS PATRIAE

Latin for "parent of the country"; refers to the traditional role of the state as guardian of persons under legal disability, such as juveniles, the insane, and incarcerated persons. The assumption is that the state acts in the best interest of those over whom the *parens patriae* relationship exists.

In *Menechino v. Oswald*[38] a prisoner argued that the New York State Board of Parole's denial of his application for parole was illegal because he had not received notice of the information to be considered, a fair parole hearing with a right to counsel, the right to cross-examine and to produce favorable witnesses, or a specification of the grounds and underlying facts upon which the denial was based. The court offered two reasons in holding that these due process rights did not apply to parole release hearings. First, the court ruled that the inmate had no legally cognizable "interest" in his parole grant, because he did not enjoy a status that was being threatened or taken away. Second, the parole board's interest in the proceeding was not adverse to that of the inmate because the board was "seeking to encourage and foster his rehabilitation and readjustment into society."[39]

Although the courts' prevailing view has been that of noninterference in parole release decisions, this has not been the only view. Abuses of discretion have been judicially reviewed, and parole boards have been found abusing their discretion, committing capricious acts, and conducting practices contrary to the general notions of fairness.[40]

In 1979 the U.S. Supreme Court directly addressed the issue of due process in parole release decision making. In *Greenholtz v. Inmates of the Nebraska Penal and Correctional Complex*[41] the inmates of a Nebraska prison brought an action alleging they had been unconstitutionally denied parole by the Nebraska Board of Parole. The inmates contested, among other things (1) the state's hearing process, (2) the board's practice when it denies parole of informing the inmates in what respect they fall short of qualifying for parole, and (3) a notice procedure of informing inmates of the month during which the parole hearing will be held in advance, and then posting notice of the exact time for the hearing on the day of the hearing.

After the lower federal courts held in favor of the inmates, the U.S. Supreme Court reversed the decision of the court of appeals. The Court stated,

> Like most parole statutes, it [the Nebraska statute] vests broad discretion in the Board. No ideal, error-free way to make parole release decisions has been developed. The whole question has been, and will continue to be, the subject of experimentation involving analysis of psychological factors combined with fact evaluation guided by the practical experience of the actual parole decision makers in predicting future behavior.[42]

The Court continued the trend of past decisions by discussing the "ultimate purpose of parole . . . rehabilitation,"[43] and stated,

> The fact that anticipation and hopes for rehabilitation programs have fallen short of expectations of a generation ago need not lead states to abandon hopes for those objectives; states may adopt a balanced approach in making parole determinations, as in problems of administering the correctional systems.[44]

Supreme Court building

The Court refused to require a hearing in all cases for every inmate as prescribed by the court of appeals, holding that such a requirement would provide, at best, a negligible decrease in the risk of error. In sum, the Court held,

> The Nebraska procedure affords an opportunity to be heard, and when parole is denied it informs the inmate in what respect he falls short of qualifying for parole; this affords the process that is due under these circumstances. The Constitution does not require more.[45]

Although the *Greenholtz* case did not extend due process as far as desired by the plaintiffs, nor as extensively as did the court of appeals, it did establish that some due process protections were available in the parole-granting process. The Court held that the methods provided for in the Nebraska statute—providing the right to an initial hearing, notice of the hearing, and articulation of the reasons for denial—were sufficient. It distinguished parole release decision making from parole revocation decision making and refused to apply the due process provisions of *Morrissey v. Brewer,* which prescribe a panoply of rights to a parolee in a revocation hearing. The Court concluded that parole release and parole revocation "are quite different" because "there is a . . . difference between losing what one has and not getting what one wants."[46]

Greenholtz, then, appears to require reasonable notice of a hearing, an initial hearing wherein the prisoner is allowed to present the case, and if parole is denied, a recitation of the reasons for denial. On the other hand, the requirement depends on the wording of the state or federal statute being interpreted. The Court concluded,

> We can accept respondent's view that the expectancy of release provided in this statute is entitled to some measure of constitutional protection. However, we emphasize that this

statute has unique structure and language and thus any other state statute provides a protectable entitlement must be decided on a case by case basis.[47]

The American Correction Association (ACA) standards require parole hearings to be conducted as fairly and equitably as possible with due process conditions maintained and all procedural safeguards assured.[48] Further, ACA standards require that the criteria for decision making are to be written in enough detail to permit consistent application in individual cases, and that the decision regarding parole release and the reasons for it are to be communicated to the prisoner orally and explained to agree with the written criteria. Applicants denied parole must be informed of an approximate future hearing date and must receive suggestions for improving their chances to receive parole by the time of the next hearing.

The ACA standards far exceed the due process requirements established by the courts, although it must be noted that the standards are not binding on any paroling authority; rather, they are only guidelines or models.

Because there is considerable disagreement regarding the amount and type of due process necessary at the parole-granting hearing, it is instructive to note that there was division on the Court in *Greenholtz* and that separate concurring opinions were written. Of particular interest is the separate opinion of Justice Powell. Powell agreed that the inmates had a right to some due process in the consideration of their release on parole, but he disagreed that the due process was conditioned on the wording of the state statute governing the deliberations of the parole board. Powell wrote that substantial liberty from legal restraint is at stake when the state makes decisions regarding probation or parole:

> Although still subject to limitations not imposed on citizens never convicted of a crime, the parolee enjoys a liberty comparably greater than whatever minimal freedom of action he may have retained within prison walls, a fact that the Court recognized in *Morrissey v. Brewer*.[49]

Because this liberty is valuable and its termination inflicts a grievous loss on the parolee, the Court concluded in *Morrissey v. Brewer*[50] that the decision to revoke parole must be made in conformity with due process standards. Powell wrote that the prisoner should justifiably expect that parole will be granted fairly and that the mere existence of a parole system is sufficient to create a *liberty interest* in the parole release decision protected by the Constitution.[51] Liberty interest refers to any interest recognized or protected by the due process clauses of state or federal constitutions.

Justice Marshall, joined by Justices Brennan and Stevens in dissenting, wrote,

> I must register my opinion that all prisoners potentially eligible for parole have a liberty interest of which they may not be deprived without due process, regardless of the particular statutory language that implements the parole system.[52]

SUMMARY

The scope of a parole board's authority and the consequences of its actions are enormous. No other part of the criminal justice system concentrates such power into the hands of so few.[53]

Parole boards select prisoners for parole and determine when revocation of parole and return to prison are necessary. In some states the parole board also supervises parolees in the community. To be effective, parole boards must have certain essential elements: (1) sentencing and parole laws must be flexible; (2) parole board members must be qualified for their jobs; (3) the parole staff must be qualified; (4) the parole board must be free from political interference; (5) parole must have a workable position in the government structure; (6) the board must employ proper parole procedures; (7) prerelease preparation must take place within the institution; (8) the public must have a proper attitude toward parole; and (9) research on the effectiveness of parole must be conducted.

Because parole selection determines the character of the organization itself, the process of selection has serious consequences for the effectiveness, and perhaps even the survival, of the entire parole system. Despite its importance to the prisoner, society, and the justice system as a whole, however, the process is a confused procedure, with little consensus regarding the proper means by which decisions are made, the grounds for decisions, and whether minimal due process should be allowed.

From the intuitive approach of the rehabilitative parole board to the justice model system with its guidelines and parole matrices, the system has not yet evolved a consistent decision-making base. Even prisoners, who are at the complete mercy of the system, do not agree on which method they prefer. One study indicates that inmates may prefer mercy to justice, as they overwhelmingly favored the intuitive approach of the Pennsylvania parole system to the guidelines approach of the federal system.

The courts, too, are at odds, although at present there seems to be a rather consistent theme that due process, if allowed at all, will be minimal and determined by the statutes of the jurisdiction. It will not be protected by the Fourteenth Amendment and thus will not be a constitutional issue.

The ACA *Manual of Correctional Standards* perhaps summarizes the issue of due process at the release hearing as well as possible:

> To an even greater extent than in the case of imprisonment, probation and parole practice is determined by an administrative discretion that is largely uncontrolled by legal standards, protections, or remedies. Until statutory and case law are more fully developed, it is virtually important within all of the correctional field that there should be established and maintained reasonable norms and remedies against the sort of abuses that are likely to develop where men have great power over their fellows and where relationships may become both mechanical and arbitrary.[54]

ENDNOTES

1. Edward E. Rhine, William R. Smith, and Ronald W. Jackson, *Paroling Authorities: Recent History and Current Practice* (Laurel, Md.: American Correctional Association, 1991), 32–33.
2. American Correctional Association, *Manual of Correctional Standards* (Washington, D.C.: 1966), 115–16.
3. National Advisory Commission on Criminal Justice Standards and Goals, *Corrections* (Washington, D.C., 1973), 397.
4. American Correctional Association, *Manual for Adult Parole Authorities,* 2nd ed. (Washington, D.C., 1980), 22.
5. ACA, *Manual of Correctional Standards,* 117, 118.
6. On some occasions this has resulted in appointments on the basis of political affiliation rather than qualifications for making parole decisions.

7. Rhine, Smith, and Jackson, *Paroling Authorities,* 37.
8. Rhine, Smith, and Jackson, *Paroling Authorities,* 51.
9. Rhine, Smith, and Jackson, *Paroling Authorities,* 36.
10. Rhine, Smith, and Jackson, *Paroling Authorities,* 51. Connecticut, Delaware, Hawaii, Minnesota, and Mississippi have full-time chairs and members who serve part-time. In Iowa and Utah the chair and at least one member are full-time, and other members serve part-time.
11. ACA, *Manual for Adult Parole Authorities,* 124.
12. George G. Killinger and Paul Cromwell Jr., eds., *Corrections in the Community: Alternatives to Imprisonment,* 2nd ed. (St. Paul: West, 1978).
13. ACA, *Manual of Correctional Standards,* 132.
14. Quoted in *The Challenge of Crime in a Free Society,* A Report of the President's Commission on Law Enforcement and Administration of Justice (1967), 274.
15. Good time (or "gain time") is awarded by prison authorities for institutional good conduct and reduces the period of sentence an inmate must serve before parole eligibility. Originally introduced as an incentive for inmates, it has become virtually automatic—being lost by misbehavior rather than awarded for good behavior. The range of good-time credits is from 5 days per month to over 30 days per month. In recent years large amounts of good time have been awarded by correctional authorities in order to reduce prison overcrowding.
16. William J. Genego, Peter D. Goldberger, and Vicki C. Jackson, "Parole Release Decision Making and the Sentencing Process," *Yale L.J.* 84 (1975): 810.
17. Elizabeth L. Taylor, *In Search of Equity: The Oregon Parole Matrix,* unpublished monograph, 1981. In 1974 the U.S. Court of Appeals for the 7th Circuit held that an inmate must be provided written notice of the reason for denial of parole. *King v. United States,* 492 F. 2d 1337 (7th Cir. 1974).
18. Genego, Goldberger, and Jackson, "Parole Release Decision Making," 820.
19. *Menechino v. Oswald,* 430 F. 2d 403, 407–408 (2d Cir. 1970), *cert. denied,* 400 U.S. 1023, 91 S. Ct. 588, 27 L. Ed. 2d 635 (1971).
20. David J. Rothman, *Conscience and Convenience: The Asylum and Its Alternatives in Progressive America* (Boston: Little, Brown, 1980), 173.
21. Rothman, *Conscience and Convenience,* 174.
22. NAC, *Corrections,* 397.
23. Later called the U.S. Parole Commission. The commission was to be phased out over eight years by the Comprehensive Crime Control Act of 1984, terminating completely in 1992, but was subsequently given five additional years before final abolition.
24. Peter B. Hoffman and Lucille K. DeGostin, "Parole Decision Making: Structuring Discretion," *Federal Probation* (Dec. 1974).
25. Peter B. Hoffman and Sheldon Adelberg, "The Salient Factor Score: A Nontechnical Overview," *Federal Probation* (March 1980).
26. Joan Petersilia and Susan Turner, "Guideline-Based Justice: Prediction and Racial Minorities," in D. Gottfredson and M. Tonry, eds., *Prediction and Classification* (Chicago: University of Chicago Press, 1987), 151–81.
27. Kevin Krajick, "Abolishing Parole: An Idea Whose Time Has Come," *Corrections Magazine* (June 1983).
28. James L. Beck, *Offender Perceptions of Parole Decision Making,* unpublished monograph, 1981.
29. Author's files.
30. *Yale L.J.* 84: 842.
31. *Yale L.J.* 84: 842.
32. *French v. Ciccone,* 308 F. Supp. 256, 257 (W. D. Mo. 1969).
33. *Anderson v. Corall,* 263 U.S. 193, 44 S. Ct. 43, 68 L. Ed. 247 (1923).
34. Charles Newman, *Sourcebook in Probation, Parole, and Pardons,* 3rd ed. (Springfield, Ill.: Charles C. Thomas, 1968), 206–207; 84 *Yale L.J.* vol. 84:843; and 45 *Minn.L.Rev.* vol. 45: 827 (1961).

35. *Scarpa v. United States Board of Parole,* 477 F. 2d 278, 281 (5th Cir. 1972), *vacated as moot;* 414 U.S. 809, 94 S. Ct. 79, 38 L. Ed. 2d 44 (1973); and *Menechino v. Oswald,* 430 F. 2d 403, 407 (2d Cir. 1970), *cert. denied,* 400 U.S. 1023, 91 S. Ct. 588, 27 L. Ed. 2d 635 (1971).
36. *Scarpa v. United States Board of Parole,* 281.
37. *Yale L.J.* 84: 843.
38. *Menechino v. Oswald.*
39. *Menechino v. Oswald.*
40. See United States *ex rel. Campbell v. Pate,* 401 F. 2d 55 (7th Cir. 1968); *Palermo v. Rockefeller,* 323 F. Supp. 478 (S.D.N.Y. 1971); and *Monks v. New Jersey State Parole Board,* 55 N.J. 238, 277 A. 2d 193 (1971).
41. 442 U.S. 1, 60 L. Ed. 2d 668, 99 S. Ct. 2100 (1979).
42. *Greenholtz v. Inmates of the Nebraska Penal and Correctional Complex,* 442 U.S. 1, 14, 99 S. Ct. 2100, 2107, 60 L. Ed. 2d 668 (1979).
43. *Greenholtz v. Inmates of the Nebraska Penal and Correctional Complex.*
44. *Greenholtz v. Inmates of the Nebraska Penal and Correctional Complex.*
45. *Greenholtz v. Inmates of the Nebraska Penal and Correctional Complex,* 16.
46. *Greenholtz v. Inmates of the Nebraska Penal and Correctional Complex,* 9–10.
47. *Greenholtz v. Inmates of the Nebraska Penal and Correctional Complex,* 12.
48. American Correctional Association, *Standards for Adult Parole Authorities,* 2nd ed. (College Park, Md.: ACA, June 1980), 242–248.
49. *Greenholtz v. Inmates of the Nebraska Penal and Correctional Complex,* 18.
50. *Morrissey v. Brewer,* 408 U.S. 471, 92 S. Ct. 2593, 33 L. Ed. 2d 484 (1972).
51. *Morrissey v. Brewer,* 19.
52. *Morrissey v. Brewer,* 22.
53. Rhine, Smith, and Jackson, *Paroling Authorities,* 32–33.
54. American Correctional Association, *Manual of Correctional Standards* (College Park, Md., June 1980), 500. See also Justice Douglas's separate opinion in *Morrissey v. Brewer.*

DISCUSSION QUESTIONS

1. Compare and contrast the autonomous, institutional, and consolidation models of parole organization. What is the pattern in your state?
2. What are the three major functions of a parole board?
3. Why is flexibility important in sentencing and in parole laws?
4. What are the primary qualifications of a good parole board member? Of a parole officer? Why are these qualities important?
5. What methods are used to select parole board members? Which method do you believe is best? Why?
6. What are the three major duties of a parole officer?
7. Define and discuss graduated release and its role in parole.
8. Why are good public relations necessary to parole's effectiveness?
9. In the final analysis, what is the most important characteristic of a parole system?
10. How is parole eligibility typically determined?

11. What is good time, and what is its relationship to eligibility for parole consideration?
12. Explain the two primary methods of parole decision making.
13. Distinguish between the matrix guidelines method and the guiding principles guidelines method.
14. Why is unstructured discretion unfair to the inmate? Give some examples.
15. What three criteria do statutes typically establish for parole release decisions?
16. What was the ruling in *Menechino v. Oswald*? How did it affect parole decision making?
17. What issues arise when seriousness of the offense is considered in parole decisions? What do you think about this issue?
18. In developing parole guidelines, what were the variables that were identified as explaining a large number of the board's decisions?
19. If you were a parole board member, what factors would you consider in attempting to arrive at a fair and just decision? Why?
20. What did James Beck find in his study on prisoners' perceptions of parole release decision making? If you were a prisoner, what method would you prefer?
21. What were the issues and what was the decision in *Greenholtz v. Inmates of the Nebraska Penal and Correctional Complex*? In light of the conservative composition of the present Supreme Court, what do you think will be the result of future decisions on these issues?
22. Where does the American Correctional Association stand on the issues covered in the previous question?

10

PAROLE CONDITIONS AND REVOCATION

What You Will Learn in This Chapter

You will learn that parole conditions imposed by parole boards are subject to the same limitations as probation conditions. Parole conditions vary from state to state, but common conditions can be found in most states. You will see that parolees have the same limitations as probationers and are also legally handicapped by diminished constitutional rights. Revocation is the ultimate sanction if parole is violated. It represents a loss of freedom; therefore, parolees are guaranteed basic due process rights prior to revocation. You will become familiar with the case of Morrissey v. Brewer, *the leading case on parole revocation.*

KEY TERMS

- **Parole conditions**
- **Standard conditions**
- **Special conditions**
- **Diminished constitutional rights**
- **Preferred rights**
- **Grace theory**
- **Contract theory**
- **Continuing custody theory**
- **"Grievous loss"**
- **Revocation hearing**
- **Hearsay evidence**
- **Preparole**

INTRODUCTION

Parole is a form of community supervision of offenders; therefore, as with probation, supervision conditions are an integral part of parole. **Parole conditions** imposed determine the amount of freedom a parolee enjoys; they also often determine whether reintegration of the offender or protecting society is the primary goal of parole in a particular state.

PAROLE CONDITIONS

The rules under which a paroling authority releases an offender to community supervision.

The two main goals of parole (reintegration of the offender and protection of society) often coexist implicitly in the variety of parole conditions imposed by the state. Whether they are consistent with each other is debatable. Some believe the approaches to these goals are different and irreconcilable; others think they can be mixed and still get desired results. Whatever may be the primary goal behind parole release, conditions imposed play a big role in achieving that goal. They also often determine whether the parolee succeeds or fails.

Parole revocation follows parole supervision if the parolee violates the conditions of parole. As with probation, revocation is not automatic in that violations can result in lesser sanctions. Revocation is important to parolees because it means losing their freedom and being brought back to jail or prison to serve time. It represents a *"grievous loss"* of liberty, so parolees have been afforded constitutional rights by the courts prior to revocation. Revocation is also important to society because the parolee will once again be under the care and custody of the state, and with that comes the high cost of keeping an offender incarcerated. It is clear that much is at stake for the parolee and the state in parole revocation.

PAROLE REVOCATION

The formal termination of a parolee's conditional freedom and the reinstatement of imprisonment.

CONDITIONS OF PAROLE

Who Imposes Parole Conditions?

Unlike probation, where conditions are set by the court, parole conditions are set by the parole board—a nonjudicial body that is usually part of the executive branch of government. Once conditions are set by the board, supervision of parole is then left to field parole officers who work either for the parole board or for another government

Halfway house for recent parolees

agency independent of the parole board, such as the parole division of a department of corrections. In these states the function of the parole board is limited to deciding whether to release an inmate on parole. Once released, the parolee is supervised by the parole division, which is independent of the parole board.[1]

As in the case of probation, where conditions are imposed by judges, parole boards also enjoy vast discretion when imposing conditions of parole. Decided cases, however, set some limitations on what parole boards can do. These limitations are similar to those in probation:

1. The condition must be clear.
2. The condition must be reasonable.
3. The condition must protect society or rehabilitate the offender.
4. The condition must be constitutional.

These limitations imply that, like inmates and probationers, parolees retain certain constitutional rights, although diminished. Because the requirements for the validity of parole conditions are similar to those for probation, the decided cases discussed in chapter 4 ("Conditions and Length of Probation") also apply to parole and will not be discussed in this chapter.

STANDARD CONDITIONS

Conditions imposed on all parolees in a jurisdiction.

SPECIAL CONDITIONS

Conditions tailored to fit the needs of a particular offender.

Types of Parole Conditions

As in the case of probation, parole conditions may be classified into two types: **standard conditions** and **special conditions.** Standard conditions are imposed on all parolees in a jurisdiction, while special conditions are tailored to fit the needs of an offender and therefore vary between offenders. The parole conditions imposed in

Massachusetts are typical of conditions imposed in other states. The Massachusetts parole conditions provide as follows:

- ▲ I will obey local, state, and federal laws and conduct myself in the manner of a responsible citizen.
- ▲ I will notify my parole officer in writing within 24 hours of any change in my employment or residence. I will notify my parole officer before applying for a license to marry. I will inform my parole officer within 24 hours if arrested.
- ▲ I will make earnest effort to find and maintain legitimate employment unless engaged in some other program approved by my parole officer.
- ▲ I will not engage in a continuous pattern of association with persons I know to have a criminal record or who are known to be engaged in a violation of the law. This prohibition does not apply where such association is incidental to my place of residence or employment or connected with activities of bona fide political or social organizations. However, the Parole Board retains authority to impose limits to these latter activities as a special condition of parole where such associations are inconsistent with my approved home plan.
- ▲ I will not leave the State of Massachusetts for a period in excess of 24 hours without securing permission from my parole officer.

Special parole conditions in various states may provide for the following:

- ▲ Prohibition against the possession of firearms or the use of a motor vehicle
- ▲ Payment of a fine or restitution
- ▲ Community service
- ▲ Residence in a community corrections center
- ▲ A period of house arrest

Table 10.1 illustrates various parole conditions and the extent to which they are imposed in selected jurisdictions.

The courts generally uphold reasonable conditions but will strike down illegal conditions or those considered unreasonable because they are impossible to meet. As in probation, appellate courts generally allow parole boards immense discretion in imposing conditions of parole. The following discussion highlights some of the recent notable court cases on the validity of parole conditions.

Some Legal Issues in Parole Conditions

Recent court cases have raised interesting legal issues involving parole conditions. For example, in one case the Tenth Circuit Court of Appeals upheld a condition that paroled Colorado sex offenders provide blood and saliva samples to create a DNA bank for easy identification should the parolee commit a similar offense.[2] The condition was challenged as violating parolees' right against unreasonable searches and seizures. The court held that this requirement was reasonable because of the significance of DNA evidence in solving sex offenses, the minimal intrusion on the inmate's right to privacy, and the inmate's diminished constitutional rights.

Similar cases have been decided in two other federal circuit courts of appeals.[3] In these cases plaintiffs argued that they were unconstitutionally required to incriminate themselves with such samples, that they were being singled out as sex offenders, thus violating their right to equal protection, and that it denied them liberty interest under the Fourteenth Amendment. The courts held the tests constitutional, saying that parole is discretionary and may be conditioned on a requirement that is itself legal.

Table 10.1 **SELECTED CONDITIONS OF PAROLE IN EFFECT IN 51 JURISDICTIONS**

Condition of Parole	Number of Jurisdictions	Percentage
Obey all federal, state, and local laws	50	98.0
Report to the parole officer as directed and answer all reasonable inquiries by the parole officer	49	96.1
Refrain from possessing a firearm or other dangerous weapon unless granted written permission	47	92.2
Remain within the jurisdiction of the court and notify the parole officer of any change in residence	46	90.2
Permit the parole officer to visit the parolee at home or elsewhere	42	82.4
Obey all rules and regulations of the parole supervision agency	40	78.4
Maintain gainful employment	40	78.4
Abstain from association with persons with criminal records	31	60.8
Pay all court-ordered fines, restitution, or other financial penalties	27	52.9
Meet family responsibilities and support dependents	24	47.1
Undergo medical or psychiatric treatment and/or enter and remain in a specified institution, if so ordered by the court	23	45.1
Pay supervision fees	19	37.3
Attend a prescribed secular course of study or vocational training	9	17.6
Perform community service	7	13.7

Source: Edward E. Rhine, William R. Smith, and Ronald W. Jackson, *Paroling Authorities: Recent History and Current Practice* (Laurel, Md.: American Correctional Association, 1991). Used with permission of the American Correctional Association.

Legal issues have also been raised concerning requirements that offenders who are on parole for sex offenses register in communities where they reside, even if the registration law was passed after the offense was committed. Some states require registration and notification in the community of the presence of sex offenders on parole. Although the validity of those statutes is likely to be upheld, no authoritative case has yet been decided by higher courts on the issue.

The Seventh Circuit Court of Appeals has upheld submission to a penile plethysmograph as a parole condition for a Michigan inmate who was convicted in federal court of kidnapping and allegedly molesting a six-year-old boy before attempting to drown him.[4] The offender in this case objected to the condition, saying that it was fundamentally unfair and therefore denied him due process. His parole was revoked. On appeal, the Seventh Circuit ruled that "the Commission may impose or modify other conditions of parole so long as they are reasonably related to the nature of the circumstances of the offense and the history and characteristics of the parolee."

The American Correctional Association (ACA), in its *Standards for Adult Parole Authorities*, recommends that general conditions that apply to all parolees should require simply that a parolee observe the law, maintain appropriate contact with the parole system, and notify the parole officer of any change of residence. Special conditions, it states, should be added "only when they are clearly relevant to the parolee's compliance with the requirements of the criminal law. Conditions should not concern . . . the lifestyle of the offender, as such, but should be tested directly against the probability of serious criminal behavior by the individual parolee."[5] The ACA also recommends that parolees be encouraged to inform the paroling authority about their views concerning the conditions that will be imposed, and should have the opportunity to appeal any request of a parole officer to impose a new condition of parole. These ACA recommendations, however, do not have the force and effect of law and may be followed or ignored by paroling authorities in various states.

Rights of Parolees While on Parole

An offender on parole does not lose all constitutional rights; however, the rights enjoyed are **diminished,** meaning that they are not as highly protected by the courts as similar rights enjoyed by nonoffenders. Even First Amendment rights (which are considered **preferred rights** because they are more highly protected than other constitutional rights) can be limited if an offender is on parole or probation. For example, in a probation case (which could just as well apply to parole) a defendant was convicted for obstructing a federal court order arising from the defendant's antiabortion activities. The court imposed as a condition of probation that defendant was prohibited from "harassing, intimidating or picketing in front of any gynecological or abortion family planning services center."[6] The defendant challenged that condition, claiming it violated her rights under the First Amendment. On appeal, the Federal Court of Appeals for the Tenth Circuit held the condition valid, saying that "conditions which restrict freedom of speech and association are valid if they are reasonably necessary to accomplish the essential needs of the State and public order."

DIMINISHED CONSTITUTIONAL RIGHTS

Constitutional rights enjoyed by an offender on parole that are not as highly protected by the courts as the rights of nonoffenders.

PREFERRED RIGHTS

Rights more highly protected than other constitutional rights.

If First Amendment rights of parolees can be curtailed in this fashion, it follows that other constitutional rights that are not as highly protected may likewise be curtailed as long as proper justification is established by the state.

The place where a parolee lives may usually be searched by the parole officer without a search warrant and without the parolee's consent. The only exception would be in states where warrantless searches are prohibited by agency rules. Some states require that the parolee, as a condition of parole, give blanket permission to search his or her place of residence. This condition has generally been upheld, although problems arise when evidence of a new crime is obtained as a result of the search. In a New York case a parole officer obtained a warrant charging a parolee with a violation and then went to the parolee's apartment. The officer charged the parolee with parole violation and conducted a two-and-a-half-hour search, which yielded narcotics. The parolee was convicted on the new charge, and the conviction was upheld. The court said, "Defendant appellant, as a parolee, was deprived of no constitutional rights by the search and seizure which was made under the circumstances of this case."[7]

In another New York case the court noted that the reasonableness standard for a search and seizure is not necessarily the same when applied to a parolee as when applied to a person whose rights are not similarly diminished, implying that Fourth Amendment protections are diminished when applied to parolees.[8]

Two recent cases from Pennsylvania, however, hold to the contrary. In a 1993 case a Pennsylvania court refused to admit drugs seized without warrant in a new criminal case against a parolee.[9] The court said that the absence of a state regulation authorizing and governing warrantless searches of parolees by parole officers, coupled with the lack of consent by the parolee, violated the parolee's constitutional rights. The court concluded that because the evidence was to be used in a new criminal case and not in a parole revocation proceeding, parole officers were in effect acting as police officers when making the warrantless search and so were bound by the warrant rule.

In 1995 another Pennsylvania court suppressed evidence against a parolee that had been obtained by virtue of a parole condition that required the parolee to submit his person, property, and residence to warrantless searches by the agents of the Pennsylvania Board of Probation and Parole.[10] Although the parolee in this case signed a search consent condition, the court said that "to allow a search of a parolee for no reason other than that the parolee accepted parole was tantamount to the parolee checking his or her Fourth Amendment rights at the door of the prison."

Note, however, that in a 1997 case the Pennsylvania Supreme Court in effect overruled the Pennsylvania lower court decisions by holding that a parolee's consent to warrantless searches by state parole agents, as specified in the conditions of release (signed by the parolee upon release from confinement, with such warrantless searches being based on reasonable suspicion that the parolee had committed a parole violation), was proper under both the Fourth Amendment and the applicable provision of the Pennsylvania constitution.[11]

These decisions show clear disagreement about the extent of the Fourth Amendment rights of parolees. This area of law is uncertain. However, most courts tend to follow the New York cases, which severely limit a parolee's Fourth Amendment rights and allow warrantless searches by parole officers as long as there is justification for the condition imposed.[12] This reiterates the dominant philosophy among courts that parolees do not have the same constitutional rights as the rest of the public.

The Power of Parole Officers to Arrest a Parolee

Many states, by law or agency policy, give a parole officer the right to arrest a parolee without a warrant. Other states require that an arrest warrant be issued by the parole board before a parole officer can make an arrest. In New York and Pennsylvania parole officers may arrest a parole violator without a warrant and receive authorization, a temporary detainer, by telephone immediately afterward. These temporary detainers must be replaced by an arrest warrant within 24 hours in Pennsylvania and 48 hours in New York. Federal probation officers, who also supervise federal parolees, may arrest a parolee without a warrant if there is probable cause to believe that the person being supervised has violated a condition of release.

Upon arrest the parolee must be taken before the court having jurisdiction over the offender or before the proper authority "without unnecessary delay."[13] Justification for these practices is found in the occasional need to take immediate action. Howard Abadinsky reports,

> When I was a parole officer in New York, it was not unusual to encounter parolees, unexpectedly, who were in serious violation of the conditions of their release. For example, heavily involved in abusing heroin (and obviously engaging in criminal acts to support the habit); prohibited from the use of alcohol (because of the dangerous nature of their behavior while under the influence) and intoxicated; child molesters found in the company of children. I could take such persons into custody immediately and use the telephone for detainer-warrant authorization.[14]

In other states, such as Texas, the parole officer must request in writing a warrant from the parole board, although emergency warrants may be obtained by telephone in limited circumstances.[15] Other states allow citations to be issued that require the parolee to appear for a hearing (Oregon), that order the parolee to appear before the parole agency supervisor for a case review (Wisconsin), or that allow the parole officer to arrest the alleged violator, take him or her before a magistrate to determine if probable cause exists that the parole conditions have been violated, and if so, issue a warrant for his or her arrest (Iowa).

ACA standards regard the arrest and detention of a parolee on violation charges as a serious act with profound implications for the parolee. The ACA therefore recommends that arrest be made only with a warrant issued by "the affirmative approval of a parole authority member or the statewide or regional director of parole supervision services." Standard 2-1107 provides as follows:

> Warrants for the arrest and detention of parolees are issued only upon adequate evidence which indicates a probable serious or repeated pattern of violation of parole conditions and a compelling need for detention pending the parole authority's initial revocation decision.

PAROLE REVOCATION

The term **revocation** refers to the formal termination of a parolee's conditional freedom and the reinstatement of imprisonment. The frequency of parole revocation has generated controversy. Some feel there are too many parole revocations; others think more parolees ought to be revoked. Too many parole revocations lead to prison congestion; too few lead to public apprehension about safety from convicted offenders. In the words of one publication, "The most pressing factor driving the concern about revocation practices today is the tremendous growth in the nation's prisons during the past decade."[16] The implication is that parole officials are reluctant to revoke if it means adding prisoners to an already overcrowded prison system. A balance must be achieved between reintegrating offenders into society and public protection.

REVOCATION

The formal termination of a parolee's conditional freedom and the reinstatement of imprisonment.

The public tends to view the rate of parole violation as indicative of parole success or failure. Criminal justice practitioners, in contrast, recognize that what may appear to be good parole statistical results can, in light of the quality and extent of supervision, indicate just the opposite. One state may report a violation rate of 8 percent, but the only indicator the state may count as a "violation" is the conviction for a new crime. This violation rate does not mean much. Another state may report a much greater rate of violation, but it may practice close, intensive supervision and have a policy of strictly enforcing all parole rules. In neither practice does the reported violation rate accurately measure the success or failure of that jurisdiction's parole system.

Three Theories of Parole and Parole Revocation

Parole practices in the past were often influenced by the theory of parole prevailing in a particular jurisdiction. Parole has variously been viewed as a form of grace, a contract, and as a different type of custody.

GRACE THEORY

The position that parole is a privilege granted by the grace or mercy of a parole board.

CONTRACT THEORY

The position that parole is a contract between the parolee and the state.

CONTINUING CUSTODY THEORY

The position that the parolee remains in the custody of either the parole authorities or the prison warden and therefore his or her constitutional rights are limited.

Advocates of the **grace theory** view parole as a privilege granted by the grace or mercy of the parole board. Under this theory parole confers no particular rights to the recipient and is subject to withdrawal at any time. The **contract theory** holds that parole is a contract between the state and the parolee. Under the contract a prisoner agrees to abide by certain conditions and terms and waives rights to a hearing in case of violation. A violation of the conditions thus represents a breach of contract, and parole can be revoked. According to the **continuing custody theory**, the parolee remains in the custody of either the parole authorities or the prison warden and therefore his or her constitutional rights are limited. Revocation is merely a change in the degree of custody and requires little, if any, due process.[17]

From a legal perspective, these theories no longer control the nature of parole revocation, however, because the U.S. Supreme Court has ruled that certain rights must be afforded the parolee prior to parole revocation, although not in the granting of parole.

Morrissey v. Brewer—The Leading Case on Parole Revocation

The U.S. Supreme Court has given parole authorities specific guidance on certain legal aspects of parole revocation. The constitutional rights given to parolees in revocation proceedings are laid out by the Court in the case of ***Morrissey v. Brewer***,[18] arguably the most important and best-known case in probation and parole. Because of its importance in parole revocation, *Morrissey* deserves an extended discussion.

The Facts

Morrissey pleaded guilty to and was convicted in 1967 of false drawing or uttering of checks. He was paroled from the Iowa State Penitentiary in 1968. Seven months later his parole was revoked for violating the conditions of his parole by buying a car under an assumed name and driving it without permission, giving false statements to the police about his address and insurance company after a minor accident, obtaining credit under an assumed name, and failing to report his residence to his parole officer. The parole officer's report also noted that Morrissey had been interviewed, had admitted to the violations, and could not explain why he had not contacted his parole officer. Morrissey's parole was revoked. He challenged the revocation, saying it was unconstitutional because there was no hearing and therefore he was deprived of due process rights. The issue brought to the U.S. Supreme Court on appeal was whether the due process clause of the Fourteenth Amendment affords a parolee certain rights before parole revocation.

GRIEVOUS LOSS

Revoking parole is a grievous loss because it involves being sent back to prison.

REVOCATION HEARING

A due process hearing which must be conducted before parole can be revoked.

PRELIMINARY HEARING

An inquiry conducted at or reasonably near the place of the alleged parole violation or arrest to determine if there is probable cause to believe that the parolee committed a parole violation.

Five Basic Rights Needed Before Revocation

The U.S. Supreme Court held that revocation represents a **"grievous loss"** of liberty, and therefore a parolee is entitled to some due process rights prior to revocation. The Court described two important stages in the typical process of parole revocation: the **preliminary hearing** and the **revocation hearing**. The preliminary hearing requires that "some minimal inquiry be conducted at or reasonably near the place of the alleged parole violation or arrest and as promptly as convenient after arrest while information is fresh and sources are available." The revocation hearing "must be the basis

Table 10-2 PROCEDURAL DUE PROCESS ROUTINELY PROVIDED AT PAROLE REVOCATION HEARINGS

	PRELIMINARY HEARING		FINAL HEARING	
Due Process Protection	#	%	#	%
Written notice of alleged violation	45	88.2	51	100.0
Disclosure of evidence of violations	42	82.4	51	100.0
Opportunity to confront and cross-examine adverse witnesses	44	86.3	47	92.2
Representation by counsel	31	60.8	40	78.4
Opportunity to be heard in person and to present evidence and witnesses	43	84.3	51	100.0
Written statement of reasons for the decision	45	88.2	48	94.1

Source: Edward E. Rhine, William R. Smith, and Ronald W. Jackson, *Paroling Authorities: Recent History and Current Practice* (Laurel, Md.: American Correctional Association, 1991), 128.

for more than determining probable cause; it must lead to a final evaluation of any contested relevant facts and consideration of whether the facts as determined warrant revocation." In *Morrissey* the Court enumerated five rights that must be afforded the parolee before revocation as the minimum requirements of due process. These rights are

1. written notice of the claimed violations of parole;
2. disclosure to the parolee of evidence against him; the opportunity to be heard in person and to present witnesses and documentary evidence;
3. the right to confront and cross-examine adverse witnesses (unless the hearing officer specifically finds good cause for not allowing confrontation);
4. a "neutral and detached" hearing body such as a traditional parole board, members of which need not be judicial officers or lawyers;
5. a written statement by the fact finders as to the evidence relied on and the reasons for revoking parole.

A survey by Edward Rhine, William Smith, and Ronald Jackson indicates that these due process rights are routinely provided at present by a great majority of states in parole revocation hearings. The survey shows that, at least in the revocation hearing, 100 percent of the states gave the parolee a written notice of the alleged violation; 100 percent disclosed evidence of violations; 92.2 percent allowed the parolee an opportunity to confront and cross-examine adverse witnesses; 78.4 percent allowed representation by counsel; 100 percent gave parolees an opportunity to be heard in person and to present evidence and witnesses; and 94.1 percent gave parolees a written statement of the reason for the decision.[19]

The Significance of Morrissey v. Brewer

Morrissey is arguably the most significant case ever to be decided by the U.S. Supreme Court in parole because for the first time the Court held that parolees are entitled to some form of due process, at least in the parole revocation process. Relying on previous nonparole cases, the Court said that "whether any procedural protections are due depends on the extent to which an individual will be 'condemned to suffer grievous loss.'" Revoking parole signifies a "grievous loss" because it means being sent back to prison, hence due process guarantees are needed.

Some writers interpret *Morrissey* to mean that parolees are also constitutionally entitled to the two-stage hearing process (the preliminary hearing and the revocation hearing) in addition to the five due process rights enumerated. Nothing in the *Morrissey* decision, however, indicates that two hearings are constitutionally required. The Court simply said that "in analyzing what is due, we see two important stages in the typical process of parole revocation," referring to the two hearings. Nonetheless, a survey shows that 45 jurisdictions conduct preliminary hearings prior to the revocation hearings.[20] Although most states have a two-stage hearing process, some states merge these two proceedings into one, with the five due process rights listed being given during the merged proceeding. The constitutionality of a merged proceeding has not been addressed by the U.S. Supreme Court, hence most states play it safe and give two hearings.

Other Legal Issues in Parole Revocation

The Constitutional Right to Counsel

In *Morrissey. V. Brewer* the Court did not address the question of the parolee's right to the assistance of retained or appointed counsel at the preliminary and revocation hearings. The Court simply said, "We do not reach or decide the question whether the parolee is entitled to the assistance of retained or appointed counsel if he is indigent." One survey shows, however, that representation by counsel is provided for in 78.4 percent of the states surveyed.[21]

In one of the first cases decided after *Morrissey*, the California Supreme Court held that a probationer was entitled to representation by retained or appointed counsel at formal proceedings for the revocation of probation. The court held that a violation of a probation condition is often a matter of degree or quality of conduct, and the point where a violation occurs is often a matter of technical judgment. It then quoted from *Goldberg v. Kelly*[22] that "trained counsel in such circumstances can help delineate the issues, present the factual contentions in an orderly manner, and generally safeguard the interests of [the] client."

The California Supreme Court decision requiring counsel is at odds, however, with a decision of the U.S. Supreme Court on the same issue involving probation. In *Gagnon v. Scarpelli*,[23] decided a year after *Morrissey*, the U.S. Supreme Court mandated a case-by-case determination of the need for counsel at probation and parole revocation hearings. The determination of the need for counsel is to be left to the discretion of the state authority responsible for administering the probation and parole system. The Court stated that in cases where a probationer's or parolee's version of a disputed issue can be fairly presented only by trained counsel, appointment of counsel for the indigent probationer or parolee should be made, "[a]lthough the presence and participation of counsel will probably be both undesirable and constitutionally unnecessary in most revocation hearings." Both the U.S. Supreme Court and the California Supreme Court refused to make the rule in *Morrissey* applicable to parole revocations that occurred before that decision.[24]

The Right to Confront Witnesses

The Court in *Morrissey* said that a parolee facing revocation has "the right to confront and cross-examine adverse witnesses (unless the hearing officer specifically finds good cause for not allowing confrontation)." Lower courts have interpreted this right to be limited, consistent with the concept of "diminished" constitutional rights. In a 1994 case,[25] for example, the Federal Eighth Circuit Court of Appeals decided that a parolee has a limited right to confront and cross-examine witnesses for the government in a parole revocation hearing. It further held that *hearsay evidence* (referring to statements offered by a witness that are based upon what someone else has told the witness and not upon personal knowledge or observation)[26] may be admitted and considered in a revocation hearing. These rules, the court said, must be properly balanced; otherwise due process is violated and the revocation of parole must be reversed. In this case no right to confrontation was given the parolee in either the preliminary or the revocation hearing despite his request to be allowed to question witnesses. Moreover, hearsay evidence was used for revocation, including violation reports, police reports, and a signed statement by the victim. The Court acknowledged that the right to confront witnesses is given to a parolee, but this right may be limited by the state if the "hearing officer specifically finds good cause for not allowing confrontation." If the government denies a parolee the right to confrontation, the government has the burden of justifying that denial. Failure to carry that burden means that a parolee's right to due process is violated, hence the revocation is invalid.

The court further said that the parolee must assert the right to confront witnesses at the preliminary hearing. If that is done then, there is no need to assert that right again in the revocation hearing. If the right is asserted, the state must allow the witnesses to be cross-examined unless the parolee waives the right or there is sufficient finding of good cause not to allow confrontation.[27] On the issue of hearsay as evidence, the court said that it is admissible in a parole revocation hearing as long as it is reliable. The court suggested questions to establish reliability:

1. Is the information corroborated by the parolee's own statements or other live testimony at the hearing?
2. Does the information fit within one of the many exceptions to the hearsay rule?
3. Does the information have other substantial indicia of reliability?

A "yes" answer to any of these above questions signifies that the hearsay is reliable and therefore may be admitted as evidence in court.

Due Process if the Board Changes its Mind Before Actual Parole Release

An issue related to parole revocation is whether the parole board must give an inmate due process if it changes its mind after informing the inmate that he or she is to be released on parole. In *Jago v. Van Curen*[28] the U.S. Supreme Court said that no due process rights are needed if the board changes its mind before actual inmate release. In that case inmate Van Curen pleaded guilty to a charge of embezzlement and was sentenced to not less than six nor more than 100 years in prison. Van Curen was interviewed in 1974 by a panel representing the parole board. The panel recommended that he be paroled "on or after April 23, 1974." The parole board approved the recommendation and the inmate was notified of this decision. Several days after Van Curen was interviewed, the parole board was informed that he had been truthful neither during the interview nor in the parole plan that he submitted to his parole officers. Van Curen had told the panel that he had embezzled $1 million when in fact he embezzled $6 million. In his parole plan Van Curen stated he would be living with his half-brother if paroled. It was discovered, however, that Van Curen actually intended to live with his homosexual lover. The parole board withdrew his early parole as a result of these revelations and, at a later meeting, formally denied Van Curen parole. At no time was Van Curen granted a hearing to explain the false statements he had given the parole authorities. He sued the parole authorities, claiming that the withdrawal of his parole without a hearing violated his constitutional right to due process.

The Court disagreed and held that the due process clause does not guarantee a hearing in cases of parole withdrawal prior to actual release on parole. The Court said,

> We would severely restrict the necessary flexibility of prison administrators and parole authorities were we to hold that any one of their myriad decisions with respect to individual inmates may . . . give rise to protected "liberty" interests which could not thereafter be impaired without a constitutionally mandated hearing under the Due Process Clause. This decision implies that withdrawal of parole prior to release is not equivalent to parole revocation after the inmate has been released and therefore does not trigger due process guarantees.

Cancellation of Provisional Release

In a 1997 case, *Lynce v. Mathis*,[29] the U.S. Supreme Court held that a Florida law canceling provisional release credits violates the *ex post facto* (penal legislation that has retroactive application) prohibition of the Constitution. Lynce was convicted of attempted murder in 1986 and sentenced to 22 years in a Florida prison. He was released in 1992 based on the Department of Corrections's determination that he had accumulated five different types of early release credits totaling 5,668 days, 1,860 of which were provisional credits given as a result of prison overcrowding. After the prisoner was released, the state attorney general issued an opinion stating that a 1992 Florida law retroactively canceled all provisional credits awarded to inmates convicted of murder or attempted murder. Lynce was rearrested and returned to prison. He went to court alleging that the retroactive cancellation of his provisional credits violated the ex post facto clause of the Constitution. The Court agreed, saying the 1992 Florida law "has unquestionably disadvantaged the petitioner because it resulted in his arrest and prolonged his imprisonment," adding that the Florida law "did more than simply remove a mechanism that created an opportunity for early release for a class of prisoners . . . rather, it made ineligible for early release a class of prisoners who were previously eligible—including some, like petitioner, who had actually been released."

Lynce is significant because it limits the applicability of newly enacted restrictive parole laws to inmates who were benefited by previous liberal laws. Restrictive parole laws can be enacted, but they apply only to inmates who have not yet earned parole credits. It cannot be applied to inmates who were benefited by and had earned release credit under a more advantageous law.

Due Process Rights of Prisoners Released under Preparole

In another 1997 decision, *Young v. Harper*,[30] the U.S. Supreme Court held that Oklahoma's preparole release program was equivalent to parole; therefore, released prisoners under **preparole** were entitled to due process rights, similar to those given in *Morrissey*, prior to being brought back to prison because their preparole had been revoked. In this case the State of Oklahoma established a preparole conditional supervision program so that when Oklahoma's prisons become overcrowded the Pardon and Parole Board could conditionally release prisoners before their sentences expired.

Upon determination of the board, an inmate could be placed on preparole after serving 15 percent of his sentence. An inmate became eligible for regular parole only after one-third of his or her sentence had elapsed.

Preparole program participants and regular parolees were released subject to similar conditions. The board reviewed Harper's criminal record and prison conduct and simultaneously recommended him for parole and released him under the preparole program. At that time he had served 15 years of a life sentence. After five months of preparole release the governor denied Harper's parole, and he was ordered by his parole officer to prison without any type of hearing. The Court held that Oklahoma's preparole release program was similar to parole, and therefore inmates released on preparole were entitled before preparole revocation to the due process rights given in *Morrissey*. In essence, the Court said that any state program for relieving prison congestion that has parole features is considered parole (regardless of what the program is called), so bringing an inmate back to prison requires due process.

Prison Time Credit for Time Served on Parole

In most jurisdictions the parolee whose parole is revoked receives no credit for the time spent on parole. In other jurisdictions the parolee receives credit on the sentence as straight time—that is, without the benefit of good-time credits. In a few states the parolee receives credit on his or her sentence equal to the time spent on parole and also earns reductions for good behavior while on parole. Generally a parolee whose parole has been revoked may be paroled again, but in some cases the revoked parolee must remain in prison for a specified time before becoming eligible for another parole.

The Right to Appeal Revocation

This issue was not addressed in *Morrissey* or in any subsequent case decided by the U.S. Supreme Court. In the absence of an authoritative decision, the answer has been no. One source reports that parolees, presumably by state law or agency policy, are entitled to appeal the revocation decision in 24 states. No such right is given in 26 states.[31]

The Time It Takes to Revoke and Outcomes

The time it takes to revoke parole varies from one jurisdiction to another. The only available data on the length of time it takes to revoke a parolee was gathered by Edward Rhine, William Smith, and Ronald Jackson. That study shows that in one state it took 10 days to revoke parole, while in 11 states it took an average of 60 days. In those 11 states, 5 states reported an average revocation time of more than 90 days. Thirty-six (76.4 percent) of the states reported that the revocation process was completed within two months.[32]

Parole revocation hearings usually result in revocation and incarceration for the original term. The same study by Rhine, Smith, and Jackson reveals that in 47 states (92.2%) the parolee may be returned to custody if parole is revoked. If the hearing shows that the parolee in fact committed the alleged violation, other sanctions are also available to the parole board:

1. No change in the parole status (used in 38 states)
2. Modification of parole conditions (used in 38 states)
3. Serve out-of-state sentence concurrently with or consecutively to the new sentence (used in 22 states)

4. Restoration to parole status, but parole term is extended (used in 21 states)
5. Incarceration for an extended term (used in 18 states)
6. Incarceration for a new term (used in 16 states)[33]

As in the case of probation, however, returning the offender to prison is usually discretionary with the board even in cases where the parolee commits a new offense. The only exception is if state law provides for automatic revocation if the parolee commits another offense. Conversely, however, a parolee may be revoked and returned to prison even if acquitted for a new offense. This is possible because while conviction for a new offense requires guilt beyond reasonable doubt, parole revocation usually requires a lower degree of certainty—either a preponderance of the evidence or reasonable suspicion that the parolee violated the terms of parole.

SUMMARY

Parole boards enjoy a lot of discretion when imposing parole conditions. The extent of authority and the limitations are basically similar to those in probation. Courts will generally uphold reasonable conditions but will strike down conditions that are impossible to meet. Parole conditions may be categorized into standard conditions and special conditions. Standard conditions are imposed on all parolees, while special conditions are tailored to fit the needs of an offender. While on parole, parolees enjoy diminished constitutional rights and therefore do not have the same rights as nonoffenders.

Revocation is the formal termination of a parolee's conditional freedom and the reinstatement of imprisonment. *Morrissey v. Brewer,* the leading case on parole revocation, holds that prior to revocation parolees must be given five basic rights. Nonetheless, these rights are not as extensive as those given to nonoffenders in criminal cases. Parolees do not have a constitutional right to counsel at a revocation hearing; this right is given on a case-by-case basis. Two recent U.S. Supreme Court decisions have given parolees more rights. One holds that a state law canceling an inmate's provisional release is unconstitutional if applied to a prisoner who was convicted before the law took effect. Another case decided that prisoners released under preparole are entitled to due process rights, similar to those granted in *Morrissey*, prior to being brought back to prison. Parolees do not have a constitutional right to appeal a revocation, but about half of the states, by law or agency policy, give parolees the right to appeal an adverse revocation decision.

ENDNOTES

1. Texas is an example where the parole board is an independent and autonomous agency that decides whether to parole an inmate. Once paroled, the parolee is under the custody and supervision of the Parole Division, which is an agency under the Texas Department of Criminal Justice.
2. *Boling v. Romer,* 101 F. 3d 1336 (10th Cir. 1996).
3. *Rise v. Oregon,* 59 F. 3d 1556 (9th Cir. 1995) and *Jones v. Murray,* 962 F. 2d 302 (4th Cir. 1992).
4. *Walrath v. Getty,* 71 F. 3d 679 (7th Cir. 1995).
5. American Correctional Association, *Standards for Adult Parole Authorities*, 2nd ed. (College Park, Md.: ACA, 1980), 28.

6. *United States v. Turner,* 44 F. 3d 900 (10th Cir. 1995).
7. *People v. Randazzo,* 15 N.Y. 2d 526 (1964). A California case reached the same result—*People v. Denne,* 141 Cal. App.2d 499 (1956).
8. *People v. Langella,* 244 N.Y.S. 2d 802 (1963). See also *DiMarco v. Greene* 385 F. 2d 556 (6th Cir. 1967).
9. *Commonwealth v. Pickron,* 535 Pa. 241 (1993).
10. *Commonwealth v. Walter,* 655 A. 2d 554 (Pa. 1995).
11. *Commonwealth v. Williams,* 1997 Pa. LEXIS 786 (1997), as cited in *The Law of Probation and Parole*, by James J. Gobert and Neil P. Cohen (1997 supplement), 315.
12. Gorbert and Cohen, *The Law of Probation and Parole,* 380. See also *Correctional Law Reporter* (October 1994), 36.
13. 18 U.S.C.A. sec. 3606.
14. *Probation and Parole: Theory and Practice*, by Howard Abadinsky, 4th ed. (Englewood Cliffs, N.J.: Prentice Hall, 1991), 224.
15. Although an emergency warrant may be issued on telephoned request from a parole officer, the board has traditionally limited the issuance of such warrants to situations that absolutely require immediate arrest and detention.
16. Edward E. Rhine, William R. Smith, and Ronald W. Jackson, *Paroling Authorities: Recent History and Current Practice* (Laurel, Md.: American Correctional Association, 1991), 123.
17. Henry Burns, *Corrections: Organization and Administration* (St. Paul: West), 308.
18. 408 U.S. 471 (1972).
19. Rhine, Smith, and Jackson, *Paroling Authorities,* 128.
20. Rhine, Smith, and Jackson, *Paroling Authorities,* 129.
21. Rhine, Smith, and Jackson, *Paroling Authorities,* 128.
22. 397 U.S. 254 (1970).
23. 411 U.S. 778 (1973).
24. *In re Prewitt,* 8 Cal. 3d 470 (1972).
25. *Belk v. Purkett,* 15 F. 3d 803 (8th Cir. 1994).
26. Wesley Gilmer, *The Law Dictionary,* 6th ed. (Cincinnati: Anderson, 1986), 160.
27. See *Correctional Law Reporter* (October 1994), 35.
28. 454 U.S. 14 (1981).
29. No. 95-7452 (1997).
30. No. 95-1598 (1997).
31. Rhine, Smith, and Jackson, *Paroling Authorities,* 129.
32. Rhine, Smith, and Jackson, *Paroling Authorities,* 129.
33. Rhine, Smith, and Jackson, *Paroling Authorities,* 131.

DISCUSSION QUESTIONS

1. What are the four limitations on the power of the parole board to impose conditions of parole?
2. What are the two types of parole conditions? Distinguish one from the other.
3. Is submission to a penile plethysmograph valid as a parole condition? Support your answer.
4. Discuss what this statement means: "Parolees have diminished constitutional rights." Does that statement apply to preferred rights? Explain.

5. May the residence of a parolee be searched by a parole officer without a search warrant and with the parolee's consent? What is the general rule?
6. "All parole officers are given authority to arrest a parolee without a warrant." Is that statement true or false? Support your answer.
7. Identify and discuss the three theories of parole and parole revocation.
8. What is the leading case on parole revocation, and what did that case say?
9. Parolees must be given five basic rights prior to revocation. What are those rights?
10. Does a parolee have a right to counsel at a revocation hearing? Justify your answer.
11. What is hearsay evidence, and is it admissible in a revocation hearing?
12. In 1997 the U.S. Supreme Court decided two cases giving parolees more rights. What do these cases say?

III

INTERMEDIATE SANCTIONS AND SPECIAL ISSUES

BURGEONING PRISON POPULATIONS AND HIGH RECIDIVISM RATES AMONG felony probationers since the early 1980s have prompted the search for alternative sanctions for certain offenders. These are the offenders for whom a sentence of imprisonment is unduly severe and regular probation is too lenient. One study of felony probation in California sounded a clarion call for the development of "intermediate sanctions." In its 1985 report *Granting Felons Probation,* the RAND Corporation stated that:

> [the] current troubles are self-perpetuating. Without alternative sanctions for serious offenders, prison populations will continue to grow and the courts will be forced to consider probation for more and more serious offenders. Probation caseloads will increase, petty offenders will be increasingly "ignored" by the system (possibly creating more career criminals), and recidivism rates will rise. In short, probation appears to be heading toward an impasse, if not a total breakdown, if substantially more funds are not made available to create more prison space. Since that is highly unlikely (and also, we believe, undesirable), alternative "intermediate" punishments must be developed and implemented.

In this section we will closely examine these problems and will discuss programs designed to more effectively deal with them. Included in the chapters that follow are issues of intermediate sanctions, juvenile justice, and loss and restoration of rights upon conviction.

In Chapter 11, "Intermediate Sanctions: Between Probation and Prison," we examine a range of intermediate sanctions, including house arrest, electronic monitoring, intensive supervision probation, restitution, community service, boot camps, and fines.

Chapter 12, "Juvenile Probation and Parole," recognizes that recent years have witnessed an increase in both the number of juvenile offenders and in the seriousness of the offenses they commit. These issues and correctional programs to deal with them are discussed in detail and recent court decisions affecting juvenile probation and parole are analyzed.

Chapter 13, "The Effectiveness of Community-Based Corrections," looks at the research on success and failure of a wide-range of community-based correctional programs.

Chapter 14, "Direct and Collateral Consequences of Crime" examines the disabilities imposed on convicted offenders that are not directly imposed by the court. Here we are concerned with losses that attach by the fact of the conviction, such as loss of right to vote, loss of the ability to hold certain jobs, and the right to own a firearm, among others.

Chapter 15, "Pardon and Restoration of Rights," considers the mechanisms by which convicted offenders may have some or all of their rights restored.

11

INTERMEDIATE SANCTIONS: BETWEEN PROBATION AND PRISON

KEY TERMS

- **Intermediate sanctions**
- **The RAND Study**
- **Intensive supervision probation (ISP)**
- **Shock incarceration**
- **Shock probation**
- **Boot camp**
- **House arrest**
- **Home confinement**
- **Electronic monitoring**
- **Restitution**
- **Community service**
- **Diversion**
- **Halfway house**
- **Day fines**

INTERMEDIATE SANCTIONS

A range of punishments that fall between probation and prison.

What You Will Learn in This Chapter

In this chapter you will examine the various alternatives to probation at one end of the correctional continuum and prison at the other. We will examine the practices of intensive supervision, house arrest and electronic monitoring, restitution and community service, halfway houses, boot camps, and fines as intermediate sanctions. Each program is discussed and analyzed.

INTRODUCTION

Recent years have witnessed the evolution of a range of **intermediate sanctions** to fill the gap between regular probation and prison. All of these new sanctions are attempts to provide increased control over offenders within the community. Until the advent of these intermediate punishments, the courts were faced with the polarized choice of either probation or prison. Criminologists Norval Morris and Michael Tonry write,

> Effective and principled punishment of convicted offenders requires the development and application of a range of punishments between prison and probation. Imprisonment is used excessively; probation is used even more excessively; between the two is a near-vacuum of purposive and enforced punishments.[1]

Morris and Tonry argue that we have been both too lenient and too severe. We have been too lenient with probationers who need tighter controls and too severe with prisoners who would present no serious threat to public safety if under supervision in the community.[2] They advocate the use of intermediate punishments such as intensive supervision probation (ISP), house arrest, electronic monitoring, restitution, community service orders, and fines. These punishments, they point out, do not exist in isolation. The fine is frequently combined with probation and incarceration. Electronic monitoring is not a sentence in itself; rather it enforces house arrest and curfews. Community service orders are combined with probation or parole. All are sometimes combined with brief jail or prison terms.[3] Morris and Tonry maintain,

> For some offenders, a substantial fine may well be combined with an order that the offender make restitution to the victim, pay court costs, and be subject to a protracted period of house arrest, monitored electronically, for which the offender pays the costs. For others, intensive probation involving regular and close supervision by a supervising officer playing a police role and also by a caseworker may be combined with a defined period of residence in a drug treatment facility, followed by regular urinalyses to ensure the offender remains drug-free, and also an obligation to fulfill a set number of hours of community service—all strictly enforced.[4]

THE RAND STUDY

The advent of widespread interest in alternative sanctions began with a report in 1976 by the U.S. Comptroller General, which concluded that probation systems were in crisis and served neither the public interest nor the offender's.[5] Other studies of the period arrived at the same conclusion.[6] Perhaps the most important of these (that is, the most heeded) and the one that precipitated serious interest in intermediate sanctions was the one conducted by the RAND Corporation for the National Institute of Justice.[7] The **RAND study** used data from more than 16,000 California felony offenders and recidivism data from a subsample of 1,672 felony probationers in Los Angeles and Alameda counties (California) in its attempt to determine the following:

RAND STUDY

Research on the effectiveness of probation conducted by the RAND Corp. in the 1980s.

- ▲ Upon what criteria do courts determine which convicted offenders will be imprisoned and which will be granted probation?
- ▲ What percentage of probationers are rearrested, reconvicted, and reimprisoned?
- ▲ How accurately can we predict recidivism?

The data revealed that a prior criminal record, drug addiction, being under community supervision at the time of arrest, being armed, using a weapon, and seriously injuring the victim were correlated with sentences to imprisonment rather than to probation. Offenders represented by private attorneys, those who pleaded guilty, and those who had obtained pretrial release were less likely to be imprisoned.

The study found that within 40 months after receiving sentences to probation, 65 percent of the offenders were rearrested; 51 percent were reconvicted; 18 percent were reconvicted of serious, violent crimes; and 34 percent were reincarcerated. Moreover, 75 percent of the official charges filed against the sample involved burglary, theft, robbery, and other violent crimes—the crimes most threatening to community safety.[8] Probationers who were like those imprisoned in terms of criminal history and seriousness of their crimes were 50 percent more likely to be rearrested than other probationers.

The RAND researchers found that the crimes and criminal records of about 25 percent of the offenders who were granted probation were indistinguishable from those of offenders who were sentenced to prison terms. They concluded that the courts have very limited ability to identify offenders who are likely to succeed on probation, and that "given the information now routinely provided to the court," the ability to predict which felon will succeed on probation "probably cannot be vastly improved."[9] The report concluded that granting felons probation poses a serious threat to public safety.

The researchers contended that the criminal justice system needs an "intermediate form of punishment for those offenders who are too antisocial for the relative freedom that probation now offers, but not so seriously criminal as to require imprisonment."[10] They recommended

> [a] sanction . . . that would impose intensive surveillance, coupled with substantial community service and restitution . . . structured to satisfy public demands that the punishment fit the crime, to show criminals that crime really does not pay, and to control potential recidivists.[11]

Citing the **intensive supervision probation** programs (ISPs) that were then being developed in several states as models for programs nationwide, the RAND researchers stated,

INTENSIVE SUPERVISION PROBATION

A form of probation that stresses intensive monitoring, close supervision, and offender control.

> Several states have experimental programs in place which indicate that an intensive surveillance program (ISP) should have intensive monitoring and supervision; real constraints on movement and action; employment; added requirements of community service, education, counseling, and therapy programs; and mechanisms for immediately punishing probationers who commit infractions.[12]

The researchers predicted that intensive supervision programs would be the most significant criminal justice experiments of the next decade.

INTENSIVE SUPERVISION PROBATION

Intensive supervision probation programs have developed rapidly around the country since the early 1980s.[13] Although ISP was originally designed to enhance rehabilitation and public safety by affording greater contact between the probation officer and the probationer, the purpose of more recent programs has been expanded to include reducing economic costs and alleviating prison overcrowding. ISPs are also seen as "socially cost-effective" because they are less likely than incarceration to contribute to the breakup of offenders' families, they allow offenders to remain employed, and they are less stigmatizing than prison. Offenders in ISP programs are thought to be deterred from committing crimes because they are under close surveillance and their opportunities for criminal activity are thus constrained. The programs vary from jurisdiction to jurisdiction, but most of them require multiple weekly contacts with probation officers, random night and weekend visits, unscheduled drug testing, and strict enforcement of probation conditions. Many require community-service restitution and some form of electronic surveillance.[14]

ISP Caseloads

Probation officers who supervise ISP clients generally have smaller caseloads than do those with regular probation caseloads. Probation and parole officers have long advocated smaller caseloads, contending that they allow the officers to give more assistance to the probationer in his or her rehabilitation efforts and provide greater protection to the community through increased surveillance and control. Whereas the average probation caseload exceeds 100 offenders, ISP officers generally supervise 25 or fewer offenders. Table 11.1 compares caseload size in selected jurisdictions. Probation officers averaged 180 cases per officer on regular probation caseloads and only 27 for ISP caseloads. Parole officers averaged 69 cases on regular caseloads and 27 on ISP caseloads.

A small but persuasive body of research indicates that reducing caseload size does *not* increase the effectiveness of adult probation or parole supervision when effectiveness is defined as the rate of recidivism.[15] In ISP programs, however, the reduced caseload size is (ideally) accompanied by more focused, extensive, and ubiquitous supervision than in regular probation.[16] Most ISP programs mandate specified levels of contact between probationer and probation officer and reduced caseload size. McCarthy and McCarthy explain:

> Each week, multiple personal contacts and collateral contacts with family and friends are employed to regulate the offender's travel, employment, curfews, drug use, and other relevant behaviors.[17]

A recent survey revealed that probation officers average 13 face-to-face contacts per year with probationers on regular supervision and 76 contacts with those on intensive supervision.[18]

The intensive supervision probation program in Georgia is one of the earliest and one of the most stringent. Georgia ISP officers supervise 25 probationers and are

Table 11.1 **AVERAGE CASELOAD PER OFFICER DURING 1996 BY TYPE**

Probation	Regular	Intensive	Electronic	Special
Arizona[1]	60	13		
Arkansas	173	15		
California[2]	900	43	43	53
Connecticut	213	25		
Dist. of Col.[3]	108	11		68.5
Florida	76	25	25	56
Georgia	218	23		
Hawaii	190	79	2.5	
Illinois	125	12		40
Kansas	71	7		
Michigan[4]	88			
Nebraska[5]	85	20		
New Jersey[6]	152	20		
New Mexico	71	20		25
Rhode Island	302	66		267
Tennessee[3]	85	21		
Texas[7]		33		40
Vermont	137			
Average	**180**	**27**	**24**	**79**

Parole	Regular	Intensive	Electronic	Special
Arizona	49		15	
Arkansas[8]	65	10		
California	88	59		35
Colorado[3]	60	20		
Connecticut[9]	50			20
Dist. of Col.	176	54		118
Georgia	60		25	
Hawaii	80	38		30
Indiana[10]	67			
Kansas[11]	63			
Massachusetts	60	15		19
Michigan[4]	95			
Nebraska	40	3		
New Jersey	86	25	16	25
New Mexico	71	20		25
New York[12]	100	40		65
Rhode Island	95		39	
South Dakota	31	15		
Tennessee[13]	54			
Texas	80	28	28	47
Vermont	10			
West Virginia	30			
Average	**69**	**27**	**25**	**43**

Table 11.1 **AVERAGE CASELOAD PER OFFICER DURING 1996 BY TYPE—*Continued***

Probation & Parole	Regular	Intensive	Electronic	Special
Alabama	165	20	20	
Alaska	59	15		
Delaware	113	40	19	20
Idaho	72		30	30
Iowa[14]	100	25		
Kentucky	87			
Louisiana	95			
Maine	152			
Maryland	98			
Minnesota	89	11		
Mississippi	118		17	
Missouri	66			
Montana	118			
Nevada	75	30	30	
New Hampshire	80	2		18
North Carolina	90	25		60
North Dakota	97	15		
Ohio	53			
Oklahoma[15]	80			
Oregon	100			
Pennsylvania	72			
South Carolina	97			
Utah[16]		22	25	55
Virginia[17]	76	28		
Washington	98			
Wisconsin	72	25		
Wyoming	69	10	10	
Federal[18]	70	26	26	
Average	**91**	**21**	**22**	**37**

[1]Int. based on answer of "2:25." [2]Reg. Supv. is 800–1000 cases. Int. supv. and elec. supv. are 25–60 cases. Spec. off. is 25–80 cases. [3]Int. incl. elec. [4]Avg. caseload is a combined quarterly avg. beginning 10/1/96–12/31/96. [5]Excl. juveniles. [6]Caseload for spec. off. varies. [7]Int. is avg. of 25–40. [8]Int. as of 12/31/96. [9]Elec. and spec. off. are 15–25. Spec. off incl. elec. [10]Incl. juvenile caseloads. [11]Based on Kansas caseload ADP (incl. probationers). Dept. leases 30 elec. monitoring units. [12]First year of parole is considered int. Time after that is considered reg. [13]Reg. supv. is the overall avg. caseload per officer. [14]Avg. reg. caseload is based on a range from 80–120. [15]Active cases only. [16]Spec. off. is avg. of 50 and 60. [17]Int. is avg. of a range from 24–32. [18]Reg. incl. parole. All fig. 1995.

Source: The Corrections Yearbook—1997.

Face-to-Face Contacts with Probation and Parole Officers during 1996

- Annually, probation officers had an average of 13 face-to-face contacts with probationers on regular supervision, 76 contacts with probationers on intensive supervision, 98 contacts with probationers on electronic monitoring, and 48 face-to-face contacts with probationers on special caseloads.
- Parole officers had an annual average of 19 face-to-face contacts with parolees on regular supervision, 62 contacts with parolees on intensive monitoring, 69 contacts with parolees on electronic monitoring, and 53 contacts with parolees on special caseloads.
- Probation and parole officers had an annual average of 30 face-to-face contacts with offenders on regular supervision, 141 contacts with offenders on intensive supervision, 115 contacts with offenders on electronic monitoring, and 67 contacts with offenders on special caseloads.

Source: The Corrections Yearbook—1997

required to make at least five face-to-face contacts with each probationer each week. Weekly unannounced alcohol and drug testing and weekly checks of local arrest records are also mandated.[19] Caseloads in Florida's intensive supervision program, called the Community Control Program (FCCP), are statutorily established at 20 or less. Supervision guidelines specify 28 contacts—24 personal and 4 collateral—per month.[20]

Evaluations of ISP

Early evaluations of ISP programs in Georgia, New York, and Texas found evidence that ISP was effective in reducing rearrests of probationers.[21] The Georgia program reported that the first 1000 participants committed only 25 serious offenses while under supervision and that by the sixth year the program had saved the state millions of dollars in correctional costs. However, because of their closer contact with probationers, ISP officers discovered more rule violations than the regular probation officers. Therefore, the intensive supervision programs had higher failure rates than regular probation even though their rearrest rates were lower.[22]

More recent evaluations question whether ISP programs were responsible for the reported successful outcomes. A 1990 study by the RAND Corporation found that judges used extra caution in sentencing offenders to the ISP programs in the early years because the programs were untested. Many programs limited participation to property offenders with minor criminal records, which undoubtedly helps to explain the lower rearrest rate.[23] When such biasing factors were controlled statistically, the researchers found no significant difference in the rearrest rates of ISP and regular probationers. Furthermore, in two of the three sites studied, there was no significant difference in the technical violation rates of regular probation and ISP participants. The findings suggest that ISP programs are not effective for high-risk offenders *if effectiveness is judged solely by offender recidivism rates.*[24] However, ISP programs are designed to serve three primary goals: (1) to relieve prison overcrowding and the costs of incarceration, (2) to keep offenders from committing crimes in the community while they are involved in the program, and (3) to impose intermediate punishment that is less severe than imprisonment but more severe than routine probation. The programs appear to be successful at imposing intermediate punishment, for which court-ordered conditions are more credibly monitored and enforced than is possible with routine probation.[25] Other studies suggest that although the costs of ISP programs are substantially greater than those of regular probation, ISP is much more cost-effective than imprisonment.[26] Some observers doubt that ISP reduces prison populations, however. Norval Morris and Michael Tonry suggest that research evidence and experience show that intermediate punishments free up many fewer prison beds and save much less money than their proponents claim. They contend that judges often hesitate to impose a new intermediate punishment on offenders who would otherwise be sentenced to prison because they doubt its ability to deliver appropriate punishment and to prevent crime. Instead, they claim, judges impose new intermediate punishments on *probation-bound* offenders.[27] Supporting this, in a study of Florida's Community Control Program, Blomberg found that 28 percent of those placed in this prison-alternative ISP program would have received probation if "community control" had not been available as a sentencing alternative.[28]

Obviously, much more research and evaluation are required in order to adequately assess the effectiveness of ISP as a correctional alternative. Unless it can be shown that ISP is more effective than regular probation in deterring criminal behavior, its greater costs may not be justifiable. However, despite findings that ISP does not reduce recidivism, these programs have enjoyed wide support from police, prosecutors, and correctional administrators. The close supervision has revitalized the reputation of probation and demonstrated probation's ability to enforce rules, support treatment programs, and ensure that offenders remain employed.[29]

SHOCK INCARCERATION AND BOOT CAMP

SHOCK INCARCERATION

A brief period of incarceration followed by a term of supervised probation. Also called shock probation, shock parole, intermittent imprisonment, or split sentence.

Shock incarceration refers to a brief period of imprisonment that precedes a term of supervised probation in hope that the harsh reality of prison will deter future criminal activity. A variety of shock incarceration formats are used, and they go by a number of names—*shock probation, shock parole, intermittent incarceration, split sentence,* and *boot camp.* The programs vary somewhat in design and organization, but all feature a short prison term followed by release under supervision. The target population is young offenders with no previous incarcerations in adult prisons.

In *shock probation* (also called *shock parole* and *intermittent incarceration*) an offender is sentenced to imprisonment for a short time (the shock) and then released and resentenced to probation. The prison experience is thought to be so distasteful that the offender will fear returning and thereafter avoid criminal behavior. The original shock probation program was established in Ohio in 1965. It was praised for limiting prison time, assisting in reintegration into the community, helping the offender to maintain family ties, and reducing prison populations and the costs of corrections.[30] The program's stated purposes were as follows:

- To impress offenders with the seriousness of their actions without a long prison sentence
- To release offenders found by the institutions to be more amenable to community-based treatment than was realized by the courts at the time of sentencing
- To serve as a just compromise between punishment and leniency in appropriate cases
- To provide community-based treatment for rehabilitable offenders while still imposing deterrent sentences where public policy demands it
- To protect the briefly incarcerated offender against absorption into the inmate culture[31]

Shock incarceration is controversial. Todd Clear and George Cole argue that it combines undesirable aspects of both probation and prison.[32] They write,

> Offenders who are incarcerated lose their jobs, have their community relationships disrupted, acquire the label of convict, and are exposed to the brutalizing experiences of the institution. Further, the release to probation reinforces the idea that the system is arbitrary in its decision making and that probation is a "break" rather than a truly individualized supervision program. It is hard to see how this kind of treatment avoids demeaning and embittering offenders.[33]

Shock probation programs have been evaluated by a number of researchers. Early studies reported success rates between 78 and 91 percent.[34] Programs were praised for limiting prison time, providing a chance for offenders to be reintegrated back into the community quickly, and for making offenders more receptive to probation supervision by illustrating the problems they will encounter if they violate the terms of their probation.[35]

However, shock incarceration was not always imposed on those for whom it was intended—young first offenders. Nicolette Parisi, in a study of federal probationers, found that a third of those who had received split sentences had previously been incarcerated on other charges, which negated the value of the "shock." Furthermore, Parisi was unable to find evidence that probationers who had first served a short period of incarceration were more successful than those who had not.[36]

Despite mixed findings on success rates, recent studies show that the use of shock probation and split sentencing is increasing nationwide.[37] McCarthy and McCarthy report that nearly a third of those placed on probation in some jurisdictions receive some sentence to confinement as well.[38]

Boot Camps

Boot camps are the most common form of shock incarceration. **Boot camps** require the convicted offender to reside in a correctional facility and participate in a program designed to instill discipline and responsibility. Most boot camp programs are designed to provide an experience much like that of military basic training with intensive physical training, hard work, and little or no free time. After a specified period, typically 90–120 days, the probationer is released to regular probation supervision. Boot camps provide the court with an alternative disposition, stricter and more structured than regular probation, yet less severe than a prison sentence.

BOOT CAMP

A form of shock incarceration that involves a military-style regimen designed to instill discipline in young offenders.

Figure 11.1 **BOOT CAMPS IN OPERATION ON JANUARY 1, 1997**

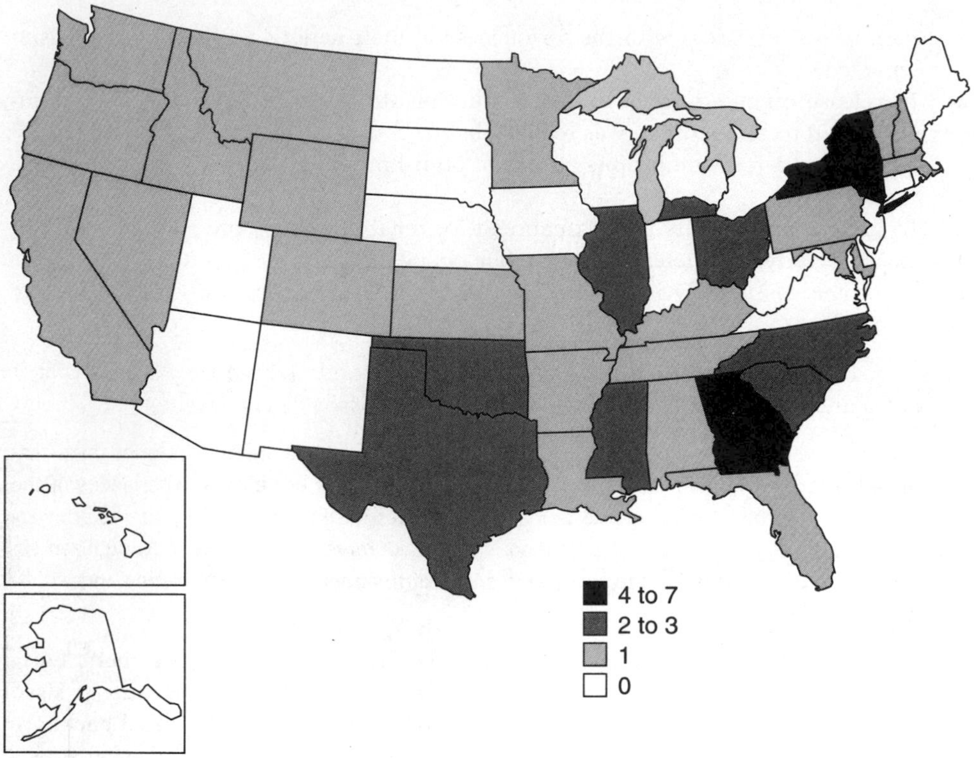

4 to 7
2 to 3
1
0

Source: The Corrections Yearbook—1997

Boot camps have strong public appeal, and their use appears to be increasing.[39] As shown in Table 11.2, by 1997 there were 54 boot camp programs operating in 33 states and the federal system.

The Harris County, Texas Boot Camp CRIPP Program

In 1991 Harris County (Houston), Texas, implemented a boot camp program for young felony offenders. The CRIPP (Courts Regimented Intensive Probation Program) boot camp program is administered jointly by the Harris County Community Corrections Department (Probation) and the Harris County Sheriff's Department, which provides drill instructors to supervise boot camp participants and provides security and custody staff for the facility.

CRIPP is based on a military model with participants grouped together in a cohort of 48 members who stay together for the full 90 days of the program. CRIPP participants are provided a range of services and program opportunities:

- *Medical services.* Participants undergo an extensive medical examination before arriving at the facility. Probationers with physical limitations are referred back to the sentencing court. Participants are also provided medical counseling services such as AIDS counseling and anonymous, voluntary HIV testing.
- *Vocational services.* Probationers can participate in vocational skills programs, including basic computer literacy skills.

Table 11.2 **BOOT CAMPS IN OPERATION AND COST PER INMATE PER DAY**

	Year First Opened	1/1/97 Boot Camps	Program Length (mos.)	1996 Daily Cost Per Inmate	Planned for 1997
Alabama[1]	1988	1	3	$21.44	0
Arkansas[1,2]	1990	1	15	$38.05	0
California	1993	1	6		0
Colorado	1991	1	3	$61.78	0
Florida[1]	1987	1	4	$50.13	1
Georgia[1]	1991	7	3	$26.00	0
Idaho[1]	1989	1	6	$38.10	0
Illinois	1990	3	4	$57.26	0
Kansas[3]	1991	1	6	$37.15	0
Kentucky[1]	1993	1	4.3	$31.56	0
Louisiana[1]	1987	1	6	$43.00	0
Maryland	1990	1	6	$39.64	0
Massachusetts[1,4]	1992	1	4	$56.01	0
Michigan[1]	1988	1	3	$68.46	0
Minnesota	1992	1	6	$149.12	0
Mississippi[1]	1985	3	5	$30.51	0
Missouri[1]	1994	1	3		0
Montana[1]	1993	1	3.5	$114.39	0
Nevada[1]	1991	1	6	$16.63	0
New Hampshire	1990	1	4	$50.96	0
New Jersey		0			1
New York[1]	1987	4	6	$64.27	0
North Carolina[1]	1989	2	3	$64.32	0
Ohio[1]	1991	2	3	$61.00	0
Oklahoma[1]	1984	2	4.5		0
Oregon[5]	1994	1	9	$65.00	0
Pennsylvania	1992	1	6	$121.39	0
South Carolina[6,7]	1987	2	3	$40.11	0
Tennessee[8]	1989	1	3.5	$64.06	0
Texas[9]	1989	2	3	$43.78	0
Vermont[1]	1993	1	4.5	$71.62	0
Washington[10]	1993	1	4	$75.85	0
Wisconsin	1991	1	6	$72.21	0
Wyoming[1]	1990	1	4	$39.00	0
Federal[1,11]	1991	3	6	$47.00	0
Average and Total	**1990**	**54**	**5**	**$56.77**	**2**

[1]Length of program is based on number of days reported. [2]Cost is FY'96. [3]County boot camp oper. with state grant. [4]Prgm. cost incl. cost to house some med. security inmates at site. [5]Length of program is 6 mo. as inmate, plus 3 mo. transition leave under inst. juris. [6]Boot camp is a program created for inmates 17–25 yrs. old sentenced under Youth Offender Act with indeterminate sentences. Boot camps reported in previous yrs. refer to shock incarceration program. [7]Shock incarceration prgm. is 3 months. [8]Length is 90–120 days. [9]Program length based on 75–90 days. [10]Work ethic camp. [11]Other programs opened in 1992, 1996.

Source: The Corrections Yearbook—1997

- *Physical training.* Physical conditioning, including drill and calisthenics, occupies the largest portion of the participants' time in the CRIPP program.
- *Social skills.* Participants may choose to participate in drug and alcohol counseling provided by counselors from the county health department and from probation staff.[40]

Upon release participants are transferred to a 90-day "superintensive" probation program. Probationers have daily contact with probation officers for the first 30 days after release, biweekly contact for the next 30 days, and one contact weekly for the following 30 days.

Velmer Burton and his colleagues evaluated the CRIPP program to determine if it changed offender attitudes. The study measured attitudinal change in the areas of coping and self-control, perceptions of boot camp staff, benefits of participating in AIDS and drug and alcohol counseling, attitudes toward the CRIPP program, perceptions of future opportunities, and the quality of relationships with family and friends.[41] They found that the CRIPP program did produce significant positive results, as measured by attitudinal change. Offenders improved their outlook on family life, and many came to realize the influence of their friends on their criminal behavior. CRIPP graduates demonstrated greater self-control and better coping skills than they had when entering the program. Additionally, they appeared to be less impulsive and more in control of their personal situations. With the exception of their attitudes regarding AIDS counseling and education, positive effects were noted in all areas.[42]

No effort was made to measure recidivism upon release from the CRIPP program and the 90-day probation term. Only if the attitudinal change resulted in long-term behavioral change can it be said that the experience was effective and cost beneficial.

New York State's Boot Camps

The New York State Department of Correctional Services (DOCS) began a shock incarceration program in 1987 and currently operates four adult facilities with a total capacity of 1,570, including 180 beds for women offenders. New York's boot camps, like almost all others, emphasize strict, military-like discipline, unquestioning obedience to orders, and highly structured days filled with hard work. However, they also focus on providing a total learning environment that fosters involvement, self-direction, and individual responsibility.[43]

The New York program has two legislatively mandated goals:

- To treat and release selected state prisoners earlier than their court-mandated minimum period of incarceration without endangering public safety
- To reduce the need for prison bed space[44]

In New York judges cannot sentence an offender directly to a shock incarceration program. DOCS staff select participants they consider suitable for the program from the inmate population. To qualify for the boot camp program in New York, offenders must be under 35 and eligible for parole within three years of admission to the DOCS. All offenders in the DOCS who are legally qualified for the boot camp program are initially sent to an orientation and screening center. At the center they are informed about the program and allowed to volunteer to participate rather than serving their full term in prison. Those who volunteer are screened for physical and mental problems that would prohibit them from participating. They are then introduced to some of the boot camp programs for a brief period. DOCS officials believe that this brief

Boot camp study points to success

A little over three months ago, Mark Alvarado thought the drill instructors at the Harris County Boot Camp were his tormenters. He believed the judge who sentenced him to 120 days in the intensive probation program was unfair.

Alvarado, 21, graduates from boot camp in two weeks.

On Thursday, he said, once is enough in the tough, military-style drill program.

At the same time, he said, it has made a difference in his outlook.

"Now, I wouldn't trade it for anything," he said.

Alvarado's experience is typical of Harris County Boot Camp graduates, according to a Sam Houston State University study released this week.

That study found graduates emerge from the demanding probation regimen with better attitudes—the key to staying out of trouble, officials said Thursday.

An improved attitude is "extremely important," said Boot Camp Director Mike Enax.

"I think the attitude that they had when they got here is what got them in trouble in the first place," Enax said.

Bob Wessels, county criminal court manager, who works as a link between judges and probation programs, said reports like the Sam Houston study help the courts know which programs work.

"We begin to match for-real—based on our experience in Harris County—programs to people," Wessels said.

"One of the things the Sam Houston study shows is you (lower recidivism rates) if you can raise their literacy, improve their job skills, teach them to read, and improve their self-esteem."

The study, by professors Velmer S. Burton Jr., James W. Marquart, Steven J. Cuvelier, Leanne Fiftal Alarid, and Robert J. Hunter, examined attitude changes in 389 probationers who completed the boot camp program.

Boot campers completing the program were more likely to accept criticism and to respect authority figures and drill instructors than when they entered the program, according to the study.

They were also more likely at the end of the program to want to avoid criminal behavior.

The study found that probationers completing boot camp had improved attitudes about drug and alcohol counseling and felt that counseling would help them beat their habits.

In addition, the study found that as boot camp residents spent time in the program, their opinions changed about the positive influence the experience was having on their lives.

Similar results were reported in probationers' attitudes about the quality of the boot camp's educational programs and about their future prospects for returning to school or securing a job.

The study reported probationers emerged with better attitudes about coping skills and self-control and that some developed more positive attitudes about family relationships.

Enax said the results square with statistics compiled by the Harris County Community Supervision and Corrections Department, which found that 85 percent of the over 2,300 men and women completing the program have not committed new crimes.

"When they first get here, they feel like it's been done as a punishment," he said.

"But after a while, they see what everybody's doing for them. Their attitude starts to be that, 'Maybe they put me here so I could learn something and get somewhere.'"

Alvarado, a convicted auto thief who was put on probation only to have it revoked later, agreed.

"When I first came in, I thought that the judge was just being unfair to me," he said.

After four months of strict discipline meted out by the boot camp instructors, Alvarado is making plans to stay out of trouble.

He wants to complete his last year at Houston Community College and begin work toward a teaching certificate at the University of Houston.

"My attitude has improved," he said.

Source: Andrea D. Greene, *The Houston Chronicle*.

Figure 11.2 **DAILY SCHEDULE FOR OFFENDERS IN NEW YORK SHOCK INCARCERATION FACILITIES**

A.M.	
5:30	Wake up and standing count
5:45–6:30	Calisthenics and drill
6:30–7:00	Run
7:00–8:00	Mandatory breakfast/cleanup
8:15	Standing count and company formation
8:30–11:55	Work/school schedules

P.M.	
12:00–12:30	Mandatory lunch and standing count
12:30–3:30	Afternoon work/school schedule
3:30–4:00	Shower
4:00–4:45	Network community meeting
4:45–5:45	Mandatory dinner, prepare for evening
6:00–9:00	School, group counseling, drug counseling, prerelease counseling, decision-making classes
8:00	Count while in programs
9:15–9:30	Squad bay, prepare for bed
9:30	Standing count, lights out

Source: National Institute of Justice: Program Focus Shock Incarceration in New York, August 1994

introduction to the activities of the program has resulted in lower failure rates among those who finally enter the program full time.

Those who are accepted into the program are assigned to one of four minimum security facilities. Male participants work in platoons of 54–60 men and proceed through the 180-day program as a unit. Figure 11.2 shows a schedule of the daily activities of participants.

While the inmate is in the facility, 41 percent of his or her time is devoted to treatment and education. Physical training and drill constitute 26 percent of the time, with hard labor on facility and community projects constituting the remaining 33 percent. This schedule with close supervision and strict discipline places strict limitations on inmates' behavior. For most such limits are new and unique. Many cannot conform to the program and drop out. Clark and her associates report that about 37 percent of those who enter shock incarceration do not complete it.

Those who successfully complete the six-month regimen are paroled and enter a postrelease phase of the program known as "AfterShock." The goal of "AfterShock" is to continue the close supervision that began in the institutional phase and to provide opportunities and programs in the community designed to improve the parolee's chances for successful integration. Each participant has two parole officers to allow increased contacts between the officers and parolees for home visits, curfew checks, and drug testing. AfterShock parolees have priority access to community services such as educational and vocational training.

The DOCS has found that the shock incarceration program saves money by reducing costs in regular prison programs and by avoiding capital costs for new prison construction. The DOCS estimates that it saves $2 million in prison costs for every 100 shock incarceration graduates. Recidivism rates for graduates 12 months after completion of the program were 10 percent compared to 15 percent for those who were screened but rejected and 17 percent for those who withdrew or were removed from shock incarceration before completion. After 24 months 30 percent of graduates had returned to prison, compared to 36 percent of the considered inmates and 41 percent of those who failed to complete the program. At 36 months shock incarceration graduates still returned to prison at lower rates, but the difference was significant only between program graduates and the considered group.[45] Clark and her associates sum the program up:

> DOCS evaluation so far indicates that the program is responding to the legislature's call for reducing prison bed space needs without increasing the public's risk. Even more important, New York's therapeutic approach may point the way for redirecting the lives of a number of young offenders, helping them stay out of the criminal justice system once they have paid their debt to society.[46]

Evaluations of Boot Camp Programs

Supporters of the boot camp concept contend that there is some evidence that the boot camp experience may be more positive than incarceration in traditional prisons. Moreover, they state, those who have completed such programs describe the experience as difficult, but constructive. They assert that recidivism rates for those who complete boot camp programs are approximately the same as for those who serve longer periods in traditional prisons or on probation.[47] After a study of existing programs, however, Merry Morash and Lila Rucker warned that boot camps hold potential for negative outcomes. Many boot camp environments are characterized by inconsistent standards, contrived stress, and leadership styles that are likely to reduce self-esteem, increase the potential for violence, and encourage the abuse of power.[48]

The National Institute of Justice recently sponsored an evaluation of eight adult boot camp programs nationwide. In all eight programs offenders participate in rigorous daily schedules involving military drill, physical training, and hard labor for 90 to 180 days. Participants were generally young males convicted of nonviolent offenses who did not have lengthy criminal records. The boot camp programs differed in a variety of ways, including length of stay, size, location (located inside a prison or in a separate facility), emphasis on treatment programming and the amount of time devoted to therapeutic programming, and the existence and intensity of postrelease supervision and programming.[49]

In five of the states evaluated (Oklahoma, Texas, Georgia, Florida, and South Carolina) the boot camp programs did not reduce recidivism. In the other three states (New York, Illinois, and Louisiana) graduates had lower rates on one measure of recidivism. In the states in which recidivism was reduced, the researchers found a strong focus on postrelease supervision and an emphasis on rehabilitation, voluntary participation, selection from prison-bound offenders, and a longer program duration. Each program had a high dropout rate. The researchers concluded that any or all of these factors "could have had an impact on offenders with or without the boot camp atmosphere."[50]

The issue of whether boot camps reduce prison crowding depends on whether the program targets prison-bound offenders. The NIJ study found that programs that allowed the Department of Corrections to select participants were most likely to alleviate prison crowding because they "maximized the probability of selecting offenders who would otherwise have been sentenced to prison."[51]

Unlike prisoners in conventional prisons, boot camp participants reported that their experiences had been positive and that they had changed for the better. These effects were stronger in programs that were voluntary or in those that provided follow-up programming and treatment after release.

The Future of Shock Incarceration Programs

Evidence at this stage of the growth and widespread use of boot camps and other shock incarceration programs seems to indicate a small but significant positive effect on recidivism and prison costs. Moreover, public demand for these programs continues. Furthermore, the Violent Crime Control and Law Enforcement Act of 1994 allowed $20 billion to create and operate more boot camps. For this reason alone boot camps will be a part of correctional practice for years to come.[52] Anderson, Burns, and Dyson conclude that boot camps are popular and continue to grow for three reasons: (1) they are cost-effective; (2) they help preserve scarce bed space; and (3) they are therapeutic in their corrective approach. However, they also argue that the potential for success is severely curtailed if aftercare provisions are not made a mandatory part of the boot camp experience. Without aftercare as an integral part of shock incarceration, any rehabilitative effects could be lost.[53]

HOUSE ARREST AND ELECTRONIC MONITORING

House arrest is not a form of probation but rather a condition of probation.[54] Electronic monitoring is a means of assuring that certain conditions of probation are met. Both have found acceptance in many jurisdictions because of their potential to satisfy the goals of imprisonment without the social and financial costs associated with incarceration.[55]

House Arrest

HOUSE ARREST

An intensive supervision program that requires the offender to remain in his or her home except during working hours or while attending court-ordered treatment programs.

House arrest, or **home confinement,** is neither a new concept nor a U.S. innovation. Galileo (1564–1642) was placed under house arrest by Church authorities for his heretical assertion that the earth revolved around the sun. More recently, Soviet physicist Andrey Sakharov (1921–1989) was confined to an apartment in Gorky for "antistate" activities.

In contemporary America house arrest is viewed as an alternative to incarceration and a means of easing prison overcrowding. For most house arrestees it is their last chance to escape a prison sentence. Programs vary, but most require that offenders remain within the confines of their home during specified hours—ranging from 24-hour-per-day confinement to imposition of late-night curfews only.

Most states and the federal system now operate some form of house-arrest program. Florida, Georgia, Oklahoma, Oregon, Kentucky, and California all make extensive use of this option. Florida's "community controlees" (those under house arrest) are required to maintain employment and to participate in self-improvement programs, such as a GED program to obtain a high school diploma, drug and alcohol counseling, or other "life skills" programs. Many are required to perform community service as well. When they are not participating in work, self-help programs, or community service, they must be at their residence.

Florida's community control officer caseloads are limited by statute to 20 offenders, and the officers work Saturdays, Sundays, and holidays. They are required to make a minimum of 28 contacts per month with each offender. Officers' schedules vary from day to day, resulting in regular but random visits with the offenders. If an offender is not where he or she should be at any particular time, a violation of community control is reported to the court.

Some contend that the intrusiveness of house arrest violates a probationer's constitutional right to privacy in his or her own home. Others argue that the program is voluntary and that the offender has given up much of this right as a result of a felony conviction. Some critics suggest that surveillance by the use of electronic monitoring may constitute unreasonable search and seizure, and that because eligibility for electronic monitoring programs requires a telephone and payment of a fee for electronic surveillance, the program discriminates against those who cannot pay the fee or afford telephone service.[56] Joan Petersilia reports that some jurisdictions have avoided this criticism by basing fees on a sliding scale or providing telephones for those who do not have them.[57]

Petersilia warns that house arrest and electronic surveillance programs are often inaugurated with unrealistic goals and expectations of success. She points out that because considerable self-discipline is required to comply with house arrest and many offenders are impulsive by nature, many offenders are likely to be unable to sustain the required behavior for long periods.[58] Several community control officers in Florida report that it is not unusual for the spouse of an individual on house arrest to complain that he or she cannot stand another day with the husband or wife at home all day. And according to the officers, several house arrestees have requested that they be sent to prison rather than continue on house arrest. One told his supervising officer, "If I have to spend any more time with my old lady, I'll probably kill her. Send me on down to Raiford [the state prison]."

House arrest may also be used for defendants awaiting trial who would otherwise be held in jail. Defendants who cannot make bail and who do not qualify for release on personal recognizance may be considered for house arrest. In Marion, Indiana, house arrest for defendants awaiting trial was instituted to relieve jail overcrowding. Although fewer than 25 percent of those referred for screening were accepted by the program, 73 percent of those accepted successfully completed the program. Of those who failed to complete the house arrest program, 13 percent were technical violators and 14 percent absconded.

Electronic Monitoring

Electronic monitoring—a correctional technology rather than a correctional program—provides verification of an offender's whereabouts. *EM,* as it is often referred to, is useful at many points on the correctional continuum, from pretrial release to parole. Figure 11.3 illustrates the key decision points where electronic monitoring is currently used. By January 1, 1997, nearly 20,000 probationers and parolees were under electronic monitoring in the United States. As shown in Table 11.3, Florida, Georgia,

ELECTRONIC MONITORING

A correctional technology that allows verification of an offender's whereabouts. The monitoring system is usually composed of a control computer located at a criminal justice agency and a transmitter worn by the offender.

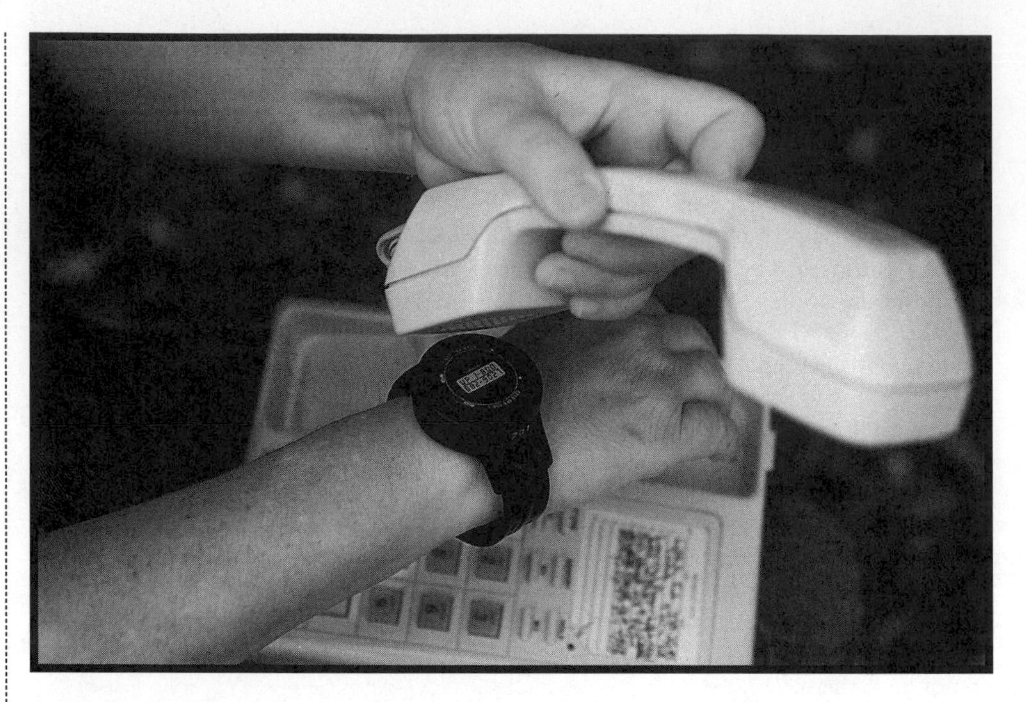

Convicted offender answers home electronic monitoring call.

Michigan, Missouri, North Carolina, Wisconsin, and the federal government make the greatest use of electronic monitoring.

The monitoring system is usually composed of a control computer located at the controlling agency and a transmitter device worn by the offender. The style of the transmitter varies; some are worn on the ankle, others on the wrist or around the neck. It monitors the presence of the offender in a vicinity during times when he or she is supposed to be there. Although the offender conceivably can remove the device by cutting the strap or stretching it and taking it off, an electronic circuit within the device detects such tampering and sends an alarm to the receiving unit. The device has been continually improved over the years and has been accepted by the scientific community as reliable and difficult for the offender to manipulate.

Legal and constitutional issues have been raised with regard to electronic monitoring, but the courts have consistently rejected them. Claims that it constitutes an unconstitutional search and seizure or that it violates the offender's right to privacy have not made much headway. Equal protection and due process arguments have also been raised without success. In sum, electric monitoring has passed constitutional muster and has become an often-used alternative to imprisonment, primarily because it is cost-effective and keeps the offender in the community.

Criticisms and Problems

Numerous criticisms have been leveled at electronic monitoring and house arrest, and various problems of implementation have been noted. Annesley Schmitt directed a major study of house arrest and electronic monitoring and observed that offenders must learn to handle the equipment properly and that their families must adapt to

Figure 11.3 **KEY DECISION POINTS WHERE ELECTRONIC MONITORING PROGRAMS ARE USED**

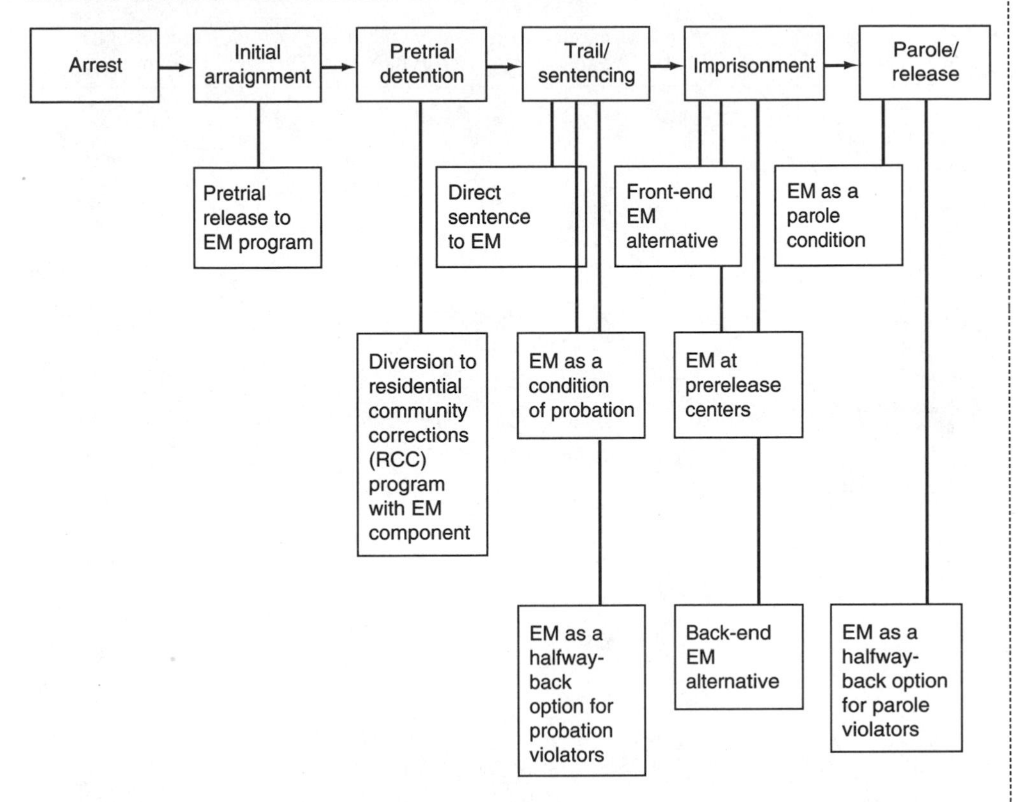

Source: James Byrne, Arthur Lurigio, and Christopher Baird, *The Effectiveness of the New Intensive Supervision Programs,* Research in Corrections Series, vol. 2, no. 2 (preliminary unpublished draft; Washington, D.C.: National Institute of Corrections, 1989).

using the telephone sparingly so that computer "calls" can be completed. Poor telephone service, bad wiring, and call-waiting and call-forwarding features on the telephone have caused technical problems. Offenders who live close to FM radio stations or transmitters have had difficulty receiving and sending the required information via the electronic devices. Correctional authorities reported unanticipated costs—for extra telephone lines, special interconnections, underestimated long-distance charges, and supplies.[59] A Texas probation agency reported that its programmed-contact computer malfunctioned and called one probationer more than 300 times in one night.[60] Charles Friel and Joseph Vaughn[61] reported other problems:

- Large metal objects, such as furnaces and refrigerators, between the transmitter and receiver have interrupted transmissions and caused false alarms.
- False alarms have occurred when offenders curled up while sleeping, positioning their bodies between the receiver and transmitter and blocking the signal.
- Probationers living in mobile homes, constructed largely of metal, have experienced transmission problems.

Table 11.3 **USE OF ELECTRONIC MONITORING DURING 1996**

Probation	Use Electr. Monitors	Number of Devices 1/1/97	Weeks Worn
Arizona	○	120	18
California	○		
Colorado	○		
Connecticut[1]	○	100	18
Dist. of Col.	○	30	12
Georgia[2]	○		
Hawaii	○	12	4
Idaho	○	50	16
Illinois	●		
Indiana	○		
Kansas	○	165	6
Massachusetts	○	100	16
Nebraska[1]	○	244	10
New Jersey	●		
New Mexico	○		16
New York[3]	○		
Tennessee	○	300	8
Texas	○		
West Virginia	○		
Wyoming	○	25	12
Total	**17**	**1,146**	
Average		**115**	**12**

Probation & Parole	Use Electr. Monitors	Number of Devices 1/1/97	Weeks Worn
Alabama	○	40	14
Arkansas[1,7]	○	5	15
Delaware	○	550	24
Florida	○	1,100	20
Iowa	○	100	5
Minnesota[8]	○	100	3
Mississippi	○	600	24
Missouri	○	1,000	
Montana	○	150	12
New Hampshire	○	50	12
New Mexico	○	140	
North Carolina	○	2,250	10
North Dakota	○	25	8
Oklahoma[9]	●		
Oregon	○	508	4
South Carolina	○	250	12
Utah	○	150	
Virginia	○	225	12
Washington	○	21	4
Wisconsin[10]	○	2,377	17
Federal[11]	○	2,000	17
Total	**20**	**11,641**	
Average		**582**	**13**

Table 11.3 ***(Continued)***

Parole	Use Electr. Monitors	Number of Devices 1/1/97	Weeks Worn
Arizona[1]	❍	285	14
California	❍	15	38
Colorado	❍	425	17
Connecticut	❍		
Dist. of Col.	●		
Georgia	❍	1,100	11
Hawaii	❍	14	12
Idaho	❍	20	16
Illinois[4]	❍	358	12
Indiana	●		
Kansas	❍	30	6
Louisiana[1]	❍	150	18
Maryland	❍		12
Massachusetts	❍		
Michigan	❍	4,000	15
Nebraska	●		
New Jersey	●		
New Mexico	❍		26
New York[5]	❍	94	17
Pennsylvania[1]	❍	375	21
Rhode Island	❍		18
South Dakota[6]	●		
Tennessee	●		
Texas	❍	711	12
West Virginia	●		
Wyoming	❍	6	12
Total	**19**	**7,583**	
Average		**623**	**15**

❍ = yes; ● = no. [1]Weeks worn is avg. [2]Elec. mon. is part of intensive prob. supv. prog. (IPS). IPS is court-mandated and not responsibility of probation div. [3]Use of elec. mon. varies by county; some use. [4]Elec. mon. used for boot camp graduates only. [5]Weeks worn est. [6]Elec. mon. currently not being used. Own/lease 6 devices and they would be worn for 8 weeks if programming is started. [7]Five units avail., number is not limited. [8]Devices est. [9]Program not used for prob. or parolees. Only use elec. mon. to supv. inm. rel. early (not considered parolees). [10]900 devices in use. [11]Admin. Office of U.S. Courts for 1995.
Source: The Corrections Yearbook—1997

Cops: Defendant hocks home monitoring unit

Evelyn Daniels, awaiting trial on drug charges, was short on cash. So, police say, she pawned the most valuable thing she had at the time—a $1,700 court-ordered home monitoring device.

The opportunity to make a few bucks was too good to pass up.

She left the monitor at a local pawnshop, telling the clerk it was an answering machine, Broward sheriff's deputies said.

"This is like someone sawing the bars off their jail cell and taking the bars to a scrap dealer," said Deputy Roger Schmorr.

The device was recovered Friday morning at the Cash King Pawnshop, 2714 W. Sunrise Blvd.

Employees at the pawnshop refused to comment.

Daniels, 27, was arrested in March on several drug-related charges, police said. Circuit Judge Melanie May placed her on pretrial release, with a monitoring device and an ankle bracelet.

When deputies didn't get a signal from the device for a week, they went looking for Daniels, sheriff's spokesman George Crolius said.

"This is definitely a unique case," Crolius said. "No one has ever tried to sell an arrest device to a pawnshop before."

Daniels, also known as Michelle Williams and Tabatha Daniel, was picked up Friday morning at a Fort Lauderdale boardinghouse at 2940 NW 11th Pl. where she had been living. She was charged with violation of pretrial release, grand theft, and dealing in stolen property.

She is now being held at the Broward County Jail. Crolius said he doesn't expect to see her with a new home monitoring device anytime soon.

Source: *Miami Herald,* June 17, 1995.

- Power outages have caused the systems to "crash."
- Batteries in the devices worn by probationers sometimes fail.

Other critics are concerned that the widespread use of house arrest with electronic monitoring may result in "net-widening." Although the program was developed as an alternative to imprisonment, it is sometimes inappropriately used with offenders who would otherwise have been placed under regular probation supervision. Friel and Vaughn caution,

> Using the technology with individuals who would be granted probation anyway is potentially abusive. It has already been pointed out that this application is likely to raise costs without necessarily increasing benefits. In addition, it widens the correctional net needlessly and is an undue invasion of privacy.[62]

Evaluations of Electronic Monitoring Programs

In view of the promise as well as the perils associated with electronic monitoring, it is essential that careful evaluation studies be undertaken.[63] One such study was conducted by J. Robert Lilly and colleagues in West Palm Beach, Florida. The Florida program, developed by Pride, Inc., a nonprofit company, began in 1984. The Pride, Inc., program was a widely publicized EM program and was a model for many others across the country. Lilly and his associates reviewed 415 cases representing all cases from the 1984 beginning through October 1989. They found that 97 percent of the offenders completed the EM period of their probation successfully, and 80 percent completed the entire term of their probation. The researchers noted,

> The EM completion rate is especially impressive in view of the fact that the likelihood of probation violations is highest earliest in the probation period [during which the electronic monitoring occurred]. When one takes into account the fact that the tighter EM control is more likely to *provoke* trouble because of the offender's resistance to authority and more likely to result in *detection* of many minor technical violations that would have escaped attention later, the low EM revocation rate is even more impressive.[64]

Other studies have also found impressive results. Evaluations in Oklahoma, Texas, California, and Illinois have produced further evidence of the value of the program. As the technology continues to improve, it is likely that EM programs will continue to expand.

RESTITUTION AND COMMUNITY SERVICE

Restitution

RESTITUTION

Restoring of property or of a right to a person unjustly deprived of it.

Restitution is defined as the restoring of property or of a right to a person who has been unjustly deprived of it. It differs from a fine in that the money paid in a fine goes not to the victim but instead to the state. Victim restitution is also different from victim compensation. The money in victim restitution is given by the offender, whereas the money given to the victim by victim compensation programs comes from the state.[65]

Restitution is a popular intermediate sanction. It may require an offender to repay the victims of his or her crime for financial losses resulting from the crime—*monetary restitution*—or to serve the community in some way as symbolic restitution—*community-service restitution.* Restitution is an act of atonement for the criminal; the money taken from him or her helps rehabilitate the victim financially. Both monetary and community-service restitution are commonly ordered as conditions of probation or parole and may also be used as diversionary devices, providing offenders the opportunity to avoid having a criminal record altogether.[66] In *diversion* situations, a first offender (usually) is ordered to perform community service or to pay monetary restitution during a period when his or her case is "continued" by the court. After the required restitution is satisfied, the court dismisses the charges.

Restitution in History

Like house arrest, restitution has a long history. The Old Testament specifies fivefold restitution for stealing and then killing an ox and fourfold restitution for stealing and killing a sheep. Double restitution is mandated for stealing (Exodus 21). Leviticus commands that restitution plus an additional fifth be made by robbers (Leviticus 6). The Code of Hammurabi, developed between 1792 and 1750 B.C., mandates thirtyfold restitution if the victim is a "god" or a "palace" and tenfold restitution if the victim is a "villein" (a low-status laborer).[67]

British philosopher Jeremy Bentham (1748–1833) prescribed restitution as an essential means of making the punishment fit the crime. In the mid-1800s Quaker prison reformer Elizabeth Fry saw restitution as a mechanism of offender rehabilitation, stating that "repayment is the first step toward reformation."[68]

During the 1960s and 1970s the various national commissions on criminal justice and the model codes of the era emphasized the value of restitution both as punishment and rehabilitation. The Model Penal Code proposed that an offender placed on probation may be required to "make restitution of the fruits of his crime or to make reparation in an amount he can afford to pay, for the loss or damage caused."[69] The National Advisory Commission on Criminal Justice Standards and Goals (1973) considered restitution as a factor that might mitigate the imposition of a prison sentence.[70] Both the American Bar Association and the National Council on Crime and Delinquency support the use of restitution as a condition of probation.

Purposes of Restitution

Burt Galaway, an early proponent of restitution as a correctional tool, delineated five purposes of restitution:

▲ Restitution provides a less severe and more humane sanction for the offender.

▲ Restitution aids the rehabilitation of the offender, and it integrates the punitive and rehabilitative purposes of the criminal law. Because the rationale incorporates the notion that punishment is related to the extent of damages done, it is perceived as just by offenders and allows them a sense of accomplishment as they complete the requirements. Restitution also provides offenders a socially appropriate, concrete way of expressing their guilt and atoning for their offenses.

▲ Restitution benefits the criminal justice system by providing an easily administered sanction that reduces demands on the system.

▲ Restitution may reduce the need for vengeance in the administration of criminal law because offenders are perceived as responsible persons taking active steps to make amends for their wrongdoing.

▲ Restitution provides redress for crime victims. Galaway suggests, however, that helping crime victims should not be the primary aim of a restitution program. Too many crimes go unsolved, and in many the arrest does not result in a conviction. Even when a conviction is secured, restitution might not be the appropriate sanction. Thus restitution will help only a small number of crime victims. He suggests, instead, a publicly funded victim compensation program.[71]

Legal Problems Associated with Restitution

Two of the legal problems associated with restitution are indigency of the defendant and the setting of the restitution amount. If the defendant is indigent and cannot pay, courts cannot cite the defendant for contempt or send the defendant to prison. However, if the defendant refuses to pay, then incarceration is valid. The restitution

Offenders perform community service by filling sand bags to protect beach homes.

amount must be set by the judge; determination of the amount cannot be delegated unless specifically authorized by statute. In some jurisdictions the judge delegates setting the amount to the probation officer as part of the probation conditions. This is constitutionally invalid. However, the judge can ask the probation officer to recommend the restitution amount, and having imposed the amount, leave the mode of payment to the probation officer. Assume that the amount of restitution is set by the judge at $500. How that amount is paid can be determined by the probation officer—in monthly installments for example.[72]

The problem of collecting restitution has always been difficult. But in 1990 the Pennsylvania Supreme Court further exacerbated the problem by holding that bankruptcy served to discharge a restitution debt.[73] The *Correctional Law Reporter* commented on the case:

> Time will tell how many offenders try to evade monetary sanctions through bankruptcy. Certainly more time and more litigation is needed to decide whether sentencing alternatives remain for a judge who sees a monetary sanction or sanctions frustrated by a bankruptcy petition.

Community Service

As we have said, community service, a form of symbolic restitution, is unpaid service to the public to compensate society for some harm done by the crime. It might consist of working for a tax-supported or nonprofit agency such as hospitals, public parks or libraries, a poverty program, or a public works program. It may involve picking up roadside litter or removing graffiti. In community-service restitution the offender repays the community he or she offended by performing some service for it rather than by making monetary reparation.

COMMUNITY SERVICE

A form of symbolic restitution that involves unpaid work for a governmental or non-profit organization.

Like monetary restitution, community-service restitution is both punitive and rehabilitative. It is punitive in that the offender's time and freedom are restricted until the work is completed. It is rehabilitative in the same way as monetary restitution: it allows offenders to do something constructive, to increase their self-esteem, to reduce their isolation from society, and to benefit society through their efforts.

Community service is distinct from monetary restitution programs. As one scholar observed,

> Community service orders are generally more applicable than restrictive programs, since they may be employed even when the victim is indemnified against loss, where no victim can be identified, and where an identified victim will not cooperate.[74]

Further, community service provides an alternative form of restitution for offenders who are unable to make meaningful financial restitution and for those whose financial resources are so great that monetary restitution has no punitive or rehabilitative effect. As the search continues for less costly and more effective methods of dealing with offenders, community service is a major trend in U.S. corrections.[75]

Effectiveness of Restitution and Community Service

The evidence of effectiveness is mixed for these programs. Research suggests that without restitution and community service programs, the vast majority of offenders who now have restitution or community service orders would have simply been placed on regular probation and the victims would have been ignored. However, evidence also shows that recidivism rates are no lower, and in some cases are higher, than those on probation with no community service or restitution orders.[76]

HALFWAY HOUSES

HALFWAY HOUSE

Residential facilities for probationers or parolees or those under ISP supervision who require a more structured setting than would be available if living independently.

Halfway houses, also known as community treatment centers or community correctional centers, are defined as residential facilities for probationers, parolees, or those under ISP supervision who require a more structured setting than would be available from living independently. Offenders live in the facility, leaving only to work or to attend school or activities such as drug treatment. Residents generally work during the day and in the evening maintain the facility, perform community service, and attend classes or counseling sessions. Most halfway houses (HWH) require residents to submit to regular drug testing.[77] Residents are gradually allowed more independence as they progress toward their goals. Prison systems make extensive use of HWHs to allow inmates a graduated release—something to fill the gap between total incarceration and absolute freedom. A three- to six-month stay in a HWH allows the inmate to decompress and adjust to freedom more readily.

There are many types of halfway houses or community correctional centers. The earliest were facilities that provided a "halfway out" residence for inmates nearing the end of their sentences or those recently paroled who needed assistance in making the transition from the prison to the free world. More recently, many jurisdictions have developed "halfway-in" houses for those who require more structure and control than that provided by probation, ISP, or even house arrest, but for whom prison is too severe a sanction. Increasingly these facilities have also been used for probationers and other offenders awaiting trial. These residential facilities have flourished over the past several decades. Prisons, probation departments, parole boards, and judges have made widespread use of these correctional alternatives. By January 1, 1997, there were 564 such facilities in operation in the United States, housing over 15,000 offenders.[78] A description follows of several different halfway house facilities.

The Minnesota Restitution Center

Minnesota provided the prototype for contemporary restitution centers. Established in 1972, the Minnesota Restitution Center (MRC) accepted adult males who had been sentenced to the Minnesota State Prison for two years or less and had served at least four months of their sentences. Recidivists, violent offenders, and professional criminals were not eligible for the program, nor were middle-class persons who could make restitution without the assistance of the center. While in prison, the inmate, with the assistance of a Restitution Center staff member, met with the victim face-to-face to establish a restitution plan. After the parole board approved the restitution plan, the offender was released on parole to the Restitution Center, where he lived, secured employment, and fulfilled the terms of the agreement. The offender could also receive additional services there, including group therapy, supervision in the community corrections center, and assistance in obtaining employment. Although the MRC was considered a success, it was closed in 1976 because the number of property offenders being sent to prison was reduced by the implementation of the state's Community Corrections Act.

The Georgia Restitution Program

Georgia based its restitution program on the Minnesota model. Unlike the Minnesota model, however, Georgia residential programs—known as *community diversion centers*—serve both probationers and parolees. Residential centers located throughout the state house 20 to 40 offenders each for up to five months. During their stay, center residents develop restitution plans, receive individual and group counseling, and are referred for a variety of other services as needed. They may also be required to work at community service projects on weekends and during evening hours. The offenders normally remain at the center until their restitution is completed.

One evaluation of the program revealed that about 85 percent of the participants were rearrested within 18 months after release. Although this does not suggest a great reduction in recidivism, the program's economic benefits are considerable. McCarthy and McCarthy state,

> During a one-year period, the residents earned a total of $128,437 in restitution payments; [and] 8,372 hours of community service were provided. Over $150,000 was paid in state and federal taxes, and over $200,000 was spent in the local communities for clothing, transportation, recreation, and personal items. In addition, the total cost of care per individual has been much less for restitution center residents than prison inmates.[79]

Texas Rehabilitation Centers

Based on the earlier models of Minnesota and Georgia, Texas established "rehabilitation centers" (formerly "restitution centers") where nonviolent offenders, as a condition of probation, live for up to one year. While there the residents work at their regular jobs. Their pay is submitted directly to the center director, who deducts the amounts for room and board, support for dependents, supervision fees, and victim restitution. The remainder is returned to the resident after release from the center. During off-work hours the residents are required to perform community service. Preliminary reports indicate that over 80 percent of residents completed their term of residence without violating their probation.

Evaluations of Halfway House Programs

As with other community-based programs, it is difficult to measure the effectiveness of halfway house programs. There is wide variation in quality of programs and in the types of offenders admitted. However, the weight of the evidence suggests that probationers and parolees who spent time in a halfway house had lower recidivism rates than similar offenders who did not reside in a halfway house. In one study, Edward Latessa and Harry Allen found that while halfway house residents are generally higher-need, higher-risk, and more likely to recidivate than ordinary probationers, no difference in outcome between the two groups could be observed. Halfway house residents generally received more treatment intervention than those on regular probation or parole. The authors concluded that such program participation may have been the critical difference.[80]

FINES AS INTERMEDIATE SANCTIONS

Fines are routinely imposed for offenses ranging from traffic violations to drug trafficking. University of Connecticut criminologist George Cole, who has conducted an extensive study of the use of fines in U.S. criminal justice, estimates that well over $1 billion in fines is collected annually by courts across the country.[81] Cole found that judges in lower courts (fines in 86 percent of cases) were more positively disposed to using fines than were those in higher courts (fines in 42 percent of cases). In recent years, however, fines have been used more often in conjunction with other penalties such as probation or imprisonment. In 1988 Ivan Boesky was fined more than $100 million and sentenced to 18 months in prison for violating Securities Exchange Commission regulations regarding insider trading. The federal Comprehensive Crime Control Act of 1984, effective November 1, 1987, specifies that for every sentence to probation the court must also order the defendant to "pay a fine, make restitution, and/or work in community service."[82]

Some judges, however, are reluctant to use fines because of the difficulty of collecting and enforcing them. As Cole points out, other branches of government enforce other penalties imposed by judges, but fines must be enforced directly by the courts, and judges have little incentive to expend their own resources to administer the collection of fines. In addition, many judges point out that offenders tend to be poor and may have no means other than additional criminal activity to obtain the funds to pay their fines. Affluent offenders, on the other hand, can "buy their way out of jail" when fines are an integral part of the sentence.[83]

Day Fines

Despite the problems associated with using fines in criminal sentencing, prison and jail overcrowding and large probation caseloads have served to direct many judges' attention to the use of fines.[84] In 1988 a court in New York initiated a program to make fines a more meaningful sentencing option. Basing their program on European precedents, judges in the New York court adjust fines to offenders' financial means. Such fines, referred to as **day fines,** are figured as multiples of the offender's daily income.[85] Thus a truck driver and a stockbroker might be fined the same multiple of a day's pay, which might make the driver's fine $500 and the stockbroker's $10,000. In this way day fines overcome many of the shortcomings associated with conventional fines. If fines are scaled to the offender's ability to pay, they may be used more often and be a more meaningful sanction.

DAY FINES

Fines that are calculated as some multiple of an offender's daily wage.

In their book *Between Prison and Probation,* Morris and Tonry note that the use of fines as punishment for crime "holds promise of a much wider swath."[86] They specify some characteristics of fines that make them the "punishment of choice for most crimes":

- Although in current practice fines are generally set in amounts too modest to be calibrated meaningfully in relation to serious crime, in principle fines can vary from small change to economic capital punishment.
- Although in current practice fines are too often haphazardly administered and collected, in principle fines can be collected with vigor and ruthlessness.
- Although in current practice fines seem unfair to the poor and unduly lenient to the rich, in principle fine amounts can be tailored to the offender's assets and income so as to constitute roughly comparable financial burdens.[87]

Presently patterns in the use of fines vary widely. Observers predict greater emphasis on fines in the future, however, both as a sentence in itself and in conjunction with other sentences.

Evaluation of Fines as Alternative Sanctions

Douglas McDonald, Judith Greene, and Charles Worzella recently evaluated the use of day fines in two jurisdictions, Staten Island, New York, and Milwaukee, Wisconsin.[88] They found that both the Staten Island and Milwaukee day fine programs indicate that a workable day fine system can be developed for regular use in courts. In Staten Island 70 percent of those assessed day fines paid in full. It was not possible to compare this figure to those assessed conventional fines as there was no control group given conventional fines. The Milwaukee project did involve a control group, and comparisons could be made. The results were somewhat disappointing. The proportions of those who failed to pay in full were 59 percent for the day fine group and 61 percent for the conventional fine group. However, the proportions of those who paid in full were 37 percent for the day fine group compared to 25 percent of the conventional group. Differences in likelihood to pay were more pronounced among the poorest offenders. Of those persons having monthly incomes less than $197, 33 percent of those given day fines paid in full, compared to 14 percent of those given conventional fines.[89]

Evaluators in the Milwaukee experiment found that within nine months of sentencing there was no significant difference in recidivism between the experimental group (day fines) and the control group (conventional fines).[90]

In Milwaukee the use of day fines reduced revenues to the county treasury, which resulted in resistance to their use. The data in the Staten Island case were not clear on this issue.[91]

Although the findings are not clear-cut, it appears that the day fine may have some positive impact; further research is needed.

SUMMARY

With more than 1.6 million persons in jails and prisons and 3.6 million on probation or parole, the criminal justice system must acknowledge the need for intermediate sanctions—alternatives to traditional sentencing options. Intensive supervision programs (ISP), electronic monitoring and house arrest, restitution, community service, and fines have been suggested as means of achieving a rational system of corrections and alleviating some of the problems associated with incarceration and probation. The importance of community-based correctional programs can best be understood by considering the consequences of imprisonment. Criminologist Harry Allen concludes,

> It is hard to identify the benefits inmates gain from prison, but the harm done there is readily seen. If you want to increase the crime problem, incite men to greater evil, and intensify criminal inclinations and proclivities, then lock violators up in prison for long periods, reduce their outside contacts, stigmatize them and block their lawful employment when released, all the while setting them at tutelage under the direction of more skilled and predatory criminals. I know of no better way to gain your ends than these.[92]

ENDNOTES

1. Norval Morris and Michael Tonry, *Between Prison and Probation: Intermediate Punishments in a Rational Sentencing System* (New York: Oxford University Press, 1990), 3.
2. Morris and Tonry, *Between Prison and Probation.*
3. Morris and Tonry, *Between Prison and Probation,* 7.
4. Morris and Tonry, *Between Prison and Probation,* 8.
5. U.S. Comptroller General, *State and County Probation: Systems in Crisis* (Washington, D.C.: Government Printing Office, 1976).
6. See J. Banks, A. L. Porter, R. L. Rardin, T. R. Silver, and V. E. Unger, *Phase I Evaluation of Intensive Special Probation Projects* (Washington, D.C.: U.S. Department of Justice, 1981); Robert M. Carter and Leslie T. Wilkins, "Caseloads: Some Conceptual Models," in Robert M. Carter and Leslie T. Wilkins, eds., *Probation, Parole, and Community Corrections,* 2nd ed. (New York: Wiley); M. Neithercutt and D. M. Gottfredson, *Caseload Size Variation and Difference in Probation/Parole Performance* (Washington, D.C.: National Institute of Juvenile Justice, 1973); Robert Martinson, "California Research at the Crossroads," Crime and Delinquency 23, no. 2 (Spring 1976).
7. Joan Petersilia, Susan Turner, James Kahan, and Joyce Peterson, *Granting Felons Probation: Public Risks and Alternatives* (Santa Monica, Calif.: RAND, 1985).
8. Petersilia et al., *Granting Felons Probation,* vi–vii.
9. Petersilia et al., *Granting Felons Probation,* viii.
10. Petersilia et al., *Granting Felons Probation,* ix.
11. Petersilia et al., *Granting Felons Probation,* ix.
12. Petersilia et al., *Granting Felons Probation,* ix.
13. Petersilia et al., *Granting Felons Probation,* iv.
14. Joan Petersilia, *Expanding Options for Criminal Sentencing* (Santa Monica, Calif.: RAND, 1987).
15. See Roger J. Lauen, *Community-Managed Corrections* (Laurel, Md.: American Correctional Association, 1988); Neithercutt and Gottfredson, *Caseload Size Variation;* Stuart Adams, *Evaluation Research in Corrections* (Washington, D.C.: Government Printing Office, 1975); Carter and Wilkins, *Probation, Parole, and Community Corrections;* and Edward E. Rhine, William R. Smith, Ronald W. Jackson, *Paroline Authori-*

ties: Recent History and Current Practice* (Laurel, Md.: American Correctional Association, 1991). Also see chapter 6, "Supervision in Probation and Parole," for a discussion of the SIPU and San Francisco Project.

16. Belinda Rogers McCarthy and Bernard J. McCarthy, Jr., *Community-Based Corrections,* 2nd ed. (Belmont, Calif.: Brooks/Cole, 1990), 122.

17. McCarthy and McCarthy, *Community-Based Corrections,* 122.

18. C. Camp and G. Camp, *The Corrections Yearbook—1997.* (South Salem, NY: Criminal Justice Institute), 148.

19. Billie S. Erwin and Lawrence A. Bennett, "New Dimensions in Probation: Georgia's Experience with Intensive Supervision (ISP)," *Research in Brief* (Washington, D.C.: National Institute of Justice, January 1987), 2.

20. Florida Department of Corrections, *An Implementation Manual for Community Control* (1983), 22.

21. Todd R. Clear and George F. Cole, *American Corrections,* 4th ed. (Belmont, Calif.: Wadsworth, 1997), 223.

22. Clear and Cole, *American Corrections,* 223.

23. Joan Petersilia and Susan Turner, *Intensive Supervision for High-Risk Probationers: Findings from Three California Studies* (Santa Monica, Calif.: RAND, November 1990).

24. Petersilia and Turner, *Intensive Supervision,* 5.

25. Petersilia and Turner, *Intensive Supervision,* 9. See also Petersilia et al., *Granting Felons Probation,* 66.

26. Howard Abadinsky, *Probation and Parole: Theory and Practice,* 4th ed. (Englewood Cliffs, N.J.: Prentice Hall, 1991), 344.

27. Norval Morris and Michael Tonry, "Between Prison and Probation: Intermediate Punishments in a Rational Sentencing System," *NIJ Reports* (January–February 1990), 9.

28. Personal communication, August 1992.

29. Clear and Cole, *American Corrections.*

30. Larry Siegel, *Criminology,* 4th ed. (St. Paul: West, 1992), 561.

31. Harry Allen, Chris Eskridge, Edward Latessa, and Gennaro Vito, *Probation and Parole in America* (New York: Free Press, 1985), 88.

32. Clear and Cole, *American Corrections,* 227.

33. Clear and Cole, *American Corrections,* 227.

34. Allen, Eskridge, Latessa, and Vito, *Probation and Parole in America,* 88.

35. Joseph J. Senna and Larry J. Siegel, *Introduction to Criminal Justice,* 5th ed. (St. Paul: West, 1990).

36. Nicolette Parisi, "A Taste of the Bars," *Journal of Criminal Law and Criminology* 72 (1981), 1109–1123. Cited in Senna and Siegel, *Introduction to Criminal Justice,* 510.

37. McCarthy and McCarthy, *Community-Based Corrections,* 127–28.

38. McCarthy and McCarthy, *Community-Based Corrections,* 127–28.

39. James F. Anderson, Jerald Burns, and Laronistine Dyson, "Effective Aftercare Provisions Could Hold the Key to the Rehabilitative Effects of Shock Incarceration Programs," *Journal of Offender Monitoring* 10(3), Summer 1997.

40. Velmer S. Burton, James W. Marquart, Steven J. Cuvelier, Leanne Fiftal Alarid, and Robert J. Hunter, "A Study of Attitudinal Change Among Boot Camp Participants." *Federal Probation* 57(3):46–52.

41. Burton et al., "A Study of Attitudinal Change," 46–52.

42. Burton et al., "A Study of Attitudinal Change," 51.

43. Cherie L. Clark, David W. Aziz, and Doris L. MacKenzie, *Shock Incarceration in New York: Focus on Treatment* (Washington, D.C.: National Institute of Justice, August 1994).

44. Clark, Aziz, and MacKenzie, *Shock Incarceration in New York,* 2. New York law permits shock incarceration graduates to be paroled before they have served the mandatory minimum prison term that would otherwise apply.

45. Clark, Aziz, and MacKenzie, *Shock Incarceration in New York,* 9.

46. Clark, Aziz, and MacKenzie, *Shock Incarceration in New York,* 11.

47. Doris Layton MacKenzie, "Boot Camp Programs Grow in Number and Scope," *NIJ Reports* (November/December 1990).

48. Merry Morash and Lila Rucker, "A Critical Look at the Idea of Boot Camp as a Correctional Reform," *Crime and Delinquency* (April 1990), 204–222.

49. National Institute of Justice, "Researchers Evaluate Eight Shock Incarceration Programs," *National Institute of Justice Update* (Washington, D.C.: National Institute of Justice, 1994). Doris L. MacKenzie and Claire Souryal of the University of Maryland conducted the study for the NIJ.

50. National Institute of Justice, "Researchers Evaluate Eight Shock Incarceration Programs," 1.

51. National Institute of Justice, "Researchers Evaluate Eight Shock Incarceration Programs," 2.

52. Anderson, Burns, and Dyson, "Effective Aftercare Provisions," 15.

53. Anderson, Burns, and Dyson, "Effective Aftercare Provisions," 16.

54. It is also called home detention and home incarceration.

55. Abadinsky, *Probation and Parole,* 347.

56. Elise Kalfayan, ed., *RAND Checklist* (Santa Monica, Calif.: RAND, January 1989), 2.

57. Petersilia, *Expanding Options for Criminal Sentencing.*

58. Petersilia, *Expanding Options for Criminal Sentencing.*

59. Petersilia, *Expanding Options for Criminal Sentencing.*

60. Personal communication.

61. Charles M. Friel and Joseph B. Vaughn, "A Consumer's Guide to Electronic Monitoring," *Federal Probation* 50(3):3–14 (September 1986).

62. Friel and Vaughn, "A Consumer's Guide to Electronic Monitoring," 12.

63. J. Robert Lilly, Richard A. Ball, G. David Curry, and Richard C. Smith, "The Pride, Inc., Program: An Evaluation of 5 Years of Electronic Monitoring," *Federal Probation* (December 1992), 42–47.

64. Lilly et al., "The Pride, Inc., Program," 45.

65. Rolando del Carmen, *Criminal Procedure: Law and Practice,* 3rd ed. (Belmont, Calif.: Wadsworth, 1995), 436.

66. Siegel, *Criminology,* 561.

67. McCarthy and McCarthy, *Community-Based Corrections,* 137.

68. McCarthy and McCarthy, *Community-Based Corrections,* 140.

69. American Bar Association Commission on Correctional Facilities and Services and Council of State Governments, *Compendium of Model Correctional Legislation and Standards,* 2nd ed. (Washington, D.C.: ABA, 1975), III-48.

70. ABA Commission on Correctional Facilities, *Compendium,* III-58.

71. Burt Galaway, "The Use of Restitution," *Crime and Delinquency* 23(1), 1977.

72. Rolando del Carmen, *Criminal Procedure,* 437.

73. *Pennsylvania Department of Public Welfare v. Davenport,* 110 S. Ct. 2126 (1990).

74. Ken Pease, "Community Service Orders," in Michael Tonry and Norval Morris, eds., *Crime and Justice: An Annual Review of Research,* vol. 6 (Chicago: University of Chicago Press, 1985), 52.

75. Rolando del Carmen, Betsy Witt, Thomas Caywood, and Sally Layland, *Probation Law and Practice in Texas* (Huntsville, Tex.: Criminal Justice Center, Sam Houston State University, 1989), 4.

76. Clear and Cole, *American Corrections,* 222.

77. Clear and Cole, *American Corrections,* 222.

78. Camp and Camp, *The Corrections Yearbook—1997* (South Salem, NY: Criminal Justice Institute), 100.

79. McCarthy and McCarthy, *Community-Based Corrections,* 154.

80. Edward Latessa and Harry Allen, *Corrections in the Community* (Cincinnati, OH: Anderson, 1997), 333.

81. George Cole, *The American System of Criminal Justice,* 6th ed. (Pacific Grove, Calif.: Brooks/Cole, 1992).

82. 18 U.S.C. 3563(a)(2).

83. Cole, *The American System of Justice.*
84. Cole, *The American System of Justice.*
85. James A. Inciardi, *Criminal Justice,* 4th ed. (Ft. Worth: Harcourt Brace Jovanovich, 1993), 445.
86. Morris and Tonry, *Between Prison and Probation,* 114.
87. Morris and Tonry, *Between Prison and Probation,* 114.
88. Douglas C. McDonald, Judith Greene, and Charles Worzella, *Day Fines in American Courts: The Staten Island and Milwaukee Experiments* (Washington, D.C.: National Institute of Justice, 1992).
89. McDonald, Greene, and Worzella, *Day Fines in American Courts,* 6–7.
90. McDonald, Greene, and Worzella, *Day Fines in American Courts,* 6–7.
91. McDonald, Greene, and Worzella, *Day Fines in American Courts,* 6–7.
92. Latessa and Allen, 1.

DISCUSSION QUESTIONS

1. What factor(s) brought about the development of intermediate sanctions?
2. What do Norval Morris and Michael Tonry mean when they say that criminal justice and corrections are both too lenient and too severe?
3. What were the conclusions of the RAND study of probation? What did the RAND researchers recommend?
4. How does intensive supervision probation (ISP) differ from regular probation?
5. Discuss the relationship between caseload size and recidivism.
6. What are the purposes of shock incarceration? How successful has it been? What are some of the problems associated with these programs?
7. Discuss the evolution and use of boot camps. What are some of the issues surrounding them?
8. What are the advantages and disadvantages of house arrest?
9. How does electronic monitoring support house arrest? What ethical and social criticisms are associated with EM?
10. How do electronic monitoring devices work? What are some of the technical problems associated with them?
11. How are restitution and community service used as a correctional tool? What are their purposes? How do monetary restitution and community service differ? How are they alike?
12. Why don't more judges use fines as intermediate sanctions? What is a day fine, and how does it overcome one of the major problems associated with fines?

12

JUVENILE JUSTICE, PROBATION, AND AFTERCARE

What You Will Learn in This Chapter

You will learn about the background, the history, and the basics of juvenile justice. The juvenile and adult systems are compared, and an overview of the juvenile justice system is presented. You will know about parens patriae *and the leading cases in juvenile law. The origin of juvenile probation is traced, and the demographics of probation officers are described. You will be familiar with two kinds of probation conditions—mandatory and discretionary. You will know the general profile of probation officers and the skills required for the job. You will learn about special programs for juveniles, particularly family counseling and boot camps. You will understand the current challenges facing juvenile probation.*

KEY TERMS

mens rea
parens patriae
family model
juvenile delinquency
CINS, CHINS, MINS, JINS
intake
adjudication
In Re Gault
disposition
aftercare
informal probation
intensive probation
boot camps
balanced and restorative justice model

INTRODUCTION

Juvenile crime has been a major problem in the United States for decades. Public perception of the problem has been fueled by mass media attention to violent juvenile crime. Sensational news reports like the following have alarmed the public and focused attention on serious and sometimes senseless juvenile crime:[1]

- Two 12-year old boys in Wenatchee, Washington, shoot and kill a migrant farm worker after he tells them to stop making noise.
- A pair of teens in Franklin, New Jersey, ages 17 and 18, gun down two pizza delivery men not for money or in an argument but (according to police) to experience the "thrill" of killing.
- Two Chicago boys, ages 10 and 11, drop a 5-year-old out of a vacant 14-story apartment because the boy refused to steal candy for them.

From the late 1980s to the early 1990s the increase in violent crime was alarming. The chairman of the House Judiciary Committee of the U.S. Congress reports that "between 1965 and 1992, the number of 12-year-olds arrested for violent crimes increased 211 percent; the number of 13- and 14-year-olds rose 301 percent; and the number of 15-year-olds rose 297 percent."[2] Although the rate of violent juvenile crime started to decline in the late 1990s, state and local governments are still seeking legislative solutions to a problem that has alarmed and mobilized the nation.

Answers do not come easily, partially because society wrestles with conflicting philosophical approaches. On the one hand there is the benevolent *parens patriae* doctrine, which seeks to do what is best for the juvenile; on the other hand is the theory of just deserts, which advocates punishing crimes based on the seriousness of the act committed and not on the personal circumstances of the offender. The public has gone through cycles of preferring punitiveness or rehabilitation. The pendulum will likely continue to swing from one side (vengeance) to the other (mercy and redemption) as long as the problem of juvenile crime exists. Right now the public is in a mood for vengeance.

BACKGROUND AND HISTORY

Mens Rea and the Juvenile

MENS REA

Criminal liability is based on the concept of *mens rea,* which is Latin for "a guilty mind." Without intent, an act is generally not considered criminal.

Criminal liability is based on the concept of ***mens rea,*** which is the Latin term for "a guilty mind."[3] Without intent an act is generally not considered criminal. A guilty mind implies that the actor knows what he or she is doing; therefore the act is punished because the actor intended for the injury to occur. Children below a certain age are presumed by law to be unaware of the full consequences of what they do. Absent *mens rea,* they should not and cannot be punished like adults.

During the latter part of the 18th century children younger than seven were deemed incapable of *mens rea* and were exempt from criminal liability. Those above seven years of age, however, could be prosecuted and sentenced to prison or given the death penalty if found guilty.[4] No state in the United States at present punishes juveniles so severely at such an early age, but the minimum age for juveniles to come under the jurisdiction of juvenile courts varies from one state to another.

The *Parens Patriae* Approach

PARENS PATRIAE

The philosophy of juvenile courts is heavily influenced by *parens patriae*—the doctrine that "the state is parent" and therefore serves as sovereign and guardian of persons under legal disability, such as juveniles.

FAMILY MODEL

A model for processing juveniles, which treats them like members of one's own family.

Juvenile courts, as they are known today, are an American creation. The first U.S. juvenile court was established in Chicago in 1899. The court was founded on the belief that a child's behavior was the product of poor family background and surroundings. It operated informally, was civil in nature, and geared toward rehabilitation.[5] The philosophy of juvenile courts was heavily influenced by ***parens patriae***—the doctrine that "the state is parent" and therefore serves as sovereign and guardian of persons under legal disability, such as juveniles. *Parens patriae* led to the **family model** of processing juveniles, which treated juveniles like members of one's family. The main concern of the juvenile court was to ensure that legal proceedings were presided over by judges who, acting as wise parents, had the best interest of the child in mind. Constitutional safeguards were minimal or nonexistent, but personal attention, love, and care were to be provided.

Over the years pure *parens patriae* declined, paving the way for greater orientation toward due process. The case that signaled the erosion of *parens patriae* was *In Re Gault* (387 U.S. 1 [1967]). In that case the U.S. Supreme Court said that "neither the Fourteenth Amendment nor the Bill of Rights is for adults alone." Since then the Court has decided other cases affording rights to juveniles they previously did not have.

Juvenile proceedings at present are still considered either civil or administrative in nature, but juveniles now have essentially the same rights as those given to adults in criminal cases. The only constitutional rights denied to juveniles are the right to a jury trial, the right to bail, the right to a public trial, and the right to a grand jury indictment. These rights, however, are usually given to juveniles by state law.

Concern about violent juvenile crime led to further decline of *parens patriae* and the enactment by state legislatures of laws that limit, if not completely withdraw, the traditional protections afforded juveniles. The National Center for Juvenile Justice has identified five themes and trends in recent laws targeting violent and other serious crimes by juveniles:[6]

1. *Diminution of jurisdictional authority of juvenile courts.* More serious and violent juvenile offenders are being removed from the juvenile justice system in favor of criminal court prosecution.

2. *Expansion of judicial disposition and sentencing authority.* More state legislatures are experimenting with new disposition and sentencing options.
3. *New correctional programming.* Correctional administrators are under pressure to develop programs as a result of new transfer and sentencing laws.
4. *Less confidentiality for juvenile court records and proceedings.* Traditional confidentiality provisions are being revised in favor of more open proceedings and records.
5. *Participation of victims of juvenile crime.* Victims of juvenile crime are being included as active participants in the juvenile justice process.

The same report says that the long-held notion of individualized disposition for juveniles, aimed at rehabilitation, has given way to greater public interest in retribution and punishing criminal juvenile behavior. The current public mood represents a shift in judicial philosophy in that dispositions are becoming more offense-based rather than offender-based.

Alarm over violent juvenile crime has had an impact on juvenile community-based corrections programs. In some jurisdictions juveniles who would have qualified for probation are being sent to institutions and kept in secure environments longer. The public seeks more intensive supervision and is more likely to fund costly projects that ensure greater safety for the community. For now, the pendulum has shifted from rehabilitation to retribution.

JUVENILE JUSTICE AND ADULT JUSTICE SYSTEMS COMPARED

The differences between the juvenile justice and adult justice processes may be summarized as follows:[7]

Adult Proceedings

1. Arrested
2. Charged
3. Accused of crime under the penal code
4. Trial
5. Formal, public trial
6. Judge is neutral
7. Found guilty of a criminal offense by an impartial judge or jury
8. Sentenced if found guilty
9. Sent to jail or prison
10. Judge or jury determines length of incarceration
11. Serves sentence for definite term, subject to parole law
12. Purpose is punishment
13. Released on parole, if eligible
14. A criminal case

Juvenile Proceedings

1. Taken into custody by police
2. Prosecutor petitions court
3. Violation comes under the juvenile code or family code
4. Adjudication
5. Usually a private, informal hearing
6. Judge acts as wise parent
7. Found to have engaged in delinquent conduct
8. Disposition
9. Committed to a state facility for juveniles
10. Youth detention authorities determine when to release
11. Committed for an indeterminate amount of time, but usually released upon reaching age of majority
12. Purpose is rehabilitation
13. Released on aftercare
14. A civil or quasi-civil case

These differences are perhaps more symbolic than substantive and have minimal real impact. For example, the difference between an arrest and a taking into custody is not all that significant because in both instances the offender is deprived of liberty. Neither is there much difference between the adult suspect being charged and the prosecutor petitioning the court for the juvenile to be adjudicated: both processes lead to hearings. Sentencing and disposition both subject the offender to lawfully prescribed sanctions. Nonetheless, society shuns the use of adult criminal law terms in juvenile proceedings and refuses to brand juveniles as criminals in hopes that rehabilitation is better served by not labeling them as such.

AN OVERVIEW OF THE JUVENILE JUSTICE PROCESS

Procedure Before Adjudication

The juvenile justice process starts in various ways, and procedures vary from state to state. Juvenile behavior that sets the process in motion may come to the attention of the government through oral or written reports from the police, probation officers, victims, parents, neighbors, school authorities, and the general public. Juvenile acts that trigger judicial intervention are generally of two types: juvenile delinquency and conduct in need of supervision (**CINS**). Each state, by law, defines the acts that come under each category. Generally **juvenile delinquency** refers to acts committed by juveniles that are punishable as crimes by a state's penal code. Examples are murder, robbery, and burglary. In contrast, conduct in need of supervision (also known in some jurisdictions as **CHINS** [children in need of supervision], **MINS** [minors in need of supervision], or **JINS** [juveniles in need of supervision]) is likely to be a status offense, meaning that it would not be punishable if committed by adults. Status offenses include such categories as truancy, running away, inhalant abuse, curfew violation, and underage drinking.

CINS, CHINS, MINS, JINS

Conduct, children, minors, or juveniles in need of supervision. Refers to juveniles who commit acts which would not be offenses if committed by adults.

JUVENILE DELINQUENCY

Juvenile delinquency refers to acts committed by juveniles that are punishable as crimes by a state's penal code. Conduct in need of supervision consists of acts that would not be punishable if committed by adults.

INTAKE

Intake is a process whereby a juvenile is screened to determine if the case should be processed further by the juvenile justice system or whether there are other alternatives better suited for the juvenile.

Often the police observe juvenile behavior that requires formal or informal action. Contact with the police can lead to a variety of actions such as taking the juvenile into custody for possible prosecution, taking the juvenile into protective custody, referral to agencies, or outright release. One publication notes that "most state statutes explicitly direct police officers to release to a parent or refer to court those juveniles who are taken into custody."[8] In practice, police officer dispositions can include outright release, warning, referral to community agency for services, referral to a "citizen hearing board," or referral to court intake.

A juvenile taken into custody by the police usually goes through the **intake** process, considered by some as "one of the most crucial case processing points in the juvenile justice system."[9] Intake is a term unique to juvenile justice, but its meaning varies from state to state. In general it refers to a process whereby a juvenile is screened to determine if the case should be processed further by the juvenile justice system or whether there are other alternatives better suited for the juvenile. It is usually done by a probation officer or other individuals designated by the court or the prosecutor. Arnold Binder, Gilbert Geis, and Dickson Bruce Jr. summarize the functions of the intake process as follows:[10]

1. Determine whether the circumstances of the case bring it within the jurisdiction of the juvenile court.

Figure 12.1 **THE STAGES OF DELINQUENCY CASE PROCESSING IN THE JUVENILE JUSTICE SYSTEM**

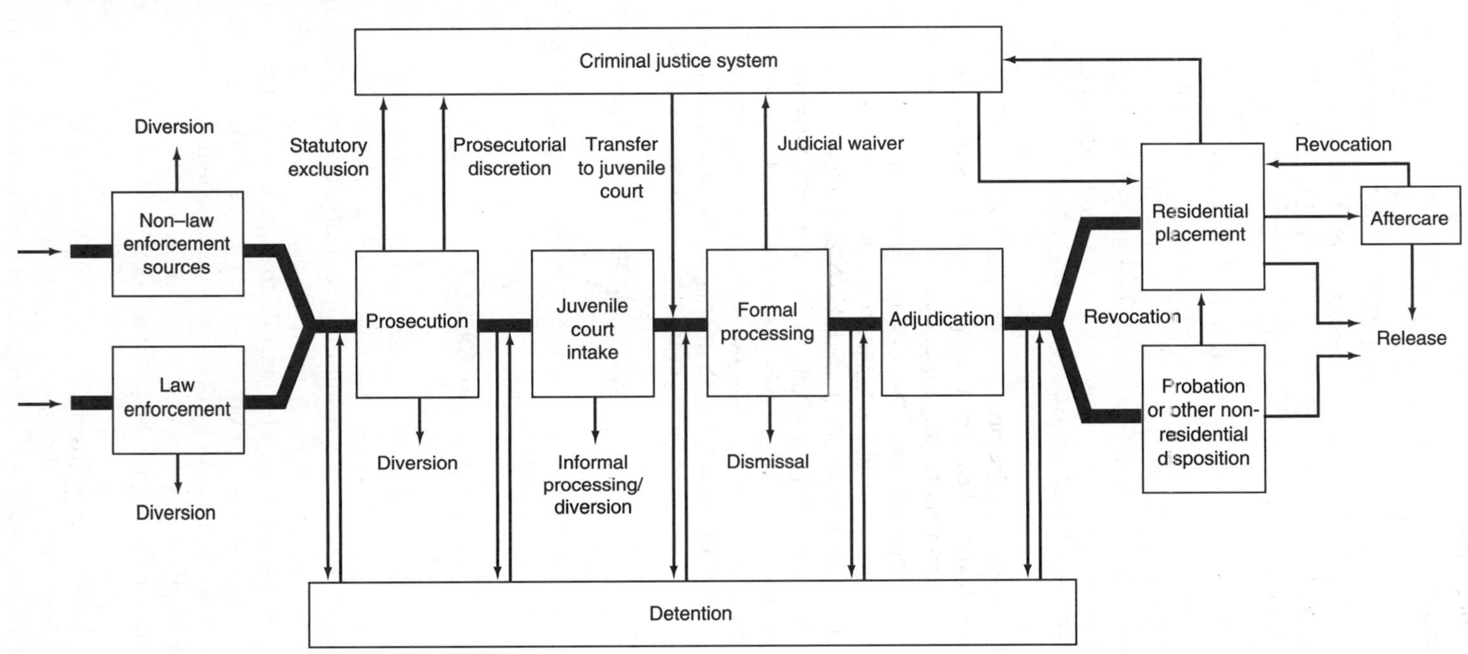

Note: This chart gives a simplified view of caseflow through the juvenile justice system. Procedures vary among jurisdictions. The weights of the lines are not intended to show the actual size of caseloads.

Source: Howard N. Snyder and Melissa Sickmund, *Juvenile Offenders and Victims: A National Report* (National Center for Juvenile Justice, Office of Juvenile Justice and Delinquency Prevention, August 1995).

2. Determine whether the evidence is sufficient to warrant a court hearing.
3. Decide whether the case is serious enough to require a court hearing.
4. Arrange for a process of informal supervision if that alternative seems desirable.

Intake may also involve detention screening, presentence investigation, crisis intervention, or other procedures mandated by the court. In short, intake does what state law or court policy intends for the process to accomplish.

A juvenile may be detained by the police, but only for a limited time. State law usually requires that a detained juvenile must be given a hearing within 24 hours after the child is placed in detention.[11] Federal rules provide that juveniles be separated from adult offenders by "sight and sound"; this assures that juveniles are detained in facilities separate from those used for adults. In the case of *Schall v. Martin* (104 S. Ct. 2403 [1984]), however, the U.S. Supreme Court held that preventive detention of juveniles (where a juvenile is detained because of the likelihood that he or she will commit other offenses) is constitutional, subject to limitations.

If the intake officer decides to refer the case to court, the prosecutor petitions the court for the juvenile to be adjudicated. Summons are then issued directing the juvenile to appear before the court at a specified time and place for an initial appearance on the petition. An arraignment is then held where the juvenile is given the opportunity to admit or deny the allegations.[12]

ADJUDICATION

Juvenile court equivalent of a trial.

Adjudication is the equivalent of a trial in adult criminal cases. However, it is less formal, and the judge takes a more active part in the hearing—including asking questions of juveniles, their parents or guardians, and witnesses. Juvenile courts were designed to be different from adult courts in that originally no lawyers were allowed, formal rules of evidence were waived, and the juvenile enjoyed no legal or constitutional protections, leading some critics to label them as "kangaroo courts." That has changed considerably; now the features of the original juvenile courts are barely recognizable. In the words of Peter Greenwood,[13]

> The informality is largely gone. Juveniles sit with their lawyers like adult defendants. Juvenile hearings or trials proceed along the same lines as criminal trials. The rules of evidence and rights of the parties are about the same, except that juveniles still do not have the right to a jury trial or to bail.

In Re Gault and Other Cases

IN RE GAULT

In Re Gault is the most significant case ever to be decided by the U.S. Supreme Court in juvenile justice. It broke the pattern of pure *parens patriae* and ushered in an era of due process for juveniles.

The leading and most important case in juvenile justice adjudication is ***In Re Gault*** (387 U.S. 1 [1967]). In that case a 15-year-old boy and a friend were taken into custody in Arizona as a result of a complaint that they had made lewd telephone calls. Gault's parents were not informed that he was in custody, nor were they shown the complaint that was filed against their son. The complainant never appeared at any hearing, and no written record was made of the hearing that was held. Gault was committed to a state institution as a delinquent until he reached the age of majority—a total of six years from the date of the hearing. Interestingly, the maximum punishment for the offense, had it been committed by an adult, was a fine of from $5 to $60 or imprisonment for a maximum of two months. Gault appealed the conviction, saying he was denied his rights during the hearing. The U.S. Supreme Court agreed.

Gault provides that juveniles must be given four basic due process rights in adjudication proceedings that can result in confinement in an institution in which their freedom would be curtailed. These rights are

1. Reasonable notice of the charges
2. Counsel, appointed by the state if the juvenile is indigent
3. The ability to confront and cross-examine witnesses
4. The privilege against self-incrimination

Gault is significant because it was the first case decided by the U.S. Supreme Court that gave due process rights to juveniles, thus signaling the erosion of the pure *parens patriae* approach to juvenile justice. *Parens patriae* is still alive in juvenile justice, but its vitality has been sapped by judicial intervention.

What led to the abandonment of pure *parens patriae*? The answer may be found in the footnote in the *Gault* case. Quoting another juvenile case decided by the Court a year earlier (*Kent v. United States,* 383 U.S. 541 [1966]), the Court said, "There is evidence . . . that there may be grounds for concern that the child receives the worst of both worlds; that he gets neither the protections accorded to adults nor the solicitous care and regenerative treatment postulated for children." Given this concern, the Court interjected due process into juvenile proceedings.

In Re Winship, decided three years after *Gault,* followed the pattern of *parens patriae* decline by holding that proof beyond a reasonable doubt, not simply a preponderance of the evidence, is required in juvenile adjudication hearings in cases in which the act would have been a crime if committed by an adult. In *McKeiver v. Pennsylvania* (403 U.S. 528 [1971]), however, the Court held back and decided that juveniles have no constitutional right to trial by jury, even in juvenile delinquency (as opposed to status offense) proceedings. But four years later, in *Breed v. Jones* (421 U.S. 517 [1975]), the Court placed juveniles in the same category as adults, holding that juveniles are entitled to the constitutional right against double jeopardy in juvenile proceedings. These cases show a roller-coaster ride for juveniles in the U.S. Supreme Court. On the whole, however, Court decisions have dealt a serious blow to the pure *parens patriae* approach.

The Disposition Stage

If a juvenile is found to have engaged in the conduct alleged in the petition, the disposition stage follows. **Disposition** is the equivalent of sentencing in adult cases, but the juvenile court judge wields greater discretion than in adult criminal trials. Because most states consider rehabilitation an integral part of juvenile corrections, the judge typically has a wide choice of available dispositions ranging from a mild reproach by the judge all the way to confinement in a state institution. Institutionalization (also known as residential commitment) is usually the most severe disposition in juvenile cases and is imposed primarily in juvenile delinquency cases. Status offenders are typically placed on probation as the maximum sanction. If probation is revoked, however, the juvenile may then be classified as a delinquent because of a violation of a court order, and he or she may be dispatched to a state institution.

DISPOSITION

Juvenile court equivalent to sentencing in an adult court.

Once the juvenile is confined in a state institution, release is left to the discretion of institutional officials, not the judge. Many states provide for **aftercare** (the equivalent of parole) for juveniles who are fit for release before serving the maximum amount of time set by state law. If released on aftercare, the juvenile is supervised, but supervision usually ceases after the juvenile reaches the age of majority—generally 18. If the provisions of aftercare are breached, after a hearing the juvenile is sent back to a state juvenile institution instead of to a state prison.

AFTERCARE

The juvenile justice equivalent to parole.

Despite the growing similarity between juvenile and adult criminal proceedings, some differences persist, the most notable being the role played by the juvenile court judge, who acts as an interested person (a wise parent) instead of an impartial arbiter. A second difference is in the imposition of the death penalty. In *Thompson v. Oklahoma* (487 U.S. 815 [1988]), the U.S. Supreme Court held that it is unconstitutional to sentence a juvenile to death if he or she was 15 years of age or younger at the time of the commission of the act, regardless of its nature. A year later, however, in *Stanford v. Kentucky* (109 S. Ct. 2969 [1989]), the Court held that it is constitutional for a state to impose the death penalty on a juvenile who was at least 16 years old at the time the crime was committed. Together the *Thompson* and *Stanford* cases hold that juveniles cannot constitutionally be given the death penalty if the crime was committed at 15 years of age, but the death penalty may be administered if the crime was committed when the juvenile was 16 years old. Thus a bright-line rule has been drawn in death penalty cases involving juveniles. The actual age at which a juvenile may be given the death penalty is, however, determined by state law. In some states the death penalty has been abolished for juveniles or adults.

Juvenile courts do not try cases involving the death penalty for juveniles. Those cases are tried in the regular criminal courts after waiver proceedings (in some states called certification or transfer proceedings) or by virtue of special state laws providing severe penalties for juveniles who commit serious crimes.

JUVENILE PROBATION AND AFTERCARE

Origin

The origin of juvenile probation is traced to John Augustus, the Boston shoemaker who in 1847 persuaded judges in Massachusetts to place wayward youth under his care. Since then juvenile probation has grown in popularity. Studies show that probation is the most widely used disposition for juveniles coming to the attention of the juvenile courts.[14] More than one-third of juvenile delinquents disposed of by American juvenile courts in 1990 were placed on probation. Moreover, 43 percent of all petitioner cases and 28 percent of cases handled informally were placed on probation.[15] One study reports that in 1993 nearly 1.5 million delinquency cases were handled by juvenile courts and that "virtually every one of those cases had contact with a probation officer at some point."[16] Clearly juvenile probation is now an integral and significant part of juvenile justice.

Structure and Administration

Juvenile probation and aftercare practices have a lot in common with their adult counterparts. Differences exist, however, in structure, philosophy, and programs. Hunter Hurst IV and Patricia McFall Torbet of the National Center for Juvenile Justice classify the structure and administration of juvenile probation and aftercare as follows:[17]

Juvenile Probation—Administration and Organization

Local and judicial	16 states and Washington, D.C.
State and judicial	7 states
Local and executive	3 states

John Augustus—planting the seeds of juvenile probation (1847)

I bailed 19 boys, from 7 to 15 years of age, and in bailing them it was understood, and agreed by the court, that their cases should be continued from term to term for several months, as a season of probation; thus each month at the calling of the docket, I would appear in court, make my report, and thus the cases would pass on for five or six months. At the expiration of this term, 12 of the boys were brought into court at one time, and the scene formed a striking and highly pleasing contrast with their appearance when first arraigned. The judge expressed much pleasure as well as surprise at their appearance, and remarked, that the object of law had been accomplished and expressed his cordial approval of my plan to save and reform.

Source: Howard N. Snyder and Melissa Sickmund, *Juvenile Offenders and Victims: A National Report* (National Center for Juvenile Justice, August 1995), 70.

State and executive	10 states
Combination	14 states

Juvenile Aftercare—Administration and Organization

Local and judicial	2 states
State and judicial	2 states
Local and executive	Washington, D.C.
State and executive	37 states
Combination	9 states

These configurations show that administration and organizational variance abounds in the structure of juvenile probation and aftercare. Variance exists on the issues of (1) whether juvenile probation and aftercare are administered locally or statewide and (2) whether the department is under judicial or executive control. The classification given does not inform us, however, whether juvenile and adult probation departments are combined or separate. Most states have separate juvenile and adult probation and aftercare departments, but in some jurisdictions, particularly in smaller counties, they are combined. In some states probation and aftercare are combined and staffed by the same officers; in other states they are separate agencies that barely interact with each other. Some states contract aftercare services out to private agencies or to local probation departments. Diversity in juvenile probation is more pervasive than in adult probation, perhaps because juvenile probation is considered primarily a local rather than a state concern.

PROBATION OFFICERS

In 1993 probation officers typically earned $20,000–$39,000 per year and had an average caseload of 41 juveniles. They are usually appointed and terminated from employment by the juvenile court judge, or a board consisting of several judges of the court.

Juvenile Probation Officers

Probation officers are the crucial players in juvenile probation. Theirs is a challenging job that is made interesting by changing philosophies, innovative programs, and an increasingly high-risk clientele. One publication reports the following data and demographics about juvenile probation officers:[18]

> There are an estimated 18,000 juvenile probation professionals impacting the lives of juveniles in the United States. Eighty-five percent of these professionals are involved in the delivery of basic intake, investigation, and supervision services at the line officer level; the remaining 15 percent are involved in the administration of probation offices or the management of probation staff.

The same publication states that juvenile probation officers are generally college-educated white males, 30–49 years of age, with five to ten years of field experience. In 1993 they typically earned $20,000–39,000 per year and had an average caseload of 41 juveniles. Most had arrest powers, but they normally did not carry weapons.[19]

Probation officers are usually appointed and also terminated by the juvenile court judge. The following provision from the State of Indiana typifies the legal provisions in most states.[20]

> The judge of the juvenile court shall appoint a chief probation officer, and may appoint other probation officers, and an appropriate number of other employees to assist the probation department. The salaries of the probation officers and other juvenile court employees shall be fixed by the judge and paid by the county, subject to the approval of the county council. In addition to their annual salary, probation officers shall be reimbursed for any necessary travel expenses incurred in the performance of their duties in accord with the law governing state officers and employees.

The standards of the National Advisory Committee on Criminal Justice Standards and Goals set the minimum educational requirement for juvenile probation officers: a bachelor's degree in one of the helping sciences, such as psychology, social work, counseling, or criminal justice.[21] Similarly, the American Correctional Association recommends that an entry-level probation officer possess a baccalaureate degree, or an equivalent in terms of experience and training, in one of the social or behavioral sciences or a related field.[22] Interestingly, the ACA believes that ex-offenders should not be categorically excluded from becoming juvenile probation officers, but adds that a criminal record check should be conducted on new employees prior to hiring.[23]

The *Desktop Guide to Good Juvenile Probation Practice* (hereinafter referred to as the *Desktop Guide*), published by the National Center for Juvenile Justice, recommends the following skills for juvenile probation officers:[24]

- Basic knowledge of pertinent law
- Skill in oral and written communication
- Ability to plan and implement investigative or supervision services
- Ability to analyze social, psychological, and criminological information objectively and accurately
- Basic knowledge of criminological, psychological, and economic theories of human behavior
- Ability to use authority effectively and constructively

INFORMAL PROBATION

Informal probation differs from regular probation in that it is used early in the juvenile justice process, even before the juvenile is adjudicated. It can take place during the intake process or just before adjudication.

Informal Juvenile Probation

It is reported that one-half of all cases referred to juvenile court intake are handled informally.[25] This includes a process called **informal probation,** which is authorized in almost every juvenile code and is commonly used in probation agencies across the

The Multifaceted Role of the Juvenile Probation Officer

An organization can, and should, set standards for ethical and professional conduct for all of the various aspects of the juvenile probation officer role. These standards represent a framework for the ideal juvenile probation officer. Only the juvenile probation officer can "flesh out" the established framework and, through his actions and demeanor, fulfill this complex, multifaceted role. The probation officer is expected to fulfill many different roles, often "taking up the slack" after judges, attorneys, social agencies, parents, and so on have met what they see as their own clearly defined responsibilities in the case and have expressed an unwillingness to extend themselves beyond these limits. Probation officers are all different in their individuality, but they share a strong, common concern for youth and the community.

A probation officer must balance many sometimes conflicting roles, often within the same time frame. He or she must understand personal priorities, values, and biases and how they coincide or conflict with those of the agency, resolving any conflicts in a manner that maintains credibility and effectiveness. The more the probation officer can be proactive in these roles, the less he or she will have to be reactive.

A short list of roles has been generated to stimulate thinking. Types of roles include diagnostician, agent of change, peace officer, and coordinator.

The Complete Juvenile Probation Officer

Cop—Enforces judge's orders
Prosecutor—Assists D.A./conducts revocations
Father confessor—Establishes helpful, trustful relationship with juvenile
Rat—Informs court of juvenile's behavior/circumstances
Teacher—Develops skills in juvenile
Friend—Develops positive relation with juvenile
Surrogate parent—Admonishes, scolds juvenile
Counselor—Addresses needs
Ambassador—Intervenes on behalf of juvenile
Problem solver—Helps juvenile deal with court and community issues
Crisis manager—Deals with juvenile's precipitated crises (usually at 2 A.M.)
Hand holder—consoles juvenile
Public speaker—Educates public regarding tasks
P.R person—Wins friends/influences people on behalf of probation

continued

country. Informal probation differs from regular probation in that informal probation is used early in the juvenile justice process before the juvenile is adjudicated. It can take place during the intake process or just before adjudication. The IJA/ABA (Institute of Judicial Administration/American Bar Association) Juvenile Justice Standards Series recommends the following guidelines for informal probation:[26]

- A contractual agreement promises that the intake officer will not file a petition in exchange for certain commitments by the juvenile and family with respect to their future conduct.
- The juvenile and parents enter into the agreement voluntarily and intelligently.
- The juvenile and parents are notified of their rights to refuse to sign and enter into the agreement and to request a formal adjudication.
- The agreement should be limited in duration.
- The juvenile and parents should be able to terminate the agreement at any time and to request formal adjudication.

The Multifaceted Role of the Juvenile Probation Officer—Continued

Community resource specialist—Service broker
Transportation officer—Gets juvenile to where he has to go in a pinch
Recreational therapist—Gets juvenile to use leisure time well
Employment counselor—Gets kid job
Judge's advisor—Court service officer
Financial advisor—Monitors payment, sets pay plan
Paper pusher—Fills out myriad forms
Sounding board—Listens to irate parents, kids, police, teachers, and so on
Punching bag—Person to blame when anything goes wrong, or kid commits new crime
Expert clinician—Offers or refers to appropriate treatment
Family counselor/marriage therapist—Keeps peace in juvenile's family
Psychiatrist—Answers question: why does the kid do it?
Banker—Juvenile needs car fare money
Tracker—Finds kid
Truant officer—Gets kid to school
Lawyer—Tells defense lawyer/prosecutor what juvenile law says
Sex educator—Facts of life, AIDS, and child support (Dr. Ruth)
Emergency foster parent—In a pinch
Family wrecker—Files petitions for abuse/neglect
Bureaucrat—Helps juvenile justice system function
Lobbyist—For juvenile, for department
Program developer—For kid, for department
Grant writer—For kid, for department
Board member—Serves on myriad committees
Agency liaison—With community groups
Trainer—For volunteer, students
Public info. officer—"Tell me what you know about probation"
Court officer/bailiff—In a pinch
Custodian—Keeps office clean
Victim advocate—Deals with juvenile's victim

Source: *Desktop Guide to Good Juvenile Probation Practice* (National Center for Juvenile Justice, Office of Juvenile Justice and Delinquency Prevention, 1993), 119–20.

- ▲ The terms of the agreement should be clearly stated in writing.
- ▲ Once a nonjudicial disposition has been made, the subsequent filing of a petition based on the events out of which the original complaint arose should be permitted for a period of three months from the date of the agreement. If no petition is filed within that period its subsequent filing should be prohibited.

Informal probation is criticized as presuming a juvenile's guilt prior to adjudication. Such criticism is muted, however, by the fact that informal probation is voluntary and entered into by the parties with the knowledge that adjudication is always an option for the juvenile; therefore, any possible coercive effect of informal probation is minimized.

CONDITIONS OF PROBATION AND AFTERCARE

In general juvenile courts enjoy immense discretion when imposing probation conditions. Hardly any state specifies the conditions that should be imposed. The setting of conditions is left to the sound discretion of the juvenile court, usually upon recommendation of the probation officer. Similarly, aftercare conditions are left to the discretion of juvenile institutional officers who are authorized to release the juvenile.

Typically conditions include provisions designed to control as well as rehabilitate the juvenile.[27] These dual goals make the imposition of conditions more challenging for the court.

Kinds of Conditions

Probation or aftercare conditions are usually of two kinds: mandatory and discretionary. Both may be specified by law or left to the discretion of the juvenile court judge or the releasing authority in the case of aftercare. Only a few states impose mandatory conditions, and where imposed, they vary from one jurisdiction to another. Mandatory conditions usually provide the following:[28]

1. Probationers may not commit a new local, state, or federal delinquent act.
2. Probationers must report as directed to their probation officers.
3. Probationers must obey all court orders.

Discretionary conditions also vary from one jurisdiction to another. As an example, the New Jersey Juvenile Statutes list the following discretionary conditions:[29]

1. Pay a fine.
2. Make restitution.
3. Perform community service.
4. Participate in a work program.
5. Participate in programs emphasizing self-reliance.
6. Participate in a program of academic or vocational education or counseling.
7. Be placed in a suitable residential or nonresidential program for the treatment of alcohol or narcotic abuse.
8. Be placed in a nonresidential program operated by a public or private agency, providing intensive services to juveniles for specified hours.
9. Be placed in any private group home with which the Department of Correction has entered into a purchase of service contract.

New Jersey law also authorizes the court to impose conditions on the parents of juveniles. About a dozen states have such laws. It is enforced through the power of the court to hold nonconforming parents in contempt.[30] How far state can go to punish parents of juveniles is unsettled. Requiring parents to pay fines, court costs, and restitution is often valid, but criminal penalties for parents usually run afoul of due process protections and are likely to be unconstitutional, particularly if they are severe.

Validity of Conditions

There are only a few court cases on the validity of conditions imposed on juveniles. These cases indicate, however, that to be valid and constitutional, the condition must have the following characteristics:[31]

1. It must be reasonably related to the offense.
2. It must aim at the offender's rehabilitation or community protection.
3. It must not unreasonably restrict constitutional rights.
4. It must be consistent with law and public policy.
5. It must be specific and understandable.

These characteristics are similar to those required for conditions in adult probation. In one case a court held that a juvenile who was borderline retarded could not be ordered to maintain satisfactory grades at school. Such a condition would have been unreasonable and unfair because failure was certain.[32] In another case an appellate court ruled that the juvenile court could not impose a fine because this was punitive. It could impose restitution, however, because restitution is rehabilitative and therefore consistent with the state's juvenile probation law and policy.[33] In another decision a state appellate court upheld 1,000 hours of community service, saying this was a reasonable condition that would help promote the goal of probation.[34] In general, *parens patriae* and the traditional wide discretion given to judges during sentencing have combined to expand the power of the juvenile court judge to impose conditions of probation. Consequently only a few conditions have been declared invalid or unconstitutional.

Aside from cases challenging the validity of probation conditions, there have also been cases questioning the constitutionality of conditions of juvenile detention. In one case a federal court in Rhode Island held that the conditions of confinement in that state's boys' training school (where juveniles were locked in cold, dark isolation cells containing only a mattress and a toilet) were anti-rehabilitative and violated the Eighth Amendment prohibition against cruel and unusual punishment.[35] In another case a federal judge in Texas held that the state's juvenile facility constituted cruel and unusual punishment and that the juveniles confined in the facility had a right to proper treatment.[36] In yet another case the Seventh Circuit Court of Appeals held that the conditions of confinement at the Indiana Boys' School, which held boys from 12 to 18 years of age, were unconstitutional.[37] Courts have generally been more protective of juveniles than adult offenders in general conditions-of-confinement cases. This is because while adult offenders are sent to prisons for punishment, juvenile offenders are usually sent to state institutions purportedly for rehabilitation, so it is believed they need better treatment.

SUPERVISION

Supervision has been called the "essence of juvenile probation."[38] The *Desktop Guide* states that "the common thread that runs through all approaches to supervision is utility; that is, that juvenile justice intervention must be designed to guide and correct the naturally changing behavior patterns of youth."[39] It adds, "Unlike adult probation, juvenile supervision views a young offender as a developing person, as one who has not yet achieved a firm commitment to a particular set of values, goals, behavior patterns, or lifestyle. As such, juvenile justice supervision is in the hopeful position of influencing that development and thereby reducing criminal behavior."[40]

Standards and Goals

As in other phases of corrections (such as jails, prisons, and parole) standards have been set by the American Correctional Association and other organizations for juvenile probation and aftercare. None of these standards, however, have been enacted into law by any state or imposed upon any juvenile probation department by court order; therefore they aim merely to persuade and remain as ideals to aspire for. One publication notes that the reason for nonadoption is that "there are no universally accepted probation standards because there is more than one way to provide probation services that observe the legal rights of minors and meet the needs for rehabilitation and safety."[41] Diversity is the rule rather than the exception in the treatment of juveniles.

The *Desktop Guide* recommends that probation departments "consider the converging interests of the juvenile offender, the victim, and the community at large in developing individualized case plans for probation supervision."[42] To reconcile conflicting goals (such as rehabilitation versus punishment, treatment versus control, and public safety versus youth development), the same publication states that probation "must endeavor to not only protect the public and hold the juvenile offender accountable, it must also attempt to meet his needs."[43] Thus the ideal form of juvenile probation supervision aims more at rehabilitation than merely meting out punishment. Standards proposed by several organizations recommend that before a juvenile is placed on probation, a needs assessment should be conducted and a service plan developed.[44] These standards further suggest that the probation officer, in conjunction with the juvenile and family, assess needs in the following areas: medical problems, proximity of the program to the youth, the capacity of the youth to benefit from the program, and the availability of placements.[45] In addition, the standards place strong emphasis on the "availability of supplemental services to facilitate the youth's participation in a community-based program."

Intensive Probation

Intensive probation is a type of supervision used in both juvenile and adult probation. It may be defined as a program of intensive surveillance of and contact with an offender and aimed at reducing criminal conduct by limiting opportunities to engage in it. Intensive supervision strategies vary from state to state, but one writer identifies the following common features in intensive supervision for juveniles:[46]

1. A greater reliance placed on unannounced spot checks; these may occur in a variety of settings including home, school, known hangouts, and job sites.
2. Considerable attention directed at increasing the number and kinds of collateral contacts made by staff, including family members, friends, staff from other agencies, and concerned residents in the community.
3. Greater use of curfew, including both more rigid enforcement and lowering the hour at which curfew goes into effect.
4. Surveillance expanded to ensure 7-day-a-week, 24-hour-a-day coverage.

Contrary to popular belief, intensive probation is usually not designed to deal with violent juvenile offenders. The majority of juveniles placed on intensive supervision are "serious and/or chronic offenders who would otherwise be committed to a correctional facility but who, through an objective system of diagnosis and classification, have been identified as amenable to community placement."[47]

Fare v. Michael C.—An Important Case in Juvenile Supervision

The only case ever to be decided by the U.S. Supreme Court on juvenile supervision is *Fare v. Michael C.* (442 U.S. 707 [1979]). This important California case helps define the relationship between a probation officer and a probationer.

Michael C., a juvenile, was taken into police custody because he was suspected of having committed a murder. He was advised of his Miranda rights (anything he said could be used against him, and he could have a lawyer). When asked if he wanted to waive his right to have an attorney present during questioning, he responded by asking for his probation officer. He was informed by the police that the probation officer would be contacted later, but that he could talk to the police if he wanted.

Michael C. agreed to talk and during questioning made statements and drew sketches that incriminated himself. When charged with murder in juvenile court, Michael C. moved to suppress the incriminating evidence, alleging it was obtained in violation of his Miranda rights. He said that his request to see his probation officer was, in effect, equivalent to asking for a lawyer. However, the evidence was admitted at trial, and Michael C. was convicted.

On appeal the U.S. Supreme Court affirmed the conviction, holding that the request by a juvenile probationer during police questioning to see his or her probation officer, after having received the Miranda warnings, is not equivalent to asking for a lawyer and is not considered an assertion of the right to remain silent. Evidence voluntarily given by the juvenile probationer after asking to see his probation officer is therefore admissible in court in a subsequent criminal trial.

The Michael C. case is significant because the Supreme Court laid out two principles that help define the supervisory role of a juvenile probation officer. First the Court stated that the communications of the accused to the probation officer are not shielded by the lawyer–client privilege. This means that information given by a probationer to the probation officer may be disclosed in court, unlike the information given to a lawyer by a client—which cannot be revealed to anyone unless the right to confidentiality was waived by both the client and the lawyer. Said the Court,

> A probation officer is not in the same posture [as a lawyer] with regard to either the accused or the system of justice as a whole. Often he is not trained in the law, and so is not in a position to advise the accused as to his legal rights. Neither is he a trained advocate, skilled in the representation of the interests of his client before police and courts. He does not assume the power to act on behalf of his client by virtue of his status as advisor, *nor are the communications of the accused to the probation officer shielded by the lawyer–client privilege.* [Emphasis added]

Second, the Court made it clear in *Fare v. Michael C.* that a probation officer's loyalty and obligation is to the state, despite any obligation owed to the probationer. The Court said,

> Moreover, the probation officer is the employee of the State which seeks to prosecute the alleged offender. He is a peace officer, and as such is allied, to a greater or lesser extent, with his fellow peace officers. He owes an obligation to the State notwithstanding the obligation he may also owe the juvenile under his supervision. *In most cases, the probation officer is duty bound to report wrongdoing by the juvenile when it comes to his attention, even if by communication from the juvenile himself.* [Emphasis added]

This statement defines where a probation officer's loyalty lies. Professionalism requires that the officer's loyalty be with the state and not with the probationer; furthermore, any communication between the probationer and the officer may be required to be divulged in court. *Fare v. Michael C.* shows that despite *parens patriae*—a doctrine based on a parent–child relationship—confidentiality of communication between the probation officer and a probationer does not exist.

REVOCATION

Violation of probation conditions leads to revocation. As in adult probation, revocation for conditions violation is largely discretionary with the juvenile court. The only exception is if revocation is mandated by law for certain serious violations.

Initiation of Revocation

As with adult probation, revocation of juvenile probation is usually initiated by the juvenile probation officer or the agency. In many jurisdictions the motion to revoke is filed in court by the prosecutor. A warrant is then issued for the juvenile's arrest. In most states the warrant is served by law enforcement officers. Some states, however, authorize juvenile probation officers to make an arrest and to conduct searches and seizures. Once arrested, the juvenile is held in custody in a juvenile facility pending a revocation hearing.

Few Rights During Revocation

Unlike adult revocation cases, where the rights during revocation proceedings are clearly laid out in the case of *Gagnon v. Scarpelli* (411 U.S. 788 [1973]), the U.S. Supreme Court has not specified the rights to which juveniles are entitled during revocation. Not many lower courts have addressed this issue, but a Michigan appellate court has decided that the juvenile revocation hearing "requires only that a certain procedural format be followed . . . the hearing is conducted only to determine whether the probation has been violated; the hearing does not result in a conviction of the underlying crime." The Michigan appellate court then held that "only a dispositional hearing was required before revoking appellant's probation; furthermore, we find that such a procedure is not violative of appellant's due process rights."[48]

The U.S. Supreme Court has not specified the rights to which juveniles are entitled during revocation. Juveniles have few rights during the revocation process.

Despite the absence of constitutional rights guarantees during revocation, at least one state appeals court has reversed revocation that was based on the "unsworn testimony of the child's probation officer, where the juvenile was given no opportunity to review any written data, reports, or records from which the probation officer testified, and where no opportunity was given the juvenile to rebut the testimony" because "the juvenile was not given the essentials of due process and fair treatment."[49] Thus, although a juvenile may not be entitled to the same rights as adults during revocation, fair treatment is required.

Standards for Revocation

The *Desktop Guide* has examined the various standards for probation revocation and concludes that if the judge determines that a violation occurred and that there is no excuse for the noncompliance, the various standards recommend three alternatives:[50]

1. A warning of the consequences of continued noncompliance and an order to comply or make up time or payment missed

2. A modification of conditions or imposition of additional conditions if it appears that a warning will be insufficient
3. Imposition of a more severe type of sanction

The judge is given immense discretion when deciding whether to revoke. These decisions are usually final and not appealable, the rationale being that the judge knows what is best for the juvenile and therefore should not be second-guessed by an appellate court. The judge has various options ranging from keeping the juvenile on probation without any change of conditions whatsoever, to imposing more severe conditions or changing treatment, to revoking probation and sending the juvenile to an institution. Judges usually rely on the recommendations of the probation officer to determine the proper action to be taken. The *Desktop Guide* recommends that the probation officer's recommendation "should not, and need not, be all or nothing," urging instead that the officer "should recommend just what is needed to produce the juvenile's compliance with his probation and no more." The implication is that revocation should be used as a last resort and not as a first option. The *Desktop Guide* then adds that ordering the juvenile to perform community work or adding curfew restriction as a condition may suffice to convince the juvenile that the effects of violation are serious.[51] Restraint, not quick revocation, is recommended.

Result of Revocation

Revocation sends the probationer to an institution for juveniles. The effect of revocation is similar to a finding of juvenile delinquency in that the juvenile may now be given the same sanctions as a juvenile delinquent, which includes being deprived of freedom and confined in a juvenile institution. Unlike adult probationers who must serve the jail or prison term originally imposed (subject to parole law), juveniles are kept in state institutions only until they reach the age of majority (adulthood). The release of a juvenile on aftercare prior to reaching the age of majority is usually determined by the juvenile authorities who run the state institution, not by the judge. In some cases, certain types of juveniles are kept beyond the age of majority by special laws that mandate harsher sanctions. However, most youth in state juvenile correctional custody are released to parole or aftercare.[52] In 1992, 69 percent of juveniles were released to parole or aftercare and therefore remained under the jurisdiction of the juvenile department. Only 15 percent were discharged without further supervision.[53]

SPECIAL PROGRAMS

Special programs are developed by juvenile probation departments to meet the needs of juveniles. They often include developing vocational skills, providing educational opportunities, and treating the mentally impaired. As is true of adult probation, juvenile programs vary between states and within a state—limited only by what local communities are willing to undertake. Variations are caused by funding levels and community receptiveness to a variety of treatment programs.

Family Counseling

A Texas state survey reveals that the most common program offered to juvenile probationers in that state is family counseling.[54] This type of counseling is important because juvenile delinquency is often traceable to bad nurture and a poor home environment. Juvenile offenders disproportionately come from dysfunctional families where there is hardly any awareness of the causes of delinquency. Consequently, family members might expect the courts to provide a panacea and "fix" the child, not realizing that family relationships and conditions are at the root of the problem. Often no amount of judicial threat or homily can make a difference; only total family commitment can. To encourage this, states authorize juvenile courts to require the family to undergo counseling and require other family members to participate in the rehabilitation process. This approach reflects the growing realization that rehabilitation efforts are doomed unless the family environment is changed for the juvenile.

Juvenile Boot Camps

One writer characterizes *boot camps* as "facilities that emphasize military drill, physical training, and hard labor."[55] Boot camps are hard to define with precision because structure and goals vary from one jurisdiction to another. One publication, however, identifies the following characteristics of boot camps:[56]

- ▲ Participation by nonviolent offenders only (to free up space in traditional facilities for violent felony offenders, meaning those who have used dangerous weapons against another person, caused death or serious bodily injury, or committed serious sex offenses)
- ▲ A residential phase of 6 months or less
- ▲ A regimented schedule stressing discipline, physical training, and work
- ▲ Participation by inmates in appropriate education opportunities, job training, and substance abuse counseling or treatment
- ▲ Provision of aftercare services that are coordinated with the program provided during the period of confinement

Corrections boot camps are of recent origin. The first modern boot camp opened in the State of Georgia in 1983.[57] Since then they have spread to other states. Boot camps are popular because they feature discipline, close supervision, and physical rigor—ingredients usually lacking in a juvenile's home environment. They are, however, expensive if managed properly. The average daily cost for a boot camp inmate in 1995 was $63.99, compared to the average cost for an adult prison inmate at $53.85.[58]

The Office of Juvenile Justice and Delinquency Prevention recently sponsored three demonstration programs in Cleveland, Denver, and Mobile to determine whether boot camps are effective and practical alternatives to juvenile institutionalization. Its key findings were as follows:[59]

- ▲ Planning and implementation met the demonstration program's goals.
- ▲ The sites formed active public–private partnerships, developed and refined coherent program rationales, and opened on schedule.
- ▲ First-year boot camp completion rates were high, ranging from 80 percent to 94 percent.
- ▲ Youths improved in educational performance, physical fitness, and behavior.
- ▲ Youths who graduated from the three-month boot camp and remained in aftercare for at least five months reported positive changes in attitudes and behavior.
- ▲ Estimates of daily costs per youth indicated that the boot camps appeared to be more cost-effective than state or local correctional facilities.

Despite these findings, the effectiveness of boot camps as a rehabilitative tool is suspect. Glowing tributes are often sporadic and anecdotal. The public, however, is enamored with the program because it stresses personal responsibility, instills discipline, and incorporates the rigors of military life. Intuitively the public perceives the program as providing a viable alternative to institutionalization that should therefore be an integral part of a juvenile's rehabilitation. Boot camps, however, have yet to live up to these high expectations. In the meantime boot camps are here to stay.

Other Programs

Other available programs are sex and drug workshops, life and job skills training, recreational opportunities, and birth control and safe sex workshops. Some states have programs aimed at developing skills in crisis intervention and mediation. Other programs are designed to address developmental and learning disabilities; there are also programs for violent and chronic juvenile offenders and special programs for youth gang members. As is the case for adult probation programs and boot camps, the effectiveness of juvenile treatment programs is open to debate and has yet to be conclusively established. The bottom line is that no silver bullet has yet been found, and perhaps never will be found, for the festering problem of juvenile delinquency and crime. What is clear, however, is that juvenile probation is a lot cheaper than placing juveniles in an institution. That alone justifies support for juvenile probation.

CHALLENGES TO JUVENILE PROBATION

A 1996 publication from the Office of Juvenile Justice and Delinquency Prevention of the U.S. Department of Justice identifies two basic problems facing juvenile probation. The first is increasing and more dangerous caseloads.[60] Because more juveniles have been brought into the system, probation caseloads have increased, and the type of juveniles under probation has changed. Juveniles who would otherwise have been sent to institutions are now being placed on probation because of space limitations. As a result officer on-the-job safety has become a problem. The same publication states that almost one-third of the respondents in a survey reported that "they had been assaulted on the job at some point in their careers." Asked whether they were ever concerned about their personal safety while performing their duties, "42 percent of the respondents reported that they were usually or always concerned."[61] Thus, says the publication, balancing juvenile probation officers' safety and the safety of the public with probationers' needs is a major challenge.

One response to the problem has been to allow juvenile probation officers to carry firearms. While this may reassure some officers, others argue that carrying firearms changes the focus of juvenile probation from rehabilitation to surveillance. That in turn may attract probation officers who are police-oriented rather than rehabilitation-oriented. Moreover, probation departments may not want to deal with legal liability issues that arise from allowing officers to carry firearms. To minimize legal liability, an officer should be allowed to carry firearms only if that officer is trained like police officers and required to enroll in continuing education programs. This is more than many juvenile departments want to do or can afford.

The second problem is whether juvenile probation should adopt a new way of looking at juvenile justice. This new paradigm suggests another way of looking at juvenile justice, one that goes beyond the traditional approaches of just deserts and treatment. The latest buzz phrases in the juvenile justice vocabulary are "balanced approach" and "restorative justice." The balanced approach "espouses the potential value of any case applying, to some degree, an entire set of principles along with individualized assessment." These are the principles of community protection, accountability, competence development, and treatment. Restorative justice, on the other hand, "promotes maximum involvement of the victim, offender, and the community in the justice process." A combination of these two concepts results in the new **balanced and restorative justice model,** which suggests that "justice is best served when the community, victim, and youth received balanced attention, and all gain tangible benefits from their interactions with the juvenile justice system."[62] This new paradigm suggests an innovative approach at a time when the public is grasping for solutions that combine the elements of retribution, rehabilitation, and fairness. It just might work. Like other concepts that have come and gone, however, the balanced and restorative model is easier proposed than implemented.

The balanced and restorative justice model suggests that justice is best served when the community, victim, and youth received balanced attention, and all gain tangible benefits from their interactions with the juvenile justice system.

A third major problem for juvenile probation is the current shift in public thinking from rehabilitation to more severe punishment, at least for certain types of offenses. Retributive justice has blurred the traditional distinctions between the juvenile justice system and adult criminal law. Whether these two approaches can coexist in a probation department needs to be further explored. It may be that probation and institutionalization will have to serve different goals—one rehabilitation and the other retribution. On the other hand, *zeitgeist* (the spirit of the times) may make surveillance the main purpose of current juvenile probation.

A fourth major problem in juvenile probation is best labeled as the "Little Kingdom" syndrome.[63] Structural fragmentation is more common in juvenile probation systems than it is in adult probation. Configurations of probation departments vary immensely from one state to another and even within a state. Many states do not have statewide probation systems. What they have instead are virtual little kingdoms managed by local agencies whose decisions are highly influenced by a juvenile court judge. Fragmentation and autonomy are justified by the assumption that juvenile justice is basically a local concern and therefore "locals" know best what should be done for their own youth. This assures flexibility, experimentation, and a degree of individualization, but it also spawns wide variations in the type of justice administered. Combined with *parens patriae,* immense discretion given to local jurisdictions can lead to abuse and neglect—abuse in the type of sanctions imposed and neglect in the kinds of programs for juveniles local communities may be willing to fund. In many cases the level of supervision and quality of treatment programs available to juveniles depend upon what the community can afford or is willing to spend. How juvenile justice can be individualized and yet collectively improved so that equal justice can be served is a continuing challenge that yields no easy answers.

SUMMARY

Juvenile justice has its roots in the concepts of *mens rea* and *parens patriae. Mens rea* denotes that only actors with guilty minds should be punished; *parens patriae* holds that the state acts as a wise parent to the child and therefore juveniles should be treated like a member of the family. Differences exist between the way we process juveniles and adults, but those differences are perhaps more symbolic than substantive.

Juvenile courts are an American creation and were founded on the belief that rehabilitation, concern, and care should be at the core of juvenile proceedings. Later, however, due process guarantees were infused into these proceedings through a series of court decisions, the most notable of which is *In Re Gault*. Two types of juvenile acts trigger judicial intervention: juvenile delinquency and conduct in need of supervision. Juvenile delinquents are minors who commit acts punishable by the state's criminal laws; conduct in need of supervision usually consists of status offenses, meaning acts that would not be punishable if committed by adults. Juvenile adjudication can result in probation. Crucial actors in juvenile probation are probation officers, who act as extensions of judicial authority and who are usually appointed and terminated by the judge. Informal probation and intensive probation are used in many juvenile jurisdictions to divert and control juveniles.

If a juvenile violates the conditions of probation, revocation ensues. Revocation is discretionary with the judge and is recommended as a last resort. Juvenile probation features many special programs, among them family counseling, boot camps, and programs designed to provide education and vocational skills. Although widely used, none of these programs has proved to be a silver bullet for the problem of juvenile crime.

ENDNOTES

1. See "Putting a Sterner Face on Juvenile Justice," *The Christian Science Monitor* (May 9, 1997), Internet edition, http://www.csmonitor.com/todays_paper/graphical/today/us/usq.2.html.
2. "Putting a Sterner Face on Juvenile Justice."
3. *Black's Law Dictionary,* 5th ed., 889.
4. Howard N. Snyder and Melissa Sickmund, *Juvenile Offenders and Victims: A National Report* (National Center for Juvenile Justice, Office of Juvenile Justice and Delinquency Prevention, August 1995), 70.
5. Rolando V. del Carmen, Mary Parker, and Francis P. Reddington, *Briefs of Leading Cases in Juvenile Justice* (Anderson, 1998), 4.
6. Patricia Torbet, Richard Gable, Hunter Hurst IV, Imogene Montgomery, Linda Szymanski, and Douglas Thomas, Executive Summary of "State Responses to Serious and Violent Juvenile Crime: Research Report" (National Center for Juvenile Justice), xi.
7. del Carmen, Parker, and Reddington, *Briefs of Leading Cases,* 9.
8. *Desktop Guide to Good Juvenile Probation Practice* (Juvenile Probation Officer Initiative Working Group, National Center for Juvenile Justice, Office of Juvenile Justice and Delinquency Prevention, 1993), 32.
9. *Desktop Guide,* 32.
10. Arnold Binder, Gilbert Geis, and Dickson D. Bruce Jr., *Juvenile Delinquency,* 2nd ed. (Anderson, 1997), 260.
11. Snyder and Sickmund, *Juvenile Offenders and Victims,* 78.
12. *Desktop Guide,* 40.
13. Peter Greenwood, "Juvenile Offenders" (National Institute of Justice, Crime File Study Guide), 1.
14. *Desktop Guide,* 43.
15. *Desktop Guide,* 43.
16. "Juvenile Probation: The Workhorse of the Juvenile Justice System" (Office of Justice Programs, Office of Juvenile Justice and Delinquency Prevention, 1996), Internet at workhors.txt at <www.ncjrs.org.>
17. Hunter Hurst IV and Patricia McFall Torbet, *Organization and Administration of Juvenile Services: Probation, Aftercare, and State Institutions for Delinquent Youth* (National Center for Juvenile Justice, 1993), 75.

18. "Juvenile Probation: The Workhorse of the Juvenile Justice System," 4.
19. "Juvenile Probation: The Workhorse of the Juvenile Justice System," 2–3.
20. Indiana Code Title 31, Article 6, Chapter 9, Section 31-6-9-4(a).
21. *Desktop Guide,* 118.
22. *Desktop Guide,* 118.
23. *Desktop Guide,* 118.
24. *Desktop Guide,* 120.
25. Snyder and Sickmund, *Juvenile Offenders and Victims,* 77.
26. *Desktop Guide,* 36.
27. Snyder and Sickmund, *Juvenile Offenders and Victims,* 135.
28. *Desktop Guide,* 16.
29. The New Jersey Juvenile Statutes 2A:4A–4B, as cited in supra note 8, 17.
30. *Desktop Guide,* 17.
31. *Desktop Guide,* 17–18.
32. *Desktop Guide,* 18.
33. *State in Interest of D.G.W.,* 361 A. 2d 513 (1976).
34. *In Re Shannon,* 483 A. 2d 363 (Md. App. 1984).
35. *Inmates of Boys Training School v. Affleck,* 346 F. Supp. 1354 (1972).
36. *Morales v. Turman,* 383 F. Supp. 53 (1974).
37. *Nelson v. Heyne,* 491 F. 2d 352 (7th Cir. 1974).
38. *Desktop Guide,* 79.
39. *Desktop Guide,* 70.
40. *Desktop Guide,* 79.
41. *Desktop Guide,* 32.
42. *Desktop Guide,* 79.
43. *Desktop Guide,* 79.
44. *Desktop Guide,* 44.
45. *Desktop Guide,* 44.
46. *Desktop Guide,* 87.
47. *Desktop Guide,* 87.
48. *Desktop Guide,* 18–19.
49. *Matter of J.B.S.,* 696 SW 2d. 223 (Tex. App. 1985).
50. *Desktop Guide,* 44.
51. *Desktop Guide,* 19.
52. *Desktop Guide,* 177.
53. *Desktop Guide,* 177.
54. Rolando V. del Carmen, Wendy Hume, Elmer Polk, Frances Reddington, and Betsy Witt, *Texas Juvenile Law and Practice* (Criminal Justice Center, Sam Houston State University, 1991), 180.
55. Clair A. Cripe, *Legal Aspects of Corrections Management* (Aspen, 1997), 371.
56. Michael Peters, David Thomas, and Christopher Zamberlan, *Boot Camps for Juvenile Offenders: A Program Summary* (Office of Juvenile Justice and Delinquency Prevention, 1997), 3.
57. Cripe, *Legal Aspects of Corrections Management,* 57.
58. Cripe, *Legal Aspects of Corrections Management,* 58.
59. "Boot Camps for Juvenile Offenders," a monograph (May 1996), internet <http://www.mcjrs.org/txtfiles/evalboot.txt>.
60. "Juvenile Probation: The Workhorse of the Juvenile Justice System," 7.
61. "Juvenile Probation: The Workhorse of the Juvenile Justice System," 7.
62. "Juvenile Probation: The Workhorse of the Juvenile Justice System," 8–9.
63. del Carmen et al., *Texas Juvenile Law and Practice,* 160–61.

DISCUSSION QUESTIONS

1. What is the *parens patriae* doctrine and how has it influenced the way we deal with juveniles?
2. Give four differences between the juvenile justice system and the adult justice system.
3. What are the adult justice equivalents for the following juvenile justice terms? Take into custody, petition, adjudication, and disposition.
4. Distinguish between juvenile delinquency and conduct in need of supervision (CINS).
5. What is intake? What does it accomplish?
6. What did the U.S. Supreme Court say in the *In Re Gault* case? Why is that case important, or is it?
7. List three other U.S. Supreme Court cases that give constitutional rights to juveniles.
8. List four skills recommended for juvenile probation officers.
9. What is informal juvenile probation? How does it differ from intensive probation?
10. What did the U.S. Supreme Court say in the case of *Fare v. Michael C.*? Why is that case significant for probation supervision?
11. "Juvenile boot camps are successful in preventing juveniles from committing other offenses." Discuss whether that statement is true or false.
12. What are the features of the balance and restorative justice model of juvenile justice?

13

THE EFFECTIVENESS OF COMMUNITY-BASED CORRECTIONS

KEY TERMS

Measures of effectiveness
Recidivism
Intermediate sanctions

What You Will Learn in This Chapter

This chapter will review the effectiveness of community corrections programs. We will look at the issue of how to measure effectiveness and at research that attempts to determine whether probation, parole, and other community-based measures actually accomplish their goals.

INTRODUCTION

Since the early 1970s public disillusionment has increased over traditional correctional treatment programs as mechanisms for controlling crime. Parole, in particular, has been widely criticized as a "revolving door" to prison that reduces the impact of criminal sentences and threatens public safety. Critics claim that studies have failed to provide any assurance that paroled inmates will not continue their criminal activities while under supervision. Media attacks on parole have focused attention on highly controversial releases such as that of Lawrence Singleton in 1988. Singleton had been convicted of raping a 15-year-old girl, cutting off both her arms, and leaving her to die on a hillside in California. When he was paroled after eight years, the public responded with outrage. The community to which Singleton was paroled refused to accept him. Alternative parole plans were thwarted by other communities. Singleton was paroled to live on the grounds of San Quentin Prison.

The Singleton case is not an isolated one. More than 700,000 felons are on parole, and the media report violent crimes committed by parolees daily. Moreover, parole has been attacked by critics from across the political spectrum—from Senator Edward Kennedy to former U.S. Bureau of Prisons Director Norman Carlson, by prisoner advocate groups, and by prisoners themselves. By 1990, in response to the widespread perception that parole was not serving the public interest, more than a dozen states had abolished parole or severely restricted their paroling authorities' discretionary power.

Probation also has been criticized. Before the "get tough on crime" era of the 1970s and 1980s, the public generally assumed that probation was reserved for less serious, nonviolent offenders, and unless some probationer committed a particularly shocking or violent crime, little attention was paid to it. However, as the flood of convicted felons began to overwhelm the prisons of most states, stopgap measures were instituted, including double- or triple-celling in established facilities, putting up "tent cities," and converting other correctional facilities into secure prisons.

As prisons became crowded, courts began to rely on probation as a disposition for greater numbers of individuals who had committed serious offenses. As probation utilization increased and more serious offenders were assigned to their caseloads, probation officers faced a crisis of quantity and quality. There were too many probationers and too few probation officers for the supervision to be effective. In the wake of these conditions, public confidence in probation and parole began to wane.

This lack of confidence in correctional programming peaked in 1974 with Robert Martinson's study of 231 correctional treatment programs across the nation. His study has been referred to as the "Nothing Works" research. Martinson concluded that, with few exceptions, the correctional programs he reviewed had no appreciable effect on recidivism.[1] In the complete report published the next year Lipton, Martinson, and Wilks concluded,

> While some treatment programs have had modest successes, it still must be concluded that the field of corrections has not as yet found satisfactory ways to reduce recidivism by significant amounts.[2]

These studies set off a national debate about the efficacy of corrections—both institutional and community-based—resulting in what one commentator called "a mixed and unsettled atmosphere regarding effectiveness."[3] The issue remains unsettled today, a quarter of a century later.

HOW IS EFFECTIVENESS MEASURED?

Much of the problem lies in the inability of researchers to agree on how to define and measure effectiveness. The most commonly used measure of effectiveness is **recidivism,** but it has no universally accepted definition:

RECIDIVISM

Failure to maintain a crime-free life after having once been convicted of an offense.

> Different studies have identified it variously as a new arrest, a new conviction, or a new sentence of imprisonment, depending on the kinds of data they had available or their project goals. As a result it is exceedingly difficult and complex to make comparisons about their results.[4]

Indeed, studies of probation and parole outcomes demonstrate that the rate of "success" depends on the definitions used by researchers. Ralph England's early study found that about 18 percent of federal probationers received new *convictions* after they were placed on probation.[5] More recently Langan and Cuniff, in a Bureau of Justice Statistics study of 79,000 felons placed on probation in 17 states, found that 43 percent were *rearrested* for a felony within three years while still on probation. However, they also found that 46 percent of the probationers that had been sent to prison or jail had absconded within the three years. Further, 71 percent had either completed their probation or were still on probation three years later. Each of these figures is correct in context. The dilemma is to determine which figure represents the rate of recidivism. As they stand, these statistics could represent either success or failure of probation.[6]

Another study of 3,995 young parolees in 22 states found that within six years of release from prison, 69 percent were *rearrested,* 53 percent were *convicted* of a new offense, and 49 percent were *reimprisoned.*[7] Although these figures represent a high rate of recidivism—whether it is defined as arrest, conviction, or return to prison—they are misleading. A closer reading reveals that only 37 percent of the sample were rearrested *while still on parole.* Consequently, it is difficult to compare these findings with those that measure recidivism within the parole period only. Moreover, there was no comparison group (control group) in this study. In evaluating parole as a release mechanism, parolee recidivism rates should be compared with the rates of persons released to mandatory supervision and those released at expiration of sentence.

We are left with the question we began with: Are probation, parole and other community-based supervision programs effective? The answer appears to be "It depends." It depends on

- how recidivism is defined,
- whether recidivism is measured only during periods of supervision,
- whether recidivism rates are compared to rates of offenders of similar age and criminal history or simply reported with no comparison group, and
- importantly, which findings in a single study are cited and for what purpose.

Langan and Cuniff's study for the Bureau of Justice Statistics, for instance, could be used to support contentions that probation is effective (71 percent were still on probation or had completed probation three years later) *or* that probation is ineffective (46 percent had been sent to prison or had absconded within three years).

The preponderance of evidence suggests that most probationers and parolees complete their term of supervision successfully. This conclusion does not, however, answer the question, Are probation and parole effective? Completion of the probation or parole term without revocation may represent the probation and parole officers' failure to adequately supervise the offenders. Violations, particularly technical violations, might not come to the attention of an officer who cannot or refuses to supervise closely. On the other hand, closer supervision would probably reveal a larger number of technical violations, which could be reflected in higher recidivism statistics; yet many of the particular offenders may not be considered failures by their supervising officers or the respective courts.

To illustrate this point, consider these examples, which would sound familiar to any experienced probation or parole officer. Which probationers and parolees are successful, and which are not?

1. The probationer or parolee has not been arrested for any offense during the term of supervision but was cited several times for technical violations, such as failure to report, failure to maintain employment, and excessive use of alcohol.
2. The parolee has no known technical violations but was arrested on two occasions for failure to pay court-ordered child support. A review of the records indicates that he got very far behind while incarcerated, but has been paying regularly since being placed under supervision. He has not been able to "catch up" the delinquent balance, however, and his ex-wife regularly files charges of delinquent child support against him.
3. The probationer or parolee has no known technical violations but was arrested for driving under the influence of alcohol two months after being placed under supervision. She agreed to enter an alcohol treatment program, and there have been no further reported violations. Her alcohol treatment counselor reports that her progress is favorable.
4. The parolee has no new crimes and no technical violations. However, he has a bad attitude and refuses to cooperate with the parole officer beyond the bare minimum required by his parole agreement.
5. The probationer is arrested and convicted for a felony committed before being placed on probation. He receives a new prison term. He has no arrests for offenses committed while on his current probation term.
6. The probationer or parolee successfully completes five years supervision with no arrests or technical violations. One year before he is scheduled to be terminated from supervision, he is arrested for a new offense. This is the first time in his adult life that he has gone more than six months without being arrested.
7. The probationer or parolee is not arrested for any new offenses, and there are no reported technical violations. However, the supervising officer has been advised repeatedly by law enforcement authorities that the probationer or parolee is heavily involved in narcotics trafficking.
8. The parolee was released from prison a year ago. He is working regularly and has no reported violations. One evening when returning from a movie with his wife he is involved in a minor traffic accident. In the ensuing events he and the other driver exchange blows, and both are arrested. He is charged with simple assault and fined $200.

Who Is on Probation?

According to a Bureau of Justice Statistics study of correctional populations in the United States in 1996:[1]

- About 55 percent of all offenders on probation had been convicted of a felony, 26 percent of a misdemeanor. About 17 percent had been convicted of driving while intoxicated, which can be considered either a felony or misdemeanor, and 2 percent for other offenses.
- Women comprised 21 percent of the nation's probationers.
- About 64 percent of adult probationers were white, 35 percent black. Hispanics, who may be of any race, comprised 15 percent of the probation population.
- Southern states generally had the highest per capita ratio of adult probationers. Texas had the largest probation population, followed by California.

Data from one study suggest that many offenders who are granted felony probation are indistinguishable in terms of their crimes or criminal record from those who are imprisoned (or vice versa).[2]

Another analysis found that 50 percent of probationers did not comply with court-ordered terms of their probation; 50 percent of known violators went to jail or prison for their noncompliance.[3] A more recent analysis indicates that 33 percent of those exiting probation failed to successfully meet the conditions of their supervision.[4] A study of a national sample of felons placed on probation found that, on any given day, about 10 to 20 percent of probationers were on abscond status, their whereabouts unknown; no agency actively invested time finding those offenders.[5]

Notes

1. Bureau of Justice Statistics, *Nation's Probation and Parole Population Reached Almost 3.9 Million Last Year*, Press Release (Washington, D.C.: U.S. Department of Justice, Bureau of Justice Statistics, August 14, 1997).
2. Joan Petersilia and Susan Turner, *Prison versus Probation in California: Implications for Crime and Offender Recidivism* (Santa Monica, Calif.: RAND, 1986).
3. Patrick Langan, "Between Prison and Probation: Intermediate Sanctions," *Science*, 1994, 264:791–93.
4. Bureau of Justice Statistics, *Nation's Probation and Parole Population Reached Almost 3.9 Million Last Year.*
5. Faye S. Taxman and James Byrne, "Locating Absconders: Results from a Randomized Field Experiment," *Federal Probation*, 1994, 58(1):13–23.

Source: Joan Petersilia, "Probation in the United States: Practices and Challenges," *National Institute of Justice Journal* (Washington, D.C.: U.S. Department of Justice, September 1997).

It is apparent that the question of which of these probationers and parolees are successful cannot be answered by arrest and conviction statistics only. A strict accounting might conclude that only #4 and #7 are successful. A subjective analysis might suggest that #4 and #7 are failures.

A REVIEW OF RESEARCH ON EFFECTIVENESS

The NILECJ Study

One of the earliest comprehensive evaluations of probation effectiveness was conducted in 1979 by the National Institute of Law Enforcement and Criminal Justice (NILECJ). The study analyzed the probation evaluation literature. The NILECJ researchers divided the literature into three groups: research that compared probation to other sentencing options, probation with no comparison, and studies that attempted to isolate the variables contributing to success on probation.[8]

Research that compared probation to other sentencing options produced mixed results. However, probationers generally had lower recidivism rates than did a group of similar offenders who had been incarcerated and then paroled. One study, which included only female offenders, found no difference in recidivism between the two groups.

Studies that examined recidivism rates for probationers with no comparison group also produced no conclusive results because they were based on diverse groups, varied definitions of recidivism, and different follow-up periods.[9]

The NILECJ attempt to isolate factors that led to success on probation was limited by the same factors that led to the mixed results in the other studies. However, significant correlations were noted between recidivism and prior criminal history, unmarried younger offenders, unemployment, low income, drug and alcohol abuse, and limited education. The fewer of these variables, the more likely the probationer was to succeed on probation.[10]

The RAND Study

One of the most notable effectiveness studies was conducted by Joan Petersilia and associates for the RAND Corporation. To study probation recidivism rates, they selected a sample of 1,672 felony probationers sentenced in Los Angeles and Alameda counties in California in 1980. The researchers followed the probationers for 40 months, recording their arrests, convictions, and incarcerations. During the 40-month period 65 percent of the probationers were rearrested, 51 percent were reconvicted, 18 percent were reconvicted of serious violent crimes, and 34 percent were reincarcerated. Moreover, they found that 75 percent of the official charges filed against the study population involved burglary or theft, robbery, and other violent crimes.[11]

Petersilia and associates then looked at the factors associated with failure on probation. They analyzed the data to determine which factors were associated with rearrest, reconviction, and success on probation.

Factors Associated with Rearrest

The likelihood of *rearrest* was increased by the number of prior juvenile and adult convictions, an original sentence of jail plus probation, and living with parents. Black probationers were more likely to be rearrested than white or Hispanic probationers. Drug offenders living with their parents and those under 21 and over 30 were more likely to be rearrested.[12]

Factors Associated with Reconviction

The probability of *reconviction* was increased by having prior juvenile and adult convictions. Property and violent offenders were more likely to be reconvicted than drug offenders.[13] The number of prior juvenile convictions was associated with *reconviction for a violent crime.* However, prior adult convictions were not correlated with reconviction for a violent crime.[14]

Factors Associated with Success on Probation

Property offenders were more likely to make a successful adjustment to probation supervision than drug or violent offenders. Older offenders and those with no prior adult or juvenile convictions were less likely to become recidivists. Those with no drug history, those who were employed, high school graduates, and those who lived with their spouse and/or children were also less likely to become recidivists.

Petersilia and her associates summarized, "In our opinion, felons granted probation present a serious threat to public safety."[15] They concluded that the criminal justice system needs an alternative intermediate punishment for serious felons—one that changes the perception of probation as a "slap on the wrist."[16] They wrote,

> The core of such an alternative must be intensive surveillance, coupled with substantial community service and/or restitution. It must be structured to satisfy public demands that the punishment fit the crime, to show criminals that crime really doesn't pay, and to control potential recidivists.[17]

Intermediate Sanctions

In the wake of research showing that traditional probation and parole were ineffective in controlling crime, many jurisdictions began to develop alternative sentencing options—**intermediate sanctions**—that stressed closer supervision and holding offenders accountable. These intermediate sanctions include intensive supervision probation (ISP), restitution and fines, community service, house arrest, and boot camps.

Intermediate sanctions are seen as a way to reduce the need for additional prison beds and to provide a continuum of sanctions that allow judges greater latitude in selecting a punishment that more closely fits the circumstances of the crime and the offender.[18] Intermediate sanctions are discussed more fully in chapter 11.

Intensive Supervision Probation (ISP)

ISP is a highly restrictive form of probation. Offenders are typically required to perform community service and/or make restitution, attend school, treatment programs, or work, submit to drug and alcohol testing, and meet with a probation officer as often as three to five times per week.[19] Caseloads for officers supervising ISP clients may be as low as 15–20 cases.

Early evaluations of ISP programs concluded that both recidivism and prison admission rates were lowered. But a study of 14 jurisdictions across the country by the National Institute of Justice indicated that ISP had not lowered the cost of correctional services and did not significantly reduce recidivism.[20] DiMascio concluded,

> recidivism among ISP participants was more often related to technical violations of the demanding conditions of intensive supervision than to new crimes. And those technical violations were more often caught because of the increased supervision.[21]

Michael Tonry and Mary Lynch reported that there are some positive findings from the ISP evaluation literature. They concluded that ISP did succeed (at some sites) in increasing participants' involvement in counseling and other treatment programs. (Table 13.1 illustrates selected ISP evaluation studies.) The drug treatment literature demonstrates that participation can reduce both drug use and crime by drug-using offenders.[22]

Despite the disappointing evaluation findings, ISP programs continue to flourish. It appears that (1) the surveillance orientation and punitive properties of ISP appeal to the public preference that penalties be demanding and burdensome and (2) ISP is seen as an appropriate midlevel punishment. Petersilia, Lurigio, and Byrne note,

> To many observers, the goal of restoring the principle of just deserts to the criminal justice system is justification enough for the continued development of intermediate sanctions.[23]

Table 13.1 **INTENSIVE SUPERVISION PROBATION EVALUATIONS AT SELECTED SITES**

Author and Year	Site	Sample	Control Groups	Contacts	Recidivism
Jolin and Stipak (1991)	Oregon	N=70 drug users	100 on EM 100 on work release Stratified random sample matched on risk	5 counseling per wk and 3 self-help per wk., plus curfew and EM	47% ISP 32% EM 33% WR
Erwin (1987)	Georgia	N=200 randomly selected from ISP	N=200 probationers N=97 prison releasees matched samples	5 per wk. ISP	40% ISP 35.5% probation 57.8% prison
Pearson (1987)	New Jersey	N=554 parolees	N=510	20 per mo.	24.7% ISP 34.6% CG
Byrne and Kelly (1989)	Massachusetts	N=227 high-risk probationers	N=834 ISP eligible offenders plus a 35% random sample of all offenders under supervision (N=2543)	10 mo. ISP 2 mo. probation	56.6% ISP 60.9% probation
Latessa (1993)	Ohio	N=317 ISP N=502 high-risk ISP	N=424 randomly selected from regular probation	4 mo. ISP 3 mo. high risk 2 mo. probation	35% ISP 43% high 34% probation
Petersilia and Turner (1993)	Contra Costa	N=170	Randomly selected offenders placed in prison, probation, or parole	12 per mo.	29% ISP 27% CG
Petersilia and Turner (1993)	Los Angeles	N=152	Randomly selected offenders placed in prison, probation, or parole	24 per mo.	32% ISP 30% CG
Petersilia and Turner (1993)	Seattle	N=173	Randomly selected offenders placed in prison, probation, or parole	12 per mo.	46% ISP 36% CG
Petersilia and Turner (1993)	Atlanta	N=50	Randomly selected offenders placed in prison, probation, or parole	20 per mo.	12% ISP 4% CG
Petersilia and Turner (1993)	Santa Fe	N=58	Randomly selected offenders placed in prison, probation, or parole	20 per mo.	48% ISP 28% CG
Petersilia and Turner (1993)	Houston	N=458 parolees	Randomly selected offenders placed in prison, probation, or parole	10 per mo.	44% ISP 40% CG

Source: Adapted from Edward Latessa and Harry Allen, *Corrections in the Community, 1997* (Cincinnati: Anderson), 318–19. Used with permission.

Boot Camps
Offenders sentenced to boot camp programs live in military-like dormitories and undergo rigorous physical and behavioral training for periods of three to six months. Boot camps are generally reserved for youthful first offenders who are viewed as more capable of changing their behaviors and attitudes than are older, more seriously involved offenders.[24] As with ISP, early evaluations of boot camp programs were positive. However, later studies have found that boot camps have no "discernable effect on subsequent offending and tend to both increase costs and crowding."[25] In a series of studies Doris Layton MacKenzie and colleagues concluded that boot camps do not reduce recidivism rates. However, they did find evidence in some jurisdictions that graduates "appear to be involved in more positive social activities than similar offenders on probation."[26]

House Arrest and Electronic Monitoring
An offender sentenced to house arrest (or home confinement) must spend the time that he or she is not working at home. Some jurisdictions enforce compliance by requiring the offender to wear a small electronic bracelet or anklet that transmits electronic signals to monitoring units. House arrest programs are operated throughout the United States. More than 45,000 offenders in all 50 states were electronically monitored in 1992. Florida alone had over 14,000 offenders under house arrest, many of whom were electronically monitored.[27] House arrest is often imposed as a condition of intensive supervision probation. It can, however, stand alone as a correctional sanction.

There are no large-scale evaluations of house arrest and electronic monitoring programs. Several small studies and two recent literature reviews stress the scantiness of the research evidence. A 1992 study by Terry Baumer and Robert Mendelsohn concluded that "the incapacitation and public safety potential of this sanction has probably been considerably overstated."[28] Michael Tonry and Mary Lynch summarize the research:

> [W]hile a fair amount has been learned about the operation and management of electronic monitoring systems, about technology, and about implementation of new programs . . . the most comprehensive review of the research observes that "we know very little about either home confinement or electronic monitoring."[29]

Community Service
Few offenders can afford to make financial restitution to their victims. Community service is a form of symbolic restitution. Community service involves ordering offenders to perform work for government or private, nonprofit agencies: painting churches, maintaining parks, collecting roadside trash, and working in nursing homes or hospitals. Community service can be used alone or in conjunction with other sanctions. Community service is an extremely popular sanction that is used in all 50 states. One study estimates that 6 percent of all felons are sentenced to perform community service, usually along with other sanctions.[30] Community service has wide public support; yet, as with other community-based correctional programs, researchers cannot show that it reduces recidivism. Douglas McDonald evaluated a large community service project funded by the Vera Institute of Justice in New York City. While he found that community service programs had little effect on recidivism, the prison diversion goals of the project were met, and the program saved taxpayers money.[31] Tonry and Lynch conclude,

> Both American and European research and experience show that community service can serve as a meaningful, cost-effective sanction for offenders who would otherwise be imprisoned.[32]

Other Outcome Measures for Evaluation

Most of the evaluation studies cited here have used recidivism as the primary or only measure of success. This has caused concern among criminal justice professionals, who suggest that one should look at other factors, including the contributions of those on probation to the overall crime problem. In a recent study Joan Petersilia wrote,

> Of all persons arrested and charged with felonies in 1992, 17 percent of them were on probation at the time of their arrest.[33]

This suggests that probationers do not represent a disproportionate share of the crime in a community.

The American Probation and Parole Association recommends to its members that they collect data on outcomes other than recidivism. They argue that factors such as the amount of restitution collected, the number of offenders employed, the amount of fines and fees collected, the number of community service hours, the number of probationers enrolled in school, and the number of drug-free days be considered as well.[34] These important outcomes are usually completely ignored by policymakers and evaluators. Tonry and Lynch argue that "for offenders who do not present unacceptable risks of future violent (including sexual crimes) crimes, a punitive sanction that costs much less than prison to implement, that promises no higher reoffending rates, and that creates negligible risks of violence by those who would otherwise be confined has much to commend it."[35]

SUMMARY

Community-based sanctions have come under attack for failing to provide any assurance that released offenders will not continue their criminal activity while under supervision. However, research has not provided conclusive evidence that these community-based correctional programs have either failed or succeeded. Determining success or failure is difficult because recidivism, the conventional measure of effectiveness, is defined differently by different researchers. Moreover, strict reliance on arrests, convictions, or reimprisonment may not provide a valid measure of success or failure.

The public demands correctional programs that satisfy both punishment and public safety objectives. For a majority of the more serious offenders—those who cannot be maintained safely under regular probation or parole supervision, yet for whom prison is too severe a sanction—a range of intermediate punishments may be safe and effective. These intermediate punishments—intensive supervision probation, house arrest with electronic monitoring, community service, and boot camps—represent the future of community corrections.

Both the public and criminal justice policymakers must come to understand that not all criminals can be locked up. Community-based correctional programs, while not able to show reduced levels of recidivism, may offer other attractive benefits such as reductions in prison admissions and lowered costs. While the public and policymakers tend to recognize that prisons and jails are expensive to build and maintain, they do not often factor in the human cost of incarceration in terms of the loss of human potentiation and stabilized families.[36] DiMascio writes,

Moreover, they [community-based sanctions] provide a means for offenders who are not dangerous to repay their victim and their communities. Intermediate sanctions also promote rehabilitation—which most citizens want, but most prisons are no longer able to provide—and the reintegration of the offender into the community. And, once the programs are in place, they do this at a comparatively low cost.[37]

Furthermore, research has shown that when the public is made aware of the possible range of punishments and given information about how they are used and with whom, they support a wide range of alternative sanctions—including community-based programs.[38]

ENDNOTES

1. Robert Martinson, "What Works? Questions and Answers About Prison Reform," *Public Interest* (Spring 1974), 25.
2. Douglas Lipton, Robert Martinson and Judith Wilks, *The Effectiveness of Correctional Treatment* (New York: Praeger, 1975), 627.
3. Ted Palmer, *A Profile of Correctional Effectiveness and New Direction for Research* (Albany: State University of New York Press, 1994), xxi.
4. Joan Petersilia, Susan Turner, James Kahan, and Joyce Peterson, *Granting Felons Probation: Public Risks and Alternatives* (Santa Monica, Calif.: RAND, 1985), 20.
5. Ralph W. England, "A Study of Postprobation Recidivism Among Five Hundred Federal Offenders," *Federal Probation* 19 (1955), 10–16.
6. Patrick A. Langan and Mark A. Cuniff, "Recidivism of Felons on Probation, 1986–1989," *Special Report* (Bureau of Justice Statistics, February 1992).
7. James J. Beck and Bernard J. Shipley, "Recidivism of Young Parolees," *Special Report* (Bureau of Justice Statistics, 1987).
8. Harry Allen, Eric Carlson, and Evalyn Parks, *Critical Issues in Adult Probation: A Summary* (Washington, D.C.: National Institute of Law Enforcement and Criminal Justice, 1979).
9. Allen, Carlson, and Parks, *Critical Issues in Adult Probation,* 36.
10. Allen, Carlson, and Parks, *Critical Issues in Adult Probation,* 37.
11. Petersilia et al., *Granting Felons Probation,* vii.
12. Petersilia et al., *Granting Felons Probation,* 52.
13. Petersilia et al., *Granting Felons Probation,* 52–56.
14. Petersilia et al., *Granting Felons Probation,* 53.
15. Petersilia et al., *Granting Felons Probation,* 53.
16. Petersilia et al., *Granting Felons Probation,* 65.
17. Petersilia et al., *Granting Felons Probation,* 65.
18. William M. DiMascio, *Seeking Justice: Crime and Punishment in America* (New York: Edna McConnell Clark Foundation, 1997).
19. DiMascio, *Seeking Justice,* 36.
20. DiMascio, *Seeking Justice,* 36.
21. DiMascio, *Seeking Justice,* 36. He cites Joan Petersilia and Susan Turner, "Evaluating Intensive Supervision Probation and Parole," in Michael Tonry and Kate Hamilton, eds. *Intermediate Sanctions in Overcrowded Times* (Washington, D.C.: National Institute of Justice, 1995).
22. Michael Tonry and Mary Lynch, "Intermediate Sanctions," in Michael Tonry, ed., *Crime and Justice: A Review of Research,* vol. 20 (Chicago: University of Chicago Press, 1996), 116.

23. Joan Petersilia, Arthur J. Lurigio, and James M. Byrne, "Introduction: The Emergence of Intermediate Sanctions." In *Smart Sentencing: The Emergence of Intermediate Sanctions* (Newbury Park, Calif.: Sage, 1992), xiv.
24. DiMascio, *Seeking Justice,* 40.
25. Tonry and Lynch, "Intermediate Sanctions," 110.
26. D. L. MacKenzie and C. Souryal, "The Impact of Shock Incarceration on Technical Violations and New Criminal Activities," *Justice Quarterly* 10: 465.
27. DiMascio, *Seeking Justice,* 40.
28. Cited in Tonry and Lynch, "Intermediate Sanctions," 122.
29. Tonry and Lynch, "Intermediate Sanctions," 122.
30. DiMascio, *Seeking Justice,* 37.
31. Cited in Tonry and Lynch, "Intermediate Sanctions," 125.
32. Tonry and Lynch, "Intermediate Sanctions," 127.
33. Joan Petersilia, "Probation in the United States," *National Institute of Justice Journal* (Washington, D.C.: United States Department of Justice), September 1977, 4.
34. Petersilia, "Probation in the United States," 5.
35. Tonry and Lynch, "Intermediate Sanctions," 127.
36. DiMascio, *Seeking Justice,* 41.
37. DiMascio, *Seeking Justice,* 41.
38. DiMascio, *Seeking Justice,* 43.

DISCUSSION QUESTIONS

1. Discuss the issue of recidivism. How is recidivism conventionally measured? What problems are related to these measures?
2. Can you suggest any other methods for determining the effectiveness of community-based corrections programs?
3. Imagine that you are the probation or parole officer supervising the eight probationers and parolees described in the chapter. In two or three sentences, evaluate each case as a success or as a failure.
4. For what kind of offender is probation an appropriate disposition? Why?
5. How might you justify parole for a violent offender who has served eight years of a ten-year sentence?
6. How do intermediate sanctions differ from regular probation and parole? What kinds of offenders would you expect to benefit most from such programs? What is the benefit to society?
7. What do you believe is the future of community-based correctional programs?

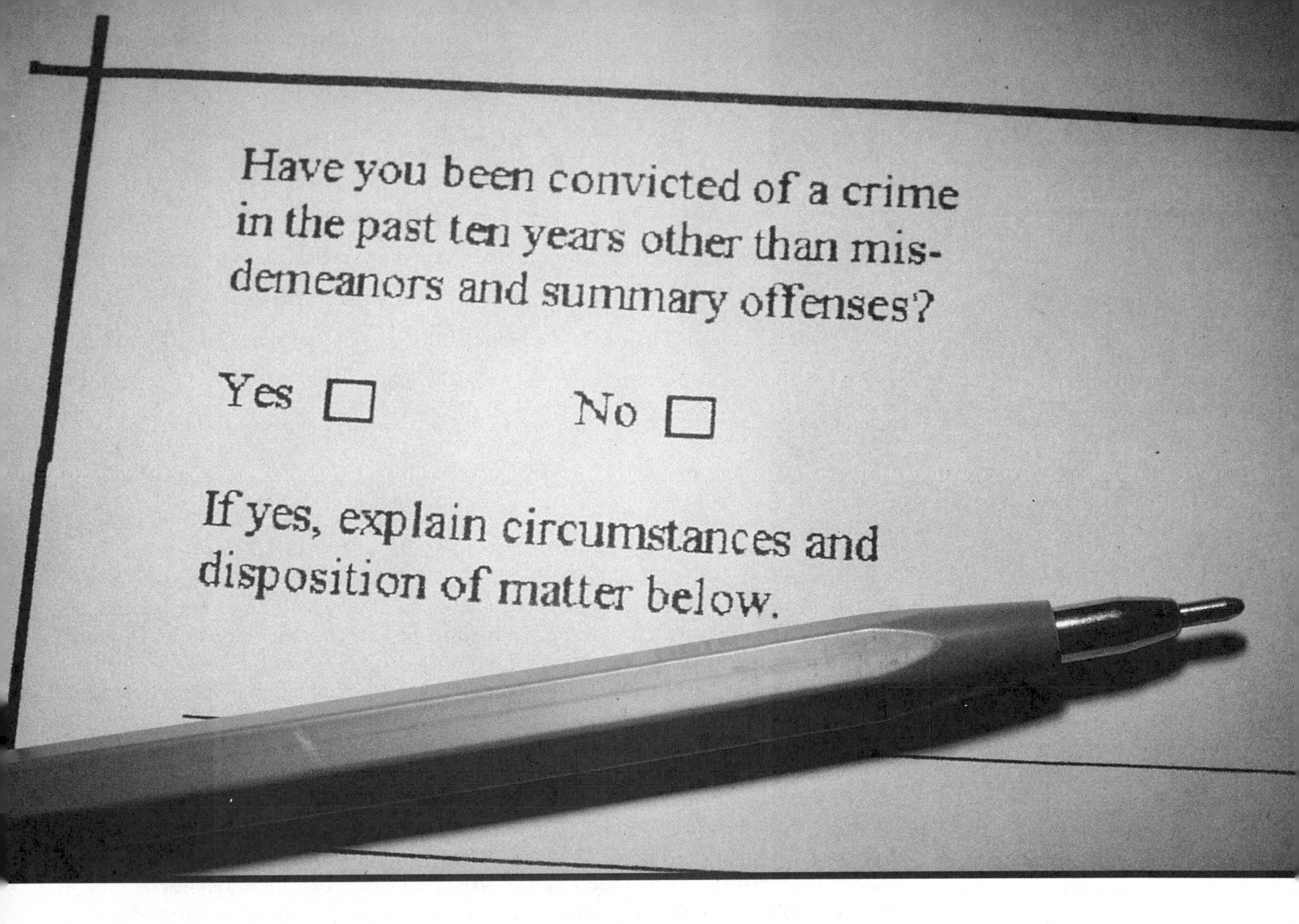

14

DIRECT AND COLLATERAL CONSEQUENCES OF CONVICTION

KEY TERMS

Direct sanctions
Collateral consequences of conviction
Civil rights
Political rights
Outlawry
Attainder
Good moral character
Moral turpitude
Public office
Public employment
Surety bond
Social stigmatization

What You Will Learn in This Chapter

Conviction brings both direct and collateral consequences. Direct consequences include fines, probation, imprisonment, or other sanctions. Collateral consequences include disabilities that are not directly imposed by the court but attach to the individual from the fact of the conviction—such as loss of the right to vote, loss of citizenship, loss of the ability to hold certain jobs, or loss of the right to own a firearm. In this chapter we examine these collateral consequences of conviction.

INTRODUCTION

The distinction between the direct and collateral consequences of conviction deserves our consideration. Conviction is usually followed by the imposition of both criminal penalties and civil disabilities. We normally think of only the *direct sanctions*—a fine, commitment to a penal or correctional institution, commitment to an institution or program for specialized treatment, probation, or some combination of these—but the imposed sanctions also include collateral consequences.

COLLATERAL CONSEQUENCES OF CONVICTION

Disabilities that follow a conviction that are not directly imposed by a sentencing court—such as loss of the right to vote, serve on a jury, practice certain occupations, or own a firearm.

Collateral consequences are disabilities that accompany conviction that are not directly imposed by the sentencing authority. They stem from the *fact of conviction* and are imposed by operation of law, the decisions of licensing or other administrative bodies, and by private individuals, such as when an employer refuses to hire an ex-convict. Most such adverse decisions of licensing bodies and private individuals result from the perception that a convicted offender lacks "good moral character." Because benefits under licensing laws are customarily restricted to persons of good moral character, this is one of the most damaging effects of conviction.

Collateral consequences also include certain incidental criminal and quasi-criminal sanctions that may follow a conviction. Examples of these are restrictions on the ownership, control, or possession of firearms; suspension or revocation of a driver's license; dishonorable discharge from the armed forces; certain criminal registration requirements; impeachment as a witness; and special requirements relating to application for pardon or other forms of executive clemency.

Thus, although collateral consequences are normally considered as the loss of *civil* rights or the imposition of civil disabilities, they may actually involve effects that have a criminal nature or that are very closely related to the criminal, rather than the civil, realm. Law professor Richard Singer has observed that "for many criminals—particularly for the 50 percent of convicted persons who are never imprisoned—[these consequences] are anything but collateral; they are, in fact, the most persistent punishments that are inflicted for crime."[1] Moreover, the number of convicted persons suffering from collateral consequences is substantial: about 14 million.[2]

The overall effects of a conviction on an offender—direct *and* collateral consequences—are the criminal and civil disabilities or penalties that the person actually suffers. This "real" sentence results from fixed legislative penalties, the sentence imposed by the sentencing authority, the operation of good-time statutes and of suspended sentence and probation and parole laws, and the disabilities that result from decisions of licensing bodies and the actions of private individuals, including the disabilities that result from loss of good moral character.

Civil and Political Rights Defined

A **civil right** is a right that belongs to a person by virtue of citizenship. **Political rights** relate to the establishment, support, or management of government. Civil rights usually include political rights, but sometimes the two kinds of rights are distinguished. For example, a resident alien may not exercise political rights, such as the right to vote or to hold political office, but has full enjoyment of civil rights.

In common usage, and in some statutes, the word *citizenship* is sometimes used to mean "civil rights." It is sometimes stated that conviction deprives the offender of citizenship, or that a pardon restores the convicted person to citizenship. This is an unfortunate use of words, for a conviction does not deprive a natural-born citizen of citizenship.

In the 1958 case *Trop v. Dulles,* the accused, convicted of desertion in time of war, was deprived of his United States citizenship. The Supreme Court declared that to deprive a man of his citizenship and thus condemn him to "statelessness" is "a penalty more cruel and punitive than torture, for it involves a total destruction of the individual's status in organized society."[3] In a later case a statute that attempted to remove citizenship from persons who leave the United States to avoid the draft was likewise declared unconstitutional.[4]

Although a person cannot be deprived of citizenship as a result of conviction, that person can and does lose civil and political rights and suffers from certain civil disabilities. The civil penalties and disabilities are seldom mentioned in a court's sentence, but the offender experiences them as a collateral consequence of conviction.

CIVIL RIGHTS

Rights that belong to a person by virtue of citizenship.

POLITICAL RIGHTS

Rights related to the establishment, support, or management of government.

History of Civil Disabilities

Civil disabilities as a consequence of crime have been traced back to ancient Greece.[5] The Greeks called the disability *infamy,* a word that found its way into Anglo-American criminal law in the term *infamous crimes.* Infamous crimes carried severe penalties as well as the additional sanctions of outlawry and attainder. **Outlawry** deemed a person outside the protection and aid of the law. In effect it established a kind of open season on the offender, who could be hunted down and killed by any citizen. This person, who was "attaint," lost all civil rights and forfeited all property to the Crown through **attainder.** The individual's entire family was declared corrupt, which made them unworthy to inherit his or her property. The theory behind both outlawry and attainder was that because the offender had declared war on the community by committing an infamous crime, the community had the right to retaliation and retribution against the offender.

The Constitution of the United States forbids "bills of attainder,"[6] and similar provisions against attainder or its effects are found in the constitutions and statutes of various states. Although the outlaw was a familiar figure in pioneer society, particularly in Western pioneer society, outlawry as a form of punishment was expressly forbidden.

OUTLAWRY

In old Anglo-Saxon law, the process by which a criminal was declared an *outlaw* and placed outside the protection and aid of the law.

ATTAINDER

At common law, the extinction of civil rights and capacities that occurred when a person received a sentence of death or outlawry for treason or another felony. The person's estate was forfeited to the Crown.

Civil Disabilities Today

In spite of constitutional and statutory provisions against outlawry and certain aspects of attainder, every state has enacted civil disability laws that affect the convicted offender. The loss of rights and the civil disabilities that result from such laws vary from state to state and crime to crime.[7] They range from statutes that deprive the criminal of all or almost all civil rights while he or she is serving a prison sentence[8] to loss of political rights, revocation of occupational licenses, and denial of employment opportunities. Such things as pension rights, rights under workers' compensation acts, and benefits under insurance policies may be lost, and marital status and the right to prevent the adoption of one's children may be affected.

Some rights are automatically lost upon conviction; others can be lost according to judicial or administrative discretion. Still others are denied by the decisions and actions of private individuals. In some cases conviction results in the loss of rights only within the particular state; in other cases the loss extends to other states, as is true for a federal offense. According to some statutes a conviction must be followed by incarceration for a specified period before rights are lost; in such cases the right is not lost if conviction is followed by probation or if the sentence to probation is not considered a conviction. Other statutes provide that conviction alone leads to forfeiture. Some rights are permanently lost and cannot be restored; others are automatically restored upon completion of the sentence or may be restored by action of the executive or a court. To determine the status of a particular convicted offender's rights, one must examine the statutory provisions, judicial decisions, administrative rulings and practices, and actions of individuals in both the state of conviction and the state in which a particular right is sought to be enforced.[9]

Extent of Loss of Rights

The civil penalty may amount to a complete denial of a right, or it may merely impose restrictions and conditions upon its exercise. In some jurisdictions, for example, the right to vote and the right to hold public office are denied for life unless they are restored by pardon or special proceeding. On the other hand, a conviction (except a conviction for perjury) generally does not completely disqualify the offender from serving as a witness—the effect is to permit the proof of the conviction to be shown in impeachment of the individual's testimony. Statutes concerning marital status may automatically give the spouse grounds for divorce, or they may give the spouse grounds for divorce only if the conviction is accompanied by imprisonment for a specified length of time. Generally in the matter of civil disabilities, the particular right must be considered in order to determine the extent of the loss.

Loss of Rights during Probation Period

The rights of the probationer during the probation period are determined basically by whether the probationer has been convicted. If the probated offender is convicted, he or she loses those rights that any convicted person in that jurisdiction loses. As we shall see, however, special statutory provisions for expunging the conviction and restoring those rights may exist. On the other hand, if probation has been ordered before the imposition of sentence, application of the narrow definition of *conviction* in particular situations may protect the probationer from the loss of civil rights. In a state where the court may grant probation in either of two ways—by suspending imposition of sentence, or by imposing a sentence and thereafter suspending its execution—some probationers lose their civil rights and others do not. Some states impose loss of rights only if the convicted person is imprisoned. In some states and the federal government, probation is a sentence in itself and is regarded as a conviction, no matter how stated. See the supplemental reading following this chapter for a state-by-state listing of rights lost by conviction.

Justification for Imposing Civil Disabilities

Many deprivations during imprisonment can be justified in that they are appropriate to the punitive aims of imprisonment. For example, holding public office, serving as a juror, and carrying on one's business are obviously incompatible with the nature of imprisonment. In addition, certain deprivations are useful as independent sanctions for criminal behavior. For example, suspending or revoking a driver's license for a conviction involving driving while intoxicated or under the influence of drugs is appropriate; it is likely to be a highly effective deterrent, and it proposes to protect society from the particular kind of danger that person poses. Few of the present laws regarding loss of civil rights upon conviction can be so justified. The laws have not been rationally designed to accommodate the varied interests of society and the individual convicted person.[10]

Such consideration prompted the American Bar Association to suggest in its *Standards Relating to Probation* that most civil rights be retained by the probationer:

> Every jurisdiction should have a method by which the collateral effects of a criminal record can be avoided or mitigated following the successful completion of a term of probation and during its service.[11]

At the very least, the statutes that authorize a sentence of probation should also address the problem of collateral disabilities and provide a method by which their effect can be individualized to the particular case.[12]

CIVIL AND POLITICAL RIGHTS AFFECTED BY CONVICTION

In this section we discuss in detail some of the most important civil and political rights that may be forfeited, restricted, or otherwise affected by virtue of conviction or imprisonment in a state penitentiary in one or more states:

- The right to claim good moral character
- The right to hold public office
- The right to vote
- The right to serve on a jury
- The right to be a witness
- Employment-related rights, such as the right to an occupational license, to public employment, to private sector employment, and to be bonded
- The right to own a firearm

Loss of Good Character

One of the most inclusive and damaging consequences of a conviction is the loss of **good character,** or as it is sometimes phrased, *good moral character.* Because good character is not a civil or political right, loss of good character is not customarily included in a list of rights lost upon conviction. In practical effect, however, this loss constitutes the basis for statutes and practices that deny the offender licenses and other employment benefits. The loss is serious, because there is considerable doubt that pardon or other proceedings to expunge a conviction restore the person's good character.

GOOD (MORAL) CHARACTER

The totality of virtues that forms the basis of one's reputation in the community.

The Right to Hold Public Office

The laws of the federal government and of many states and municipalities disqualify all convicted persons or persons convicted of certain crimes from holding public office. A public office has been defined as an "agency for the state, the duties of which involve in their performance the exercise of some portion of the sovereign power, great or small."[13]

State prohibitions take two forms:

1. Most states' statutes expressly bar persons convicted of felonies, infamous offenses, or specified offenses from holding public office.
2. Some states indirectly bar convicted felons from holding public office by requiring that a holder of public office be a qualified voter. Most states disqualify convicted felons as voters, which precludes them from holding public office.[14]

Federal statutes and the U.S. Constitution also contain provisions that exclude certain offenders from holding certain positions in the government of the United States. With the limited exception of Section 3 of the Fourteenth Amendment,[15] the Constitution does not bar offenders from holding any position in the federal government. Congress, however, may bar ex-felons from holding any nonconstitutional public office.[16] The U.S. Pardon Attorney notes that Congress has passed statutes that exclude persons convicted of specified offenses from holding any nonconstitutionally created federal office. These offenses include falsifying, destroying, or removing public records or documents; receiving compensation in matters affecting the government; rebellion; and treason.[17] Conviction for treason disqualifies the defendant from holding "any office under the United States."

Every state except Alaska and Vermont imposes restrictions on holding public office after a conviction. Some states permanently restrict the right to hold public office after a felony conviction unless the convicted person receives a pardon or is otherwise restored to full franchisement. Some states return the right to hold public office after discharge from probation, parole, or prison. A few states permit probationers to hold public office while still on probation.[18] See the supplemental reading following this chapter for a state-by-state listing of rights lost after conviction.

The thrust of the *National Advisory Commission Standards* would seem to prohibit holding public office only during a period of actual confinement, and presumably would permit the holding of a public office during a period of probation that did not involve confinement.[19]

The Right to Vote

Although the right to vote is considered a fundamental right of citizenship, it is generally held that it can be denied to convicted felons. The provisions of the constitutions and laws of 50 states and the District of Columbia that remove or limit the convicted offender's right to vote vary widely. Disfranchisement may follow convictions of a felony, an infamous crime, a crime involving moral turpitude, and specified other offenses.[20]

The California Supreme Court, in a case decided in 1973, declared that the provisions of the California constitution and statutes that deprived the convicted felon of the right to vote violated the equal protection clause of the U.S. Constitution.[21] The case was overruled by the U.S. Supreme Court in the case of *Richardson v. Ramirez,* which held that a state may strip ex-felons who have fully paid their debt to society of their fundamental right to vote without running afoul of the Fourteenth Amendment.[22]

A cherished freedom which can be lost by a conviction.

Nothing in *Richardson v. Ramirez* requires a state to deny the vote to the person on probation or parole or to the convicted felon, however. Thus some states disqualify persons only during a period of imprisonment, which may result in preserving the right of a person on probation to vote. Currently the right to vote is lost in all but three states (Maine, Massachusetts, and Vermont). Utah restricts the right to vote only for defendants convicted of election crimes or treason. A minority of states permanently deny convicted felons the right to vote unless they are pardoned (or restored to citizenship through some other method). The other jurisdictions vary widely in their handling of convicted persons' voting rights. About half of the remaining jurisdictions deny the vote only while the felon is under correctional supervision (prison, probation, or parole).[23]

The Right to Serve on a Jury

The exclusion of convicted persons from jury service has its origin in common law. Most states have enacted the common law rule and exclude persons from jury duty if they have been convicted of felonies, infamous crimes, crimes involving moral

A conviction may exclude a person from jury duty.

turpitude, or certain specified crimes.[24] The right to serve on a jury is deprived in all but five states (Colorado, Illinois, Iowa, Maine, and New Hampshire). Some states permit felons to serve on juries after they have fully completed their sentences. Others suspend the right only until the offender is released from incarceration. In some others the right may be restored by pardon.[25] The federal rule is that citizens are not competent to serve on a federal grand or petit (trial) jury if they have been convicted of a crime punishable by imprisonment for more than one year.[26] A statute that says only citizens having good character can serve on a jury also disqualifies the person with a criminal record. If the law requires that only persons who are qualified electors can serve on a jury, loss of the right to vote following a conviction carries with it the right to serve on a jury.

The Right to Be a Witness

Common law disqualified as a witness any citizen convicted of treason, felony, or crimes involving fraud or deceit. This absolute disqualification extends today in a few states to persons convicted of perjury or subornation of perjury.[27] The usual situation today, however, is that a person who has been convicted of a crime is permitted to testify, but the fact of the conviction may be shown to impeach (discredit) his or her testimony. The theory behind both absolute disqualification and impeachment is that a person who has been convicted of a crime cannot be trusted to give truthful testimony; thus the court and the jury are entitled to take the conviction into account. The witness can be asked if he or she has been convicted of a felony or other crime and must answer truthfully. Opposing counsel is then at liberty to argue that because the witness is a convicted offender the testimony should not be believed. This does not mean, of course, that the jury (or the court) will disbelieve the witness. The jury or the

The right to be a witness may be affected by a conviction.

judge may decide that the convicted offender is indeed telling the truth and give the individual's testimony the weight accorded to the testimony of any other witness.

The Supreme Court in *Davis v. Alaska* placed the constitutional right of confrontation by a defendant in a criminal case above any considerations that might protect the offender on probation against impeachment.[28] At issue in the case was whether an adjudication of delinquency could be shown against a prosecution witness, although the statutes of Alaska, like those of many states, provide that an adjudication of delinquency is not a conviction. The Court held that the right of the defendant to confront the witness and to inquire into all circumstances that might affect the witness's credibility was paramount over the statutory policy against permitting the use of an adjudication of delinquency for impeachment purposes.[29]

The Right to an Occupational License

Federal, state, and local governments throughout the United States restrict entry into more than 350 occupations and professions through licensing requirements.[30] These restrictions—of which there are in excess of 2,000—affect more than ten million people.[31] For example, the state of California has passed legislation requiring the licensing of automobile mechanics.[32]

In all of the states and in the federal government, the right to obtain or hold an occupational license is affected by a criminal record, and similar provisions restrict the convicted offender's right to hold jobs covered by the licensing regulations of cities and towns. Disqualification may result from the express words in general statutes—as for example in the business or professional code—or from the licensing acts governing the particular trade or profession. Both the renewal and initial granting of a license are affected by a criminal record, and power to revoke an existing license is granted to the licensing agency as well as to the courts. Even without express words,

Occupations That Require a License in Many Jurisdictions

Embalmer
Junk dealer
Midwife
Liquor dealer
Taxicab operator
Solicitor and canvasser
Vocational nurse
Watchmaker
Guide dog trainer
Tourist camp operator
Inhalation therapist
Dental hygienist
Massage parlor operator
Water well contractor
Operator of a "public cart"
Psychiatric technician
Trading stamp dealer
Night clerk
Practical nurse
Seller of horse meat
Minnow dealer
Fur dealer
Sewage work operator
Florist
Photographer
Seller of lightning rods
Weigh master
Fish and game guide
Surveyor
Manicurist
Milk dealer
Operator of hotel, lodge, or home for the aged
Anthracite coal mine inspector
Mine foreman
Police officer
Oil and gas inspector
Forester
Money lender
Motor car dealer
Manufacturer of narcotics
Seller of hearing aids
Operator of driver training school
Hospital administrator
Threshing machine operator and dealer
Tile layer
Yacht salesperson
Tree surgeon
Pest controller
Well digger
Potato grower
Hypertrichologist (hair remover)
Dealer in scrap tobacco
Landscape architect
Billiard hall owner and operator

Source: D. Rudenstine, *The Rights of Ex-Offenders* (New York: Avon, 1979).

statutory or even administrative requirements that a license may be issued only to persons of good moral character effectively exclude the convicted person.[33]

The exact provisions of licensing statutes vary from state to state, from occupation to occupation, and even within occupations. The criminal record that disqualifies may be a felony, a misdemeanor, a felony with moral turpitude, a crime with moral turpitude, or an infamous crime. The conviction that disqualifies may be interpreted according to the narrow or the broad definition of *conviction.*

Unfortunately rehabilitation—whether evidenced by a pardon, successful completion of probation, certificate of good conduct, expungement proceedings, sealing of the record of conviction, or otherwise—does not effectively open the door to professional and occupational licenses. This is true not only in the imprisoning state; it is also inevitable if the offender moves to a different state. The lack of uniformity in the laws and practices of the various states and localities makes it almost impossible for persons with criminal records to determine where they might be allowed to apply their training and skills, whether they acquired them in or out of prison.

The Requirement of Good Character

The most serious obstacle to the offender who seeks to enter a licensed occupation arises from the fact that many, if not most, licensing statutes require that the licensee possess good character. It is almost universally assumed that a person who has been convicted of a criminal offense is not of good character. The obstacles created by the provisions and assumptions about good character are all the more serious because there is considerable doubt that there is any way for a convicted person to restore his or her good character. Although pardon and other forms of wiping out convictions may remove particular civil disabilities and, for example, permit the convicted person to vote or serve on a jury, such a pardon or expungement proceeding does not necessarily, or even by implication, restore good character.[34]

Most, if not all, professions require that the applicant for licensing prove good character. This requirement is usually statutory, but even when the provision is not expressed, courts have found that the licensing authority has the implied power to bar persons who are "morally unfit" from being licensed.[35] Conviction of a crime is generally held to be evidence that the offender lacks the requisite character for the professional license.[36] In some instances, however, the rule is that the fact of conviction is evidence only of *loss of* good character, and additional inquiry is made to determine if the offense involved **moral turpitude**—conduct that is offensive to society.

MORAL TURPITUDE

An act of baseness, vileness, or depravity in the private and social duties a person owes to other humans or to society in general that is contrary to the accepted, customary rule of right and duty between persons. A grave infringement of the moral sentiment of the community. A felony or a misdemeanor that is contrary to the public's moral standards.

Because the public's moral standards vary with place and time, it is impossible to know which crimes involve moral turpitude. The terms *good moral character* and *good character* are also susceptible to changing meanings. Thus, as a practical matter, licenses are refused or revoked according to the meanings licensing agencies place on such terms. In general, however, a licensing agency regards a conviction as conclusive evidence of bad character, and such decisions are seldom overruled by the courts.[37]

The Right to Public Employment

The term *public employment* is often used interchangeably with the term *public office,* although there are certain technical distinctions between the two. Elective positions in federal, state, and municipal governments as well as some appointive positions are generally regarded as *public offices*. A public office may not be compensated, as for example positions on a school board or even positions on a municipal council. *Public employment,* on the other hand, is paid employment with some type of governmental agency. The vast majority of government jobs are considered public employment.

Most state statutes permit public employment for persons convicted of a felony. Some statutes allow employment after completion of sentence. Others allow convicted felons public employment, but they give the hiring agency or the civil service commissioner the right to deny public employment to a convicted offender on the sole basis of his or her felony conviction. In a few states a felony conviction may not be the sole grounds for denial of public employment unless the offense bears a direct relationship to the position sought. Additionally, a small number of states apply a direct relationship test *and* consider other factors such as rehabilitation, the time lapse since offense, the offender's age at the time of conviction, and the nature and seriousness of the offense. Most jurisdictions, however, permit public employment after final completion of sentence because civil rights are restored at this time. There are no statutory restrictions on public employment of convicted persons in the District of Columbia, Maine, Utah, or Vermont.[38]

Private Employment

A job applicant with a criminal record faces almost insurmountable barriers to private employment. It is difficult to identify the nature and extent of these barriers because of the complexity and diversity of private employment and because of the reluctance of some private employers to admit that they discriminate against ex-convicts. Discrimination based on age, sex, or race is unlawful, and it has been held that a private employer's refusal to hire a job applicant because of his or her arrest record violates the applicant's civil rights.[39] This protection does not extend to persons who have been convicted of a criminal offense, however. The distinction between "conviction" and "criminal offense" is left almost completely to the private employer's discretion. The probationer, regardless of his or her technical legal status, is a convicted person as far as the general public is concerned.

Some business and trade organizations and private employers make a point of providing jobs to convicted offenders. The Solution to Employment Problems (STEP) program of the National Association of Manufacturers is one such effort.[40] In this and similar programs employers provide equipment and instructors to train offenders while they are in prison and then guarantee them jobs upon their release.

The Right to Be Bonded

A bond is a certificate or evidence of an obligation. A simple bond is signed only by the person who is bonded, the *principal.* A *surety bond* is signed by the principal and by other persons, known as *sureties,* who promise to pay money in the event that the *assured,* the party in whose favor the bond is written, suffers damage because the principal fails to perform as agreed. A bail bond, for example, guarantees the appearance of the accused (the principal) for trial. If the accused fails to appear, the bail bondsman (the surety) must either locate the principal and return him or her for trial or forfeit the amount of the bond to the state (the assured).

Almost any kind of job where the employee handles money or merchandise may require the employee to be bonded. Thus a person who cannot be bonded cannot work in a bank, a store, or a warehouse. That person cannot become a truck driver, responsible for valuable shipments of goods, if the job specifications require the posting of a bond. Similarly, collection agents, bookkeepers, door-to-door canvassers, ticket-takers, ice cream vendors, and holders of milk routes each may need a surety bond before they will be allowed to assume their duties.

Private individuals are sometimes sureties on bonds for friends or relatives, but most surety bonds are written by insurance and bonding companies that are in the business of writing bonds. In the typical situation the employee (or sometimes the employer) pays a fee for the bond, and in return the insurance company agrees to pay any losses to the employer occasioned by the dishonesty or unlawful acts of the employee.

No bonding company is required by law to furnish a bond to all applicants. The decision to write or deny a bond is with the surety. The company carefully investigates all persons who request bonds and refuses to bond persons they consider to be poor risks. Because they refuse to bond poor risks, the saying goes that "bonding companies bond only those who don't need it." The loss of the right to be bonded that follows a criminal conviction is not so much a loss of the *right* to be bonded as it is the loss of the *ability* to get a bond. This is because almost without exception, a person with a criminal record is considered a poor risk. Irrespective of any other obstacle, this inability to be bonded may constitute the final barrier to employment.

The U.S. Department of Labor, through the Employment and Training Administration, offers fidelity bonding coverage for job applicants. The coverage is available to persons who cannot obtain suitable employment because they have police, credit, or other records that prevent their being covered by the usual commercial bonds. Ex-offenders are eligible for the bonds if (1) they are qualified and suitable for the particular position and (2) they are not commercially bondable under ordinary circumstances. The applicant applies for the bond through a state employment office, and the bond becomes effective when the applicant has begun work and the manager of the local employment service office or other authorized representative of the state agency has certified the bond.[41]

Unfortunately, few ex-offenders seek to take advantage of this program. Both employers and prospective employees seem to lack information about the bonding that is available through state employment agencies. It is a sad fact that ex-offenders generally refrain from applying for jobs that require bonding.

The Right to Own a Firearm

The right to own a firearm is possibly the most restrictive of all civil disabilities lost by conviction. Federal law independently restricts convicted felons from possessing any firearms, yet every state except Vermont (which relies on federal law) has additional statutory restrictions.[42] As Burton, Cullen, and Travis point out, "The rationale behind this restriction, of course, is to keep weapons out of the hands of dangerous individuals and to protect an unsuspecting public."[43] Thirty-six states restrict firearm ownership for persons convicted of any felony. Others restrict the possession of firearms to those convicted of violent and/or drug-related crimes.[44]

SOCIAL STIGMATIZATION OF EX-OFFENDERS

Stigmatization and loss of social status are probably the most severe of the collateral consequences of a felony conviction. The status degradation that follows a person with a court record extends beyond the offender's discharge from the correctional process. This is particularly true when the person is committed to a state or federal correctional institution after conviction.

A kind of circular effect can be observed in the assignment of such a status. Ex-offenders suffer from civil disabilities that bar them from jobs and entry into professions. Society thus limits their occupational choices to jobs considered menial. The public then views all ex-offenders as holding menial jobs and characterizes them as members of a lower stratum of society. Membership in the lower strata of society forecloses opportunities for more prestigious jobs, and the possibility of movement into the upper levels of society is restricted. The result is the creation of a permanent class of outcasts who can never be assimilated into the mainstream of community life.[45]

It is, of course, an open question whether the removal of continuing civil disabilities would change community attitudes toward the offender. Attention must also be paid to the proposition that the public has a right to know of the previous criminal record in order to protect itself against the recidivist offender. It is probable that removal of civil disabilities will not in itself change the public attitude toward the offender, but distinctions must be made. The imposition of civil disabilities should bear some rational relationship to the offense committed and to the function to be performed. Different treatment must be accorded the hard-core recidivist offender and the rehabilitated offender, and a way must be found to distinguish one from the other. Procedures for removing disabilities must be simplified and provide for a restoration of good character when circumstances warrant. Most important of all, affirmative education efforts must involve the public in corrections and in the welfare of the ex-offender. Professionals in law enforcement and corrections and the leaders of the bench and bar must concern themselves with removing the inconsistencies and inequities that characterize the consequences of conviction today.

SUMMARY

Conviction is followed by both direct and collateral consequences. Direct consequences include fines, probation, imprisonment, and other sanctions imposed by the court. Collateral consequences are disabilities that follow a conviction that are not directly imposed by a court, such as loss of civil and political rights and loss of good moral character. The overall effects of a conviction are thus direct and collateral sanctions.

The particular rights lost by conviction depend on the crime for which the offender was convicted and the jurisdiction in which the conviction occurred. There is little agreement among states as to which rights are lost by conviction or the manner by which the rights may be restored, if they may be restored at all.

Apart from the loss of rights by operation of law or from interpretations by administrative bodies and licensing agencies, the convicted individual also loses social status and suffers social stigmatization. He or she is usually thought to have lost good moral character, a loss that often results in further collateral sanctions—such as the loss of employment opportunities. Procedures for removing disabilities should be simplified and should provide for restoration of good moral character when circumstances warrant.

ENDNOTES

1. Richard Singer, "Conviction: Civil Disabilities," in Stanford Kadish, ed., *Encyclopedia of Crime and Justice* (New York: Free Press, 1983), 243–48.

2. Velmer S. Burton Jr., Francis T. Cullen, and Lawrence F. Travis III, "The Collateral Consequences of a Felony Conviction: A National Study of State Statutes," *Federal Probation* (September 1987), 52.

3. *Trop v. Dulles,* 356 U.S. 86, 78 S. Ct. 590, 2 L. Ed. 2d 630 (1958).

4. *Kennedy v. Mendoza-Martinez,* 372 U.S. 144, 83 S. Ct. 554, 9 L. Ed. 2d 644 (1963).

5. R. Damaska, "Adverse Legal Consequences of Conviction and Their Removal: A Comparative Study,"*J. Crim. L. C. & P. S.* 59:347 (1968).

6. U.S. Const. art. 1.

7. Much of the material on the current status of civil disabilities of convicted persons for this chapter was obtained from *Civil Disabilities of Convicted Felons: A State by State Study* prepared by the Office of the United States Pardon Attorney (October 1996) and from Burton, Cullen, and Travis, "The Collateral Consequences of a Felony Conviction"; and Velmer S. Burton Jr., Lawrence F. Travis III, and Francis T. Cullen, "Reducing the Legal Consequences of a Felony Conviction: A National Survey of State Statutes," *International Journal of Comparative and Applied Criminal Justice* 12(1):101–109 (Spring 1988).

8. For an early study on collateral consequences of a conviction, see "The Collateral Consequences of a Criminal Conviction," *Vanderbilt Law Review* 23(5) (Oct. 1970). The authors acknowledge their substantial obligation to that publication for much of the philosophical and historical material set out in this chapter. More recent publications relied on include Joseph G. Cook, *Constitutional Rights of the Accused,* 2nd ed. (San Francisco: Bancroft-Whitney, 1986); Burton, Cullen, and Travis, "The Collateral Consequences of a Felony Conviction"; and Burton, Travis, and Cullen, "Reducing the Legal Consequences of a Felony Conviction."

9. The most complete and current listing with which we are familiar is U.S. Pardon Attorney, *Civil Disabilities of Convicted Felons.*

10. Burton, Cullen, and Travis, "The Collateral Consequences of a Felony Conviction."

11. ABA, *Standards Relating to Probation,* Standard 4.3.

12. ABA, *Standards Relating to Probation,* 54–65.

13. *Yaselli v. Goff,* 12 F. 2d 396 (2d Cir. 1926).

14. D. Rudenstine, *The Rights of Ex-Offenders* (New York: Avon, 1974).

15. "No person shall be a Senator or Representative in Congress, or elector of President or Vice President, or hold any office, civil or military, under the United States, or under any state, who, after having previously taken an oath of a member of Congress, or as any officer of the United States, or as a member of any state legislature, or as an executive or judicial officer of any state, to support the Constitution of the United States, shall have engaged in insurrection or rebellion against the same, or given aid or comfort to the enemies thereof. But Congress may by a vote of two-thirds of each house, remove such disability." U.S. Constitution, Fourteenth Amendment.

16. It is ironic that the Constitution would not disqualify a convicted felon from serving as President, Vice President, or in either house of Congress. However, the Constitution does provide that the "President, Vice President and all civil officers of the United States, shall be removed from Office on Impeachment for, and Conviction of, Treason, Bribery, or other high Crimes or Misdemeanors," U.S. Constitution, Art. 2, Sec. 4, and further provides that a judgment in the case of impeachment may include removal from office and "disqualification to hold and enjoy any Office of honor, Trust or Profit under the United States" U.S. Constitution, Art. 1, Sec. 3.

17. U.S. Pardon Attorney, *Civil Disabilities of Convicted Felons,* 7.

18. U.S. Pardon Attorney, *Civil Disabilities of Convicted Felons.*

19. *National Advisory Commission Standards,* Standard 16.17.

20. U.S. Pardon Attorney, *Civil Disabilities of Convicted Felons.*

21. *Ramirez v. Brown,* 9 Cal. 3d 199, 107 Cal. Rptr. 137, 507 P. 2d 1345 (1973).

22. *Richardson v. Ramirez,* 418 U.S. 24, 94 S. Ct. 2655, 41 L. Ed. 2d 551 (1974).

23. U.S. Pardon Attorney, *Civil Disabilities of Convicted Felons.*

24. Rudenstine, *The Rights of Ex-Offenders,* 120, 121.

25. U.S. Pardon Attorney, *Civil Disabilities of Convicted Felons,* Appendix A.

26. 28 U.S.C.A. § 1865 (b) (5).

27. *Subornation of perjury* means to procure or induce another to commit perjury.

28. *Davis v. Alaska,* 415 U.S. 308, 94 S. Ct. 1105, 39 L. Ed. 2d 347 (1974).

29. *Davis v. Alaska.*

30. Rudenstine, *The Rights of Ex-Offenders,* 82–83.

31. Rudenstine, *The Rights of Ex-Offenders,* 82–83.

32. Florida has recently enacted a similar statute (1993).

33. Rudenstine, *The Rights of Ex-Offenders,* 83–85.

34. New York issues a certificate of good conduct to convicted persons after five years of good conduct. A few New York licensing statutes require recognition of the certificate.

35. *Dorf v. Fielding,* 20 Misc. 2d 66, 18,197 N.Y.S. 2d 280 (1948). A person convicted for running a house of prostitution was denied a license to sell secondhand goods.

36. *Application of Brooks,* 57 Wash. 2d 66, 355 P. 2d 840 (1960), *cert. den.* 365 U.S. 813, 81 S. Ct. 694, 5 L. Ed. 2d 692 (1961).

37. Some decisions require a hearing before denial of license, particularly if the criminal record is remote. *Peterson v. State Liquor Authority,* 42 A.D. 2d 195, 345 N.Y.S. 2d 780 (1973).

38. The current status of restrictions on public employment was obtained from Burton et al., "The Collateral Consequences of a Felony Conviction," 56.

39. *Gregory v. Litton Systems, Inc.,* 316 F. Supp. 401 (C.D. Cal. 1970). An employer was enjoined from denying a job to a black applicant because of his arrest record on the ground that blacks are arrested more frequently than whites.

40. The National Association of Manufacturers operates its S.T.E.P. (Solutions to Employment Problems) in correctional institutions as part of work-release programs in certain federal institutions.
41. U.S. Department of Labor, *Guidebook for Operation of the Federal Bonding Program* (November 1990).
42. U.S. Pardon Attorney, *Civil Disabilities of Convicted Felons,* Appendix B.
43. Burton, Cullen, and Travis, "The Collateral Consequences of a Felony Conviction," 58.
44. U.S. Pardon Attorney, *Civil Disabilities of Convicted Felons,* Appendix B.
45. E. Sutherland and D. Cressey, *Principles of Criminology* (Philadelphia: Lippincott, 1966).

DISCUSSION QUESTIONS

1. Distinguish between civil and political rights.
2. What were the facts and the holding in *Trop v. Dulles*? How is this case related to question 1?
3. Compare and contrast the concepts of *outlawry* and *attainer.*
4. What is the general trend with regard to loss of civil rights upon conviction? Why do you think this is so?
5. Discuss the loss of rights during probation. What are the issues?
6. What are the justifications for imposing civil disabilities on convicted persons?
7. What is the current status of loss of the right to vote as a civil disability upon conviction? How have the courts ruled on this issue?
8. Assuming that ex-offenders want to obtain honest work, how do laws that restrict employment and licensing affect recidivism?
9. In what respects is social stigma a civil disability?

Loss and Restoration of Rights to Vote, to Hold State Office,* and to Serve on a Jury as a Result of Felony Conviction

STATE	RIGHTS LOST	HOW RIGHTS ARE RESTORED
Alabama	vote, jury (for crime of moral turpitude), office	Rights restored by pardon only. Federal felons eligible for state pardon.
Alaska	vote (for felony involving moral turpitude), jury	Rights restored automatically upon unconditional discharge or by pardon. Federal felons ineligible for state pardon. Set-aside procedure available for certain state convictions.
Arizona	vote, jury, office	Rights automatically restored upon completion of sentence for first offenders; recidivists must apply to court upon discharge from probation or two years after discharge from imprisonment, or obtain pardon. Set-aside procedure available for certain state offenders. Federal offenders ineligible for state pardon but may obtain automatic restoration or court relief.
Arkansas	vote, jury, office	Right to vote automatically restored upon completion of sentence; right to serve on jury restored by pardon; right to hold office not restored, even by a pardon, but may be restored by expungement. Federal felons eligible for state pardon. Deferred adjudication and expungement procedures available to some state offenders.
California	vote, jury, office	Right to vote lost only if imprisoned, and restored automatically upon completion of sentence, including parole. Other rights restored by pardon only. Federal offenders ineligible for state pardon. Set-aside procedure available for state offenders sentenced to probation.
Colorado	vote, office	Right to vote lost only if incarcerated, and automatically restored upon completion of sentence, including parole. For certain offenses, right to hold office lost only if incarcerated and restored upon completion of sentence or while on release from actual confinement on conditions of probation; for other offenses, right restored by pardon. Federal felons ineligible for state pardon.
Connecticut	vote, jury, office	Rights to vote and hold office restored upon proof of discharge from sentence, including parole or probation and payment of fine. Right to serve on jury automatically restored seven years after conviction (unless defendant is then incarcerated). Federal felons ineligible for state pardon.
Delaware	vote, jury, office	Rights to vote and serve on a jury restored by pardon; right to hold office not restored. Federal felons ineligible for state pardon.
District of Columbia	vote, jury, office	Rights to vote and to hold many offices lost only during incarceration and restored automatically upon release from incarceration. Right to serve on a jury restored automatically one year after completion of sentence upon certification under jury plan. Right to hold certain offices restored by pardon, which only President may grant for both federal and D.C. offenders.
Florida	vote, jury, office	Rights restored by pardon or restoration of rights. Federal felon may obtain restoration of rights but not state pardon.

continued

*"Office" generally refers to both elective and appointive office, but may apply only to elective office depending on the state.

STATE	RIGHTS LOST	HOW RIGHTS ARE RESTORED
Georgia	vote, jury (disqualification from grand jury service applies only to state felons convicted after 1976), office (for felony involving moral turpitude)	Right to vote automatically restored upon completion of sentence. Right to hold office restored if civil rights restored and 10 years have passed since completion of sentence and no further conviction of felony involving moral turpitude. Right to sit on a jury restored by pardon or restoration of rights. Restoration of rights but not state pardon available to federal offenders. Sentence without adjudication available for certain state first offenders.
Hawaii	vote, jury, office	Right to vote lost only if incarcerated, and automatically restored upon release from confinement. Right to hold office (except for certain crimes) restored upon final discharge. Right to serve on jury restored by pardon. Federal offenders ineligible for state pardon. Conditional discharge and deferred adjudication procedures available to certain state offenders.
Idaho	vote, jury, office	Rights lost only if imprisoned, and restored automatically upon final discharge. Federal felons ineligible for state pardon. Withheld judgment and probation procedure available to most state offenders; amendment of conviction from felony to misdemeanor available for many state offenses when prison sentence is imposed but suspended.
Illinois	vote, office	Right to vote lost only if imprisoned, and automatically restored upon release from incarceration. Right to hold public office automatically restored upon completion of sentence (except for certain election-related offenses). Federal offenders ineligible for state pardon.
Indiana	vote, jury, office	Right to vote lost only if imprisoned, and automatically restored upon release from incarceration. Right to serve on a jury restored upon completion of sentence. Right to hold office restored only by pardon (court-imposed disqualification for certain misdemeanors cannot exceed 10 years). Federal offenders ineligible for state pardon.
Iowa	vote, felons may be challenged for cause as jurors, office	Rights restored by pardon or restoration of rights, both by Governor. Federal offenders eligible for restoration of rights but ineligible for state pardon. Deferred judgment procedure available to some state offenders.
Kansas	vote, jury, office	Rights lost only if imprisoned, and automatically restored upon completion of sentence or final discharge. Federal offenders ineligible for state pardon. Expungement procedure available for many state convictions.
Kentucky	vote, jury, office	Rights restored by gubernatorial pardon or restoration of rights ("partial pardon"). Federal offenders eligible for restoration of rights but not full state pardon.
Louisiana	vote, jury, forfeiture of office	Rights to vote and to hold office lost only if under an order of imprisonment and automatically restored upon termination of supervision. Right to serve on a jury apparently restored by pardon. "First-offender pardon" available for state offenders; Board of Pardons has discontinued processing requests for "first-offender pardon" for federal offenders. Regular state pardon not available to federal offenders.
Maine	court may order forfeiture of office	Pardon presumably does not restore forfeited office. Federal felons ineligible for state pardon.
Maryland	vote, jury, office	For first offenders, rights automatically restored upon completion of sentence, except, as to right to hold office and right to serve on jury, for certain offenses. Otherwise and for other offenders, rights restored by pardon. Federal offenders ineligible for state pardon. Probation without adjudication procedure available to certain state offenders.

STATE	RIGHTS LOST	HOW RIGHTS ARE RESTORED
Massachusetts	jury, forfeiture of office	Right to serve on a jury automatically restored seven years after completion of sentence. Federal felons eligible for state pardon. Sealing of records procedure available to certain state offenders.
Michigan	vote, jury, forfeiture of office, and disqualification for certain offenses	Right to vote lost only if incarcerated, and automatically restored upon release from confinement. Right to hold public office (except for certain offenses) restored upon completion of sentence; although felons not ineligible for jury service after completion of sentence, may still be challenged for cause. Federal offenders ineligible for state pardon. Certain state offenders eligible for set-aside procedure.
Minnesota	vote, jury, office	Rights automatically restored upon discharge from sentence. Federal offenders ineligible for state pardon. Set-aside procedure available for certain state offenders.
Mississippi	vote (for specified offenses), jury, office	Right to vote may be restored by legislature, by administrative procedure for certain veterans, by pardon, or by executive order for certain probationers. Right to serve on a jury automatically restored five years after conviction. Right to hold office restored only by pardon. Federal offenders ineligible for executive order or state pardon.
Missouri	vote, jury, office	Right to vote automatically restored upon final discharge (except for election crimes); right to hold office restored upon completion of sentence. Right to serve on a jury restored by pardon. Federal offenders ineligible for state pardon.
Montana	vote, jury, office	Right to vote lost only if imprisoned, and automatically restored upon release from incarceration. Right to hold office restored upon completion of sentence. Right to serve on a jury apparently lost and apparently restored by pardon. Federal offenders ineligible for state pardon.
Nebraska	vote, jury, office	Rights restored by certificate or warrant of discharge for state offenders. Federal offenders ineligible for certificate or warrant of discharge or state pardon. Set-aside procedure available for state offenders sentenced to probation or payment of fine only.
Nevada	vote, jury, office	Rights restored by court or administrative procedure or by pardon (except right to hold office for certain offenses). Administrative or court relief and state pardon apparently not available to federal offenders. Sealing procedure available to certain state offenders.
New Hampshire	vote, office	Right to vote lost only if incarcerated, and automatically restored upon release from confinement. Right to hold office restored upon final discharge from sentence. Federal offenders ineligible for state pardon. Annulment procedure available to many state offenders.
New Jersey	vote, jury, forfeiture of office, and disqualification from office for certain offenses	Right to vote automatically restored upon completion of sentence. Right to serve on a jury and right to hold office restored by pardon or order of governor. Federal offenders ineligible for state pardon. Expungement procedure available to certain state offenders. Certificate of good conduct available to state offenders to prevent disqualification or discrimination in licensing decision based on conviction.
New Mexico	vote, jury, office	Rights restored by gubernatorial restoration of rights or by pardon. Federal offenders ineligible for state pardon but may regain rights to vote and to hold office by gubernatorial restoration of rights.

STATE	RIGHTS LOST	HOW RIGHTS ARE RESTORED
New York	vote, jury, forfeiture of office; disqualification from office only in certain circumstances	Right to vote lost only if incarcerated, and automatically restored upon expiration of sentence or discharge from parole. Right to sit on a jury and to hold office (if lost) restored by pardon or by administrative or court restoration of rights. Administrative relief available to federal offenders, but not state pardon.
North Carolina	vote, jury, office	All rights automatically restored upon filing of certificate of unconditional discharge from sentence in court of county of conviction for state offenses or residence for federal offenses. Federal offenders ineligible for state pardon but eligible for restoration procedure.
North Dakota	vote, jury, office	Rights to vote and hold office lost only if imprisoned, and automatically restored upon release from incarceration. Right to sit on a jury lost during period of ineligibility to vote (unless special provision of law renders offender ineligible). Federal offenders ineligible for state pardon. Reduction of conviction from felony to misdemeanor or procedure for vacating conviction available to certain state offenders.
Ohio	vote, jury, office (for federal offenses, these rights lost only for convictions after 1973)	Right to vote lost only if incarcerated and automatically restored upon release from incarceration. Rights to hold office and to serve on a jury restored by serving sentence of community control sanction or of confinement not followed by postrelease control or by final release by parole authority. (Some disqualifications terminate after seven years.) Not clear whether restoration procedures apply to federal offenders. Federal offenders ineligible for state pardon. Sealing procedure for state records only available to certain state and federal offenders, which restores rights.
Oklahoma	vote, jury, office	Right to vote automatically restored after period of time equal to sentence. Right to hold office restored 15 years after completion of sentence unless specific permanent bar applies. Right to serve on a jury restored by pardon. Federal offenders ineligible for state pardon. Deferred judgment and expungement procedures available to certain state offenders.
Oregon	vote, jury, office	Rights lost only if incarcerated, and automatically restored upon release from confinement, except for disqualification relating to state legislative office, which is restored upon completion of sentence. Not clear whether federal offenders eligible for state pardon.
Pennsylvania	vote, jury, office	Right to vote lost only if incarcerated, and automatically restored upon release from confinement. Rights to hold public office and to serve on a jury restored through pardon. Federal offenders ineligible for state pardon.
Rhode Island	vote, jury, office	Rights to vote and to serve on a jury automatically restored upon completion of sentence. Right to hold office restored three years after completion of sentence. Not settled whether federal offenders eligible for state pardon. Expungement available to certain state offenders.
South Carolina	vote, jury, office	Rights to vote and to hold public office restored upon completion of sentence (except for conviction of felony embezzlement of public funds, which disqualifies felon from holding office unless disability is removed by 2/3 vote of legislature upon payment of sum embezzled and interest). Right to serve on a jury restored only by pardon. Federal offenders ineligible for state pardon.

STATE	RIGHTS LOST	HOW RIGHTS ARE RESTORED
South Dakota	vote, jury, office	Rights lost only if sentenced to imprisonment, and automatically restored upon release from confinement (or, when execution of sentence suspended, upon termination of sentence). Not clear whether federal offenders eligible for state pardon. Probation without adjudication procedure available to state offenders.
Tennessee	vote, jury (for certain offenses), office	Right to hold office for certain offenses lasts until civil rights are restored; otherwise, rights lost only if incarcerated and restored by court action for convictions before July 1, 1986; rights restored by pardon, service or expiration of maximum sentence, or final release from incarceration for convictions after July 1, 1986, except right to vote not restored to certain felons. Federal felons eligible for automatic and court restoration but not for state pardon.
Texas	vote, jury, office (for certain offenses)	Right to vote restored two years after receiving certificate of discharge, two years after completing probation, or by pardon. Other rights restored by restoration of civil rights granted by governor to certain felons after completion of sentence, and at least three years after conviction. Federal felons are ineligible for state pardon, but certain federal felons may have rights restored by governor. Deferred adjudication, set-aside, and expungement procedures available for certain state offenders.
Utah	vote (for treason and election crimes), jury, forfeiture of certain offices, and disqualification for treason and election crimes	Rights restored by pardon. State pardon unavailable to federal offenders. Expungement procedure available for certain state offenses.
Vermont	jury	Right lost only if sentenced to imprisonment, and restored only by pardon. Not settled whether federal offenders are eligible for state pardon.
Virginia	vote, jury, office	Rights restored by removal of political disabilities, or pardon, both by governor. Federal offenders eligible for removal of political disabilities but not for state pardon.
Washington	vote, jury, office	Rights restored by pardon or by restoration of civil rights from governor without a pardon. Federal offenders may obtain restoration of right to vote and to hold office from Clemency and Pardons Boards, but ineligible for state pardon. For state offenses after July 1, 1984, rights restored by final discharge from court; for earlier state offenses, restoration of rights by sentencing court or administrative agency, depending on sentence. Right to serve on a jury for federal offenders must be restored by presidential pardon.
West Virginia	vote, jury, office	Rights to vote and to hold office (except for bribery of state officer, which is permanently lost) restored upon completion of sentence. Right to serve on a jury presumably restored by pardon. Federal felons ineligible for state pardon.
Wisconsin	vote, jury, office	Rights to vote and to serve on a jury automatically restored upon completion of sentence. Right to hold office restored only by pardon. Federal offenders eligible for state pardon.
Wyoming	vote, jury, office	Rights restored by parson or by restoration of rights upon expiration of sentence, both by governor. Federal offenders eligible for restoration of rights but ineligible for state pardon.

Source: United States Pardon Attorney, *Civil Disabilities of Convicted Felons* (Washington, D.C.: United States Department of Justice, 1996).

Summary of State Law Firearms Disabilities Imposed Upon Conviction

The reader should be aware that federal firearms laws independently prohibit convicted felons from possessing any firearm. For federal offenders, this disability is removed by a full presidential pardon or by obtaining relief from the Bureau of Alcohol, Tobacco, and Firearms (BATF) pursuant to 18 U.S.C. § 925(c); the latter remedy, however, has not been funded by Congress since fiscal year 1992. Accordingly, federal felons currently must obtain a full presidential pardon in order to have their federal firearms disability removed. A presidential pardon (unless restricted in effect by its terms) will also remove state firearms disabilities arising from the conviction of the pardoned offense; accordingly, the state restoration methods summarized below are not currently meaningful for federal offenders. If, however, the restoration procedure under 18 U.S.C § 925(c) is funded in the future, methods for removing the state firearms disabilities of federal offenders will be of interest.

For state offenders, the federal firearm disability may be removed by restoration of civil rights provided the restoration does not expressly restrict firearms privileges. These charts do not purport to answer the complex legal question of the extent to which a state offender in each of these states remains subject to the federal firearms disability for convicted felons. Rather, the chart describes only the state law pertaining to the loss and restoration of firearms privileges upon conviction. Please consult Section 3 of the summary of federal law in the survey for further details. States marked with an asterisk permit restoration of state firearms privileges when the offender obtains relief under 18 U.S.C. § 925(c); however, as noted, that remedy is not currently funded.

This chart highlights some of the more detailed information set forth in the firearms section of each state's entry in the survey, solely to facilitate comparison of various state laws. The terms "felonies," "violent crimes," "drug crimes," and "handguns" are all used in their colloquial, nontechnical sense for the purposes of summarization. The exact scope of each state's disability is determined by technical definitions, which are discussed in more detail in each state's summary. While a state pardon in many states will remove state firearms disabilities, the column marked "Only by State Pardon" is meant to signify those circumstances in which a state pardon is the only method for removing state firearms disabilities. For the reader's convenience, the symbol ‡ denotes those states in which a state pardon is available to federal offenders.

STATE	ALL FELONIES		VIOLENT CRIMES		DRUG CRIMES		RESTORATION METHODS			EXCEPTIONS/ EXPLANATIONS
	BANS ALL GUNS	BANS HANDGUNS	BANS ALL GUNS	BANS HANDGUNS	BANS ALL GUNS	BANS HANDGUNS	BY PASSAGE OF TIME (YRS)	BY ADMIN./ JUDICIAL PROCEDURE	ONLY BY STATE PARDON	
Alabama				X					X	
Alaska		X (concealable firearms)					X (10 yrs from discharge for felonies not against the person)		X (for felonies against the person)	
Arizona	X							X (except for "dangerous offenses," 10 yrs after discharge for "serious" offenses, 2 yrs for other offenses)	X (for "dangerous offenses")	
Arkansas	X							X (8 yrs for offenses involving use of a weapon)	X‡ (otherwise)	
California	X		X						X (non-weapons offenses only)	No restoration for offenses involving use of dangerous weapon.
Colorado	X								X	
Connecticut	X (except certain felonies)								X	Felons also lose the right to obtain permit to carry a handgun or to purchase firearms.
Delaware	X		X		X					Apparently no restoration procedure under state law.
District of Columbia	X		X		X					Restoration only by presidential pardon.

STATE	ALL FELONIES		VIOLENT CRIMES		DRUG CRIMES		RESTORATION METHODS			EXCEPTIONS/ EXPLANATIONS
	BANS ALL GUNS	BANS HANDGUNS	BANS ALL GUNS	BANS HANDGUNS	BANS ALL GUNS	BANS HANDGUNS	BY PASSAGE OF TIME (YRS)	BY ADMIN./ JUDICIAL PROCEDURE	ONLY BY STATE PARDON	
Florida	X							X (8 yrs after completion of sentence)		Felons also prohibited from obtaining license to carry a concealed weapon.
Georgia	X							X (for antitrust and trade offenses, and persons granted relief under 18 U.S.C. § 925(c))	X	First offender discharged without adjudication relieved of disability upon discharge; felons prohibited from obtaining license to carry handguns.
Hawaii	X		X		X				X	
Idaho	X (if sentence of custody)		X (enumerated crimes)		X (enumerated crimes)		X (except enumerated crimes, upon final discharge)	X (5 yrs for enumerated crimes)		Restoration not available for first- or second-degree murder and certain felonies involving use of firearms. Felons and violent misdemeanants barred from carrying a concealed weapon outside the home or fixed place of business.
Illinois	X							X (20 yrs for forcible felony; 5 yrs for certain assault crimes)		
Indiana		X							X	Ban applies to possession of handgun outside home, property, or fixed place of business.

STATE	ALL FELONIES		VIOLENT CRIMES		DRUG CRIMES		RESTORATION METHODS			EXCEPTIONS/ EXPLANATIONS
	BANS ALL GUNS	BANS HANDGUNS	BANS ALL GUNS	BANS HANDGUNS	BANS ALL GUNS	BANS HANDGUNS	BY PASSAGE OF TIME (YRS)	BY ADMIN./ JUDICIAL PROCEDURE	ONLY BY STATE PARDON	
Iowa	X								X	Restoration not available for forcible felony, felony drug crime involving firearm, or certain weapons offenses. Felons also banned from obtaining a pistol permit.
Kansas	X		X (person felony)		X		X (5 yrs for nonperson felony not involving firearm; 10 yrs for person felony not involving firearm, and nonperson felony involving firearm)		X (person felony involving firearm)	"Person felony" is state sentencing classification.
Kentucky	X	X							X‡	
Louisiana			X (if felony)		X (if felony)		X (10 yrs)	X (after completion of sentence)		Ban applies to persons convicted of certain enumerated offenses and to carrying a concealed weapon.
Maine	X		X					X (5 yrs after discharge)		Also bans felons from obtaining permit to carry a concealed weapon; right restored only by pardon.
Maryland		X (and assault weapons)		X (and assault weapons)	X (for felony)				X	Felons also denied permit to carry a handgun.

STATE	ALL FELONIES		VIOLENT CRIMES		DRUG CRIMES		RESTORATION METHODS			EXCEPTIONS/ EXPLANATIONS
	BANS ALL GUNS	BANS HANDGUNS	BANS ALL GUNS	BANS HANDGUNS	BANS ALL GUNS	BANS HANDGUNS	BY PASSAGE OF TIME (YRS)	BY ADMIN./ JUDICIAL PROCEDURE	ONLY BY STATE PARDON	
Massachusetts	X				X		X (5 yrs for long guns)		X (hand-guns)	Bans apply outside home or business.
Michigan	X						X (3 yrs after completion of sentence for nondrug, nonviolent crimes)	X (5 yrs after completion of sentence for most drug and violent crimes)		"Felony" defined as crime punishable by imprisonment for 4 or more yrs. Felons also denied permit to purchase, carry, or transport pistol.
Minnesota	X		X		X		X (10 yrs after expiration of sentence or restoration of rights for violent crimes; upon discharge of sentence for other felonies and drug crimes)			Persons convicted of certain assault offenses prohibited from having pistols for 3 yrs.
Mississippi	X							X (except license to carry)		Felons also banned from carrying a concealed handgun or fully automatic firearm outside home or place of business; right restored by pardon.
Missouri				X (dangerous felony)			X (5 yrs after conviction or release from confinement)			Indefinitely bans all felons from obtaining permit to acquire concealable firearms.

STATE	ALL FELONIES		VIOLENT CRIMES		DRUG CRIMES		RESTORATION METHODS			EXCEPTIONS/ EXPLANATIONS
	BANS ALL GUNS	BANS HANDGUNS	BANS ALL GUNS	BANS HANDGUNS	BANS ALL GUNS	BANS HANDGUNS	BY PASSAGE OF TIME (YRS)	BY ADMIN./ JUDICIAL PROCEDURE	ONLY BY STATE PARDON	
Montana			X (if firearm used to commit crime)					X		Court may impose firearms restrictions for other felonies, with restoration upon completion of sentence. Felon also banned from obtaining permit to carry concealed weapon.
Nebraska	X								X	
Nevada	X								X	
New Hampshire			X (if felony)		X (if felony)			X		Unsettled whether state pardon restores state firearms privileges.
New Jersey			X		X				X	Also bans acquisition or transfer of all firearms for all felonies.
New Mexico	X						X (10 yrs, except for deferred sentence upon completion of sentence)			
New York	X							X (first offenders only)	X (for other offenders)	
North Carolina		X (and fully automatic weapons)							X	Ban applies outside home or business.

STATE	ALL FELONIES		VIOLENT CRIMES		DRUG CRIMES		RESTORATION METHODS			EXCEPTIONS/ EXPLANATIONS
	BANS ALL GUNS	BANS HANDGUNS	BANS ALL GUNS	BANS HANDGUNS	BANS ALL GUNS	BANS HANDGUNS	BY PASSAGE OF TIME (YRS)	BY ADMIN./ JUDICIAL PROCEDURE	ONLY BY STATE PARDON	
North Dakota	X						X (10 yrs from conviction or release from prison or probation for violent felony; 5 yrs for nonviolent felony)			Ban also applies to violent class A misdemeanors with automatic restoration after 5 yrs.
Ohio			X (if felony)		X			X		
Oklahoma		X (and concealable firearms and machine guns)								No existing state procedure for removing firearms disability.
Oregon	X						X (15 yrs after discharge, except for homicide, crime involving a gun, and recidivists)			Felons cannot obtain permit to carry concealed handgun.
Pennsylvania			X		X (if punishable by more than 2 yrs)			X (10 yrs and relief granted under § 925(c))		Felons and violent and drug offenders also banned from obtaining license to carry concealed handgun outside home or fixed place of business; restoration by pardon.

STATE	ALL FELONIES		VIOLENT CRIMES		DRUG CRIMES		RESTORATION METHODS			EXCEPTIONS/ EXPLANATIONS
	BANS ALL GUNS	BANS HANDGUNS	BANS ALL GUNS	BANS HANDGUNS	BANS ALL GUNS	BANS HANDGUNS	BY PASSAGE OF TIME (YRS)	BY ADMIN./ JUDICIAL PROCEDURE	ONLY BY STATE PARDON	
Rhode Island			X		X				X	Unsettled whether federal offenders eligible for state pardon.
South Carolina				X					X	
South Dakota			X				X (15 yrs after discharge)			Felons, violent offenders, and drug offenders in past 2 yrs banned from obtaining permit to carry concealed pistol.
Tennessee				X		X (if felony)				Apparently no restoration procedure under state law.
Texas	X						X (5 yrs after release from prison or supervision; restores right to possess in home only)			Unless based on innocence, pardon will not remove firearms disability.
Utah	X (while on probation or parole)	X	X						X	Exception for hunting (state law appears not to prohibit felon from obtaining hunting license). Felons also banned from obtaining permit to carry concealed weapon.
Vermont										Firearms restrictions may be imposed as condition of probation.
Virginia	X							X		

STATE	ALL FELONIES		VIOLENT CRIMES		DRUG CRIMES		RESTORATION METHODS			EXCEPTIONS/ EXPLANATIONS
	BANS ALL GUNS	BANS HANDGUNS	BANS ALL GUNS	BANS HANDGUNS	BANS ALL GUNS	BANS HANDGUNS	BY PASSAGE OF TIME (YRS)	BY ADMIN./ JUDICIAL PROCEDURE	ONLY BY STATE PARDON	
Washington	X		X					X (except certain offenders)		Felons also banned from obtaining permit to carry concealed weapon unless restoration by state procedure or § 925(c) relief. Ban does not apply to certain nonviolent, nondrug offenses for which probation and dismissal of charges granted.
West Virginia	X							X		Persons convicted of crime involving use of a deadly weapon banned from obtaining permit to carry concealed deadly weapon other than on own premises.
Wisconsin	X									
Wyoming			X						X‡ X	Felons also banned from obtaining permit to carry concealed handgun.

15

PARDON AND RESTORATION OF RIGHTS

KEY TERMS

- Pardon
- Absolute (full) pardon
- Conditional pardon
- Commutation
- Automatic restoration of rights
- Certificate of discharge
- Expungement
- Certificate of rehabilitation
- Sealing
- Certificate of relief from disabilities
- Certificate of good conduct
- Good moral character
- Direct relationship test

What You Will Learn in This Chapter

In this chapter you will learn the history and philosophy of pardons. You will also learn the various types of pardons, how they are obtained, and the legal consequences of a pardon. We also examine alternative ways by which a conviction might be set aside—automatic restoration of rights, expungement, and sealing. And we look at court decisions on the issue of restoring good moral character. Finally, we provide an overview of the status of restoration of civil rights after conviction.

INTRODUCTION

We have seen that a conviction for a criminal offense or an adjudication of delinquency is followed by direct consequences in the form of criminal sanctions and collateral consequences in the form of loss of civil rights. The rights affected by a conviction include voting rights, the right to hold public office, employment opportunities, and judicial rights such as the rights to sue, execute legal instruments, serve on a jury, and testify without impeachment. Certain marital and parental rights also may be lost, and some rights relating to property—including insurance, workers' compensation, and pension benefits—may be impaired.

The direct consequences of conviction—the criminal sanctions—end with the completion of the sentence. Generally a sentence is completed on the day the offender is released from an institution or discharged from probation or parole supervision. In contrast, the collateral effects of a conviction or adjudication—the loss of civil rights, employment opportunities, and so on—generally continue for the offender's lifetime or until some affirmative act occurs that by law prevents the continuance of the civil disabilities or serves to "wipe out" or reduce them. As we will see, these affirmative acts are of limited value: some because they are not intended to completely reduce or wipe out the conviction, others because they cannot reach occupational licensing practices or the private employer. Almost all procedures for restoring civil rights have the additional weakness of not wiping out a criminal conviction or adjudication of delinquency; they do not restore "good character." In this chapter we examine some of the methods used to minimize the effects of a conviction or adjudication of delinquency.

The methods of removing the collateral consequences of a conviction or adjudication include pardon, automatic restoration of rights upon application, expungement, sealing, court decisions, governors' executive orders, and legislative acts. Unfortunately, the methods in use do not seal, expunge, nullify, or restore in any practical, effective way.

PARDON

An executive act that mitigates or sets aside punishment for a crime. The power to pardon is generally vested in state governors, but the president has the power to pardon for federal offenses. Pardons are either conditional or absolute (full).

PARDON

Operating as a distinct subsystem of the criminal justice process, **pardon** fulfills a necessary function. Yet despite its importance to a well-balanced system of justice, it has received little scholarly attention. This lack of study has led to its misapplication and to confusion about its nature and function.

Even the courts have been misled into ambiguous and insupportable holdings. Some jurisdictions have held that a pardon wipes out the crime as though it never happened. Other jurisdictions have held that for some purposes a pardon does not wipe out the fact of a conviction. Thus the recipient of a pardon is regarded not as a "new person" but as a convicted criminal. This is true, for example, when the pardoned criminal takes the stand as a witness in a trial; his or her testimony may be impeached by the fact of the previous conviction even though a pardon has been granted.

Ideally the pardon's effect should reflect the grounds for which it is granted. A pardon that is granted because later evidence shows the convicted person to be innocent should wipe out the crime for all purposes, whereas a pardon granted because a prisoner helped stop a prison riot probably should not.

COMMUTATION

Changing a punishment to one which is less severe, as from execution to life imprisonment.

The Power to Pardon

Historically the power to pardon belonged to the king or sovereign. Because a crime was considered to be an offense against the king, he was deemed to have the power to forgive it. In early American law, however, the power to pardon was generally given to the legislature. When it was granted to the executive, it was severely restricted. By the time the Constitution was written, the older rule was again followed. The president was given the power of pardon except in cases of impeachment.[1] In most states today the power to pardon is given to the governor, acting either alone or in conjunction with some official or board.[2]

When granted to the governor, the power may be either without limitation or restricted. In a number of states the governor's power to pardon does not extend to treason and impeachment. When the governor's power is restricted in this manner, these excepted crimes may usually be pardoned by the legislature. Normally the power to pardon does not extend to violations of municipal ordinances; it extends only to offenses against the state. In some states the power to pardon permits a pardon at any time after charge or indictment; in others the power can be exercised only after conviction. Other states forbid pardon until the minimum sentence or a certain length of sentence has been served, or until after a stated number of years of successful parole. Where state law so provides, both absolute and conditional pardons may be issued.

Objectives of Pardon

The pardoning power was originally seen as a method of righting legal wrongs and of freeing the innocent. Later a commutation of sentence, or a pardon, became an acceptable way to correct unduly severe sentences or to recognize mitigating circumstances that were not taken into consideration at the trial. The divergent views concerning the death penalty have often been expressed in the use of the power of executive clemency to reduce the sentence to life imprisonment. Prisoners who are old, infirm, or have a fatal illness are often pardoned for humanitarian reasons, and escaped prisoners who have rehabilitated themselves after their escape are occasionally pardoned in recognition of their exemplary lives during the period of freedom. The pardoning power is sometimes used to prevent deportation of an alien and sometimes—in the form of amnesties or general pardons—to achieve political purposes.[3] President Carter, for instance, granted amnesty to Vietnam-era draft evaders who fled to Canada.

The pardoning power, used either alone or in connection with special statutory proceedings, is now frequently used to remove the civil disabilities that are a collateral consequence of a conviction. Its use for this purpose of restoring civil rights is our chief concern in this chapter.

Kinds of Pardons

FULL PARDON

A pardon that frees the criminal without any condition whatever. It reaches both the punishment prescribed for the offense and the guilt of the offender.

CONDITIONAL PARDON

A pardon that becomes operative when the grantee has performed some specific act(s) or that becomes void when some specific act(s) transpires.

Pardons generally are either full (absolute) or conditional. A **full pardon** freely and unconditionally absolves an individual from the legal consequences of his or her crime and conviction. A **conditional pardon** does not become operative until certain conditions are met or after the occurrence of a specified event. A conditional pardon generally does not restore the full civil rights of the offender unless there is express language to that effect in its proclamation.

Delivery and Acceptance of Pardons

A pardon is not effective until it is delivered, and until delivered, it may be revoked. An absolute pardon need not be accepted by the prisoner.[4] A conditional pardon, however, must be accepted, because a prisoner may prefer to serve out his or her sentence rather than accept the conditions attached to the pardon.

Revocation

A full pardon, once delivered, cannot be revoked. A conditional pardon may be revoked for violation of the conditions imposed. Some courts have attempted to restrict the right of the governor to revoke a conditional pardon by prohibiting revocation without some sort of determination that the person pardoned has violated the conditions.

Procedure for Obtaining a Pardon

The procedure for obtaining a pardon is fixed by statute or by regulations of the pardoning authority. Generally the convicted person must apply for a pardon, and some time must elapse after release from confinement or discharge on parole before the offender may apply.[5] When the offender makes application he or she is required to notify certain persons, typically the prosecuting attorney, the sheriff, and the court of conviction. Posting—publication of a public notice—may be required. There may be limitations on repeated applications for pardon, such as a minimum time interval between applications. In most cases the pardoning authority conducts an investigation. A hearing on the application may be held, which is open to the public in some states.[6]

Legal Effects of a Pardon

The most important question the offender asks about a pardon is, What rights are restored by a pardon? The general answer is that a pardon restores certain civil rights that were lost upon conviction. To determine the precise legal effects of a pardon, one must examine both statutory and case law in the jurisdiction where the pardon is granted. This section discusses the general rules with respect to the question.

There are two points of view as to whether a pardon wipes out guilt. The classic view, which represents the minority position today, was expressed by the U.S. Supreme Court over a century ago:

> A pardon reaches both the punishment prescribed for the offense and the guilt of the offender; and when the pardon is full, it releases the punishment and blots out the existence of the guilt, so that in the eyes of the law the offender is as innocent as if he had never committed the offense. If granted before conviction, it prevents any of the penalties and disabilities consequent upon conviction from attaching; if granted after conviction, it removes the penalties and disabilities and restores him to all his civil rights; it makes him, as it were, a new man, and gives him new credit and capacity.[7]

The opposite and majority view, stated in *Burdick v. United States,* is that a pardon is an implied expression of guilt and that the conviction is not obliterated.[8] Depending on which view prevails in a given state, the relevant statutory or constitutional provisions, and the reasons for the granting of a pardon in a particular case, a number of consequences follow.

Enhancement of Punishment

Depending on the statutory provisions and court interpretations, an offense for which the offender has been pardoned may or may not be counted in enhancement-of-punishment procedures for declaring the offender a "habitual offender." The minority position is that if the pardon is held to have wiped out the offender's guilt, or if it was issued on the basis of a finding or belief that the offender was in fact innocent of the offense, then it will probably not be used for enhancement. The majority position, however, is that inasmuch as the pardon does not wipe out guilt for the underlying offense but, indeed, implies guilt, the conviction remains and may serve to enhance punishment at the trial of a subsequent offense.[9]

Rights to Vote, Serve on a Jury, Hold Public Office, and Be a Witness

A full pardon generally restores the ordinary rights of citizenship, such as the rights to vote and hold public office. The effect of the pardon may be set out in the state constitution or statutes or in the regulations of the pardoning authority. Pardon restores eligibility for public office, but it will not restore a person to any public office he or she held at the time of conviction. A commutation or a conditional pardon, however, does not restore rights or remove disqualifications for office.[10] Generally, a conviction for which a witness has been conditionally pardoned can also be used to impeach him or her. Some states bar the showing of a conviction that has been pardoned, however, and even those that do not will allow the fact of the pardon to be offered in rebuttal.

Licensing Laws

Generally, where an occupational licensing law disqualifies persons convicted of crime, a pardon does not remove the disqualification, nor does it automatically restore a license that has been revoked on the grounds of a criminal conviction. Some decisions have indicated that although loss of a professional license is a penalty, the proceedings to revoke a license are not penal.[11] The revocation of professional license is thus not a conviction for which the executive has the power to pardon. The California statute provides generally that a pardon shall

> operate to restore to the convicted person all the rights, privileges, and franchises of which he has been deprived in consequence of said conviction or by reason of any matter involved therein.

However, the statute also states,

> [N]othing in this article shall affect any of the provisions of the Medical Practices Act, or the power or authority conferred by law on the Board of Medical Examiners therein, or the power or authority conferred by law upon *any* board which permits any person or persons to apply his or their art or profession on the person of another [emphasis added].[12]

AUTOMATIC RESTORATION OF RIGHTS

In 1996 the United States Pardon Attorney's Office published a state-by-state survey entitled *Civil Disabilities of Convicted Felons*. The study reported that 33 states have laws for **automatic restoration of rights** upon completion of sentence. The remainder require some affirmative action on the part of the offender.[13] The supplemental reading in chapter 14 contains a state-by-state listing of rights that are lost and the means by which they are restored.

The New Hampshire statute, which provides automatic restoration by virtue of a **certificate of discharge,** reads, in part,

> the order, certificate, or other instrument of discharge, given to a person sentenced for a felony upon his discharge after completion of service of his sentence or after service under probation or parole, shall state that the defendant's rights to vote and to hold any future public office of which he was deprived by this chapter are thereby restored and that he suffers no other disability by virtue of his conviction and sentence except as otherwise provided by this chapter.[14]

The laws of the other states that grant automatic restoration of rights are basically similar, but the provisions differ somewhat. The Illinois Unified Code of Corrections, for example, contains this language:

> On completion of sentence of imprisonment or on a petition of a person not sentenced to imprisonment, all license rights and privileges granted under the authority of this State which have been revoked or suspended because of conviction of an offense shall be restored unless the authority having jurisdiction of such license rights finds after investigation and hearing that restoration is not in the public interest.[15]

The Wisconsin statute is one of the oldest and most comprehensive statutes providing that every person who has been convicted of a crime obtains a restoration of his or her civil rights by serving out the term of imprisonment or otherwise satisfying the sentence. The statute reads, in part,

> *Civil rights restored to convicted persons satisfying sentence.* Every person who is convicted of crime obtains a restoration of his civil rights by serving out his term of imprisonment or otherwise satisfying his sentence.[16]

Most courts consider the effect of automatic restoration of rights to be equivalent to that of a pardon. Typically the conviction can be considered in any subsequent criminal action and under the enhancement statutes. The ex-offender is not restored to eligibility to receive an occupational or professional license and must report the conviction on job application forms.

EXPUNGEMENT

Purpose of Expungement Statutes

The word *expunge* means "erase." Thus the purpose of **expungement** statutes is to allow the record of a crime to be erased as if it never happened. Says one author,

> It is not simply a lifting of disabilities attendant upon conviction and a restoration of civil rights. . . . It is rather a redefinition of status, a process of erasing the legal event of a conviction or adjudication, and thereby restoring to the regenerate offender his status quo ante.[17]

EXPUNGEMENT

("An erasure") Process by which the record of a criminal conviction (or juvenile adjudication) is destroyed or sealed after expiration of time.

The typical expungement statute does not specify automatic restoration of rights because it requires affirmative action by the offender. Expungement differs from the issuance of "certificates of relief of good conduct" (as in New York) in that the issuance of the certificates restores rights without attempting to wipe out the criminal record. A study of expungement statutes reported in 1988 that 28 states have some method of judicial restoration of civil rights.[18] Eligibility for expungement, however, varies widely. In some states expungement statutes apply only to probationers. Other states expunge records only for nonviolent offenses or low-grade felonies. Some others allow expungement of felony offenses only for first offenders. California permits the conviction for a felony to be set aside and issues a *certificate of rehabilitation.*[19]

Expungement after Successful Completion of Probation

Adult probation laws of many states contain procedures that permit the probationer, either after completion of probation or after a specified period on probation, to apply for an order that terminates the probation and wipes out the conviction. Texas statutes, for instance, provide that at any time after the defendant has satisfactorily completed one-third of the original probationary period or two years of probation, whichever is less, the court may reduce or terminate the period of probation.[20]

The American Bar Association *Standards Relating to Probation* recommend,

> Every jurisdiction should have a method by which the collateral effects of a criminal record can be avoided or mitigated following the successful completion of a term on probation and during its service.[21]

Two approaches are taken by present statutes on the subject:

1. Deferring formal adjudication of guilt through the period of probation and discharging the defendant following successful service without ever declaring the defendant guilty
2. Permitting withdrawal of a guilty plea and dismissal of the charges following the successful service of all or part of the probation term

The ABA advisory committee cites with approval the Maryland procedures that permit placing a consenting defendant on probation after the determination of guilt but before a formal entry of judgment. Such a provision allows the offender—upon successful completion of probation—to avoid the disabilities that attach to a felony conviction.[22]

All of the statutes and model codes and standards discussed in this section serve at least a limited purpose of mitigating the effects of a conviction, but they apply only to probationers. Some states, such as California, have enacted statutes that also extend opportunities for expungement to offenders who have not been placed on probation.

SEALING

SEALING

The legal concealment of a person's criminal (or juvenile) record such that it cannot be opened except by order of the court.

Sealing statutes have the same objective as expungement statutes in that they seek to erase the record of a conviction. However, they go further; they attempt to actually *conceal* the fact of conviction. Typically these statutes relate to juveniles or to persons who were under the age of 21 when they committed a crime. Sealing statutes are defended on the basis of public policy, which demands that certain documents and records be treated as confidential and therefore not be open to indiscriminate inspection even though they are in custody of a public officer or board and are of a public nature. Examples of such documents include those kept on file in public institutions concerning the condition, care, and treatment of inmates and those in offices charged with the execution of laws relating to the apprehension, prosecution, and punishment of crimes. Nevertheless, only a few states have sealing statutes; the statutes that exist tend to be limited in scope, and the procedures for sealing cumbersome.

Sealing provisions in juvenile court statutes must be read with reference to other provisions in those statutes that restrict access to juvenile records to persons with a legitimate interest in the protection, welfare, or treatment of the child and that provide for the destruction of fingerprints. Also related are (1) the juvenile code provisions that specifically state that neither an adjudication of delinquency nor a commitment is a conviction and (2) the statutes that give the juvenile court the authority to dismiss a petition and set aside findings. The sealing statutes operate to provide additional protection.

RESTORATION OF RIGHTS UPON APPLICATION

Removal of Disabilities

Some states provide by statute for procedures the offender can initiate to remove the disabilities that follow a conviction. These procedures differ from expungement procedures in that they do not attempt to wipe out the conviction. They are more or less straightforward attempts to remove the disabilities that are collateral consequences of conviction. Typically the certificate or other document that is furnished upon completion of the proceedings specifies the rights that are restored.

New York provides for two main ways of regaining some of the rights lost upon conviction. A first offender, or a former offender who has been convicted of more than one misdemeanor in addition to one felony, can apply for a *certificate of relief from disabilities.*[23] The *certificate of good conduct,* available to all offenders, is granted five years after release from custody, subject to certain conditions.[24] An ex-offender must possess one of these certificates in order to apply for a job or license barred by virtue of a criminal conviction. As we have said, California provides a certificate of rehabilitation to all offenders who complete their sentence. The purpose of the certificate is to facilitate employment opportunities and to assist in occupational or professional licensing.

These certificates and the order of the court usually restore the ex-offender to such political rights as the right to vote and provide him or her with a document that is some evidence of his or her good conduct since release from custody. Nonetheless, they do not prevent a prospective employer or a licensing agency from taking the conviction into account in deciding whether to give the offender a job or a license.

COURT DECISIONS

Elsewhere in this book we have discussed the broad and narrow definitions of *conviction*. It is clear that in many cases in which the broad definition was adopted (that is, where sentencing constitutes a conviction), the purpose and the effect of the decision were to protect the defendant's right to practice his or her profession or engage in other licensed occupation.[25] As one author has noted, the difference between two burglars on probation in California can be dramatic. Whereas the sentenced burglar (broad definition) has lost all civil rights, the unsentenced burglar (narrow definition) is a provisional or conditional felon and, as such, retains his or her civil rights and is subject to no disabilities except those prescribed in the terms of probation.[26]

Similar attempts to minimize the effects of a conviction can be seen in cases that narrow the definition of *moral turpitude* or *infamous crime*.[27] Some of these cases are forerunners of the "reasonable relationship" statutes, which require that a reasonable relationship exist between conviction and the rights or privileges the convicted person is deprived of. In the *Otsuka* case,[28] where the issue was the right to vote, the court limited the meaning of *infamous crime* to offenses where the elements of the crime are such that the person who committed it may reasonably be deemed to pose a threat to the integrity of the elective process.

An important Supreme Court case decided the issue of whether an ex-convict can possess good moral character as generally required in licensing statutes. In the case of *Schware v. Board of Bar Examiners*[29] the evidence showed that the applicant for the New Mexico bar examination had used several aliases in the 20 years prior to his application, had been arrested but never tried or convicted, and had been a member of the Communist Party 17 years earlier. The State Board of Bar Examiners refused to permit him to take the bar exam on the ground that he had not shown good moral character. The Court reversed the decision of the board, stating that a state cannot exclude a person from the practice of law or from any other occupation in a manner or for reasons that contravene the due process or equal protection clause of the Fourteenth Amendment. The Court emphasized that the applicant had done nothing in the 15 years preceding the application to reflect adversely on his character.[30]

A significant decision was handed down by the District of Columbia Court of Appeals in the case of *Miller v. District of Columbia*.[31] The agency involved had denied a vendor's license to an applicant, a former offender, because it found that he was not rehabilitated. Reversing the agency and finding that the applicant was rehabilitated, the court not only ordered the agency to grant the applicant a license but also went on to express "serious concern" about the agency's lack of standards. The court said, in part,

> Unless there are some standards relating the prior conduct of an applicant to the *particular* business activity for which he seeks a license, the power to deny a license inevitably becomes an arbitrary, and therefore, unlawful, exercise of judgment by one official, a graphic example of which is so clearly revealed by the record in this case.

RESTORING GOOD MORAL CHARACTER

GOOD (MORAL) CHARACTER

The totality of virtues that forms the basis of one's reputation in the community.

None of the methods and procedures we have examined in this chapter for removing or reducing the collateral consequences of a criminal conviction restores **good moral character** to the ex-offender. They all suffer from this overriding deficiency. Because licensing statutes almost universally require that the holders of a professional or occupational license be of good character, and many private employers of nonlicensed workers impose the same requirement, the effect is, to quote one author, "to close the door of hope to a person once sentenced for a crime, frustrating his chances for rehabilitation in a useful occupation for which he is trained."[32]

One of the problems in applying the standard of good moral character is, of course, the vagueness of the term. The Supreme Court in *Konigsberg v. State Bar* noted that

> the term [*good moral character*] by itself is unusually ambiguous. It can be defined in an almost unlimited number of ways, for any definition will necessarily reflect the attitudes, experiences, and prejudices of the definer. Such a vague qualification, which is easily adapted to fit personal views and predilections, can be a dangerous instrument for arbitrary and discriminatory denial of the right to practice law.[33]

Yet the rule remains as it was when announced by the Supreme Court in 1898:

> [The state] may require both qualifications of learning and of good character, and if it deems that one who has violated the criminal laws of the state is not possessed of sufficient good character, it can deny to such a one a right to practice medicine, and further, it may make the record of a conviction conclusive evidence of the fact of the violation of the criminal law and of the absence of the requisite good character.[34]

This rule has been generally observed in subsequent legislation and court decisions.[35]

Bad Character

The early law on restoring good moral character developed in the law of pardons. The general rule there seemed to be that all disqualifications that are imposed solely because of bad character—which may be incidentally evidenced by a conviction for a crime—are unaffected by a pardon. According to this rule a pardoned felon was thus restored the rights to vote, serve on a jury, receive a pension, and testify in court because the individual had not lost these rights simply because of bad moral character. When the exercise of a right is associated with a character requirement, however, the result is different. In that case the conviction may be evidence, even conclusive evidence, of bad character, unaffected by the pardon, and by extension of the same reasoning unaffected by certificates of rehabilitation and similar procedures.[36]

Thus when a qualification of good moral character is written into a licensing statute or into a statute prescribing qualifications for public office, it has been held to be within the power of the legislature to require that weight be given to the fact of a criminal conviction as evidence of bad character. An Ohio court stated,

> Whatever the theory of the law may be with regard to a pardon, it cannot work such moral changes as to warrant the assertion that a pardoned convict is just as reliable as one who has constantly maintained the character of a good citizen.[37]

The Direct Relationship Test

Although the authority of legislatures to impose civil disabilities on offenders and of licensing authorities to consider convictions in determining good character has not been seriously eroded, the trend is to impose what is becoming known as the **direct relationship test.** In a case in which the California Supreme Court declared that several convictions for participating in civil rights demonstrations did not determine an applicant unfit to admission to the bar, the court stated the fundamentals of this test:

> The nature of these acts, moreover, does not bear a *direct relationship* to petitioner's fitness to practice law. Virtually all of the admission and disciplinary cases in which we have upheld decisions of the State Bar to refuse to admit applicants or to disbar, suspend, or otherwise censure members of the bar, have involved acts which bear upon the individual's manifest dishonesty and thereby provide a *reasonable basis* for the conclusion that the applicant or attorney cannot be relied upon to fulfill the moral obligations incumbent upon members of the legal profession.[38]

THE STATUS OF CIVIL DISABILITIES TODAY

Civil disability statutes in general, and licensing statutes in particular, are being attacked in the courts on several grounds. The authors of "The Collateral Consequences of a Criminal Conviction"[39] effectively summarized the problems and proposed solutions. They argued as follows:

1. Civil disability laws are overbroad in that the laws of most jurisdictions provide for the blanket imposition of disabilities upon a criminal conviction.
2. The laws are inconsistent.
3. Although most jurisdictions provide for the eventual restoration of convicted criminals' rights, these procedures are of limited effectiveness; as a result many ex-convicts suffer disabilities long after deprivation is justifiable.
4. Among the disabilities suffered, the loss of employment opportunity is one of the most onerous. This is increasingly true as the number of licensed occupations continues to increase. Under existing laws discrimination against convicted criminals by private employers is perfectly legal.
5. Although regulations of many public and licensed occupations are necessary, many of the regulations are unreasonable, and procedures with respect to denial and revocation of licenses are not fair.

Attacks on the constitutionality of civil disability laws are being made on the following grounds:

1. Civil disability laws are bills of attainder.
2. Imposition of civil disabilities is cruel and unusual punishment.
3. Procedures with reference to the imposition and application of civil disability laws violate due process.
4. Civil disability laws deny equal protection.

In addition, these laws achieve none of the objectives of modern correctional theory and actually impede offenders' rehabilitation, both within the correctional institution and in the community. Recommendations to ameliorate these situations include

1. elimination of unnecessary restrictions,
2. reasonable application of necessary restrictions,
3. adoption of the direct relationship test,
4. greater participation by the sentencing court in determining the civil disabilities to be imposed on the individual defendant, and
5. automatic restoration of rights and privileges five years after the convict's release into the community.

SUMMARY

Although the direct consequences of a conviction end with the completion of the sentence, most of the collateral consequences continue for the lifetime of the offender—unless some affirmative act takes place to prevent the civil disabilities from attaching or reduce them. The methods used to restore rights include pardons, automatic restoration of rights, expungement, sealing, and restoration of rights upon application. None of these, however, has the effect of restoring good moral character, a requirement of all professional and occupational licensing boards and many private employers. This has the effect of denying employment to many ex-offenders and thereby frustrates their chances for rehabilitation in a meaningful occupation.

Civil disability laws achieve none of the goals of modern corrections. Although reasonable restrictions on some ex-offenders are justified—where there is a direct relationship between the crime committed and the functions and responsibilities of the licensed business or profession—the arbitrary barring of convicted persons from most licensed occupations serves no realistic public purpose and may, in fact, have negative consequences for society.

ENDNOTES

1. U.S. Const. art. II, § 2, cl. 1. ". . . and he (the president) shall have the power to grant reprieves and pardons for offenses against the United States except in cases of impeachment." The president has no power to pardon a state offender. *In re* Bocchiaro, 49 F. Supp. 37 (W.D.N.Y. 1943).

2. In California, by virtue of its constitution, the general authority to grant reprieves, pardons, and commutations of sentence is with the governor. Calif. Const. art. V, § 8, Cal. Penal Code § 4800, *et seq.* The Board of Prison Terms has replaced the Advisory Pardon Board as the investigative/advising agency. Cal. Penal. Code § 4801. In New York the power to pardon lies with the governor by constitutional provision. N.Y. Const. art. IV, § 4. In Texas the application for pardon is directed to the Board of Pardons and Paroles, and the governor may not grant a pardon unless it has been recommended by the board. However, the governor may refuse to grant a recommended pardon. Tex. Const. Art. IV, § 11. Texas Admin. Code, Title 37, § 143.1.

3. Other forms of executive clemency that are utilized to carry out these purposes include commutation of sentence, reprieve of execution, emergency medical reprieve, and remissions of fines and forfeitures. Rudenstine, 141–42 (1979).

4. In *Biddle v. Perovich,* 274 U.S. 480, 47 S. Ct. 664, 71 L. Ed. 1161 (1927), the Supreme Court, in a case where the president had commuted a death sentence to life imprisonment, held that an acceptance of the pardon was not necessary. The Court held that a pardon is not an act of grace but a tool for the public good. Justice Holmes wrote that a pardon is not an act of grace but a "determination of the ultimate authority that the public welfare will be better served" by a pardon.

5. In Texas, for example, an applicant must show a minimum of one year of good behavior after release from prison and completion of his or her sentence before an application can be made. A pardon will not be considered for an inmate still in prison unless his or her innocence has been established beyond a reasonable doubt, nor will a pardon be issued to a dead person.

6. The hearings are open in New York and closed in California. No hearings are provided for in Texas.

7. *Ex parte* Garland, 71 U.S. 333, 18 L. Ed. 366 (1867).

8. *Burdick v. United States,* 236 U.S. 79, 59 L. Ed. 476 (1915).

9. *State v. Walker,* 432 So. 2d 1057 (La. Ct. App. 1983); *Durham v. Wyrick,* 665 F. 2d 185 (8th Cir. 1981).

10. *Ex parte* Lefors, 303 S.W. 2d 394 (Tex. Crim. App. 1957).

11. *Marlo v. State Board of Medical Examiners,* 112 Cal. App. 2d 276, 246 P. 2d 69 (1952); *Murrill v. State Board of Accountancy,* 97 Cal. App. 2d 709, 218 P. 2d 569 (1950).

12. Cal. Penal Code § 4853 (West).

13. U.S. Pardon Attorney, *Civil Disabilities of Convicted Offenders* (Washington, D.C.: U.S. Department of Justice, 1996).

14. N.H. Rev. Stat. Ann. § 607-A:5.

15. Illinois Unified Code of Corrections, § 1005-5-5(d).

16. Wis. Stat. Ann. § 57.078.

17. Gouth, "The Expungement of Adjudication Records of Juvenile and Adult Offenders: A Problem of Status," *Wash.L.O.* 149 (1966).

18. Burton et al., 105–106.

19. Burton et al. report that the certificates are generally granted after completion of the sentence in order to facilitate employment or licensing. New York has a similar procedure.

20. Tex. Code Crim. Proc. Ann. art. 42.12, § 7 (Vernon).

21. American Bar Association, *Standards Relating to Probation,* § 4.3.

22. American Bar Association, *Standards Relating to Sentencing Alternative and Procedures,* 68–69.

23. McKinney's Consol. Laws on N.Y., Correction Law (Chicago, n.d.) §§ 701–703.

24. N.Y. Exec. Law § 242(3) (McKinney).

25. *State Medical Board v. Rodgers,* 190 Ark. 266, 79 S.W. 2d 83 (9135).

26. "The Effect of Expungement on a Criminal Conviction," *S.Calif.L.Rev.* 40:127–47 (1967).

27. *Otsuka v. Hite,* 51 Cal. Rptr. 284, 414 P. 2d 412 (1966). The court held that a burglar no longer would be considered as convicted of an infamous crime for purposes of disfranchisement.

28. *Otsuka v. Hite.*

29. *Schware v. Board of Bar Examiners,* 353 U.S. 232, 77 S. Ct. 752, 1 L. Ed. 2d 796 (1957).

30. *Schware v. Board of Bar Examiners.* See also *Mindel v. United States Civil Service Commission,* 312 F. Supp. 485 (N.D. Cal. 1970); and *Morrison v. State Board of Education,* 82 Cal. Rptr. 175, 461 P. 2d 375 (1969).

31. *Miller v. District of Columbia,* 294 A. 2d 365 (D.C. App. 1972).

32. "Entrance and Disciplinary Requirements for Occupational License in California," *Stan.L.Rev.* 18:533–50 (1962).

33. *Konigsberg v. State Bar,* 353 U.S. 252, 77 S. Ct. 722, 1 L. Ed. 2d 810 (1957).

34. *Hawker v. New York,* 170 U.S. 189, 18 S. Ct. 573, 42 L. Ed. 1002 (1898).

35. In 1960 the Supreme Court itself refused to overturn a civil disability law. *De Veau v. Braisted,* 363 U.S. 144, 80 S. Ct. 1146, 4 L. Ed. 2d 1109 (1960).

36. See, generally, "Note, Constitutional Law—Power of Legislature to Exclude a Pardoned Felon from a Civil Service Position," Iowa L.Rev. 27:305–309 (1942).
37. State *ex rel. Attorney General v. Hawkins,* 44 Ohio St. 98, 5 N.E. 228 (1886).
38. *Hallinan v. Committee of Bar Examiners,* 65 Cal. 2d 447, 55 Cal. Rptr. 228, 421 P. 2d 76 (1966).
39. This summary relied heavily on the definitive study of loss and restoration of civil rights by convicted offenders, "The Collateral Consequences of a Criminal Conviction," *Vanderbilt Law Review* 23:929 (1970).

DISCUSSION QUESTIONS

1. Compare and contrast the two types of pardon.
2. Who has the power to pardon, and under what circumstances may a pardon be granted?
3. What are the legal effects of a full pardon? Does a pardon wipe out guilt? What are the two major positions on this issue?
4. How does a pardon affect the right to vote? The right to serve on a jury? The right to hold public office? The right to serve as a witness?
5. Does a pardon restore a person's license to practice a profession? Explain.
6. How do various states deal with the issue of automatic restoration of rights upon completion of sentence? What is the trend?
7. What is expungement, and how do the various states handle this issue? What is the American Bar Association position?
8. How are sealing and expungement alike and different?
9. Discuss sealing in juvenile court.
10. How do various jurisdictions address the issue of restoration of rights following a conviction?

GLOSSARY

abjuration An oath to forsake the realm forever taken by an accused person who claimed sanctuary.

advisory board Panel of citizens, judges, or other public officials who act as advisors to the judiciary in setting broad general policy or in determining other aspects of probation services and administration.

amercement A monetary penalty imposed on a person for some offense, he being "in mercy" for his conduct, imposed arbitrarily at the discretion of the court or the person's lord. *Black's Law Dictionary* distinguishes between amercements and fines as follows: fines are certain, are created by some statute, and can only be assessed by courts of record; amercements are arbitrarily imposed.

American Correctional Association (ACA) The ACA was founded in 1870 with the stated primary purpose of "exert[ing] a positive influence on the shaping of national correctional policy and . . . promot[ing] the professional development of persons working within all aspects of corrections." It also develops standards for correctional practice, accredits agencies, and provides technical assistance.

American Probation and Parole Association (APPA) The professional association for probation, parole, and community corrections workers. The APPA disseminates information about probation, parole, and community corrections to its members; provides technical assistance to community corrections agencies and governing bodies; conducts training; establishes and monitors professional standards; and provides a forum for a broad range of correctional issues and controversies.

annulment To nullify, make void, abolish. An act that deprives a criminal conviction of all force and operation.

attainder In common law, the extinction of civil rights and capacities that occurred when a person who had committed treason or a felony received a sentence of death or outlawry for his crimes. The effect was that all his estate was forfeited to the crown.

autonomous model of parole organization An organizational pattern in which parole decisions are made within an autonomous body not affiliated with other agencies of the criminal justice system. Most common pattern for adult paroling authorities.

---

benefit of clergy An exemption for members of the clergy that allowed them to avoid being subject to the jurisdiction of secular courts.

boot camp A residential correctional program designed to instill discipline and responsibility that resembles military basic training.

---

civil rights Rights that belong to a person by virtue of citizenship.

classification Determination of the level of needed supervision (usually in terms of minimum, medium, maximum) based on the probationer/parolee's risk of recidivism and need for services.

collateral consequences of conviction Disabilities that follow a conviction that are not directly imposed by a sentencing court—such as loss of the right to vote, serve on a jury, practice certain occupations, or own a firearm.

community service A special condition of probation that requires offenders to perform unpaid work for civic or nonprofit organizations. Community service may be regarded as a substitute for financial compensation to victims or as symbolic restitution.

consolidation model of parole organization An organizational pattern in which parole decisions are made by a central authority that has independent powers but that is organizationally situated in the overall department of corrections.

continuing custody theory The view that the parolee remains in custody of either the parole authorities or the prison and that his/her constitutional rights are limited. Release on parole is merely a change in the *degree* of custody.

contract theory The view that parole represents a contract between the state and the parolee by which a prisoner agrees to abide by certain conditions and terms in return for his/her release. Violation of the conditions represents a breach of contract that allows parole to be revoked.

---

deferred adjudication A form of probation that, after a plea of guilty or *nolo contendere,* defers further proceedings without an adjudication of guilt.

determinate sentence A sentence to imprisonment for a fixed period of time as specified by statute. Also known as **flat, fixed,** or **straight sentence.**

---

electronic monitoring The use of small electronic transmitters attached to offenders' bodies to monitor their movement and thus enhance probation officers' surveillance capabilities.

en banc A French term designating a session of court in which all judges participate.

expungement "Erasure"; process by which the record of a criminal conviction (or juvenile adjudication) is destroyed or sealed after expiration of time.

---

filing A procedure by which an indictment is "laid on file," or held in abeyance without either dismissal or final judgment, in cases where justice does not require an immediate sentence.

---

good (moral) character The totality of virtues that forms the basis of one's reputation in the community.

good time Reduction in sentence for institutional good conduct.

grace theory The view that parole is a privilege and a matter of grace (mercy) by the executive; parole confers no particular rights on the recipient and is subject to withdrawal at any time.

---

house arrest Confinement of an offender in his/her residence instead of a correctional institution.

---

indeterminate sentence A sentence to imprisonment in which the duration is not fixed by the court but is left to be determined by some other authority (usually a parole board or other agency) after some minimum period is served. The basis of parole.

institutional model of parole organization An organizational pattern in which parole release decisions are made primarily within the institution. Advocates of the institutional model believe that because institutional staff are most familiar with the offender and his/her response to institutional programs, they are most sensitive to the optimal time for release. Most commonly used in the juvenile field.

intensive supervision probation (ISP) A probation program of intensive surveillance and supervision in the community as an alternative to imprisonment.

intermediate sanction Alternative punishments that fall between probation and incarceration, including house arrest, electronic monitoring, community service, restitution, fines, shock probation, and intensive probation supervision.

Interstate Compact for the Supervision of Parolees and Probationers An agreement among the states to supervise probationers and parolees for each other.

---

jail time Credit allowed on a sentence for time spent in jail awaiting trial or mandate on appeal.

judicial reprieve Withdrawal of a sentence for an interval of time during which the offender is at liberty and imposition of other sanctions is postponed.

just deserts The concept that the goal of corrections should be to punish offenders because they deserve to be punished and that punishment should be commensurate with the seriousness of the offense.

justice model The correctional practice based on the concept of *just deserts.* The justice model calls for fairness in criminal sentencing; all persons convicted of a like offense will receive a like sentence. Prisons are viewed as a place of even-handed punishment, not rehabilitation. This model of corrections relies on determinate sentencing and abolition of parole.

---

mandatory release Conditional release to the community that is automatic at the expiration of the maximum term of sentence *minus* any credited time off for good behavior.

mark system Credits for good behavior and hard work; one of the historical foundations of parole. In Alexander Maconochie's mark system on Norfolk Island, convicts could use credits or *marks* to purchase either goods or time (reduction in sentence). In this system, the prisoner progressed through stages from strict imprisonment through conditional release to final and complete restoration of liberty, with promotion based on the marks accredited.

medical model The concept that given the proper care and treatment, criminals can be changed into productive, law-abiding citizens. This approach suggests that people commit crimes because of influences beyond their control, such as poverty, injustice, and racism. Also called the **rehabilitation model.**

Model Penal Code A criminal code developed by the American Law Institute as a simpler, more consistent statement of the law that states could use as a model, if they wished, whenever they undertook to revise or modernize their criminal codes.

---

net widening The tendency for social control mechanisms to encompass a larger (or a different) population than originally planned.

---

offender-based presentence investigation report A presentence investigation report that seeks to understand the offender and the circumstances leading to and surrounding the offense and to evaluate the potential of the offender as a law-abiding, productive citizen.

offense-based presentence investigation report A presentence investigation report that focuses primarily on the offense that was committed, the offender's culpability, and the offender's criminal history.

outlawry In old Anglo-Saxon law, the process by which a criminal was declared an *outlaw* and placed outside the protection and aid of the law.

---

pardon An executive act that mitigates or sets aside punishment for a crime. The power to pardon is generally invested in state governors, but the President has the power to pardon for federal offenses. Pardons are either conditional or absolute (full).

conditional pardon: A pardon that becomes operative when the grantee has performed some specific act(s) or that becomes void when some specific act(s) transpires.

full pardon: A pardon that frees the criminal without any condition whatever. It reaches both the punishment prescribed for the offense and the guilt of the offender.

parole The conditional release, by an administrative act, of a convicted offender from a penal or correctional institution under the continued custody of the state, to serve the remainder of his or her sentence in the community under supervision.

parole d'honneur French for "word of honor," from which the English word *parole* is derived.

parole guidelines Guidelines to be followed in making parole release decisions. Most guidelines prescribe a "presumptive term" for each class of convicted inmate depending on both offense and offender characteristics.

paroling authority An administrative body (usually 3–19 members) empowered to decide whether inmates shall be conditionally released from prison before the completion of their sentence, to revoke parole, and to discharge from parole those who have satisfactorily completed their terms.

presumptive sentence A statutorily determined sentence convicted offenders will *presumably* receive if convicted. Offenders convicted in a jurisdiction with presumptive sentences are assessed this sentence unless mitigating or aggravating circumstances are found to exist.

pretrial diversion A form of probation imposed before a plea of guilt that can result in dismissal of the charges; used primarily with offenders who need treatment or supervision and for whom criminal sanctions would be excessive.

probation, regular The release of a convicted offender by a court under court-imposed conditions for a specified period during which the imposition or execution of sentence is suspended.

probation, term of The length of probation.

probation conditions The rules or terms under which a court releases an offender to community supervision. Conditions of release fall into two categories, standard and special. **Standard conditions** are imposed on all probationers in a jurisdiction. **Special conditions** are tailored to fit the particular needs of an individual offender.

---

recognizance Originally a device of preventive justice that obliged persons suspected of future misbehavior to stipulate with and give full assurance to the court and the public that the apprehended offense would not occur. Recognizance was later used with convicted or arraigned offenders with conditions of release set. Recognizance is usually entered into for a specified period.

restitution A condition of probation that requires offenders to compensate their victims for damages or monetary losses incurred as a result of their crimes.

revocation The withdrawal of either probation or parole because the behavior of the offender was in violation of the conditions agreed upon. Revocation requires the offender to begin or continue serving his or her sentence.

risk assessment Determination of an offender's risk of recidivism and appropriate classification and case management strategies. This is most often accomplished by using actuarial prediction scales based on variables shown to be empirically correlated with success or failure on probation or parole.

Salient Factor Score The parole guidelines developed and used by the U.S. Parole Commission for making parole release decisions; served as the model for parole guidelines developed in many other jurisdictions.

sealing The legal concealment of a person's criminal (or juvenile) record so that it cannot be opened except by order of the court.

security for good behavior A recognizance or bond given the court by a defendant before or after conviction conditioned on his being "on good behavior" or keeping the peace for a prescribed period.

sentencing guidelines Standardized instruments designed to provide clear and explicit direction to the court in determining the appropriate sentence. Guidelines typically consider offense severity and the offender's prior record. A matrix that relates these factors may be used.

shock probation A brief period of incarceration—typically 30–120 days—followed by resentencing to a term of probation supervision.

supervision The oversight that a probation and/or parole officer exercises over those who are placed in his/her charge during a term of probation or parole. There are several models or approaches to supervision, including:

> **casework model** the probation/parole officer serves primarily as a counselor, dispensing "treatment" to "clients" in a one-on-one therapeutic relationship.
>
> **brokerage model** the probation/parole officer attempts to determine the needs of the probationer/parolee and refers him/her to the appropriate community agency for services. Also called the **community resource management model.**
>
> **community resource management team (CRMT) model** a form of brokerage model in which caseloads of probationers/parolees are "pooled" and served by more than one officer, each specializing in one or more areas, such as drug/alcohol services or employment. The officer specializing in a particular area develops linkages to the community agencies that provide those services. Thus, a drug/alcohol specialist would assess the probationer's needs in the area of substance abuse, refer him/her to community agencies that provide substance abuse services, and monitor the probationer's progress in this area.
>
> **justice model** supervision is geared to helping offenders comply with the conditions of their release. The traditional rehabilitative function is voluntary and is brokered through the appropriate community agencies.

suspended sentence An order of the court after a verdict, finding, or plea of guilty that suspends or postpones the imposition or execution of sentence during a period of good behavior.

---

technical violation Infractions of a probation or parole condition not involving violation of a law.

ticket-of-leave A license or permit given to a convict as a reward for good conduct, originally in the penal settlements, which allowed him to go at large and labor for himself before his sentence expired, subject to certain restrictions and revocable upon subsequent misconduct. A forerunner of parole.

ticket-of-leave man A convict who has obtained a ticket-of-leave.

transportation The forced exile of convicted criminals. England "transported" convicted criminals to the American colonies until the Revolution and afterward to Australia. The foundations of the transportation system are found in the law of 1597, 39 Eliz. c.4, "An Acte for Punyshment of Rogues, Vagabonds, and Sturdy Beggars." The act declared that obdurate idlers "shall . . . be banished out of this Realm . . . and shall be conveyed to such parts beyond the seas as shall be . . . assigned by the Privy Council."

---

victim impact statement Information in a presentence investigation report about the impact of the offense on identifiable victims or the community.

TABLE OF CASES

INDEX

J

K

L

M

Credits

10 Corbis-Bettmann Archives; **14** Stock Montage; **28** Bob Daemmrich; **37** Bob Daemmrich; **50** AP/WideWorld Photo; **56** John Boykin/PhotoEdit; **79** A. Ramey/PhotoEdit; **95** A. Ramey/Woodfin Camp & Associates; **106** Paul Merideth/Tony Stone Images; **134** Kevin Horan/Stock Boston; **159** William Campbell/Sygma; **161** Lionel J-M Delevingne/Stock Boston; **185** Corbis-Bettmann Archives; **210** Corbis-Bettmann Archives; **215** Bob Daemmrich/The Image Works; **228** Corbis-Bettmann Archives; **234** © 1990 Forest McMullin/Black Star; **236** Douglas Burrows/Liaison International; **253** A. Ramey/Woodfin Camp & Associates; **270** Gilles Mingasson/Liaison International; **277** A. Ramey/Woodfin Camp & Associates; **286** Tony Savino/The Image Works; **311** James L. Shaffer/PhotoEdit; **323** Tony Freeman/PhotoEdit; **329** Tony Freeman/PhotoEdit; **330** Jim Pickerell/Stock Boston; **331** Bob Daemmrich/The Image Works; **353** W. McNamee/Sygma